Register of Educational Research in the United Kingdom
Volume 9: 1991–93

The *Register of Educational Research in the United Kingdom* lists all the major research projects being undertaken in Britain in the period under review. This volume, number 9, covers research which was on-going during 1991, the whole of 1992 and the early months of 1993.

Each entry provides names and addresses of the researchers, a detailed abstract, the source and amount of the grant (where applicable), the length of the project – or the fact of its continuance, and bibliographic details of publicised material about the research. Comprehensive author and subject indexes enable the reader to use the Register to its best advantage and to obtain accurate information with both speed and ease. The subject index is based on keywords selected from the British Education Thesaurus. Each entry is listed against all its keywords.

The National Foundation for Educational Research is the leading educational research body in the United Kingdom, carrying out a varied programme of research into many aspects of education.

Register of Educational Research in the United Kingdom
Volume 9: 1991–93

National Foundation for Educational Research in England and Wales

London and New York

First published 1994
by Routledge
11 New Fetter Lane, London EC4P 4EE

Simultaneously published in the USA and Canada
by Routledge
29 West 35th Street, New York, NY 10001

Typeset in Times by LaserScript, Mitcham, Surrey
Printed and bound in Great Britain by
Antony Rowe Ltd., Chippenham, Wiltshire

British Library Cataloguing in Publication Data
A catalogue record for this book is available from the British Library

ISBN 0–415–10664–8

Contents

How to use the Register

The Register entries are arranged alphabetically according to the name of the institution at which the research was carried out; within each institution, the entries are arranged alphabetically by department and within the department by researcher. The entries are also consecutively numbered.

Name and subject indexes appear at the back of the volume. The subject index is based on keywords which have been selected from the British Education Thesaurus. Each entry is listed against all of its keywords.

Although every effort has been made to check that the details of the entries supplied by the researchers are correct, there may be some errors and inconsistencies, for which we apologise.

The details of the research projects contained in this Register are stored on an IBM microcomputer at the National Foundation for Educational Research (NFER) and entries are continuously updated and new material is added as it is received. Therefore, it is possible to provide Register users with printouts of more up-to-date information. A modest charge is made for this service, which is available from:

Register of Educational Research in the UK
National Foundation for Educational Research
The Mere
Upton Park
Slough
SL1 2DQ
Berkshire
Telephone: (0753) 574123

Aberdeen University

9/0001

Department of Education, Taylor Building, King's College,
Aberdeen AB9 2UB
0224 272000
Flett, M. Ms; Watt, J. Dr; Nisbet, J. Prof.
Young families now: a focus for learning in the community
Abstract: 'Young Families Now' is an action research project based
in an area of rapid social change within the city of Aberdeen. The
focus of the work is the development of educational opportunities for
young children and their parents, particularly their mothers. The
project aims to respond to educational needs as these are defined by
the community. It supports existing groups in the field of early
childhood care and education and helps local people identify new
needs and establish new forms of provision for children and their
mothers. The project also aims to bring together parents and professionals to look at new ways of working and to open up discussion on
how local childcare services in health, social work and education can
better meet the needs of young families. As an action research project,
it also tries to bring together the community's expertise in developing
an action programme with the University's expertise in research.
Status: Sponsored project
Source of Grant: Bernard Van Leer Foundation – The Hague £600,000
Date of Research: 1986-1991
*KEYWORDS: access to education; community education; mother's;
preschool education; young children*

9/0002

Department of Education, Taylor Building, King's College,
Aberdeen AB9 2UB
0224 272000
Thorp, J. Mr; *Supervisor:* Nisbet, J. Prof.
Curriculum and staff development in small rural schools
Abstract: In many areas of Britain the distribution of schools is at, or
close to, the irreducible minimum. Small schools find themselves
once again under threat resulting from both the requirement of the
Education Reform Act 1988 to deliver the National Curriculum with
the limited expertise of two or three teachers and from formula
funding which emphasises their high staffing costs. To meet their
legal obligations it is widely thought that small schools need 'support'. Ten detailed case studies of support in action are presented,
including Education Support Grant funded support projects, non-
funded teacher self-help groups and individual school solutions. The
case studies report the fieldwork undertaken in each of the ten areas
and have been completed from interviews, observations and documentary analysis. Analyses of individual cases reveal first a series
of tensions among approaches to support while further analysis
indicates the substantive themes of the research, teacher empowerment, autonomy and control.
Status: Individual research
Date of Research: 1985-1991
*KEYWORDS: cooperation; curriculum development; education sup-
port grants; rural schools; school support; small schools; staff
development*

9/0003

Department of Psychology, Taylor Building, King's College,
Aberdeen AB9 2UB
0224 272000
Pont, H. Mr; *Supervisor:* Shepherd, J. Mr
Cognitive assessment of maladjusted children
Abstract: A cognitive social learning approach to assessment is based
on the belief that social behaviour is determined by the individual's
expectations and beliefs about a situation, and is under the control of
mediating processes such as self control or reflective ability. The need
therefore is to focus on what a person constructs in specific situations,
rather than to infer general explanatory traits merely to describe
behaviour. Within the terms of the above approach several areas of
cognitive social functioning were identified as being of particular
significance in the study of behaviourally and/or emotionally disturbed children, e.g. self perception, perception of problem behaviour, perception of others and inter-personal problem-solving skills.
The present study includes an in depth assessment of 40 children in
a residential special school for emotionally/behaviourally disturbed
children in the above areas together with a full professional and

current behaviour assessment. Performance of the target group is
compared with normal controls and a group of problem behaviour
controls from a List D setting to identify differences in functioning.
Status: Individual research
Date of Research: 1985-1991
*KEYWORDS: cognitive development; cognitive measurement; emo-
tional disturbances; psychological evaluation*

Anglia Polytechnic University

9/0004

Anglia Business School, Centre for Higher Education
Management, Danbury Park Conference Centre, Danbury
Park, Chelmsford CM3 4AT
0245 225511
Davies, J. Prof.
**Evolution of the role, structure and operations of senior
management groups in universities**
Abstract: The research aims to: (1) monitor the evolution of senior
management teams in 5 universities over a 3 year period; (2) produce
a classification of types of senior management teams; (3) identify the
situational factors underpinning the development of the various
types; and (4) indicate the operational characteristics associated with
each type, and the consequences for institutional processes. The
research is based on 5 universities engaged in the transformation of
its senior management structures and processes, using a combination
of case study and action research methods, with the principal inves-
tigator acting as participant observer in the change process. The
principal types of structure that have been identified are: (1) traditional model; (2) general management academic sector model; (3)
loose brief troubleshooter model; (4) functional policy coordinator
model; (5) functional executive/presidential model. Differences are
apparent in terms of the role and style of vice-chancellor; the power
and authority of pro-vice-chancellors; the style of operation of team;
institutional processes for planning, resource allocation; and interaction with academic units and administration.
Status: Sponsored project
Source of Grant: Anglia Business School and five institutions concerned £ 25,000
Date of Research: 1988-1991
*KEYWORDS: management teams; universities; university adminis-
tration*

9/0005

Anglia Business School, Centre for Higher Education
Management, Danbury Park Conference Centre, Danbury
Park, Chelmsford CM3 4AT
0245 225511
Davies, J. Prof.; Kells, H. Prof.
**The management and development of mechanisms of
university/industry collaboration in European and Latin
American universities**
Abstract: The research aims to: (1) assess the state of the art univer-
sity/industry relations in terms of technology transfer and continuing
education in 14 European universities; (2) identify and evaluate the
significance of factors facilitating and inhibiting these developments;
(3) develop perspectives on the strategics and processes needed to
improve universities' adaptability and responsiveness to industry and
the internal mechanisms of managing and sustaining such change;
and (4) assess the relevance of these findings to developments in this
field in Latin America. The research is based on 14 European universities in Spain, Portugal, Italy, France, Switzerland, Netherlands,
Belgium and the United Kingdom. The analysis is carried out by
teams of visiting Latin American rectors and academics using a
tightly structured framework based on prior research by the principal
researcher carried out for the Organisation for Economic Cooperation
and Development (OECD). This case study method draws on institutions of different sizes, traditions, disciplinary configurations, and
environmental stimuli.
Published Material: 'Managing quality and the links with the productive sector' (1990). In: the report entitled 'In the Wake of Colum-
bus': European Rectors' Conference, Geneva.
Status: Sponsored project
Source of Grant: European Community; UNESCO; European Rectors' Conference, Geneva (CRE); Participating universities £75,000

Date of Research: 1989-1991
KEYWORDS: comparative education; entrepreneurship; industry higher education relationship; technology transfer; universities

9/0006

Anglia Business School, Centre for Higher Education Management, Danbury Park Conference Centre, Danbury Park, Chelmsford CM3 4AT
0245 225511
Anglia Business School, Victoria Road South, Chelmsford CM1 1LR
0245 412141
Kells, H. Prof.; *Supervisor:* Davies, J. Prof.
Models and theories of self-regulation in higher education: a multi-national study
Abstract: This is a multi-stage, fifteen year project to describe, understand and improve higher education self-regulation processes. Earlier stages were empirical; later stages qualitative and theory building. Focus was on North America and Western Europe. In the early stages, retrospective descriptive and correlational studies of self-evaluation processes were employed in North America. In the middle stages, qualitative case analyses, propositional in nature, were conducted in Holland and North America.
Published Material: KELLS, H.R. & KIRKWOOD, R.J. (1979). 'Institutional self-evaluation processes', Educational Record, pp.22-45.; KELLS, H.R. (1988). Self-study processes. New York and London: Macmillan.; KELLS, H.R. & VAN VUGHT, F.A. (1988). 'Theoretical and practical aspects of a self-regulation and quality control system for Dutch higher education', Tijdschrift Voor Hoger Onderwijs, Vol 6, No 1, pp.15-20., February.; KELLS, H.R. (1990). 'The inadequacy of performance indicators', Higher Education Management, November. ; KELLS, H.R. (1990). 'The use of incentives in program review and planned change'.Paper given at European Association for Institutional Research, Lyon, September. Higher Education Management, Vol 3, No 2, 1991.
Status: Individual research
Date of Research: 1990-1992
KEYWORDS: comparative education; higher education; institutional evaluation; self evaluation – groups

9/0007

Department of Arts and Letters, East Road, Cambridge CB1 1PT
0223 63271
Tallack, M. Mrs; *Supervisor:* Baxter, D. Mr
Anglia Polytechnic University critical studies project
Abstract: Anglia Polytechnic University Art History Division staff at Cambridge, are working with two hundred year 5 and year 6 pupils and their teachers, following these pupils through their school career until 1995. The staff provide: (1) expertise in and outside the classroom in Critical Studies work. Working alongside the primary and secondary teachers in schools, galleries, museums and other locations; (2) in-service classes for primary and secondary teachers; (3) visual and other resources for cross-curricular critical studies work drawn from Anglia Polytechnic University's own due resources, galleries, museums and the community. The aims of this Critical Studies research project are: (1) to introduce pupils to as wide a variety of art objects as possible in order to: (i) generate understanding of the cultural, historical, formal and other ways of engaging with art objects; (ii) improve their artwork; (iii) extend their critical vocabulary to enable them to critically evaluate their own artwork; (2) to familiarise teachers with the innumerable ways in which Critical Studies work can enrich many areas of the school curriculum; (3) to develop and extend teachers' confidence and abilities in relation to Critical Studies work; (4) to test, and refine, cross curricular strategies, teaching methods and assessment procedures in relation to Critical Studies work in primary and secondary schools in the context of the National Curriculum.
Status: Sponsored project
Source of Grant: Caloustie Gulbenkian Foundation £5,000; Eastern Arts Association £900
Date of Research: 1990 - continuing
KEYWORDS: art activities; art education; criticism; cross curricular approach

9/0008

Department of Geography, East Road, Cambridge CB1 1PT
0223 63271
Fitzgerald, M. Ms
Education for sustainable development in the third world
Abstract: The aims are to determine the origin of and reasons for environmental education programmes (EEP) and to assess their contribution to sustainable development and disaster mitigation. A pilot EEP in Ethiopia has been evaluated. A 45% sample of participating centres has been visited and interviews conducted with students, farmers, teachers and education officers at district, regional and ministerial level. It is concluded that there are contradictions between the centralisation of programme planning and the need for environmental education to be location-specific and between the goals of providing relevant education and meeting the demand for qualifications. These arise from northern-inspired interpretations of sustainable development. They limit the potential of environmental education to produce the values and behaviour required for sustainable development.
Published Material: FITZGERALD, M. (1990). 'Education for sustainable development: decision-making for environmental education in Ethiopia', The International Journal of Educational Development, Vol 10, No 4, pp.289-302.; FITZGERALD, M. (1990). 'Environmental education in Ethiopia: the sources of decision-making'. In: BANDHU, D., SINGH, H. & MAITRA, A.K. Environmental education and sustainable development. New Delhi: Indian Environmental Society.; FITZGERALD, M. (1991). 'Education for sustainable development: a long-term strategy for famine prevention in Ethiopia', Occasional Paper in Rural Studies, No 9, Anglia Polytechnic, Division of Geography.
Status: Individual research
Date of Research: 1987 - continuing
KEYWORDS: developing countries; development education; environmental education

9/0009

Department of Geography, East Road, Cambridge CB1 1PT
0223 63271
Fitzgerald, M. Ms
The contribution of geography to environmental education
Abstract: The aim is to evaluate geography's contribution to education for sustainable development. The proposed method is an analysis of school syllabuses and assessment procedures in the United Kingdom and California. Initial research suggests that geography's separation of the 'human' and the 'physical' undermines its potential to synthesise ecology and environment in the ways needed to bring about new environmental ethics.
Published Material: FITZGERALD, M. (1990). 'Education for sustainable development: decision-making for environmental education in Ethiopia', The International Journal of Educational Development, Vol 10, No 4, pp.289-302.; FITZGERALD, M. (1990). 'Environmental education in Ethiopia: the sources of decision-making'. In: BANDHU, D., SINGH, H. & MAITRA, A.K. Environmental education and sustainable development. New Delhi: Indian Environmental Society.; FITZGERALD, M. (1990). 'Education for sustainable development: a long-term strategy for famine prevention in Ethiopia', Occasional Paper in Rural Studies, No 9, Anglia Polytechnic, Division of Geography.
Status: Individual research
Date of Research: 1991 - continuing
KEYWORDS: environmental education; geography

9/0010

Faculty of Health and Social Work, Victoria Road South, Chelmsford CM1 1LL
0245 493131
Wakeham, M. Mr
Information needs and information seeking behaviour of nurses
Abstract: The objectives of the study are to identify the kinds of information sought by student nurses, trained staff and students on post-basic courses. The researchers have sought by means of a questionnaire, to investigate the ways in which information is sought, particularly in libraries. One thousand questionnaires were distributed within the four health districts with which Anglia Polytechnic University has links via its Departments of Nursing and Midwifery Education. A response rate of around 50% was obtained. The replies have been analysed through the SPSS PC program and

the results are being collated.
Status: Sponsored project
Source of Grant: British Library £1,850
Date of Research: 1991-1991
KEYWORDS: information needs; information seeking; nurse education; nurses

9/0011
   Sawyers Hall Lane, Brentwood CM15 9BT
   0277 264504
   Sussex University, Institute of Continuing and Professional
   Education, Sussex House, Falmer, Brighton BN1 9RH
   0273 606755
   Turner, M. Mr; *Supervisor:* Lacey, C. Prof.; Lewin, K. Dr
**The management of teacher probation and induction in
primary schools**
Abstract: The pilot and main study investigated approaches to the
management of teacher probation and induction in five local education authorities, chosen to represent rural, suburban and urban perspectives. Overall, 11 schools were used and interviews were
conducted with all participants within them of the management of
probation and induction on five occasions during a year (Headteacher, Deputy, designated support teachers, probationers). The
methodology was of partially structured but open ended interviews
which were recorded by the interviewer, and transcribed and analysed
for key factors. The research analysis is proceeding in an attempt to
identify significant patterns and models in the management of probation and induction.
Status: Individual research
Date of Research: 1987-1992
KEYWORDS: primary schools; probationary teachers; teacher induction

Associated Examining Board

9/0012
   Stag Hill House, Guildford, Surrey GU2 5XJ
   0483 506506
   Delap, M. Dr; Eason, S. Mr; Macdonald, H. Dr; Taylor, M.
   Mr ; *Supervisor:* Cresswell, M. Mr
Examinations research programme
Abstract: The research and statistics group carries out a continuing
program of research into fundamental problems associated with
educational measurement together with work on specific examinations. Particular areas of study pursued in 1992 and 1993 are:-
grading processes; reliability of moderation; gender differences;
differentiated assessment; aggregation. The research group is also
involved in development work associated with the assessment of the
National Curriculum. A further aspect of the work involves collaborative studies with the other United Kingdom Examining Boards and
Groups to ensure that all the General Certificate of Secondary Education (GCSE) and General Certificate of Education (GCE) examinations are set, marked and graded to comparable standards.
Published Material: GOOD, F.J. & CRESSWELL, M.J. (1988). 'Can
teachers enter candidates appropriately for examinations involving
differentiated papers?', Educational Studies, Vol 14, No 3, pp.289-
297.; GOOD, F.J. & CRESSWELL, M.J. (1988). Differentiated
assessment: grading and related issues. London: Secondary Examinations Council.; GOOD, F.J. & CRESSWELL, M.J. (1988). Grading
the GCSE. London: Secondary Examinations Council.; GOOD, F.J.
& CRESSWELL, M.J. (1988). 'Placing candidates who take differentiated papers on a common grade scale', Educational Research,
Vol 30, No 3, pp.177-189.; GOOD, F.J. (1989). 'Setting common
examination papers that differentiate', Educational Studies, Vol 15,
No 1, pp.67-82.
Status: Sponsored project
Source of Grant: Associated Examining Board
Date of Research: 1983 - continuing
*KEYWORDS: assessment; evaluation; examinations; moderation –
marking; National Curriculum; sex difference*

Aston University

9/0013
   Department of Modern Languages, Aston Triangle,
   Birmingham B4 7ET
   021 359 3611
   Young, A. Miss; *Supervisor:* Ager, D. Prof.
**Sociolinguistic factors affecting attitudes and motivation in
foreign language learning at school: an Anglo-French
comparative study**
Abstract: This study will attempt to identify the differing attitudes
held by English and French school children towards foreign language
learning with particular reference to their sociolinguistic environment. The issue will be considered from a sociolinguistic, rather than
from a psycholinguistic perspective, giving primary importance to
environmental, as opposed to individual factors. In particular, emphasis will be placed upon the differing sociolinguistic environments
of the two areas concerned (Mulhouse, France and Walsall, England),
in an attempt to shed light upon the linguistic attitudes, orientations
and motivation of the children living within these communities and
to identify the underlying factors which may consequently affect
motivation. Three aspects of the pupils' sociolinguistic environment
– parental opinion, peer pressure and the learning environment are
believed to exert significant influence and will be given special
attention, as it is believed that they play an important role in the
formation of attitudes. A structured sample drawn from pupils attending schools in Mulhouse and Walsall will supply the data base for
this research. The main thrust of the study will be quantitative in
approach, involving the distribution of about 500 questionnaires to
pupils in both towns. This will be followed up by the use of qualitative
methods, in the form of indepth interviews with an individually
matched sample of 50 French/English pupils, whose purpose will be
to modify and check the quantitative data.
Status: Sponsored project
Source of Grant: Aston University
Date of Research: 1991 - continuing
*KEYWORDS: comparative education; modern language studies;
pupil attitudes*

9/0014
   Department of Modern Languages, Aston Triangle,
   Birmingham B4 7ET
   021 359 3611
   Upward, C. Mr
The reform of English spelling by omission of redundant letters
Abstract: Proposals for rationalising English orthography date back
to the sixteenth century. Modern proposals have assumed that reform
merely required consistent representation of Received Pronunciation,
but they took little account of the psychological and administrative
practicalities of introducing a visually revolutionary system. One
such proposal, the Simplified Spelling Society's 'New Spelling'
(1948), formed the basis for Sir James Pitman's 'Initial Teaching
Alphabet', which proved the educational benefits of regularised
spelling, but was unsuited for a general reform of written English. In
1982, Valerie Yule published on the concept of 'Cut Spelling', which
meant reform by omitting redundant letters rather than introducing
new letters to words. The aim of the project is to systematise the
concept of Cut Spelling, explore its linguistic implications, and
develop a coherent reform proposal based on it. The concept of Cut
Spelling has been reduced to 3 main rules: (1) omission of letters
irrelevant to pronunciation; (2) extended use of syllabographic l, m,
n, r in post-accentual syllables, with morphophonemic regularisation
of inflections; (3) simplification of doubled consonants. The implications of such a system have been explored under a number of
headings: (i) degree of visual disruption resulting from different kinds
of spelling change; (ii) reduction of grapheme-variety; (iii) avoidance
of spelling error; (iv) economy of representation; (v) homophones
and homographs; (vi) phonographic and graphotactic innovation;
(vii) diachronic tendencies towards Cut Spelling in English and other
European languages. In conclusion, Cut Spelling offers a practicable
new approach to the modernisation of English spelling, combining
compatibility with traditional orthography, enhanced regularity, and
significant economy in use.
Published Material: UPWARD, C. (1989). 'Conflicting eficiency
criteria in Cut Speling-2', Journal of the Simplified Spelling Society,
Vol 3, No 1, pp.21-29.; UPWARD, C. (1989). 'The initial teaching
alphabet and spelling reform', UK i.t.a. Federation Newsletter, pp.13-18,

Spring.; UPWARD, C. (1989). 'Recent developments in 're-regulating' written German', Journal of the Simplified Spelling Society, Vol 3, No 1, pp.15-17.; UPWARD, C. & GREGERSEN, E. (1989). 'Morfemes and cut spelling', Journal of the Simplified Spelling Society, Vol 3, No 1, pp.25-29.; UPWARD, C. (1992). approximately 40 articles in The Oxford Companion to the English Language. Oxford: Oxford University Press. A full list of publications is available from the researcher.
Status: Sponsored project
Source of Grant: Aston University: Department of Modern Languages; The Simplified Spelling Society
Date of Research: 1982-1992
KEYWORDS: *English; literacy; reading; spelling*

Bath College of Higher Education

9/0015
Newton Park, Newton St Loe, Bath BA2 9BN
0225 873701
Gomersall, M. Dr
The Tudors & Stuarts through information technology (IT): history & information technology in the primary school
Abstract: The project is concerned with the development of curriculum materials for primary school history, using information technology. Subject content is focused on the Tudors and Stuarts, a National Curriculum Core Study Unit for primary school history at key stage 2, and also recognises cross-curricular learning opportunities. The research is school based, with materials being developed by curriculum tutors within the Faculty of Education at Bath College of Higher Education in association with local teachers and their pupils.
Status: Sponsored project
Source of Grant: National Council for Educational Technology £3,000; Bath College of Higher Education £3,000
Date of Research: 1991-1992
KEYWORDS: *history; information technology; primary school curriculum*

9/0016
Newton Park, Newton St Loe, Bath BA2 9BN
0225 873701
Towler, L. Ms; *Supervisor:* Broadfoot, P. Prof.
Profiling in the primary school: extension of self-assessment in primary schools 1989-1991 – collaborative approach to assessment
Abstract: This project investigates the background and issues surrounding the introduction of Records of Achievement, or profiles, to the primary school and, in particular, the principle of involving children and parents as partners, with teachers, in the assessment process. It explores the contribution made by the literature and research into Records of Achievement in the secondary context, in order to develop both a rationale for, and a critique of, self-assessment and examines ways in which these may prove applicable to primary children. The issues examined inlcude the development of skills necessary for effective review and analysis of achievement and the extent to which young children may be empowered through ownership of their profile. The effect of individual differences in respect of age, gender, attainment and culture are also explored, and the implications for school policy on assessment considered. A qualitative case study of the introduction of profiling in one primary school was carried out in order to determine the extent to which children of ten and eleven years may be capable of taking responsibility for their own learning and benefit from involvement in their own self-assessment. The research also included using questionnaires and interviews, to gain the reaction and response of parents to the introduction of profiles as a method of reporting on achievement and to the request for their involvement in the process. The conclusions drawn indicate that a coherent school policy for assessment, which is supported by the commitment of teachers and parents, can ensure that the principle of assessment as first and foremost the responsibility of the learner is both valid and can be realistically applied in education from the early years.
Published Material: BROADFOOT, P., et al (1991). 'Implementing National Assessment: issues for primary teachers', Cambridge Jour-
nal of Education, Vol 21, No 2, pp.153-168.; TOWLER, L. & BROADFOOT, P. (1992). 'Self-assessment in the primary school', Educational Review, Vol 44, No 2, pp.137-151.
Status: Individual research
Date of Research: 1993 - continuing
KEYWORDS: *assessment; primary schools; profiles; pupil responsibility; records of achievement; school reports; self evaluation – individuals*

9/0017
Newton Park, Newton St Loe, Bath BA2 9BN
0225 873701
Bristol University, School of Education, 35 Berkeley Square, Bristol BS8 1JA
0272 303030
Feiler, A. Mr; *Supervisor:* Webster, A. Dr
Support arrangements for primary school children who experience difficulty learning to read – help or hinderance?
Abstract: One aim of this research will be to establish how much help is provided for children with reading difficulties in primary schools and the nature of this help. A related aim will then be to establish the effect that internal and external arrangements for helping such children have on the amount and quality of support provided. In other words does the presence of 'special arrangements' (either internal or external to the school) result in class teachers providing levels of support similar to those before these arrangements were made, more help, or less? A related aim will be to explore the quality of support once help is provided. Does this tend to result in children being given tasks that are less stimulating, where the emphasis is on de-coding and on processing texts for information rather than on reading texts that are imaginative and expressive? It is intended that teachers and children from 6 primary schools will participate in this investigation – which will be carried out by interviewing, observation and analysing school records.
Status: Individual research
Date of Research: 1992 - continuing
KEYWORDS: *primary education; reading difficulties; reading teaching; remedial programmes; remedial reading; special educational needs*

9/0018
Newton Park, Newton St Loe, Bath BA2 9BN
0225 873701
London University, Institute of Education, Department of International and Comparative Education, 20 Bedford Way, London WC1H OAL
071 436 2186
Coulby, D. Dr; Jones, C. Mr
Urban civic culture and the school curriculum
Abstract: The research identifies two possible directions for curricular systems in the European Community (EC) in the light of developing European Civic Culture. The first of these – the traditional – seeks to identify European achievement in the arts and science and conflate these with human achievement per se. The second – the international – looks to the way in which European achievement in science and the arts has been influenced by forces beyond Europe. It further identifies scientific and artistic achievement entirely beyond Europe. The research seeks to investigate this polarity in curricular in EC countries. It seeks to establish ways in which international views of European civic culture may be encouraged.
Published Material: COULBY, D. (1992). 'European civic culture and education'. In: COULBY, D. & JONES, C. (Eds). (1992). The world yearbook of education in 1992: urban education. London: Kogan Page.
Status: Individual research
Date of Research: 1991 - continuing
KEYWORDS: *cultural activities; curriculum; European Community; sciences*

9/0019
Newton Park, Newton St Loe, Bath BA2 9BN
0225 873701
London University, Institute of Education, Department of Mathematics, Statistics and Computing, 20 Bedford Way, London WC1H OAL
071 580 1122
Harries, T. Mr; *Supervisor:* Sutherland, R. Dr

LOGO and the development of algebraic skills
Abstract: The main aim of the research is to develop an understanding of the algebraic perceptions of pupils who are perceived to be 'low attainers' in mathematics. This involves investigating not only their algebraic perceptions but also their understanding of numbers and how this understanding can be used to articulate numerical algorithms. Some of the specific questions being investigated are: (1) Is algebraic thinking closed to some of the pupils in our schools or is their lack of understanding more a reflection of the environment in which they are introduced to it? (2) Is the apparent lack of understanding of algebraic symbols due in part to a lack of facility with numbers? (3) Is it possible to create an environment within LOGO which will enable pupils to explore numbers, and naturally build up a facility to generalise and use variables? The research is being carried out over a period of 4 terms, with year 8 pupils in two different schools. The progress of the pupils as they work through a series of activities will be monitored through observation and the use of 'dribble' files. Also there will be regular individual structured interviews.
Status: Individual research
Date of Research: 1992 - continuing
KEYWORDS: *algebra; computer uses in education; logo; low achievement; mathematics education*

Bath University

9/0020
　　School of Education, Claverton Down, Bath BA2 7AY
　　0225 826826
　　Ritchie, R. Mr; *Supervisor:* Denley, P. Dr
Evaluating the effectiveness of a practitioner's use of a constructivist approach for developing scientific knowledge and understanding in primary students during their initial training and primary teachers on inservice courses
Abstract: Implementing the National Curriculum for Science requires primary teachers to develop pupils' knowledge and understanding in science, particularly through exploration and investigation, and assess their progress. For many teachers this is proving difficult because they lack appropriate background knowledge and understanding in science themselves. Recent research (Kruger & Summers, 1989) has confirmed that many primary teachers have no formal qualifications in science. Present recruits to teacher training are not required to have a qualification in science and existing cohorts in institutions include many students with limited scientific backgrounds. Consequently, the training of teachers and successful inservice education of teachers (INSET) requires trainers to adopt approaches that will develop scientific knowledge and understanding in teachers. Considerable research in the secondary sector, and limited research in the primary sector have shown the importance of adopting a constructivist approach to science education. The purpose of the research is to examine the effectiveness with adult learners of the use of such an approach. Focused observation and analysis of personal practice results in modifications to teaching and evaluation of changes. Effectiveness is assessed in terms of improved knowledge and understanding of scientific ideas. The project will look for evidence of improved understanding and the impact of this on the learning opportunities provided for children in the classroom. Formal and informal methods have been used to validate the research.
Status: Individual research
Date of Research: 1989 - continuing
KEYWORDS: *inservice teacher education; preservice teacher education; primary education; science education; student teachers*

9/0021
　　School of Education, Claverton Down, Bath BA2 7AY
　　0225 826826
　　Jamieson, I. Prof.; Harris, A. Ms
Evaluation of the Economic Awareness in Teacher Training project (EcATT)
Abstract: Evaluation of the Economic Awareness in Teacher Training project. The evaluation uses a progressive focusing model to analyse the project's initial design, the local education authorities, with which it is involved, the schools with which it is working and finally the classrooms in which it operates. The evaluation should throw light on the concept of economic awareness, universities as

centres for curriculum change and the operation of cross curriculum themes in the National Curriculum.
Status: Sponsored project
Source of Grant: Department of Education and Science £20,000; Banking Information Service; Unilever £10,000
Date of Research: 1990-1991
KEYWORDS: *curriculum development; economics education; enterprise education; evaluation; teacher education*

Berkshire County Council

9/0022
　　Education Department, Information Technology
　　Management, Shire Hall, Shinfield Park, Reading RG2 9XD
　　0734 233425
　　Reece, D. Mr
Analysis of examination results
Abstract: Information is received from the National Consortium for Examination Results (NCER) and examination results are analysed by subject, sex and school and a combination of the three. These are in the form of detailed tabulations, summary measures of performance and 'profiles' for schools. Results for examinations taken at different times are matched together to produce overall summaries of attainment. Information on the ethnic origin of candidates is added to the results, which are also analysed by ethnicity.
Status: Sponsored project
Source of Grant: Berkshire County Council
Date of Research: 1981 - continuing
KEYWORDS: *examination results; institutional evaluation; performance indicators*

9/0023
　　Education Department, Information Technology
　　Management, Shire Hall, Shinfield Park, Reading RG2 9XD
　　0734 233425
　　Reece, D. Mr
Survey of recruitment and staffing difficulties in secondary schools
Abstract: The need to form a full picture of the staffing problems in schools has prompted the development of a systematic monitoring of the recruitment process and the resulting teaching force. A system is in place for incorporating the collection of information on attempts to recruit into the routine of administration.
Status: Sponsored project
Source of Grant: Berkshire County Council
Date of Research: 1986 - continuing
KEYWORDS: *secondary schools; teacher recruitment; teacher supply and demand*

9/0024
　　Education Department, Information Technology
　　Management, Shire Hall, Shinfield Park, Reading RG2 9XD
　　0734 233425
　　Reece, D. Mr
Literacy screening analyses
Abstract: Each year a survey of the literacy capabilities of children in the 7+ and 9+ year groups is undertaken: (1) to identify those children in need of particular help; and (2) to use the results at school level as an index of educational needs in the school. This index is combined with indices of social needs, based on census variables and free school meals, to give a score for the school. This is used to help allocate discretionary teaching resources.
Status: Sponsored project
Source of Grant: Berkshire County Council
Date of Research: 1986 - continuing
KEYWORDS: *ability identification; educational planning; literacy; pupil needs*

9/0025
　　Education Department, Information Technology
　　Management, Shire Hall, Shinfield Park, Reading RG2 9XD
　　0734 233425
　　Reece, D. Mr

Berkshire school pupil forecasting system
Abstract: The objective of the Berkshire school pupil forecasting system is to predict numbers of pupils of each age group in every Berkshire school, for up to 10 years ahead. The basic approach in forecasting is the 'cohort trend' method, where changes observed to cohorts of pupils over previous years are applied in the future. Recent enhancements to the system include: (1) the prediction of primary school entry (i.e. 5 year old) age pupils by relating intakes to the past and predicted resident population of the school catchment area, using data from the Research and Intelligence Unit's Population Estimation and Projection Models; and (2) prediction of intakes to secondary schools by using data from the Education Department's computerised Secondary School Allocation System. Forecasts are produced annually using pupil numbers in January.
Status: Sponsored project
Source of Grant: Berkshire County Council
Date of Research: 1976 - continuing
KEYWORDS: *long range planning; prediction; pupil numbers; regional planning*

9/0026
Education Department, Information Technology Management, Shire Hall, Shinfield Park, Reading RG2 9XD
0734 233425
Reece, D. Mr
Careers service analyses
Abstract: A cohort study is made annually to study the experiences of young people in finding employment and to provide information about their career preferences and outcomes.
Status: Sponsored project
Source of Grant: Berkshire County Council
Date of Research: 1984 - continuing
KEYWORDS: *career choice; careers service; employment opportunities; youth employment*

Birmingham University

9/0027
School of Education, Edgbaston, Birmingham B15 2TT
021 414 3344
Davies, L. Dr; Harber, C. Dr
School management in conditions of stringency
Abstract: Managers of schools in countries with limited or declining budgets for education face conditions and problems in their institutions which are rarely addressed by conventional educational administration literature. Shortages of resources of all kinds (teachers, training, textbooks, equipment, furniture), levels of pay which can compromise full commitment to the work of teaching, and communication and transport problems may characterise a number of Third World countries as well as some declining First World ones. Together with widely divergent expectations of authority and the role of the headteacher, this may mean that images of school management are called for which are radically different from the models in much administrative theory. There is little systematically collected evidence either about problems faced by schools operating in economically constrained circumstances or about the management strategies which are actually used for coping with them. However, it is probable that the internal reality of very tightly budgeted schools will depart significantly from the prescriptions for 'effective' management found in Western-based management textbooks. The research aims to gather case-study evidence on the reality of school organisation in selected Third World countries. Clearly, there can be no single objective and valid view of how a school operates. Rather, the same features of school organisation will be viewed and assessed by different participants in the process. The research therefore uses qualitative methods to examine the perceptions of key participants within school management – headteachers, deputies and senior teachers. A cumulative bank of such case studies of schools can develop a grounded theory around themes relevant for future management training. The aim is therefore to encourage portrayal of the real contexts of school life in order to (a) critically challenge the imposition of western based educational administration principles; and (b) derive relevant management images and strategies which do not necessarily rely on full levels of school financing.
Published Material: DAVIES, L. (1990). Equity or efficiency?

school management in an international context. London: Falmer Press.; HARBER, C. (1989). Politics in African education. London: Macmillan.
Status: Sponsored project
Source of Grant: Birmingham University
Date of Research: 1990 - continuing
KEYWORDS: *developing countries; educational administration; educational environment; educational finance*

9/0028
School of Education, Edgbaston, Birmingham B15 2TT
021 414 3344
Bullock, A. Dr; Thomas, H. Dr; *Supervisor:* Thomas, H. Dr
The funding of schools after the 1988 Education Reform Act
Abstract: The principal aims of this study are to describe and analyse the pattern of resource distribution in local education authorities; to examine the change in priorities as the system moves from one method of funding to another; to investigate the relationship between the resource priorities of the local education authority and those of the school and inquire into the rationale of resource decisions. The methods used are: quantitative analysis of local education authority budgetary data and school level budgetary data; and interviews and self-completed question schedules with personnel in schools.
Published Material: THOMAS, H. & BULLOCK, A.D. (1992). 'School size and local management funding formulae', Educational Management and Administration (forthcoming).; THOMAS, H. & BULLOCK, A.D. (1991). 'The flawed formulae', Vol 1, No 3, pp.5-6.
Status: Sponsored project
Source of Grant: Leverhulme Trust £42,000
Date of Research: 1990 - continuing
KEYWORDS: *educational finance; financial policy; financial support; local management of schools*

9/0029
School of Education, Edgbaston, Birmingham B15 2TT
021 414 3344
Arnott, M. Ms; Bullock, A. Dr; Thomas, H. Dr; *Supervisor:* Thomas, H. Dr
The impact of local management of schools
Abstract: The project aims to describe and analyse the impact of Local Management of Schools. This includes the immediate impact in relation to local education authority approaches to delegation, and the impact on roles of headteachers and deputy headteachers. The methods to be used are quantitative analysis of a questionnaire sent to 2000 headteachers in England and Wales and qualitative analysis of interviews with school personnel.
Status: Sponsored project
Source of Grant: National Association of Head Teachers £62,000
Date of Research: 1991 - continuing
KEYWORDS: *educational change; headteachers; local management of schools; school based management*

9/0030
School of Education, Edgbaston, Birmingham B15 2TT
021 414 3344
Miller, C. Ms; *Supervisor:* Upton, G. Prof.
Development of a distance learning course for teachers of children with speech and language disorders
Abstract: The aims of the research are to investigate teachers' needs regarding speech and language disorders and to develop a distance learning course based on the identified needs. The questionnaire used to identify needs and discussions with trainers lead to modifications in the balance of the syllabus for the course.
Published Material: MASON, H. & MILLER, C. (1991). 'Training teachers of children with special needs at a distance'. In: UPTON, G. (Ed). Staff training and special educational needs: innovatory strategies and models of delivery. London: David Fulton.
Status: Sponsored project
Source of Grant: Department of Education and Science £76,000
Date of Research: 1981-1991
KEYWORDS: *communication disorders; course content; distance education; language handicaps; speech handicaps; teacher education*

9/0031
School of Education, Edgbaston, Birmingham B15 2TT
021 414 3344
Lock, R. Dr; Millett, K. Ms
Animals and science education: pupils' knowledge, attitudes and behaviour with respect to animals and the uses which are made of them
Abstract: The aim of the research is to investigate the knowledge, attitudes and behaviour of 14-16 year old students towards the uses of animals. The findings of the research will inform the development of curriculum materials relevant to the use of animals as described by the National Curriculum (Science) with particular reference to Key Stage 4. Data will be gathered by means of a self-completion questionnaire to be completed by a sample of 14 year old students across the country. The questionnaire will survey student knowledge, attitudes and behaviour with respect to animals and their use both in the classroom and in the wider context of the students' everyday lives.
Status: Sponsored project
Source of Grant: Research Defence Society Charitable Trust £33,000
Date of Research: 1990-1991
KEYWORDS: *animals; laboratory animals; National Curriculum; pupil attitudes; science education*

9/0032
School of Education, Edgbaston, Birmingham B15 2TT
021 414 3344
Berry, J. Mr; Supervisor: Evans, W. Mr
Genre theory and writing functions
Abstract: The research arises out of current debates about genre theory and its appropriateness to English education. The aim is to examine the theory and its applicability to English classroom situations. Examination of samples of writing done in classrooms in four or five contrasting schools will attempt to establish the number of functions of writing commonly covered by children at National Curriculum Key Stages 1 and 2 in those schools, and whether they can be related to any identifiable genres. Depending on these results, specific teaching ploys might be invented to test genre ideas and apply them to the teaching of writing. The usefulness of the ideas, the need for action (or otherwise) and the nature and outcome of the experiments will be discussed with statements of the National Curriculum (Writing) in mind. Australian genre teaching materials and the experience of Australian self-help groups will enter into the study for consideration and to provide a framework for experiment.
Status: Individual research
Date of Research: 1991 - continuing
KEYWORDS: *creative writing; English studies curriculum; literary genres; National Curriculum; writing – composition; writing skills*

9/0033
School of Education, Edgbaston, Birmingham B15 2TT
021 414 3344
Layton, L. Mrs; Supervisor: Upton, G. Prof.
A pilot study to test a programme for training nursery school children to attend to the sounds in words
Abstract: The objectives of this pilot study are: 1) to select, from existing techniques, a battery of tests which will assess certain phonological awareness skills in pre-school children who are currently attending nursery school classes or playgroups; 2) using these tests to identify about six children aged between three and a half to four years old with deficiencies in phonological awareness; 3) to design a set of graded procedures which can then be applied using the targeted group; and 4) to assess the suitability of the tests and procedures with a view to including them in a major training study. The object of this would be the improvement of phonological awareness skills in targeted children and an assessment of the effect of such improvement on the children's later written language skills. However it is hoped that the pilot study will also yield a set of games and activities which would have wider application within the typical nursery school routine.
Status: Sponsored project
Source of Grant: Children's' Research Charity via Hereford & Worcester Dyslexia Association £10,000
Date of Research: 1990-1991
KEYWORDS: *dyslexia; language handicaps; nursery schools; phonics; phonology; preschool children; speech tests*

9/0034
School of Education, Edgbaston, Birmingham B15 2TT
021 414 3344
Layton, L. Mrs; Supervisor: Upton, G. Prof.
Phonological awareness of nursery-school children
Abstract: The project aims at the development and evaluation of a structured programme of phonological training materials designed to enhance phonological awareness in pre-school aged children in general and in particular those children whose phonological skills are under-developed. The first phase of the project involved assessing the phonological skills of a group of 50 pre-school aged children and a detailed examination of phonological training in a sample of 10 nursery schools. The second phase involves the development of the training pack and the evaluation of its effectiveness. The pack is being designed for use with all children but a particular focus of the study will be on its use with children whose phonological skills are under-developed and who are considered to be at risk of developing a specific learning difficulty. A follow-up of these children is planned two years after the completion of the present study.
Published Material: LAYTON, L. & UPTON, G. (1991). 'Phonological training and the pre-school child', Links, Spring.; LAYTON, L. & UPTON, G. (1991). 'In my view', Child Education, Vol 68, No 9.
Status: Sponsored project
Source of Grant: Department of Education and Science; Oak Foundation; Via Hereford and Worcester Dyslexia Association £54,000
Date of Research: 1991 - continuing
KEYWORDS: *nursery schools; phonology; preschool children; preschool education; speech handicap*

9/0035
School of Education, Edgbaston, Birmingham B15 2TT
021 414 3344
Connors, M. Ms; Supervisor: Fraser, B. Mr
The integration experiences of hearing impaired children: the transition from primary to secondary schooling
Abstract: The project aims to describe the educational and social experiences of hearing-impaired pupils in mainstream settings as they transfer from primary to secondary schools and to identify those practices which facilitate transition. Sample size will be not more than 12. These pupils will come from a variety of integrated settings, will be using a range of communication methods, will be from different ethnic backgrounds and will be situated in both rural and urban areas. An ethnographic approach will be used to study the following: pupils' own experiences and needs; access to the curriculum; social aspects of transfer; parental issues; implications for specialist and mainstream staff.
Status: Sponsored project
Source of Grant: National Deaf Children's Society
Date of Research: 1990-1992
KEYWORDS: *deafness; educational experience; hearing impairments; mainstreaming; primary secondary education; social experience; special educational needs; transition education*

9/0036
School of Education, Edgbaston, Birmingham B15 2TT
021 414 3344
Shepherson, D. Mr; Supervisor: Thomas, H. Dr
Economic decision-making models on non-advanced further education
Abstract: An investigation of the relationship between resource decisions and curriculum decision processes will be examined in the context created by the local authority role in creating a framework for strategic planning, as influenced by the Local Authority Act and the Education Reform Act. At the centre of the analysis will be an opportunity cost model of decision making. It is expected that quantitative data will be collected reflecting commonly used performance indicators. This will be analysed in the context of qualitative data, based upon interviews, relating to the perceptions of individuals on their valuations of resource and curriculum alternatives.
Status: Individual research
Date of Research: 1989 - continuing
KEYWORDS: *educational finance; educational planning; local education authorities*

9/0037
School of Education, Edgbaston, Birmingham B15 2TT
021 414 3344
Richmond, J. Mr; Supervisor: Thomas, H. Dr

Problems and possibilities of managing small secondary schools (circa 400) as a result of the Education Reform Act 1988

Abstract: The Education Reform Act 1988 has implications for the management and size of schools within a local authority, Her Majesty's Inspectorate having suggested that four-form entry schools may be the minimum under Local Management of Schools yet many secondary schools fall below this minimum. In order to examine the problems and possibilities for the management of such schools, the proposed research will be both qualititative and quantitative in approach. Key issues of the 1988 Act will be reviewed and consideration given to the requirements of the Government through the Department of Education and Science, those of the local education authority as well as the needs of small schools themselves.
Status: Individual research
Date of Research: 1990 - continuing
KEYWORDS: Education Reform Act 1988; local management of schools; school size; small schools

9/0038
School of Education, Edgbaston, Birminghm B15 2TT
021 414 3344
Hull, J. Prof.
A study of the rhetoric used in the public debates about religious education in England and Wales 1987-1990
Abstract: This research looked at the rhetoric used in debates about religious education in Britain. Examples of the imagery of mixed, inappropriate or disgusting food (mish-mash, hotch-potch) when describing the use of world religions in education were gathered from debates in the Houses of Parliament 1988 and from newspapers. The imagery of food disgust was traced back into childhood and through Western culture and the background of food distaste in biblical thought was studied. It is concluded that the use of these expressions indicates tribalistic and racist prejudice.
Published Material: HULL, J.M. (1991). Mish-mash: religious education in multi-cultural Britain: a study in imagery. Derby: CEM.
Status: Sponsored project
Source of Grant: Birmingham University: Faculty of Education and Continuing Studies Research Grant £500
Date of Research: 1990-1991
KEYWORDS: imagery; multicultural education; religious differences; religious education

9/0039
School of Education, Edgbaston, Birmingham B15 2TT
021 414 3344
Grove, J. Mrs; Spencer, L. Ms; *Supervisor:* Hull, J. Prof.; Grimmitt, M. Dr
Religion in the Service of the Child (RiSC) project
Abstract: Drawing upon phenomenological and hermeneutical theory, the Religion in the Service of the Child (RiSC) project has developed a strategy for teaching explicit religious material to primary pupils. The strategy has been developed through action research in classrooms. Many specific religious items, called numena, have been presented to pupils in National Curriculum Key Stages 1 and 2 in 39 schools in the West Midlands in a variety of situations. These trials have been closely observed, many through video recordings. Pupil reaction has been monitored and used to inform pedagogical development and to identify criteria for choice of content. The strategy is designed to foster a deep approach to learning and encourages pupils to be their own meaning makers. Pupils are facilitated to make use of the religious material, presented to them in all its power and holiness, to illuminate their understanding of their own lives and experiences. Numena are chosen particularly for their potential to raise and address issues of concern to children. In the interaction between pupil and content facilitated by the strategy, those concerns, often unconscious, can be allowed to surface and be addressed with security. Such an encounter with the religious world can promote deep reflection on the child's part into his or her own life world. The research has shown that, contrary to accumulated professional wisdom of the past 20 years, young pupils are able to respond imaginatively and holistically to the beauty and mystery of religious material in modes which are natural to them and in ways which benefit their development.
Published Material: GRIMMITT, M.H., GROVE, J., HULL, J.M. & SPENCER, L. (1991). A gift to the child: Religious education in the primary school. Hemel Hempstead: Simon & Schuster.; GRIMMITT, M.H. (1991). Religion in the Service of the Child: Interim

Report. CREDAR Lecture Series. University of Birmingham.; HULL, J.M. (1991). God-talk with young children: notes for parents and teachers. CEM.; GRIMMITT, M.H. (1991). 'The use of religious phenomena in schools: some theoretical and practical considerations', British Journal of Religious Education, Vol 13, No 2, pp.77-88.; GROVE, J.E. (1991). 'Religion in the Service of the Child: a new strategy for primary religious education', Planning RE in Schools.
Status: Sponsored project
Source of Grant: Church related charitable trusts and industry £74,600
Date of Research: 1989-1992
KEYWORDS: educational materials; religious education

9/0040
School of Education, Edgbaston, Birmingham B15 2TT
021 414 3344
Ranson, S. Prof.; Thomas, H. Dr; Ribbins, P. Dr; *Supervisor:* Ranson, S. Prof.
The new government and management of education
Abstract: The implementation of the 1988 Education Reform Act over four to five years provides a unique opportunity to study the emergence of a new system of government for education. This research proposes to develop knowledge and understanding of the new system of government for education. It will focus upon understanding the tension within the new system between its principal characteristics of administrative regulation and public choice and accountability. The research will analyse the emerging patterns of administration (financial staffing and curriculum procedures) and public choice (open enrolment, opting out and accountability systems) in the new system of government as it is implemented. A theoretical model will be developed which seeks to explain the development and change of the new system of government by identifying key factors; their purposes and strategies; their resource ownership and interests; their roles and relationships in the system; patterns of conflict and cooperation; and the emerging structure of power, influence and control. The unique opportunity to study a system as it develops over time requires a longitudinal research design which enables the team to understand 'diachronic' as well as 'synchronic' characteristics of the emerging system. This research intends to clarify types of emergent system of educational government and will enable a study of how the nature of institutional management may be shaped by the context in which they are located. This subsequent study will wish to investigate the effects of the changes on the roles of governors, headteachers and staff, the distribution of educational opportunities and standards of pupil achievement.
Status: Sponsored project
Source of Grant: Economic and Social Research Council £54,000
Date of Research: 1990 - continuing
KEYWORDS: Education Reform Act 1988; educational administration; educational change; educational finance; grant maintained schools; open entry; parent choice; school-based management

9/0041
School of Education, Edgbaston, Birmingham B15 2TT
021 414 3344
McCall, S. Mr; Stone, J. Mrs; *Supervisor:* McCall, S. Mr; Stone, J. Mrs
Moon as a route to literacy for blind children with learning difficulties
Abstract: The project is concerned with investigating the teaching of literacy to blind children with additional learning difficutlies. Moon is an alternative to Braille, a tactile code based on a simplified raised line version of the Roman print alphabet rather than on dots. The characters are large and bold and Moon has traditionally found a valuable role amongst elderly blind people, many of whom cannot cope with the demands of learning braille but go on to read fluently through Moon. There has been very little research done into the question of whether Moon presents access to literacy for blind children with learning difficulties who are unable to manage braille. Although a few teachers have attempted to experiment with Moon, their efforts have inevitably been hampered by the lack of appropriate material and information and the results of their efforts have not been evaluated. The general aim of the project is to investigate whether Moon offers a viable alternative to braille in the teaching of literacy to educationally blind children and young people who have additional learning difficultes. Specifically the project will address the following objectives: (1) to investigate current practices in the teaching of reading and writing to blind children with additional learning diffi-

culties; (2) to develop packages of materials for the teaching and learning of Moon; (3) to trial and refine these materials with the assistance of teachers and children from a variety of educational settings; and (4) to evaluate the effectiveness of Moon in developing the literacy of blind children and young people with learning difficulties.
Status: Sponsored project
Source of Grant: Leverhulme Trust £51,000
Date of Research: 1992 - continuing
KEYWORDS: *blindness; braille; learning disabilities; literacy education; raised line drawings; sensory aids; special educational needs*

9/0042

School of Education, Edgbaston, Birmingham B15 2TT
021 414 3344
Wade, C. Dr
Perceptions of children with special educational needs
Abstract: The clients in education are infrequently consulted; where the clients are designated as having special educational needs consultation is rare. The investigation presumes that what such pupils can tell us about their feelings and attitudes to their educational experiences will be of valid use in determining educational provision. Approximately 135 children have answered (written, verbal, scribed) questionnaires and a similar number have answered a sentence completion instrument. This sample is a mix of hearing impaired, visually impaired, physically handicapped, mentally handicapped and learning difficulties pupils aged 7-16. In depth interviews complement the surveys and these are drawn from Australia and New Zealand as well as the United Kingdom.
Published Material: WADE, C.B. (1988). 'Whose problem is it anyway? Resources for handicapped pupils in the mainstream class', OIDEAS, No 33, pp.71-81.
Status: Sponsored project
Source of Grant: Leverhulme Foundation Fellowship £7,150
Date of Research: 1989-1991
KEYWORDS: *educational experience; exceptional persons; pupil attitudes; special educational needs*

9/0043

School of Education, Edgbaston, Birmingham B15 2TT
021 414 3344
Lacey, P. Mrs; *Supervisor:* Upton, G. Prof.
The workings of multidisciplinary teams in special education
Abstract: This is an investigation into the workings of multidisciplinary teams in special education. The emphasis will be on how they function, the amount of collaboration possible, the way in which the curriculum is influenced by such a team and the training necessary for effective cross-discipline work. The main aims for the research are: (1) to investigate the workings of multidisciplinary teams in the field of special education; and (2) to draw together examples of good practice for dissemination through courses and written work. Methods of research will include observation and interview of team members and pupils in schools and local education authorities. Questionnaires will also be used but the main emphasis will be on case studies and accounts. As the 1988 Education Reform Act is likely to have a considerable effect upon the financing of specialist professionals in special education, there will be due emphasis on the changes monitored over the four years given to this research.
Status: Sponsored project
Source of Grant: Birmingham University: School of Education
Date of Research: 1991 - continuing
KEYWORDS: *cross curricular approach; special education teachers; special educational needs; support services; team teaching*

9/0044

School of Education, Edgbaston, Birmingham B15 2TT
021 414 3344
Mason, H. Ms; Hull, T. Mr; *Supervisor:* Mason, H. Ms
The speed of tactile information processing for blind pupils
Abstract: The major aim of this research is to develop and field trial a tactile speed of information processing test based on a sighted version of the existing print version of the British Ability Scales. This is to be standardised on the blind population, aged 5-17, of England, Wales and Northern Ireland, Scotland and Eire.
Status: Sponsored project
Source of Grant: Leverhulme Trust £38,050
Date of Research: 1990-1992

KEYWORDS: *blindness; tactual perception; tactual visual tests; visual impairments*

9/0045

School of Education, Edgbaston, Birmingham B15 2TT
021 414 3344
Harber, C. Dr; Davies, L. Dr
Educational management in developing countries
Abstract: This is a qualitative research project that uses observation, semi-structured interviews and documentation to explore the realities of school management in developing societies. It pays particular attention to the social, economic, political and cultural context in which schools operate and the ways in which this affects the attitudes and behaviour of key participants including headteachers, teachers, parents and pupils.
Published Material: DAVIES, L. (1990). Equity and efficiency: school management in an international context. London: Falmer Press.; HARBER, C. (1989). Politics in African education. London: MacMillan.; DADEY, A. & HARBER, C. (1991). Training and professional support for Headship in Africa. London: Commonwealth Secretariat.
Status: Individual research
Date of Research: 1990 - continuing
KEYWORDS: *developing countries; educational administration; educational policy; politics education relationship; school systems*

9/0046

School of Education, Edgbaston, Birmingham B15 2TT
021 414 3344
Merrett, F. Dr; *Supervisor:* Merrett, F. Dr
Behavioural approach to teaching project
Abstract: Empirical research has been employed to investigate the kinds of behaviours that teachers find most troublesome and the sort of responses they make to these behaviours. This has been extended to include samples from Hong Kong and Singapore. Packages used to teach teachers' methods of classroom behaviour management based on surveys and on experimental work in primary and secondary classrooms have recently been revised and upgraded. Observational research is now being focused upon the differential response rates of male and female teachers to boys and girls and the effects brought about on pupil on-task behaviour by manipulation of teachers' response ratios (i.e. the ratio between their positive and negative response rates). Another new move is the application of correspondence training to the improvement of pupils' social behaviour at the secondary level.
Published Material: MERRETT, F. & WHELDALL, K. (1990). 'Positive teaching in the primary school', (Research Paper). London: Paul Chapman.; WHELDALL, K. & MERRETT, F. (1991). General manual for the positive teaching packages. Cheltenham: Positive Products.; WHELDALL, K. & MERRETT, F. (1991). Teaching manual for the positive teaching package (primary version). Cheltenham: Positive Products.; MERRETT, F. & WHELDALL, K. (1991). Teaching manual for the positive teaching package (secondary version). Cheltenham: Positive Products.; MERRETT, F. & WHELDALL, K. (1991). 'Teachers' use of praise and reprimands to boys and girls', Educational Review, (in press).
Status: Individual research
Date of Research: 1980 - continuing
KEYWORDS: *behaviour problems; classroom discipline; classroom management; pupil behaviour; teacher behaviour; teacher pupil relationship*

9/0047

School of Education, Edgbaston, Birmingham B15 2TT
021 414 3344
Thomas, H. Dr; *Supervisor:* Thomas, H. Dr
Using management development packages in schools: an action research programme aimed at encouraging the wider use of school managed training materials for professional development
Abstract: The aims of the project are to: (1) evaluate different training modes when using a package of materials for management development; (2) assess these training modes using two packages from a set identified by Task Force; (3) draw lessons from the use of these materials which would contribute to the development of nationally prepared guidelines, for dissemination to schools, on the use of management development packages; (4) use the project as a means

for developing a regional support network of information and methodology on the use of packages of materials on the development of school management; (5) encourage local education authorities to support the maintenance of these networks beyond the lifetime of the project and the Task Force. The materials will be used in 10 schools, and data will be collected using interview schedule.
Published Material: THOMAS, H. (1992). Using management development packages in schools: a report on the training materials project for the West Midlands consortium of the School Management Task Force. Birmingham: Birmingham University.
Status: Sponsored project
Source of Grant: Department of Education and Science – School Management Task Force £24,000
Date of Research: 1991-1992
KEYWORDS: educational materials; management development; management in education

9/0048

School of Education, Edgbaston, Birmingham B15 2TT
021 414 3344
British Institute of Learning Disabilities, Wolverhampton Road, Kidderminster, Worcestershire DY10 3PP
0902 850251
Cook, M. Mrs; *Supervisor:* Upton, G. Prof.; Harris, J. Dr
Developing school-based services for children with severe learning difficulties and challenging behaviour
Abstract: The general aim of the project is to improve the quality of school-based services for children with severe learning difficulties who present various forms of challenging behaviour. More specifically it involves: a) collaboration with teachers and care staff in special schools for children with severe learning difficulties in the design and implementation of a range of strategies for the management and amelioration of challenging behaviour in schools; b) monitoring and evaluating different intervention strategies to identify those which can be most effectively employed in schools; and c) developing an in-service training programme which will assist teachers and other staff in working more effectively with children with challenging behaviour. The study is being carried out in two phases. In the first phase five schools are involved in the development of the intervention strategies which will be evaluated in phase two in a further five schools.
Status: Sponsored project
Source of Grant: Mental Health Foundation £62,000
Date of Research: 1992 - continuing
KEYWORDS: behaviour modification; behaviour problems; severe learning difficulties; special education teachers; special educational needs; special schools

9/0049

School of Education, Centre for Religious Education Development and Research, Edgbaston, Birmingham B15 2TT
021 414 3344
Hull, J. Prof.; Reeve, J. Miss
Cathedrals through touch and hearing
Abstract: The aim of the project is to explore the problems of presenting architecture to visually handicapped people. Cathedrals in England are being equipped with special facilites including wooden models, ground plans, tactile illustrations, cassette recordings and braille guides. The project was mainly confined to West Midlands cathedrals during 1988/89 but will work in more than 20 cathedrals nationwide during the following years. The work is sponsored by the Archbishop of York.
Published Material: HULL, J.M. (1990). Touching the rock: an experience of blindness. London SPCK (Society for the Promotion of Christian Knowledge).; HULL, J.M. (1990). 'On being a whole body seer: an epistemic condition for the education of the blind', British Journal of Visual Impairment, pp.62-63, Summer.; HULL, J.M. (1990). 'The God of the blind', The New Beacon, Vol 74, No 877, pp.200-204, June.; REEVE, J. (1991). 'Keeping in touch with cathedrals', British Journal of Visual Impairment, Autumn.
Status: Sponsored project
Source of Grant: Industrial and charitable sources £162,179
Date of Research: 1986 - continuing
KEYWORDS: architectural education; blindness; educational equipment; special educational needs; visual impairments

9/0050

School of Education, Centre for Religious Education Development and Research, Edgbaston, Birmingham B15 2TT
021 414 3344
Hull, J. Prof.
The education of the church and the pleasures of capitalism
Abstract: The project has to do with the education of the religious consciousness of adults under the conditions of industrial modernity and late capitalism. The approach is multi-disciplinary, drawing particularly upon sociology, social psychology and theology to create an understanding of the barriers to religious maturity for modern adults. Special emphasis is placed upon ideology and false consciousness, and resources are being drawn from Marxist and Freudian theory (critical theory).
Published Material: HULL, J.M. (1983). What prevents Christian adults from learning? London: SCM Press.
Status: Individual research
Date of Research: 1985 - continuing
KEYWORDS: adult education; capitalism; Christianity; church and education; religious education; secularisation

9/0051

School of Education, Edgbaston, Birmingham B15 2TT
021 414 3344
Open University, Faculty of Mathematics, Walton Hall, Milton Keynes MK7 6AA
0908 274066
Hewitt, D. Mr; *Supervisor:* Mason, J. Dr
The principle of economy in learning and teaching mathematics
Abstract: This research concerns the recognition of economy as a factor in the learning and teaching of mathematics. Economy, in this context refers to the personal use of one's time and energy in order to achieve a particular aim, ability or understanding. Very young children learn skills and develop abilities before entering the formal environment of a classroom; they learn at a rate that adults consider impressive and much of their learning remains learnt for the rest of their life. The researcher has identified aspects of the way in which young children use themselves in gaining these abilities, and compare these with ways pupils are often asked to work in mathematics classrooms. The research is mainly based on observations of children both in and out of classroom situations. Conclusions are likely to identify ways children use themselves in learning efficiently and the consequences these may have on styles of teaching mathematics.
Published Material: HEWITT, D. (1987). 'Memory', Mathematics Teaching, No 118, pp.18-20, March.; HEWITT, D. (1987). 'Gaining time', Mathematics Teaching, No 119, pp.9-11, June.; HEWITT, D. (1988). 'Fickle', Mathematics Teaching, No 125, pp.14-15, December.; HEWITT, D. (1989). 'Forcing awareness', Micromath, Vol 5, No 1, pp.27-29, Spring.
Status: Individual research
Date of Research: 1987-1992
KEYWORDS: learning theories; mathematics education; teaching methods; time factors – learning

9/0052

School of Education, Research Centre for the Education of the Visually Handicapped, Edgbaston, Birmingham B15 2TT
021 414 3344
Tobin, M. Dr; Hill, E. Mrs; *Supervisor:* Tobin, M. Dr
Visually impaired people in their mid-twenties: educational, vocational, and personal ambitions and needs
Abstract: This research forms part of a project concerning young visually handicapped people and those over the age of 60. It is a five year investigation into the changing skills, abilities, ambitions, lifestyles, and needs of such people with a visual handicap. The methodology consists of postal questionnaires, telephone and face-to-face interviews. Initially a core group of some 50 to 100 subjects will be assembled. The sample will be increased from time to time to deal with specific, *ad hoc* topics of concern to the population of visually impaired people.
Status: Sponsored project
Source of Grant: Guide Dogs for the Blind Association; Royal National Institute for the Blind; Birmingham University
Date of Research: 1990 - continuing
KEYWORDS: aspiration; lifestyle; skills; special educational needs; visual impairments; vocational education

9/0053

School of Education, Research Centre for the Education of the Visually Handicapped, Edgbaston, Birmingham B15 2TT
021 414 3344
Tobin, M. Dr; Mason, H. Ms

Speed of visual information processing

Abstract: The aim of this research is to measure the speed of visual information processing of partially sighted pupils on tasks similar to those used with their fully sighted peers. Preliminary findings have indicated a large discrepancy between the average performances of the partially sighted and the published norms for the fully sighted. Further work is now being undertaken with a larger sample of partially sighted children with a view to reducing normative data for the population of partially sighted pupils. Trials are also being conducted on a test to measure speed of tactile information processing.

Published Material: TOBIN, M.J. & MASON, H. (1986). 'Speed of information processing and the visually handicapped child', British Journal of Special Education, Vol 13, No 2, pp.69-70, June (Research Supplement).
Status: Sponsored project
Source of Grant: Birmingham University; Royal National Institute for the Blind
Date of Research: 1985 - continuing
KEYWORDS: cognitive processes; partial vision; visual impairments; visual learning

9/0054

School of Education, Research Centre for the Education of the Visually Handicapped, Edgbaston, Birmingham B15 2TT
021 414 6733
Tobin, M. Dr

Reading by the blind: Braille and Moon

Abstract: A series of experiments are being undertaken on various aspects of tactile reading by blind children and adults. Experimental comparisons are being made among alternative letter shapes with the aim of producing a more legible tactile code for older adults and for those with poor tactual ability. For Braille, measurements are being made of Braille reading speed, accuracy, and comprehension among blind school children; experimental comparisons are also being made to evaluate alternative 'papers' on to which Braille can be embossed. Trials are also being conducted on methods to enable sighted adult volunteers to teach reading and writing of Moon-type to newly-blinded adults.

Published Material: COOPER, A., DAVIES, B.T., LAWSON-WILLIAMS, N. & TOBIN, M.J. (1985). 'An examination of natural and synthetic papers for embossing Braille', The New Beacon, Vol LXIX, No 823, pp.325-328, November.; TOBIN, M.J., BURTON, P., DAVIES, B.T. & GUGGENHEIM, J. (1986). 'An experimental investigation of the effects of cell size and spacing in Braille – with some possible implications for the newly-blind adult learner', The New Beacon, Vol LXX, No 829, pp.133-135, May.; TOBIN, M.J. & HILL, E.W. (1989). 'Harnessing the community: Moonscript, the Moon-writer and sighted volunteers', British Journal of Visual Impairment, Vol VII, No 1, pp.3-5.
Status: Sponsored project
Source of Grant: Birmingham University; Royal National Institute for the Blind
Date of Research: 1985 - continuing
KEYWORDS: blindness; braille; reading teaching; sensory aids; tactile adaptation; tactual perception

9/0055

School of Education, Research Centre for the Education of the Visually Handicapped, Edgbaston, Birmingham B15 2TT
021 414 6732
Bozic, N. Mr; Campbell, S. Mr; Vallender, M. Mr;
Supervisor: Tobin, M. Dr

Development of microcomputer software for educational and vocational applications (for blind and partially sighted persons)

Abstract: The Research Centre has a programme of individual research and development projects concerned with using and adapting microcomputer technology to allow visually handicapped children and adults to have access to databases, educational materials, and word processing systems. Software has been developed so that output can be produced in Braille, large print, computer graphics and synthetic speech. Details of software are provided by means of regular newsletters, information sheets, and software documentation, all of which is available on request from the Research Centre.

Published Material: SPENCER, S. & ROSS, M. (1988). 'Visual stimulation using microcomputers', European Journal of Special Needs Education, Vol 3, No 3, pp.173-176.; SPENCER, S. & ROSS, M. (1989). 'Closing the gap, facilitating integration: microcomputer technology and the handicapped learner', Special Children, Vol 28, pp.20-21.; SPENCER, S. & ROSS, M. (1989). 'Assessing functional vision using microcomputers', British Journal of Special Education, Vol 16, No 2, Research Supplement, pp.68-70.; SPENCER, S. & ROSS, M. (1989). 'Software packages for the young visually handicapped', Special Children, No 31, pp.20-21.; BOZIC, N., TOBIN, M.J. & VALLENDER, M. (1991). 'New developments in visual stimulation', Visability, Vol 3, pp.18-19, Autumn.
Status: Sponsored project
Source of Grant: Royal National Institute for the Blind
Date of Research: 1983 - continuing
KEYWORDS: blindness; computer assisted reading; computer software; computer system design; educational materials; partial vision; visual impairments

9/0056

School of Education, Research Centre for the Education of the Visually Handicapped, Edgbaston, Birmingham B15 2TT
021 414 6732
Tobin, M. Dr

Longitudinal investigation of cognitive development and educational achievement in blind and partially sighted children

Abstract: This investigation, begun in 1973, aims to monitor aspects of the psychological and educational development of blind and partially sighted children attending special schools for the visually handicapped in England and Wales. The sample of 120 is estimated as constituting some 47% of the age group, the visual activities of the children ranging upwards from nil to 4/36 plus (as measured on the Snellen chart). The subjects are tested at least once every year by the researcher and a team of assistants. Among the major variables being measured are: (1) print and Braille reading; (2) mathematics attainment; (3) short-term memory; (4) verbal and non-verbal reasoning; (5) speed of information processing; (6) various 'Piagetian' constructs; (7) personality and self-concept. Degree of residual vision, cause of visual defect, age of onset and social class constitute some of the major independent variables.

Published Material: TOBIN, M.J. (1979). 'A longitudinal study of blind and partially sighted children in special schools in England and Wales', Insight, Vol 1, No 1, Summer.; TOBIN, M.J. (1987). 'Visually handicapped teenagers' opinions about special and mainstream schooling', The New Beacon, January.
Status: Sponsored project
Source of Grant: Birmingham University; Royal National Institute for the Blind
Date of Research: 1973 - continuing
KEYWORDS: academic achievement; blindness; cognitive development; longitudinal studies; outcomes of education; partial vision; special schools; visual impairments

9/0057

School of Education, Edgbaston, Birmingham B15 2TT
021 414 3344
Sandwell Metropolitan Borough Council, Child Guidance Centre, 12 Grange Road, West Bromwich, West Midlands B70 8PD
021 553 7411
Bovair, K. Mr; Smith, C. Mr; Watts, P. Mr; *Supervisor:* Upton, G. Prof.

Disruptive behaviour in schools: post Elton Project Sandwell Initiative

Abstract: The aim of this project is to collect quantitative and qualitative data, in order to further illuminate the nature, causes and consequences of disruptive behaviour in schools. An assessment will be made of the impact of the Elton Report (Discipline in schools: the report of the Committee of Enquiry chaired by Lord Elton. Department of Education and Science, 1989) on responses to disruptive behaviour in schools. A detailed examination of developments in one local education authority over a period of one school year will be carried out. The study will combine survey and case study analyses. The consequences of disruption will be examined in terms of school/LEA responses and subsequent pupil placements.

Status: Sponsored project
Source of Grant: Birmingham University: School of Education £2,000
Date of Research: 1991 - continuing

KEYWORDS: *antisocial behaviour; discipline; disruptive pupils; pupil behaviour; pupil placement*

9/0058
School of Psychology, Edgbaston, Birmingham B15 2TT
021 414 3344
Cochrane, R. Prof.; *Supervisor:* Bairstow, P. Dr
An evaluation of conductive education
Abstract: The Foundation for Conductive Education in conjunction with the Peto Institute in Budapest has set up a pilot project to bring the Hungarian system for treating children with cerebral palsy to Britain. An Institute has been set up in Birmingham which has admitted a number of children and trainee Conductors and exposed them to Conductive Education from 1 January 1988. A research evaluation of the effectiveness of Conductive Education in improving motor abilities, intellectual functioning and social functioning is being undertaken at the same time. Three main questions are being addressed: (1) what are the key principals underlying Conductive Education?; (2) does the Birmingham Project faithfully replicate the original Hungarian scheme of Conductive Education?; (3) does Conductive Education produce more benefits for the disabled than traditional therapies?
Status: Sponsored project
Source of Grant: Department of Education and Science £469,847
Date of Research: 1987-1992
KEYWORDS: *Cerebral Palsy; conductive education; evaluation; motor development; psychomotor skills*

9/0059
School of Psychology, Edgbaston, Birmingham B15 2TT
021 414 3344
Stones, E. Prof.
Psychology and pedagogy: investigations into the relationships between principles of psychology of human learning and practical teaching and the supervision of practical teaching in teacher training
Abstract: The work comprises a variety of investigations by experienced teachers into different aspects of pedagogy and employing different approaches. Qualitative as well quantitative data are sought for. Surveys of current practice are complemented by empirical work exploring the effects of theory based practical pedagogical intervention into the teaching of a wide variety of subjects. Experiments are predominantly naturalistic, clinical, learning based and outcome-oriented case studies involving small groups of teachers or student teachers and their pupils.
Published Material: STONES, E. (1984). Supervision in teacher education: a counselling and pedagogical approach. London: Methuen.; STONES, E. (1987). 'Teaching practice supervision: bridge between theory and practice', European Journal of Teacher Education, Vol 10, No 1, pp.67-69.; STONES, E. (1989). 'Pedagogical studies in the theory and practice of teacher education', Oxford Review of Education, Vol 15, No 1, pp.3-15.; A full list of publications is available from the researcher.
Status: Individual research
Date of Research: 1983 - continuing
KEYWORDS: *educational theories; learning theories; psychology; teacher education; teaching experience; teaching practice; teaching process*

Bishop Grosseteste College

9/0060
Newport, Lincoln LN1 3DY
0522 527347
Ducker, P. Mr; *Supervisor:* Wilson, J. Ms
Quality in initial teacher training – an examination of course structure within selected institutions
Abstract: This research involves an examination of the present initial teacher training course structure that exists within Bishop Grosseteste College and similar institutions. It will examine methods of delivery within the course, and the use of teaching staff to facilitate a more cost-effective course structure that allows a flexible arrangement (with regard to the group tutor system and the need to provide specialist inputs) within a four year BEd (Bachelor of Education) and

one year PGCE (Post Graduate Certificate of Education) programme. The research process involves action research methods through the examination of a sample of teaching groups within Bishop Grosseteste College and other institutions, the collection of data through observation and field notes, interviews, questionnaires and the use of statistical evidence from similar research, if available. The researcher aims to identify, monitor and evaluate elements which affect the quality of student-teacher education.
Status: Sponsored project
Source of Grant: Bishop Grossesteste College
Date of Research: 1991-1992
KEYWORDS: *course evaluation; education courses; education curriculum; preservice teacher education; teacher*

9/0061
Newport, Lincoln LN1 3DY
0522 527347
Liverpool University, Department of Education, PO Box 147, Liverpool L69 3BX
051 794 2000
Hopkins, S. Mr; *Supervisor:* Thomas, D. Mr
The constructs teachers use to evaluate their own classroom practice
Abstract: The research is aimed at eliciting the constructs used by primary teachers when they evaluate a teaching/learning episode as successful and/or unsuccessful. 120 teachers and 120 student teachers completed an open-ended questionnaire which was used to elicit, from a content analysis, indicators which teachers or student teachers use to categorise teaching/learning as successful and/or unsuccessful, and the influences which determine, in their view, the presence or absence of these indicators. A comparison of teachers and student teachers is related to the expert-novice literature. A model to support reflective-pedagogy, generated from the empirical findings of the study, is suggested.
Status: Sponsored project
Source of Grant: Bishop Grosseteste – Governing Body
Date of Research: 1986-1991
KEYWORDS: *performance indicators; student teachers; teacher effectiveness; teacher evaluation; teachers*

Bradford University

9/0062
Centre for Continuing Education, 12 Claremont, Bradford BD7 1DP
0274 309835
Field, J. Dr; *Supervisor:* Field, J. Dr
Lifestyle, values and educational participation among adults
Abstract: Most studies of participation in adult education focus upon socioeconomic and demographic factors, such as social class, age or gender. However, participation rates also vary widely within categories, and this study is concerned to discover whether lifestyle patterns can be related to educational participation among the adult population. Two major methods will be used to explore the extent to which educational participation can be explained with reference to life cycle patterns. They are: (a) surveys of adult learners in personal development courses and in craft-based courses, using an established lifestyle analysis; and (b) semi-structured interviews to explore the degree of inner-directedness within adult learners' value systems, and to investigate the role of material factors in influencing decisions to participate. Outcomes will be analysed using a conceptual framework that will draw upon the work of Pierre Bourdieu as well as of market research theorists and critics of post-modernist sociology.
Published Material: FIELD, J. (1991). 'Out of the adult hut: Institutionalisation, individuality and new values in the education of adults'. In: RAGGATT, P. & UNWIN, L. (Eds). Change and intervention: vocational education and training. London: Falmer Press.
Status: Individual research
Date of Research: 1992 - continuing
KEYWORDS: *adult education; lifestyle; participation*

9/0063
Centre for Continuing Education, 12 Claremont, Bradford BD7 1DP

0274 309835
Warwick University, Faculty of Educational Studies,
Department of Continuing Education, Continuing Education
Research Centre, Coventry CV4 7AL
0203 523523
University of Wroclaw, Instytut Pedagogiki, 50 527
Wroclaw, Poland
Field, J. Dr; *Supervisor:* Field, J. Dr; Duke, C. Prof.

Active citizenship and adult learning

Abstract: Questions of citizenship are high on the political agenda, and are controversial conceptually. In Britain, initiatives such as the Speakers' Commission report 'Encouraging Citizenship', and the Guidance Note on 'Education for Citizenship' issued by the National Curriculum Council have sought to promote active citizenship through the formal schooling system. At the same time, developments within the framework of the European Community, and changes in the systems of government in Eastern and Central Europe, have highlighted the cognitive, behavioural and attitudinal prerequisites of active participation in public debate and decision-making among the adult population. This project is concerned to examine citizenship within the adult education curriculum; learning within citizen movements; and the changing relation between civil society and state as manifested through the governance of the education system. Within the British context, this involves a series of case studies of citizen organisations (Women's' Institute, Credit Union Movement, Amnesty International, Greenpeace support groups, Neighbourhood Watch, Football Supporters' Association) and of measures designed to delegate powers over the educational system (community education). Interviews with those involved are being supplemented by observation, literature review and small-scale surveys. Comparative studies are being conducted in Poland, through the University of Wroclaw; negotiations are under way for a further comparative study in Sweden, conducted through the University of Linkoping as part of its inquiry into 'The Swedish Study Circle in the Year 2002'.
Published Material: FIELD, J. (Ed). (1991). Active Citizens as adult learners. University of Warwick.; PAYNE, J. (1991). Adult learning and active citizenship in Inner London. University of Warwick.; FIELD, J. (1991). 'Questions about research that makes a difference', Convergence, Vol XXIV, No 3, pp.71-78.
Status: Sponsored project
Source of Grant: Universities Funding Council £43,000; Tempus, European Community £1,230
Date of Research: 1990 - continuing
KEYWORDS: *adult education; citizenship education; community education; comparative education*

9/0064
Department of Social & Economic Studies, Richmond Road,
Bradford BD7 1DP
0274 733466
Neville, C. Mr; *Supervisor:* Glandon, N. Dr

The experience of working class men in further and higher education

Abstract: The research aims to explore the backgrounds and motivations of working-class men who choose to return to non-vocational education via Access Courses. It will explore their experiences on the Access Courses, particularly how they deal with topics that may challenge or threaten their self-images, e.g. gender/race. It will chart their progress from Access Course into higher education and explore changes in values/attitudes that may result. The research will attempt to summarise the range of traits and motivations for study displayed by the same group. The methods include a survey of all Access students in West Yorkshire via questionnaires to highlight gender differences; discussion with Access Course tutors; and individual/group discussion with male Access students. The results may have implications for (a) marketing Access Courses and (b) teaching mixed groups of adults.
Status: Individual research
Date of Research: 1991 - continuing
KEYWORDS: *Access programmes; educational experience; mature students; men; motivation; working class*

9/0065
Management Centre, Emm Lane, Bradford BD9 4JL
0274 733466
Holmes, G. Ms; *Supervisor:* Gilding, D. Dr; Peacock, A. Dr;
Welford, R. Dr

Learning resource centres for executive development

Abstract: This project will develop and evaluate different forms of flexible delivery of management education, that allow structured self-learning. A pilot 'Learning Resource Centre' will be established with an industrial partner. The project will study: (1) the place of student centred learning in the management development process; (2) the design and production of suitable modules of learning material; (3) the 'learning and technology' required; (4) the physical facilities needed; (5) the management of learning resource centres.
Status: Sponsored project
Source of Grant: Bradford University £60,000
Date of Research: 1991 - continuing
KEYWORDS: *educational technology; learner-centred methods; learning resources centre; management development; management studies*

9/0066
Management Centre, Emm Lane, Bradford BD9 UJL
0274 733466
Marsland, J. Mr

Comparison of examination results of Business Studies students who have/have not intercalated a year to see if the extramural experience affects results

Abstract: This research is a comparison of the results of courses run by the Management Centre at Bradford University. For several years the department has run both traditional and 'sandwich' undergraduate courses in parallel. Direct comparison of results from the two is difficult since the syllabuses are not identical. However, in recent years an appreciable number (10-15%) of the three-year course students have voluntarily intercalated a year of industrial experience. Examination marks and degree classifications will be examined to see whether performance in the final year of the course is affected by the break for practical experience.
Status: Individual research
Date of Research: 1989 - continuing
KEYWORDS: *attendance patterns; business education; course evaluation; examination results; outcomes of education; sandwich courses; undergraduate study*

Bristol University

9/0067
School of Education, Centre for Assessment Studies, 22
Berkeley Square, Bristol BS8 1JA
0272 251537
Grant, M. Dr; Came, F. Mr; Bowker, P. Mr; Noble, J. Mrs

Special educational needs and the GCSE

Abstract: A programme of research and development work will review the efficacy of existing General Certificate of Secondary Education (GCSE) provision for pupils with special educational needs and low-attaining pupils, and show how better access to assessment and certification can be achieved. In September 1991, the project was expanded to include approaches adopted by a sample of examining bodies, other than GCSE examining groups, to provision made for pupils with special educational needs. Methods to be used include a questionnaire survey of 55 mainstream schools in England and Wales; interviews in 30 special schools; interviews with a range of representatives of examining groups, examining bodies, special educational needs (SEN) interest groups/interested parties and in depth research and development work in two case study local education authorities (LEAs). The research report will identify developments in practice which have improved opportunities for pupils with special educational needs to gain accreditation at 16+. The report will be accompanied by support materials designed to provide techniques and procedures through which teachers and examiners can monitor and improve aspects of their assessment strategies. The project centres upon five National Curriculum subjects: English; mathematics; science; technology; and geography.
Status: Sponsored project
Source of Grant: School Examinations and Assessment Council £340,000
Date of Research: 1991 - continuing
KEYWORDS: *assessment; examinations; general certificate of secondary education; low achievement; special educational needs*

9/0068

School of Education, 35 Berkeley Square, Bristol BS8 1JA
0272 303030
Acker, S. Dr; Hill, T. Mr; Black, E. Ms
Students, supervisors and the social science research training process
Abstract: This project is one of four qualitative studies funded by the Economic and Social Research Council to investigate the experiences of research students in social science departments. The project's theoretical contributions will be to greater understanding of the social science research student supervision process, through collecting data on policies, practices, experiences and expectations from both students and supervisors. The supervisor-student relationship is conceptualised as a teaching-learning interaction embedded in a framework of contextual factors, including structures and cultures of departments and disciplines. An additional anticipated outcome is a practical contribution to academic staff development. In the British model of social science graduate education the supervisor plays a key role, yet training for supervisors is minimal. This project will help discover from experienced supervisors what, in their opinion, is 'good practice' and from less experienced ones, what they would like to learn. The main part of the study will consist of in depth interviews with a sample of supervisors and research students in eight or nine departments. A particular focus will be upon the disciplines of psychology and education, although several other subjects will be represented. The approach is qualitative; the data will be combed for themes with the aid of a suitable microcomputer and software package.
Status: Sponsored project
Source of Grant: Economic and Social Research Council £36,972
Date of Research: 1990-1991
KEYWORDS: *graduate study; social science research; student research; supervision*

9/0069

School of Education, Centre for Assessment Studies,
22 Berkeley Square, Bristol BS8 1JA
0272 303030
Squirrell, G. Ms; *Supervisor:* Broadfoot, P. Prof.
Youth Development Projects
Abstract: Forty seven Youth Development (YDPs) have been funded by the Employment Department for a three year period 1989-1992. These YDPs were funded to develop increased awareness of working life, enhanced careers guidance and higher level skills. The overall aim for all YDPs was to consider mechanisms for, and the barriers to, increasing the coherence of young people's experiences of the various sectors of education, training and employment. The YDPs are run and delivered by Careers Service staff, school and college teachers, training providers and employers. The young people involved are aged 14 – 19 taking mainstream school, college and training courses and those receiving special education and training needs provision.
Published Material: SQUIRRELL, G. (1991). Individual action planning: development work with 14-19 year olds. CAS/TEED.; SQUIRRELL, G. (1991). Youth Development Project Directory. TEED.; SQUIRRELL, G. (1992). Report on the Youth Development Project Initiative, TEED.
Status: Sponsored project
Source of Grant: Department of Employment
Date of Research: 1989-1992
KEYWORDS: *career education; school to work transition; youth opportunities; youth programmes*

9/0070

School of Education, Centre for Assessment Studies,
22 Berkeley Square, Bristol BS8 1JA
0272 303030
Squirrell, G. Ms; *Supervisor:* Broadfoot, P. Prof.
Piloting the personal competence model in secondary schools
Abstract: The project is in two phases. The first is concerned with evaluating the method of implementation and accessibility of a Model of Personal Competence commissioned by the Employment Department. This phase lasts from July 1991 to May 1992. During the second phase from May 1992 to August 1992 training and guidance materials for school staff and pupils will be written. The guidance materials arise from the findings of the early pilot project. Nine schools in England and Scotland are piloting the Model with young people in years 10 -13. The Model is used within pupils pursuing a personal and social education programme, general studies per-em-ployment and Certificate of Pre-Vocational Education (CPVE). The research process is that of formative evaluation. A case study of implementation is being compiled for each institution piloting the Model. The Model aims to encourage greater personal effectiveness in young people in a number of areas; for example, handling emotions and stress, making effective use of information and getting on well with others. Four parallel projects are also piloting the Model in other educational institutions in further and higher education and with a number of employers.
Status: Sponsored project
Source of Grant: Department of Employment
Date of Research: 1991-1992
KEYWORDS: *affective education; competence; individual development; social skills*

9/0071

School of Education, Centre for Assessment Studies,
22 Berkeley Square, Bristol BS8 1JA
0272 303030
Bristol Polytechnic, Department of Education, Redland Primary Centre, Redland Hill, Bristol BS6 6UZ
0272 741251
Osborn, M. Ms; Abbott, D. Ms; *Supervisor:* Broadfoot, P. Prof.; Pollard, A. Prof.; Croll, P. Prof.
Primary assessment, curriculum and experience
Abstract: The project aims to describe and analyse the responses of pupils and teachers in infant schools and infant departments to the National Curriculum and related innovations. This includes a consideration of the views of headteachers and teachers of the new reforms and their impact on the school and, in particular, an analysis and evaluation of the development of strategies for change. The study aims to contribute to theoretical perspectives on teacher professionalism and on the control and impact of educational change. It is designed also to consider the impact of the National Curriculum on the curriculum and pedagogy of the infant school. Issues of teacher aims and expectations, curriculum content and time allocation, teaching methods and pupil classroom experience, are being addressed. As well as considering the impact of the National Curriculum on teachers and pupils, the study will provide baseline data on contemporary infant practice. The project will also evaluate materials in action and their impact on pupils. The operation of the assessments in classrooms will be studied and pupil responses to the assessment tasks considered. Conflicting claims about pupil perceptions of, and reactions to, being tested are being considered. The research involves interviews with 150 teachers drawn from 48 schools in 8 local education authorities plus four rounds of detailed classroom studies in a sub-sample of nine classrooms to study curriculum change and pupil experience in more depth. Classroom studies are also being conducted during the implementation of the first unreported and reported Standard Assessment Tasks in these nine schools.
Published Material: BROADFOOT, P., ABBOTT, D., CROLL, P., OSBORN, M. & POLLARD, A. (1991). 'The conduct and effectiveness of primary school assessment', (PACE Working Paper 6), AERA Conference, Chicago.; BROADFOOT, P., ABBOTT, D., CROLL, P., OSBORN, M., POLLARD, A. & TOWLER, L. (1991). 'Implementing national assessment: issues for primary teachers', Cambridge Journal of Education, Vol 21, No 2.; POLLARD, A., OSBORN, M., ABBOTT, D., BROADFOOT, P. & CROLL, P. 'The child's place in a conflict of interests'. In: ASPE Conference Papers. (forthcoming).; BROADFOOT, P., ABBOTT, D., CROLL, P., OSBORN, M. & POLLARD, A. (1991). 'Look back in anger? Primary teachers' experience of SATs', (PACE Working Paper 8).; POLLARD, A. 'Balancing priorities: children and curriculum in the 90's. In: CAMPBELL, R.J. (Ed). Breadth and balance in the primary curriculum. London: Falmer Press.
Status: Sponsored project
Source of Grant: Economic and Social Research Council £149,973
Date of Research: 1989 - continuing
KEYWORDS: *educational change; infant school curriculum; infant school education; National Curriculum; primary school curriculum; standard assessment tasks*

9/0072

School of Education, National Development Centre for Education Management and Policy, 35 Berkeley Square, Bristol BS8 1JA
0272 303030
Wallace, M. Dr; *Supervisor:* Bolam, R. Dr

Planning for change in multiracial primary schools
Abstract: The aim of this research is: (1) to explore how multiracial schools in the primary sector plan to implement multiple innovations in a context of cultural diversity; and (2) to identify the processes and procedures which appear to be effective. Planning for change is likely to be especially problematic in a situation where different groups in the local community have different expectations about the direction for school development. The research will be conducted in 3 local education authorities. In each LEA headteachers of 8 schools will be interviewed and case studies will be carried out in 2 of these schools.
Status: Sponsored project
Source of Grant: Leverhulme Trust £55,000
Date of Research: 1990-1992
KEYWORDS: educational administration; educational change; educational innovation; educational planning; multicultural education; primary schools

9/0073
School of Education, National Development Centre for Educational Management & Policy, 35 Berkeley Square, Bristol BS8 1JA
0272 303030
Bolam, R. Dr; McMahon, A. Ms; Pocklington, K. Mr; Weindling, R. Mr ; *Supervisor:* Bolam, R. Dr
Models of effective management in schools
Abstract: The research will aim to: (i) identify examples of management structures and processes which staff of these schools have recognised as effective practice; (ii) identify international comparisons of management structures and processes which add to our understanding of effective practice. The research falls into two distinct phases. Phase 1 is a questionnaire survey of staff in a sample of 40 primary and 20 secondary schools. In Phase 2, 12 of these schools will be selected for detailed case study. Information about international school management structures and processes will be gathered mainly through a review of the relevant literature.
Status: Sponsored project
Source of Grant: Department of Education and Science – School Management Task Force £31,506
Date of Research: 1991-1992
KEYWORDS: educational administration; management in education; school effectiveness; school organisation

9/0074
School of Education, National Development Centre for Educational Management & Policy, 35 Berkeley Square, Bristol BS8 1JA
0272 303030
Wallace, M. Dr; *Supervisor:* Bolam, R. Dr
The role of the senior management team in secondary schools
Abstract: The aim of this research is to examine how senior management teams manage secondary schools within a context of educational reform and to identify approaches to teamwork which appear to be effective. Senior managers in secondary schools may face a greater need than hitherto to co-ordinate their work so as to effectively orchestrate the implementation of multiple innovations. The research will be conducted in two local education authorities (LEAs). In each LEA, case studies were carried out during the summer of 1991 in 3 schools where all members of the senior management team express a strong commitment to teamwork. A longitudinal case study will be undertaken in 1 of these schools.
Status: Sponsored project
Source of Grant: Economic and Social Research Council £57,000
Date of Research: 1991 - continuing
KEYWORDS: educational administration; educational change; management teams; school-based management; secondary schools

Brunel University

9/0075
Centre for the Study of Human Learning, Uxbridge UB8 3PH
0895 274000
Kingston University, Faculty of Education, Kingston Hill Centre, Kingston Hill, Kingston upon Thames KT2 7LB
081 549 1141

Johnson, G. Mr; *Supervisor:* Harri-Augstein, S. Mrs; Thomas, L. Prof.
Teaching competence – a personal construct investigation
Abstract: The research involves the elicitation of personal constructs of teaching competencies from teacher training staff and students with a view to re-designing teaching/school experience criteria for assessment. The major research tool is repertory grids and feedback for learning programmes linked to learning conversations between staff (c.12) and students (c.50).
Status: Individual research
Date of Research: 1990 - continuing
KEYWORDS: competence; competency-based teacher education; discussion – teaching technique; personal construct theory; repertory grid tests; teacher effectiveness

9/0076
Department of Education and Design, Runnymede Campus, Englefield Green, Egham TW20 0JZ
0784 431341
Reid, J. Mrs; *Supervisor:* Thomas, J. Mr; Down, B. Dr
The effectiveness of implementing a multicultural and antiracist education
Abstract: The research reviews the effective changes in school practices of the LEAs (local education authorities) policies. It traces the changing trends and concerns regarding the amount of take-up, the process and impact of which are qualitatively and quantitatively assessed. The research objectives are threefold. First, to establish what is recognized as multicultural and antiracist education in local education authorities and schools. Second, to establish whether there are differences in provisions between the LEAs and schools and third, whether multicultural and antiracist education practices at the primary level help the performances/achievements at secondary level. The introductory section, a historical perspective, discusses the rise of multicultural and antiracist education awareness. Issues on prejudices and institutional racism are included. A survey of the literature and a review of other researches are undertaken in order to base the similarities and differences of this research. The investigation is three dimensional, analysing the LEAs policies, the primary and secondary schools policies and comparing/contrasting the schools objectives according to needs. The methodologies are ethnographic – the 'involved' observer, questionnaires and interviews. The implications of the Education Reform Act 1988 are also discussed, particularly equal opportunity and education for all in relation to cross-curricular dimensions – is it a policy which will permeate an education for a multicultural society? The results are assessed and the outcomes discussed and summarized according to the underlying hypothesis – have LEAs and schools policies effected positive changes?
Status: Individual research
Date of Research: 1988-1992
KEYWORDS: antiracism education; educational policy; equal education; local education authorities; multicultural education

9/0077
Department of Education and Design, Runnymede Campus, Englefield Green, Egham TW20 0JZ
0784 431341
Jonietz, P. Mrs; *Supervisor:* Harris, N. Prof.
International education in international schools: developing a consensus of opinion
Abstract: This research explores how international schools appear diverse in location, size, population, funding and governing body, but are similar in goals, objectives, and curricula. It will then enquire whether teachers, administrators, and parents can reach consensus on the thesis that international schools establish an educational system because they are similar to each other and different from national systems. Schools in Frankfurt, London, and Washington, D.C. each serve as research sites. This is because they each have a well established community base, an experienced multinational faculty, a multinational, multicultural student body, English as the language of instruction, and European Council of International Schools accreditation. They have also adopted the International Baccalaureate diploma to cut across cultures and boundaries. The research employs triangulation through archive review, interviews, and questionnaires to demonstrate consensus on how these international schools are related to traditional definitions of international education, as well as to a larger organizational system of international education.
Status: Individual research
Date of Research: 1987-1992

KEYWORDS: *intercultural programmes; international baccalaureate; international education; international schools; multicultural education*

9/0078

Department of Government, Uxbridge UB8 3PH
0895 274000
Bennett, N. Dr; *Supervisor:* Kogan, M. Prof.
The implementation of local education authority curriculum policies in two metropolitan authorities
Abstract: This study examines the impact of local education authority (LEA) curriculum policies on teachers' practice in two metropolitan LEAs, working from literature on policy-making and implementation, curriculum theory and school improvement. 66 teachers in 6 schools, 3 from each LEA, discussed in extended semi-structured interviews the influences they took account of, or were aware of as an influence, when deciding on programmes of study, setting work or working in the classroom. The 6 headteachers and the 2 LEA Chief Inspectors were also interviewed. The sample of teachers was stratified by seniority and subject area, and balanced so far as possible for gender across seniority. The schools were selected as 'matched pairs' across the LEAs, which were themselves selected for their comparable size, location, and sociopolitical character. LEA curriculum policies were found to have little impact, due to their general character but more importantly to the low professional status and lack of policing authority of their advisers/inspectors. Public examinations were more important, and had caused major reviews of departmental and individual practice. Parental interest in examination results was seen to have influenced this. Most significant were internal school factors. Departmental characteristics influenced its importance and impact as a basic unit of institutional allegiance. The degree of trust between senior and junior staff affected how far teachers would surrender their perceived classroom privacy, autonomy and discretion. The study concludes that external requirements need strong policing or strong internal support if they are to have a significant impact on teacher practice.
Status: Individual research
Date of Research: 1984-1991
KEYWORDS: *curriculum development; educational planning; local education authorities; teaching process*

9/0079

Department of Government, Uxbridge UB8 3PH
0895 274000
Sussex University, Institute of Continuing and Professional Education, Sussex House, Falmer, Brighton BN1 9RH
0273 606755
Kogan, M. Prof.; Becher, R. Prof.; Henkel, M. Ms
Graduate education in the United Kingdom
Abstract: The research concerns developments in British higher education at two levels. The recent history of the policy of graduate education is reviewed with a view to creating a policy analysis in which the conflicting objectives of graduate education are analysed; the governmental machinery for generating policy in graduate education described; and the relationship between graduate education and staffing of higher education put under scrutiny. This part of the study leads to the critique of existing policies and proposals for its improvement. The second level of the study is that of micro-analyses of graduate education in different disciplinary areas. The analysis includes a summation of the essential characteristics of the discipline concerned, the way in which it recruits its students, the extent to which there is pre-requisite structured training before research is undertaken; the expectations within the discipline, and the relationship between graduate training and recruitment for higher education staffing and cognate professions. The methods involved are a study of secondary sources and interviews at both levels.
Published Material: CLARK, R.B. The research foundations of graduate education. Los Angeles: University of California. (forthcoming).
Status: Sponsored project
Source of Grant: The Nuffield Foundation
Date of Research: 1991-1992
KEYWORDS: *educational policy; graduate study; higher education*

9/0080

Department of Human Sciences, Uxbridge UB8 3PH
0895 56461

Stafford, C. Dr
Education and the family in Taiwan and China
Abstract: Anthropological fieldwork was carried out in Taiwan to investigate the relationship between families and the state. Particular attention was paid to education and to family religion as competing discourses within a small fishing village. The schools promote identification with the nation, and encourage sacrifice to the point of martyrdom for national goals. Families, through religious practices involving spirit mediums, seek to protect children from all harm for the sake of the family goals. The researcher is in the process of writing articles based on this fieldwork, and in the next year will expand the project to include material from mainland China.
Published Material: STAFFORD, C. (1992). 'Good sons and virtuous mothers: kinship and Chinese nationalism in Taiwan', MAN, June. (forthcoming).
Status: Sponsored project
Source of Grant: Wenner-gren Foundation £4,286; Taiwan History Field Research Project £7,143; University of London Central Research Fund £1,000
Date of Research: 1991 - continuing
KEYWORDS: *family life; nationalism; religion; state schools*

9/0081

Department of Human Sciences, Uxbridge UB8 3PH
0895 56461
Richardson, J. Prof.
Cognitive processes in student learning
Abstract: Over the last 20 years, cognitive psychologists have made considerable advances in the development of theories of human learning and memory. Nevertheless, it is commonplace that such models cannot easily encompass the sort of learning that occurs in real life situations. During the same period, researchers into higher education have carefully investigated the knowledge and skills relevant to a variety of academic disciplines. Their findings have major implications for policy and practice in higher education, but they need to be interpreted within clearly articulated models of the cognitive processes underlying student learning. This research attempts to integrate these two areas of investigation. It will provide cognitive psychologists with a rich and qualitatively different body of evidence against which to evaluate the validity and generality of their theories of human learning and development; it will provide researchers into higher education with sophisticated theoretical descriptions of the strategies and processes employed in academic contexts; and it will provide teachers in higher education with statements of the practical applications of this research.
Published Material: RICHARDSON, J.T.E. (1983). 'Student learning in higher education', Educational Psychology, Vol 3, Nos 3 & 4, pp.305-311.; RICHARDSON, J.T.E., EYSENCK, M.W. & PIPER, W.D. (Eds.) (1987). Student learning: research in education and cognitive psychology. Guildford: SRHE & Open University Press.
Status: Individual research
Date of Research: 1983 - continuing
KEYWORDS: *cognitive processes; cognitive psychology; epistemology; higher education; learning processes; memory*

9/0082

Faculty of Social Sciences, Uxbridge UB8 3PH
0895 274000
Cave, M. Prof.; Hanney, S. Mr; Kogan, M. Prof.
Performance measurement in higher education
Abstract: Against a background of growing interest in output and performance measurement in higher education (and the public sector in general) a need emerged for a critical analysis of the developing policy and practice being encouraged by the Government. The aims included: (i) to make a systematic and critical survey of the existing literature of performance indicators for higher education, within the context of more general literature of performance indicators; (ii) to analyse the range of models of performance indicators that might be applied. The literature review covered official reports and considerable material on subjects (including first destinations, bibliometrics and student evaluations of teaching) not specifically developed within the context of performance indicators (PIs). Some came from North America. The analysis therefore focused on how far it was appropriate to adopt this material to produce PIs which met the various criteria identified as being important in any successful model of PIs. The research revealed weaknesses in the set of PIs that the Committee of Vice Chancellors and Principals and University Grants Committee had been persuaded to propose. However, provided PIs were de-

veloped for both the major functions of higher education – teaching and research – the analysis concluded they had a potential role within models of evaluation at several levels including: (i) the funding body which makes inter-institutional comparisons; (ii) the institutions, where detailed and planning budgeting occurs. The research has continued to monitor and analyse the rapid expansion of policy and practice in performance measurement in the United Kingdom and other western countries.
Published Material: CAVE, M., HANNEY, S., KOGAN, M. & TREVETT, G. (1988). The use of performance indicators in higher education: a critical analysis of developing practice. London: Jessica Kingsley.; CAVE, M., KOGAN, M. & HANNEY, S. (1989). 'Performance measurement in higher education', Public Money and Management, Vol 9, No 1, pp.11-16, Spring.; CAVE, M., KOGAN, M. & HANNEY, S. (1990). 'The scope and effects of performance measurement in British higher education'. In: DOCHY, F. et al (Eds). Management information and performance indicators in higher education: an international issue. Van Gorcum.; CAVE, M. & HANNEY, S. (1990). 'Performance indicators for higher education and research'. In: CAVE, M., KOGAN, M. & SMITH, R. (Eds). Output and performance measurement in government: the state of the art. London: Jessica Kingsley.
Status: Sponsored project
Source of Grant: Brunel University £5,900
Date of Research: 1986-1991
KEYWORDS: higher education; performance indicators

Cambridge University

9/0083
Department of Experimental Psychology, Downing Site, Downing Street, Cambridge CB2 3EB
0223 333550
Goswami, U. Dr
Vowel sounds in reading
Abstract: The aim of this research is to discover whether a child's awareness of the linguistic units of the onset (initial consonants) and the rime (vowel and final consonants) affects learning about vowels in reading. The first phase of the project involved recognition of common vowels in spoken words when the vowel was either part of the rime (tap, LEG, pack), or constituted the entire rime (tree, flee, CLUE). 5- and 6-year-old children found it more difficult to recognise shared vowels within rimes, suggesting that it is hard to distinguish the vowel sound independently of the context provided by the final consonant/s. The second phase will test whether this recognition problem is reflected in learning to recognise vowel sounds in reading. The prediction was that shared vowels would be learned where rimes were common between words (e.g. beak-peak), but not where the vowel was shared but the rime differs (e.g. beak-heap). This prediction was found to hold true at all ages (5-, 6- and 7-year-olds).
Status: Sponsored project
Source of Grant: Spencer Post-Doctoral Fellowship, The Spencer Foundation, USA £; 21,429
Date of Research: 1990-1992
KEYWORDS: phonetics; reading research; reading skills; vowels

9/0084
Institute of Education, Shaftesbury Road, Cambridge CB2 2BX
0223 69631
Southworth, G. Mr
Management information services
Abstract: The objectives of the study were to discover how staff in schools were encountering and responding to information technology and its impact on school management: to analyse and report the main finding emerging from this data; and to outline some conclusion and directions for further investigation. The study investigated headteachers' and secretaries' views concerning Management Information Services (MIS) in a sample of 20 small primary schools across East Anglia. Research was undertaken by 4 fieldworkers using structured interviews. The study focused on equipment, training and support, problems and challenges, in-school effects, financial and school management. Emerging themes were lack of storage space: the isolation of school secretaries; problems of finding sufficient time to

familiarise oneself with the equipment; the way implementation relies upon the goodwill of the secretary, changing role and responsibility of the secretary and, to a lesser degree, the headteacher.
Published Material: SOUTHWORTH, G. (1991). Management Information Services for small primary schools: a report for School Management Task Force. Chelmsford: East Anglia Regional Curriculum.
Status: Sponsored project
Source of Grant: Department of Education and Science £5,340
Date of Research: 1991-1991
KEYWORDS: headteachers; management information systems; office atuomation; school organisation; school secretaries

9/0085
Institute of Education, Shaftesbury Road, Cambridge
CB2 2BX
0223 69631
Ainscow, M. Mr; Hopkins, D. Dr; Southworth, G. Mr; West, M. Mr
Improving the quality of education for all
Abstract: The aim of this study is to prodce and evaluate a model of school development, and a programme of support, that strengthens a schools' ability to provide quality education for all its pupils. Currently the project involves 25 schools in the South East of England and in Yorkshire. The team from Cambridge provide training and support for school coordinators who, in turn, support project activities in other schools. Current research questions are: (1) What strategies facilitate policy development in schools?; (2) what are the social experiences that characterise the cultures of 'moving schools'?; (3) What is the impact of our intervention? Work is also going on to explore new methodologies to map the process of change in schools.
Published Material: AINSCOW, M. & HOPKINS, D. (1992). 'Aboard the 'moving school'', Educational Leadership, Vol 50, No 3, pp.79-83.; HOPKINS, D., AINSCOW, M. & WEST, M. (1993). School improvement in an era of change. Poole: Cassell. (in press).
Status: Sponsored project
Source of Grant: Local Education Authority contributions; Participating schools; Cambridge University: Institute of Education
Date of Research: 1990 - continuing
KEYWORDS: educational improvement; educational innovation; educational quality; school effectiveness

9/0086
Institute of Education, Shaftesbury Road, Cambridge
CB2 2BX
0223 69631
Ainscow, M. Mr
Special needs in the classroom
Abstract: The aim of this project is to develop and disseminate teacher education materials that can be used to help student teachers and experienced teachers cater for pupil diversity in mainstream schools. The research involves an international resource team. Intensive action research was carried out in 1990-91 in 8 countries. This has led to the development of a resource pack, video programmes and a coordinators guide. On the basis of this formative research the materials are now being used in over 30 countries. Major national action research projects involving the project materials and ideas are currently underway in China, India, Spain and Thailand. Developments are also being introduced in the Middle East, South America and Africa. All of these developments involve further action research to refine the theoretical basis of the materials.
Published Material: AINSCOW, M. (1990). 'Special needs in the classroom: the development of teacher education resource pack', International Journal of Special Education, Vol 5, No 1, pp.13-20.; AINSCOW, M. (1993). 'Teacher education as a strategy for developing inclusive schools'. In: SLEE, R. (Ed). The politics of integration. London: Falmer Press.; AINSCOW, M. (1993). 'Teacher development and special needs: some lessons from the UNESCO project 'Special needs in the classroom''. In: MITTLER, P. et al (Eds). World yearbook of education. London: Kogan Page.; AINSCOW, M. (1993). Special needs in the classroom: a teacher education guide. Paris: UNESCO.
Status: Sponsored project
Source of Grant: UNESCO
Date of Research: 1988 - continuing
KEYWORDS: comparative education; educational materials; mainstreaming; special educational needs; teacher education

9/0087

Institute of Education, Shaftesbury Road, Cambridge CB2 2BX
0223 69631
James, M Dr; Conner, C. Dr

Moderation at National Curriculum Key Stage 1 across four local education authorities in 1992

Abstract: The study was intended to focus upon the moderation of National Curriculum assessment at Key Stage One in four local education authorities (LEAs) in the Eastern Region, particularly addressing the issues of consistency and standards. Two moderators in each of the four LEAs were observed being trained, whilst training in their 'moderation schools' and during school visits. Interviews were undertaken with moderators, teachers and headteachers in the schools visited. The evidence suggests that one of the major difficulties moderators faced was how to interpret and balance the various expectations placed upon them. Particular concern emerged regarding reliability and validity. Unless National Curriculum assessment is demonstrably reliable and valid it will have very little credibility and value. Current governmental concern stresses consistency (reliability) yet gives insufficient attention to the arguably more important question of validity.
Published Material: JAMES, M. & CONNER, C. (1993). 'Are reliability and validity achievable in National Curriculum assessment? Some observations on moderation at Key Stage One in 1992', The Curriculum Journal, Vol 4, No 1, Spring.
Status: Sponsored project
Source of Grant: Four local education authorities, jointly £14,000
Date of Research: 1991-1992
KEYWORDS: *assessment; moderation – marking; National Curriculum; reliability; school-based assessment; validity*

9/0088

Institute of Education, Shaftesbury Road, Cambridge CB2 2BX
0223 69631
Ainscow, M. Mr; Hart, S. Ms

Developing successful learning

Abstract: This is an action research project which is seeking to develop effective approaches to school-based staff development. The work was prompted by concerns about how to support teachers in meeting the needs of all pupils within the National Curriculum. Specifically the research is exploring the use of partnerships within which teachers support one another in reflecting upon and developing their professional practice. Currently the findings of the research are now being introduced into a further group of schools using materials that have been developed. Experience so far suggests that adopting a partnership approach to professional development helps to create a collaborative culture in schools.
Published Material: AINSCOW, M. & HART, S. (1992). 'Moving practice forward', Support for Learning, Vol 7, No 3, pp.115-120.
Status: Sponsored project
Source of Grant: Bedfordshire Local Education Authority; Sharnbrook School ; Samuel Whitbread School; Cambridge University: Institute of Education
Date of Research: 1990 - continuing
KEYWORDS: *cooperative learning; staff development; teacher development*

9/0089

Institute of Education, Shaftesbury Road, Cambridge CB2 2BX
0223 69631
Gibson, R. Dr; *Supervisor:* Gibson, R. Dr

Shakespeare: from school to higher education

Abstract: A study of the continuity of the Shakespeare experience of students moving from school, sixth form college or further education into higher education. The research arises out of the work of the Shakespeare and Schools project based at the University of Cambridge, Institute of Education. A considerate amount of data has been collected for the period 1986-1993. This will be analysed together with data on teaching methods and students' experience in the period April 1993-July 1994.
Published Material: GIBSON, R. (1993). 'Teaching Shakespeare'. In: BRINDLEY, S. et al (Eds). Teaching English. Milton Keynes: Open University Press.; GIBSON, R. (1993). 'A black day will it be to somebody', Cambridge Journal of Education, Vol 23, No 1, (in press).
Status: Individual research
Date of Research: 1992 - continuing
KEYWORDS: *developmental continuity; English literature; higher education; sixteen to nineteen education; teaching methods*

9/0090

Institute of Education, Shaftesbury Road, Cambridge CB2 2BX
0223 69631
Dadds, M. Dr

The nature and use of the enquiry project in short award-bearing courses for primary school teachers

Abstract: The research is exploring the variety of classroom and school development issues upon which primary school teachers focus when conducting their self-chosen project on short courses at the Cambridge Institute of Education. The research is also studying the practical links that teachers make between their self-chosen projects and the work of colleagues in their schools where links are being made, the research looks at the demands which this places on the inservice teachers as disseminators and change agents. It is seeking to understand what knowledge, personal skills, personal qualities and competencies are needed for teachers to make successful links. The research also seeks to identify factors within the inservice course and the school that support, or hinder, teachers in these demands. Questionnaires have raised data from students on four short award-bearing courses. Follow-up interviews with a small sample of teachers are being conducted over a period of a year. Interviews will be sought with a small sample of colleagues in the inservice teachers' schools.
Status: Sponsored project
Source of Grant: Cambridge University: Institute of Education £3,530
Date of Research: 1992 - continuing
KEYWORDS: *inservice teacher education; primary school teachers; teacher development*

9/0091

Institute of Education, Shaftesbury Road, Cambridge CB2 2BX
0223 69631
Bradley, H. Mr

Evaluation of a mentor scheme for headteachers

Abstract: There are three phases, containing 16, 32 and 96 mentor/mentee pairs respectively. By questionnaire and interview, the mentors are followed through their training. Then by interview of a sample of both mentors and mentees, the implementaion of the mentor programme will be monitored. In Phase 1 about a 50% sample is being followed for evaluation purposes, reducing to about 25% in Phase 2 and 10% in Phase 3.
Status: Sponsored project
Source of Grant: School Management Task Force; Department for Education; Local Education Authorities, jointly £220,000
Date of Research: 1992 - continuing
KEYWORDS: *headteachers; management in education; mentors*

9/0092

Institute of Education, Shaftesbury Road, Cambridge CB2 2BX
0223 69631
Sweetingham, P. Ms; *Supervisor:* Rouse, M. Mr; Ainscow, M. Mr

Towards a reconceptualisation of support teaching

Abstract: This thesis covers the ways in which special needs and subject specialist teachers work together in secondary schools. It explores through a series of case studies the developmental process through which relationships grow or are inhibited from growing. The study has implications for special needs provision in all ordinary schools and will suggest ways in which there needs to be a reconceptualisation of roles and responsibilities in mainstream education.
Status: Individual research
Date of Research: 1990 - continuing
KEYWORDS: *mainstreaming; secondary schools; special educational needs; support staff*

9/0093

Institute of Education, Shaftesbury Road, Cambridge CB2 2BX
0223 69631
Rouse, M. Mr; *Supervisor:* Rouse, M. Mr; Balshaw, M. Ms

Special needs in primary schools

Abstract: This project investigates the effects of the government funded National Priority Area (NPA) courses designed to help schools in meeting special educational needs. A collaborative initiative was established six years ago between higher education (Cambridge Institute of Education) and a number of local education authorities (LEAs). The initiative linked individual development for teachers with institutional development for their schools with the

active participation of the LEAs. Follow up evaluation by survey, case study and other ethnographic methods across five LEAs has indicated successful implementation of school change and growth for individual participants.
Published Material: ROUSE, M. & BALSHAW, M. (1991). 'Collaborative INSET and special educational needs'. In: UPTON, G. (Ed). Staff development for special educational needs. London: David Fulton.; ROUSE, M. (1991). 'Effective INSET: the role of the outsider'. In: McLAUGHLIN, C. & ROUSE, M. (Eds). Supporting schools. London: David Fulton.
Status: Sponsored project
Source of Grant: Six participating Local Education Authorities
Date of Research: 1989 - continuing
KEYWORDS: local education authorities; mainstreaming; primary schools; special educational needs; teacher development

9/0094
Institute of Education, Shaftesbury Road, Cambridge CB2 2BX
0223 69631
McLaughlin, C. Ms
Evaluation of teacher appraisal in Havering
Abstract: The project aims to evaluate the training and implementation of teacher appraisal in a London Borough. The schools in the Borough were divided into 2 cohorts and the evaluation covers both cohorts. Headteacher appraisal is also being evaluated. The methods used were as follows: Questionnaires to all participants and then interviews in the sample schools. In Cohort 2 sample schools volunteers also kept diaries of the process. In Cohort 1 the interviewed sample was 4 out of a total of 20 primary schools, 1 special school and 2 out of a total of 4 secondary schools. The same sample was in Cohort 2. The evaluation is still in progress.
Status: Sponsored project
Source of Grant: Havering Borough Council
Date of Research: 1992 - continuing
KEYWORDS: teacher effectiveness; teacher evaluation

9/0095
Institute of Education, Shaftesbury Road, Cambridge CB2 2BX
0223 69631
Greenwich University, Avery Hill Campus, Bexley Road, Eltham, London SE9 2PQ
081 316 8000
Hart, S. Ms; *Supervisor:* Oliver, M. Dr; Dalton, T. Dr
Curriculum innovation, professional development and special educational needs
Abstract: The research takes the form of a case study investigation of an instance of curriculum innovation which in principle presents the opportunity to combine the process of meeting 'special educational needs' with the process of improving curriculum provision on behalf of all pupils. The question which the research seeks to address is as follows: if general curriculum improvement is a means of meeting 'special educational needs', is there a meaningful distinction to be maintained between 'ordinary' and 'special' education and, if so, on what basis is that distinction now to be made? The area of new approaches to the teaching of writing has been selected as a focus for the investigation. Intensive fieldwork has been carried out in a 3rd-4th year junior class over a period of a year in order to monitor the writing development of 6 pupils representing a wide range of 'needs' and attainments. The material collected through participant observation together with samples of children's writing is being analysed in order to explore how individual needs are accommodated on a week-by-week basis and the significant features of individual development over time. It is intended that the research should yield insights relating to children's learning in the substantive field of enquiry and also provide the basis for a rearticulation of the relationship between 'ordinary' and 'special' education grounded in sociological and curriculum theory, knowledge and research.
Status: Individual research
Date of Research: 1988-1992
KEYWORDS: curriculum development; individual needs; mainstreaming; mixed ability; special educational needs; writing teaching

9/0096
Institute of Education, Shaftesbury Road, Cambridge CB2 2BX
0223 69631
University of East Anglia, School of Education, Centre for Applied Research in Education, Norwich NR4 7TJ

0603 56161
Southworth, G. Mr; *Supervisor:* Nias, J. Dr; Macdonald, B. Prof.
Primary school headship: an analysis derived from an ethnographic study of a single headteacher
Abstract: An ethnographic study was conducted into the work of a single, male headteacher. Using participant observation and interviews over the course of a school year (one day per week) data were collected and then analysed and written-up as a case study. The case study offers a portrait of the headteacher at work. Whilst a number of themes emerge from the study the main issue centres upon the power of the headteacher. The researcher is critical of the headteacher's power in the school and analyses why the headteacher is powerful, and how this might be altered and headship reconceptualised.
Status: Individual research
Date of Research: 1987 - continuing
KEYWORDS: headteachers; primary schools; school organisation; teaching profession

9/0097
Institute of Education, Shaftesbury Road, Cambridge CB2 2BX
0223 69631
University of East Anglia, School of Education, Centre for Applied Research in Education, Norwich NR4 7TJ
0603 56161
Dadds, M. Dr; *Supervisor:* Elliott, J. Prof.
Validity and award-bearing teacher action research
Abstract: At the heart of this research is a case study of one inservice teacher (A middle school teacher attending the action research based two year part-time Advanced Diploma course at the Cambridge Institute of Education). The teacher's three assessed action research studies are analysed to show how they relate to her professional work in school. The impact of the research on her colleagues and on their curriculum development is also explored. The case study shows the importance of her professional commitment and deep-rooted personal experiences in formulating, developing and using her research. It also shows the powerful effect of her personal qualities on her effectiveness as a change agent. Her influence on the research and on school colleagues was equally well supported by conducive management strategies and processes and by collegial attitudes towards curriculum and professional development. The case study explores the importance of these features of the receiving inservice climate and culture in school. Successful implementation of inservice is thus seen to be related to the context in which the teacher is working. The research also considers the role of the written assessed text in action research based inservice work. Alternative ways of presenting research findings may, it is suggested, be crucial for developing texts for school audiences and school purposes. Alternative texts are shown to help teachers to develop further action outcomes from their award-bearing action research work.
Published Material: DADDS, M. (1992). 'Thinking and being in teacher action research'. In: ELLIOTT, J. (Ed). Reconstructing teacher education. Lewes: Falmer Press.; DADDS, M. (1992). 'Can INSET essays change the world for children?' In: CONSTABLE, H. (Ed.) Change in classroom practice. Lewes: Falmer Press.
Status: Individual research
Date of Research: 1986-1991
KEYWORDS: action research; inservice teacher education; teacher development

9/0098
Institute of Education, Shaftesbury Road, Cambridge CB2 2BX
0223 69631
University of Utah, Department of Special Education, Milton Bennion Hall, Salt Lake City, Utah 84112, USA
0101 801 581 8122
University of Maryland, College Park, Department of Special Education, Maryland 20742, USA
0101 301 405 1000
Rouse, M. Mr; Florian, L. Dr; Hardman, M. Dr; *Supervisor:* Rouse, M. Mr
Towards the effective inclusive school
Abstract: The State of Utah (USA) has been committed for a number of years to the development of inclusive schools in which all pupils, regardless of disability will be educated. This evaluation and research project by the State investigated the outcomes of the initiative and the progress made to full inclusion. Initial findings indicate progress in a range of significant areas in certain parts of the State. Barriers to

change, as well as an account of innovative practice, are included in the final report.
Published Material: FLORIAN, L. & ROUSE, M. (1993). 'Utah's inclusive schools'. A report to the Utah State Department of Education, Salt Lake City, Utah.
Status: Sponsored project
Source of Grant: State of Utah £8,451
Date of Research: 1992 - continuing
KEYWORDS: disabilities; institutional evaluation; mainstreaming; special educational needs; United States of America

Cardiff Institute of Higher Education

9/0099
Faculty of Education, Cyncoed Centre, Cardiff CF2 6XD
0222 551111
University of Wales College of Cardiff, School of Education, 42 Park Place, Cardiff CF1 3BB
0222 874000
Rowlands, M. Mr; *Supervisor:* Sutton, R. Dr
Student teachers' conception of the nature of science and learning
Abstract: The aim of this research is to investigate any interrelationship between the construction of primary school student teachers' conceptions of the nature of science and the construction of their conceptions of teaching and learning. Case studies will be carried out of a small number of primary school student teachers during the period of their four-year teacher training course. Triangulation will be achieved by employing several techniques, including: observation of classroom interactions; interviews; and analysis of journals and teaching materials. Results will generate theories grounded in the data and illuminated by developments in the history, philosophy and sociology of science and science education.
Status: Individual research
Date of Research: 1992 - continuing
KEYWORDS: philosophy of science; preservice teacher education; science education; scientific literacy; student teachers

9/0100
School of Physical Education, Sport and Leisure, Cyncoed Centre, Cardiff
0222 551111
University of Wales College of Cardiff, School of Education, Senghenaydd Road, Cardiff CF2 4AG
0222 874000
Lancey, K. Mr; *Supervisor:* Durojaiye, S. Dr
Gender differences in motor performance from infancy to adolescence
Abstract: The aim of the research is to identify gender differences in the motor performance of children of primary school age, and to account for those differences.
Status: Individual research
Date of Research: 1990 - continuing
KEYWORDS: motor development; primary school pupils; sex differences

Charlotte Mason College

9/0101
Ambleside, Cumbria LA22 9BB
0539 433066
Light, R. Mr
Mathematics – shape & space: mathematics & art
Abstract: The project looks at cross-curricular links for mathematics and art, studying children's' spatial development in the context of both their mathematics and drawing abilities, the development of spatial representation within art history and their relationship with cognitive development.
Status: Individual research

Date of Research: 1991 - continuing
KEYWORDS: art; art history; cognitive development; cross curricular approach; mathematics; spatial ability

9/0102
Department of Professional Studies, Ambleside, Cumbria LA22 9BB
0539 433066
Hegarty, P. Dr; Hegarty, P. Mrs; *Supervisor:* Hegarty, P. Dr; Hegarty, P. Mrs
The Two Degrees – a comparative study of former students and first post headteacher satisfaction with initial teacher education at Charlotte Mason College
Abstract: The Council for the Accreditation of Teacher Education (CATE) criteria for primary initial teacher education have occasioned very significant changes in B. Ed. applied teacher education courses. This study aims to illuminate the levels of student and first post headteacher satisfaction with students' initial training. The methods include surveys of the whole output from Charlotte Mason College of the last two cohorts of Applied B. Ed. and the first two cohorts of Subject Studies B. Ed., and observations and interviews with a small sample each year.
Status: Sponsored project
Source of Grant: Charlotte Mason College £300
Date of Research: 1989 - continuing
KEYWORDS: B. Ed. degrees; participant satisfaction; preservice teacher education; probationary teachers; student teachers; teaching experience

9/0103
Development Unit, Ambleside, Cumbria LA22 9BB
0539 433066
Alker, D. Mr; *Supervisor:* Postle, M. Dr
The identification of prerequisites for effective teacher mobility between Germany and the United Kingdom
Abstract: The project will develop, implement, monitor and evaluate a training programme in consultation with local education authorities (LEAs) for the induction and transfer training of European Community (EC) trained teachers. The aims of the training programme are: (1) to introduce an appropriate range of teaching methods and styles to obtain a better match in teaching approaches; (2) to familiarise EC teachers with the National Curriculum; (3) provide support in meeting the language demands in both general communication skills and the language of the classroom; (4) develop confidence in coping with the demands of cultural and social difference. A major focus of the training programme will be school-based training in association with participating schools and LEAs
Status: Sponsored project
Source of Grant: Department of Education and Science £20,000
Date of Research: 1989 - continuing
KEYWORDS: European Community; Germany; teacher mobility; teacher transfer; training

Chartered Institute of Public Finance and Accountancy (CIPFA)

9/0104
The LMS Initiative, 3 Robert Street, London WC2N 6BH
071 895 8823
Coopers & Lybrand Deloitte, Plumtree Court, London EC4A AHT
071 212 2018
National Foundation for Educational Research, The Mere, Upton Park, Slough SL1 2DQ
0753 574123
Thompson, Q. Mr; Keys, W. Dr; *Supervisor:* Evans, M. Mr
Local management in schools: the three year review
Abstract: A study into the formula funding of schools and the related management issues that currently face local education authorities (LEAs), to provide them with timely and practical information on the issues they will wish – and be required – to review as part of the three

year review of Local Management of Schools (LMS) schemes due to be completed in autumn 1992. The study will look forward to examine the delegation of responsibilities and the management issues from both the LEAs viewpoint and from the perspective of schools. This will include the scope and means of delegation, the facility for sending policy signals to schools, and the mechanisms for monitoring performance and for operating quality control. It will also cover formula funding in depth as a distribution mechanism, in terms of its impact on education policy in schools and by reference to its technical construction.
Published Material: The LMS Initiative (1992). Local management of schools: a study into formula funding and management issues. Prepared by Coopers & Lybrand Deloitte and NFER. London: CIPFA.
Status: Sponsored project
Source of Grant: Department of Education and Science; Consortium of Local Education Authorities £25,000
Date of Research: 1991-1992
KEYWORDS: educational change; educational finance; educational policy; local education authorities; local management of schools; school-based management

Cheltenham & Gloucester College of Higher Education

9/0105
Oxstalls Campus, Oxstalls Lane, Gloucester GL2 9HW
0452 426700
Bray, S. Mrs
The transferability of current insurance qualifications within the European Community
Abstract: The aims and objectives of this research are to investigate the various insurance qualifications within the European Community, their level, the recognition they receive within individual Member States and how they compare with the insurance qualifications elsewhere in the European Community. It is also intended to enquire how transferable these qualifications are in the light of 1992, also how qualifications which have been gained in the United Kingdom can be applied to jobs in the European community and the implications for business studies/language courses. How applicable are qualifications which have been gained in other European countries to work in the United Kingdom insurance industry? The investigation will be carried out in European countries where insurance features most prominently. Methodology will include desk research, data collection, contacting professional bodies from each country, insurance companies, Chambers of Commerce and The National Council for Vocational Qualifications (NCVQ). No definite conclusions have been drawn.
Status: Sponsored project
Source of Grant: Cheltenham & Gloucester College of Higher Education £900
Date of Research: 1990-1992
KEYWORDS: credit transfer; European Community; insurance occupations; qualifications; transfer policy

9/0106
Faculty of Business and Finance Management, Oxstalls Campus, Oxstalls Lane, Gloucester GL2 9HW
0452 426700
Cowley, V. Mrs; *Supervisor:* Lewis, P. Mr
A working arrangement: student work experience placements
Abstract: This is an investigation into student work experience placements. Employers are being asked what they get out of work experience arrangements; who, in their view benefits most from them; and how far their expectations of students are realised. They are also being invited to describe how they plan in advance for work placements, and how they believe colleges can best assist them in this task and in making the arrangements work well for all parties.
Status: Sponsored project
Source of Grant: Cheltenham & Gloucester College of Higher Education
Date of Research: 1990-1991
KEYWORDS: employer attitudes; job placement; student employment; work experience

9/0107
Faculty of Business and Finance Management, Oxstalls Campus, Oxstalls Lane, Gloucester GL2 9HW
0452 426700
Hall, J. Mrs; *Supervisor:* Williams, C. Mrs
The role of information technology in business, finance and management
Abstract: The aims of this project are to: (1) ascertain the information technology skills and knowledge required by business and industry of a Business Studies graduate; (2) identify the types of hardware and software and the applications for which they are used in industry today, with particular reference to the micro-computer. The research will be carried out by semi-structured interviews with a selection of local organisations.
Status: Individual research
Date of Research: 1990-1991
KEYWORDS: business; computers; industry; information technology

9/0108
Faculty of Education and Health, The Park, Cheltenham GL50 2QF
0242 532700
Cutting, E. Ms; Fahey, W. Mr
Expectations of school health services: part 4 'What teenage students expect from the school health service'
Abstract: Given the current emphasis on making services 'more responsible to the consumer' (HMSO, 'Primary health care – an agenda for discussion'), and the client-centred approach of the Cumberlege report and other recent reports, the authors are examining a series of samples of parents, teachers and pupils as to their expectations of school health services. With the assistance of students on school nurse courses the two authors are investigating the expectations of various groups of randomly chosen respondents (up to 200). A two-part quantative and qualitative questionnaire is prepared each session. The findings reported in 1991 are concerned with pupil expectations.
Published Material: CUTTING, E. & FAHEY, W.S. (1987). 'What parents expect from the primary school health service', Health at School, June.; FAHEY, W.S. & CUTTING, E. (1988). 'What parents expect from the secondary school health services', Health at School, June.; FAHEY, W.S. & CUTTING, E. (1989). 'What teachers expect from the school health services', Health at School, June.
Status: Individual research
Date of Research: 1990-1991
KEYWORDS: pupil attitudes; school health services

9/0109
Faculty of Education and Health, The Park, Cheltenham GL50 2QF
0242 532700
Noyes, P. Dr
A study of teaching methods in a college of higher education
Abstract: This research will identify the teaching needs of new members of academic staff in the Faculty of Education and Health at Cheltenham & Gloucester College of Higher Education, by means of paired observation and discussion groups. Action research techniques are then being used to develop and monitor teaching methods. 9 academic staff are involved and the direction of the project will depend upon identified needs and decisions reached during discussion.
Status: Sponsored project
Source of Grant: Cheltenham & Gloucester College of Higher Education
Date of Research: 1990-1991
KEYWORDS: colleges of higher education; individual needs; staff development; staff orientation; teaching methods

9/0110
Faculty of Education and Health, The Park, Cheltenham GL50 2AF
0242 532700
More, C. Dr
History of Cheltenham Training College 1847-1947
Abstract: This research will trace the history of Cheltenham Training College (later the separate colleges of St Paul and St Mary) which was the largest Evangelical training college and at times the largest

college in the country. The history will focus on eight areas: the foundation of the College; its management over the succeeding century in the light of national changes in the educational and religious framework; the qualifications, pay and conditions of staff; the origins and destinations of students; the syllabus; the expectations of students while training, and the formation and characteristics of the student ethos; sport and physical exercise; and the relationship between old students and the College. The study will use a full range of sources: e.g. annual reports, governors' minute books, inspectors' reports, staff and student registers, student magazines, reminiscences and photographs.
Status: Sponsored project
Source of Grant: Cheltenham & Gloucester College of Higher Education £ 24,000
Date of Research: 1990-1991
KEYWORDS: colleges of education; educational history; teacher education

9/0111
Faculty of Education and Health, The Park, Cheltenham
GL50 2QF
0242 532700
Davidson, J. Ms; *Supervisor:* Lewis, E. Dr; Noyes, P. Dr
Computer assisted learning in the teaching of reading
Abstract: This research will develop and evaluate a computer aided learning system for the teaching of reading incorporating recent advances in digitised speech output. This simulates the usual reading instruction process where the teacher provides individual assistance to the learner by spoken prompts. Scanning techniques now enable pages of reading books already in use in primary classrooms to be displayed on a microcomputer and a child's voice is recorded, digitised and used to provide the speech. These prompts are issued when the child highlights words or whole pages with which he or she may be having difficulty. This system has the advantage of providing additional reading practice with an infinitely patient non-judgemental listener and avoids the humiliation that some children experience when seen to fail in front of a skilled reader. The initial reaction from pupils and teachers has been favourable, largely due to the clarity of the voice and the fact that teachers can use books which are already used in their schools and do not therefore need to change dramatically their approach to reading. The results of initial trials undertaken in Gloucestershire primary schools comparing groups of children using the system with control groups have shown the system to be of benefit in the teaching of reading. These comparisons are made by recording improved performance in standardised reading tests and measurements of sight vocabulary. The improvement goes beyond the immediate situation and evidence suggests it influences general reading attainment. Work has now started in the area of helping children who have had difficulty in learning to read.
Status: Individual research
Date of Research: 1988-1992
KEYWORDS: computer-assisted reading; computer uses in education; reading teaching

9/0112
Faculty of Education and Health, The Park, Cheltenham
GL50 2QF
0242 532700
Gemie, S. Dr
The State and women's schooling in France, 1815-1914
Abstract: This research will test recent theoretical models of the State and women's relationships to public power structures by reference to the experience of schoolmistresses and schoolgirls in nineteenth century France. To assess the effects of the presentation of official role models of ideal feminine types on female students at teacher training colleges. To further understanding of the effects of limited entry into public positions on women's mentalities and to analyse women's ability to re-formulate official ideas in the light of their experience – in particular, their relationship to feminist, anarchist and socialist sub-cultures following their entries into the teaching profession. The research sample was based on archive research in Lyon, Caen, Bordeaux, Lille and Paris, and may involve reference to a database of the careers of some 200 schoolmistresses. Methods involved social and cultural historical investigation, with some guidance from recent works by feminist and critical theorists.
Published Material: GEMIE, S. (1991). 'The schoolmistress's revenge: secular schoolmistresses, academic authority and village conflicts in France, 1815 to 1948', History of Education, No 20, pp.203-17.

Status: Sponsored project
Source of Grant: Cheltenham & Gloucester College of Higher Education £ 1,500
Date of Research: 1988-1992
KEYWORDS: educational history; educational policy; france; teaching profession; women's education

9/0113
Faculty of Education and Health, The Park, Cheltenham
GL50 2QF
0242 532700
Fahey, W. Mr
The identification of the needs of lesbian and gay students in higher education
Abstract: From a self selected sample of at least 50 lesbians and gay students currently taking courses in 10 separate institutions of higher education, the authors in this study aim to, examine students' perceptions of their needs, explore the extent to which these needs are currently being met within educational institutions, and develop a strategy to reduce or eliminate inequalities in higher education related to student sexuality. Methodology will include a postal questionnaire followed by a selection of semi-structured interviews with quantitative and qualitative aspects.
Status: Individual research
Date of Research: 1991-1992
KEYWORDS: higher education; homosexuality; lesbianism; student needs

9/0114
Faculty of Education and Health, The Park, Cheltenham
GL50 2QF
0242 532700
Noyes, P. Dr
A survey of student expectations and perceptions of higher education
Abstract: This research was carried out to identify the nature of student expectations of the college. The major source of these expectations were discovered, and an investigation into how they had changed was conducted, especially at the time of most impact, i.e. the first two weeks at college, and after one year at college. Areas where the college fell short of student expectation were identified. Issues for further research and areas of college practice which needed to be adapted were recommended. Links were established with the quality assurance study of the induction process. The link between expectations, academic performance and satisfaction were investigated. There was also a contribution to the debate on the efficacy of expectation theory in explaining human behaviour. All students who entered the college in September 1990 were surveyed by questionnaire: firstly, before they arrived at college to monitor initial expectations, secondly, immediately after the induction process to ascertain immediate changes in perceptions after the initial impact of coming to college had been experienced and thirdly, after a year at college, to measure perceptions of that time. Expectation Theory was used as a means of examining the process of attitude change that occurred during the year, and outcome measures were collected by means of satisfaction indices calculated from questionnaire responses and academic performance indicated by college grades.
Status: Sponsored project
Source of Grant: Cheltenham & Gloucester College of Higher Education
Date of Research: 1990-1992
KEYWORDS: expectation; higher education; student attitudes; student experience

9/0115
Faculty of Education and Health, The Park, Cheltenham
GL50 2QF
0242 532700
Charlton, A. Dr; Leo, E. Ms; Indoe, D. Mr; James, J. Ms
Evaluation of a teacher training package designed to enhance pupils' self-image
Abstract: The research involves an evaluation of an inservice teacher training package constructed by the researchers. The package – EASI Teaching Package (Enhancement Approaches with the Self-Image) – is designed to assist teachers to improve the self-image of their pupils. Evaluation will incorporate a pre-/post-intervention design. Seventy-two teachers (drawn from nine primary schools) are to

constitute the intervention group. They will receive the EASI Teaching Programme (four one-and-a-half-hour meetings) over a 4 week period. A comparison group (similar size/type to the intervention group) will receive no special treatment. Pre-/post-evaluations will utilise indices of teachers' classroom behaviour, and pupils' self-image reports and behavioural functioning.
Status: Individual research
Date of Research: 1990 - continuing
KEYWORDS: *inservice teacher education; programme evaluation; pupil development; self concept*

9/0116
Faculty of Education and Health, The Park, Cheltenham
GL50 2QF
0242 532700
Attilar Joszef University, Department of Sociology, Saeged
6722, Petofi Sandor Str., 30/34, Hungary
010 36 62 21 611
Cowen, H. Mr; Rosie, A. Dr; Gabor, K. Mr
A comparative study of student youth social and political lifestyles in Hungary and England
Abstract: The research project builds upon an international youth study already carried out in Hungary, Germany and the Netherlands. Its focus is on the social profiles, social and political orientation and lifestyles of student youth in localities in Hungary and England, comparing how student youth are living through Europe's economic and political changes. Student bodies in Sopron and Kosseg, Hungary, and Cheltenham and Gloucester, England will be the subject of interviews by questionnaire. Students will be selected under three basic categories: older, secondary school students; further education and technical college students; students in higher education. They will be questioned on a series of central issues relating to: patterns of social orientation; most important life events; perspectives and attitudes towards personal and societal futures; political interest and participation; group activities. Findings will be compared and then considered in the light of current youth and educational policies in each country.
Status: Sponsored project
Source of Grant: Hungarian Academy of Social Science
Date of Research: 1991-1992
KEYWORDS: *cross cultural studies; economic change; lifestyle; political attitudes; social change; students*

9/0117
Faculty of Education and Health, The Park, Cheltenham
GU50 2QF
0242 532700
Leeds University, School of Education, Leeds LS2 9JT
0532 431751
Brown, B. Miss; *Supervisor:* Sugden, D. Dr
An examination of teaching and learning strategies for children with movement learning difficulties
Abstract: In this research, 50 children aged 2 to 11 years with movement learning difficulties have been examined for 6 years in a movement learning context whilst they have been engaged in developing rudimentary and fundamental movement abilities. The children's movement development has been examined in the context of their total development. The teaching considerations surrounding the teacher's role, curriculum content, teaching strategy and learning environment have been critically analysed in the context of the movement learning experience of the children. The children were taught in segregated and integrated settings.
Status: Individual research
Date of Research: 1984-1991
KEYWORDS: *moderate learning; motor development; movement education; special educational needs; teaching process*

9/0118
Faculty of Education and Health, The Park, Cheltenham
GL50 2QF
0242 532700
Oxford University, Department of Experimental Psychology, Wellington Square, Oxford OX1 2JD
0865 270360
Huxford, L. Mrs; *Supervisor:* Terrell, C. Dr; Bradley, L. Dr
The relationship between the phonological strategies employed in the early stages of reading and spelling
Abstract: This research comprises longitudinal and intervention studies aimed at examining young children's developing phonological strategies in reading and spelling. It contributes to the growing body of data on the connections between reading and spelling. Fifty-six children between three and a half and five and a half years, who had satisfied a minimum requirement of phonological ability were included in the sample for the longitudinal study. A combination of standardised tests and tasks specifically devised and refined for the study have been used. A battery of eight tests were constructed to compare reading and spelling, controlling for alphabet and use of visual and contextual strategies. In order to assess children's phonological development against other factors of experience and ability, measures of age, reading spelling, alphabetical knowledge, intelligence, memory and hearing were taken. The pattern of results from forty-three of the children supports the claim that children appear to acquire a phonological strategy in spelling before an equivalent strategy. Forty-two children in two experimental groups and a control group are taking part in the intervention study. The effects on reading acquisition of two different approaches to writing are being measured.
Published Material: HUXFORD, L., TERRELL, C. & BRADLEY, L. (1991). 'The relationship between the phonological strategies in reading and spelling', Journal of Research in Reading, Vol 14, No 2, pp.99-105.; HUXFORD, L., TERRELL, C. & BRADLEY, L. 'Invented spelling and learning to read'. In: STERLING, C. & ROBSON, C. (Eds). Psychology, spelling and education. Clevedon: Multilingual Matters, (forthcoming).
Status: Individual research
Date of Research: 1987-1992
KEYWORDS: *child development; phonology; reading skills; spelling*

Chester College of Higher Education

9/0119
Cheyney Road, Chester CH1 4BJ
0244 375444
Alston, P. Dr; Ellis, V. Mrs; McQueen, A. Mr; Derby, J. Mrs; Boxall, V. Mrs; *Supervisor:* Alston, P. Dr
Music for the generalist primary teacher, with reference to the National Curriculum
Abstract: The aim of the project is to develop a model for combined skill, concept and affective learning in listening, performing and composing. This theoretical model will then be translated into classroom practice by the devising of materials to assist the generalist primary teacher to cope with the demands of the National Curriculum in Music at key stage 1 and key stage 2. All materials will be on trial in classrooms before being published. This work will then feed back into the theoretical model which will need to be revised and refined. A final report will comment on the practicability of teaching the National Curriculum in Music at key stage 1 and key stage 2 through a model of skill, concept and affective learning.
Published Material: A list of publications is available from the researchers.
Status: Sponsored project
Source of Grant: University of Liverpool Board of College Studies £565; Chester College £200
Date of Research: 1990 - continuing
KEYWORDS: *music education; National Curriculum; primary school teachers*

9/0120
Cheyney Road, Chester CH1 4BJ
0224 375444
Alston, P. Dr; Carhart, J. Rev.; Robertson, D. Mr; Pegg, R. Dr; Major, D. Mr; Jackson, S. Dr; Lunt, P. Dr; *Supervisor:* Alston, P. Dr
Work based learning for academic credit
Abstract: The aim of the project is to work in collaboration with three higher education institutions (Chester College of Higher Education, Liverpool Polytechnic and Liverpool University), to develop the use of work placements as academic components of first degree programmes as an option for students not on designated sandwich courses. The project will: (1) provide them with experience of the

world of work, opportunities for taking initiatives and developing their independence; (2) provide them with the opportunity of gaining academic credit towards their degree from learning derived from experience in an employer site; (3) provide additional examples of ways to extend the range of main stream curricula with higher education to meet the requirements of employment; and (4) to enhance partnerships between higher education and employers.
Status: Sponsored project
Source of Grant: Learning from Experience Trust
Date of Research: 1990 - continuing
KEYWORDS: credits; experiential learning; industry higher education relationship; job placement; work-education relationship

9/0121
　　　Cheyney Road, Chester CH1 4BJ
　　　0244 375444
　　　Pickford, A. Mr
Developing information technology in a primary Post Graduate Certificate of Education course
Abstract: The aim of the project is to identify the factors affecting student competence in information technology in relation to the teaching practice experience of Post Graduate Certificate of Education (PGCE) students. The research will also consider the kinds of positive interventions which can be made by a teacher training institution and those personal characteristics of students which might lead to the development of information technology capability. The sample size is approximately 50 PGCE students (primary). The study uses questionnaires and direct observation by tutors.
Status: Individual research
Date of Research: 1992 - continuing
KEYWORDS: information technology; preservice teacher education; student teachers; teaching practice

9/0122
　　　Cheyney Road, Chester CH1 4BJ
　　　0224 375444
　　　Exeter University, Department of Education, St Luke's,
　　　Exeter EX1 2LU
　　　0392 76311
　　　Heaney, S. Mrs; *Supervisor:* Golby, M. Dr
Graduates becoming primary teachers: a study of the development of reflective professionalism by graduates following a school-based one year primary course in initial teacher education
Abstract: Case study material will be assembled in order to examine the development of reflective professionalism in graduates following a one year school-based course of initial teacher training. Work will be done with sequential intakes, over three or more years, of 25 in number.
Status: Individual research
Date of Research: 1987-1991
KEYWORDS: preservice teacher education; probationary teachers; professional development; student teachers; teaching profession

City University

9/0123
　　　Northampton Square, London EC1V OBH
　　　071 477 8000
　　　Golombok, S. Dr; Rust, J. Dr
Pre-school activities inventory
Abstract: The Pre-School Activities Inventory is a psychometrically constructed questionnaire for the measurement of sex-role behaviour in children. It is completed by the child's parents, teacher or nursery staff. The questionnaire contains 28 items, and is divided into three areas: toys and games, activities and characteristics. It has been validated by comparing parents responses on the questionnaire with teacher's ratings of masculinity and femininity.
Status: Individual research
Date of Research: 1988-1992
KEYWORDS: early childhood education; preschool children; sex differences; sex role

9/0124
　　　Centre for Continuing Education, Northampton Square,
　　　London EC1V OHB
　　　071 477 8000
　　　Parry, G. Mr; Thompson, A. Dr
Access coordinators in institutions of higher education in the United Kingdom
Abstract: This is a one year research project investigating the role of access coordinators in higher education who have responsibility for extending and supporting the participation of mature and non-traditional students. The first phase used a questionnaire to heads of continuing education in all universities, polytechnics and colleges to collect baseline data on patterns of provision and activity. The second phase involved the identification of a small number of institutions for more qualitative and detailed investigation using case study methods. A final report would be made available to responding institutions and to others on request.
Published Material: THOMPSON, A. & PARRY, G. (1992). Access coordinators in higher education. London: City University.
Status: Sponsored project
Source of Grant: Universities Funding Council £15,000
Date of Research: 1990-1991
KEYWORDS: access to education; coordinators; higher education; mature students; re-entry students; student participation

9/0125
　　　Centre for Continuing Education, Northampton Square,
　　　London EC1V OHB
　　　071 477 8000
　　　Parry, G. Mr; Davies, P. Ms
Evaluation of the introduction of a national framework for the recognition of Access courses to higher education in England and Wales and Northern Ireland
Abstract: This research will be a twenty month study of the introduction of the CNAA/CVCP (Council for National Academic Awards/Committee of Vice Chancellors and Principals) national framework for the recognition of Access courses to higher education. The research project aimed to trace the origin, development and impact of the framework as a means of extending opportunities for adults without conventional qualifications to participate in higher education. The first phase focused on the first round of approvals of authorised validating agencies and involved content analysis of published documents and interview and observational studies of the central body. The extended phase focused on subsequent rounds of approvals and case studies of selected authorised validating agencies to monitor the impact of the framework at local level and in relation to Access course providers and students. The study involved both formative and summative evaluation and results and conclusions were to be disseminated through an interim and final report.
Published Material: PARRY, G. & DAVIES, P. (1991). Framing Access. Leicester: UDACE.; PARRY, G. & DAVIES, P. (1991). 'The National Evaluation Study: some issues from the first report', Journal of Access Studies, Vol 6, No 1, pp.65-71.; DAVIES, P. & PARRY, G. (1992). 'Central intentions and local interpretations: implementing national arrangements for the recognition of Access Courses', Journal of Access Studies, Vol 7, No 1, pp.42-60.; PARRY, G. & DAVIES, P. (1992). Kitemarking Access. London: DEU.
Status: Sponsored project
Source of Grant: TEED; FEU; DES; UDACE £63,000
Date of Research: 1990-1991
KEYWORDS: Access programmes; higher education; programme evaluation

Coopers & Lybrand Deloitte

9/0126
　　　Plumtree Court, London EC4A 4HT
　　　071 583 5000
　　　Thompson, Q. Mr; *Supervisor:* D'Armenia, M. Ms
Investment appraisal of Education Support Grant XXX for the training of youth leaders in the inner cities in England and in the valleys in Wales
Abstract: The Department of Education and Science has commissioned Coopers and Lybrand Deloitte to carry out an investment appraisal of Education Support Grant (ESG) XXX for the training of

youth leaders in the inner cities in England and in the Valleys in Wales. The appraisal will: estimate the total investment in the local scheme; assess the extent of support from other sources; compare costs with those of other forms of youth worker training; assess the costs and benefits of the schemes; and evaluate the efficiency of the ESG mechanism. This is one of a number of evaluation exercises of the ESG, the combined results of which will allow the Department to assess the overall value of the programme and its viability as a model for future youth training.
Status: Sponsored project
Source of Grant: Department of Education and Science £53,500
Date of Research: 1991 - continuing
KEYWORDS: *financial support; inner city; investment; training; youth leader; youth service*

Council for Environmental Education

9/0127
> Reading University, Faculty of Education and Community Studies, National Environmental Resource Base, London Road, Reading RG1 5AQ
> 0734 756061
> Gayford, C. Dr

Inservice Education of Teachers programmes in environmental education
Abstract: This project involves the production of inservice teaching approaches suitable for use by local authorities, schools or colleges. The emphasis is on interactive methods both for educating teachers and giving suggestions for ways in which environmental education can be integrated into the curriculum. Extensive trialling will occur in several invited local authorities on a partnership basis. The following modules for inservice use will be available from 1992: (1) Introducing Environmental Education; (2) Science; (3) English.
Status: Sponsored project
Source of Grant: Central Electricity Generating Board £50,000
Date of Research: 1988-1992
KEYWORDS: *environmental education; inservice teacher education*

9/0128
> Reading University, Faculty of Education and Community Studies, National Environmental Resource Base, London Road, Reading RG1 5AQ
> 0734 756061
> Field Studies Council, Central Services, Preston Montford, Montford Bridge, Shrewsbury SY4 1HW
> 0743 850674
> Hale, M. Ms; Hindon, J. Dr

Charging for out of classroom activities in schools
Abstract: The aim of the research is to discover the impact of the charging aspects of the Education Reform Act – 1988 on out of school activities, in particular, fieldwork related to geography and science. The investigation had three stages: (1) 1989/90 – a questionnaire sent to approximately 400 Field Study Centres to assess the impact of charging; (2) 1990/91 – a repeat of the 1989/90 survey; and (3) questionnaire sent to all schools in 8 selected local education authorities.
Status: Sponsored project
Source of Grant: Field Studies Council; Council for Environmental Education; Department of Education and Science £1,500
Date of Research: 1989-1991
KEYWORDS: *extracurricular activities; fees; field study centres; geography education; science education*

9/0129
> Reading University, Faculty of Education and Community Studies, National Environmental Resource Base, London Road, Reading RG1 5AQ
> 0734 756061
> Loughborough University of Technology, Department of Information and Library Studies, Loughborough LE11 3TU
> 0509 263171
> Midgley, C. Ms

Building support for environmental education (Phase I)
Abstract: The overall aim is to improve the provision and use of support for environmental education. The main objectives of the project are to: (1) increase awareness amongst practitioners of the sources of support; (2) encourage discerning use and evaluation of information by users; (3) improve and extend the means of dissemination of/access to information; (4) improve the applicability of the support provided; (5) establish mechanisms for maintaining the currency of information disseminated; and (6) recommend further initiatives, depending on the results of the research. Phase I will focus on a survey of the information needs of environmental education practitioners which will be carried out by questionnaire and semi-structured interviews. The results of this survey will dictate the format of a subsequent survey of current provision, the findings of which will be used to compile a directory of information sources.
Status: Sponsored project
Source of Grant: Department of the Environment: Environmental Grant Fund £ 45,000; Esso UK plc £3,000
Date of Research: 1991-1992
KEYWORDS: *educational resources; environmental education; information needs; information sources*

Coventry University

9/0130
> Priory Street, Coventry CV1 5FB
> 0203 631313
> Corness, P. Mr; Deepwell, F. Ms

TIGER project (Translating Industrial German) – Computer-based training in German technical translation
Abstract: Computer-assisted training packages in German-English translation are being developed for application in industry. The packages are at beginners, intermediate and advanced (degree) levels. Design is based on contrastive analysis of German and English, and the learning materials focus on problems of translation from German to English caused by interference from native-language structures. At the advanced level, there is an additional module for training in the use of a computer-assisted translation system ('Alpnet TSS'). The translation training, which will make use of an appropriate combination of computer-based and printed course materials, will be applied on courses in technical translation at Coventry University and will be supplied together similar institutions and to industry. On-line German-English technical glossaries, which are being developed in cooperation with industrial firms, and which are to form a component of the training course, will also be available as self-standing products.
Published Material: CORNESS, P.J. (1986). 'The ALPS computer-assisted translation system in an academic environment'. In: PICKEN, C. (Ed). 1986. Translating and the computer 7. London: Aslib.
Status: Sponsored project
Source of Grant: Training, Enterprise and Education Directorate
Date of Research: 1990-1992
KEYWORDS: *computer-assisted language learning; educational software; German; translation*

9/0131
> Priory Street, Coventry CV1 5FB
> 0203 631313
> Hocking, B. Dr

Developing a joint BA Honours course in International Studies and Business Studies
Abstract: The purpose of the project is to develop a course which focuses on the international context in which modern business operates and, thereby, provides a broader educational experience than is the case with most undergraduate courses in business studies.
Status: Sponsored project
Source of Grant: Coventry University Staff Development Programme
Date of Research: 1990-1992
KEYWORDS: *business education; international studies; undergraduate study*

9/0132
> Priory Street, Coventry CV1 5FB
> 0203 631313
> Hocking, B. Dr

Developing teaching materials on the international politics of the environment
Abstract: The aim of the project is to develop teaching materials on the subject of the environment as an issue on the international agenda. These will comprise a bibliography and a course guide which can be used in the context of traditional courses or self-learning environments.
Status: Sponsored project
Source of Grant: Coventry University: Learning Systems Development Fund
Date of Research: 1990-1991
KEYWORDS: educational materials; environmental education; international education; politics

9/0133
Centre for Communication Studies, Gosford Street, Coventry CV1 5RZ
0203 631313
French, D. Mr
Industrial placements in Belgium
Abstract: The project investigates student experience of industrial placements and the perception of the value, operational problems, etc. of such placements on the part of students, academic staff and placement hosts. It concentrates on communication/media studies but its conclusions have more general application.
Status: Sponsored project
Source of Grant: Belgian Government; European Community COM-METT Programme ; University of Liege; Coventry University
Date of Research: 1989-1991
KEYWORDS: industry-education relationship; job placement; student experience

9/0134
Centre for Communication Studies, Gosford Street, Coventry CV1 5RZ
0203 631313
Worcester College of Higher Education, Henwick Grove, Worcester WR2 6AJ
0905 748080
French, D. Mr; Richards, M. Prof.
Student experience of European exchange
Abstract: The project examines, using individual and group interviews, students perceptions of the changes in their attitude and competences consequent upon the experience of study abroad. Results, even provisional, are not yet available but should be of importance in formulating future policies on student mobility. Initial interviews are with students from Britain and Belgium and the initial sample is small.
Status: Individual research
Date of Research: 1991-1992
KEYWORDS: student attitudes; student exchange programmes; student experience; study abroad

9/0135
Department of Languages, Politics and History, Priory Street, Coventry CV1 5FB
0203 631313
Taylor, K. Mr
Material for a literature and politics course
Abstract: This research will involve collecting course materials for a new third year undergraduate course on literature and politics, with particular reference to Britain and Europe in the contemporary period, and also to changing ideas and values in view of the rapid changes in East/West Europe.
Status: Sponsored project
Source of Grant: Coventry University
Date of Research: 1990-1991
KEYWORDS: educational materials; higher education; literature; politics; undergraduate study

9/0136
School of Art & Design, Priory Street, Coventry CV1 5FB
0203 631313
Bevan, R. Mr; *Supervisor:* Richards, C. Dr
Conceptualisation design and orientation in complex multimedia structures
Abstract: The aim of this research is to develop more intuitive and creative methods of designing and representing interlinked information in interactive, non-linear multimedia structures, providing simple and effective means of orientation and navigation within such structures.
Status: Sponsored project
Source of Grant: Apple Computer UK Ltd £23,000
Date of Research: 1989-1992
KEYWORDS: computer-assisted design; educational media; multimedia approach

9/0137
School of International Studies and Law, Priory Street, Coventry CV1 5FB
0203 631313
Corness, P. Mr
ALPS (Automated Language Processing Systems) computer-assisted translation system as a language learning tool
Abstract: Computer-assisted translation (CAT) systems are being increasingly used in translation departments in business and industry. It is felt that it is vitally important to incorporate such advances in information technology into its degree courses at this institution. In the BA Modern Languages Degree scheme, work with ALPS now features in the First Year Approaches to Language Studies, in the Information Technology Option in the Second and Final Year in translation work at all levels, and the Translation Option includes a more advanced practical application of ALPS. Work with ALPS is also incorporated into the language modules in European Engineering Studies and other degree courses. This is seen as a natural development of the successful Computer Assisted Language Learning programme. ALPS was selected from among a number of different systems because of its interactive approach, which makes possible new types of computer-assisted language learning activities and text analysis facilities, in addition to familiarising students with up to date tools of the modern practising translator.
Published Material: CORNESS, P. (1986). 'The ALPS computer assisted translation system in an academic environment'. In: PICKEN, C. (Ed). (1986). Translating and the computer, 7. London: ASLIB.
Status: Sponsored project
Source of Grant: Coventry University
Date of Research: 1985-1992
KEYWORDS: computer-assisted learning; modern language studies; translation

9/0138
School of International Studies and Law, Priory Street, Coventry CV1 5FB
0203 631313
Jones, D. Mr; Orsini-Jones, M. Mrs
Multi-media course in Italian language
Abstract: The aim is to prepare a course for the teaching of Italian language which would be suitable for use in this institution. It will need to make use of audio and video recording facilities and computer programs as well as written material, and to be usable with limited input from teaching staff. Work is currently progressing on a beginners course, but it is hoped ultimately to produce an integrated course for three years.
Status: Sponsored project
Source of Grant: Coventry University
Date of Research: 1986 - continuing
KEYWORDS: course content; educational materials; Italian; modern language studies; multimedia approach

Create Consultants

9/0139
109 West End Lane, London NW6 4SY
071 328 8619
Weindling, R. Mr
Current developments in the preparation and support of principals in the United States
Abstract: The study consisted of a review of the current literature concerning United States school principals' management roles, functions and competencies. The aim was to present a description of

research and practice, together with critical comment and recommendations to assist the Department of Education and Science School Management Task Force. The first section of the study covered the phases of pre-service prior to being appointed as a principal including State certification: Induction – the support given during the first years of the principalship; and Inservice – the various types of management development for established principals. The second section examined various national initiatives such as the 'Lead' programme which established a leadership centre in each State. Two national research centres have also been established. Section three looked at competency-based approaches, particularly assessment centres. (The first UK one has been opened in Oxford). The elaborate and detailed system in Florida is described, as well as a summary of the research on which it is based. The fourth section provides details of six methods of supporting principals, including mentoring and shadowing. The study also offers recommendations about the applicability of the various systems to this country.
Status: Sponsored project
Source of Grant: Department of Education and Science £5,175
Date of Research: 1991-1991
KEYWORDS: *headteachers; management development; principals; United States of America*

Crewe & Alsager College of Higher Education

9/0140
     Hassall Road, Alsager, Stoke on Trent ST7 2HL
     0270 500661
     James, M. Mr; *Supervisor:* Seymour, R. Mr
Managing the implementation of the National Curriculum
Abstract: This research examines the introduction of the National Curriculum as an exercise in the management of change. Literature reviews have been carried out on curriculum theory, a centrally controlled curriculum and various perspectives on the National Curriculum as well as educational change. The question of cross curricularity and subject overlap has emerged as extremely important. Five secondary schools will be studied. Interviews with the headteacher and deputy and the heads of science, geography and technology will take place. Data will then be collated and analysed to compare 'real world' perceptions and problems with the theoretical perspectives of the literature review. It is hoped that 'good practice' guidelines and additional knowledge on the management of change will emerge.
Status: Individual research
Date of Research: 1990 - continuing
KEYWORDS: *core curriculum; curriculum development; educational administration; educational change; educational development; interdisciplinary approach; national curriculum*

9/0141
     Department of Education Management, Hassall Road,
     Alsager, Stoke on Trent ST7 2HL
     0270 500661
     Hemmings, N. Mr; *Supervisor:* Seymour, R. Mr
Self managing schools – a practical way forward for secondary schools
Abstract: The research aims to consider some of the practical effects of school management in the light of the Education Reform Act 1988 (ERA). In particular focusing upon the ways secondary schools have adapted to the new challenges that ERA has presented. A case study of representative schools has begun.
Status: Sponsored project
Source of Grant: Stoke on Trent Local Education Authority £150
Date of Research: 1990 - continuing
KEYWORDS: *educational administration; educational change; Educational Reform Act – 1988; local management of schools; school-based management; secondary schools*

9/0142
     Department of Education Management, Hassall Road,
     Alsager, Stoke on Trent ST7 2HL
     0270 500661
     Braund, C. Mr

Education management training and development in Europe
Abstract: The aim of this project is to chart education management training in Europe and to analyse different models in use. Research methodology will involve a literature survey, general survey and various visits.
Status: Sponsored project
Source of Grant: Crewe & Alsager College of Higher Education
Date of Research: 1990-1992
KEYWORDS: *comparative education; management development; management in education; training*

9/0143
     Department of Education Management, Hassall Road,
     Alsager, Stoke on Trent ST7 2HL
     0270 500661
     West-Burnham, J. Mr; *Supervisor:* Seymour, R. Mr;
     James, L. Dr
The applicability of total quality management to the management of schools
Abstract: Total Quality Management (TQM) has emerged in the 1980s as the most powerful tool for organisational review and development. This research seeks to explore the extent to which the principles of TQM are applicable to school management. The research model is based on the researcher's book (WEST-BURNHAM, J. (1992). Managing quality in schools: a TQM approach, Longman), as a basis for examining perceptions of quality, identifying and analysing existing relevant practice and developing a model that is applicable in schools. The book includes an invitation to respond to the writer – this will generate an opportunity sample. The writer has been engaged by a number of local education authorities to run courses on quality management – participants in these courses will be used as a sample for follow-up work in order to review the principles and practices identified in the book.
Published Material: WEST-BURNHAM, J. (1992). Managing quality in schools: a TQM approach. Harlow: Longman Press.
Status: Individual research
Date of Research: 1990 - continuing
KEYWORDS: *educational quality; management in education; school based management*

9/0144
     Health Research and Development Unit, Hassell Road,
     Alsager, Stoke on Trent ST7 2HL
     0270 500661
     Heathcote, G. Dr; *Supervisor:* Heathcote, G. Dr
Training for special educational needs in Sandwell and Coventry
Abstract: Action research conducted in two Metropolitan districts to improve the 'match' between training opportunities and special educational needs.
Status: Sponsored project
Source of Grant: Replan; National Institute for Adult Education; Training, Enterprise & Education Directorate £7,000
Date of Research: 1990-1991
KEYWORDS: *access to education; action research; opportunities; special educational needs; training*

9/0145
     Hassall Road, Alsager, Stoke on Trent ST7 2HL
     0270 500661
     Turnock, J. Mr; *Supervisor:* Tolly, B. Dr
The role of the Church of England in the provision of education at Worfield Endowed Church of England (Aided) Primary School from 1546 to 1991 in the light of the 1988 Education Reform Act with particular reference to the governors' responsibility for curriculum, funding and building
Abstract: The aim of this research is to clarify the purpose and application of educational endowments from the Brierley Charity of 1609, Lloyd and Parker Charity of 1613 and other trust deeds which were later amalgamated into the Worfield United Charities. It will also try to establish the changing role of the Church of England and the provision of free education. The project will look at the changes which took place in local thinking and to examine the influences of the major educational reform acts of the last 150 years. The researchers will establish whether the Foundation Governors' income from endowment is still regulated by the 1909 scheme, or whether subsequent variations have been legitimised by the Charity Commissioners. Links will be established between the elected Church Foun-

dation Governors and their associated endowments with other members of the Governing Body in order to clarify responsibility for the curriculum and the ownership of the land and buildings of Worfield Primary School. It is also hoped to clarify the powers of the whole Governing Body in the light of new legislation under the 1988 Education Reform Act.
Status: Sponsored project
Source of Grant: Shropshire Local Education Authority £395
Date of Research: 1991 - continuing
KEYWORDS: church education relationship; educational history; educational legislation; financial support; free education; school governors

9/0146
Department of Education Management, Hassall Road, Alsager, Stoke on Trent ST7 2HL
0270 500661
Seymour, R. Mr
Learning styles and education management
Abstract: This research uses the work of Honey and Mumford on learning styles and applies it to the education sector. Education management norms have been derived to compare with other management groups. Follow-up work has been carried out on a sample from the original research group to analyse individual changes and review these against the background of learning development and organisational environment. A learning diagnostic questionnaire was used and important indicators were found for the training and development of middle managers in schools. Further work is in progress on the use of learning styles in relation to students' study choices within a flexible, negotiated programme for the M.Sc. degree in Education Management.
Published Material: SEYMOUR, R. & WEST-BURNHAM, J. (1989). 'Learning styles and education management: part one', International Journal of Educational Management, Vol 3, No 4, pp.19-25, December.; SEYMOUR, R. & WEST-BURNHAM, J. (1990). 'Learning styles and education management: part two', International Journal of Educational Management, Vol 4, No 4, pp.22-26, December.
Status: Sponsored project
Source of Grant: Crewe and Alsager College of Higher Education
Date of Research: 1988-1992
KEYWORDS: cognitive style; learning strategies; management in education

Dartington Social Research Unit

9/0147
Foxhole, Dartington Hall, Totnes, Devon TQ9 6EB
0803 862231
Bristol University, Department of Social Policy and Planning, 8 Woodlands Road, Bristol BS8 1TN
0272 251424
Cleaver, H. Mrs; *Supervisor:* Millham, S. Prof.
A continued evaluation of 'Catch 'em Young'
Abstract: The study will explore the possible long term benefits for children who were involved in 'Catch 'em Young', a 3 year scheme established to prevent delinquency and behaviour problems in secondary school children. The report submitted to the Department of Education and Science in 1989 scrutinised children's behaviour as they transferred from primary to secondary school. The long term follow up study allows us to focus on the study group of 495 children as they pass through school, make important career decisions and enter the adult world. The previously applied methodology, which used both extensive and intensive dimensions, will be utilised. Thus, the research will continue to combine an overview resulting from a survey of the experiences of the study children with insights and perceptions of a small group of children, their teachers and parents. When linked with the earlier research findings, it will provide an opportunity to explore how family, school and peer group influences interact in the transitions of adolescents.
Published Material: CLEAVER, H. (1991). Vulnerable children in schools: a study of Catch 'em Young – a project helping 10 year olds transfer school. Aldershot: Dartmouth Publishing Company.
Status: Sponsored project
Source of Grant: Department of Education and Science £30,000
Date of Research: 1990 - continuing

KEYWORDS: antisocial behaviour; behaviour problems; delinquency prevention; longitudinal studies; secondary school pupils; transfer pupils

De Montford University

9/0148
PO Box 143, Leicester LE1 9BH
0533 551551
Mason, R. Dr; Maughan, C. Mr; Bruntlett, S. Mr
Artists-in-education training project
Abstract: This pilot project was set up in 1990 by the Arts Council working with three regional arts associations and Leicester Polytechnic (now De Montford University). The aims were 'to provide performing artists, visual artists, craftspeople, writers and composers with the skills and knowledge they need to work with confidence in education today'. The programme developed and implemented early in 1991 covered a 10-day period and included residential training weekends staffed by a combination of artists, teachers and educators, and six day placements in primary or secondary schools. The progress of the project was systematically documented and evaluated by a project officer specifically appointed for this purpose. His evaluation report identified strengths and weaknesses of the training programme and of the residencies in terms of their contribution to teachers' and pupils' learning in the arts and the impact of artists on school arts programmes.
Published Material: ILLSLEY, R. (1991). The Artists-in-Education Training Project: an evaluative report. Leicester Polytechnic.
Status: Sponsored project
Source of Grant: Arts Council of Great Britain £35,000
Date of Research: 1990-1991
KEYWORDS: artists; arts education; training

9/0149
Department of Education, Scraptoft Campus, Scraptoft, Leicester LE7 9SU
0533 431011
Bennett, R. Dr; *Supervisor:* Allison, B. Prof.; Denscombe, M. Dr; Huxley, M. Mr
The significance of dance in community based projects
Abstract: Following a broad survey of the national, regional and local policies for the promotion of dance, the research follows a case study approach using a combination of observation, participant observation and interview techniques to look at the effects of gender, race and class on the take-up of community based dance initiatives.
Status: Individual research
Date of Research: 1987 - continuing
KEYWORDS: community programmes; dance

9/0150
Department of Education, Centre for Postgraduate Teacher Education, Scraptoft Campus, Scraptoft, Leicester LE7 9SU
0533 431011
Kypreou, I. Miss; *Supervisor:* Allison, B. Prof.; Mason, R. Dr
The assessment of art at first degree level: a comparative study of the principles and methods underlying assessment of fine art students in Athens and Leicester
Abstract: The study sets out to determine: (a) the role theories of art criticism play in the assessment of fine art students at first degree level; (b) whether assessment procedures in two fine art institutions (Leicester – documented procedures, Athens – non-documented procedures) can be described relative to major theories of art criticism; and (c) the extent to which the differing procedures of assessment utilised in the two institutions are subject to or are affected by the theoretical positions adopted by individual examiners. Fieldwork (observation, interview and questionnaire) will be carried out in the two institutions.
Status: Individual research
Date of Research: 1988 - continuing
KEYWORDS: art education; comparative education; criticism; degrees – academic; fine arts; Greece

9/0151

Department of Education, Centre for Postgraduate Teacher Education, Scraptoft Campus, Scraptoft, Leicester LE7 9SU
0533 431011
Iwano, M. Miss; *Supervisor:* Mason, R. Dr; Denscombe, M. Dr

Curriculum reform in Japanese art education: the case of multiculturalism

Abstract: This research will investigate, analyse and evaluate Japanese art curriculum at primary, secondary and high school levels. It will explore the possibility of curriculum reform in Japanese art education with reference to theory and practice of multicultural education. Since multicultural education has been applied in non-western societies, the study will aim also to identify key principles which might be taken into account or underpin an international concept and application of multicultural education.

Status: Individual research
Date of Research: 1989-1992
KEYWORDS: art education; curriculum development; Japan; multicultural education

9/0152

Department of Education, Centre for Postgraduate Teacher Education, Scraptoft Campus, Scraptoft, Leicester LE7 9SU
0533 43101
Rawding, M. Mr; *Supervisor:* Mason, R. Dr; Allison, B. Prof.

Relationship between works of literature and works of art with reference to interpretation theory and implications for school curricula

Abstract: The investigation seeks answers to three related questions. First, what is available in art educational literature that relates both to the particular concept of artistic intention and the broader area of controversy which has arisen in connection with the theoretical relationship of art and criticism? Second, what insights can the study of the concept of artistic intention provide regarding conceptual issues associated with the theoretical relationship of art and criticism? Third, what steps are required to 'bridge the gap' between philosophy of art (ref. critical theory) and the philosophy of education (ref. curriculum theory) in order to translate theoretical materials arising from the study of the concept of artistic intention into a coherent pedagogy of art criticism? It is anticipated that the study will render the nature of controversy in philosophical aesthetics more readily available to the field of education by providing a framework for a theoretically coherent and consistent pedagogy of criticism. Hence the study will conclude with recommendations for curriculum development that includes reference to the synthesis of subject content, methods of teaching and learning, and curricular aims and objectives.

Status: Individual research
Date of Research: 1985 - continuing
KEYWORDS: art education; curriculum development; literature

9/0153

Department of Education, Centre for Postgraduate Teacher Education, Scraptoft Campus, Scraptoft, Leicester LE7 9SU
0533 431011
Tyers, J. Mr; *Supervisor:* Allison, B. Prof.

The personality and other attributes, qualities, abilities and opinions of A-level design students

Abstract: The project is designed to ascertain the personality characteristics of General Certificate of Education (GCE) students and to compare them with other A-level students. It is anticipated that the research will show the extent to which, if any, the design course affects attitudes and working processes.

Status: Individual research
Date of Research: 1987 - continuing
KEYWORDS: A-level examinations; design education; learner characteristics; personality

9/0154

Department of Education, Centre for Postgraduate Teacher Education, Scraptoft Campus, Scraptoft, Leicester LE7 9SU
0533 551551
Joetsu University of Education, Joetsu-Shi, Niigata-Ken 943, Japan
Mason, R. Dr; *Supervisor:* Mason, R. Dr; Nakase, N. Prof.

Art education in Japanese high schools: a case study

Abstract: This project was carried out in a junior high school in Joetsu City over a three-month period in Autumn 1990. The aim was to describe and explain meanings and systems of organised behaviour making up a specifically Japanese culture of teaching and learning in art through ethnography. Fieldwork data are currently being analysed. An ethnographic account of art teaching in a Japanese high school is thought to be of practical relevance for British art teachers for the following reasons: (1) Japan has a highly centralized education system with a National Curriculum which includes art. The high level of general education achievement is currently the envy of the developed world. Information derived from systematic observation of Japanese schooling is understood as having potential to generate useful comparative data about core curriculum content and standards of achievement in art; (2) Modern Japan provides a unique example of a culture which has adopted western ideals but to a remarkable degree has retained its unique artistic identity. An ethnography of Japanese art education is likely to be of practical assistance in contemporary debates about multicultural curriculum in art in the British educational context.

Status: Sponsored project
Source of Grant: Ministry of Education, Japan £7,000
Date of Research: 1990-1992
KEYWORDS: art education; comparative education; cross cultural studies; ethnography; Japan

9/0155

School of Arts, PO Box 143, Leicester LE1 9BH
0553 551551
Rice, J. Mrs; O'Sullivan, T. Mr; Saunders, C. Ms; *Supervisor:* Rice, J. Mrs

Communication and professional competencies in a modular humanities programme

Abstract: The Communication and Professional Studies (CPS) programme plays a key role in the degree scheme in arts and humanities (DSAH) at De Montfort University. In brief, its function is two-fold: (1) it is designed to equip students with the core skills necessary to participate effectively within a flexible, modular arts degree; and (2) it begins to develop in students some of the key vocational and future career skills relevant to their undergraduate studies. The aims of this project are to: (1) research, design and produce open learning packages for key elements of the CPS programme in the school of arts; (2) research and develop the necessary tutoring and student centred delivery skills for staff teaching on the DSAH; (3) provide research evidence of the teaching and learning requirements generated by the DSAH; (4) provide staff development to support the teaching and learning requirements generated by the DSAH; (5) provide an opportunity to address broader issues of coherence and progression by developing CPS skills in the subject modules; and (6) provide a model for development for open learning packages on the Level 1 DSAH programme. Project development will take two forms: (1) Curriculum audit and research – this will include research to identify the teaching and learning experiences of staff and students on the DSAH with reference to the CPS Level 1 module; and staff development workshops to address the issues identified in audit; (2) Open learning packs – this will include development of supported self-study packs for selected elements of the CPS course; and staff development workshops to disseminate the process of their generation (i.e. information technology skills) and the teaching skills necessary for their implementation.

Status: Sponsored project
Source of Grant: De Montford University £19,000
Date of Research: 1991 - continuing
KEYWORDS: communication skills; competency-based education; humanities; minimum competencies; modular courses; open education

9/0156

PO Box 143, Leicester LE1 9BH
0533 551551
University of Central England in Birmingham, Perry Barr, Birmingham B42 2SU
021 331 5000
Eastwood, J. Ms; Supervisor: Mason, R. Dr; Denscombe, M. Dr; Shute, C. Dr

An investigation into the therapeutic relationship and implications for speech language therapy training

Abstract: Student training in speech-language therapy comprises theoretical and practical components. Theories are largely borrowed from other disciplines such as psychology, linguistics and medicine, but practical work with communicatively-impaired in-

dividuals is an important part of training. The theory of therapy is, however, poorly understood. This research will examine the theory or philosophy and practice of therapy in the literature and in a variety of *in situ* settings where communicatively-impaired individuals receive treatment from speech-language therapists. The aim of the research is to analyse and clarify existing theories of therapy and to develop new systems and methods or models for training speech-language therapy students.
Published Material: EASTWOOD, J. (1988). 'Qualitative research methodology – an additional research method for speech pathology?', British Journal of Disorders of Communication, Vol 23, No 2, pp.171-184.; SHUTE, C., EASTWOOD, J., FREEMAN, M. & WHITEHOUSE, J. (1989). Supervised work experience in speech therapy. Birmingham Polytechnic.; C.N.A.A. Briefing Paper No. 23 (1990). A survey of supervised work experience in speech therapy.
Status: Individual research
Date of Research: 1990 - continuing
KEYWORDS: *speech therapy; speech training; therapists; training methods*

Derbyshire College of Higher Education

9/0157
Western Road, Mickleover, Derby DE3 5GX
0332 47181
Roberts, R. Dr; Dolan, J. Mr
Economic and industrial awareness in the primary school
Abstract: Research is continuing into both the perceptions primary school children have of 'work' and the ways in which teachers can make use of these perceptions to design curricular responses. However, the publication of National Curriculum Council's 'Education for economic and industrial understanding: curriculum guidance 3 and 4' has given an additional dimension to the research concerning the effective management of EIU (Economic and Industrial Understanding) as a cross curricular theme within the National Curriculum. Over the past year a research base has been established in about 30 local primary schools whose headteachers have an interest in cross curricular themes in general and EIU in particular. It is proposed to investigate children's' perceptions, school curricular responses and the management issues that these generate in the coming year. Additionally a group of 15 students completing initial teacher training will be undertaking exploratory research based topics with the network. A comparison group and network is being established with Dr J. Ahier at Homerton College, Cambridge. Alongside this work with primary children a parallel investigation is beginning into perception and awareness of EIU held by students training to be primary teachers with a view to establishing data which can then be reflected in the design of more effective EIU modules, and the further development of cross curricularity within B. Ed. (Bachelor of Education) and PGCE (Post Graduate Certificate of Education) courses.
Published Material: ROBERTS, R.J. & DOLAN, J. (1989). 'Children's' perception of work'', Educational Review, Vol 41, No 1, pp.19-28.; DOLAN, J. & ROBERTS, R.J. (1989). 'Unpacking the knapsack', Primary Teaching Studies, Vol 4, No 3, pp.259-267, Summer.; DOLAN, J. & ROBERTS, R.J. (1990). 'Consultancy led INSET: the case of economic awareness education', British Journal of In-Service Education, Vol 16, No 2, pp.91-96.
Status: Sponsored project
Source of Grant: Derbyshire College of Higher Education
Date of Research: 1987-1992
KEYWORDS: *cross curricular approach; employment; enterprise education; preservice teacher education; primary education; pupil attitudes*

9/0158
Western Road, Mickleover, Derby DE3 5GX
0332 47181
Wallace, G. Dr
Local management of schools: database of research
Abstract: The aim of this research is to establish and maintain a database of Local Management of Schools (LMS) related research with the objective of: (a) ensuring ready access to an overview of

LMS research and findings for British Educational Research Association (BERA) members and other researchers; (b) widening such access beyond what is normally published, e.g. dissertations, and theses at Masters level; (c) identifying and disseminating successful practice; (d) identifying and disseminating issues of interest or concern to policy makers and the media.
Published Material: WALLACE, G. (Ed.) (1991). Local management of schools. London: Multilingual Matters. British Educational Research Association. (BERA Dialogues Series, No 6).
Status: Sponsored project
Source of Grant: Derbyshire College of Higher Education £3,700; British Educational Research Association £600
Date of Research: 1990 - continuing
KEYWORDS: *databases; local management of schools; research*

9/0159
Western Road, Mickleover, Derby DE3 5GX
0332 47181
Roberts, R. Dr; McKean, R. Mrs; *Supervisor:* Littler, G. Prof.; Dale, A. Mr
Evaluation of Derbyshire College B. Ed. (Hon) Initial Degree
Abstract: The aims of this research project are to evaluate the B. Ed. Hons degree at Derbyshire College for a number of different research perceptions, and in doing so to provide the faculty and the validating body with data upon which sound judgements can be made about the standing and the future of the degree; and to provide course management with data upon which valid course development can be used. The evaluation is based on the experience of the cohort of 1987 entry students and associated staff within the college and off-site, in particular teaching practice schools. The mode of enquiry is through 'whole college evaluation' and 'research based teaching' together with 'process evaluation' facilitated by the employment of a research assistant. The case study will cover approximately 120 students and 30+ staff.
Status: Sponsored project
Source of Grant: Derbyshire College of Higher Education
Date of Research: 1987-1991
KEYWORDS: *bachelors degrees; course evaluation; preservice teacher education*

9/0160
Western Road, Mickleover, Derby DE3 5GX
0332 47181
South Bank University, Department of Education, Diary House, 77-79 Borough Road, London SE1 OAA
071 378 7355
Liverpool University, Department of Education, PO Box 147, Liverpool L69 3BX
051 794 200
King, J. Ms; *Supervisor:* Wallace, G. Dr; Weiner, G. Miss; Hamilton, D. Prof.
Gendered expectations and the primary school curriculum
Abstract: The central question of this project was whether gender discrimination continues to operate in primary schools in the planning and delivery of topic work. The research examined whether there was: gender bias in the topic choices of teachers and pupils; gender bias in the reasons teachers give about their topic choices; gender bias in the organisation and delivery of topic lessons; and gender bias in the value given to achievements by pupils. Gender bias is defined as any consistent pattern of differentiated behaviour in the way pupils are treated. The research was conducted in two parallel junior school classes in a rural and suburban primary school. The methods used included participant observation, interviews, questionnaires, and records, children's work and documents. The evidence shows that in spite of equal opportunities rhetoric, differential gender expectations condition teachers' reactions to pupils' work. Teachers have the power to convert these expectations into graded hierarchies of ability that continue to affect pupils' life chances.
Published Material: KING, J. 'Gendered expectations and the primary school curriculum'. Paper presented at British Educational Research Association (BERA) Conference, August 1990.
Status: Individual research
Date of Research: 1987-1991
KEYWORDS: *gender equality; primary education; projects – learning activities; sex differences*

Dundee University

9/0161

Centre for Continuing Education, Dundee DD1 4HN

0382 23181

Orbell, S. Dr

Description and evaluation of an educational intervention to assist learning disabled adults into employment and independent living

Abstract: The aim of this project is to describe the experiences of the first group of trainees entering a newly opened training centre. It will describe: (1) the needs of trainees; and (2) the activities undertaken by trainees, identifying the methods and difficulties associated with operationalising supported employment training. The project will also longitudinally assess the outcomes of training including: (a) employment; (b) independent living; (c) perceived competence; and (d) self-esteem. The sample used was 39 adults, aged 16 – 25, with mild or moderate mental handicap. Data collected included project records and staff assessments. Personal interviews with trainees were of two kinds: (a) semi-structured interviews to identify living skills, social activities, aspirations, work motivation; and (b) quantitative instruments designed to measure perceived competence, self-esteem, social comparisons.

Status: Sponsored project

Source of Grant: Scottish Office Home and Health Department

Date of Research: 1990-1992

KEYWORDS: adult basic education; competence; employment potential; life skills; mental retardation; moderate learning difficulties; special educational needs; supporting studies

9/0162

Centre for Continuing Education, Dundee DD1 4HN

0382 23181

Hartley, J. Dr

An analysis of government policy for teachers' professional development in Scotland: 1979-1990

Abstract: An analysis of government documentation and research on teachers' continuing professional development, informed by critical theory.

Published Material: HARTLEY, J.D. (1986). 'Structural isomorphism and the management of consent in education', Journal of Education Policy, Vol 1, No 3, pp.229-237.; HARTLEY, J.D. (1990). 'Tests, tasks and Taylorism: a model T approach to the management of education', Journal of Education Policy, Vol 5, No 1, pp.67-76.; HARTLEY, J.D. (1989). 'Beyond collaboration: the management of professional development in Scotland', British Journal of Education for Teaching, Vol 10, No 2, pp.253-261.; HARTLEY, J.D. (1990). 'Beyond competency: a socio-technical model of continuing professional education', British Journal of Inservice Education, Vol 16, No 1, pp.66-70.

Status: Individual research

Date of Research: 1986 - continuing

KEYWORDS: academic staff development; educational policy; inservice teacher education; professional development; Scotland

9/0163

Centre for Continuing Education, Dundee DD1 4HN

0382 23181

Kaskaris, I. Mr; *Supervisor:* Hartley, J. Dr

The Gramscian theory of education: a critical study of the development of educational theory

Abstract: This research aims to generate a theory of education which: first, provides a critical analysis of the positivism underlying much educational theory; second, analyses the post-modern semiotic reaction to this, with a view to pointing up its largely de-politicised, ahistorical essence; and third, suggests a convergence of Gramscian theory and critical theory.

Status: Individual research

Date of Research: 1988 - continuing

KEYWORDS: educational theories; sociology of education

9/0164

Centre for Continuing Education, Dundee DD1 4HN

0382 23181

Murray, R. Mr; *Supervisor:* Hartley, J. Dr

The development of managerialism in Scottish education since 1945

Abstract: The study examines the increasing tendency in Scottish education to use industrial and corporate modes of management in education since 1945.

Status: Individual research

Date of Research: 1988 - continuing

KEYWORDS: educational history; management in education; Scotland

9/0165

Centre for Continuing Education, Dundee DD1 4HN

0382 23181

Gerver, E. Prof.

Trends and issues in gender and education in Scotland

Abstract: This study will analyse patterns and trends in gender differences in Scottish education and training, including continuing education. It will focus on gender as an issue in education management.

Published Material: GERVER, E. (1994). Gender and the democratic intellect. Edinburgh: Scottish Academic Press, (forthcoming).

Status: Individual research

Date of Research: 1991-1992

KEYWORDS: educational administration; educational trends; Scotland; sex differences

9/0166

Centre for Medical Education, Ninewells Hospital and Medical School, Dundee DD1 9SY

0382 6011

Mulholland, H. Dr; *Supervisor:* Mulholland, H. Dr

Assessment of competence in general practice

Abstract: The research was designed to improve the reliability and validity of the Membership Examination of the Royal College of General Practitioners (RCGP). Results of the last five years were analysed (for approximately 2,000 candidates each year) and recommendations made as to changes in numbers and types of questions in the existing papers. Two new types of test were developed: (1) The Critical Reading Paper in which candidates have to read, critically evaluate and discuss applications of scientific journal articles and of printed material of a variety of forms; (2) The simulated surgery in which candidates are placed in conditions which simulate as far as possible real surgery conditions and are assessed on their competence in consultation. This part of the research is now being continued with funding from the European Community. The second stage of the project is to develop a method of assessing consultation skills in general practice. This part of the project is being carried on in conjunction with the Department of General Practice at the University of Leicester and the Free University of Amsterdam.

Published Material: LOCKIE, C. (Ed.) (1990). 'The MRCGP Examination', Occasional Paper, No 46. London Royal College of General Practitioners.

Status: Sponsored project

Source of Grant: Royal College of General Practitioners; Department of Health; European Community

Date of Research: 1988 - continuing

KEYWORDS: assessment; competence; examinations; medical education; medicine; physicians

9/0167

Centre for Medical Education, Ninewells Hospital and Medical School, Dundee DD1 9SY

0382 60111

McAleer, S. Dr; *Supervisor:* Harden, R. Prof.; Laidlaw, J. Miss

A programme to encourage and facilitate doctors' participation in clinical audit

Abstract: The need for audit as one aspect of clinical practice is now generally accepted throughout the medical profession. Its adoption requires a change in behaviour of doctors – one which will be successful and long lasting. This distance learning programme intends to provide a more in depth training about audit by using a 5 stage approach – awareness, interest, appraisal, trial and adoption. The programme will be designed to relate audit to the doctor's (both hospital and community) day-to-day practice and encourage further learning about audit on-the-job. It comprises a resource book which contains key information about audit. In addition participants will receive a series of 'doctors' diaries' in which audit activities will be

described in a problem based format. Responses to these problems will be collected and feedback provided – using comparisons between decisions made and those of colleagues. There will also be a number of practical audit activities linked to the diaries. The programme will be offered on a national basis.
Status: Sponsored project
Source of Grant: Scottish Office Home and Health Department
Date of Research: 1991-1992
KEYWORDS: distance education; institutional evaluation; medical services; professional continuing education

9/0168

Centre for Medical Education, Ninewells Hospital and Medical School, Dundee DD1 9SY
0382 60111
Rudland, J. Miss; *Supervisor:* Harden, R. Prof.
Practical psychiatry in primary care
Abstract: This programme is being developed with the aim of improving the practical psychiatry skills of medical practitioners (GPs). It comprises resource booklets containing sections on depression and anxiety, alcohol abuse, marital and sexual problems, the difficult patient and special problems. The booklets will utilise latent image printing to offer immediate feedback to the participants. Participants will also receive a series of management problems in which decisions have to be taken concerning diagnosis and treatment. Participants' responses to these problems will be returned on a pre-printed card to the Centre for Medical Education. On receipt of the card a personalised commentary on the given responses will be sent to the participants.
Status: Sponsored project
Source of Grant: SmithKline Beecham Pharmaceuticals Ltd
Date of Research: 1991-1992
KEYWORDS: distance education; medical education; professional continuing education; psychiatry

9/0169

Centre for Medical Education, Ninewells Hospital and Medical School, Dundee DD1 9SY
0382 60111
Abdel-Fattah, A. Dr; Thomas, M. Ms; *Supervisor:* Harden, R. Prof.
Assessment of the educational needs of health professionals in palliative care of patients with advanced cancer, and their families
Abstract: The aim of this project is to assess the learning needs of the health care professionals in palliative care of patients with advanced cancer, and their families. The first phase, concluded in 1990, has targeted general practitioners and included a print programme, patient management challenges and a computer programme. The current phase is targeting junior hospital doctors in a hospital ward environment. Different educational strategies are being used to facilitate the learning needs in this area.
Status: Sponsored project
Source of Grant: Cancer Relief Macmillan Fund
Date of Research: 1986-1992
KEYWORDS: cancer; doctor-patient relationship; health personnel; medical education; medical services; professional continuing education

9/0170

Centre for Medical Education, Ninewells Hospital and Medical School, Dundee DD1 9SY
0382 60111
Blicharski, J. Mr; *Supervisor:* Harden, R. Prof.
Distance learning in Central Nervous Systems (CNS) psychiatry
Abstract: As part of Glaxo's continued research in the field of central nervous system pharmacology, Glaxo have commissioned the Centre for Medical Education, Dundee to develop a distance learning programme aimed at senior managers within Glaxo. This programme will inform managers of the pharmacological significance of a new drug, ondansetron, and how it can be used in a variety of disorders. Development of an educational strategy to explain often complex theories and terminology will be accompanied by assessments for each topic module. Information will be presented at four levels of complexity allowing readers to obtain information at a level appropriate to their needs.

Status: Sponsored project
Source of Grant: Glaxo Group Research Ltd
Date of Research: 1991-1992
KEYWORDS: distance education; management development; medical education; pharmacology; psychiatry

9/0171

Centre for Medical Education, Ninewells Hospital and Medical School, Dundee DD1 9SY
0382 60111
Lindsay, G. Mr; Hesketh, A. Mrs; *Supervisor:* Harden, R. Prof.
An individualised patient education programme for community pharmacy practice
Abstract: This project aims to develop and study a practical system to provide patient education via the community pharmacy. This will involve the use of new technology to provide user-friendly interactive patient education materials. An important aspect of the project will look at ways of developing and studying a liaison between pharmacists, general practitioners, and patients.
Status: Sponsored project
Source of Grant: Scottish Office Home and Health Department
Date of Research: 1990 - continuing
KEYWORDS: health education; medical services; patient education; pharmacists; pharmacy

9/0172

Centre for Medical Education, Ninewells Hospital and Medical School, Dundee DD1 9SY
0382 60111
Thomson, L. Mrs; *Supervisor:* Harden, R. Prof.
Diploma in advanced nursing studies
Abstract: The Diploma Course aims to equip the individual with the knowledge and ability necessary to provide a high standard of individualised nursing care which is research based and reinforces individual accountability of the practitioner. Furthermore, the course aims to embrace the dynamics of change and emphasise the necessity for continuing professional updating and educational development.
Status: Sponsored project
Source of Grant: University of Dundee; Tayside Health Board
Date of Research: 1990 - continuing
KEYWORDS: distance education; nurse education; professional continuing education; professional development

9/0173

Centre for Medical Education, Ninewells Hospital and Medical School, Dundee DD1 9SY
0382 60111
Davis, M. Dr; *Supervisor:* Harden, M. Prof.
The Wound Programme
Abstract: The Wound Programme is a learning resource for medical undergraduates in the UK, Europe and North America. It comprises a resource book, a student study guide and a teachers' guide. It is designed to inform undergraduates about recent advances in the field of skin wound healing and can be employed by medical schools wishing to implement one or more of the following curriculum strategies, student centred learning, problem based learning and integration of the curriculum, both horizontal and vertical. The resource book employs a new format, based on a hypertext layout, and a new approach to the assessment of patients with wounds – the wound healing matrix.
Status: Sponsored project
Source of Grant: ConvaTec
Date of Research: 1990 - continuing
KEYWORDS: educational materials; learning strategies; medical education; medical students

9/0174

Department of Epidemiology and Public Health, Ninewells Hospital and Medical School, Dundee DD1 9SY
0382 60111
Tayside Educational Psychology Service, St Mary's Lane, Lochee, Dundee
0382 621976
Abraham, C. Dr; Cross, J. Ms; Smith, E. Mrs; Kirkaldy, B. Mr
What dimensions are used to describe special educational needs?
Abstract: There is evidence that, despite the recommendations of the

Warnock Report, professionals continue to rely heavily on the use of handicap categories when describing children's' special educational needs (SENs). This project aims to investigate current definitions of special educational needs by psychologists and doctors in Records of Needs within Tayside Region, with a view to evaluating progress towards a needs model. A content analysis will be carried out on the 100 most recently opened Records of Needs in Tayside Region. A content analysis coding frame will be designed on the basis of a detailed analysis of a sub-sample of 25-30 records. The coding categories and method of analysis will be tested by independent coders and by deriving inter-coder reliability scores. There will also be comparison with the findings of other researchers.
Status: Sponsored project
Source of Grant: Scottish Office Education Department £6,781
Date of Research: 1992-1992
KEYWORDS: disabilities; doctors; groups; needs; psychologists; special educational needs

9/0175
　　Department of Social Work, Dundee DD1 4HN
　　0382 23181
　　Kendrick, A. Dr; Fraser, A. Dr
An examination of the factors that promote the development of an integrated child care strategy
Abstract: This is an overview study of current policies and developments in Scottish Social Work Departments which relate to the integration of residential and community child care services between agencies (particularly Social Work and Education) and with Social Work Departments. The study will be carried out by content analysis of policy and planning documents and by interviews with key social work personnel. In three selected local authorities the nature of the integration of child care services will be studied in more detail over two years. A cohort study will look at career patterns of children in care and will focus on the outcomes of particular social work placements. Collection of data will be by questionnaire, analysis of case files and interviews with children and young people. Interviews will be carried out with personnel involved with the cohort of children to examine the relationship between organisational structures policies and practice as perceived by social work staff, Children's Panel Members and Reporters to the Children's Panel. To provide information about the level of inter-agency integration, educational staff will be interviewed. A questionnaire survey of residential establishments used for children in the care of Social Work Departments will be carried out to establish the extent and range of residential services in Scotland and their links with complementary child care services.
Status: Sponsored project
Source of Grant: Social Work Services Group £200,000
Date of Research: 1990 - continuing
KEYWORDS: child welfare; community services; residential care; Scotland; social services; social work

Durham University

9/0176
　　Department of Sociology and Social Policy, Elvet Riverside 11, New Elvet, Durham DH1 3JT
　　091 374 2329
　　Corr, H. Dr
Teachers and the politics of gender 1800-1914: a comparative study of England and Scotland
Abstract: The research is primarily designed to historically document the social construction of gender roles and inequalities in the teaching profession and within wider educational structures. It aims to show how successive state educational policies sought to promote gender differences in the curriculum and in the teacher training system as the nineteenth century progressed. The study compares and contrasts the position of the sexes under English and Scottish educational, religious, and political systems. Particular themes focus on the following:- the feminisation of teaching 1800-1914; occupational and sex segregation in the teaching labour force; liberal upper and middle class feminism and the campaign to introduce the teaching of housework in state schools; sexual politics in teachers' unions – the National Union of Teachers (NUT) and the Educational Institute of Scotland (EIS). The research is based on archive sources and official parliamentary papers, school board records and church records.

Status: Individual research
Date of Research: 1986 - continuing
KEYWORDS: educational history; sex differences; sex role; women teachers; women's education

9/0177
　　Department of Theology, Abbey House, Palace Green, Durham DH1 3RS
　　091 374 2060
　　McCann, J. Mr; *Supervisor:* Hulmes, E. Prof.
A theological critique of Christian education, with special reference to developments in Northern Ireland since 1944
Abstract: The thesis has three principal aims: (1) to provide justification for a confident Christian education in an increasingly secular and agnostic world; (2) to evaluate the development and present status of Christian education in Northern Ireland in the light of its sectarian history and current situation of community conflict; (3) to consider the remit of Christian education and its role in promoting societal harmony. The thesis consists of seven chapters and includes: the issue of Christian education in the Northern Ireland context; a validation of Christian education; and a criticism of analytical philosophy and positivist influences in contemporary liberal education, especially where these have affected conceptions of religious education. In addition it promotes Christian apologetics as both a viable and needed response to relativistic agnosticism. The scope of the thesis embraces: considerations of Northern Ireland confessionalism; the influence of ideologies; the separate schools system; the question of integrated education; the historical background to the divided communities; the challenge of the great Christian imperatives of love and forgiveness in respect of community reconciliation and of implementing a Christian education fully alive to its responsibilities; the assumptions and values of Christian eduction; the nature of religious education; theistic belief and the Christian tradition. The concluding chapter confronts practical issues and suggest models and approaches in Christian education with outreach towards reconciliation.
Status: Individual research
Date of Research: 1988-1992
KEYWORDS: Christianity; church and education; community relations; educational history; interfaith relations; religious conflict; religious differences; social change

9/0178
　　School of Education, Leazes Road, Durham DH1 1TA
　　091 374 2000
　　Breet, F. Ms; *Supervisor:* Byram, M. Dr; Thompson, L. Ms
Verbal interaction in mathematics lessons in four secondary schools in Anglophone Cameroon
Abstract: The study examines the role of classroom language in the learning mathematics through English as a second language. Teachers of English and mathematics will be trained to work together and change classroom practices. Consequences for children's learning will be monitored.
Status: Sponsored project
Source of Grant: Overseas Development Administration
Date of Research: 1990 - continuing
KEYWORDS: Cameroon; cross curricular approach; English – second language; language of instruction; mathematics education

9/0179
　　School of Education, Leazes Road, Durham DH1 1TA
　　091 374 2000
　　Dexter, G. Mr; *Supervisor:* Gilliland, J. Mr; McGuiness, J. Mr
Training in communication skills and counselling techniques and its influence on participants' personal constructs
Abstract: A study of the effectiveness of counsellor training, involving a review of intentions, content and processes involved in counsellor training courses. The research, in its early stages, will sample a range of short and long courses. The effects and effectiveness of courses will be evaluated by use of a range of qualitative measures including structured interviews, personal diaries, with some pre- and post-structured assessment, possibly involving the use of repertory grid techniques and where appropriate, case studies.
Status: Individual research
Date of Research: 1989 - continuing
KEYWORDS: communication skills; counselling techniques; counsellor training; course evaluation

9/0180
School of Education, Leazes Road, Durham DH1 1TA
091 374 2000
Gott, R. Dr; Feasey, R. Ms; *Supervisor:* Gott, R. Dr
Exploration of science
Abstract: The research project has three aims. Firstly a questionnaire to be used to ascertain teachers' (in primary and secondary schools) perceptions of the nature and purpose of practical work in science. Secondly a series of practical investigations which lead to information on progression in this key area of the National Curriculum. Finally a series of case studies of curriculum elements will be produced and finalised in schools. The work will result in a series of reports to the National Curriculum Council, INSET (Inservice Teacher Education) materials for schools and research publications.
Status: Sponsored project
Source of Grant: National Curriculum Council £158,000
Date of Research: 1990-1991
KEYWORDS: *curriculum development; National Curriculum; practical science; science education*

9/0181
School of Education, Leazes Road, Durham DH1 1TA
091 374 2000
Gott, R. Dr; Phipps, R. Mr; Feasey, R. Ms
Measurement in science in the primary classroom
Abstract: As part of work for the National Curriculum Council (NCC) on the implementation of the investigative work of Attainment Target 1 in Science, the issue of the availability of measuring equipment came to be seen as a matter of some concern to those interviewed as part of the research, and to the research team. As a consequence the science team in Durham undertook a survey independently of the NCC, of the availability of such equipment in a sample of primary schools drawn from a nationwide random sample. A paper based on this research is in preparation.
Status: Individual research
Date of Research: 1990-1992
KEYWORDS: *measurement; measurement equipment; primary schools; science activities; science education*

9/0182
School of Education, Leazes Road, Durham DH1 1TA
091 374 2000
Davis, A. Dr
Inquiry into key psychological concepts used to characterise features of learning and teaching, especially in mathematics
Abstract: This research argues that learning may be seen as the acquisition of knowledge and understanding, and/or the acquisition of abilities, capacities and skills. Research into the degree to which the curriculum offered to pupils 'matches' their current level of knowledge etc., relies on certain conceptions of knowledge, belief, understanding, ability, skill, and so on. Ideas behind the National Curriculum, especially with regard to assessment, also rely upon certain characteristics of the changes in pupils that occur when learning takes place. The research consists of a wide ranging conceptual/philosophical investgation into the adequacy of these conceptions and characterisations. Empirical research of others is sometimes reviewed and referred to but the argument being pursued is that at least some of this research is an expensive irrelevance, based tacitly on conceptually inadequate foundations.
Published Material: DAVIS, A.J. (1986). 'Learning and belief', Journal of Philosophy of Education, Vol 20, No 1.; DAVIS, A.J. (1988). 'Ability and learning', Journal of Philosophy of Education, Vol 22.; DAVIS, A.J. (1990). 'Logical defects of the TGAT Report', British Journal of Educational Studies, Vol XXXVIII, No 3, pp.237-250.; DAVIS, A.J. 'Matching and assessment', Journal of Curriculum Studies, (forthcoming).
Status: Individual research
Date of Research: 1987 - continuing
KEYWORDS: *cognitive processes; learning processes; learning theories; mathematics education*

9/0183
School of Education, Leazes Road, Durham DH1 1TA
091 374 2000
Robson, M. Ms; *Supervisor:* Cook, P. Mr; Gilliland, J. Mr
Stress in children
Abstract: The aim of this research is to investigate stress as it is perceived by adolescents in secondary schools and to build a paradigm of this perception. It is also proposed to design an intervention system that could be used in schools to teach adolescents to cope more successfully with stress. The cognitive paradigm that is useful in understanding the stress process seems incomplete without an acknowledgement of the role of unconscious learning and perception and this research aims to extend the model to include this. It is hoped that the role played by our unconscious in the perception of, and reaction to, stress may be incorporated in the model of the stress process as well as in the intervention system. The size and composition of the sample has not yet been established although exploratory pilot studies suggest that stress is a meaningful concept in the adolescents' world. From these exploratory studies, stressors seem many and various and the individual's perception of the stress appears to rest upon factors which include learned responses, social support and personality. Coping strategies are also many and various and likewise appear to rest upon the same mediating factors, as well as the individuals perceived control over the stressors.
Status: Individual research
Date of Research: 1990 - continuing
KEYWORDS: *secondary school pupils; stress – psychological; stress management*

9/0184
School of Education, Leazes Road, Durham DH1 1TA
091 374 2000
Goumandakoye, A. Mr; *Supervisor:* Byram, M. Dr;
McPartland, M. Mr
English language curriculum development in Niger: Niger educational development 1960-1992 with particular reference to English language teaching
Abstract: The present study concerns itself with a critical analysis of formal education in the Niger Republic from independence to the present, and the extent to which the experience gained in English Language Teaching could be beneficial for the rest of the curriculum, to the enhancement of the whole system. Hence, this piece of work should not only reveal achievements but also pinpoint the major setbacks of the educational system; more importantly, it should suggest ways and means which could lead to an improvement of the current system through a contrastive analysis of the major components, i.e. French, mathematics, and English, which is felt to be a dynamic and successful subject. The present study offers a comprehensive description of the evolution of Nigerian formal education, thus contributing to the enhancement of education awareness in Niger; it is hoped that the findings will not only give insight and provide skills useful to the Ministry, but also bring about positive change in one of the main components of any educational system, i.e. the curriculum.
Status: Sponsored project
Source of Grant: British Council
Date of Research: 1990-1992
KEYWORDS: *curriculum development; educational history; English – second language; Nigeria; second language teaching*

9/0185
School of Education, Leazes Road, Durham DH1 1TA
091 374 2000
Abu-Jalala, F. Mrs; *Supervisor:* Byram, M. Dr
The cultural dimension of English as a Foreign Language in the Arabian Gulf States
Abstract: The research aims to examine the possibility of introducing English as a foreign language (EFL) together with its western culture in an Arabic/Islamic culture, and to what extent. The study falls into two branches. Firstly, investigating the experts' (university staff, English language Inspectors, the curriculum planning department and teachers) opinion using the 'Delphi Technique', questionnaire method. Secondly, pupils at the secondary stage are involved in interviews and questionnaires to give their opinions about the same issue. The size of the sample is governed by the size of the population of teachers and pupils – this will include English language staff in secondary schools and the University of Qatar, and secondary school pupils.
Status: Sponsored project
Source of Grant: British Council in Doha £1,700
Date of Research: 1989 - continuing
KEYWORDS: *Arab states; English – second language; second language teaching*

9/0186

School of Education, Leazes Road, Durham DH1 1TA
091 374 2000
Lo, A. Mrs; *Supervisor:* Byram, M. Dr
An examination of Language Experience Approach (LEA) to teaching reading development and its use in second language learning
Abstract: A critical survey of the literature on language experience approaches to reading development and writing with particular reference to their use in second language learning. The research includes a case study of the introduction and development of language experience approaches with students in a secondary school in Hong Kong. The evaluation of the study utilises a range of qualitative approaches, observations, self-reporting, written materials and some formal and informal assessments of attainment.
Status: Individual research
Date of Research: 1986-1991
KEYWORDS: language experience approach; reading comprehension; reading teaching; second language learning; teaching methods

9/0187

School of Education, Leazes Road, Durham DH1 1TA
091 374 2000
Grace, G. Prof.; McGuiness, J. Mr
Headteachers: the impact of radical reform upon senior professionals
Abstract: An empirical and theoretical study of changing conceptions of leadership in English schooling with reference to transitions from the headteacher (as moral leader), the headteacher (as senior professional) and the headteacher (as chief executive). The study is based upon taped interviews with a sample of infant, junior and secondary headteachers in the north-east of England. A target sample of 100 is proposed. Accounts will be analysed in relation to LEA (local education authority) locations, level of school and possible gender differences in reaction to the development of managerialism in education.
Status: Sponsored project
Source of Grant: Durham University: Research and Initiatives Committee
Date of Research: 1990 - continuing
KEYWORDS: headteachers; leadership; leadership styles; local management of schools; management in education; school-based management

9/0188

School of Education, Leazes Road, Durham DH1 1TA
091 374 2000
Khuwaileh, A. Mr; *Supervisor:* Byram, M. Dr
English language teaching in higher education in Jordan: Syllabus design for English for Specific Purposes (ESP) courses
Abstract: A needs analysis in the use of English for learning science and technology in higher education in Jordan will be carried out, using questionnaires and interviews. This will lead to development of a syllabus and recommendations for curriculum change.
Status: Sponsored project
Source of Grant: Jordanian Government
Date of Research: 1990-1992
KEYWORDS: curriculum development; English – second language; English for specific purposes; higher education; Jordan; science education; technology education

9/0189

School of Education, Leazes Road, Durham DH1 1TA
091 374 2000
Byram, M. Dr; *Supervisor:* Byram, M. Dr
Culture and civilisation studies for advanced language learners – an experiment in French and English schools
Abstract: The purpose of the research is to develop curricula, teaching and assessment methods for advanced language learning with reference to cultural studies, i.e. acquiring knowledge and understanding of the way of life and thinking of a foreign people and country. The research takes place in England and France and is based on existing approaches to teaching culture at GCE 'A' level and Baccalaureat. The design involves, in both countries, a team of teachers and researchers who develop, operate and evaluate an experimental curriculum and assessment. The curriculum has two main emphases: that learners should acquire knowledge and understanding of selected

dimension of French/English culture (defined as above); and that learners should acquire the research tools – largely those of ethnography – to carry out their own investigations of a foreign culture. The cooperation of teams working in parallels in France (at the Institut National de Recherche Pedagogique) and in England provides for mutual information on research and development methods, on teaching techniques and on evaluation. The report will include, as well as a description of the research process, a specimen curriculum and materials to illustrate the principles underpinning the experiment.
Status: Sponsored project
Source of Grant: Leverhulme Trust £90,700
Date of Research: 1990 - continuing
KEYWORDS: comparative education; cultural education; educational materials; second language learning; teaching methods

9/0190

School of Education, Leazes Road, Durham DH1 1TA
091 374 2000
Alnajjar, A. Mr; *Supervisor:* Gilliland, J. Mr; McGuiness, J. Mr
The needs and individual coping responses of adolescents in the United Arab Emirates
Abstract: This research consists of a survey of models of adjustment and coping relevant to the investigation of adolescents' perceived needs and coping responses. The research includes a pilot study and the main study of adolescents in the United Arab Emirates (UAE). The pilot study involving approximately 60 students elicited a range of perceived needs and responses by means of written replies to open ended statements. A questionnaire based on the results of the pilot study has been administered to approximately 700 students throughout all of the States of the UAE. These results are currently being analysed.
Status: Sponsored project
Source of Grant: United Arab Emirates Embassy
Date of Research: 1986-1991
KEYWORDS: adolescents; Arab states; coping; needs

9/0191

School of Education, Leazes Road, Durham DH1 1TA
091 374 2000
Qattous, K. Mr; *Supervisor:* Byram, M. Dr
English language teaching – an evaluation of an industrial training programme
Abstract: The English for Specific Purposes (ESP) course for workers in the Aramco petroleum company will be analysed and evaluated as an example of programme development and ESP in industrial settings.
Status: Individual research
Date of Research: 1988 - continuing
KEYWORDS: Arab states; English – second language; English for specific purposes; programme evaluation

9/0192

School of Education, Leazes Road, Durham DH1 1TA
091 374 2000
Northern Council for Further Education, 5, Grosvenor Villa, Grosvenor Road, Newcastle upon Tyne NE2 2RU
091 281 3242
Stoker, S. Mr; Reece, I. Mr; *Supervisor:* Stoker, S. Mr
Evaluation of further education college governor training
Abstract: The aim of the project is to evaluate the Further Education Governor Training Programme run by the Northern Council for Further Education at Newcastle upon Tyne based on: observation of teaching sessions; assessment of materials used; and interviews with governors and tutors.
Status: Sponsored project
Source of Grant: Northern Council for Further Education £4,000
Date of Research: 1990-1992
KEYWORDS: further education; governing bodies; programme evaluation; training

9/0193

School of Education, Leazes Road, Durham DH1 1TA
091 374 2000
Davies, C. Mrs
Young children as musicians: a study of musical processes in the invented songs of children aged 3-7

Abstract: The young child using language uses infantile forms of sentences, yet as soon as language is used at all it shows that the child is aware of relationships between elements of language and of the meanings conveyed by these relationships. But the view often taken of learning music is that young children acquire the 'building blocks' of music and only at a later stage do they synthesise these, and that not until then can it be said that they are making music. The researcher believes that in like manner, children are absorbing music holistically from the beginning, developing an intuitive awareness of the relationships inherent in music's structure. The research involves collecting invented songs of 33 children aged 5-7 and analysing them to see what evidence there is that children have a sense of the wholeness of music (as derived from Langer's account of music as time). The analysis so far, shows that even while they are still acquiring the materials for music-making, children are using these as musicians do.
Published Material: DAVIES, C.V. (1986). 'Say it till a song comes', British Journal of Music Education, Vol 3, No 3, pp.279-293.
Status: Individual research
Date of Research: 1988-1992
KEYWORDS: *learning; music; music education; songs; young children*

9/0194

School of Education, Leazes Road, Durham DH1 1TA
091 374 2000
Gates, J. Mrs; *Supervisor:* Smith, R. Mr
Professional development of teachers
Abstract: This is a qualitative research project using case study method. It focuses upon a small group of primary school teachers at varying career stages and in differing cultural settings. Using research strategies of action research, biographical and journal writing and career profiles, the growth of reflectivity is examined. The research aims to identify the explicit and implicit values, attitudes and assumptions that govern the rationale of teachers in both their 'talk about teaching' and their practice. From an analysis of these it is planned to move to a consideration of implications in terms of initial and inservice teacher training.
Status: Individual research
Date of Research: 1990 - continuing
KEYWORDS: *primary school teachers; professional development; teacher attitudes*

9/0195

School of Education, Leazes Road, Durham DH1 1TA
091 374 2000
Al-Marzooki, A. Mr; *Supervisor:* Stoker, S. Mr; Lawless, R. Dr
The role and development of technical and vocational education in Qatar
Abstract: This research is examining the social, political and religious environment of Qatar in the context of its changing economic situation. It will also look at past policies of vocational education and training in Qatar in an attempt to assess the compatibility of such schemes with the country's manpower requirements and will pay special attention to the pace of industrialisation in Qatar.
Status: Individual research
Date of Research: 1989-1992
KEYWORDS: *Qatar; technical education; vocational education; work education relationship*

9/0196

School of Education, Leazes Road, Durham DH1 1TA
091 374 2000
Byram, M. Dr; *Supervisor:* Byram, M. Dr
Education for international understanding through foreign language teaching: a German – British collaborative project
Abstract: The purpose of the project is to investigate the contribution of foreign language teaching to international understanding through the images of a country purveyed in language teaching. The focus is on the images purveyed by textbooks for teaching English in Germany and German in England. The design involves a team of teachers and researchers at the Universities of Durham and Braunschweig (Germany). Working in German-English pairs, the teams analyse the images of German-English life portrayed in textbooks for secondary schools according to criteria including representativity, accuracy, realism and appropriateness to learners. Each textbook analysis includes a detailed account of the content of the book as well as an evaluation. The project also involves theoretical development of criteria for evaluation and discussion of the relationship between language teaching and teaching for international understanding or 'politische Erziehurig'.
Published Material: DOYE, P. (Ed). (1990). Grossbritannien: seine Darstellung in duetschen Schulbuchern fur den Englischunterricht. Frankfurt: Deisterweg.
Status: Sponsored project
Source of Grant: Durham University £2,000; British Council £2,800
Date of Research: 1990 - continuing
KEYWORDS: *cultural awareness; English – second language; German; modern language studies; textbook evaluation*

9/0197

School of Education, Leazes Road, Durham DH1 1TA
091 374 2000
Guernina, Z. Dr; *Supervisor:* Byram, M. Dr; Lawless, R. Dr; McPartland, M. Mr
Student supply and the expansion of Arabic studies in higher education
Abstract: In 1986 the Parker Report (PARKER, Sir Peter (1986). 'Speaking for the future': a review of the requirements of diplomacy and commerce for Asian and African languages and area studies. University Grants Committee) drew attention to the need to increase available expertise in Oriental and African languages and associated area studies in order to meet the growing demands of industry, commerce and diplomacy. Yet the university system which has been the traditional source of this expertise has experienced difficulties and a gradual reduction of resources, especially in Arabic. Furthermore the Parker Report did not examine the implications of its recommendations with respect to the school system. Where are the increased numbers of students to come from? How are school pupils to be encouraged to take up Arabic Studies? How is the decline in applications for Arabic Studies over the last decade to be reversed? The purpose of this project is therefore to examine the factors which influence school pupils' perceptions of Arabic Studies and their potential interest and to gather the information required to initiate change in Arabic Studies in higher education. The project includes a nation-wide survey of sixth formers, of undergraduates currently studying Arabic and of admissions tutors in Arabic departments. It also includes an analysis of sixth form curricula (Religious Education, Geography, History) which might have an influence on perceptions and attitudes towards the Arabic-speaking world. The project will thus provide data on the relationship between sixth form and university studies with respect to recruitment for Arabic Studies. It will also make recommendations as to possible changes which might promote an expansion of Arabic Studies in the future.
Status: Sponsored project
Source of Grant: Economic and Social Research Council £28,620
Date of Research: 1989-1991
KEYWORDS: *Arabic studies; higher education; pupil attitudes; sixth forms*

9/0198

School of Education, Leazes Road, Durham DH1 1TA
091 374 2000
Stockdale, C. Mr; *Supervisor:* French, M. Mr
The Mechanics Institution movement in the North East of England
Abstract: This research looks at the history of the development of the Mechanics Institutions in the North East of England between 1820 and 1902. It includes comparisons of contemporary and recent literature about the Movement. The Movement's activities will be evaluated within the context of the social and economic climate of the period, together with the legacy of educational, literary and social development in terms of failure and success. The research includes consultation of contemporary records existing within the region and also those of institutions in other parts of the country. Standard texts have been used to support the political, social, economic and cultural background against which the Movement evolved.
Status: Individual research
Date of Research: 1990 - continuing
KEYWORDS: *adult education; educational history; mechanics institutes*

9/0199

School of Education, Leazes Road, Durham DH1 1TA
091 374 2000
Ashton, E. Miss; *Supervisor:* Minney, R. Mr; Day, D. Mr

Religious education and primary school children
Abstract: The research project arose out of observations of primary school children's modes of thinking and ways in which they conceptualize. Wide reading, at the moment, is being carried out in the fields of educational psychology, philosophy and theology. Practical teaching projects and schemes of work are to be planned and executed in the classroom, which will be assessed according to certain evaluation criteria. It is anticipated that the research will lead to the publication of educational material for both teachers and children.
Status: Individual research
Date of Research: 1991 - continuing
KEYWORDS: primary education; religious education

9/0200
    School of Education, Leazes Road, Durham DH1 1TA
    091 374 2000
    Awiria, O. Mr; *Supervisor:* Gilliland, J. Mr; McGuiness, J. Mr
Comparative study of disruptive behaviour and discipline in schools in the United Kingdom and Kenya
Abstract: This study, in its early stages, seeks to examine aspects of disruptive behaviour and discipline in selected secondary schools in the United Kingdom and Kenya. In both countries, disruption in schools is currently an issue of considerable concern to teachers, parents and government (e.g. 'Discipline in schools': report to the Committee of Enquiry chaired by Lord Elton, HMSO, 1989). The present study will examine aspects of definition, theory and explanation as they apply to different levels of organisation in the two countries. Data collection will be by means of sample surveys of attitudes among administrators, teachers, student teachers and pupils. It is hoped to include qualitative data obtained through individual and group interviews. Other research techniques are likely to be used as the project develops.
Status: Sponsored project
Source of Grant: St Christopher's Trust £4,000; British Foreign Schools Society £1,400; The Leathersellers' Company £1,000
Date of Research: 1991 - continuing
KEYWORDS: behaviour problems; comparative education; discipline; disruptive pupils; Kenya; secondary schools

9/0201
    School of Education, Leazes Road, Durham DH1 1TA
    091 374 2000
    Cornelius, M. Mr
Use of games in the teaching of mathematics
Abstract: This research is concerned with the history of games and their use in investigational work in the teaching of mathematics. The aim of the research is to stimulate pupil investigations in mathematics through the use of board games. Details of board games from a wide range of civilisations and periods have been identified and described. Mathematical activities based on these games have been devised and piloted with pupils. Methods used included classroom trials with investigations based on games.
Published Material: BELL, R. & CORNELIUS, M.L. (1988). Board games around the world: a resource book for mathematical investigations. Cambridge: Cambridge University Press.; CORNELIUS, M.L. & PARR, A. (1991). What's your game?: a resource book for mathematical activities. Cambridge: Cambridge University Press.
Status: Sponsored project
Source of Grant: Durham University Research Committee
Date of Research: 1985-1991
KEYWORDS: educational games; learning activities; mathematics education

9/0202
    School of Education, Leazes Road, Durham DH1 1TA
    091 374 2000
    Cornelius, M. Mr; *Supervisor:* Cornelius, M. Mr
Graduate numeracy
Abstract: This is an investigation into the mathematical needs of new graduates in employment. The methods used include a sample of new graduates being investigated through employers via questionnaires and interviews to ascertain what mathematical skills are needed in employment and what deficiencies exist. The conclusions are likely to be of interest to both institutions of higher education and employers.
Published Material: CORNELIUS, M.L. (1991). 'Numeracy in a university and beyond', Education and Training, Vol 33, No 3, pp.28-31.; CORNELIUS, M.L. (1991). 'Just a few questions', Times

Higher Education Supplement, April.; CORNELIUS, M.L. (1991). 'Degree of panic', Times Educational Supplement, May.; CORNELIUS, M.L. (1991). 'Graduate numeracy', Teaching Mathematics and its Applications, Vol 10, No 4, pp.151-153.
Status: Sponsored project
Source of Grant: Enterprise in Higher Education
Date of Research: 1990 - continuing
KEYWORDS: employer attitudes; graduate employment; graduates; mathematical ability; numeracy; work education relationship

9/0203
    School of Education, Leazes Road, Durham DH1 1TA
    091 374 2000
    Ridley, L. Miss; *Supervisor:* Coffield, F. Prof.
Young people and illicit drugs
Abstract: The aims of the research are: (1) to produce a clear picture of young people's knowledge and attitudes towards illicit drug taking; (2) to identify the main sources of their information; (3) to assess the major influences in determining whether they accept offers of drugs and become engaged in experimental use. As a result of the information gained, a health promotion publicity campaign will be devised, aimed at the primary prevention of illicit drug use among young people. Our method is ethnographic in principle and uses the research technique of single sex discussion groups. The participants are young people at three age levels of 12/13, 14/15 and 16/18. The discussion groups are taped and held in contrasting areas within Tyneside, Durham, Cumbria and Cleveland.
Status: Sponsored project
Source of Grant: Department of Health and Northern Regional Health Authority £44,355
Date of Research: 1991-1992
KEYWORDS: adolescents; drug abuse; drug education; health promotion; illegal drug use

9/0204
    School of Education, Leazes Road, Durham DH1 1TA
    091 374 2000
    Thompson, L. Ms; *Supervisor:* Byram, M. Dr
Social networks and ethnic identity in an urban nursery: a sociolinguistic analysis of preferred language use
Abstract: The aim of the research is to describe the preferred language use of a group of 12 Punjabi-English speaking children during their first term in nursery education where they constitute a linguistic minority. Data were gathered using audio-tape recorders. Three hours of naturally occurring discourse data were collected from each informant. These were complemented by observations of 'thick' (Geertz, 1975) contextual data. The analysis describes the linguistic behaviour of these bilingual children in terms of Hymes' (1974) taxonomy of communicative competence: when they chose to speak; with whom; the preferred language (Panjabi or English) of each interaction; the contribution to the discourse as initiator, sustainer or terminator of the interaction. Initial insights and observations from the analyses suggest that preferred language use functions as an act of ethnolinguistic identity (Le Page and Tabouret-Keller, 1985) that consolidates in-group membership of social networks. Social networks (Milroy, 1980) analysis offer a non-ethnocentric research method for observing language use.
Status: Sponsored project
Source of Grant: Durham University Research and Initiatives Committee £800
Date of Research: 1987-1992
KEYWORDS: bilingual pupils; ethnic group; ethnicity; language usage; linguistics; nursery schools; Punjabi; social networks

9/0205
    School of Education, Leazes Road, Durham DH1 1TA
    091 374 2000
    Taylor, S. Ms; *Supervisor:* Byram, M. Dr
Constructing culture: a study of teacher-pupil talk in French language lessons
Abstract: This research was started as a result of work undertaken on an ESRC (Economic and Social Research Council) funded project to determine the effects of foreign language teaching on young people's perceptions of other cultures. The aims of this research are to: (1) apply the conversation analysis approach to the study of foreign language lessons; (2) explore and describe ways in which foreign culture is constructed through tak in foreign language lessons; (3)

consider the implications of this process for children's perceptions of other cultures. The work is based upon detailed analysis of taped lessons using conversation analysis. The tapes were made over two terms and include lessons of first, second and third year pupils in a comprehensive school. This work is supported by observations and interviews with teachers in two schools.
Status: Individual research
Date of Research: 1986-1992
KEYWORDS: classroom communication; cultural awareness; foreign culture; modern language studies

9/0206

School of Education, Leazes Road, Durham DH1 1TA
091 374 2000
Constantinides, A. Mr; *Supervisor:* Booth, I. Dr
The provision of education in the middle school years in Cyprus
Abstract: The aim of this study is to examine the type of education offered during the middle school years in Cyprus. At first an attempt is made to define middle school years and relate this concept to the educational system of Cyprus and other countries. The history of education in Cyprus is briefly surveyed to set the background against which the Gymnasium, a distinct educational unit catering for the middle school years, has evolved and reached its present form. The aims, objectives, structure and content of the Gymnasium are examined in detail. The role of the Gymnasium within the educational system and the degree to which this role is successfully accomplished are investigated in two studies conducted among students and teachers of the Gymnasium. The results reveal that on the whole the role, content and time span of the Gymnasium are satisfactory. There is, however, a strong feeling that there is scope for improvement in the content of the curriculum in order to make it more effective. Finally certain recent developments in the educational system of Cyprus and their implications for the future of the Gymnasium are discussed.
Status: Individual research
Date of Research: 1983-1992
KEYWORDS: Cyprus; middle school education

9/0207

School of Education, Leazes Road, Durham DH1 1TA
091 374 2000
Palmer, J. Dr
Emergent environmentalism: subject knowledge and concern for the environment
Abstract: Phase One of this project is currently proceeding and has led to the accumulation of a substantial amount of data. Questionnaires have been circulated to environmental educators throughout the UK asking for information and supporting autobiographical statements explaining key factors influencing the development of personal concern for the environment. The aim is to identify significant life events/life experiences which have contributed towards people's concern for and interest in environmental matters. If a major goal of environmental education is to produce informed and environmentally active citizens, then presumably environmental educators should know the kinds of learning experiences which help to influence the development of environmental care and concern. Statements have been collected from a sample of over 200 educators. They will be used to make recommendations on the implications of significant learning experiences for the designing of educational programmes and approaches to the inclusion of environmental education in the formal curriculum. The pilot study for Phase Two of the project will involve the collection of autobiographical (audio taped) statements/discussion from nursery children in the USA on their understanding of common environmental issues (ranging from the immediate environment to global concerns). Analysis of this should reveal issues for further investigation, suggest preliminary categories of response and allow for subsequent comparison with nursery age children in the UK.
Status: Sponsored project
Source of Grant: Durham University £3,412
Date of Research: 1991 - continuing
KEYWORDS: conservation – environment; environmental education; natural resources

9/0208

School of Education, Leazes Road, Durham DH1 1TA
091 374 2000

Cotton, P. Ms; *Supervisor:* McGuiness, J. Mr; Gilliland, J. Mr
Comparative study of writing development in French and English primary schools
Abstract: This research will be looking at the effect of early visual exposure to cursive script on children's writing, and is a comparative study of writing development in England and France. From this it is hoped to add theoretical substance to the rapidly increasing desire for schools to change from print to joined writing when children begin school. Initially, theoretical aspects of the differences between print and cursive script will be investigated, looking at the theoretical rationale of French researchers such as Lilian Lurcat and her influence on children's writing in France. These will be compared with research that has influenced British children's writing, beginning with Edward Johnson in 1913, who wanted all children to print because he thought it would help with their reading. Practical aspects will be observed from school entry until the later primary years. Children will be carefully monitored in terms of their attitudes to writing and their self-image as writers. Specific areas to be targeted will be legibility, speed, accuracy, spelling, flow of ideas, creativity, and handwriting as part of the whole writing process. A small sample of about six schools will be monitored in detail over a period of about three years. This will necessitate involvement with all classes in all schools. Alongside this, a nationwide developmental survey will be conducted, and a National Register set up of all schools who are introducing or have already introduced joined writing on school entry. This development has been prompted by the numerous responses from an article written in 'Child Education'.
Published Material: COTTON, P. (1988). Handwriting Review, p.15.; COTTON, P. (1990). Handwriting Review, p.57.; COTTON, P. (1990). United Kingdom Reading Association Journal, Vol 24, No 1, p.2, April.; COTTON, P. (1991). United Kingdom Reading Association Journal, Vol 25, No 1, p.27, April.; COTTON, P. (1992). Child Education, p.53, April.
Status: Sponsored project
Source of Grant: Kingston University
Date of Research: 1990 - continuing
KEYWORDS: comparative education; creativity; France; handwriting; writing research; writing skills

9/0209

School of Education, Leazes Road, Durham DH1 1TA
091 374 2000
Morrison, K. Mr; *Supervisor:* Gilliland, J. Mr
Developing emancipatory curricula in primary schools
Abstract: The study critiques the work of Jurgen Habermas and indicates how it may be used to inform a debate on developing emancipation through primary school curricula. Issues in the sociology of knowledge are addressed which bridge the gap between Habermasian theory and school curricula. A case study of the National Curriculum of England and Wales is undertaken, focussing particularly on cross-curricular issues. A short empirical research is undertaken to attempt to complete an analysis of the contribution of Habermas to curriculum theory and practice.
Published Material: MORRISON, K. (1989). 'Bringing progressivism into a critical theory of education', British Journal of Sociology of Education, Vol 10, No 1, pp.3-18.
Status: Individual research
Date of Research: 1990 - continuing
KEYWORDS: educational theories; primary school curriculum

9/0210

School of Education, Leazes Road, Durham DH1 1TA
091 374 2000
Ramzi, A. Dr; *Supervisor:* Minney, R. Mr; Day, D. Mr
Islamic education in the understanding of present day Muslim educationists
Abstract: This study is an attempt to introduce a whole view of the understanding of present day Muslim educationists in respect of Islamic education within its Islamic context and Muslim conceptions. The problem the study explores and tries to underline is the kind of crisis that is hypothesized to exist in the understanding of Muslim educationists. The crisis is supposed to take the form of uncertainty and/or obscurity in the experience of Muslim educationists and thinkers that affects their understanding. The definition of this gap in conception, its existence, the factors that affect it and its exploration are present in the study. A historical background is given of both Islamic and non-Islamic education in the experience of Muslim educationists. The investigation has been conducted to answer one of

the six questions raised in exploring the areas of thought in which the crisis appears more acute. The sample of respondents includes 100 Muslim educationists who were sent a questionnaire on four categories of concepts. Owing to its nature the study suggests a certain set of strategies or broad lines of practicalities to help Muslim present day educationists bridge this gap in the light of what is changeable and unchangeable in Islamic thought.
Status: Individual research
Date of Research: 1988-1992
KEYWORDS: *educational theories; Islamic education; religion and education*

9/0211
> School of Education, Leazes Road, Durham DH1 1TA
> 091 374 2000
> Dunford, J. Mr; *Supervisor:* Goodings, R. Mr

The modern inspectorate: HM Inspectorate of schools 1944-91
Abstract: The twin aims of Her Majesty's Inspecorate (HMI) – advice and inspection – have dominated the work of HMI since 1944, but the balance between the two aims has frequently shifted. This study chronicles the history of HMI since 1944, placing it in the context of its earlier history and studying its effect on other parts of the education system – schools, colleges, local education authorities, higher and further education institutions and the Department of Education and Science (DES). The relationship between HMI and the DES is studied with particular reference to the independence of HMI. The research included interviews with senior inspectors and local authority officials.
Published Material: GOODINGS, R.F. & DUNFORD, J.E. (1990). 'Her Majesty's Inspectorate of Schools, 1939-1989: the question of independence', Journal of Educational Administration and History, Vol XXII, No 1, pp.1-8.
Status: Individual research
Date of Research: 1987-1992
KEYWORDS: *educational history; inspection; inspectors – of schools*

9/0212
> School of Education, Leazes Road, Durham DH1 1TA
> 091 374 2000
> Mahmoud, T. Mr; *Supervisor:* Galloway, D. Prof.

Making efficient use of microcomputers in teaching mathematics to gifted children in the Jordanian primary schools
Abstract: The study offers a critical examination of concepts of giftedness, in the context of mathematics. It presents a framework for the development of computer based programmes of individualized education for the mathematically gifted. It tests the framework by pilot studies in a sample of schools in Jordan.
Status: Individual research
Date of Research: 1989 - continuing
KEYWORDS: *computer uses in education; gifted; individualised methods; Jordan; mathematics; primary education*

9/0213
> School of Education, Leazes Road, Durham DH1 1TA
> 091 374 2000
> Harvey, P. Dr; *Supervisor:* McPartland, M. Mr;
> Saunders, A. Dr

The role and value of A-level geography fieldwork: a case study
Abstract: The study aims to analyse the role and value of a residential fieldwork experience in geographical learning for advanced level geography students (i.e. students aged 16-19): to compare and contrast the respective assessments of the student and teacher of fieldwork's purpose; and to explore frameworks and methods for evaluating the effectiveness of field instruction as a learning process. The research uses qualitative research strategies in a case-study to describe and analyse the holistic process of learning in action from the perspectives of its participants. Four themes are explored in depth: skills-based learning; affective learning; learning transfer; and geography fieldwork as environmental education. Results show that learning is affected by a tension of purpose between teaching for theoretical exemplification, technical competency and investigative skills, and environmental awareness. Stage-management in hypothesis-testing aimed at developing students' conceptual understanding is the predominant teaching method but despite this emphasis successful transfer of learning is low. The technical competency emphasis is propositioned as moving fieldwork towards utilisation of a technocentric ideology in addressing environmental issues in geography. This is regarded as devaluing an individual's environmental experience, personal commitment, and political obligation which are seen as important aspects of an environmental education. Fieldwork is seen to be most valuable in the affective domain: producing self- and subject-motivation through *inter alia* novelty of milieu, self-concept enhancement, productive role-modelling, and changing students' 'scripts' for learning. The links between these affective dimensions and fieldwork's role in students' cognitive development offer profitable avenues for further research.
Published Material: McPARTLAND, M.F. & HARVEY, P.K. (1987). 'A question of fieldwork?', Teaching Geography, Vol 12, No 4, pp.162-164.
Status: Sponsored project
Source of Grant: Economic and Social Research Council
Date of Research: 1984-1991
KEYWORDS: *A-level examinations; field studies; geography education; learning activities*

9/0214
> School of Education, Leazes Road, Durham DH1 1TA
> 091 374 2000
> Gilliland, J. Mr; Steele, J. Mr

A survey of computer literacy in initial teacher education
Abstract: Nationally, information technology (IT) has been given an increasingly high profile in schools, from the early Department of Education and Science/Department of Trade and Industry initiatives and the Microelectronics in Education Project (MEP) to its inclusion now as a cross-curricular issue in the National Curriculum. Schools of Education are required therefore to offer computer literacy courses which meet professional school orientated needs and also enhance personal skills through IT in response to computer literacy programmes in higher education. This research is gathering survey data from students following courses of initial teacher education and students following some higher degree courses. Access, confidence and competence are assessed on entry to the course and the project seeks to monitor changes in these three aspects during and on exit from the course. First results from pre- and post-course surveys show differences between groups and positive effects of introductory courses and the IT environment made available to students in the School of Education of Durham University. The range of competence, confidence and experience on entry is extremely wide and creates educational and logistic problems for the delivery and management of courses in IT and the IT environment. Activities, responses and results to date suggest the need for an application of more sophisticated models of teaching and instruction.
Published Material: GILLILAND, J. & STEELE, J. (1990). 'Computer literacy in an initial teacher training student population'. In: McCARTAN, A. (Ed). Computer literacy for every graduate – strategies and challenges for the early 1990s, pp.30-33. Oxford: CTISS Publications.
Status: Sponsored project
Source of Grant: Durham University: School of Education
Date of Research: 1989 - continuing
KEYWORDS: *computer literacy; computer uses in education; information technology; preservice teacher education*

9/0215
> School of Education, Leazes Road, Durham DH1 1TA
> 091 374 2000
> Hull University, School of Education, Cottingham Road,
> Hull HU6 7RX
> 0482 46311
> Warburton, P. Mr; Sleap, M. Mr; Cale, L. Mrs

Physical activity patterns of primary school children
Abstract: There is now wide recognition of the positive effect regular exercise can have on our health. The main aim of this observation study is to monitor the exercise activity levels of children aged between 5 and 11 years. This observation study forms part of a wider evaluation of the Happy Heart Resource Materials which was undertaken between February 1991 and June 1992. The method of observation to be used will be based on a paper presented by O'Hara and Colleagues (1988) which validated a minute by minute observation procedure against heart rate. Between 60 and 70 children were observed in the spring of 1991 and again during the same period in 1992. Half of the children will act as a control group whilst the other half will receive regular input from the Happy Heart Resource

Materials. The children will be observed both in school and at home. The results from the study will be used to assess the impact of the Happy Heart Resource Materials with regard to possible changes in children's activity patterns.
Status: Sponsored project
Source of Grant: Health Education Authority £16,000
Date of Research: 1990-1992
KEYWORDS: educational materials; exercise; health activities; health promotion; heart rate; physical activities; primary school pupils

9/0216
School of Education, Leazes Road, Durham DH1 1TA
091 374 2000
Hull University, School of Education, Cottingham Road, Hull HU6 7RX
0482 46311
Warburton, P. Mr; *Supervisor:* Sleap, M. Mr
An investigation into the physical activity levels of primary school children
Abstract: The aim of the research is to evaluate a two year dissemination programme presently being undertaken by the Happy Heart Resource project team at Hull University. This dissemination programme is centred on the resource materials produced by the project. The evaluation aims to: (1) establish views of teachers regarding usage of resource packs; (2) assess the activity levels of a sample of children experiencing Happy Heart resources in comparison to a matched group of children not involved in the project.
Status: Sponsored project
Source of Grant: Health Education Authority £14,000
Date of Research: 1991 - continuing
KEYWORDS: educational materials; exercise; health activities; health promotion; physical activities; primary school pupils

9/0217
School of Education, Leazes Road, Durham DH1 1TA
091 374 2000
Hull University, School of Education, Cottingham Road, Hull HU6 7RX
0482 465406
Aubrey, C. Ms; *Supervisor:* McNamara, D. Prof.
An investigation of teachers' mathematical subject knowledge and the processes of instruction in reception classes
Abstract: This research looks at the teaching of mathematics in infant classes. The main phase of the project (1991-1992) will be a direct follow-on to existing research which has been established for 3 years. The aims are to: (1) investigate teachers' pedagogical subject knowledge, in particular in terms of its influence on beliefs and the content and processes of mathematical instruction in reception classes. (This is an area with a small, but mainly US research interest, which has concentrated on addition and subtraction word problems); (2) take existing data on children's informal knowledge in key areas of mathematics at school entry, as a starting point for accessing teachers' understanding of how children think about mathematics, and knowledge about their own pupils' thinking. These data are available already from work carried out by the researchers with previous grants; (3) consider the co-ordination and utilisation of teacher and pupil knowledge within the complex world of classrooms. (Only limited research attention has been paid to this area); (4) consider the implications of the study for the mathematics curriculum for children's first year at school. The early part of the project involved devising, piloting and revising complex mathematical assessment interviews for young children entering school. Data have been collected for around 90 children. The main phase of the project will entail observing some of the previously assessed children through their first year in school, using field notes, tape recorded interactions, interviews with class teachers, and re-assessment of the children at the end of May, 1992. Observational data will allow generation of suitable categories, validation and interpretation. Audio recording will allow checking and validation of observer records and more detailed analysis of selected extracts of transcriptions of pupil and teacher discourse. All data collected from mathematics sessions will be transcribed and written up as a case record of the event. These will provide detailed descriptions of the content and processes of mathematics instruction in infant classrooms. The case records may form the basis for further analysis. The teacher interviews will document teachers' own descriptions of subject matter knowledge, their planning, their strategies and their means of instruction. Data so far

analysed, suggest children bring into school a range of flexible, informal strategies and an overlapping, less stable conventional knowledge where a concern for accuracy is not always strong. Children's strategies suggest that, as in language acquisition, a rule-governed approach is operating from the start. Teachers' aims for early instruction seem, however, to be derived from a pre-school ideology which emphasises play, choice and practical activity rather than reflecting the way children think about mathematics.
Published Material: A full list of publications is available from the researcher.
Status: Sponsored project
Source of Grant: Durham University £8,500
Date of Research: 1989-1992
KEYWORDS: early childhood education; infant school teachers; mathematics education

9/0218
School of Education, Leazes Road, Durham DH1 1TA
091 374 2000
Ministry of Education, PO Box 80, Doha, Qatar, Arabian Gulf Galalah, A. Mr; *Supervisor:* Byram, M. Dr
English in the State of Qatar: an analysis of perceptions and attitudes
Abstract: The research is conducted to verify the actual position of English in the Qatari society, among the student population in the Qatari school system, and among the adults who represent the Qatari workforce. The research is addressing the fact-finding stage of syllabus design, which is considered the base for the other stages of specifying the objectives, tailoring the materials and then the evaluation of the final course material. The study aims at assessing the facts regarding the perception of the target language status in the society through the study of the attitudes of the respondents. The study sample consists of three cross sections, namely 659 students from both the preparatory and secondary levels, 460 adults representing most professions and nationalities in the country. In addition, 10 interviews with prominent decision makers were undertaken. Two main areas were subject to assessment, facts and perceptions of respondents regarding the status of English and the attitudes regarding the target language and the peoples who speak it as a mother language. Findings revealed that English is the language of wider communication in Qatar in addition to extremely positive attitudes. Non-parametric statistics were employed in data analysis. Nationality among other variables showed significant differences.
Status: Sponsored project
Source of Grant: British Council; per annum £750
Date of Research: 1987-1992
KEYWORDS: Arab states; English – second language; English for specific purposes; English studies; second language learning

9/0219
School of Education, Leazes Road, Durham DT1 1TA
091 374 2000
University of Qatar, Doha, PO Box 2713, Qatar
010 974 83-2222
Hassan, F. Mr; *Supervisor:* Byram, M. Dr
Sociocultural aspects of teaching English to Arabic speaking students
Abstract: In foreign language learning the learner's affective variables seem to be playing a very crucial role. For example, the learner's own attitude towards learning the target language can be influenced by his/her attitudes towards the native speakers of this language and their culture. There is accumulating evidence that prejudice or active dislike diminishes motivation and interferes with learning. The attitudes of the Arab students in the Gulf towards the English language people and culture have never been investigated before. In doing so, the present research aims to find out: (a) if these students come into the English language class with already acquired perceptions of the target language, people and culture and what these perceptions are; (b) what the students' attitudes towards the English people and culture are and whether these tend to be stereotypical; (c) if there is an association between these perceptions and attitudes and if the association is significant; and (d) investigate the relationship between the students' attitudes and perceptions on the one hand, and the learners' achievement in the target language on the other. the study sample consists of 60 male and 120 female students starting their first year in Qatar University. The research tools are self-report writing, questionnaires, interviews, semantic differential tests and results of final achievement examinations kept in the university records.

Status: Individual research
Date of Research: 1989 - continuing
KEYWORDS: *Arab states; cultural awareness; English – second language; foreign culture; native speakers; second language learning*

9/0220
University Business School, Old Shire Hall, Durham DH1 3HP
091 374 2000
McLean, M. Mr
Enterprise in vocational education and training
Abstract: The aim of this project is to research, develop, pilot and disseminate active-learning materials to embed enterprising approaches to the delivery of vocational courses in further education. Fourteen colleges of further education were involved in the piloting of the materials. Information was gathered by observation of lecturers and students in the classroom situation and feedback was also given during workshop sessions. Initially a review of literature was undertaken, followed by in-depth interviews with 'enterprise' practitioners.
Status: Sponsored project
Source of Grant: Training, Enterprise & Education Directorate; British Steel
Date of Research: 1988-1991
KEYWORDS: *enterprise education; experiential learning; training; vocational education*

Edinburgh University

9/0221
Centre for Educational Sociology, 7 Buccleuch Place,
Edinburgh EH8 9JT
031 650 1000
McPherson, A. Prof.; Raffe, D. Mr; Bagnall, G. Dr
Deprivation research – Phase 2
Abstract: This project uses data from the Scottish Young People's Survey to investigate the effect of social disadvantages on education.
Published Material: A full list of publications is available from the Research Administrator
Status: Sponsored project
Source of Grant: John Watson's Trust £10,000
Date of Research: 1991-1992
KEYWORDS: *academic achievement; disadvantaged environment; school effectiveness; social status*

9/0222
Centre for Educational Sociology, 7 Buccleuch Place,
Edinburgh EH8 9JT
031 650 1000
Raffe, D. Mr; Lamb, J. Dr; Middleton, L. Ms; *Supervisor:* McPherson, A. Prof.
Survey of 50% of Grampian Leavers
Abstract: The research team will conduct a survey of 50% of pupils in the Grampian Region in S4 in session 1989-90 to provide reliable information on education and training.
Published Material: A full list of publications is available from the Research Administrator
Status: Sponsored project
Source of Grant: Grampian Regional Council £28,000
Date of Research: 1990-1991
KEYWORDS: *labour market; school leavers; school to work transition; secondary education; training; vocational education*

9/0223
Centre for Educational Sociology, 7 Buccleuch Place,
Edinburgh EH8 9JT
031 650 1000
Paterson, L. Dr; *Supervisor:* McPherson, A. Prof.
The efficient use of talent in the expansion of Scottish higher education
Abstract: The object of the research is to investigate the scope for exploiting untapped talent among young people (aged under 20) as a result of the fundamental changes affecting Scottish higher education.
Published Material: A full list of publications is available from the Research Administrator

Status: Sponsored project
Source of Grant: The Leverhulme Trust £25,632
Date of Research: 1992 - continuing
KEYWORDS: *access to education; educational change; further education; higher education; sixteen to nineteen education*

9/0224
Centre for Educational Sociology, 7 Buccleuch Place,
Edinburgh EH8 9JT
031 650 1000
Raffe, D. Mr; Howieson, C. Ms; *Supervisor:* Raffe, D. Mr
The effectiveness of new curriculum models for initial vocational training
Abstract: The purpose of this research is to investigate the main objectives for modularisation and related reforms such as certification in different countries, and to assess the variation of the success of such policies across different institutional contexts and different national circumstances.
Status: Sponsored project
Source of Grant: European Community PETRA Programme £16,387
Date of Research: 1991-1992
KEYWORDS: *certification; comparative education; curriculum; labour market; modular courses; vocational education*

9/0225
Centre for Educational Sociology, 7 Buccleuch Place,
Edinburgh EH8 9JT
031 650 1000
Raffe, D. Mr; Lamb, J. Dr; Jones, G. Dr; Hughes, J. Miss; Brannen, K. Mrs; Fairgrieve, J. Mrs; Middleton, L. Ms; *Supervisor:* McPherson, A. Prof.
Spring 1991 and autumn 1991 Scottish Young People's Surveys
Abstract: Three further postal surveys in the Scottish Young People's Survey (SYPS) series will be conducted. A 10% national sample of young people who started S4 in 1989, and an overlapping 10% sample of leavers from the 1989/90 session, will be surveyed in spring 1991. The latter will extend the biennial sequence of leavers surveys since 1977. A 10% sample of young people who started S4 in 1987, which was surveyed in the spring 1989 SYPS, will be surveyed again in autumn 1991.
Published Material: A full list of publications is available from the Research Administrator
Status: Sponsored project
Source of Grant: Scottish Office Education Department; Department of Employment; Industry Department for Scotland; Training, Enterprise & Education Directorate £425,337
Date of Research: 1990-1992
KEYWORDS: *cohort analysis; further education; labour market; longitudinal studies; school leavers; secondary education; surveys; vocational education*

9/0226
Centre for Educational Sociology, 7 Buccleuch Place,
Edinburgh EH8 9JT
031 650 1000
Paterson, L. Dr; Lamb, J. Dr; Howieson, C. Ms; Croxford, L. Ms; Middleton, L. Ms; Raffe, D. Mr; *Supervisor:* McPherson, A. Prof.
Scottish Young People's Survey
Abstract: Regular multi-purpose surveys of school leavers and young people in Scotland, which collect data on their secondary, further and higher education, training, employment and unemployment, and on the various transitions among them. The surveys also cover the family backgrounds of young people, their household formation and other aspects of the transition to adulthood, and various attitudes. A postal survey, the Scottish Young People's Survey (SYPS) currently comprises two arms: a biennial survey, conducted in the spring of each odd-numbered year, of school leavers from the previous session; and a biennial series of longitudinal survey of school year groups, each of which is first contacted in the spring after fourth year and followed up after about 30 months at age 19-plus. Samples for the leavers survey and the (first-sweep) year-group survey overlap. Sample fractions are usually 10% giving target samples of about 7,000 for each survey arm, and achieved samples of about 5,500. The basic survey design is periodically enhanced to boost coverage in particular regions or for groups of interest (e.g. TVEI students).
Status: Sponsored project

Source of Grant: Scottish Office Education Department; Industry Department for Scotland; Department of Employment; Economic and Social Research Council
Date of Research: 1971 - continuing
KEYWORDS: *further education; higher education; school to work transition; unemployment; vocational education; youth employment*

9/0227
Centre for Educational Sociology, 7 Buccleuch Place, Edinburgh EH8 9JT
031 650 1000
Paterson, L. Dr; Raffe, D. Mr
The changing impact of a policy initiative: a multilevel analysis of TVEI
Abstract: The purpose of this research is to examine the effects of the pilot Technical and Vocational Education Initiative (TVEI) on attainment, truancy, staying-on, employment, training and attitudinal outcomes. The study will use data from the Scottish Young People's Survey.
Status: Sponsored project
Source of Grant: Economic and Social Research Council
Date of Research: 1990-1991
KEYWORDS: *achievement; attitude formation; school to work transition; sixteen to nineteen education; technical education; truancy; vocational education*

9/0228
Centre for Educational Sociology, 7 Buccleuch Place, Edinburgh EH8 9JT
031 650 1000
Raffe, D. Mr; Croxford, L. Ms; Howieson, C. Ms;
Supervisor: McPherson, A. Prof.
Young people's experience of National Certificate Modules
Abstract: The project will analyze data from the Scottish Young People's Surveys (1985-1989) to ascertain the impact and development of the 16+ programme among young people. The analyses will cover five broad areas: National Certificate models in context, whether educational, social, occupational or geographical; trends between the first and third Action Plan year groups; progression into, within and out of the modular system; attitudes to the National Certificate; and modules within schools.
Published Material: a full list of publications is available from the Research Administrator, Joan Hughes at Edinburgh University
Status: Sponsored project
Source of Grant: Scottish Education Department £62,075
Date of Research: 1988-1991
KEYWORDS: *curriculum research; modular courses; national certificate – Scotland; Scotland; secondary education; sixteen to nineteen education*

9/0229
Centre for Educational Sociology, 7 Buccleuch Place, Edinburgh EH8 9JT
031 650 1000
McPherson, A. Prof.; Raffe, D. Mr; Lamb, J. Dr; Jones, G. Dr; Middleton, L. Ms
Continuation of Scottish Young People's Survey
Abstract: The biennial series of surveys of Scottish school leavers is to be continued.
Published Material: A bibliography of published work is available from the Research Administrator.
Status: Sponsored project
Source of Grant: Scottish Education Department £120,000
Date of Research: 1990-1992
KEYWORDS: *cohort analysis; school leavers; school to work transition; Scotland; sixteen to nineteen education; surveys; youth employment*

9/0230
Centre for Educational Sociology, 7 Buccleuch Place, Edinburgh EH8 9JT
031 650 1000
Raffe, D. Mr; McPherson, A. Prof.; Paterson, L. Dr
The changing impact of a policy initiative: a multilevel analysis of TVEI
Abstract: The project aims to examine the effects of the pilot TVEI

on attainment, truancy, staying-on, employment, training and attitudinal outcomes. The study will use data from the Scottish Young People's Survey.
Published Material: A bibliography of published work and further details of the project are available from the Research Administrator, Joan Hughes.
Status: Sponsored project
Source of Grant: Economic and Social Research Council £33,174
Date of Research: 1990-1991
KEYWORDS: *outcomes of education; pupil attitudes; technical education; vocational education*

9/0231
Centre for Educational Sociology, 7 Buccleuch Place, Edinburgh EH8 9JT
031 650 1000
Raffe, D. Mr; McPherson, A. Prof.
Sample enhancement for the 1991 Scottish Young People's Survey
Abstract: The project aims to support enhancement of the sampling fraction of the 1991 Scottish Young People's Survey.
Published Material: A bibliography of published work and further details of the project are available from the Research Administrator, Joan Hughes.
Status: Sponsored project
Source of Grant: Economic and Social Research Council £25,725
Date of Research: 1990-1991
KEYWORDS: *cohort analysis; school leavers; school to work transition; Scotland; sixteen to nineteen education; surveys; youth employment*

9/0232
Centre for Educational Sociology, 7 Buccleuch Place, Edinburgh EH8 9JT
031 650 1000
Middleton, L. Ms; McPherson, A. Prof.; Lamb, J. Dr; Jones, G. Dr; Hughes, J. Miss; Brannen, K. Ms; Fairgrieve, J.Mrs;
Supervisor: Raffe, D. Mr
Spring 1991 and Autumn 1991 Scottish Young People's Surveys
Abstract: Three further postal surveys in the SYPS (Scottish Young People's Survey) series will be conducted. A 10% national sample of young people who started S4 in 1989, and an overlapping 10% sample of leavers from the 1989/90 session, were surveyed in Spring 1991. The latter will extend the biennial sequence of leavers' surveys since 1977. A 10% sample of young people who started S4 in 1987, which was surveyed in the Spring 1989 SYPS, were surveyed again in Autumn 1991.
Published Material: A bibliography of published work and further details of the project are available from the Research Administrator, Joan Hughes.
Status: Sponsored project
Source of Grant: Scottish Education Department; Department of Employment; Industry Department for Scotland; Training Agency £425,337
Date of Research: 1990-1992
KEYWORDS: *cohort analysis; school leavers; school to work transition; Scotland; sixteen to nineteen education; surveys; youth employment*

9/0233
Centre for Educational Sociology, 7 Buccleuch Place, Edinburgh EH8 9JT
031 650 1000
McPherson, A. Prof.; Raffe, D. Mr; Lamb, J. Dr; Middleton, L. Ms
Continuation of Scottish Young People's Survey
Abstract: The biennial series of surveys of Scottish school leavers is to be continued.
Published Material: A bibliography of published work is available from the Research Administrator, Joan Hughes, at Edinburgh University.
Status: Sponsored project
Source of Grant: Scottish Education Department £120,000
Date of Research: 1990 - continuing
KEYWORDS: *school leavers; school to work transition; Scotland; secondary education; surveys*

9/0234
Centre for Educational Sociology, 7 Buccleuch Place,
Edinburgh EH8 9JT
031 650 1000
Cohen, G. Mr; *Supervisor:* McPherson, A. Prof.; Raffe, D. Mr
Economic and Social Research Council Survey link scheme (2)
Abstract: The research examined the problems of the measurement
of socio-economic status using hierarchical linear models; missing
data and modelling educational attainment.
Published Material: A bibliography of published work is available
from the Research Administrator, Joan Hughes, at Edinburgh University.
Status: Sponsored project
Source of Grant: Economic and Social Research Council
Date of Research: 1991-1992
KEYWORDS: *academic achievement; measurement; models; performance; surveys*

9/0235
Department of Artificial Intelligence, 80 South Bridge,
Edinburgh EH8 9YL
031 650 1000
Howe, J. Prof.; Brna, P. Dr
**Computer aided recognition of misconceptions about simple
electrical circuits**
Abstract: It is desirable to have a more detailed understanding of how
faulty beliefs (misconceptions) arise, how they are maintained, and
how new beliefs effectively replace old ones. The long term goal is
to use this understanding to guide the researchers in the development
of exploratory regimes which can assist students to improve their
grasp of some domain. Consequently, the ability is needed to recognize that one or more misconceptions are held by a given student and
to characterize this set of beliefs. This project is concerned with the
problem of recognizing misconceptions as students are in the process
of constructing simple electrical circuits. The method of investigation
entails the construction of a number of student models. These are
computational representations of the beliefs associated with simple
electrical circuits. Various interpreters of these computational models
are being constructed. The information obtained from the student's
behaviour in constructing a circuit, the circuit's actual behaviour, and
the student's exploratory activity will be the basis for exploring the
diagnostic issues.
Status: Sponsored project
Source of Grant: Science and Engineering Research Council; Economic and Social Research Council; Medical Research Council
£89,380
Date of Research: 1989-1992
KEYWORDS: *cognitive processes; comprehension; learning activities; misconceptions; science education*

9/0236
Department of Business Studies, William Robertson
Building, 50 George Square, Edinburgh EH8 9JY
031 650 1000
Macauley, C. Ms; *Supervisor:* Brown, A. Dr; Webb, J. Dr
**The higher education route to the labour market for women
returners**
Abstract: The project explored the aspirations and achievements of
those women returners who re-enter the labour market via the higher
education route; and compared the labour market experience of
mature women graduates from Scottish universities with men who
also gain a university degree for the first time at the same age.
Preliminary research using data from the Universities Statistical
Records Office had already been conducted before the project began.
This was supplemented by a postal questionnaire for all contactable
Scottish university graduates who entered university at the age of 25
or over and graduated in the period 1985-1990. The response rate was
51.2%. 541 usable responses were received. The majority (90%) of
respondents were satisfied with their university course. A relatively
high proportion (one third) however graduated with ordinary degrees.
Significantly more women than men had other domestic commitments while at university. Older graduates were successful in attaining occupational mobility, although more men than women obtained
the highest status jobs (11.4% women; 27.7% men). Mature graduates were more likely than young graduates to work in the public
sector. The private sector was more likely to recruit younger graduates and mature male graduates than mature female graduates. One
third of respondents felt that they had been discriminated against on
grounds of age.

Published Material: BROWN, A. & WEBB, J. (1990). 'The higher
education route to the labour market for mature students', British
Journal of Education and Work, Vol 4, No 1, pp.5-21.
Status: Sponsored project
Source of Grant: Universities Funding Council £15,000
Date of Research: 1990-1991
KEYWORDS: *employment opportunities; graduate employment;
higher education; labour market; mature students; women's employment*

9/0237
Department of Education, 10-12 Buccleuch Place, Edinburgh
EH8 9JT
031 650 1000
Davis, J. Mr; *Supervisor:* Donn, G. Dr
**Sport for all?: an investigation into the factors that motivate a
child not to participate in sport**
Abstract: An investigation into the factors that motivate a child not
to participate in sport. At present there has been great concern by such
organisations as the Sports Council that the number of school children
taking up sport is falling. In carrying out this study the researcher will
attempt to discover how culture is involved when a child makes the
every day choice not to participate in sport at school and if the new
educational policies that are being implemented by the Scottish
Office are in any way reversing this process. By looking at what
results in non-participation, this study will differ from previous ones
in this field which have mostly been concerned with describing the
process through which participation comes about (i.e. socialisation).
That is, rather than recognising that children take every day decisions
concerning sports participation, previous works tend to view children's sports participation as being determined by external factors.
Moreover, the research will investigate in what way, if any, educational policy changes affect the everyday choices of children in terms
of sports participation.
Status: Sponsored project
Source of Grant: Carnegie Trust £1,100
Date of Research: 1991 - continuing
KEYWORDS: *educational policy; participation; physical education;
pupil participation; social influences; sports*

9/0238
Department of Education, CALL Centre, 4 Buccleuch Place,
Edinburgh EH8 9JT
031 650 1000
Aitken, S. Dr; Millar, S. Ms; Nisbet, P. Mr; Sutherland, E.
Ms; *Supervisor:* Entwistle, N. Prof.
Communication Aids for Language and Learning (CALL)
Abstract: This is a research and development project, including
service delivery, offering help in assessing what communication aids
or teaching programmes are needed for learners with disabilities.
Development work includes investigation of how these aids might be
incorporated within, and contribute towards, curriculum development. Research is carried out into a wide range of aspects of communication difficulty and technology, with development of a new
microelectronic and computing systems to exploit new technologies.
Support is given to clients and carers in tailoring and using the chosen
system. Activities cover a Scotland-wide assessment service; information, demonstrations and advice and loan services. Training is
offered through the media of seminars, awareness training, short and
long term secondments for training of professionals including teachers, psychologists, social workers, programmers and technicians.
1991/92 projects include assessment related work; training related
work; smart wheelchair-related work; and functional communication
related work.
Published Material: AITKEN, S. (1987). 'Me and my therapists',
The Scottish Child, Winter, pp.16-17.; AITKEN, S. (1988. 'Computer aided instruction with the multiply impaired', Journal of Mental
Deficiency Research, No 32, pp.257-263.; BUULTJENS, M. &
AITKEN, S. (1987). 'Assessment of vision in multiply impaired
children', British Journal of Special Education, No 14, pp.112-114.;
A comprehensive report pack and a set of research papers are available from the researcher.
Status: Sponsored project
Source of Grant: Scottish Office Education Department £110,000
Date of Research: 1986 - continuing
KEYWORDS: *communication aids – for disabled; disabilities; educational materials; special educational needs*

9/0239

Department of Education, 10-12 Buccleuch Place, Edinburgh
EH8 9JT
031 650 1000
Wu, L. Miss; *Supervisor:* Entwistle, N. Prof.

An exploratory study on school readiness, with special reference to the school-aged children in Taiwan

Abstract: The aim of the present research is twofold. First, to explore the reality of school readiness in progress, and second to discover the causes for the difference in children's readiness. The sample comprises thirty-six school-age entrants and their parents and four primary 1 teachers in Taiwan. Open-ended interviewing and fieldnote observations are the major methods employed in fieldwork.

Status: Sponsored project
Source of Grant: The Republic of China, Ministry of Education
Date of Research: 1986-1991
KEYWORDS: *school entrance age; school readiness; Taiwan*

9/0240

Department of Education, 10-12 Buccleuch Place, Edinburgh
EH8 9JT
031 650 1000
Smith, C. Mr; *Supervisor:* Entwistle, N. Prof.

Understanding in educational contexts

Abstract: Understanding is a much used term in education but what it is to understand in an educational context has received surprisingly little attention to date. If an aim of education is that students should achieve understanding, it seems that this deficit should be remedied. In fact, a growing interest in the nature of understanding is beginning to emerge. A difference in conceptualisation between authors can be detected in which understanding is described either as a phenomenon of personal experience or as a target set in some way by the contextual conditions around the individual. A more appropriate description for education seems to require some sort of combination of these two views in which the relationships between the targets for understanding set by the curriculum and the experiences of the students can be examined. Accordingly, an attempt has been made to develop a conceptualisation of understanding which enables this type of issue to be examined and attention is now being turned to examining the relationship between the target for understanding set by the curriculum (in terms of course outlines and aims, assessment materials and course delivery) and the understanding experiences of the students (probably by surveying responses to assessments and interviews).

Status: Individual research
Date of Research: 1991 - continuing
KEYWORDS: *comprehension; learning*

9/0241

Department of Education, 10-12 Buccleuch Place, Edinburgh
EH8 9JT
031 650 1000
Percy, S. Ms; *Supervisor:* Donn, G. Dr; King, K. Dr

Curriculum and Assessment in Scotland: A Policy for the 90s', impact of this initiative in a rural secondary and primary school

Abstract: This research aims to trace the process of change and the impact on assessment and teaching of English language in Scottish schools following the publication of Scottish Office Education Department (1987) Curriculum and Assessment in Scotland: A Policy for the 90s. Using a rural secondary school (510 pupils and 44 staff) and its feeder primary school (220 pupils and 11.8 staff) as a sample, the study involves oral history, ethnographic interviews, documentation and participant observation.

Status: Individual research
Date of Research: 1990 - continuing
KEYWORDS: *curriculum development; educational assessment; educational change; English studies; Scotland*

9/0242

Department of Education, 10-12 Buccleuch Place, Edinburgh
EH8 9JT
031 650 1000
Weiyuan, Z. Mr; *Supervisor:* King, K. Dr; Thomson, G. Dr

Comparative research on career guidance between Britain and China

Abstract: Career guidance is increasingly becoming an important task in a changing world. The aim of this research is to compare students' career needs, including students' value criteria and choices of various occupations; the relationship between their career goals and school activities; and their needs in regard to career choice. In China, the researcher has selected and surveyed four junior-senior secondary schools (grades 7-12) and two junior secondary schools (grades 7-9). In each of these schools, classes were randomly chosen from each grade level. The total participants in the study were 674 students, 722 parents, and 127 teachers. A further study will select and survey using the same questionnaire, similar schools and students, parents and teachers, in Scotland. Through comparative research on need assessment between British students and Chinese students, the study will discuss problems and give recommendations on how career guidance can be best implemented.

Published Material: A full list of publications is available from the researcher.
Status: Individual research
Date of Research: 1991 - continuing
KEYWORDS: *career counselling; China; comparative education; Scotland; vocational guidance*

9/0243

Department of Education, 10-12 Buccleuch Place, Edinburgh
EH8 9JT
031 650 1000
Morris, J. Mr; *Supervisor:* Entwistle, N. Prof.; McPherson, A. Prof.; Raab, C. Mr

The work of the Scottish Council for Research in Education 1928-1992

Abstract: This is a study of the Scottish Council for Research in Education which was one of the earliest research councils to be found in Europe. Its history is traced from total independence relying on voluntary but professional labour, to that of a group of professional researchers still having independence but within the bounds of a market economy. The main themes will be: testing shading into assessment; outreach i.e. dissemination of findings to the teaching force and in international activity; policy where customer-contractor and even negotiated research works within a range of constraints. The methodology will be that of archive search with the Founder Institutions, the Education Institute of Scotland and the Association of Directors of Education, Scotland, and other appropriate bodies such as the Scottish Office Education Department, the Public Record Office, West Register House, Edinburgh and the archive of the Council itself. It will include taped interviews with leading Council Members and officials, past and present. Four of its five Directors and all its Chairmen for the past 40 years are still alive. The researcher has had an association with the Council, first as a subject in one of its projects in 1932 and subsequently in a variety of roles including that of assessor.

Status: Individual research
Date of Research: 1991 - continuing
KEYWORDS: *educational history; educational research; Scotland*

9/0244

Department of Education, 10-12 Buccleuch Place, Edinburgh
EH8 9JT
031 650 1000
Davis, J. Mr; *Supervisor:* Donn, G. Dr; Thomson, G. Dr

Sport for all in education: an inquiry into PE and sport in schools, what constitutes good practice and its relation to the role of culture and culture within schools

Abstract: The project can be separated into two sections. The first is policy based and aims to outline teaching methods, lesson structure, share of the curriculum, methods of evaluation and other areas that relate to physical education (PE) in schools. It will describe how these affect and are perceived by children of different age, sex and ethnic background. In doing so it will illustrate the present aim of PE policy, how this relates to children at different stages of development and how this is affected by issues such as time and resources. In short the present practice existing in schools with regard to PE, will be brought forth with the aim of defining good practice in PE as viewed by parents, teachers and pupils. The second part of the proposal will use the first section as a practical core around which to develop the theoretical nature of the project. By viewing the school as a social microcosm the project will illustrate PE as it relates to other areas of the school and is affected by the structure of the school. Central to this will be the examination of the role of culture and cultures within the school.

Status: Sponsored project

Source of Grant: Carnegie Trust for Universities of Scotland £2,275; Scottish Office Education Department £10,750
Date of Research: 1991 - continuing
KEYWORDS: educational policy; educational practices; physical education; sports

9/0245
Department of EducationCentre for Research on Learning and Instruction, 10-12 Buccleuch Place, Edinburgh EH8 9JT
031 650 1000
Tait, H. Ms; Thompson, S. Mrs;
Supervisor: Entwistle, N. Prof.

Improving student achievement through promoting effective learning

Abstract: By promoting effective learning, student achievement should be improved. A significant part of this project involved producing a set of guidelines for teaching staff in higher education to allow them to explore alternative ideas and approaches to entry qualifications, previous knowledge, study skills, syllabus content, teaching methods, assessment and institutional policies for supporting teaching and learning. The guidelines are not intended to be in any way prescriptive, but rather to provide an opportunity for staff to reflect on their current policies and practices in light of the latest research findings. A separate part of the project aimed to develop an approach to studying inventory which could be used mid-way through the first term of a first year course to identify students who may be at risk of failing due to inappropriate study habits and inadequate skills. A computer program was developed to display scores on three dimensions graphically, and to identify students at risk of failure by means of a 'prediction function'. Further development work of the inventory is underway, and is planned for the computer program 'StudentView', if funding becomes available.
Published Material: ENTWISTLE, N.J., TAIT, H. & THOMPSON, S. (1992). 'Improving student achievement through promoting effective learning'. Final Report to the Scottish Office Education Department. Available from Edinburgh University, Centre for Research on Learning and Instruction.; ENTWISTLE, N.J., THOMPSON, S. & TAIT, H. (1992). 'Guidelines for promoting effective learning in higher education'. Final Report to the Scottish Office Education Department. Available from Edinburgh University, Centre for Research on Learning and Instruction.; ODOR, P. 'StudentView – an interactive graphical system for analysing and exploring student questionnaire data'. User handbook, demonstrator version. Available from Edinburgh University, Centre for Research on Learning and Instruction.
Status: Sponsored project
Source of Grant: Scottish Office Education Department £40,000
Date of Research: 1990-1991
KEYWORDS: educational innovation; higher education; learning strategies; teaching methods

9/0246
Department of Education, Centre for Research on Learning and Instruction, 10-12 Buccleuch Place, Edinburgh EH8 9JT
031 650 1000
Entwistle, N. Prof.; Napuk, A. Mrs; Dickie, S. Ms;
Normand, B. Mrs

English language monitoring

Abstract: The main aim is to assess national standards of attainment across the language modes of reading, writing, listening, talking and interaction. A representative national sample will be drawn from P4, P7 and S2 and assessed using appropriate test materials. Some tests used in the 1989 survey will be repeated to provide a basis of comparison.
Status: Sponsored project
Source of Grant: Scottish Education Department £132,000
Date of Research: 1991 - continuing
KEYWORDS: assessment; attainment tests; English studies; language tests; Scotland

9/0247
Department of Education, Centre for Research on Learning and Instruction, 10-12 Buccleuch Place, Edinburgh EH8 9JT
831 650 1000
Entwistle, N. Prof.; Supervisor: Entwistle, N. Prof.

Understanding understanding

Abstract: This is an exploratory interview study in which the revision strategies of students who have recently finished their final examinations were discussed. In the context of revision, students explained how they had sought understanding, and how they used their understanding to answer examination questions. Qualitative analysis of the transcripts produced categories of description which elucidated the nature of understanding, the development of understanding, and the differing forms of understanding reached. These forms of understanding affected the ability of students to answer different kinds of question. Narrow, specific questions could be answered by reproducing the structure of the topic provided by the lecturer, while broader questions required a broader and more flexible, personal understanding. Complications for teaching and assessment in higher education are considered.
Published Material: ENTWISTLE, N.J. & ENTWISTLE, A.C. (1991). 'Contrasting forms of understanding for degree examinations: the student experience and its implications', Higher Education, Vol 22, pp.205-227.; ENTWISTLE, A.C. & ENTWISTLE, N.J. (1992). 'Experiences of understanding in revising for degree examinations', Learning and Instruction, Vol 2 (in press).; ENTWISTLE, N.J., ENTWISTLE, A.C. & TAIT, H. (1992). 'Academic understanding and contexts to enhance it: a perspective from research on student learning'. In: DUFFY, T. & JONASSEN, D. (Eds). Designing Environments for Constructive Learning. (preliminary title – publisher to be decided).
Status: Sponsored project
Source of Grant: Godfrey Thomson Trust Fund (internal departmental support) £2,000
Date of Research: 1990-1991
KEYWORDS: comprehension; examination techniques; higher education; learning

9/0248
Department of Mathematics and Statistics, James Clerk Maxwell Building, King's Buildings, Mayfield Road, Edinburgh EH9 3JZ
031 650 1000
Triadafillidis, T. Mr; Supervisor: Searl, J. Dr; Entwistle, N. Prof.

Practical work in the mathematics classroom

Abstract: This research arises from the oft asserted claim that practical activities are an essential element in creating a learning environment in the mathematical classroom. A number of practical activities have been developed for pupils aged 12-14 and these, together with activities developed elsewhere, are being evaluated in a number of schools. The illuminative evaluation approach will be used.
Status: Individual research
Date of Research: 1990 - continuing
KEYWORDS: learning activities; mathematical applications; mathematics education; secondary education

9/0249
Department of Mathematics and Statistics, James Clerk Maxwell Building, King's Buildings, Mayfield Road, Edinburgh EH9 3JZ
031 650 1000
Searl, J. Dr; Supervisor: Searl, J. Dr

Mathematics 16-20

Abstract: This project will analyse the different patterns of learning and teaching adopted in school and university (and polytechnics) for mathematics. The reasons for undergraduates abandoning their mathematical studies will be examined by means of personal interview and questionnaire. Students will be matched by sex, age and qualification in an attempt to elucidate the factors which contribute to success in mathematics in tertiary education.
Status: Individual research
Date of Research: 1991 - continuing
KEYWORDS: higher education; learning motivation; learning strategies; mathematics achievement; sixteen to nineteen education; undergraduate study

9/0250
Edinburgh Centre for Social Welfare Research, 23 Buccleuch Place, Edinburgh EH8 9JT
031 650 4637
Scottish Council for Research in Education, 15 St John Street, Edinburgh EH8 8JR
031 557 2944

Arnott, M. Ms; *Supervisor:* Adler, M. Mr; Munn, P. Mrs; Raab, C. Mr

The devolved management of schools: a comparative study of the impact of parental participation and the local management of schools in Scotland and England

Abstract: Separate legislation in Scotland and England provides a strategic opportunity for comparative research on parental participation and the local management of schools. In Scotland, every school is expected to establish its own School Board. Parents have a majority of places but the Board's 'baseline' powers are quite limited. This contrasts with the situation in England where parents have one-third of the places on governing bodies but these have more extensive powers. For example, they receive budgets from the local authority to cover most of their running costs which they are free to spend as they wish. The research will attempt to examine and inform the arguments of supporters and critics of these developments by studying the management of four secondary schools in each of three education authorities. These authorities have contrasting policies towards devolved management: Authority 1 has sought to retain a dominant position in the management of its schools; Authority 2 is experimenting with a greater degree of delegated managment of resources; while Authority 3 is strongly committed to devolved school management. The research will be based upon documentary analysis, observation of meetings, interviews with key actors in the policy process at national, local and school levels, and a parents survey.

Status: Sponsored project
Source of Grant: Economic and Social Research Council £159,000
Date of Research: 1992 - continuing
KEYWORDS: *comparative analysis; local management of schools; parent participation; school boards – Scotland; school governing bodies*

9/0251

Old College, South Bridge, Edinburgh EH8 9YL
031 650 1000
Scottish Council for Research in Education, 15 St John Street, Edinburgh EH8 8JR
031 557 2944
Adler, M. Mr; Raab, C. Mr; Munn, P. Mrs

Devolved management of schools

Abstract: This project aims to compare the impact of parental participation and Local Management of Schools on parents, teachers, education authorities and government in England and Scotland. It will also analyse the changes in relationships between those involved, and assess their significance for educational provision.

Status: Sponsored project
Source of Grant: Economic and Social Research Council £100,000
Date of Research: 1992 - continuing
KEYWORDS: *central administration; educational change; educational policy; local education authorities; local management of schools; parent participation; parent-school relationship; school-based management*

Essex University

9/0252

Contemporary Japan Centre, Wivenhoe Park, Colchester
CO4 3SQ
0206 872543
Neary, I. Prof.; *Supervisor:* Okazaki, T. Mr

Teaching and testing Japanese and similar languages in schools

Abstract: The aim of this research project is to undertake an investigation into methodologies appropriate for the teaching of 'hard languages', such as Japanese, Chinese and Arabic in schools in the UK. In the course of the research the Research Fellow will develop teaching materials, schemes of work and assessment techniques which will be used initially in the teaching of Japanese to groups of children from three schools in Colchester, namely the Sixth Form College, the Royal Grammar School and the County High School for Girls. The first stage of the research will consist of a survey of the courses already being used to teach Japanese, Chinese and Arabic in this country. New teaching materials for experimental Japanese classes will be devised according to the results of the preliminary

survey, then they will be modified in response to the experiences within the classroom throughout the three year project.

Status: Sponsored project
Source of Grant: Department of Education and Science £90,000
Date of Research: 1991 - continuing
KEYWORDS: *Arabic; Chinese languages; educational materials; Japanese; non western languages; second language learning*

Exeter University

9/0253

Department of Psychology, Washington Singer Laboratories, Exeter EX4 4OG
0392 264626
Mitchell, D. Dr; *Supervisor:* Mitchell, D. Dr

Cognitive analysis of fluent reading and learning to read

Abstract: The aim of the research is to determine the cognitive processes underlying fluent reading and learning to read. The methods are experimental and often involve speeded responses and groups of words or sentences presented on a screen under the control of a microcomputer. Specific tasks that have been used include lexical decision tasks, subject placed reading tasks, tachistoscopic recognition tasks and mind-recall tasks. To date the researchers have carried out work on word-recognition, sentence parsing and text integration with particular reference to the influence of context or prior knowledge at all levels. Some of the most recent work concerns the role of lexical and pragmatic effects of parsing. Contributions from PhD students include work on automatic processing of word meaning, the use of script-knowledge in comprehension, the use of plans goals in comprehension, and individual differences in reading skills.

Status: Sponsored project
Source of Grant: Economic and Social Research Council £42,000; Nuffield Foundation £2,500; British Council £1,100
Date of Research: 1989-1992
KEYWORDS: *beginning reading; cognitive processes; reading comprehension; reading rate; reading tests*

9/0254

School of Education, St Lukes, Heavitree Road, Exeter
EX1 2LU
0392 263263
Ross, M. Mr; *Supervisor:* Ross, M. Mr; Radnor, H. Ms

Assessing achievement in the arts

Abstract: This research report addresses the role of subjectivity in assessment in the arts. Perhaps it would be more accurate to speak of two, interacting subjectivities: that of the pupil and that of the teacher. Subjectivity has traditionally been regarded as invalidating the legitimacy of aesthetic appraisal, on the one hand the pupil's subjective experience has been seen both as inaccessible to the teacher and as private to the pupil. On the other hand the subjective judgements of teachers have often been thought to be irrelevant and alien to their pupils' artistic purposes. Claims for validity and reliability in arts assessment are most often made to rest upon the twin notions of connoisseurship and consensus: teachers, by virtue of their experience and expertise, coming together to provide an agreed yardstick of aesthetic value, applied more or less exclusively to the impact of the pupil's artwork or product. The researchers have sought to offer a contrary view: to focus upon process rather than product, upon pupil understanding rather than product impact, to promote the pupil as the principal assessor, and talk as a medium not only of aesthetic communication but of artistic insight and judgement. Above all the researchers argue the case for the recognition of the proper and indispensible function of subjectivity in artistic appraisal and have attempted to demonstrate, through the case studies, how the interplay of subjective responses, expressed in dynamic conversation, can yield substantial qualitative evidence for both formative and summative assessments in arts education. The whole study rests upon a process model of aesthetic understanding that identifies a sequence of four transitional operations characterising each aesthetic encounter in terms of the two complementary dimensions of 'realization' and 'display'. This model (adapted from the work of Rom Harre) also serves as the instrument of data analysis and to articulate an argument in favour of qualitative assessment in the arts. Arts teachers are urged to make greater use of conversational talk in teaching and assessment and to allow greater emphasis upon contemplation and reflection in

promoting aesthetic understanding in their classes. Incidentally, the study reveals the disturbing extent to which arts teachers currently may be neglecting children's aesthetic, creative and expressive development – those very elements they often claim to be their principal concerns. The arts encourage individual creative responses, whether in the course of art production or appreciation. These forms of response lend themselves to the assessment of individual achievement against personal past performance and within the context of an unfolding personal biography – rather than in more traditional normative and comparative terms. Much current practice is reductionist and fails to take account of the personal, expressive – as distinct from the collective, instructional – objectives of arts curricula. The present project focuses upon National Curriculum Key Stage 3 and attempts: (i) to formulate an approach to assessment suitable for expressive and creative work in the arts at Key Stage 3 as a collective domain within the curriculum; (ii) to develop a framework for mapping the expressive and creative across the full range of the arts in education; (iii) to facilitate pupil self-assessment as a significant element in the formal assessment process. Work began in the schools in January 1990 and was concluded in June 1991. Field work was carried out in a number of secondary schools in Cornwall, Devon and Dorset.
Status: Sponsored project
Source of Grant: Leverhulme Trust £50,000
Date of Research: 1990-1991
KEYWORDS: aesthetic education; arts; assessment; evaluative thinking; verbal communication

9/0255
> School of Education, St Luke's, Heavitree Road, Exeter
> EX1 2LU
> 0392 263263
> Treharne, D. Dr

Tower Hamlets project: communication between Tower Hamlets Local Education Authority and school governing bodies
Abstract: Now in the second year of research, this project is evaluating communication between the Tower Hamlets Education Authority, schools and governing bodies. The particular focus of this study has been a primary school and a secondary school, both in different neighbourhoods. The interim report dealt with the period of transition between Tower Hamlets as part of division five of the Inner London Education Authority, and Tower Hamlets Local Education Authority in its first year of operation. It outlined the problems encountered by the local authority establishing a working network for information, and the difficulties encountered by governing bodies in promoting this as practice. Phase two of the study will evaluate the change from the provision of centrally based services, to provision through neighbourhoods. It will also focus on the relationship between a new headteacher, the governing body, and the newly devolved neighbourhood services. Reporting of this phase will take place in Autumn 1992.
Status: Sponsored project
Source of Grant: London Borough of Tower Hamlets
Date of Research: 1991-1992
KEYWORDS: educational planning; governing bodies; local education authorities; neighbourhoods

9/0256
> School of Education, St Luke's, Heavitree Road, Exeter
> EX1 2LU
> 0392 263263
> Carre, C. Mr; *Supervisor:* Wragg, E. Prof.; Bennett, S. Prof.

The Leverhulme Primary Project
Abstract: The nature and quality of teacher education is the subject of much current debate and research has highlighted the importance of the quality of classroom activity and of teacher competences. An initial national survey reflected current concerns amongst teachers' views of their competences to teach the National Curriculum. The project's research programme into various aspects of primary education is divided into two strands: (1) The classroom management strand has as its major aim to conduct research into teachers' professional skills, by studying teachers both in class and under experimental conditions. Several hundred lessons have been observed and a cluster of studies conducted. These have considered such matters as: teachers' first encounters with new classes, either at the beginning of the year or at the start of teaching practice; the handling of disruption; the management of professional skills like questioning and explaining; strategies used by supply teachers; pupils' views of discipline;

teachers' management of their subject knowledge. Techniques used include live observation of lessons, interviews, questionnaires and the use of photographs to analyse decision making strategies; (2) The development of the teacher competence strand, questions the role of teacher knowledge in teaching quality, defined in terms of competences. Research was conducted on student-teachers (N=59) taking the Post Graduate Certificate in Education and were from four specialisms, Maths, Science, Music and Early Years. A sample (N=24) was randomly selected for in-depth observation and interview. A number of data-gathering formats were used to collect information on changes in student-teachers understanding of three knowledge bases (i.e. subject knowledge, pedagogical subject matter, beliefs and ideologies). The impact of teaching experiences and the course has been monitored. A follow-up study is being conducted on a small sample, through the first year of teaching.
Published Material: TROTTER, A. & WRAGG, E.C. (1990). 'A Study of Supply Teachers', Research Papers in Education, Vol 5, No 3, pp.251-276.; DUNNE, E. & BENNETT, N. (1990). Talking and Learning in Groups. London: Macmillan.; BENNETT, S.N., WRAGG, E.C. & CARRE. C.G. (1991). 'Primary Teachers and the National Curriculum', Junior Education, Vol 15, No 11, November.; CARTER, D.S.G. & CARRE, C.G. (1991). 'Gender differences in primary teachers' self estimates of their competence to teach National Curriculum Science', Australian Educational Researcher, Vol 18, No 2.; BENNETT, S.N., WRAGG, E.C., CARRE, C.G. & CARTER, D. (1992). 'A longitudinal study of primary teachers' perceived competence in, and concerns about, National Curriculum implementation', Research Papers in Education, Vol 7, No 1.
Status: Sponsored project
Source of Grant: The Leverhulme Trust £268,700
Date of Research: 1989-1992
KEYWORDS: classroom management; competence; preservice teacher education; teacher development; teacher effectiveness

9/0257
> School of Education, St Luke's, Heavitree Road, Exeter
> EX1 2LU
> 0392 263263
> Preece, P. Dr

Learning and the pace of lessons
Abstract: An algebraic model relating the rate of learning to the pace of teaching and to pupil ability has been developed. The model accounts well for prior data on learning at different speeds and accurately predicts the learning deficit for able pupils taught in heterogeneous classes. The model can predict the changes of pace and learning from lesson to lesson. A direct investigation of the interrelationship of learning, ability and pace has been carried out with 40 undergraduate education students, using foreign language vocabulary items. Some qualitative features of the theoretical model were supported.
Published Material: PREECE, P.F.W. (1990). 'Learning and the pace of lessons: a theoretical model', British Journal of Mathematical and Statistical Psychology, Vol 43, pp.1-6.; PREECE, P.F.W. (1990). 'Imitatio Physicae', British Educational Research Journal, Vol 16, pp.297-304.; PREECE, P.F.W. (1991). 'Foreign language vocabulary learning and the pace of instruction', The Teacher Trainer, Vol 5, No 2, pp.21-22.
Status: Individual research
Date of Research: 1989 - continuing
KEYWORDS: ability; learning; mixed ability; pacing; time factors – learning

9/0258
> School of Education, St Luke's, Heavitree Road, Exeter
> EX1 2LU
> 0392 263263
> Bloomer, M. Dr

Life in post-compulsory classrooms
Abstract: Despite massive changes to the 14-19 curriculum, classroom life in the post-compulsory (16-19) sector of education is vastly under-represented in research literature and a great deal of what does exist is informed as much by inferences from grand curriculum designs ('it is planned to happen, therefore it happens') as by any systematic study. This study is the first stage of a research programme which aims to gain insights into students' and teachers' experiences of teaching and learning, and to provide evidence of the effects of 'educational planning/provision' upon student learning. The aims are: (1) to enable the researchers to deepen their insights into teachers'

and students' experiences of classroom life in order that a more substantial project can be planned; (2) to develop such materials and skills as will be necessary to discharge the full project; and (3) to establish a network of teacher fieldworkers. The pilot study will be based at a tertiary college. Initially, it will focus on A-level students but will broaden out to include other types of course. Semi-structured observations of class meetings and follow-up interviews with students and teachers will yield the data for this exploratory, pilot study. In addition, certain information will be obtained from college records. These data will inform and guide the choice of concepts, categories and hypotheses that will shape the full project. A number of teachers at the college will participate in the project as field workers and, ultimately as full partners in the research.

Status: Sponsored project
Source of Grant: Exeter University: School of Education Research Fund £650
Date of Research: 1991-1992
KEYWORDS: classroom environment; classroom research; educational planning; learning; sixteen to nineteen education

9/0259

School of Education, St Luke's, Heavitree Road, Exeter
EX1 2LU
0392 263263
Davis, N. Dr; Wright, B. Mr; Tearle, P. Ms; *Supervisor:* Davis, N. Dr

ISDN2 and computer networks to enhance initial teacher training
Abstract: Exeter University School of Education has recently built a Media and Resources Centre which contains a TV studio and three information technology (IT) rooms (two on 24 hour access), with extensive ethernet network and many of the PCs are on this network. The University of Virginia will provide computer conferencing and mail software (TIM) plus consultancy on its installation. Exeter will become the first international node in the emerging K12 network for the USA (Bull and Harris, 1990). British Telecom will install several ISDN2 nodes in this building and one in a local school's resource centre/library. Other nodes are in Martlesham and Anglia College of Higher Education's Xploratorium. The second phase of the project during Lent and Trinity terms 1992 will trial these links with student teachers. These trials would be an assessed part of an IT course. At the same time the ISDN2 link will be in use with one or two students placed in the secondary school for teaching practice. Again this is an assessed part of their course. The project officers, who are experienced IT tutors with expertise in multimedia and communications including databases on CD, will assist permanent tutors implement this. The third phase of the project will document these case studies in the form of published papers, video and student work. The database of IT applications discussed by large groups of students could provide stimulating reflections on future use of IT in education. At this stage the data gathered on costs and learning issues (using action research methods) will be carefully analysed.

Status: Sponsored project
Source of Grant: Employment Department – Learning Technology Unit £80,000
Date of Research: 1991-1992
KEYWORDS: computer uses in education; educational media; information technology; learning resources centres; preservice teacher education

9/0260

School of Education, St Luke's, Heavitree Road, Exeter
EX1 2LU
0392 263263
Fox, R. Dr

Investigating teachers' assessment of children's writing at National Curriculum Key Stage 2
Abstract: The main aim of the project is to investigate primary teachers' methods of assessing the writing of children for National Curriculum Key Stage 2. A second aim is the production of computer software to enable teachers and students to practise such assessment within a framework provided. The investigation involves observation and interviews with local teachers in up to six primary schools in Devon. An important contextual feature is the need for teachers to develop their practice in this area in order to assess children in the National Curriculum for English at Key Stage 2.

Status: Sponsored project
Source of Grant: Exeter University: School of Education £750; Exeter University Research Fund £4,000

Date of Research: 1991-1992
KEYWORDS: assessment; English studies; National Curriculum; primary education; writing evaluation; writing skills

9/0261

School of Education, St Luke's, Heavitree Road, Exeter
EX1 2LU
0392 263263
Naughton, C. Mr

Exeter Music Technology Project
Abstract: The Exeter Music Technology Project (EMTP) is an investigation into the use of a Roland 'Sampler' with a group of students from the School of Education and Exeter College of Further Education. The project is therefore concerned with students knowing how to use 'computer equipment'.

Status: Individual research
Date of Research: 1991-1992
KEYWORDS: computer uses in education; educational technology; music education

9/0262

School of Education, St Luke's, Heavitree Road, Exeter
EX1 2LU
0392 263263
Naughton, C. Mr

Devon Music Technology Project
Abstract: The Devon Music Technology Project (DMTP) is a county-wide investigation based initially on a survey of what provision there is in the county. The use of 'Sampler' packages in primary schools in a cross-curricular manner is the basis of this project.

Status: Individual research
Date of Research: 1991-1992
KEYWORDS: computer uses in education; educational technology; music education

9/0263

School of Education, St Luke's, Heavitree Road, Exeter
EX1 2LU
0392 263263
Somers, J. Mr; *Supervisor:* Somers, J. Mr

The nature of learning in educational drama
Abstract: There is very little evidence of the nature of learning which takes place in the arts. At a time when the place of the arts in education is under scrutiny, it seems timely that we should attempt to discover what kind of learning takes place during and following specific drama experiences. Teachers have devised five lesson packages which they are reshaping as a result of using them within their own teaching. The next phase is for teacher-researchers to be brought out of their schools so that they can observe other teachers using the material. After final redrafting of the lesson packages, drama teachers across the country will be asked to use the material. Results will be collated in Exeter and published. The project uses attitude scales, observation schedules, interviews and analysis of written work to evaluate the nature of the pupils' experiences. Lessons are on: (1) old age; (2) Downs Syndrome; (3) gender; (4) photograph as stimulus; (5) legend as stimulus.

Status: Sponsored project
Source of Grant: Exeter University Research Fund £3,000
Date of Research: 1989 - continuing
KEYWORDS: curriculum development; drama; educational materials; learning experience

9/0264

School of Education, St Luke's, Heavitree Road, Exeter
EX1 2LU
0392 263263
Trend, R. Dr; *Supervisor:* Stephenson, J. Mr; Chamberlain, P. Dr; Peacock, A. Dr

Earth Science and Physical Geography in the secondary school curriculum: a study of current practice in one English local education authority
Abstract: A study of the geography/science interface, focusing on curriculum content, teacher cooperation, disciplines, school subjects and the relationships between the emerging National Curriculum and current practice in the schools of one English local education authority. The thesis is developed around the Earth science and physical

geography content of science and geography curricula at 11 to 14 years. Philosophical and historical elements are strongly represented. The empirical research initially involved the questionnaire survey of 270 geography and science teachers in the 67 schools of one English local education authority in order to examine content selection. Earth science was found to be closely associated with integrated science schemes, and physical geography with separate subject courses (as opposed to combined humanities). 15 'key schools' were identified from the questionnaire data, and 43 teachers were interviewed to identify critical factors in content selection. Various 'models of' Earth science content selection are proposed: one based on science, one on geography and one comprising a combined science/geography course, labelled 'Earth/Studies'. National Curriculum content is used to develop a fourth 'model for' Earth Studies at 11 to 14 years: it incorporates all relevant content from the geography and science curriculars. The conclusions address geography/science links in terms of both current practice and the opportunities provided by the National Curriculum. Earth science content selection is portrayed as essentially problematic because it straddles the geography/science interface.
Status: Individual research
Date of Research: 1985-1991
KEYWORDS: *curriculum; earth science; National Curriculum; physical geography; science curriculum; secondary education*

9/0265
School of Education, St Luke's, Heavitree Road, Exeter
EX1 2LU
0392 263263
Preece, P. Dr
Student attitudes regarding effective teaching behaviours – a teaching practice study
Abstract: An anglicized version of the Teaching Behaviours Questionnaire is to be given to 200+ Post Graduate Certificate in Education (PGCE) secondary students before teaching practice (TP). After TP, quantitative ratings on each student for each category on the standard assessment schedule will be obtained. This should permit the investigation of the factorial structure of the instrument and provide TP performance scores for correlating with scores on the attitude inventory. In a related intervention exercise, half of the science student group will receive feedback on the research evidence concerning teaching behaviour covered in the inventory. By using the other half of the group as a control, the effect of the intervention on TP performance will be investigated.
Status: Sponsored project
Source of Grant: Exeter University: School of Education
Date of Research: 1991 - continuing
KEYWORDS: *Postgraduate Certificate in Education; preservice teacher education; student attitudes; student teacher evaluation; teacher behaviour; teaching practice*

9/0266
School of Education, St Luke's, Heavitree Road, Exeter
EX1 2LU
0392 263263
Burn, R. Dr; *Supervisor:* Vamos, P. Prof; Burghes, D. Prof
Teaching and learning undergraduate mathematics
Abstract: Although there is much current innovation in relation to other aspects of mathematics teaching in higher education, there is virtually none relating to the basic 'bread and butter' courses in the first and second year of an honours degree in mathematics. The research compared teaching and learning in the first and second year courses at an English university and an English polytechnic. The method was to conduct half-hour interviews, using one set of questions for staff and one for students. Sixty-eight students were interviewed and thirty-two staff, slightly more than half of each being from the university. The results showed (in the students' opinion) significant advantages in two aspects of polytechnic practice (i.e. not making a sharp distinction between the use of class time for lectures or problems, and the prescription of a set book or lecture notes for the course). There were widespread complaints that lecturers went too fast and none that lecturers went too slowly. It also became clear that students following up recommendations for further reading in the library are frustrated and not helped by the recommendation. Finally there was a lack of awareness on the part of lecturers of the length of a student's working week; overestimated by university lecturers and underestimated by polytechnic lecturers.
Status: Sponsored project

Source of Grant: Exeter University £2,500
Date of Research: 1990-1991
KEYWORDS: *higher education; mathematics education; student attitudes; student evaluation of teacher performance; teaching methods*

9/0267
School of Education, St Luke's, Heavitree Road, Exeter
EX1 2LU
0392 263263
Fines, J. Dr; Nichol, J. Dr
Enquiry into teaching history to over sixteens (ETHOS)
Abstract: Enquiry into teaching history to over sixteens (ETHOS) has developed an A and AS level syllabus consisting of 60% coursework. The syllabus gives control of the curriculum back to history teachers, and they mediate their courses from their perspective as trained academic historians. A new approach to resourcing which sees the student carrying on a dialogue with an academic has been produced. This is linked to initiatives in pedagogy.
Status: Sponsored project
Source of Grant: Nuffield Foundation £150,000
Date of Research: 1987-1992
KEYWORDS: *A level examinations; A level examinations – AS; curriculum development; history; teaching process*

9/0268
School of Education, St Luke's, Heavitree Road, Exeter
EX1 2LU
0392 263263
Fines, J. Dr; Nichol, J. Dr
Primary history project
Abstract: The primary history project is enquiring into possible approaches to implementing the national history curriculum in 25,000 primary schools where there is little expertise.
Status: Sponsored project
Source of Grant: Nuffield Foundation £20,000
Date of Research: 1991 - continuing
KEYWORDS: *history; National Curriculum; primary education*

9/0269
School of Education, St Luke's, Heavitree Road, Exeter
EX1 2LU
0392 263263
Hughes, M. Dr; *Supervisor:* Hughes, M. Dr
Feedback, peer-interaction and adult-intervention in initial logo learning
Abstract: The overall aim of the research is to increase our understanding of children's learning, and of the effects on learning of outside agencies such as feedback, peers and adults. The research will study children learning to control the Logo Turtle in view of the theoretical and curricular relevance of this activity. The specific research objectives are: (1) to compare children learning in four conditions: (a) alone; (b) with a peer; (c) with an adult; and (d) with an adult and a peer, looking at the effects of these conditions on task performance and on aspects of learning; (2) to examine the nature of the feedback provided by the system and to look at its effect on children's learning in the individual condition; (3) to analyse the interaction taking place within the peer and adult conditions, looking in particular at interaction concerned with planning and feedback, and to assess its effects on learning; (4) to examine the effects of age and gender on the above issues, by using children aged 4, 7 and 11, and by including same-sex and mixed-sex pairs in the peer conditions.
Status: Sponsored project
Source of Grant: Economic and Social Research Council £90,550
Date of Research: 1990 - continuing
KEYWORDS: *computer uses in education; feedback; interaction; learning processes; peer teaching; teacher-pupil relationship*

9/0270
School of Education, St Luke's, Heavitree Road, Exeter
EX1 2LU
0392 263263
Golby, M. Dr; *Supervisor:* Golby, M. Dr
Perspectives on the government of schools at local level
Abstract: The School Governors Research Group and the Governors Support Centre mounts a range of research conducted both by ind-

ividual members of the Group and as a collective. The research includes local studies, regional studies and international comparative studies. Central interests are in the extent of parental involvement, the internal processes of deliberation and judgement and the relation to local education authorities. Theoretical work on key constructs underpins the work.
Published Material: GOLBY, M. (1990). The new governors speak: Exeter papers in school governorship No 1. Tiverton: Fairway Publications.; GOLBY, M. (1990). 'In their own words', School Governors, pp.11-18, April.; GOLBY, M. & APPLEBY, R. (1991). School governors today: in good faith. Tiverton: Fairway Publications.
Status: Sponsored project
Source of Grant: Leverhulme Trust; Universities Funding Council; Exeter University Research Fund; Exeter Society for Curriculum Studies
Date of Research: 1986 - continuing
KEYWORDS: educational administration; school governing bodies; school governors

9/0271
School of Education, St Luke's, Heavitree Road, Exeter
EX1 2LU
0392 263263
Copley, T. Mr
Forms of assessment in religious education (FARE)
Abstract: This is an action research topic carried out for South Western local education authorities, which uses teachers in the contributing authorities to investigate and trial appropriate ways of assessing religious education at each Key Stage compatible with current practice in National Curriculum subjects and current thinking in religious education.
Published Material: CODDINGTON, V., COPLEY, T., PRIESTLEY, J. & WADMAN, D. (1991). A fare deal for RE. Exeter: School of Education, Exeter University.
Status: Sponsored project
Source of Grant: St Matthias Trust £15,000; Sarum St Michael Educ'n Charity £3,000; St Luke's Coll Found'n Trust £40,000; Jerusalem Trust £ 60,000; SW LEA's £8,000
Date of Research: 1989-1991
KEYWORDS: assessment; National Curriculum; religious education

9/0272
School of Education, St Luke's, Heavitree Road, Exeter
EX1 2LU
0392 263263
Ernest, P. Dr
A social constructivist theory of mathematics
Abstract: This is a basic, theoretical research project extending a previous project which concerned the philosophical foundations of the mathematics curriculum and mathematical pedagogy (see ERNEST, P. (1991). 'The philosophy of mathematics education'). The current project is intended to extend the theoretical foundations. The contributions of Imre Lakatos and Ludwig Wittgenstein form a basis, but parallels in educational, psychological, sociological (e.g. constructivism) are drawn upon and utilised. The central thesis is that mathematics is a human construction, which is fallible, corrigible and ever changing. The project concerns working out this theory rigorously.
Published Material: ERNEST, P. (1991). The philosophy of mathematics education. London: Falmer Press.
Status: Sponsored project
Source of Grant: Leverhulme Research Fellowship £11,400
Date of Research: 1991 - continuing
KEYWORDS: educational philosophy; mathematics

9/0273
School of Education, St Luke's, Heavitree Road, Exeter
EX1 2LU
0392 263263
Hazlewood, P. Mr; *Supervisor:* Wragg, E. Prof.
The influence of teacher appraisal on secondary school management
Abstract: The imminent introduction of formal teacher appraisal into schools based on the premises that appraisal would monitor teacher performance, improve practice and enhance the overall management of schools provides a platform for considerable debate. The principal aim of this investigation is to consider the influence that teacher

appraisal has on the management of secondary schools. A range of hypotheses relating to management of schools are being tested. Based on case studies of four similar sized secondary schools (for 11-16 age group) in similar localities, the research used unstructured interview as the primary methodology. Validity is currently being established through group discussion and other methods. A detailed questionnaire is being utilized to test hypotheses arising from the interviews. Approximately 45 teachers in various management positions were interviewed and questionnaires were sent to a range of 198 teachers in six schools. The results are currently being analyzed.
Status: Sponsored project
Source of Grant: Wiltshire Local Education Authority; Pool School
Date of Research: 1989 - continuing
KEYWORDS: educational administration; secondary schools; teacher evaluation

9/0274
School of Education, St Luke's, Heavitree Road, Exeter
EX1 2LU
0392 263263
Watson-Broughton, A. Mrs; *Supervisor:* Copley, T. Mr; John, M. Prof.
The aims of the Education Reform Act, 1988 for acts of worship in secondary schools
Abstract: The aim of this research is to discover the most practical, sensitive, interesting, dynamic, relevant way to deliver the aims of the Education Reform Act, 1988 with reference to daily acts of worship. To promote the spiritual aspects of a balanced curriculum in the secondary school, a working definition of 'spiritual' needs to be drawn. This needs to address the current secular nature of society. Since symbols have always played an important role in religion it was thought useful to pursue research in the area of aesthetics. A study of National Curriculum art documents was made which was very beneficial. Particular artists from history were highlighted and their ideas, aims and aspirations related to recent legislation on acts of worship in schools. A distinction was drawn at all times between ecclesiastical worship and educational worship.
Status: Sponsored project
Source of Grant: College of St Hild and St Bede Durham Bursary £2,000
Date of Research: 1991 - continuing
KEYWORDS: Education Reform Act 1988; religion and education; school worship; symbolism

9/0275
School of Education, St Luke's, Heavitree Road, Exeter
EX1 2LU
0392 263263
Desforges, C. Prof.; Hughes, M. Dr; *Supervisor:* Desforges, C. Prof.; Hughes, M. Dr
Parents and assessment at National Curriculum Key Stage 1
Abstract: The aim of the proposed research is to study the effect that parents' conceptions of teaching, learning and assessment may have on the assessment and reporting procedures currently being introduced into schools, and to study the effect that these procedures may in turn have on parents. It is hypothesised that two important mediating factors could be the accuracy of teachers' perceptions of parents' views, and the extent to which parents are directly involved in the assessment process. The specific research questions to be addressed are: (1) What are parents' conceptions of teaching, learning and assessment? (2) How accurately are these conceptions perceived by teachers? (3) How far do teachers' perceptions of parents influence their actual assessment behaviour? (4) How far do teachers actually involve parents in the assessment process, and to what effect? (5) What do teachers select to report to parents at the end of the assessment process? (6) What do parents make of these reports, and what effects do they have on their conceptions of teaching, learning and assessment, and on their relationship to the school? (7) What effects do the assessment and reporting processes have on teachers' perceptions of parents' conceptions, and on teachers' classroom practice?
Status: Sponsored project
Source of Grant: Economic and Social Research Council £55,943
Date of Research: 1991 - continuing
KEYWORDS: academic record; parent aspiration; parent-school relationship; school-based assessment

9/0276
School of Education, St Luke's, Heavitree Road, Exeter
EX1 2LU
0392 263263
Hughes, M. Dr; *Supervisor:* Hughes, M. Dr
Parents and the National Curriculum
Abstract: The focus of the research is on the relationship between parents and schools as the National Curriculum is implemented in the early years of school. The research has two main objectives: (1) to obtain baseline data on the perceptions of parents and teachers as the first children entered Key Stage 1; (2) to monitor the changing perceptions of parents and teachers as these children progress through Key Stage 1, culminating in the first national standardised assessments of 7-year-olds in 1991. In order to achieve these objectives a cohort of 150 children in 11 schools has been followed through Years 1 and 2 of the National Curriculum. Annual interviews have been carried out with their parents and teachers. Further information has been obtained from a wider sample of 80 headteachers who have also been interviewed annually.
Published Material: HUGHES, M., WIKELY, F. & NASH, T. (1990). 'Business partners', Times Educational Supplement, pp.20-21, 5 January.; HUGHES, M. (1991). 'Parents and the National Curriculum', Early Education, No 3, pp.8-9.; HUGHES, M. (1991). 'Parents and the National Curriculum', Proceedings of the Conference, 'Young Children Learning', Thames Polytechnic.; HUGHES, M., WIKELY, F. & NASH, T. 'Parents in the new era'. In: MERTENS, R. & VASS, J. (Eds). Impact issues: discursive interruptions in curriculum practice. Brighton: Falmer Press. (in press).
Status: Sponsored project
Source of Grant: Leverhulme Trust £83,500
Date of Research: 1989-1992
KEYWORDS: *infant school education; National Curriculum; parent-school relationship*

9/0277
School of Education, St Luke's, Heavitree Road, Exeter
EX1 2LU
0392 263263
Trotter, A. Mrs; Bennett, S. Prof.; *Supervisor:* Bennett, S. Prof.
Differential provision for children with special educational needs in ordinary schools
Abstract: The aim of the study is to investigate the effects of various kinds of provision made for children with special educational needs at secondary level. Three main systems were investigated – the support base, withdrawal, and in-class support. Children were selected at primary level who were deemed to be in need of special educational needs provision at secondary school. Their entry into secondary school and subsequent performance was closely monitored. Along with details of their academic performance, the research includes the views of their parents and the children themselves.
Status: Sponsored project
Source of Grant: Economic and Social Research Council
Date of Research: 1986 - continuing
KEYWORDS: *mainstreaming; secondary education; special educational needs; support services*

9/0278
School of Education, St Luke's, Heavitree Road, Exeter
EX1 2LU
0392 263263
Kennett, D. Mr; Al-seaidy, H. Mr; *Supervisor:* Burghes, D. Prof.; Kennett, D. Mr
Further development on interactive video
Abstract: The main aim of the research is to evaluate a mathematics teaching interactive video package called School Disco. The evaluation concentrates on the motivational and attainment based aspects. For the purpose of conducting the evaluation process, several tests have been applied. Technical and educational points which might have a direct or indirect effect on pupil motivation have been detected. Other aims of the research are to explore the extent to which interactive video material could be employed within an educational system.
Status: Sponsored project
Source of Grant: Exeter University £2,000
Date of Research: 1990 - continuing
KEYWORDS: *interactive video*

9/0279
School of Education, St Luke's, Heavitree Road, Exeter
EX1 2LU
0392 263263
Savage, J. Mrs; *Supervisor:* Desforges, C. Prof.
The role of informal assessment in teachers' practical action
Abstract: The main aims of the research are to: (1) understand more about the way in which informal assessment is generated from teachers' intuitive theories; and (2) understand more about the way that this influences teaching acts. An opportunity sample of nine or ten teachers, who are working with 5-7 year olds, is being used. There will be several parts to the research. Firstly, the teachers will record some classroom action on videotape. Nine pieces of action of not more than 20 minutes in length will be recorded by each teacher. Secondly, each teacher will reflect upon this action, through the method of stimulated recall, in order to gain their informal assessments. Unstructured interviews will be used. Thirdly, these informal assessments will be organised and related to each teacher's views of teaching and learning. A more structured interview will then take place. Fourthly, the data will be analysed in terms of whether or not any action is taken as a result of the informal assessments. This data will include both the classroom action on videotape and teachers' reflections of that action on audiotape. The research is examining and analysing two types of process – teachers' thinking (the processes in their heads) and the processes that occur over a period of time in terms of action.
Status: Individual research
Date of Research: 1989 - continuing
KEYWORDS: *assessment; classroom observation techniques; teacher response*

9/0280
School of Education, St Luke's, Heavitree Road, Exeter
EX1 2LU
0392 263263
Greenhough, P. Ms; *Supervisor:* Hughes, M. Dr; Preece, P. Dr
The inter-relationship of cognitive abilities, attitudes, social interaction and performance in early logo learning
Abstract: This research investigates the interrelationship of cognitive abilities, attitudinal factors, social interaction and performance in young children. The context of the research is paired learning with a computer and in the first instance focuses on early Logo activities. Seventy-two, Year 3 children worked either in same-sex or mixed pairs for five sessions with the floor Turtle on drawing or driving activities. They also worked for two sessions individually. Prior to the work with the Turtle, the children were assessed on five British Abilities Scales. Prior, during and after the sessions their attitudes to the task, their partner, and gender stereotypes were assessed. All sessions were videotaped and the social interaction transcribed.
Status: Sponsored project
Source of Grant: Nuffield Foundation £25,000
Date of Research: 1990 - continuing
KEYWORDS: *cognitive ability; computer-assisted learning; interaction; logo; turtles – robots*

9/0281
School of Education, St Luke's, Heavitree Road, Exeter
EX1 2LU
0392 263263
Peacock, A. Dr
Parents' understanding of science in the National Curriculum
Abstract: The research is a longitudinal study of parents of children entering school in Autumn 1989 in 11 representative primary schools in one local authority. The sample is identical to that being used for a larger study (Parents and the National Curriculum, sponsored by Leverhulme Trust, director Dr M. Hughes) and the current study works closely with Dr Hughes' team. The study uses semi-structured interviews on a serial basis with parents, teachers and head teachers, to ascertain the flow of information to parents about their children's science work at National Curriculum Key Stage 1, and to evaluate parents' understanding of the information received. The study has so far highlighted clear differences of perception between parents and teachers about what parents know and need to know; and is currently investigating parents' interpretations of the reports received after the 1991 Standard Assessment Tasks.
Published Material: PEACOCK, A. & BOULTON, A. (1991). 'Parents' understanding of science at Key Stage 1', Education 3-13, Vol 19, No 3, pp.26-29, October.

Status: Sponsored project
Source of Grant: Exeter University Research Committee Grant £5,000
Date of Research: 1990 - continuing
KEYWORDS: National Curriculum; parent attitudes; parent-school relationship; primary education; science education

9/0282

School of Education, St Luke's, Heavitree Road, Exeter
EX1 2LU
0392 263263
Cousins, J. Ms; Supervisor: Desforges, C. Prof.; Hughes, M. Dr

The place of reflection in teachers' processes of change

Abstract: This is an ethnographic study of teachers' theories about the language of young children when they start school and how these influence their classroom practice. It is based on a piece of action research carried out with 10 reception teachers for a year and examines the development of their own theories and the courses of change.
Status: Individual research
Date of Research: 1986 - continuing
KEYWORDS: change; child language; classroom management; teacher attitudes

9/0283

School of Education, St Luke's, Heavitree Road, Exeter
EX1 2LU
0392 263263
Wragg, C. Ms; Supervisor: Wragg, E. Prof.; Ackland, J. Mr

Management in the primary school class

Abstract: This research into classroom management is based upon a study of over 200 lessons given by teachers in the South West of England, Manchester and London. It includes over 400 interviews with pupils and an analysis of over 1,000 teacher questions and responses.
Status: Individual research
Date of Research: 1990-1992
KEYWORDS: classroom management; classroom research; primary schools

9/0284

School of Education, St Luke's, Heavitree Road, Exeter
EX1 2LU
0392 263263
Macleod, F. Ms; Supervisor: Hughes, D. Dr; Bennett, S. Prof.

Parental involvement in reading programmes

Abstract: The study is investigating whether there are potentially important differences in parental involvement in reading programmes and that parental involvement in reading is causally related to increments in reading development as measured by reading tests and that this in turn is causally related to later scholistic achievement.
Status: Individual research
Date of Research: 1985-1992
KEYWORDS: parent participation; reading improvement; reading skills

9/0285

School of Education, St Luke's, Heavitree Road, Exeter
EX1 2LU
0392 263263
Wikeley, F. Mrs; Supervisor: Hughes, M. Dr; Golby, M. Dr

Parental choice of school

Abstract: This research involves the use of case study to identify criteria used by parents in choosing schools and to explore how these can help schools in marketing themselves.
Status: Individual research
Date of Research: 1991 - continuing
KEYWORDS: institutional advancement; marketing; parent choice; parent-school relationship; selection

9/0286

School of Education, St Luke's, Heavitree Road, Exeter
EX1 2LU
0392 263263
Hughes, M. Dr; Supervisor: Hughes, M. Dr; Golby, M. Dr

Parents and National Curriculum: criteria of parental choice of primary school

Abstract: In the present political climate it is becoming increasingly important for schools to make themselves attractive to parents. In order to do this it would be advantageous for them to know how parents choose a school and on what criteria that choice is based. The research will concentrate on parental choice of primary school. It will select from the sample being used by the wider research project 'Parents and the National Curriculum', some parents for a case study approach. The whole sample consists of a wide range of parents in differing socioeconomic circumstances. They all have a child who started school in the year 1988/89 and have been interviewed four times over the past two years. The complete interview, which was semi-structured, covered several aspects of the changes taking place in their children's schooling at the present time. This research will look in depth at the criteria they used, and how those criteria were chosen in their decision as to which primary schools their children would attend. It is hoped that by looking closely at the cases of a few parents it will be possible to identify differences in the choice process. In this way it is hoped to develop a paradigm which illuminates the process and would enable schools to better target potential parents.
Published Material: HUGHES, M., WIKELEY, F. & NASH, P. (1990). Parents and the National Curriculumm: an interim report. Exeter University.; HUGHES, M., WIKELEY, F. & NASH, P. (1991). Parents and SATs: a second interim report from the project Parents and the National Curriculum. Exeter University; HUGHES, M., WIKELEY, F. & NASH, P. (1991). 'Parents in the new era: myth and reality'. In: MERTHENS, F. & VASS, J. (Eds). Impact Issues: Discursive Interruptions in Curriculum Practice. London: Falmer.; HUGHES, M., WIKELEY, F. & NASH, P. (1990). 'Business partners', Times Educational Supplement, 5 January.
Status: Sponsored project
Source of Grant: Leverhulme Trust
Date of Research: 1989 - continuing
KEYWORDS: access to education; Education Reform Act 1988; parent choice; primary schools

9/0287

School of Education, St Luke's, Heavitree Road, Exeter
EX1 2LU
0392 263263
Viant, R. Dr; Supervisor: Golby, M. Dr

School governorship as democratic participation

Abstract: This work seeks to illuminate how far school governorship can be a democratic and participatory activity undertaken as a public service through 'active citizenship'. Recent legislation has opened up such possibilities even though it has not been unequivocally intended to do so. The introductory section places the work in context and attention is initally directed towards the historical origins of school governorship and shows how, through the post-war period, it became a merely cermonial institution. The legal, educational and philosophical contexts are then explored. The empirical work forms a detailed case study of one governing body – 'The Everyday Story of Governorfolk'. The research programme which supports the case study is qualitative in style, and centres round non-participant observation of governors' meetings and in depth interviews with four governors. As the research proceeds the focus is progressively refined to concentrate on emerging issues which relate to key democratic principles – participation, responsibility, representation, independence of mind and accountability. There emerges a picture of one example of governorship which is subsequently compared and contrasted with different governing bodies by means of a review of other research in this field. The findings from the case study reveal that in certain respects opportunities for democratic participation exist and are taken up. In many other respects this governing body is not found to be particularly democratic. The work concludes with recommendations for changes in governors' training and for amendments to the legislation.
Published Material: APPLEBY, R. & GOLBY, M. (1992). School governors: end of term report. Tiverton: Fairway Publications.
Status: Individual research
Date of Research: 1990-1992
KEYWORDS: governing bodies; participative decision making; school governors

9/0288

School of Education, St Luke's, Heavitree Road, Exeter
EX1 2LU
0392 263263

Neather, E. Mr; *Supervisor:* Neather, E. Mr
Foreign language training for initial teacher training (ITT) students
Abstract: The aim of this project is to: (1) establish a detailed register of current language experience and competence amongst all undergraduate and Post-Graduate Certificate of Education (PGCE) students at the School of Education; (2) enquire into the aspirations and wishes of students in terms of foreign language learning, and their perception of the place of foreign languages in their careers, and in the future lives of the children they teach; (3) relate the pattern of such wishes and aspirations to the pattern of main subject courses followed by students with a view to establishing what language courses could best be offered to which groups of students; (4) investigate the resources and timetabling of access courses for students wishing to pursue individual programmes of less common languages, such as Greek and Portuguese, for which class tuition might not be available; (5) discuss with course tutors the role and function of foreign languages in the course profile of students with a view to integrating foreign language modules into the overall course structure on a rational and planned basis; (6) investigate the practice followed by other institutions of teacher training, and to make comparisons with foreign languages in teacher training establishments in other countries of the European Community; and (7) explore the needs and aims of foreign languages teaching in primary and middle schools in Devon. It is proposed that the project should last three terms from October 1992. This would give time to carry out surveys and put in place a carefully considered pilot scheme at the start of the new academic year in October 1993. Proposals and recommendations would then be made in December 1993 for possible implementation of a full programme in October 1994. The research will involve questionnaire surveys and interviews with students (sample=420 postgraduate students and 917 undergraduate students) and staff colleagues; visits to other institutions and attendance at European conferences.
Status: Sponsored project
Source of Grant: Department for Education £4,590
Date of Research: 1992 - continuing
KEYWORDS: *modern language studies; preservice teacher education; student teachers*

9/0289
    School of Education, St Luke's, Heavitree Road, Exeter
    EX1 2LU
    0392 263263 Bermuda Ministry of Education, Department of Education, PO Box HM 1185, Hamilton HM EX, Bermuda
    Hocking, C. Mr; *Supervisor:* Burghes, D. Prof.; Harvard, G. Mr
The nature of relationships between teachers' attitudes and beliefs about educational change in Bermuda and other personal, psychological and educational variables
Abstract: The aim of this study is to determine whether there exists a relationship, and the nature of any possible relationship, between teachers' attitudes to educational changes taking place in Bermuda and other personal, psychological or educational variables. The research uses questionnaire investigation to gather data on teachers' age, experience, sex, training, etc., their current feelings about teaching as a job, their preferred psychological functioning and their attitudes to change. The background of educational change against which teachers' attitudes are assessed includes abolition of selection at 11+, introduction of middle level education, non-selective secondary education, and mainstreaming of special children.
Status: Individual research
Date of Research: 1989-1992
KEYWORDS: *Bermuda; educational change; teacher attitudes*

9/0290
    School of Education, Physical Education Association
    Research Centre, St Luke's, Heavitree Road, Exeter EX1 2LU
    0392 263263
    Biddle, S. Dr; Fox, K. Dr; Armstrong, N. Dr
Psychological aspects of children and physical activity
Abstract: 11-12 year old children (N=250) have been tested on physical activity and psychological constructs to see if activity levels and choices can be related to the psychology of the child. Preliminary evidence indicated that more active boys were intrinsically motivated towards physical education and sport, whereas girls required more extrinsic motivation. Active and less active children could also be discriminated on the basis of motivational orientations and physical self-perceptions. Ongoing research is following up these findings and

is investigating achievement cognitions and self-perceptions.
Published Material: BIDDLE, S. & ARMSTRONG, N. 'Children's physical activity: An exploratory study of psychological correlates', Social Science and Medicine. (in press)
Status: Sponsored project
Source of Grant: Exeter University £4,000; Northcott Medical Foundation £14,000
Date of Research: 1990 - continuing
KEYWORDS: *child psychology; health; physical activities; physical activity level*

Further Education Unit

9/0291
    Spring Gardens, Citadel Place, Tinworth Street, London
    SE11 5EH
    071 962 1280
    Carroll, S. Ms; *Supervisor:* Dixon, K. Mr; Haldane, A. Mr
Access to learning and accreditation in Work Related Further Education
Abstract: A substantial number of projects related to flexible learning have been supported by the Work Related Further Education Development Fund and its predecessors. Most have encouraged innovative developments locally but some could provide extra benefits through wider dissemination of outcomes. Recent studies have shown colleges making progress and generally positive staff attitudes, but that further help would accelerate the process of embedding flexible learning. The need for colleges to be responsive to the requirements of individual learners, emphasised by the introduction of National Vocational Qualifications and the possibility of a 'common core' curriculum, has led many colleges to commence the transition from conventional modes of delivery to the implementation of flexible learning across the curriculum and across institutions. The aims of this project are: (a) to provide the information base on which a national overview of the Work Related Further Education flexible learning developments programme might be taken; (b) to give detailed consideration to the strategy required to achieve the implementation of this overview approach. It will provide information and an analysis in order to assess how the Work Related Further Education Development Fund might operate more effectively to promote speedier advances in flexible learning across the country; and ensure coherence within the Fund and with likely future local education authority and Training and Education Council strategies.
Status: Sponsored project
Source of Grant: Training, Enterprise and Education Directorate
Date of Research: 1990-1991
KEYWORDS: *flexible learning; further education; work education relationship*

9/0292
    Spring Gardens, Citadel Place, Tinworth Street, London
    SE11 5EH
    071 962 1280
    Clyde, A. Mr
Key technologies – potential developments and their implications for vocational education and training
Abstract: The aims of this project are to: (1) identify trends in the development of key technologies that might be incorporated into education and training curricula to prepare trainees for future developments; (2) identify methods whereby such trends can be reviewed regularly so that curricula can be updated by appropriate bodies (e.g. in the United Kingdom, by the examining and validating bodies, industrial lead bodies and education and training institutions); (3) support proposed research into key technologies at the Technical and Further Education (TAFE) National Centre for Research and Development in Australia. The term 'key technologies' was used by the Engineering Council (EC) in 'A Call to Action' (EC, 1986), to describe those technologies which had a significant potential to increase 'added value' in industry. This document listed examples of key technologies under the general headings of materials, components and processes. These ideas and their curriculum implications were developed further in 'The Key Technologies – some implications for education and training' (FEU/EC, 1988). This report also indicated that potential key technologies varied with company circumstances, and could not always be easily recognised, although they

were likely to have interdisciplinary implications. Subsequent FEU work, published as 'The Concept of Key Technologies' (FEU, 1989), suggested that an understanding of the 'added-value' and interdisciplinary aspects could best be fostered through student assignments. 'Training for the Future' (FEU, 1990) provides guidelines and model assignments. Current work under the title 'Training in Context' aims to prepare and disseminate materials to assist in the delivery of the concept in industry, colleges and training centres. The FEU has also supported curriculum development in several potential key technology areas, e.g. transputers and quality assurance, but such work has not concentrated on this aspect of the technology. TAFE (in Australia) has also undertaken work in this area.

Status: Sponsored project
Source of Grant: Further Education Unit
Date of Research: 1990-1991
KEYWORDS: *industry-education relationship; technology education; vocational education*

9/0293
Spring Gardens, Citadel Place, Tinworth Street, London
SE11 5EH
071 962 1280
Herrman, S. Ms; Johnson, M. Mr; *Supervisor:* Williets, D. Mr
The impact of the Education Reform Act – 1988 on the further education curriculum
Abstract: The purpose of this project is: (i) to analyse and appraise the changes in the further education curriculum over an initial 3-year period; and (ii) throughout the period of the project, to keep local education authorities and colleges informed of significant developments and outcomes, either generally or on specific curricular issues. The Education Reform Act – 1988 is one of a number of significant influences on the further education curriculum. It requires every local education authority to prepare and submit for the Secretary of State's approval a scheme providing for: (i) the principles and procedures which the authority will use to plan the educational provision to be made in the further and higher education colleges which it maintains or substantially assists; (ii) the determination of an annual budget for each of those colleges; and (iii) the delegation by the authority of the management of the budget to the governing body of the college, where such delegation is required or permitted under the scheme. The general criteria which the Secretary of State expects to apply in considering the schemes submitted will include the following: (i) that each scheme should give colleges as much freedom as possible to manage their affairs and allocate their resources as they think best within the strategic framework set by the local education authority; (ii) that each scheme should promote responsiveness by colleges to the changing needs of students, employers and the local community; (iii) that each scheme should give colleges appropriate incentives to earn additional income by providing course and other services and facilities for the local community, including in particular the business community. The Further Education Unit's remit is to review and evaluate the further education curriculum and to determine priorities and recommend improvements. In this context and in line with the Further Education Unit's current strategies on curriculum planning, management and evaluation, and on market penetration, the Unit proposes to undertake an analysis of the curriculum impact of the Education Reform Act. The project aims to assess the changes in the range, balance, processes and perceived quality of the post 16 curriculum which occur during the first 3-year period of operation of measures derived from the Education Reform Act. Whilst it is recognised that the legislation is one significant influence on the further education curriculum, there are other influences. Interim bulletins or guidance notes on formative issues, will be disseminated by the Further Education Unit at appropriate times throughout the project and a final report will assess the development of the further education curriculum during the early years of the implementation of the Education Reform Act in further education.
Status: Sponsored project
Source of Grant: Further Education Unit
Date of Research: 1990-1992
KEYWORDS: *curriculum development; Education Reform Act 1988; educational change; further education*

Glamorgan University

9/0294
Business School, Pontypridd, Mid Glamorgan CF37 1DL
0443 480480
Trotman-Dickenson, D. Prof.
Professional bodies: education and training; and the labour market
Abstract: This research is concerned with professional education and training in the United Kingdom and other countries in Europe. Comparisons with France and Germany have been made and implications of a free market in professional services in the European Community are being examined. The research has been extended to study the market for professional services in Central and Eastern Europe.
Published Material: TROTMAN-DICKENSON, D.I. (1989). 'The response of professional bodies to changing needs', Higher Education Review, Vol 22, No 1, pp.47-62.; TROTMAN-DICKENSON, D.I. (1991). 'Developing and measuring competence', Proceedings of the Association of Education and Training Technology.; TROTMAN-DICKENSON, D.I. (1990). 'Professional bodies and poicies in the anticipation and the aftermath of 1992', The Royal Bank of Scotland Quarterly Review 29, September.; TROTMAN-DICKENSON, D.I. (1993). 'Challenges and opportunities for professionals in the UK and Central and Eastern Europe of the emergence of new market economies', European and Business Research (forthcoming).
Status: Individual research
Date of Research: 1989 - continuing
KEYWORDS: *comparative education; France; Germany; labour market; professional associations; professional education; professional services*

9/0295
Business School, Pontypridd, Mid Glamorgan CF37 1DL
0443 480480
Thomas, R. Ms
The impact of the introduction of staff appraisal on women academics' career opportunities in higher education
Abstract: Staff appraisal is new to higher education and its introduction can be seen to reflect wider changes in public sector industrial relations. Stemming from the 23rd Report from Committee A (Committee of Vice Chancellors and Principals (CVCP, 1987)), appraisal is being presented to staff as a formal procedure for staff development, '...directed towards developing staff potential, assisting in the improvement of performance and enhancing career and promotion opportunities...' (para 43). The assumption arising from this is that the introduction of staff appraisal will serve to improve women's opportunities of gaining senior positions due to the bureaucratisation of the promotion process and the provision of career planning. However, to some, its introduction is being heralded as an extension of managerial control which at best will have little impact on women's career opportunities and at worse will be detrimental to them, merely formalising and legitimising existing discriminatory practices. Longitudinal research of in depth case studies in higher education institutions, accompanied by wider questionnaire analysis, aims to establish women academics' experience of appraisal and its impact on their careers.
Status: Individual research
Date of Research: 1990 - continuing
KEYWORDS: *career development; institutes of higher education; teacher evaluation; teaching profession; women teachers; women's employment*

9/0296
Business School, Pontypridd, Mid Glamorgan CF37 1DL
0443 480480
Farrell, C. Miss; *Supervisor:* Boyne, G. Dr; Baker, C. Prof.
Territorial justice and nursery education provision in England and Wales
Abstract: The aim of this project is to measure the need for, and the provision of, nursery education facilities in local authority areas in England and Wales. This involves the construction of a model of service need and service provision, and the evaluation of the extent of territorial justice. This assessment is based on a statistical analysis of the relationship between service need and service provision. The

project examines the reasons for spatial variations in provision and assesses the impact of local financial resources, party politics, private sector provision and day care services upon the level of local authority provision of nursery education.
Status: Individual research
Date of Research: 1990 - continuing
KEYWORDS: *early childhood education; nursery school education; preschool education; regional characteristics; regional planning*

9/0297
> Department of Behavioural and Communication Studies,
> Pontypridd, Mid Glamorgan CF37 1DL
> 0443 480480
> Beynon, W. Dr; Middlehurst, R. Mr

Learning outcomes and competences in English/Communication Studies
Abstract: Since November 1989 there has been participation in a Department of Education and Science/Training Agency-funded research project organised by the Unit for the Development of Adult and Continuing Education (UDACE) and sited in Communication Studies, Polytechnic of Wales (now Glamorgan University); the English Department, Lancaster University; and the School of Humanities, Newcastle Polytechnic (now University of Northumbria at Newcastle). The research identified competences and learning outcomes associated with Communication/Cultural Studies (thus contextualised as 'English'). The research was of great significance both to students (who were fully involved in the research and were extensively interviewed, etc.) and staff teaching and planning courses in the area of Communication/Cultural Studies. The competences were arrived at after full liaison with prospective employers.
Published Material: A list of working papers and reports is available from the researchers.
Status: Sponsored project
Source of Grant: Department of Education and Science; Training Agency
Date of Research: 1989-1991
KEYWORDS: *competence; English studies; learning; literacy; outcomes of education*

9/0298
> Department of Property and Development Studies,
> Pontypridd, Mid Glamorgan CF37 1DL
> 0443 480480
> Jiang, L. Mr; Plimmer, F. Ms; *Supervisor:* Plimmer, F. Ms; Hibberd, P. Prof.; Gronow, S. Mr

Education and training of property valuers in China
Abstract: In the light of China's economic reform and the development of an 'open policy', the emergence of a property market has produced the need for property valuation skills in China. The research has investigated the needs of China for property valuation skills and, based on United Kingdom experience, is investigating ways in which computer-aided teaching can be used to provide appropriate professional education and training for valuers in China.
Published Material: JIANG, L., PLIMMER, F., HIBBERD, P. & GRONOW, S. (1993). 'Land reform in China', Journal of Property Management (forthcoming).; JIANG, L., PLIMMER, F., HIBBERD, P. & GRONOW, S. (1993). 'Education and training of valuers in China', Journal of Property Research (forthcoming).
Status: Sponsored project
Source of Grant: Royal Institution of Chartered Surveyors
Date of Research: 1991 - continuing
KEYWORDS: *China; housing; professional education*

9/0299
> Department of Property and Development Studies,
> Pontypridd, Mid Glamorgan CF37 1DL
> 0443 480480
> Williams, T. Mr; Hughes, T. Mr; *Supervisor:* Hughes, T. Mr; Hibberd, P. Prof.; Gronow, S. Mr

The application of quality management principles to learning
Abstract: In vocational courses there are two principle customers whose needs are to be satisfied: the students and the employers. Research has shown that these needs are difficult to define and equally difficult to satisfy. The aims of the research are therefore to: (1) identify the key personal and technical skills necessary in professional quantity surveying practice; (2) develop a simulation based teaching vehicle on the basis of (1) above; and (3) use quality

management principles to monitor and improve the learning experience.
Published Material: HUGHES, T. & WILLIAMS, T. (1991). Quality Assurance, a Framework to Build on. Oxford: Blackwell Scientific Publications.; HUGHES, T. & WILLIAMS, T. (1991). 'Learning by experience: integrated learning materials based on a construction project', Building Technology and Management, Vol 18, pp.56-64, Kuala Lumpur, Building Technology Society.
Status: Sponsored project
Source of Grant: Department of Employment: Enterprise in Higher Education; Initiative £9,000
Date of Research: 1991 - continuing
KEYWORDS: *educational quality; industry-higher education relationship; quality control; vocational education; work-education relationship*

9/0300
> Enterprise Unit, Pontypridd, Mid Glamorgan CF37 1DL
> 0443 480480
> Saunders, D. Mr

Student and peer tutoring in Wales
Abstract: The student and peer tutoring in Wales initiative involves four higher education centres which are sending their students into schools to help teachers in the delivery of the curriculum as well as provide positive role models for pupils. The project examines assessment issues and strategies emerging from student and peer tutoring, as well as numerous other developments emerging out of links between universities or institutes and local schools.
Published Material: SAUNDERS, D. (1992). 'Peer tutoring in higher education', Studies in Higher Education, Vol 17, No 2, pp.211-217.
Status: Sponsored project
Source of Grant: BP (Chemicals) Baglan Bay £30,000
Date of Research: 1991 - continuing
KEYWORDS: *peer teaching; role models; student-school relationship; Wales*

9/0301
> Enterprise Unit, Pontypridd, Mid Glamorgan CF37 1DL
> 0443 480480
> Saunders, D. Mr; *Supervisor:* Saunders, D. Mr

Developing a portfolio of personal development
Abstract: A cross-section of students is engaged in a longitudinal study involving self-assessment of study and transferable skills. Academic and personal achievement are also recorded, and the final stage of the project involves the preparation of one-page profile sheets for use with curriculum vitae.
Published Material: SAUNDERS, D. (1990). 'The assessment of prior experiential learning', Simulation Games for Learning, Vol 20, No 1, pp.76-85.; SAUNDERS, D. (1992). 'Profiling in higher education', Journal of the National Association for Staff Development, No 26, pp.51-57.
Status: Sponsored project
Source of Grant: Department of Employment: Enterprise in Higher Education Initiative
Date of Research: 1990 - continuing
KEYWORDS: *higher education; profiles; records of achievement; resumes – personal; self evaluation – individuals; skill development*

Glasgow University

9/0302
> Department of Education, Glasgow G12 8QQ
> 041 339 8855
> Dunn, W. Mr; Holroyd, C. Mr

National standards for training and development within masters programmes in education: Glasgow University
Abstract: The project aims to assess the appropriateness of incorporating the National Standards for Training and development with Masters Degrees in Education. Work at the feasibility stage has shown that students on M.Ed courses recognise the Training and Development Lead Body (TDLB) key roles, units and elements of competence as applicable within their work as education professionals. In 1992-1993 two courses within the Glasgow M.Ed programme will be developed in ways which allow students to demonstrate which

of the TDLB standards they meet; it is intended that it will be clarified which parts of M.Ed provision cannot be described in terms of the TDLB competences/standards.
Status: Sponsored project
Source of Grant: Department of Employment
Date of Research: 1991 - continuing
KEYWORDS: competency-based education; education courses; higher education; masters courses; qualifications; standards

9/0303
    Department of Sociology, Lilybank House, Glasgow G12 8RT
    041 339 8855
    Littlewood, P. Mr; *Supervisor:* Littlewood, P. Mr
A sociological evaluation of the relationship between expectations and outcomes concerning parental inclusion on School Boards
Abstract: The establishment of School Boards in Scotland under the Education Reform Act 1988 took place amid considerable controversy as to the possible consequences of so increasing the participative role of parents in decision making and policy formulation of schools. The study seeks to assess the nature and extent of the impact of this increased participation, and how the perceptions of the principal actors have been affected by the first two years of School Board activity. The study is based on a sample of 6 secondary schools in Glasgow, and involves: a) sustained observation of their meetings; b) interviews and questionnaires with all members and head teachers of the school in the sample; and c) collection of data from the Regional and Scottish Education Departments regarding policies relating to School Boards.
Published Material: LITTLEWOOD, P. (1990). 'The return of the board? 'Parent power' and participation in the Scottish school system',Critical Social Policy, No 27, pp.96-109, Winter.
Status: Sponsored project
Source of Grant: Glasgow University: John Robertson Bequest £755
Date of Research: 1990 - continuing
KEYWORDS: parent control; parent school relationship; school boards – Scotland; school governing bodies

Harris City Technology College

9/0304
    The Dyslexia Centre, 9 Maberley Road, Upper Norwood, London SE19 2JH
    081 771 2261
    Canterbury Christ Church College, North Holmes Road, Canterbury CT1 1QU
    0227 767700
    Tod, J. Ms; *Supervisor:* Jones, L. Mr; Abbott, P. Mr
Dyslexia research project
Abstract: A three year research project has been set up at the Dyslexia Centre of Harris City Technology College in Upper Norwood, South London. The research body is Harris City Technology College in conjunction with Christchurch College, Canterbury. The aim of the new centre is the development of best practice in the teaching of dyslexic students. The provision of special teacher training in this area of learning difficulty and the undertaking of research and development in the use of technology and materials appropriate to the teaching of dyslexic students. The aims of the project are: (1) to measure the progress over three academic years of a group of pupils entering the Harris CTC in September 1990, diagnosed as having the specific learning difficulty known as dyslexia, using a range of approaches designed to enable these pupils to participate fully and effectively in the City Technology College curriculum which includes access to the National Curriculum; (2) to devise new approaches and resource materials in order to test their value for pupils in the Harris CTC and to enable the Centre to develop resource materials for a wide use with the CTC age group (11-18); (3) to develop the use of information technology and work with dyslexic pupils in the Harris CTC and to disseminate good practice in this respect. The project runs from 1 November 1990 to 31 October 1993.
Status: Sponsored project
Source of Grant: Department for Education £250,000
Date of Research: 1990-1993

KEYWORDS: city technology colleges; dyslexia; educational materials; learning disabilities; special educational needs; teaching methods

Heriot-Watt University

9/0305
    Department of Business Organisation, Riccarton Campus, Currie, Edinburgh EH14 4AS
    031 449 5111
    Edinburgh University, Department of Business Studies, William Robertson Building, 50 George Square, Edinburgh EH8 9JY
    031 650 1000
    Newton, T. Dr; *Supervisor:* Keenan, A. Prof.
Final analysis of the data collected on the work experience of graduate engineers
Abstract: The project analysed the engineering education, business training of engineers, work difficulties and work experience of young graduate engineers. The study was based on a longitudinal analysis of the work of 798 engineers, who were followed up from their penultimate term at university until four years into employment. Data collection was through questionnaire and semi-structural interview. Good response rates were obtained throughout the study. The findings suggest: (1) notable mis-matches between the career expectations of engineering students and their subsequent work experience; (2) deficiencies in the higher education of engineers, particularly in relation to management studies; (3) a dissatisfaction with the business training of graduate engineers, again particularly in relation to managerial skills; (4) that work difficulties in relation to report writing, information handling and dealing with people were more common than those relating to lack of technical expertise.
Published Material: A full list of publications is available from the researcher.
Status: Sponsored project
Source of Grant: Economic and Social Research Council
Date of Research: 1979-1991
KEYWORDS: engineering education; engineers; graduate employment; work-education relationship

9/0306
    Department of Business Organisation, Riccarton Campus, Currie, Edinburgh EH14 4AS
    031 449 5111
    Keenan, A. Prof.; *Supervisor:* Keenan, A. Prof.
Career outcomes of engineers and their relationships to education, training and early work experiences
Abstract: The research follows up a sample of several hundred professional engineers into mid career. Extensive data are already held on them from a previous study covering the first five years at work. The investigation will look at the predictive power of the earlier data in terms of a variety of career outcomes.
Status: Sponsored project
Source of Grant: Science and Engineering Research Council £72,982
Date of Research: 1992 - continuing
KEYWORDS: career development; engineering education; engineers; training; work-education relationship

Heriot-Watt University Moray House Institute of Education

9/0307
    Moray House Institute of Education, Holyrood Road, Edinburgh EH8 8AQ
    031 556 8455
    Tymms, P. Mr
Development of performance indicators for client satisfaction
Abstract: The aims of the research are: (1) to develop instrument(s) for the regular monitoring of client satisfaction; and (2) consider the evaluation of teaching and learning.

Status: Sponsored project
Source of Grant: Moray House Institute of Education
Date of Research: 1990-1992
KEYWORDS: *evaluation; participant satisfaction; performance indicators; teacher effectiveness*

9/0308
Moray House Institute of Education, Holyrood Road,
Edinburgh EH8 8AQ
031 556 8455
Jackson, S. Dr
Implications of moving towards a more resource based approach to teaching
Abstract: The aim of the research is to examine the implications of a move towards a more resource based teaching approach. This will include looking at the implications for: (i) the role of the teacher; (ii) departmental and school administration; (iii) development of materials; and (iv) assessment. The research will look at the extent to which similar or different implications can be identified in different subject areas. The project also involves the preparation of teaching materials and this includes a video package for preservice and inservice courses. The package is based upon a case study (The James Young High School, Livingston) outlining how the Design Technology Department have implemented a resource based approach. During the production of these materials there has been collaboration with British Petroleum (B.P.) who have used some of the material to produce a video package highlighting the high quality design and craft work taking place at the school.
Published Material: JACKSON, S. & BARRETT, P. (1991). 'Resource based learning – what does it mean in terms of Standard Grade teaching across the curriculum', Scottish Educational Research Association (SERA) Conference, St Andrews University.
Status: Sponsored project
Source of Grant: Moray House Institute of Education
Date of Research: 1990-1992
KEYWORDS: *educational innovation; resource-based learning; resource materials; teaching methods*

9/0309
Moray House Institute of Education, Holyrood Road,
Edinburgh EH8 8AQ
031 556 8455
Francis, E. Mrs; *Supervisor:* Perfect, H. Mr
Research on values education (ROVE)
Abstract: The project is concerned with the identification of approaches to teaching and learning which are beneficial to the development of values education for students over the age of 16 years. The aim of the project is to highlight the philosophical and methodological issues which should be addressed whenever the development of a values curriculum is contemplated. The focus will be the language currently used by educationalists in curriculum guidelines and educational settings which conveys a sense of values and approaches to teaching and learning which enable values education. The enquiry is being conducted with: teachers; lecturers in teacher education and other academic disciplines; curriculum developers; and educational adminstrators in central and local government. A network committed to the study of values in education will be created to enhance discussion of values education in Scotland for the 16+ age group. A number of unpublished working papers are available on request from the project team.
Status: Sponsored project
Source of Grant: Gordon Cook Foundation £40,000
Date of Research: 1991 - continuing
KEYWORDS: *curriculum development; sixteen to nineteen education; values education*

9/0310
Moray House Institute of Education, Holyrood Road,
Edinburgh EH8 8AQ
031 556 8455
Turner, D. Mr; Kidd, J. Dr; Adams, F. Mr
B. Ed. Primary and Scottish Wider Access Programme – monitoring student progress
Abstract: The study is intended to establish a formative baseline for a subsequent study of a cohort of Scottish Wider Access Programme students over the duration of a college B. Ed. Primary course. It will attempt to examine the course experience of Access students in terms

of: (a) teaching, learning and assessment/placement demands; (b) social integration and participation in collegiate life; and (c) academic and other forms of counselling. It will also attempt to draw comparisons with the experiences of Access students across colleges and across professions e.g. nursing. The project will use a combination of: (a) empirical study of product data relating to entry and transit (eventually exit) characteristics; and (b) illuminative approaches. These will include questionnaries and interviews for students and providers within and without college.
Status: Sponsored project
Source of Grant: Moray House Institute of Education
Date of Research: 1991-1992
KEYWORDS: *Access programmes; B. Ed. degrees; cohort analysis; mature students; preservice teacher education; student development*

9/0311
Moray House Institute of Education, Holyrood Road,
Edinburgh EH8 8AQ
031 556 8455
Tymms, P. Mr; Cosford, B. Mr; Dunnett, A. Mrs; Draper, J. Mrs; Knowles, I. Mr
Institutional ethos
Abstract: The aim of the project is to investigate the 'ethos' of the Institute with a view to: (a) establishing how people who work in it experience the Institute, with a particular emphasis on how shared or distinct perceptions of ethos are; and (b) identifying a set of performance indicators upon which a long term strategy to monitor Institutional ethos can be designed. Data was initially collected through interview from a range of people including students and academic and support staff. This interview data has been analysed to highlight key issues and as the basis for the development of questionnaires on ethos issues which will be circulated to: (a) Institute staff (academic and support); (b) Institute students; (c) staff and students at two other institutions (one a university, one a two campus college) for comparative purposes. Associations will be sought between views on the Institute regarding relationships, academic atmosphere and social opportunities role within the organisation and other, individual characteristics.
Status: Sponsored project
Source of Grant: Moray House Institute of Education
Date of Research: 1991 - continuing
KEYWORDS: *attitude measures; institutes of higher education; institutional environment; organisational climate; student's attitudes; teacher's attitudes*

9/0312
Moray House Institute of Education, Holyrood Road,
Edinburgh EH8 8AQ
031 556 8455
Diniz, F. Mr; Reid, G. Mr
Specific learning difficulties (Dyslexia) project
Abstract: The aims of the research are to investigate the potential for developments in teacher education to meet the needs of those concerned about the education of children with specific learning difficulties associated with dyslexia.
Status: Sponsored project
Source of Grant: Scottish Dyslexia Trust
Date of Research: 1990 - continuing
KEYWORDS: *dyslexia; learning disabilities; reading difficulties; special educational needs; teacher education*

9/0313
Moray House Institute of Education, Holyrood Road,
Edinburgh EH8 8AQ
031 556 8455
Crowther, N. Mr
Development of curriculum based resources
Abstract: Since 1982 a series of filmstrips for schools have been published under the collective title 'Habitats in Scotland'. Each is accompanied by a teacher's booklet. Initially the publications were made to meet the curriculum resource needs of specialist teachers of outdoor and environmental education. Increasingly in recent years the resource needs of primary teachers, identified by the Primary Education Development Project (PEDP) has been a major outlet for sales. Work continues on reprinting and updating previous titles in addition to the completion of the remaining titles in the series. The

focus of continuing research is the production of teaching resources for the 5-14 Environmental Studies Syllabus.
Published Material: CROWTHER, N. (1984). Seashore and coastal habitats. Edinburgh: Moray House.; CROWTHER, N. (1985). Mountains and moorlands. Edinburgh: Moray House.; CROWTHER, N. (1987). Freshwater habitats. Edinburgh: Moray House.; CROWTHER, N. (1988). Woodlands in Scotland. 2nd edition. Edinburgh: Moray House.
Status: Sponsored project
Source of Grant: Resources for Environmental and Social Studies Teaching (RESST); Moray House Institute of Education
Date of Research: 1982 - continuing
KEYWORDS: *educational materials; environmental education; outdoor education; publications; resource materials*

9/0314

Moray House Institute of Education, Holyrood Road,
Edinburgh EH8 8AQ
031 556 8455
Masterton, T. Mr; Simpson, A. Mr
Environmental Development Unit and Resources for Environmental and Social Studies Teaching (RESST)
Abstract: The aims of the Environmental Development Unit are to: (1) act as a non-course related focus for environmental developments with the Institute; (2) create and manage an Institute environmental and social studies publications system; (3) assist with help – products specific to particular courses.
Published Material: A full list of RESST publications and videos can be obtained from the researchers on request.
Status: Sponsored project
Source of Grant: Moray House Institute of Education
Date of Research: 1983 - continuing
KEYWORDS: *educational materials; environmental education; publications; social studies*

9/0315

Moray House Institute of Education, Holyrood Road,
Edinburgh EH8 8AQ
031 556 8455
Watson, J. Dr; McAree, R. Ms
Reading with young deaf children in the home
Abstract: This research will examine the reading habits of young deaf children at home at the pre-school stage, with special attention given to what happens when parents and children read together. The transition from home to school will be monitored, reading at school will be observed if possible and an attempt will be made to determine difficulties and their causes – whether a deafness or teaching and learning issue.
Status: Sponsored project
Source of Grant: Moray House Institute of Education
Date of Research: 1988-1992
KEYWORDS: *deafness; early reading; hearing impairments; home-school relationship; pre-reading experience; pre-school children; reading; reading difficulties*

9/0316

Moray House Institute of Education, Holyrood Road,
Edinburgh EH8 8AQ
031 556 8455
Thornton, R. Mr
A comparison of the internal organisation of proportions within English and French discourse and its bearings on the teaching of English to native speakers of French
Abstract: This research aims to provide a basis for the production of learning activities and materials for native speakers of French learning English as a second language.
Status: Sponsored project
Source of Grant: Moray House Institute of Education
Date of Research: 1989-1992
KEYWORDS: *English – second language; French people; second language learning*

9/0317

Moray House Institute of Education, Holyrood Road,
Edinburgh EH8 8AQ
031 556 8455

Grassie, M. Mr
Critical activity and its effect on the art and design curriculum
Abstract: The aims of the research are to: (1) study the effect of the Scottish Certificate of Education new Standard Grade Critical Activity Units on the Art and Design Curriculum especially in S1 and S2; (2) prepare slide packs, display boards and appropriate visual material as backup for Critical Activity Units in Expressive and Design Areas and to see if these can be adapted for use in the common course; and (3) consider the new Higher Art and Design and the Critical Activity element proposed, in relationship to present Standard Grade development.
Status: Sponsored project
Source of Grant: Moray House Institute of Education
Date of Research: 1990-1992
KEYWORDS: *art education; criticism; curriculum development; design education; Scottish certificate of education; standard grade examinations*

9/0318

Moray House Institute of Education, Holyrood Road,
Edinburgh EH8 8AQ
031 556 8455
Hill, A. Mr
Group textual study of fiction in primary school
Abstract: The aims of the project are: (1) to explore the potential for educational development in the group discussion of children's fiction texts; and (2) to make the resulting insights and developed expertise available to teachers. The project originated in a perceived need, in an area of Scotland, for the encouragement of oral work and the use of fiction as more than a Friday afternoon relaxation. It rests upon the following beliefs: (1) That imagination (defined as mental operation upon the possible, as distinct from the actual) is an important aspect of intelligence; (2) That good children's fiction, as a product of imagination, might have an important role in fostering imagination, and responses to imaginative stimuli, in children; (3) That structured discussion might: (a) expand children's understanding and appreciation of what is being read by enabling them to share insights and responses, developing their ability to take literal and inferred meaning from text; (b) enhance children's enjoyment of a text through sharing insights and responses; (c) actively motivate less committed readers by demonstrating the wider varieties of enjoyment and response contained within a text; and (d) promote children's language development, firstly by giving them an experience which is both common (the novel) and individually differentiated (subjective reading and responses), and secondly by presenting occasions when they need to express and articulate their own understandings and perceptions, and listen to and consider the responses and opinions of others in the group. To various extents, according to circumstances, observations by the researcher and by teachers suggest that these beliefs are valid. The resulting materials work well.
Published Material: HILL, A.G. (1985). Group textual study of fiction in the primary school. Edinburgh: Moray House.; HILL, A.G. (1988). Exemplar on, 'The battle of bubble and squeak'. Edinburgh: Moray House.; HILL, A.G. (1989). Exemplar on, 'I am David'. Edinburgh: Moray House.; HILL, A.G. (1990). Recommended titles for the group textual study of fiction in primary schools. Edinburgh: Moray House.; HILL A.G. (1991). Exemplar on Two Banana Books: 'Scaredy Cat' and 'Conker'. Edinburgh: Moray House. A full list of publications is available from the author.
Status: Individual research
Date of Research: 1983-1992
KEYWORDS: *children's literature; fiction; primary schools; story reading*

9/0319

Moray House Institute of Education, Holyrood Road,
Edinburgh EH8 8AQ
031 556 8455
Diniz, F. Mr
Moray House Institute of Education policy on equal opportunities (disability and race): curricular implementation
Abstract: The main aim of this research is to monitor the curricular implementation of the Institute's policy on Equal Opportunity (Disability and Race). The curricular dimension is regarded as a major strategy for students and staff to develop critical perspectives on discrimination, in relation to disability and race.
Status: Sponsored project
Source of Grant: Moray House Institute of Education

Date of Research: 1990-1992
KEYWORDS: *access to education; curriculum development; disabilities; educational discrimination; equal education; higher education; race*

9/0320

Moray House Institute of Education, Holyrood Road,
Edinburgh EH8 8AQ
031 556 8455
Grant, C. Mr
Computers in nursery schools
Abstract: The aim of the research is to examine the use of computers in the context of the nursery classroom whether in a nursery school or a nursery class attached to a primary school. This will involve: (1) establishing the policy of Her Majesty's Inspectorate (HMI) as regards the use of computers in the nursery classroom context; (2) establishing regional policy/guidelines on the use of computers in nursery classrooms; (3) establishing the number of nursery classrooms where computers are used, identifying the type of computer used and times available; (4) identifying the degree of computer training given to teachers of nursery classes by the colleges where they originally trained; (5) examining the amount and nature of inservice training offered by Scottish regions; and (6) examining the amount and nature of inservice offered by colleges.
Status: Sponsored project
Source of Grant: Moray House Institute of Education
Date of Research: 1989-1992
KEYWORDS: *computer uses in education; nursery schools*

9/0321

Moray House Institute of Education, Holyrood Road,
Edinburgh EH8 8AQ
031 556 8455
Lloyd, G. Ms
Problem girls
Abstract: The aim of the research is to explore the nature of school based deviance in adolescent girls and the responses of schools to such deviant behaviour.
Published Material: LLOYD, G. (Ed). (1992). 'Chosen with care? – Responses to disturbing and disruptive behaviour'. Edinburgh: Moray House.
Status: Sponsored project
Source of Grant: Moray House Institute of Education
Date of Research: 1990-1992
KEYWORDS: *adolescents; antisocial behaviour; discipline policy; discipline problems; disruptive pupils; girls*

9/0322

Moray House Institute of Education, Holyrood Road,
Edinburgh EH8 8AQ
031 556 8455
Drame, M. Mr; *Supervisor:* Dickinson, L. Mr;
McMichael, P. Dr
An investigation of an interactive process model for implementing an English Language Teaching (ELT) syllabus in secondary schools in French speaking Africa
Abstract: In post-independence Africa there is concern about the mismatch between educational curricula and inappropriate teaching materials used to implement them. For example, in Senegal a national syllabus has been designed and yet the incongruity between this syllabus which teaches English as communication and the inappropriate audio-lingual textbook used for its implementation remains an urgent issue to be addressed. The project aims to address this issue and proposes to investigate an interactive process model for syllabus implentation. A draft set of materials appropriate to the Senegalese threshold level communicative syllabus will be designed. This package of materials will be trialled, revised and retrialled in Senegal with a view to investigating a proposed model for teacher development on syllabus implementation. The project will include three stages: (1) a planning phase (1991-1992) in which a draft set of materials suitable to the Senegalese syllabus will be developed in addition to the data collection instruments (observation schedules, questionnaires, interviews) to be used during the implementation phase to take place in Senegal during the second year; (2) an implementation phase (1992-1993) in which the draft set of materials will be trialled, revised and retrialled in Senegal with a view to investigating the effectiveness of the proposed interactive process model for syllabus implementation;

and (3) an evaluation and reporting phase (1993-1994) in which all data including questionnaires, interviews, observation schedules, teachers' diaries and samples of pupils' test scores will be collected and analysed qualitatively and quantitatively with the objective of assessing the empirical validity of the proposed procedure. The research findings will be assessed and the possible applications considered with regard to the educational context in Senegal in particular and in French speaking Africa in general.
Status: Sponsored project
Source of Grant: The British Council
Date of Research: 1991 - continuing
KEYWORDS: *curriculum development; educational materials; English – second language; second language teaching; Senegal*

9/0323

Moray House Institute of Education, Holyrood Road,
Edinburgh EH8 8AQ
031 556 8455
Draper, J. Mrs; Fraser, H. Mrs; Taylor, W. Mr; Smith, D. Dr
A study of probationers
Abstract: The project was designed to collect data on views of training held by beginning teachers, and on the experience of those teachers of their induction, support and assessment. Data was also collected on their recruitment experiences. The data was collected over a two year period from a national sample of over 300 probationer teachers employed across Scotland, and from their headteachers. A longitudinal database on the experiences of probationer teachers was constructed. This was analysed in conjunction with data from an end-of-training profile, and reports compiled by headteachers after one year and after two years of probationary teaching. The results suggest that there is a broad range of views of training, and varied experiences of recruitment induction support and assessment. The project report highlights experiences found by probationers to support their professional development and identifies issues requiring debate and resolution. Implications of the findings for appraisal and the evaluation of probation 'as an experience' fostering development are key concerns in the project.
Published Material: DRAPER, J., FRASER, H., SMITH, D.J. & TAYLOR, W. (1989). 'Shaping the new teacher in school: the insider's view'. Report of 5th meeting of the Forum of Educational Research in Scotland, 1989, Scottish Council for Research in Education.; DRAPER, J., FRASER, H., SMITH, D. & TAYLOR, W. (1991). 'The induction of probationer teachers: implications of an industrial model', Scottish Educational Review, Vol 23, No 1, pp.23-31.; DRAPER, J. & SMITH, D. (1991). 'Primary probationers and discipline', Summary reports from Control and Discipline Seminar, Craigie College, Ayr, June 1991, pp.7-8.
Status: Sponsored project
Source of Grant: Scottish Office Education Department £60,000
Date of Research: 1988-1991
KEYWORDS: *preservice teacher education; probationary teachers; teacher attitudes; teacher induction; teaching experience*

9/0324

Moray House Institute of Education, Holyrood Road,
Edinburgh EH8 8AQ
031 556 8455
Wait, A. Mr
The introduction of 'Management' to the secondary curriculum
Abstract: This two year project seeks to examine the problems associated with the introduction of the new Scottish Certificate of Education higher grade course in 'Management and Information Studies', which commenced in 1991. This is a brand new subject area in secondary education and a stand-alone higher with no equivalent standard grade. The aim is to research the preparedness and ability of Business Studies teachers to deliver the course, and to examine the problems associated with learning and teaching approaches and assessment structure. The research will establish: (a) the current level of preservice training; (b) the requirements for inservice training, and (c) the problems associated with the introduction of the course.
Status: Sponsored project
Source of Grant: Moray House Institute of Education
Date of Research: 1990-1992
KEYWORDS: *business education; curriculum development; higher grade examinations; management studies; Scottish Certificate of Education; secondary curriculum*

9/0325

Moray House Institute of Education, Holyrood Road,
Edinburgh EH8 8AQ
031 556 8455
Frame, B. Ms

An investigation into techniques for the teaching of non-fiction in schools

Abstract: The first aim of this research is to describe the present use of non-fiction. To find out what non-fiction is used by teachers of pupils aged 9-12 years of age in two primary schools. To find out how the non-fiction is used by describing teaching methods and pupil tasks. The second aim is to compare this with the suggested programmes of study for reading as set out in Scottish Office Education Department (SOED) English language 5-14, comparing the findings of the first aim with what has been recommended in the SOED document under Reading: Strand 3 – Reading for Information; Strand 5 – Finding and handling information; and Strand 6 – Awareness of Genre – all under (1) programmes of study and (2) attainment targets. The comparison will draw out differences relating to teaching methods and pupil tasks.

Published Material: 'Non-fiction in Primaries 6-7 English Language 5-14: Report', Edinburgh: Moray House.
Status: Sponsored project
Source of Grant: Moray House Institute of Education
Date of Research: 1990-1992
KEYWORDS: English studies; literature studies; nonfiction; reading

9/0326

Moray House Institute of Education, Holyrood Road,
Edinburgh EH8 8AQ
031 556 8455
Dickinson, N. Ms

The identification of the feasibility of the preparation of Master of Arts (MA) Dissertations in distance mode in developing countries

Abstract: The aims of the research are: (a) to identify the feasibility of preparing and writing Master of Arts (MA) dissertations in distance mode; and (b) to identify the areas of difficulty in writing dissertations in distance mode in respect of resources, local supervision, external (Moray House) supervision, and time factors. The project aims to identify difficulties inherent in distance learning and in country dissertation mixing and to seek solutions.

Status: Sponsored project
Source of Grant: Moray House Institute of Education
Date of Research: 1990-1992
KEYWORDS: developing countries; distance education; Masters degrees; Masters dissertations

9/0327

Moray House Institute of Education, Holyrood Road,
Edinburgh EH8 8AQ
031 556 8455
Page, C. Dr

Transition to college

Abstract: This research will provide evidence about the nature of the transition to Moray House, as experienced by new students, which could help this Institute (and other colleges) make wise decisions on future planning in the areas of teaching and learning, advising and counselling, residence, college ethos and health education. The researcher will also address such questions as: to what extent does the new student experience homesickness? how is this related to links with home (e.g. letters, home events missed, vacations etc.)? what preparation for the transition was experienced? and in what ways does homesickness affect course work?

Status: Sponsored project
Source of Grant: Moray House Institute of Education
Date of Research: 1990-1992
KEYWORDS: college students; colleges of higher education; student behaviour; student problems

9/0328

Moray House Institute of Education, Holyrood Road,
Edinburgh EH8 8AQ
031 556 8455
Hamilton, J. Dr

Language medium teaching

Abstract: The aim of the research is to examine the effects of language medium teaching on learner motivation and foreign language proficiency within the Scottish context.

Status: Sponsored project
Source of Grant: Moray House Institute of Education
Date of Research: 1990 - continuing
KEYWORDS: learning motivation; modern language studies; Scotland; second language teaching

9/0329

Moray House Institute of Education, Holyrood Road,
Edinburgh EH8 8AQ
031 556 8455
Bain, W. Mr

Analysis of reports on curriculum

Abstract: The years between 1945-1990 have been a period of major change in school curriculum, assessment, and certificates as well as in advisory groups such as Her Majesty's Inspectorate (HMI) and the Scottish Examination Board (SEB), Scottish Vocational Education Council (SCOTVEC), Scottish Consultative Council on the Curriculum (SCCC) and the General Teaching Council (GTC). The researcher is analysing the processes of decision making which led to specific reports and their implementation or shelving, in both primary and secondary education. In addition, the analysis considers teachers' and others' involvement in working parties and bodies such as the GTC and SCCC, and the expanding of certification in secondary schools. A range of reports and primary sources are being studies for this work.

Published Material: BAIN, W.H. (1988). '29 steps to standard grade', Times Educational Supplement Scotland, No 1113, 4 March, pp.12.; BAIN, W.H. (1989). 'The Sera conference reports', Times Educational Supplement Scotland, 6 October, pp.5.
Status: Individual research
Date of Research: 1988-1992
KEYWORDS: curriculum; educational history; educational innovation; Scotland

9/0330

Moray House Institute of Education, Holyrood Road,
Edinburgh EH8 8AQ
031 556 8455
Crawford, E. Dr

Fitting into institutions

Abstract: The aims of the research are to: (1) examine the experience of teacher education students in placement schools; (2) examine the experience of schools accepting students; (3) identify institutional factors (as opposed to personal factors) which affect the experience of both parties; (4) evaluate these factors with regard to beneficial and detrimental aspects of the experiences; and (5) develop induction and preparation procedures and compare with present preparation techniques.

Status: Sponsored project
Source of Grant: Moray House Institute of Education
Date of Research: 1990-1992
KEYWORDS: preservice teacher education; student placement; student teachers; teaching experience; teaching practice

9/0331

Moray House Institute of Education, Holyrood Road,
Edinburgh EH8 8AQ
031 556 845
Crawford, E. Dr

Specific aspects of curriculum or Values Education and the understanding of science

Abstract: To explore the attitudes of science teachers which affect practice regarding teaching of science and understanding of the nature of science.

Status: Sponsored project
Source of Grant: Moray House Institute of Education
Date of Research: 1991-1992
KEYWORDS: science education; science teachers; scientific literacy; values education

9/0332

Moray House Institute of Education, Cramond Campus,
Cramond Road North, Edinburgh EH4 6JD
031 312 6001

McDonald, F. Ms; *Supervisor:* Carlisle, B. Mr; Adams, F. Mr
Aspects of new paradigm research and nontraditional learning: innovative approaches to performance excellence in sport
Abstract: This study seeks to establish new parameters for training and performance in sport and the terms and conditions of a new paradigm research and development method in action. The project aims to: (1) offer a critique of training theory; (2) analyse performance in terms of key concepts, underlying values and performance goals; (3) develop a methodology for working within the parameters of what has come to be known as 'New Paradigm Research'; (4) establish what is nontraditional as opposed to traditional learning; (5) spot emergent training parameters and consider general applications; (6) establish the broad features of a new training system.
Status: Sponsored project
Source of Grant: Moray House Institute of Education £1,000
Date of Research: 1988-1992
KEYWORDS: *models; nontraditional education; performance; physical education; sports; teaching methods*

9/0333
Moray House Institute of Education, Cramond Campus, Cramond Road North, Edinburgh EH4 6JD
031 312 6001
Hosie, D. Mr; Turner, M. Ms
Comparative study of children with a hearing impairment
Abstract: This is a preliminary study to assess the merits of 3 distinct models of teaching children with a hearing impairment.
Status: Sponsored project
Source of Grant: Moray House Institute of Education
Date of Research: 1990-1992
KEYWORDS: *deafness; hearing impairments; special educational needs; teaching methods*

9/0334
Moray House Institute of Education, Holyrood Road, Edinburgh EH8 8AQ
031 556 8455
Macrae, S. Mrs
An investigation into how pupils perceive and react to stressful situations in school
Abstract: The study aims to find how young people in school identify and respond to situations which they perceive as stressful. A longitudinal study was carried out with children from junior classes, from the transition from primary/secondary and from SIV. The researcher was involved with these pupils in discussions and in observing their behaviour to discover individual stressors. In the first year, the researcher concentrated on this identification process in a small number of schools, probably in Edinburgh. Thereafter, the task was to design appropriate measures so that stress might be alleviated. The research focused on children and their perceptions of stressful situations. The researcher was required to interact with children from different age groups and having identified stressors, conceptualise and implement measures which would allow them to be reduced. The pupils themselves were encouraged to evaluate the new procedures.
Status: Sponsored project
Source of Grant: Health Promotion Trust/Economic and Social Research Council £3,150
Date of Research: 1987-1991
KEYWORDS: *pupil behaviour; stress – psychological; stress management; stress variables*

9/0335
Moray House Institute of Education, Holyrood Road, Edinburgh EH8 8AQ
031 556 8455
Jarvie, M. Mrs
Peer group counselling in upper primary
Abstract: One of the issues identified in the Committee on Primary Education (Scotland) (COPE) Position Paper, 'Primary Education in the Eighties', as not having been adequately addressed is 'the conscious and coherent development of aspects of Personal and Social Education'. The research will address this issue. Its aim is to ascertain if training P7 pupils in group counselling skills increases their ability to: (a) listen to and be empathic with peers; (b) be confident and assertive; (c) engage in value clarification and decision-making; and (d) cope with change.
Status: Sponsored project

Source of Grant: Moray House Institute of Education
Date of Research: 1990-1991
KEYWORDS: *group counselling; individual development; peer counselling; primary education; social development*

9/0336
Moray House Institute of Education, Holyrood Road, Edinburgh EH8 8AQ
031 556 8455
Jones, C. Mr; Van der Kuyl, T. Mr; Johnston, M. Mr
Interactive video project for the hearing impaired
Abstract: The project aims to research and identify the priority areas for development of education for the deaf and to produce high quality interactive courseware to meet the variety of needs of hearing impaired children and adults. Due to problems faced by deaf children on their transfer from primary to secondary schools, the first multimedia courseware will be focused on the upper primary children (ages 8 to 12). A Shopping Microworld is being designed and developed to enable children to organise their own shopping lists, and browse round the food and children's clothing departments of a large high street store. Various pedagogical activities and cognitive strategies are being incorporated into this Microworld. These include LOGO activities, unit pricing, money handling and conservation of measure.
Status: Sponsored project
Source of Grant: Scottish Office Education Department
Date of Research: 1989-1991
KEYWORDS: *computer-assisted learning; deafness; hearing impairments; interactive video; special educational needs*

9/0337
Moray House Institute of Education, Holyrood Road, Edinburgh EH8 8AQ
031 556 8455
Francis, E. Mrs; Jackson, S. Dr; Morrison, A. Mr
Scottish Enterprise Consortium: Moray House Institute of Education
Abstract: The aim of the research is to develop a range of enterprise projects within a centrally funded college and across a consortium of higher education institutions. These will include: (i) a process innovative network; (ii) an Enterprise model for the Postgraduate Certificate of Education (PGCE); (iii) a video project on enterprise awareness; and (iv) consultancy for an evaluation project.
Status: Sponsored project
Source of Grant: Training, Enterprise and Education Directorate
Date of Research: 1989-1991
KEYWORDS: *enterprise education; higher education*

9/0338
Moray House Institute of Education, Holyrood Road, Edinburgh EH8 8AQ
031 556 8455
Tymms, P. Mr; *Supervisor:* Tymms, P. Mr
The long term influence of effective and ineffective A level departments
Abstract: The short-term effectiveness of schools can be measured by immediate outputs such as examination results, attitudes and aspirations. But what about the long-term effects of schools? The project will extend an existing database to answer that question.
Status: Sponsored project
Source of Grant: Economic and Social Research Council £10,000
Date of Research: 1992 - continuing
KEYWORDS: *A level examinations; accountability; examination results; outcomes of education; performance indicators; programme effectiveness; school effectiveness*

9/0339
Moray House Institute of Education, Holyrood Road, Edinburgh EH8 8AQ
031 556 8455
Cosford, B. Mr
Preparing teachers for student placement
Abstract: An investigation of the feasibility and effectiveness of a programme designed to prepare teachers for having a student on placement. In particular to test the Planning, Implementation, Evaluation (PIEC) model, within a context as a framework for developing the teacher's role on placement.

Status: Sponsored project
Source of Grant: Moray House Institute of Education £1,000
Date of Research: 1990-1991
KEYWORDS: *student teacher supervisors; student teachers; supervisory training; teacher education; teaching experience; teaching practice*

9/0340
Moray House Institute of Education, Holyrood Road,
Edinburgh EH8 8AQ
031 556 8455
Macintyre, C. Dr
Action research in initial teacher training
Abstract: The aims of this research at Moray House Institute of Education are to: (a) develop written and visual materials; (b) help student teachers become effective action researchers in the classroom; (c) help the teachers who have responsibility for overseeing the students to guide and support them appropriately; and (d) help college tutors to supervise the students' action research. This is being done by studying the experiences and evaluations of four cohorts of final year students, their teachers and their supervisors and constantly producing and amending materials to facilitate and enrich their task.
Status: Sponsored project
Source of Grant: Moray House Institute of Education £1,900
Date of Research: 1989-1991
KEYWORDS: *preservice teacher education; programme development*

9/0341
Moray House Institute of Education, Holyrood Road,
Edinburgh EH8 8AQ
031 556 8455
Quickfall, M. Mr; *Supervisor:* Tymms, P. Mr
Value added measures
Abstract: Input and output measures are available for all students who have completed degrees in all colleges of education in Scotland. These data are being examined with a view to establishing value added measures for courses in these colleges.
Status: Individual research
Date of Research: 1991-1992
KEYWORDS: *degrees – academic; higher education; measurement objectives; organisational effectiveness; performance indicators; programme effectiveness*

9/0342
Moray House Institute of Education, Holyrood Road,
Edinburgh EH8 8AQ
031 556 8455
Carver, D. Mr; Dickinson, L. Mr
Developing deep processing strategies in academic interaction
Abstract: This research at Moray House Institute of Education is in three phases and involved in 1988-89 creating and trialling a set of materials designed to enable academic counselling to proceed on a structured basis; and in 1989-90 analysing transcripts of academic oral interaction in order to classify strategies and sources of breakdown. The aim of this research is to create and test a teaching module designed to develop students' ability to interact in the academic setting.
Status: Sponsored project
Source of Grant: Moray House Institute of Education
Date of Research: 1989-1991
KEYWORDS: *higher education; interaction; student participation*

9/0343
Moray House Institute of Education, Holyrood Road,
Edinburgh EH8 8AQ
031 556 8455
Macintyre, C. Dr
Student teachers' perceptions of stressful situations in schools
Abstract: Most student teachers expect to have anxious, even stressful times during their weeks on school placement as they build relationships with teachers, children and tutors, learn to teach and have continuous assessment. Some cope very well; they may even find short periods of anxiety or stress stimulating if there is a fairly immediate and successful outcome. But others find that stress builds to an unacceptable level, that of distress and they fail to cope. This can have devastating and possibly long lasting results. What then are the factors which cause student teachers stress/distress? Are there ways (coping strategies) in which they can be helped to cope? This research intends to address these questions by asking student teachers to reflect on their practice and report their level of anxiety stress/distress, to articulate if they can name the factors that caused them stress and to evaluate the coping strategies they used. Having identified the students' perceptions and their successful coping strategies the research will then find if these can usefully be shared with other students to alleviate their problems. Finally the student teachers in the next cohort at Moray House will be asked whether knowledge of coping strategies helped them to select appropriately and so helped them to reduce the level of stress to at least an acceptable degree.
Status: Sponsored project
Source of Grant: Moray House Institute of Education
Date of Research: 1991 - continuing
KEYWORDS: *preservice teacher education; stress – psychological; stress variables; student teachers; teaching experience; teaching practice*

9/0344
Moray House Institute of Education, Cramond Campus,
Cramond Road North, Edinburgh EH4 6JD
031 312 6001
Dick, A. Mrs
Attitudes to and perceptions of Scottish primary school children to physical activities
Abstract: The aims of this research are to: (i) set up an exploratory pilot study to clarify appropriate methodology for the collection of data; (ii) explore the data with reference to gender, multicultural issues, social class, environment and preferred physical activities amongst Scottish school children; and (iii) reflect on the implications of the above in regard to content of Expressive Arts, physical education (PE).
Status: Sponsored project
Source of Grant: Moray House Institute of Education £460
Date of Research: 1989 - continuing
KEYWORDS: *physical activities; physical education; primary schools; Scotland*

9/0345
Moray House Institute of Education, Holyrood Road,
Edinburgh EH8 8AQ
031 556 8455
Lyle, J. Mr; Lynn, A. Mr; Messenger, G. Miss; McLeod, C. Mr
National Coaching Centre
Abstract: This is a consultancy service offered to coaches and coach educators. The services are grant-aided by the Scottish Sports Council and the National Coaching Foundation. Services include performance monitoring, courses, conferences and hire of facilities. A report is published annually.
Status: Sponsored project
Source of Grant: Scottish Sports Council; National Coaching Foundation; Reebok UK £86,650
Date of Research: 1987-1991
KEYWORDS: *sports; sports coaching*

9/0346
Moray House Institute of Education, Holyrood Road,
Edinburgh EH8 8AQ
031 556 8455
McMichael, P. Dr; Draper, J. Mrs
Short-term secondments
Abstract: Stimulated by an increase in short term (23 months) appointments to college lectureships together with a policy of secondments to posts at both regional and national level from within the teaching profession this project aims to examine the experience of secondment and to discover ways in which transitions from job to job can be facilitated in order to maximise a sense of personal control as well as productivity. The project will attempt to discover: (1) Why secondees apply for secondments and what their expectations about secondment might be; (2) What form of induction was provided; (3) How this was perceived; (4) How initial adjustments were made; (5) What balance was achieved between fitting the job and developing the job; (6) Whether exiting from secondment was 'managed' and, if so, how; (7) What effects the secondment had on perceptions of self and on future employment. Interviews will be conducted with 25

secondees completing full-time secondments during 1991 in colleges, the Scottish Office Education Department, the Scottish Consultative Council on the Curriculum, and regional authorities. Questionnaires based on analysis of the invterviews will be circulated to a wider sample of secondees. Selected secondees are teachers, headteachers, advisers and college lecturers.
Status: Sponsored project
Source of Grant: Scottish Office Education Department £2,000
Date of Research: 1991-1992
KEYWORDS: secondments; staff development; teacher development

9/0347
Moray House Institute of Education, Holyrood Road,
Edinburgh EH8 8AQ
031 556 8455
Glasgow University, Department of Psychology, Glasgow
G12 8QQ
041 339 8855
Reid, G. Mr; *Supervisor:* Hinton, J. Dr
Teacher stress and organisational climate
Abstract: The results from four pilot studies already undertaken show a need for examination of teacher stress from the perspectives of personal organisation, school organisation and organisational climate. The study will, therefore, develop some strands identified in the pilot studies including the following: (1) the implications of personal organisation for inservice programmes including aspects such as time management, staff support and staff training; (2) the effect of school organisation on communications, staff support, interpersonal links, role factors, curriculum development and curriculum and organisational changes; (3) the nature of the school organisational climate and its importance in relation to school management – staff morale, motivation, sociability and efficiency. Reading has revealed stress factors such as role overload; time management; administration; fragmentation; interpersonal relations; interpersonal support; openness of staff discussions; leadership skills; school communications network; role conflict and locus of control. The problem, it appears, with identifying stress contributory factors such as the list above, is that it is acknowledged that teacher stress is a multi-facted phenomenon and the identification of isolated factors can be misleading and unhelpful for the development and delivery of a school inservice stress management programme. The study examines the theme of organisation, aiming to support the following hypothesis: (a) personal organisation, school organisation and organisational climate are influential factors in stress generation among teachers in schools; (b) stress management inservice programmes need to address these issues for enhanced effectiveness; and (c) the theoretical model of psychological stress (Hinton 1991) is a valid model of examining perceived stress among teachers.
Published Material: REID, G. (1991). 'Supporting the support teacher: stress factors in teaching children with specific learning difficulties', Links, Vol 16, No 3, pp.18-20.
Status: Individual research
Date of Research: 1989 - continuing
KEYWORDS: educational environment; institutional environment; stress – psychological; stress management; stress variables; teacher morale

9/0348
Moray House Institute of Education, Scottish Centre for
Education Overseas, Holyrood Road, Edinburgh EH8 8AQ
031 556 8455
Ahrens, P. Mrs
An investigation into the difficulties of introducing innovation in English language teaching in developing countries
Abstract: This research grew out of work for a presentation at the British Council Dunford House Conference in 1990 on the topic of sustainability in the design of English language teaching projects. A database of difficulties was compiled in consultation with overseas Master of Arts (MA) students and used at the conference. This will be expanded and put into a hierarchy, in consultation with current overseas students, to form a questionnaire which will be sent to previous students, now seeking to introduce various innovative practices in their home systems. The results will be an ordered list of difficulties actually encountered by practitioners in the field. Later research might seek to identify ways of coping with these difficulties.
Status: Sponsored project
Source of Grant: Moray House Institute of Education £250
Date of Research: 1992 - continuing

KEYWORDS: developing countries; English – second language; second language teaching

9/0349
Moray House Institute of Education, Scottish Centre for
Education Overseas, Holyrood Road, Edinburgh EH8 8AQ
031 556 8455
Dickinson, L. Mr
A survey of learner training for language learning
Abstract: Learner training is concerned with helping learners consider the factors that affect their learning and with helping them to discover the learning strategies which suit them best. It focuses learners' attention on the process of learning so that the emphasis is on how to learn rather than what to learn. Though this is a relatively new development in language teaching and learning, there are indications that there is a growing interest in many parts of the world. This research aims to survey a broad sample of language teaching institutions to gauge the interest in learner training, to discover the varying meanings given to the term and to establish a network of individuals and institutions with an interest in learner training.
Status: Sponsored project
Source of Grant: Moray House Institute of Education £500
Date of Research: 1991-1992
KEYWORDS: learning processes; learning strategies; metacognition; second language learning

9/0350
Moray House Institute of Education, Scottish Centre for
Education Overseas, Holyrood Road, Edinburgh EH8 8AQ
031 556 8455
Ahrens, P. Mrs; Dickinson, N. Mrs
Teaching foreign languages at primary level
Abstract: This piece of research looks at English language teaching in Europe and at the teaching of foreign languages in Scotland at the primary level. It relates to the increased interest in and demand for foreign language learning at primary level. Data has been collected and is still in the process of being collected on the problems teachers of a foreign language at primary level face. From existing data a checklist of common difficulties has been designed. This has been trialled and refined. Copies of this checklist have been sent to contacts in various countries. The data from the checklists will be analysed. Visits have been made within Edinburgh to selected primary schools where a foreign language is being taught. A report will be written on the different models of teaching a foreign language at primary level in use and teachers will be asked to fill in a checklist about their specific problems. The analysis of the data should show the main areas that cause problems to teachers at this level. Further research will set out to identify and collect teachers' coping strategies.
Status: Sponsored project
Source of Grant: Moray House Institute of Education £500
Date of Research: 1991 - continuing
KEYWORDS: modern language studies; primary education; problems; second language teaching; teaching methods

9/0351
Moray House Institute of Education, The National Centre for
PLAY, Cramond Campus, Cramond Road North, Edinburgh
EH4 6JD
031 312 6001
Ovens, N. Mrs
Play provision for children and young people in Scotland aged 5-15: what is happening?
Abstract: Following the investigative study 'Working for PLAY' in 1988 in Scotland, and the research undertaken by the School for Advanced Studies at Bristol University and the production of the Action Plan 1991/1992 of Play Wales, there would appear to be a need to analyse the lack of comparable developments in Scotland. In Scotland, play is provided through both region and district local authority functions but in the local government restructuring, certain functions were not clearly allocated leading to some areas of confusion. Some authorities are single purpose authorities. Voluntary agencies' local units therefore may lack clearly identified communication links with the local authorities. Interviews with key bodies such as the Scottish Office Education Department and Social Work Services Group, the Convention of Scottish Local Authorities, the Scottish Play Council and others, will be conducted. A report will be prepared on the findings.

Published Material: 'Working for PLAY' – an investigative study on provision for play in Scotland, 1988, Funded by Save the Children, Moray House Institute of Education: National Centre for PLAY.
Status: Sponsored project
Source of Grant: Moray House Institute of Education £600
Date of Research: 1991-1992
KEYWORDS: *community resources; community services; local government; play; recreational facilities; Scotland*

Hertfordshire University

9/0352

School of Humanities and Education, Wall Hall Campus, Aldenham, Watford WD2 8AT
0707 279000
Hull, B. Mrs; *Supervisor:* Gipps, C. Dr
The effects of the National Curriculum on infant teachers and their practice
Abstract: The research aims to investigate the extent to which infant teachers respond to change, in particular the requirements of the National Curriculum. Case studies involving six teachers in two schools were carried out, employing techniques of participant observation and interviewing over a two year period. The results are currently being evaluated and set in a context which looks at the image of teachers of young children through history and literature. This theme is developed into an examination of the growth of professionalism with regard to infant teachers, and with particular reference to gender inequalities in education, posing the hypothesis that infant teaching has suffered from low status because of its relationship to the education of girls and the social position of women in society.
Published Material: HULL, B. (1990). 'The National Curriculum: its effects on infant teachers and their practice', Early Years, Vol 2, No 1, pp.39-44. Autumn.
Status: Sponsored project
Source of Grant: Hatfield Polytechnic £2,500
Date of Research: 1989-1992
KEYWORDS: *infant school teachers; National Curriculum; professional recognition; teaching profession*

9/0353

School of Humanities and Education, Wall Hall Campus, Aldenham, Watford WD2 8AT
0707 279000
Powell, S. Dr; Jordan, R. Ms
Investigation of the development of social cognition and the subsequent effectiveness of cognitive curricular approaches to meeting individual needs
Abstract: This research investigates the development of social cognition with special regard to individuals who fall within the autistic continuum. The researchers have conducted experimental studies with individuals with autism on the development of a 'theory of mind'. Action research is being conducted into ways in which individual learning can be facilitated within the curriculum by means of cognitive approaches. Computer programs were used to derive principles that underpin the pedagogy of a 'cognitive curriculum', that encompasses the needs of all children. The programs were evaluated in an experimental study with autistic individuals and the principles are being evaluated through classroom-based action research in a variety of educational settings.
Published Material: POWELL, S.D. & JORDAN, R.R. (1990). 'Thinking about autistic children thinking'. In: Collected Papers – International Conference on Experimental Psychology and the Autistic Syndromes. (Durham) Sunderland: Sunderland Polytechnic; JORDAN, R.R. & POWELL, S.D. (1990). 'Autism and the National Curriculum', British Journal of Special Education, Vol 17, No 4, pp.140-142.; JORDAN, R.R. & POWELL, S.D. (1991). 'Teaching thinking – the case for principles', European Journal of Special Needs Education, Vol 6, No 2, pp.112-124.; RIDING, R.J. & POWELL, S.D. (1991). Learn to think – Stage two (Special Education Version), Birmingham, Learning and Training Technology.; POWELL, S.D. & JORDAN, R.R. (1991). 'A psychological perspective on identifying and meeting the needs of exceptional pupils', School Pyschology International, Vol 12, pp.315-327. A full list of publications is available from the researcher.

Status: Sponsored project
Source of Grant: Inge Wakehurst Trust £500
Date of Research: 1987 - continuing
KEYWORDS: *autism; cognitive ability; curriculum research; individual needs; social cognition*

9/0354

School of Humanities and Education, Wall Hall Campus, Aldenham, Watford WD2 8AT
0707 279000
Thornton, M. Ms; *Supervisor:* Young, M. Mr
Subject specialisation and the primary school curriculum
Abstract: A critical examination of the effects of an increasing centralist emphasis upon subject specialism in the primary school and the implications this might have: (a) for the tradition of generalist class teaching in the primary school sector; (b) for the curriculum as experienced by primary aged pupils; and (c) the teaching methods and organisational features through which it is transmitted. School based investigations took place in the autumn of 1988. The sample included 22 infant, junior and JMI (junior mixed infants) schools in one division of a local education authority. In each school curriculum guidelines were examined, the headteacher and a selection of teaching staff interviewed (determined by age of pupils taught, i.e. Reception, Year 2, Year 3 and Year 6), and classroom observations made on the basis of teaching staff interviewed.
Published Material: THORNTON, M. (1990). 'Primary specialism', Early Years, Vol 11, No 1, pp.34-38, Autumn.; THORNTON, M. (1991). 'Why a full explanation is needed', Times Educational Supplement, 13 December.
Status: Sponsored project
Source of Grant: Hertfordshire University
Date of Research: 1986-1992
KEYWORDS: *curriculum research; primary school curriculum; specialisation*

9/0355

School of Humanities and Education, Wall Hall Campus, Aldenham, Watford WD2 8AT
0707 279000
Campbell, R. Prof.
Hearing children read
Abstract: Now in its second phase, this study aims to explore the effectiveness of various teacher responses to the mistakes of early beginning readers. An in depth case study of two children reading to their teacher throughout a school year has been conducted. Interactions were audio-recorded and subsequently transcribed. Results have suggested that a word cueing strategy was particularly helpful to the reader. However, effectiveness needs to be explored at various levels and recent articles have debated this topic.
Published Material: CAMPBELL, R. (1986). 'Social relationships in hearing children read', Reading, Vol 20, No 3, pp.157-167, December.; CAMPBELL, R. (1987). 'Oral reading errors of two beginning readers', Journal of Research in Reading, Vol 10, No 2, pp.144-155, September.; CAMPBELL, R. (1988). 'Is it time for USSR, SSR, SQUIRE, DEAR or ERIC?', Education, Vol 16, No 2, pp.3-13, June.; CAMPBELL, R. (1988). Hearing children read. London: Routledge.; CAMPBELL, R. (1992). Reading real books. Buckingham: Open University Press.
Status: Individual research
Date of Research: 1980 - continuing
KEYWORDS: *beginning reading; early reading; oral reading; reading skills; teacher-pupil relationship*

9/0356

School of Humanities and Education, Wall Hall Campus, Aldenham, Watford WD2 8AT
0707 279000
Miller, L. Mrs; *Supervisor:* Campbell, R. Prof.; Trendall, C. Dr
The share-a-book project
Abstract: The project has arisen from the growing awareness of insights on learning to read to be gained by observing young children's earliest interactions with print and the increasing recognition of the role of the home environment and parental involvement in promoting early literacy development. A successful initiative in this area has been the introduction of shared reading schemes in primary schools, which recognise the importance of parents reading to and sharing books with their children. The share-a-book scheme has been

extended into pre-school. The principles embodied in the concept of shared reading schemes could be viewed as a pre-cursor to such a scheme. The research focused upon the implementation and evaluation of a share-a-book scheme in a community playgroup and involved a group of 40 preschool children and their parents. Evaluation relates to the children's emerging literacy skills and linked features of the home background. The viability of the scheme was evaluated for Cambridgeshire library service. Quantitative and qualitative methods of data collection were used. These included: (i) recording the number of books loaned and parental comments on these; (ii) a pre/post questionnaire relating to the children's emerging literacy skills and related features of the home background; (iii) pre and post testing of the children's concepts about print. The first phase of the project has been completed. A further phase is concerned with the continuity of literacy experiences between the preschool and the beginning of primary school.
Published Material: MILLER, L. (1990). 'Sharing books in the pre-school: what is it all about?', Early Years, Vol 11, No 1, pp.13-17.; MILLER, L. (1991). 'Literacy development in young children: continuities between home and school', Early Education, No 4, Autumn.
Status: Individual research
Date of Research: 1988 - continuing
KEYWORDS: *home environment; paired reading; prereading experience; preschool children*

9/0357
School of Humanities and Education, Wall Hall Campus, Aldenham, Watford WD2 8AT
0707 279000
Campbell, R. Prof., Scrivens, O. Mrs, Mangan, M. Mr
An investigation of sustained silent reading in the primary school
Abstract: Following the strong recommendations that there should be more emphasis on silent independent reading in primary schools there is limited evidence that the procedure defined as SSR (sustained silent reading) can have a beneficial effect on children's attitudes to reading and reading achievement when used with a course of reading instruction. The aim of the study is: (i) to identify schools using SSR within the local division and/or county by means of a questionnaire; (ii) to explore and analyse how SSR is organised within some of these schools; (iii) to investigate how the activity is perceived by teachers, children and parents by means of triangulation methods and interviews; (iv) to ascertain any possible gains in reading performance or attitudes to reading assessed within the schools; (v) to discover any particular problems these schools might experience in the use of SSR. If this project is extended it will follow the form of an investigation of an adaption of SSR named 'Book-Time' which would be set up in one or more nursery schools or playgroups. There is very little evidence to date of the organisational difficulties which might occur or of the benefits to 3-5 year old children. This study would, therefore, be providing a contribution to knowledge about pedagogical practices.
Published Material: CAMPBELL, R. (1988). 'Is it time for USSR, SSR, SQUIRT, DEAR or ERIC?', Education 3-13, Vol 16, No 2, pp.22-25, June.; CAMPBELL, R. (1989). 'The teacher as a role model during sustained silent reading', Reading, Vol 23, No 3, pp.179-183, November.; CAMPBELL, R. (1990). Reading together. Buckingham: Open University Press.; CAMPBELL, R. (1992). Reading real books. Buckingham: Open University Press.
Status: Individual research
Date of Research: 1988-1992
KEYWORDS: *primary schools; reading strategies; silent reading; sustained silent reading*

9/0358
School of Humanities and Education, Wall Hall Campus, Aldenham, Watford WD2 8AT
0707 279000
Jackson, A. Dr
Microcomputer use in the primary school
Abstract: This is an extension of research commenced at postgraduate level. It investigates some of the psychological variables which influence children's performance during microcomputer based problem solution when working alone or in groups. It also considers the current uses of microcomputers in primary education, and factors which affect use. Previous surveys have revealed that microcomputers are primarily used for group rather than individualised instruction in the primary school. This research addresses the question of why,

and whether groups of children show superior performance compared to children working alone on a series of mathematical problems. All experiments have been, and will be conducted in primary schools working with 10- to 11- year old children. Performance is examined in terms of: (1) time to problem solution; (2) number of moves to solution; (3) types of moves made. Over 300 children have been tested in 5 experiments so far. Initial results indicate that groups of 3 children do show superior on-task decision making to individuals. There was an indication that group interaction could be more beneficial for performance over and above the provision of a software based 'help-facility'. Further investigations will include: (1) differences in decision making strategy between groups and individuals; and (2) the conditions under which intragroup discussion is beneficial to performance.
Published Material: JACKSON, A., FLETCHER, B.C. & MESSER, D.J. (1986). 'A survey of microcomputer use and provision in primary school', Journal of Computer Assisted Learning, Vol 2, No 1, pp.45-55.; MESSER, D.J., JACKSON, A. & MOHAME-DALI, M. (1987). 'Influences on computer based problem solving: help facilities, intrinsic orientation, gender and home computing', Educational Psychology, Vol 7, No 1, pp.33-46.; JACKSON, A., FLETCHER, B.C. & MESSER, D.J. (1988). 'Effects of experience on microcomputer use in primary schools: results of a second survey', Journal of Computer Assisted Learning, Vol 4, No 4, pp.214-226, December.; JACKSON, A. (1988). 'Are three heads better than one? An investigation of children solving microcomputer based problems', Paper presented to the XXIV International Congress of Psychology, Sydney, Australia, August.; JACKSON, A., FLETCHER, B.C. & MESSER, D.J. (1991). 'When talking doesn't help: an investigation of microcomputer based group problem solving', Invited paper for Special Issue of International Journal of Educational Research. A full list of publications is available from the researchers.
Status: Individual research
Date of Research: 1988 - continuing
KEYWORDS: *computer uses in education; group work; microcomputers; primary schools; problem solving*

Hull University

9/0359
School of Education, Cottingham Road, Hull HU6 7RX
0482 46311
McNamara, D. Prof.; *Supervisor:* McNamara, D. Prof.
Focused mentoring for the National Curriculum
Abstract: The study aims to explore the contributions which teacher trainers (tutors) and teachers responsible for the student teachers during periods of school practice (mentors) make to students' practical preparations for teaching. The study will focus upon the teaching of mathematics at all four key stages of the National Curriculum. A case study design is being adopted, supplemented by classroom observation and focused interviews.
Status: Sponsored project
Source of Grant: Paul Hamlyn Foundation £8,000
Date of Research: 1992-1992
KEYWORDS: *mathematics education; National Curriculum; student teacher supervisors; teacher education; teaching practice*

9/0360
School of Education, Cottingham Road, Hull HU6 7RX
0482 46311
McClelland, V. Prof.
History of the Roman Catholic involvement in education in England and Wales since 1935. (Within a general history of the Roman Catholic church in England and Wales since 1935)
Abstract: The project re-evaluates the origins of the dual system in education since 1944 and locates educational policy in the Roman Catholic church in England and Wales within the general ecclesiastical development of ther period since 1935. The work will estimate the effect of the Second Vatican Council upon educational development and will examine the social upheaval within the Catholic community since 1965. It will also provide indications of the future of the current partnership between church and state in educational provision.
Published Material: McCLELLAND, V. (1991). 'Gravissimum Educationis'. In: HASTINGS, A. (Ed). Modern catholicism: Vatican

II and after, pp.172-174. London: S.P.C.K.; McCLELLAND, V. (1991). 'The effect of the Council on catholicism: Great Britain and Ireland'. In: HASTINGS, A. (Ed). Modern Catholicism: Vatican II and after, pp.365-376. London: S.P.C.K.; McCLELLAND, V. (1988). 'Sensus Fidelium': the developing concept of Roman Catholic effort in education in England and Wales'. In: TULASIEWICZ, W. & BROCK, C. (Ed). Christianity and educational provision. London: Routledge.
Status: Sponsored project
Source of Grant: The National Catholic Fund
Date of Research: 1989-1992
KEYWORDS: *Catholic schools; church and education; church state relationship; educational history; educational policy; Roman Catholic church*

9/0361

School of Education, Cottingham Road, Hull HU6 7RX
0482 46311
Richmond, M. Mr; *Supervisor:* Brock, C. Mr
The transition to democracy and educational change in contemporary Chile and post-Franco Spain
Abstract: Located within two main sub-fields of educational inquiry (comparative education and the politics of education), the study aims to ascertain and understand the effects of transitions to democracy upon education and also the role of education within such transitions. Given its vital involvement in social and cultural reproduction, education may reveal itself to be a particularly sensitive field for registering the changes associated with a shift away from authoritarianism towards more democratic forms of polity. This sensitivity (its extent and character) will constitute the primary focus of the study. An examination of Chile and Spain affords an opportunity to explore whether or not there are structural similarities or parallels within the process of democratic transition and associated educational change in different countries. Study of the two national experiences is further justified by the possibility that Spain's transition may have furnished lessons for later transitions in Latin America in particular, such as that in Chile. Fieldwork in both countries will focus upon the main primary and secondary written sources of information and upon interviews with government officials and significant personnel within non-governmental organisations.
Status: Individual research
Date of Research: 1990-1992
KEYWORDS: *change; comparative education; democracy; development education; politics education relationship*

9/0362

School of Education, Cottingham Road, Hull HU6 7RX
0482 46311
Owen, D. Mr; *Supervisor:* McClelland, V. Prof.
Economy, education and ecumenism 1931-1984
Abstract: The contribution of the churches to education has been conspicuous by a pattern of discord, even hostility, from the earliest years of the last century, when the setting for their work was permeated by division. Social division, political division and religious division formed a perpetuating circle. The question was posed by Russell that perhaps it was necessary to have several different and separate churches and chapels to reach out to several different social classes. Could a united church have served a divided society? By the middle of the twentieth century a number of the denominational schools were giving concern to the local authorities; many of the buildings were old and considered inadequate to modern educational requirements. The chief concern was that most of the religious bodies lacked the financial means to maintain their schools. The research considers the approaches of the education authorities and the religious bodies towards the provision of education in parts of Lincolnshire by the establishment of joint Anglican and Methodist controlled schools.
Status: Individual research
Date of Research: 1988-1991
KEYWORDS: *aided schools; church and education; church-state relationship; controlled schools; economics-education relationship; educational administration; educational history; local education authorities; voluntary schools*

9/0363

School of Education, Cottingham Road, Hull HU6 7RX
0482 46311

Ridzuan, A. Dr; *Supervisor:* Wilkinson, J. Dr
Factors relating to achievement of high school students in Kuching City, Malaysia
Abstract: This study aims to contribute towards a greater understanding of high-school student learning, with a view to determining remedial action to be taken to upgrade academic achievement, improving learning and teaching strategies and environment, and assisting in national curriculum development. The research used survey and demographic questionnaire techniques looking at a sample study of 925 seventeen-year old lower sixth formers in the eight high schools of Kuching City, Sarawak, Malaysia. The data were analysed using t-tests, stepwise regression and correlation-statistical techniques to establish what correlation could be found between the educational achievements (SPM results) of the pupils in those groupings and the learning approaches, learning styles, school motivation and psychological attitudes (e.g. optimism, locus of control). It was found that there were considerable correlations between predictors and the overall achievement in each of the classification groups. However, the best predictors of achievement varied significantly from group to group. Achievement in individual subjects of the curriculum was also studied in relation to aspects of the teaching-learning environment, student attitudes and demographic factors. This too provided evidence of significant correlation between achievement and certain factors for each discipline, but a wide range of variation between the predictors for achievement in different disciplines. On the basis of conclusions drawn from the analysis of the data, recommendations are made for remedial actions and strategic planning to be undertaken to improve students' achievement and enhance the institutional teaching-learning environment. Scope for further research comprising longitudinal studies, wider samples, and different methodologies is indicated, which could lead to a better understanding of high-school students' learning in this developing third-world country.
Status: Sponsored project
Source of Grant: Government of Malaysia
Date of Research: 1988-1991
KEYWORDS: *academic achievement; cognitive style; educational environment; learning motivation; learning strategies; locus of control; secondary school pupils*

9/0364

School of Education, Cottingham Road, Hull HU6 7RX
0482 46311
Costello, P. Dr; Andrews, R. Mr; Mitchell, S. Ms;
Supervisor: Costello, P. Dr; Andrews, R. Mr
Improving the quality of argument: sixth forms and higher education
Abstract: This project is inter-related with 'Improving the quality of argument: schools'. The project is cross-curricular and runs for three years. In year one, the focus is on sixth forms; this shifts in years two and three to higher education (Humberside University and Hull University). The aim of this project is to explore argument action in various subjects and to devise materials to improve the qualtiy of arguing. The research is grounded to begin with and then is more focused and applied.
Status: Sponsored project
Source of Grant: Leverhulme Trust £89,000
Date of Research: 1991 - continuing
KEYWORDS: *argument; criticism; higher education; sixth form education; writing processes; writing skills*

9/0365

School of Education, Cottingham Road, Hull HU6 7RX
0482 46311
Costello, P. Dr; Andrews, R. Mr; Mitchell, S. Ms;
Supervisor: Costello, P. Dr; Andrews, R. Mr
Improving the quality of argument: schools
Abstract: This project is inter-related with 'Improving the quality of argument: sixth forms and higher education'. The project explores the learning and teaching of argument at key stages 2, 3 and 4 in the National Curriculum. Operating in ten primary and ten secondary schools in Humberside and Lincolnshire, its aim is to improve the quality of argument and to record evidence of this improvement. The approach is one of action research.
Published Material: ANDREWS, R. (1991). 'Argument in the primary school', Language Matters, No 1, pp.34-35, Autumn.
Status: Sponsored project
Source of Grant: Esmee Fairbairn Charitable Trust £52,000

Date of Research: 1991-1992
KEYWORDS: argument; criticism; learning; National Curriculum; teaching methods; writing processes; writing skills

9/0366

School of Education, Cottingham Road, Hull HU6 7RX
0482 46311
Abangma, P. Mrs; *Supervisor:* Brock, C. Mr

A comparative study of secondary school curricula in England and Wales and the Republic of Cameroon: issues of breadth, balance and relevance

Abstract: Issues of breadth, balance and relevance seem to dominate educational debate in the twentieth century. These concepts are considered as curriculum planning principles which will lead to the development of every pupil (intrinsic values) and equip him/her with skills, knowledge and working life (extrinsic values) which will boost the economy of any nation. The problem is the controversy that surrounds the usage and application of these concepts. While it is very important to mention such issues, it is worth noting that no curriculum has ever existed without these concepts even if they are not mentioned; and also, their usage will differ within nations. An analysis of the existing literature and empirical data will reveal the relativity and limits within which they could be applied. The following are to be considered: (1) The possibility of a country discovering the appropriate curriculum for future employment; (2) The stage/level at which one realises breadth, balance and relevance within the school curriculum; (3) Areas of similarities or overlap and differences within the curricula of the countries in question. The research centres on the secondary school curriculum in England/Wales and the Republic of Cameroon. This comparison is necessary especially as both countries operate a national curriculum.
Status: Individual research
Date of Research: 1989-1991
KEYWORDS: comparative education; curriculum development; educational objectives; educational philosophy; National Curriculum; work-education relationship

9/0367

School of Education, Cottingham Road, Hull HU6 7RX
0482 46311
Bennett, J. Mr; *Supervisor:* Webster, D. Rev.

Personal, social, moral and religious education in primary schools. The impact and implications of the Education Reform Act 1988 and the National Curriculum

Abstract: The introduction of the National Curriculum and the implications of the Education Reform Act 1988 have serious consequences for the formal subject curriculum in primary schools, and for the informal curriculum defined to some degree as moral, personal and social education. Alongside this status of religious education in the basic curriculum, but not the National Curriculum, and the legal standing of the subject in the light of the Education Reform Act poses problems and possibilities for the subject within the curriculum as a whole. An analysis of these four interconnected areas of the curriculum will provide insights into their place and purpose in the primary school curriculum and a backdrop for an explanation of the impact of recent changes in education. The following will be considered: (a) the natures of the four subject areas, aims, objectives and philosophical implications in primary schools; (b) the implications and effects of the Education Reform Act 1988; (c) the implications and effects of the National Curriculum; and (d) the interconnective nature of the four subject areas.
Status: Individual research
Date of Research: 1989 - continuing
KEYWORDS: Education Reform Act 1988; individual development; moral education; National Curriculum; primary schools; religious education; social development

9/0368

School of Education, Cottingham Road, Hull HU6 7RX
0482 46311
Okpanachi, J. Mr; *Supervisor:* Mawer, M. Mr; Hornby, G. Mr

Integrated education for children with special educational needs in physical education programmes in Nigerian primary schools

Abstract: The 20th century has witnessed many educational innovations aimed at improving the quality of life for all children. The significant improvement among these is the education of handicapped children who for so long have been neglected and even forgotten. With several legislative acts and through the support of various philanthropic organisations, handicapped children are moving towards taking their proper place in society. To begin with, special schools were built to cater for the welfare of these children but with time it has been realised that special schools can only serve those with severe difficulties while others could be integrated into ordinary schools. Children with special educational needs have greater problems in physical education than other school subjects because of difficulties in movement. The main concern of the research is to find out how best these children can be helped to overcome their movement difficulties and how others with different problems can also be helped. Participation and enjoyment are not only goals for these children; their acceptance by others is another. Through integrated programmes all children should be able to work, play and learn together successfully.
Status: Individual research
Date of Research: 1990 - continuing
KEYWORDS: disabilities; mainstreaming; physical education; special educational needs

9/0369

School of Education, Cottingham Road, Hull HU6 7RX
0482 46311
Smith, J. Mr; *Supervisor:* McClelland, V. Prof.

The educational influence of the Methodist church in the second half of the 19th century (1850 – 1902)

Abstract: A survey of the influence of the Methodist church on education in the second half of the 19th century, with particular reference to the work of Dr J.H. Rigg. The influence of Methodist thought and pressure groups on the framing of legislation relating to education between 1870 and 1902.
Status: Individual research
Date of Research: 1991 - continuing
KEYWORDS: church and education; church state relationship; educational history; educational legislation; nonconformity; religion and education

9/0370

School of Education, Cottingham Road, Hull HU6 7RX
0482 46311
Tydeman, M. Mr; *Supervisor:* Spence, B. Dr

Preparing teachers for organisational change: an evaluation of a programme of compulsory inservice training in readiness for the re-organisation of a school system

Abstract: In September 1988 the organisation of the school system in the city of Hull was changed from transferring children between phases of education at the ages of 9 to 13 to transfer at 11 and 16. This reorganisation involved the simultaneous reallocation into different types of school of 2,000 teachers employed in the city in August 1988. The local education authority recognised that the effective implementation of this reorganisation could only be achieved with the aid of a coordinated and sustained inservice education of teachers (INSET) programme for all affected staff. The programme lasted from 1985 to 1988 and it was remarkable in the history of INSET in five main respects: (1) it involved the sustained daily release of 3% of the teaching force in the city; (2) it was a compulsory programme for all the teachers; (3) it was a systematic programme which was based upon, and supportive of, a city-wide philosophy and policy; (4) it was a centralised programme; and (5) it was planned as an integral part of the pre re-organisation preparation. Large scale INSET programmes have not been adequately researched before. This evaluation of Hull reorganiation INSET aims to provide information of value to decision makers who are involved in the planning, negotiation and delivery of large scale INSET programmes based upon a description of the programme, judgements of the extent to which it achieved its stated objectives and the teachers' views of its value to them.
Status: Individual research
Date of Research: 1989 - continuing
KEYWORDS: change; evaluation; inservice teacher education; school organisation

9/0371

School of Education, Cottingham Road, Hull HU6 7RX
0482 46311
Warner, M. Mr; *Supervisor:* Webster, D. Rev.

Developmental concepts of Christianity in a person with a mental handicap

Abstract: The majority of the research in this particular field, and to a large extent in the field of Christianity and education, has been done from a western, secular, academic approach. It is the intention of the study to 'plug this gap' by having the emphasis on Christianity and the development of thinking in terms of Faith, Jesus, God, Heaven, Hell, Holy Spirit, Salvation, death, angels, demons etc., in a person with a mental handicap. Gilliford, an authoritative work in this field, highlights the concern. He quotes in this work a study by D. Answorth (1961) 'it is likely that until 9 or 10 years of age, any story (biblical and in particular parables) will probably be interpreted literally, and that the details of the text and incidents of the story will be of paramount importance to the child'. The research hypothesises that this highlights a child's Faith; Matthew's Gospel chapter 18, v. 3 states, 'Assuredly, I say to you, unless you are converted and become as little children, you will by no means enter the Kingdom of Heaven' NKJ. This implies a simplicity of Faith uncomplicated by adult intellect and doubt. The research starts from the premise that if a child can accept love, then they can accept the love of God. No child/adult, irrespective of the degree of intellectual handicap, is unable to receive love. Secondly, if we accept that we are body, soul and spirit in 'design', then a person with a mental handicap is injured in body and soul. However, God communicates through the spirit, hence the experience they have of God is as real as my own. The problem is that they may be unable to express this experience in the physical. The intention of this research is to establish what is understood by such a person, to identify the development of thinking in this area, and propose ways in which we might teach and encourage their Beliefs and Faith.
Status: Individual research
Date of Research: 1991 - continuing
KEYWORDS: *beliefs; Christianity; mental retardation; religious education; special educational needs*

9/0372
School of Education, Cottingham Road, Hull HU6 7RX
0482 46311
Biggs, M. Mr; *Supervisor:* Brock, C. Mr
Education in the United Arab Emirates: an examination of selected themes and issues with reference to the 'small country' context
Abstract: The United Arab Emirates (UAE) is a group of seven small sheikdoms, previously known as the Trucial States whilst under British tutelage. Since their independence in 1971, and aided by the oil wealth of certain emirates, the UAE has undergone a period of unprecedented growth and modernisation. It has progressed from relative obscurity and poverty into a modern well serviced country of international recognition with one of the highest per capita incomes in the world. Education has always been assigned an important role in this process of modernisation. This research outlines educational provision in the UAE in both an historical and contemporary context. It further discusses important factors that influence the style of educational provision at all levels in both the state and private sectors such as Islam; demography, gender; manpower, pluralism; and 'small country' issues.
Status: Individual research
Date of Research: 1989-1992
KEYWORDS: *Arab states; developing countries; development of education; educational policy*

9/0373
School of Education, Cottingham Road, Hull HU6 7RX
0482 46311
Andrews, R. Mr; *Supervisor:* Protherough, R. Dr
An analysis of the structural relationships of narrative and argument in the writing of Year 8 schoolchildren
Abstract: Research has shown that children in secondary school write argument less well than narrative, and that teachers concentrate on narrative forms in their teaching at the expense of argumentative forms. This study attempts to ask the question: Is there a path from narrative to argument via the structure of the two modes, so that children in schools might be helped to write argument? Traditionally, the two modes are seen as being at opposite poles of a rhetorical model. This study questions that model, and instead offers a model in which the two modes have much more in common than has been assumed.
Status: Individual research

Date of Research: 1987-1991
KEYWORDS: *narration; persuasive discourse; secondary education; writing – composition; writing research*

9/0374
School of Education, Cottingham Road, Hull HU6 7RX
0482 46311
Pereiro, J. Rev.; *Supervisor:* McClelland, V. Prof.
Church, State and education: a study of the educational philosophy of Henry Edward Manning, 1865-92
Abstract: H.E. Manning's years as Archbishop of Westminster coincided with a renewed interest in the 'Education Question'. The civilizing value of education, the social and economic benefits which would follow from its wider extension, were themes dear to Victorian England. The interest in education and the rapid nationwide development of the educational structures soon led to an all important debate about the respective roles of the individual, the Church and the State in this area. H.E. Manning played a prominent part in the 'Education Question'. On the one hand, he made a considerable contribution to the setting up of the Catholic Educational System. He also intervened quite decisively in the above-mentioned debate through his connections with men in power and his involvement in the official commissions set up to examine present policy and to offer solutions to the educational problems of the times. The research concentrates on the philosophical principles from which he draws his suggestions to solve the problems and tensions of the age, as well as for the setting up of the educational system on a proper basis to assure its greater effectiveness.
Status: Individual research
Date of Research: 1990 - continuing
KEYWORDS: *church education relationship; educational history; educational philosophy*

9/0375
School of Education, Cottingham Road, Hull HU6 7RX
0482 46311
Waugh, D. Mr; *Supervisor:* Gorwood, B. Dr
A study of the management and implementation of educational change in primary schools
Abstract: The research involves a study of primary schools of different sizes, but is concerned principally with those with 100 pupils or fewer. Case studies will be made and a questionnaire has been used to enable comparisons to be drawn between schools of varying sizes and the effects of educational reform upon them. The following will be considered: management of curriculum change; collaboration with other schools; resources and facilities; scope for delegation of responsibility by headteachers; the role of the headteacher; professional development of teaching staff; secretarial and other ancillary assistance; and classroom and school organisation.
Status: Individual research
Date of Research: 1990 - continuing
KEYWORDS: *educational change; primary schools*

9/0376
School of Education, Cottingham Road, Hull HU6 7RX
0482 46311
Lanade, J. Mr; *Supervisor:* Spence, B. Dr
An investigation into parent teacher association activities and their effectiveness in secondary schools in Kwara State, Nigeria
Abstract: The concept of parents and teachers working together for the mutual benefit of the schools and the pupils has only recently been applied formally to the administration of secondary schools in Nigeria. This study of a sample of secondary schools in Kwara State, Nigeria, by means of a battery of questionnaires for school principals, teachers, parents and pupils, aims to develop criteria for the more effective development of the associations, and to determine the relationship, if any, between currently active parent teacher associations and the general educational welfare and development of the pupils and the schools' academic success and reputation in the community.
Status: Individual research
Date of Research: 1989-1992
KEYWORDS: *Nigeria; parent-school relationship; parent-teacher associations; secondary schools*

9/0377

School of Education, Cottingham Road, Hull HU6 7RX
0482 46311
Uzoigwe, F. Mrs; *Supervisor:* Brock, C. Mr

Education and social change with special reference to Nigerian women (particularly the Igbo)

Abstract: Nigeria embraced western style education in the early 1940s. Unlike many developing countries, Nigeria is a very big country with a population of well over a million people. There are over 300 languages in Nigeria and the main ethnic groups are: the Hausa/Fulani in the north, the Yoruba in the west and the Igbo in the east. Since the advent of western education no serious study has been undertaken with a view to determining whether or not Nigerian women and girls have had the same educational opportunities as men and boys, and also whether western style education has enhanced or jeopardised the status of women in Nigeria. In this study, therefore, a vigorous attempt is being made to assess the educational status of women – firstly in global terms, in order to understand and appreciate more realistically the Nigerian situation; bearing in mind the findings of the United Nations, which show that women constitute the greater percentage of the world's illiterates and that the rate is much higher among the women in the developing countries. In the case of Nigeria for instance, in 1984 the Federal Ministry of Education indicated that the adult illiteracy rate stood at 65%. It should, however, be borne in mind that in Nigeria a number of factors including heavy domestic chores and child marriages have, over the years, militated against the formal education of women and girls. Generally, the women in the northern part of Nigeria have lagged behind their counterparts in other parts of the country educationally, because the north is predominantly Moslem and certain demands are made on the women. For example, some women have to go into purdahs and some girls are withdrawn from educational institutions at puberty. However, it is noteworthy that any measures designed to reduce female illiteracy rates in Nigeria (there are more illiterate women than men) must take into account informal methods of education, such as adult education, especially with regard to rural women.

Status: Individual research
Date of Research: 1989 - continuing
KEYWORDS: Nigeria; women's education

9/0378

School of Education, Cottingham Road, Hull HU6 7RX
0482 46311
Gonzalez, B. Mr; *Supervisor:* Brock, C. Mr

The teaching and learning of geography in schools in Gibraltar

Abstract: Examination results over the last 10 years have given much concern in Gibraltar with regard to geography. There have been several visible trends which suggest a decrease in importance and status of the subject in the school curriculum. The research aims to identify the factors which have been responsible for this downward trend. In British schools geography is one of the more popular subjects and the results obtained compare quite favourably with the results obtained in other diciplines. Why is there such a marked contrast with the results obtained in Gibraltar? The research will concentrate on the learning of the subject and the importance of environmental stimulus or lack of it, and an in-depth analysis of the existing geographical curriculum taught in schools at all levels.

Status: Individual research
Date of Research: 1989-1992
KEYWORDS: geography education; Gibraltar

9/0379

School of Education, Cottingham Road, Hull HU6 7RX
0482 46311
Stopper, M. Mr; *Supervisor:* Spence, B. Dr

A cross-case study of actors' perceptions of key aspects of policy realization in sixth-form colleges

Abstract: The growth of the sixth-form college as a focus for post-16 provision, has created opportunities for examining what given institutions appear to have achieved from the perspective of both students and staff. Studies of the sixth-form have been related hitherto to areas such as: students' views of what the aims and objectives of sixth-form education ought to be; what they regard as the aims and objectives actually pursued by teachers; and the views of teachers as to the importance of particular aims and objectives. Little work has, however, been done on comparing the views of staff and students towards what has actually been achieved in these terms. The present research concentrates upon two key areas: (1) general education; (2) pastoral

provision, which represent dimensions of the common concern for educating the 'whole person'. It draws upon multiple data sources and methods, including documentary analysis, unstructured interview, participant observation and questionnaire and seeks to represent actors' construction of reality in selected institutions.

Status: Individual research
Date of Research: 1989-1992
KEYWORDS: general studies; pastoral care – education; pupil attitudes; sixth form colleges

9/0380

School of Education, Cottingham Road, Hull HU6 7RX
0482 46311
Douglas, F. Mr; *Supervisor:* McClelland, V. Prof.

A study of pre-school education in the Republic of Ireland with particular reference to those pre-schools which are listed by the Irish Pre-School Playgroups Association in Cork City and County

Abstract: Over the years there has been protracted discussion on the provision of preschool education for children in the Republic of Ireland. Generally this has proceeded without prior knowledge of what actually goes on within the various pre-school establishments yet with the number of working mothers ever on the increase it is of the utmost importance that information be available to parents and educators alike. This thesis is an attempt to redress this lack of understanding with respect to preschool children in Cork City and County. It is intended to: (1) obtain information; (2) answer practical questions on pre-school provision; and (3) study the effects of present preschool facilities on children. It is intended also to offer recommendations for future development. The methodology of the study is ethnographic and is based on observation in 24 pre-schools in Cork City and County. A nationwide questionnaire is used to lace these observations in context.

Status: Individual research
Date of Research: 1989-1992
KEYWORDS: Ireland; preschool education

9/0381

School of Education, Cottingham Road, Hull HU6 7RX
0482 46311
Tydeman, M. Mr; *Supervisor:* Spence, B. Dr

INSET for school reorganisation in Hull: analysis and evaluation

Abstract: In September 1988 the organisation of the school system in the city of Hull was changed from transferring children between phases of education at the ages of 9 and 13 to transfer at 11 and 16. This reorganisation involved the simultaneous reallocation into different types of school of more than 2,100 teachers employed in the city in August 1988. The LEA (local education authority) recognised that the effective implementation of this reorganisation could only be achieved with the aid of a coordinated and sustained INSET (in service education and training) programme for all affected staff. The programme lasted from 1985 to 1988 and it was instituted as a compulsory INSET programme for all teachers. Large scale INSET programmes have not been adequately researched before. This analysis and evaluation of Hull reorganisation INSET aims to provide information on four topics of value to decision makers who are involved in the planning, negotiation and delivery of large scale INSET programmes: the extent to which the programme achieved its stated objectives; its replicability; its effectiveness; its value for the teachers involved.

Status: Individual research
Date of Research: 1989 - continuing
KEYWORDS: inservice teacher education; programme evaluation; school organisation

9/0382

School of Education, Cottingham Road, Hull HU6 7RX
0482 46311
Sleap, M. Mr; *Supervisor:* Sleap, M. Mr

Effects of introducing small equipment into primary schools for use at playtimes

Abstract: The physical environment of primary schools can provide an immense resource for the all-round development of children. At present only a fraction of the full potential is utilised. The aim of the project is to evaluate the effects of introducing a range of inexpensive, readily available items of small equipment into primary schools for

use at playtimes. The sample consists of six different types of primary school. The project will last for 12 weeks during Autumn term 1991, with written evaluations and follow-up interviews conducted with children, teachers, and dinner supervisors.
Status: Sponsored project
Source of Grant: Learning Through Landscapes £2,840
Date of Research: 1991-1992
KEYWORDS: educational environment; educational equipment; educational facilities; play; playgrounds; primary schools; recreational facilities

9/0383
    School of Education, Cottingham Road, Hull HU6 7RX
    0482 46311
    Andrews, R. Mr; *Supervisor:* Protherough, R. Dr
A study of narrative and argument writing in three Beverley comprehensive schools
Abstract: The aim of the study is to explore the connection between narrative and argument, with particular reference to the teaching of the 'essay' form. The hypothesis is that narrative structures underpin those of the argument and that a clarification of this relationship might well provide a basis for helping students of all ages to write essays more readily. The study will limit itself to writing in all the primary and secondary schools in one town: Beverley in East Yorkshire, where there are three large comprehensives. Methods used will include interviews, questionnaires and, most importantly, analysis of scripts, as well as observation of teaching methods. The study will draw on the various disciplines of literature, psychology of child development, linguistics and education.
Published Material: ANDREWS, R. (1989). Narrative and argument. Buckingham: Open University Press.
Status: Sponsored project
Source of Grant: Hull University £685
Date of Research: 1987-1991
KEYWORDS: argument; criticism; narration; persuasive discourse; writing – composition; writing research; writing skills; writing teaching

9/0384
    School of Education, Cottingham Road, Hull HU6 7RX
    0482 46311
    Waugh, D. Mr; *Supervisor:* Gorwood, B. Dr
Implementing educational changes in primary schools with particular reference to small schools
Abstract: The research takes the form of questionnaire and survey work on the methods used, and problems encountered, when primary schools attempt to meet the requirements of the 1988 Education Reform Act. A survey of around 200 schools has been undertaken and a number of case studies made. The aim of the research is to determine whether school size affects the ability to implement change. It is hoped that recommendations can be made, which will draw upon examples of 'good practice', to enable schools to fulfil legal requirements in an educationally acceptable way.
Status: Individual research
Date of Research: 1990 - continuing
KEYWORDS: Education Reform Act 1988; educational change; educational legislation; educational planning; primary schools; school size; small schools

9/0385
    School of Education, Cottingham Road, Hull HU6 7RX
    0482 46311
    McCalman, L. Mr; *Supervisor:* Andrews, R. Mr
The supplementary school and its role in inner city London
Abstract: The study hopes to achieve two goals. Its primary objective is to explain the role of Afro-Caribbean Supplementary Schools in inner city London. Their funding, curriculum, opportunities for assessment and profiling, and education direction in terms of policy will be looked at. Emphasis will be placed on the curriculum of these schools, the recruitment of pupils, the quality of staff and measures for assessing the programme. The second objective of the study is to show that with the implementation of the National Curriculum, the Supplementary Schools will have to expand their roles to encompass changes in education.
Status: Individual research
Date of Research: 1988-1991
KEYWORDS: Afro-Caribbean youth; inner city; supplementary education

Institute of Child Health

9/0386
    The Wolfson Centre, Mecklenburgh Square, London
    WC1N 2AP
    071 837 7618
    Pennington, L. Ms; *Supervisor:* McConachie, H. Dr; Jolleff, N. Ms; Wisbeach, A. Ms
Putting training into practice: evaluating 'My Turn to Speak'
Abstract: The current project has two parts to it. Firstly, the development team for 'My Turn to Speak' will run study days to familiarise speech therapists, teachers and others who might wish to use the published training package. The study days will include some of the activities of the workshop, and discussion on how best to implement the approach in various schools and with children who have various levels of severity of physical disorder. The second part of the current project involves evaluating the workshops that have been run by the development team, and comparing their process and outcome with workshops run by new tutors, often past participants. One aim of the package is to facilitate the setting up of a rolling programme of training throughout a school. In addition a multiple baseline, single case study is being undertaken to look at the implementation of the team approach to communication with one child.
Published Material: PENNINGTON, L., JOLLEFF, N., McCONACHIE, H., WISBEACH, A. & PRICE, K. (1993). My Turn to Speak: A Team Approach to Augmentative Communication. London: Institute of Child Health, distributed by Winslow Press.
Status: Sponsored project
Source of Grant: The Viscount Nuffield Auxiliary Fund £11,683
Date of Research: 1993 - continuing
KEYWORDS: communication aids – for disabled; communication disorders; programme evaluation; special educational needs; workshops

9/0387
    The Wolfson Centre, Mecklenburgh Square, London
    WC1N 2AP
    071 837 7618
    Pennington, L. Ms; *Supervisor:* McConachie, H. Dr; Jolleff, N. Ms; Wisbeach, A. Ms
My Turn to Speak
Abstract: My Turn to Speak is a workshop training package designed for use in schools for children with severe physical disabilities. The package is being developed in response to concern about the fragmented approach to communication development often observed in following up children assessed at The Communication Aids Centre, The Wolfson Centre, London. The workshop aims to facilitate the development of functional communication of users of communication aids in schools by creating a collaborative approach between teachers and therapists. The workshop is being trialled in four schools. Two children in each school are targeted for observation and intervention. The children use a variety of communication aids. Evaluation of their communication development is undertaken using objective techniques. Workshops are being undertaken and results will be given on their completion.
Status: Sponsored project
Source of Grant: The Nuffield Foundation £25,492; The Baring Foundation £19,000
Date of Research: 1991-1992
KEYWORDS: communication aids – for disabled; communication disorders; physical disabiities; special educational needs; workshops

Jordanhill College of Education

9/0388
    Division of Business & Computer Education, Southbrae Drive, Jordanhill, Glasgow G13 1PP
    041 950 3000
    Munro, R. Mr; *Supervisor:* Munro, R. Mr
Cross phase continuity and progression project: transition from primary to secondary school
Abstract: The aims of this project are to: (1) improve the social and

educational links between secondary schools and their associated primary schools and with senior classes of these primary schools; (2) promote social and educational links between secondary school departments; (3) create an educational structure that will motivate pupils and enhance learning; (4) evaluate the effects of computer technology as an aid to learning; (5) ease the transition between primary and secondary schools. Various software packages and teaching materials have been produced by the pilot project which will now be tested (and refined) in a number of invited schools in Glasgow.
Status: Sponsored project
Source of Grant: Apple Computer UK; Strathclyde Regional Council
Date of Research: 1990-1992
KEYWORDS: primary to secondary transition; transitional education

9/0389
Division of Business & Computer Education, Southbrae Drive, Jordanhill, Glasgow G13 1PP
041 950 3000
Kirkwood, M. Mrs; *Supervisor:* Kirkwood, M. Mrs
Programming in Scottish Standard Grade Computing Studies
Abstract: The aim of this project is to develop and trial individualised learning materials on programming in Scottish Standard Grade Computing Studies within the framework of a staff development project.
Status: Sponsored project
Source of Grant: Jordanhill College of Education
Date of Research: 1990 - continuing
KEYWORDS: computer science education; material development

9/0390
Division of Business & Computer Education, Southbrae Drive, Jordanhill, Glasgow G13 1PP
041 950 3000
Munro, R. Mr; Ramsay, A. Mrs; *Supervisor:* Munro, R. Mr
Information technology in initial teacher training
Abstract: This is an assessment of the impact on and influence of information tehcnology in the delivery and methodology of Jordanhill College courses in initial teacher training and the formulation and refinement of strategies to exploit the education potential and enhance the educational effectiveness of this resource.
Status: Sponsored project
Source of Grant: Jordanhill College of Education £225
Date of Research: 1990-1991
KEYWORDS: computer uses in education; information technology; preservice teacher education

9/0391
Division of Business & Computer Education, Southbrae Drive, Glasgow G13 1PP
041 950 3000
Winch, J. Mr; *Supervisor:* Winch, J. Mr
Information technology development programme for teachers
Abstract: This is a programme for staff development in schools dealing with awareness and perspectives on applying information technology (IT) in classrooms; managerial skills and classroom strategies in IT; and professional skills in the methodology of IT. Various booklets and education materials will be produced.
Status: Sponsored project
Source of Grant: Training, Enterprise and Education Directorate £46,000
Date of Research: 1989-1992
KEYWORDS: computer uses in education; information technology; staff development

9/0392
Division of Business & Computer Education, Southbrae Drive, Jordanhill, Glasgow G13 1PP
041 950 3000
Northern College of Education, Computer Education Department, Dundee Campus, Gardyne Road, Dundee DD5 1NY
0382 453433
Munro, R. Mr; Lamont, M. Mrs; *Supervisor:* Munro, R. Mr
SPRITE (Supporting and Promoting Information Technology in Education)

Abstract: The aim of this project is to improve, enhance and encourage the use of information technology (IT) by college staff (throughout Scotland) and assist the permeation of IT use in college courses.
Status: Sponsored project
Source of Grant: Jordanhill College of Education; Northern College; Scottish Office Education Department
Date of Research: 1991 - continuing
KEYWORDS: colleges; computer uses in education; information technology

9/0393
Division of Community Education, Southbrae Drive, Glasgow G13 1PP
041 950 3000
Rowlands, C. Mr; *Supervisor:* Rowlands, C. Mr
Community education graduates at Jordanhill – survey of appointments
Abstract: This began out of an interest to acquire an accurate picture of the employment of past students especially when related to the present national employment figures. Similar research has been completed each year since 1981. Within Scotland as a whole and especially within the colleges of education, much concern has been expressed at the numbers of newly qualified teachers who have been unable to obtain employment in their chosen profession. Within the Jordanhill Division of Community Education it has always been assumed that ex-students have been more fortunate in this respect. In an effort to gain a realistic assessment of the situation, this research was undertaken. The purpose of the research was: (1) to investigate the employment situation of youth and community work students who qualified from June 1981 onwards from Jordanhill; (2) to investigate the jobs obtained by students according to certain criteria, i.e. sex, length of course followed; (3) to investigate the degree of difficulty experienced by students in gaining employment; and (4) to investigate the types of employment accepted.
Status: Sponsored project
Source of Grant: Jordanhil College – Community Education Sub-Committee
Date of Research: 1991-1992
KEYWORDS: graduate employment; graduate surveys

9/0394
Division of Community Education, Southbrae Drive, Glasgow G13 1PP
041 950 3000
McMellin, I. Mr; *Supervisor:* McMellin, I. Mr
The benefit from the Focus Learning Centre
Abstract: The study aims to identify the benefits adult participants perceive they have gained by undertaking educational opportunities at the Focus Community Learning Centre, by reflecting back at least one year since initial participation. Interviews will be carried out and analysis of these undertaken.
Status: Sponsored project
Source of Grant: Jordanhill College; Ayr Division, Strathclyde Local Education Authority £575
Date of Research: 1990-1992
KEYWORDS: adult education; community education; outcomes of education

9/0395
Division of Education and Psychology, Southbrae Drive, Jordanhill, Glasgow G13 1PP
041 950 3000
MacBeath, J. Dr; McAndrew, L. Ms; *Supervisor:* MacBeath, J. Dr
To evaluate the response of teacher, parents and pupils to new forms of reporting introduced in the 5-14 development programme
Abstract: This project will examine the usefulness of new styles of reporting to parents, their implication for teachers and the degree to which pupils find them helpful and formative.
Status: Sponsored project
Source of Grant: Scottish Office Education Department £111,000
Date of Research: 1991 - continuing
KEYWORDS: assessment; parent-pupil relationship; profiles; school reports

9/0396

Division of Education and Psychology, Southbrae Drive, Jordanhill, Glasgow G13 1PP
041 950 3000
Peck, B. Mr; *Supervisor:* Peck, B. Mr

Management and organisation of teaching 'The European Dimension' in schools (International network with representatives from The Netherlands, Belgium, Germany, Greece and Denmark)
Abstract: This is a comparative study of the introduction and teaching of 'The European Dimension' in schools, with particular focus upon management issues and organisation. The outcome will be the publication of a book on the experiences of the six participating countries.
Status: Sponsored project
Source of Grant: European Community; Jordanhill College £6,000
Date of Research: 1990-1992
KEYWORDS: comparative education; European studies

9/0397

Division of Education and Psychology, Southbrae Drive, Glasgow G13 1PP
041 950 3000
MacBeath, J. Dr; Thompson, W. Mr; *Supervisor:* MacBeath, J. Dr; Thompson, W. Mr

Study of School Boards in Scotland
Abstract: The aim of this project is to evaluate the work of School Boards in Scotland.
Status: Sponsored project
Source of Grant: Scottish Office Education Department £60,000
Date of Research: 1990-1992
KEYWORDS: school boards – Scotland; school governing bodies

9/0398

Division of Education and Psychology, Southbrae Drive, Glasgow G13 1PP
041 950 3000
MacBeath, J. Dr; Weir, A. Mr; *Supervisor:* MacBeath, J. Dr

OECD (Organisation for Economic Co-operation and Development) education indicators on attitudes and expectations
Abstract: The aims of this project are to: (1) examine surveys and polls of attitudes to and expectations of schooling in Britain with a view to identifying key performance indicators of international relevance; and (2) produce a digest and bibliography of the research based on parents', pupils' and teachers' expectations of schools.
Status: Sponsored project
Source of Grant: Scottish Office Education Department £11,400
Date of Research: 1990-1992
KEYWORDS: attitude measures; educational attitudes; educational objectives; performance indicators; school effectiveness

9/0399

Division of Education and Psychology, Southbrae Drive, Glasgow G13 1PP
041 950 3000
Bryce, T. Dr; Stark, R. Mrs; Walker, A. Dr; Dalziel, H. Mrs; *Supervisor:* Bryce, T. Dr; Stark, R. Mrs

Monitoring of achievement in science: second round
Abstract: The aim of this project was to assess the achievement of Scottish pupils at the P4, P7 and S2 stages in certain aspects of science. The approach and methodology was based on that of the monitoring exercises undertaken at Jordanhill College between 1985-1988. The exercise involved minor revision of the assessment framework: design and pilot testing of new and amended assessment materials; a testing programme carried out in summer 1990, marking and analysis of completed tests; writing a project report for the Scottish Office Education Department and draft dissemination materials for teachers. Advice and assistance on aspects of test design and data analysis was provided by the Assessment of Achievement Programme Central Support Unit. Account was taken of the 5-14 curriculum and assessment development programme.
Published Material: AAP Science (based on the findings of the 1987 survey) (1990). Edinburgh: HMSO.; AAP Feedback. Science P4 and P7 (1990). SED/AAP.; AAP Feedback. Science P7 and S2 (1990). SED/AAP.; STARK, R., BRYCE, T.G.K., DALZIEL, H. & WALKER, A. (1991). 'Monitoring of Achievement in Science' – Report of AAP Science (Second Round, 1990) submitted to SOED, September.

Status: Sponsored project
Source of Grant: Scottish Office Education Department £141,000
Date of Research: 1989-1991
KEYWORDS: achievement tests; assessment; science education

9/0400

Division of Education and Psychology, Southbrae Drive, Glasgow G13 1PP
041 950 3000
Heriot-Watt University, Moray House Institute of Education, Holyrood Road, Edinburgh EH8 8AQ
031 556 8455
Craigie College of Education, Beech Grove, Ayr KA8 0SR
0292 260321
MacBeath, J. Dr; Thompson, W. Mr; Arrowsmith, J. Mrs; Forbes, D. Mr; *Supervisor:* MacBeath, J. Dr; Thompson, W. Mr

School self-evaluation
Abstract: The aim of this project is to develop materials which can be used to gather parent, pupil and teacher perspectives on their own school.
Status: Sponsored project
Source of Grant: Scottish Office Education Department £5,592
Date of Research: 1990-1992
KEYWORDS: material development; parent attitudes; pupil attitudes; school effectiveness; self evaluation – groups; teacher attitudes

9/0401

Division of Inservice Training, Southbrae Drive, Jordanhill, Glasgow G13 1PP
041 950 3000
Robertson, P. Mrs; McGinley, L. Mrs; MacDonald, D. Mr; *Supervisor:* Smith, I. Mr; Rand, J. Mr

The training the trainers approach to staff development project
Abstract: The 'trainer of trainers' approach has been widely used in educational innovation in Scotland, however, there has been no formal evaluation of this approach. In response to this the Scottish Office Education Department has funded an evaluative study to ascertain the effectiveness of the model within education. The aim of the project is to identify, and further test by action research, a set of factors which contribute to the effective management and operation of 'training of trainers' staff development strategies. The project is designed in three stages. The initial stage being a detailed literature survey, a survey of recent and current course provision, research into the pilot School Board Initiative, intensive study of several cases, the forming of hypotheses to be used in consultancy and action research with School Board Initiatives. The second stage consists of consultancy involvement with three major courses and post-course evaluations. Finally there will be post-course follow-ups with participants and others in client relationships with course providers. Outcomes of the project will include papers designed for education personnel who plan or present staff development programmes, a project bulletin – a Checklist for Training of Trainers Programmes, and a final report for the Scottish Office Education Department.
Status: Sponsored project
Source of Grant: Scottish Office Education Department £62,691
Date of Research: 1988-1991
KEYWORDS: inservice education; staff development; trainers; training methods

9/0402

Division of Inservice Training, Southbrae Drive, Glasgow G13 1PP
041 950 3000
McCall, C. Dr; Ellis, S. Mrs; Grant, M. Mrs; Hughes, A. Mrs; *Supervisor:* McCall, C. Dr

Philosophical inquiry in values education
Abstract: This project aims to disseminate the method of philosophical inquiry in values education and to use this in staff development in values education.
Status: Sponsored project
Source of Grant: Gordon Cook Foundation £40,000
Date of Research: 1991 - continuing
KEYWORDS: moral education; philosophy; values education

9/0403

Division of Inservice Training, Southbrae Drive, Glasgow
G13 1PP
041 950 3000
Semple, S. Mrs; *Supervisor:* Semple, S. Mrs

Scottish Young People's Survey – transition issues

Abstract: The purpose of this project was to create briefing papers on young people's views on further and higher education, manufacturing industry and reasons for leaving school. The study used data already existing in the Scottish Young People's Survey that had not been previously assessed. The six briefing papers on transition issues created are: (1) Further Education: Scottish School Leavers' Views; (2) Higher Education: Scottish School Leavers' Views; (3) Returning to School: Scottish School Leavers' Views; (4) Making Decisions: Scottish School Leavers' Views; (5) Parents and Young People: Some Perceptions of Parental Influence; and (6) Manufacturing Industry: Scottish School Leavers' Views.

Status: Sponsored project
Source of Grant: BP Exploration plc £3,000
Date of Research: 1990-1991
KEYWORDS: *attitudes; further education; higher education; industry; opinions; school leavers; school to work transition; surveys*

9/0404

Division of Inservice Training, Southbrae Drive, Glasgow
G13 1PP
041 950 3000
Rand, J. Mr; *Supervisor:* Rand, J. Mr

TVEI local evaluation

Abstract: The college has been responsible for the local evaluation of former Technical and Vocational Education Initiative (TVEI) pilot projects. The format and nature of the research tasks have varied from project to project, the primary focus has been to help projects identify development needs.

Status: Sponsored project
Source of Grant: Individual Scottish local authorities; per annum approx £ 240,0000
Date of Research: 1986-1992
KEYWORDS: *programme evaluation; technical education; vocational education*

9/0405

Division of Inservice Training, Southbrae Drive, Glasgow
G13 1PP
041 950 3000
Semple, S. Mrs; *Supervisor:* Semple, S. Mrs

BP Exploration Fellowship in vocational education and guidance

Abstract: The overall aim of this project is to improve the preparation young people receive for their transition from school to employment and further and higher education. Specifically it aims to: devise and pilot careers education materials for pupils and their parents; develop careers education and information videos where needed; provide inservice support to teachers using careers education and involved in vocational guidance and education/industry links; provide inservice support to careers service staff and others working in the field; influence the content of initial teacher training to ensure student teachers are briefed on vocational education and guidance; and contribute to staff development in the college on vocational education and guidance. The outcome of the project will be the production of six briefing papers on young people's views of transition issues; a video and teaching pack 'Going to College' on non-advanced further education; a careers education resource base; materials for inservice courses in: (a) careers education; (b) evaluating careers interviews; (c) work related curriculum; (d) influencing the curriculum; and materials for preservice courses in careers and the work-related curriculum.

Status: Sponsored project
Source of Grant: BP Exploration plc £40,000
Date of Research: 1990-1992
KEYWORDS: *career awareness; educational guidance; school leavers; school to work transition; transitional education; vocational guidance*

9/0406

Division of Language and Literature, Southbrae Drive,
Glasgow G13 1PP
041 950 3000

Williams, W. Mr; *Supervisor:* Williams, W. Mr

Scottish Standard Grade Beginners Latin Course: design of a course book

Abstract: The aim of this project is to design a beginners Latin course book based on the elements of the Scottish Standard Grade.

Status: Sponsored project
Source of Grant: Jordanhill College £500
Date of Research: 1988 - continuing
KEYWORDS: *educational materials; Latin; textbook preparation*

9/0407

Division of Language and Literature, Southbrae Drive,
Glasgow G13 1PP
041 950 3000
McGonigal, J. Dr; Lawson, J. Mr; Lovett, R. Mr; *Supervisor:* McGonigal, J. Dr

Spoken English (Scottish Standard Grade) for pupils with language difficulties

Abstract: This project will develop and test in field trials teaching and assessment materials for pupils with specific language difficulties who are to follow a proposed Scottish Standard Grade Course in Spoken English.

Status: Sponsored project
Source of Grant: Scottish Office Education Department £5,227.40
Date of Research: 1991-1991
KEYWORDS: *English; language handicaps; material development*

9/0408

Division of Mathematics, Southbrae Drive, Glasgow
G13 1PP
041 950 3000
Meechan, R. Mr; Robertson, I. Mrs; Clarke, D. Mr;
Supervisor: Meechan, R. Mr; Robertson, I. Mrs

Assessment of Achievement Programme (AAP) Mathematics: third round Monitoring Project

Abstract: The aim of this project is to assess achievement in various aspects of mathematics at the P4, P7 and S2 stages of Scottish schools, providing a description of what pupils know and can do at each stage and allowing valid comparisons to be made between stages and with results of the Scottish Office Education Department (SOED) Mathematics survey (1988). The exercise involves: a reappraisal of the assessment framework to take account of the 5-14 Development Programme and current curriculum; the development of new test items, both written and practical; a main programme of assessment in May/June 1991; marking completed tests; defining analyses to be undertaken; a project report for SOED with a summary for use in disseminating the results. Advice and assistance has been provided by the Assessment of Achievement Programme (AAP) Central Support Unit of the Scottish Council for Research in Education (SCRE) on aspects of test design, carrying out of data preparation and analysis, liaison with schools and distribution and collection of written tests.

Status: Sponsored project
Source of Grant: Scottish Office Education Department £99,000
Date of Research: 1990-1992
KEYWORDS: *achievement tests; assessment; mathematics education*

9/0409

Division of PE, Sport and Outdoor Education, Southbrae
Drive, Glasgow G13 1PP
041 950 3000
Sharp, R. Dr; *Supervisor:* Sharp, R. Dr

Computing in physical education

Abstract: This project aims to identify the computing requirements of physical education (PE) teachers in Scotland with regard to the AppleMac computer.

Status: Sponsored project
Source of Grant: Jordanhill College £580
Date of Research: 1991-1992
KEYWORDS: *computer uses in education; physical education teachers; Scotland*

9/0410

Division of PE, Sport and Outdoor Education, Southbrae
Drive, Glasgow G13 1PP
041 950 3000

Walden, N. Mr; *Supervisor:* Walden, N. Mr
Students' environmental knowledge and attitude
Abstract: The aim of this project is to examine the relationships between environmental knowledge and environmental attitude among student teachers in Jordanhill College.
Status: Sponsored project
Source of Grant: Jordanhill College £265
Date of Research: 1991-1991
KEYWORDS: conservation – environment; environmental education; student teacher attitudes

9/0411
Division of PE, Sport and Outdoor Education, Southbrae Drive, Glasgow G13 1PP
041 950 3000
McWilliam, A. Dr; *Supervisor:* McWilliam, A. Dr
The demands for a teaching qualification in Outdoor Education
Abstract: A survey of headteachers of Scottish schools will be carried out to determine their attitudes towards the demands for a teaching qualification in Outdoor Education.
Status: Sponsored project
Source of Grant: Jordanhill College £150
Date of Research: 1991-1992
KEYWORDS: outdoor education; teacher education; teacher qualifications

9/0412
Division of Primary Education, Southbrae Drive, Jordanhill, Glasgow G13 1PP
041 950 3000
Twiddle, B. Mr; MacDonald, D. Mr; Semple, S. Mrs; Cantlay, D. Mr; *Supervisor:* Twiddle, B. Mr
Enterprise Education: Scottish Enterprise funded package writing
Abstract: This project aims to prepare two packages: (1) to examine the previous 'industrial' experience of students and to prepare a self study package to enable them to make best use of their experiences; (2) to examine the scope for Enterprise Education in 5-14.
Status: Sponsored project
Source of Grant: Scottish Enterprise £15,000
Date of Research: 1991-1992
KEYWORDS: educational materials; enterprise education; work education relationship

9/0413
Division of Primary Education, Southbrae Drive, Jordanhill, Glasgow G13 1PP
041 950 3000
Andrews, J. Mrs
Three primary school boards: the first years
Abstract: This project will use three case studies to establish how a school and its community perceive: (a) their role in the new school board, and its functions; (b) their feelings of preparedness for participation in the boards; and (c) how these perceptions alter over the first year of school boards.
Status: Sponsored project
Source of Grant: Jordanhill College of Education £335
Date of Research: 1989-1991
KEYWORDS: primary schools; school boards – Scotland; school-community relationship; school governing bodies

9/0414
Division of Primary Education, Southbrae Drive, Glasgow G13 1PP
041 950 3000
Ellis, S. Mrs; *Supervisor:* Ellis, S. Mrs
Primary science: children planning investigations
Abstract: The aims of this project are to look at teaching strategies which help children plan scientific investigations and how these relate to their scientific knowledge and understanding.
Status: Sponsored project
Source of Grant: Jordanhill College £100
Date of Research: 1990-1991
KEYWORDS: primary education; science education; science experiments

9/0415
Division of Primary Education, Southbrae Drive, Glasgow G13 1PP
041 950 3000
Graham, I. Miss; *Supervisor:* Graham, I. Miss
The use of concepts as a planning framework for environmental studies
Abstract: This project will show how a concept framework can be used in the selection of knowledge, skills and attitudes to be developed in an environmental study in the primary classroom.
Status: Sponsored project
Source of Grant: Jordanhill College £100
Date of Research: 1991-1991
KEYWORDS: concept teaching; environmental education

9/0416
Division of Science, Southbrae Drive, Glasgow G13 1PP
041 950 3000
Stark, R. Mrs; *Supervisor:* Stark, R. Mrs
Monitoring of achievement in science
Abstract: This is a review of the Assessment of Achievement Programme (AAP) science survey linking it with the 5-14 Development Programme.
Status: Sponsored project
Source of Grant: Scottish Office Education Department £15,500
Date of Research: 1991-1992
KEYWORDS: achievement; assessment; science education

9/0417
Division of Secondary and Curricular Studies, Southbrae Drive, Glasgow G13 1PP
041 950 3000
Mair, J. Mr; Weir, A. Mr; *Supervisor:* Weir, A. Mr
Sponsorship in Scottish colleges of further and higher education
Abstract: The aim of this project is to investigate the entrepreneurial activities of colleges with particular reference to their success in attracting commercial sponsorship. In particular it will examine: (1) how funding is attracted; (2) what are the objectives of customers and contractors and what benefits they perceive; (3) what particular or distinctive activities result and what are the consequences of these for the contractor's institutional profile; and (4) what internal structures characterise contractors who are successful in attracting sponsorship.
Published Material: MAIR, J.D. (1991). Colleges and sponsorship. Glasgow: Jordanhill College.
Status: Sponsored project
Source of Grant: Scottish Office Education Department £5,000
Date of Research: 1990-1991
KEYWORDS: corporate support; educational finance; industry-further education relationship; industry-higher education relationship; sponsorship

9/0418
Division of Secondary and Curricular Studies, Southbrae Drive, Glasgow G13 1PP
041 950 3000
Weir, A. Mr; *Supervisor:* Weir, A. Mr
School self-evaluation: personnel training
Abstract: The aim of this project is to train and evaluate the senior personnel of schools in undertaking school self-evaluations.
Status: Sponsored project
Source of Grant: Grampian, Highland, Tayside Regions £10,000
Date of Research: 1991-1992
KEYWORDS: school effectiveness; self evaluation – groups; staff development

9/0419
Division of Social Studies, Southbrae Drive, Jordanhill, Glasgow G13 1PP
041 950 3000
Munro, R. Mr; Hillis, P. Dr; *Supervisor:* Hillis, P. Dr
Computers in teaching history
Abstract: The aims of the project are: (1) to provide a range of curricular material to help primary and secondary schools use census databases; (2) and to compile a rateable value database for parts of Glasgow in 1881 for use with Scottish Vocational Education Council (SCOTVEC) modules.

Status: Sponsored project
Source of Grant: Scottish Office Education Department £6,500
Date of Research: 1991-1992
KEYWORDS: computer uses in education; databases; history

9/0420
Division of Social Work, Southbrae Drive, Jordanhill,
Glasgow G13 1PP
041 950 3000
Cameron, K. Mrs
Law improvement project
Abstract: The aim of this project is to improve the standards of law
teaching on social work courses throughout Britain.
Status: Sponsored project
Source of Grant: Central Council for Education and Training in
Social Work £3,500
Date of Research: 1990-1992
KEYWORDS: law related education; social work studies

9/0421
Division of Social Work, Southbrae Drive, Glasgow G13 1PP
041 950 3000
McCullough, D. Mr; *Supervisor:* McCullough, D. Mr
**Central Regional Council (Scotland) Youth Strategy – an
evaluative study of school liaison groups**
Abstract: The study aims to establish the extent to which school
liaison groups are effective in helping to maintain children in their
own communities, and in encouraging inter-agency cooperation for
the assessment of children's needs and the provision of appropriate
resources.
Published Material: McCULLOUGH, D.R. (1991). Developing a
Strategy – a review of school liaison groups in Central Region.
Central Regional Council, December.
Status: Sponsored project
Source of Grant: Central Regional Council; Jordanhill College
Date of Research: 1990-1991
*KEYWORDS: community involvement; groups; school-community
relationship*

9/0422
Division of Special Educational Needs, Southbrae Drive,
Jordanhill, Glasgow G13 1PP
041 950 3000
Hewitt, C. Mrs; Hamill, P. Mr; Robertson, P. Mrs;
Supervisor: Hewitt, C. Mrs
Below average attainment project
Abstract: This project aims to describe and evaluate the variety of
services designed to support the progress of pupils with learning
difficulties and social disadvantage.
Status: Sponsored project
Source of Grant: Scottish Office Education Department £69,638
Date of Research: 1991 - continuing
*KEYWORDS: disadvantaged; moderate learning difficulties; special
educational needs; support services*

9/0423
Division of Speech Therapy, Southbrae Drive, Glasgow
G13 1PP
041 950 3000
MacKenzie, C. Ms; *Supervisor:* MacKenzie, C. Ms
Survey of aphasia service provision
Abstract: This project aims to establish the nature and variation of
aphasia service provision in the United Kingdom.
Published Material: MACKENZIE, C. (1991). 'Speech therapy ser-
vices to aphasic adults in the United Kingdom', Paper presented at
British Aphasiology Society Conference, September, Sheffield.;
MACKENZIE, C. (1991). 'Pattern of aphasia services in the United
Kingdom, with special reference to Scotland', Paper presented to
joint study day of Care of the Elderly Special Interest Group/British
Aphasiology Society, December, Glasgow.
Status: Sponsored project
Source of Grant: Jordanhill College
Date of Research: 1990-1991
*KEYWORDS: aphasia; language handicaps; learning disabilities;
services; special educational needs*

9/0424
Division of Speech Therapy, Southbrae Drive, Glasgow
G13 1PP
041 950 3000
McCartney, E. Miss; *Supervisor:* McCartney, E. Miss
Newly qualified entrants to the speech therapy profession
Abstract: The aims of this project are to: (1) investigate the experi-
ences of newly-qualified graduates entering speech therapy services
in Great Britain; (2) implement a package of supportive measures for
Grade A therapists in conjunction with one Area Health Board
(Ayrshire and Arran, the 'Good Practice' Area); and (3) relate the
performance (management objectives) and morale (personal objec-
tives) of Grade A therapists to their first post experiences.
Status: Sponsored project
Source of Grant: Scottish Office Home and Health Department;
Jordanhill College £5,000
Date of Research: 1990-1991
KEYWORDS: graduate employment; speech therapy; therapists

9/0425
Scottish Centre for Children with Motor Impairment,
Southbrae Drive, Jordanhill, Glasgow G13 1PP
041 950 3000
MacKay, G. Dr; McCartney, E. Miss; Cheseldine, S. Dr;
McCool, S. Miss; *Supervisor:* MacKay, G. Dr
Scottish Centre for Children With Motor Impairment
Abstract: This project will undertake evaluation of children's progress,
development of curriculum, implementation of policy, and costs/benefits
of the Scottish Centre for Children with Motor Impairment.
Status: Sponsored project
Source of Grant: Scottish Office Education Department £170,000
Date of Research: 1991 - continuing
*KEYWORDS: motor development; special educational needs; spe-
cial schools*

9/0426
Scottish School for Further Education, Southbrae Drive,
Glasgow G13 1PP
041 950 3000
Robertson, I. Mr; Gordon, A. Mr; Blake, J. Mrs; *Supervisor:*
Robertson, I. Mr
System for accessing modular information project
Abstract: The aims of the project are to: (1) develop, maintain, and
market a computerised information system for Scottish vocational
qualifications; and (2) develop an enhanced system for Youth Train-
ing (YT) and Employment Training (ET) provision.
Status: Sponsored project
Source of Grant: Training, Enterprise and Education Directorate;
Scottish Office Education Department £65,000
Date of Research: 1990-1991
*KEYWORDS: computer system design; information systems; quali-
fications; vocational education; youth opportunities*

9/0427
Scottish School of Further Education, Southbrae Drive,
Jordanhill, Glasgow G13 1PP
041 950 3000
Soden, R. Dr; Holmes, S. Mrs; Dumbleton, P. Mr;
Supervisor: Soden, R. Dr
**Improving the problem solving skills of learners in vocational
programmes**
Abstract: This project aims to illuminate the staff development
required to enable further education lecturers to provide a 'thinking
curriculum' in catering, hairdressing, text processing and electrical
circuit work.
Status: Sponsored project
Source of Grant: Scottish Office Education Department; Training,
Enterprise & Education Directorate £52,000
Date of Research: 1991-1992
*KEYWORDS: curriculum development; problem solving; staff devel-
opment; thinking skills; vocational education*

9/0428
Scottish School of Further Education, Southbrae Drive,
Glasgow G13 1PP
041 950 3000

Niven, S. Mr; McQueenie, E. Mrs; Finlay, I. Mr; *Supervisor:*
Niven, S. Mr
Management issues in nursing/midwifery education
Abstract: The aim of this project is to promote active research into
management issues in nursing/midwifery education for the directors
of nursing/midwifery education.
Status: Sponsored project
Source of Grant: Jordanhill College; Scottish Office Home and
Health Department £2,500
Date of Research: 1991-1992
KEYWORDS: management studies; nurse education

9/0429
The Library, Southbrae Drive, Glasgow G13 1PP
041 950 3000
McLelland, D. Mrs; Millar, K. Miss; Harrison, M. Mrs;
Supervisor: McLelland, D. Mrs
Bibliography of Scottish education 1970-1990
Abstract: The aim of this project is to collect and list on a computer
database all material on Scottish education published or issued be-
tween 1970 and 1990.
Status: Sponsored project
Source of Grant: Leverhulme Trust £30,700
Date of Research: 1991-1992
KEYWORDS: data collection; educational research; Scotland

Keele University

9/0430
Department of Education, Keele, Staffordshire ST5 5BG
0782 621111
Wakelin, M. Mrs; *Supervisor:* Brighouse, T. Prof.;
Wringe, C. Dr
**The use of performance indicators in the evaluation of
educational institutions**
Abstract: Current use of performance indicators is to be surveyed and
evaluated in relation to currently proposed educational aims. Their
validity as a measure of educational effectiveness and their affect on
the performance of teachers and institutions will be assessed.
Status: Individual research
Date of Research: 1989-1992
*KEYWORDS: educational objectives; institutional evaluation; or-
ganisational effectiveness; performance indicators*

9/0431
Department of Education, Keele, Staffordshire ST5 5BG
0782 621111
Bale, J. Mr
**International recruiting of student-athletes by American
universities**
Abstract: The project seeks to identify the extent of recruitment of
foreign student-athletes by US universities and the experience of such
recruits while resident in the United States of America.
Published Material: BALE, J.R. (1988). 'The international recruiting
game: foreign student athletes in American universities'. In: BONDI,
E. & MATTHEWS, H. (Eds). Educational society: social, political
and geographical perspectives. London: Routledge.; BALE, J.R.
(1987). 'Alien student-athletes in American higher education; loca-
tional decision-making and sojourn abroad', Physical Education
Review, Vol 10, No 2, pp.81-93.; BALE, J.R. (1988). 'Foreign
students in NCAA Division 1 universities; an empirical study of six
men's sports', Journal of Comparative Physical Education and Sport,
Vol 10, No 1, pp.21-31.; BALE, J.R. (1991). The Brawn Drain:
foreign student-athletes in American universities. Urbana: University
of Illinois Press.
Status: Individual research
Date of Research: 1985-1991
*KEYWORDS: athletes; overseas students; selective admission; stu-
dent recruitment; United States of America; universities*

9/0432
Department of Education, Keele, Staffordshire ST5 5BG
0782 621111

Sang, J. Mr; *Supervisor:* Bale, J. Mr
School, sport and society in Kenya
Abstract: This project seeks to explore the development of athletics
in Kenya by adopting a world systems approach. The role of educational organisations both inside Kenya and abroad will be fully
evaluated but it is recognised that other agencies in a very wide range
of cultures and nations cannot be ignored in explaining the emergence
of sport in a 'developing' nation.
Status: Individual research
Date of Research: 1990 - continuing
KEYWORDS: Kenya; sports

9/0433
Department of Education, Keele, Staffordshire ST5 5BG
0782 621111
Corden, R. Mr; *Supervisor:* Evans, T. Mrs
**An investigation of the collaborative interaction and talk of
children in relation to their perception of teacher audience,
task purpose and learning context**
Abstract: The study is of task related, or work focused discourse of
small groups of 12 to 13 year old pupils working within the naturalistic settings of the classroom. The research is concerned with the
way in which children engage in a variety of tasks using spoken
language to interact and collaborate in the learning process when the
teacher is not in a central, authoritative position (physically), and
when the discussion has the 'potential' to be negotiable and not
dominated by one omnipotent figure. The study will attempt to
identify the way in which pupils engage in discussion in relation to
their perception of teacher audience and the subsequent perceptions
of contextual learning conditions and task purpose. The study adopts
an ethnographic, or ethnomethodological approach and makes extensive use of audio and video recordings. The use of retrospective
analysis and triangulation will be adopted in order to try and encompass the 'whole' group interaction and to be sensitively aware of
contextual factors and particularly, the way in which the pupils'
perceptions of 'audience' (as projected by the teacher) affects the
interactional process and use of language in the learning process.
Status: Individual research
Date of Research: 1987-1991
*KEYWORDS: classroom communication; discussion – teaching;
group work; speech communication; teacher pupil relationship;
technique*

9/0434
Department of Education, Keele, Staffordshire ST5 5BG
0782 621111
Burgess, R. Mr; *Supervisor:* Gleeson, D. Prof.
**Research and evaulation of Cheshire LEA's Technical and
Vocational Education Initiative (TVEI), Inservice Education of
Teachers (INSET) & Education Support Grant (ESG)
programmes**
Abstract: The aim is to provide an up-to-date case study analysis of
a small group of schools (secondary, primary and special) and a
further education institution, in order to evaluate the impact of
Technical and Vocational Education Initiative (TVEI), Inservice
Education of Teachers (INSET) and Education Support Grant (ESG)
initiatives on staff development and teaching and learning processes.
Status: Sponsored project
Source of Grant: Cheshire Local Education Authority £35,000
Date of Research: 1989-1991
*KEYWORDS: education support grants; inservice teacher education;
programme evaluation; technical education; vocational education*

9/0435
Department of Education, Keele, Staffordshire ST5 5BG
0782 621111
Gough, G. Dr; Glover, D. Mr; Gleeson, D. Prof.; *Supervisor:*
Gleeson, D. Prof.; Brighouse, T. Prof.
**Technical and Vocational Education in Initial Teacher
Training**
Abstract: An action oriented study of the Technical and Vocational
Education Initiative (TVEI) in Initial Teacher (IT) education which
adopts a qualitative approach looking at management of change and
developmental perspectives.
Published Material: GLEESON, D. (1989). The Paradox of Training.
Buckingham: Open University Press.; GLEESON, D. (1991). Train-
ing and its Alternatives. Buckingham: Open University Press.;

GLEESON, D. & BRIGHOUSE, T.R.P. 'How to manage change in colleges', Polytechnics & Colleges: an illustrative study. London: Training, Enterprise Education Directorate.
Status: Sponsored project
Source of Grant: Training, Enterprise & Education Directorate £30,000
Date of Research: 1991 - continuing
KEYWORDS: change; preservice teacher education; technical education; vocational education

9/0436
Department of Education, Keele, Staffordshire ST5 5BG
0782 621111
Russell, V. Mr; Gleeson, D. Prof.; *Supervisor:* Gleeson, D. Prof.
Evaluation of a local education inspectorate
Abstract: This project involves an investigation of the changing role of the inspectorate in one local education authority using interview and observation approaches.
Status: Sponsored project
Source of Grant: Hereford & Worcester Local Education Authority
Date of Research: 1989 - continuing
KEYWORDS: inspection; inspectors – of schools; local education authorities

9/0437
Department of Education, Keele, Staffordshire ST5 5BG
0782 621111
Russell, V. Mr; Gleeson, D. Prof.; *Supervisor:* Gleeson, D. Prof.
Evaluation of Technical & Vocational Education Initiative developments
Abstract: This is an evaluation of the Technical & Vocational Education Initiative (TVEI) in a local education authority, with the specific purpose of initiating and supporting practitioner research.
Status: Sponsored project
Source of Grant: Hereford & Worcester Local Education Authority
Date of Research: 1989 - continuing
KEYWORDS: technical education; vocational education

9/0438
Department of Education, Keele, Staffordshire ST5 5BG
0782 621111
McLean, M. Mrs; Siggers, T. Mr; *Supervisor:* Gleeson, D. Prof.
Technical and Vocational Education Initiative (TVEI) evaluation project
Abstract: The aim of the study is to evaluate the county-wide extension of Technical and Vocational Education Initiative (TVEI) in Staffordshire and to provide independent and impartial assessment of a cluster based strategy, how it affects school and college curriculum, organization, community, links with employers and other support services across the county. The research adopts an action oriented approach to evaluation, involving formative methods of reporting.
Status: Sponsored project
Source of Grant: Training, Enterprise and Education Directorate; Staffordshire LEA
Date of Research: 1988 - continuing
KEYWORDS: technical education; vocational education

9/0439
Department of Education, Keele, Staffordshire ST5 5BG
0782 621111
Powell, G. Mr
The order of knowledge
Abstract: The study will offer a radical re-assessment of the development of education, especially since the Renaissance. It will involve a new interpretation of the significance of Plato's analysis of the classical conceptual system which has dominated our education.
Status: Individual research
Date of Research: 1988 - continuing
KEYWORDS: educational history; educational theories; philosophy

9/0440
Department of Education, Keele, Staffordshire ST5 5BG
0782 621111
Thompson, D. Mr
The history of geological and earth-science education in the United Kingdom
Abstract: The history of geological and earth science education in the United Kingdom reveals the important part that geology, geologists and the geological profession played in the early days of the growth of science education from 1830 to 1900 in both schools and vocational courses, e.g. of the Department of Science and Arts. The wives of geologists were in the van of women's education and extra mural education. A decline to a nadir in the 1930s has been followed by a steady rise in the growth of interest, culminating in the formation of the Association of Teachers of Geology (1967) (now the Earth Science Teachers' Association (1988)) and the acceptance of Earth Science in the National Science Curriculum (1989).
Published Material: THOMPSON, D.B. (1991). 'MIMCU, Geoff Cox and the future of the Ecton Hill Education Centre', Geoscientist, Vol 1, No 5, pp.12-17.
Status: Individual research
Date of Research: 1970 - continuing
KEYWORDS: earth science; educational history; geology education; physical sciences; science education

9/0441
Department of Education, Keele, Staffordshire ST5 5BG
0782 621111
Marques, L. Mr; *Supervisor:* Thompson, D. Mr
Children's alternative ideas about earth-science concepts, e.g. continental drift and plate tectonics
Abstract: Children's alternative ideas relating to earth-science concepts have been only modestly researched. Following work on children's ideas of the origin of the earth, the origin of life and the nature and origin of volcanoes, the research has now turned to children's views of the origin of continents, oceans and the possible wandering of the former. Following a pilot study with pupils and teachers and in-depth interviews with pupils, a questionnaire survey of the views of 300 Portuguese children has been administered. It is conjectured that the many garbled ideas of students accrue from watching television, reading newspapers and attempting to use ideas drawn from science and geography lessons at school. So far 30 or so alternative ideas have been noted and curriculum strategies which challenge many of them been developed and trialled.
Status: Individual research
Date of Research: 1989 - continuing
KEYWORDS: comprehension; earth science; oceanography; physical sciences; plate tectonics

9/0442
Department of Education, Keele, Staffordshire ST5 5BG
0782 621111
Thompson, D. Mr
Curriculum materials for earth-science teaching in the National Curriculum
Abstract: Earth Science is new to the science curriculum in the United Kingdom. Curriculum materials need to be written, trialled and published quickly. Trials are to be carried out on whole classes of 20-30 pupils. Materials are designed for variety and balance of approach and a concentration on pupil activity including practical experimental work. Publication is via the Earth Science Teachers' Association 'Science of the Earth' and 'Project Earth'.
Published Material: A list of Earth Science Teachers Association publications is available from Geo Supplies Ltd, 11 Station Road, Chapeltown, Sheffield S30 4XH.
Status: Individual research
Date of Research: 1988 - continuing
KEYWORDS: earth science; educational materials; material development; National Curriculum; physical sciences; science education

9/0443
Department of Education, Keele, Staffordshire ST5 5BG
0782 621111
Brighouse, T. Prof.; Gough, G. Dr; Johnson, M. Mr; Glover, D. Mr; Walton, W. Mr
Successful schooling
Abstract: The project aims to establish further information and knowledge about 'successful schooling', by means of questionnaires and in-depth interviews in 15-18 core study schools.
Status: Sponsored project
Source of Grant: Local Education Authorities £25,000
Date of Research: 1990 - continuing
KEYWORDS: outcomes of education; school effectiveness; success

9/0444

Department of Education, Keele, Staffordshire ST5 5BG
0782 621111
Mardle, G. Mr; Colclough, P. Mr; Shain, F. Ms; Modiba, M. Ms; *Supervisor*: Mardle, G. Mr
Equal opportunities policies in schools and colleges post local management developments from the 1988 Education Act
Abstract: In the past, policy initiation in the education system has in general been the responsibility of either the government or the local education authority. Under the 1988 Education Act this has changed. Secondary schools and further education colleges now have control over their budgets and also a far higher degree of control over certain policy initiatives. Within the context of many other pressures this has led to a degree of inertia in certain areas. In particular, the development of equal opportunity policies has been affected. The aim of this investigation is to examine, via questionnaire and case study material, the effects of current legislation on the area of equal opportunity policy in schools and colleges. The focus of attention starts with the political aspects of the problem. It then goes on to examine the way in which such policy in the areas of gender, race and disability is seen by the participants, developed in the institutions and the methods deployed in putting it into practice. It is hoped the results and conclusions of the study will enable more institutions to develop and implement such policies.
Status: Individual research
Date of Research: 1991 - continuing
KEYWORDS: *educational policy; equal education; gender equality; nondiscriminatory education*

9/0445

Department of Education, Keele, Staffordshire ST5 5BG
0782 621111
Tolley, J. Ms; *Supervisor*: Wringe, C. Dr
Evaluation of foreign language teaching objectives (with particular reference to the teaching of French)
Abstract: An empirical investigation of factors determining the choice of objectives for the teaching of French at school level. These include pupil motivation and communication needs for the individual and for industry and commerce.
Status: Individual research
Date of Research: 1986 - continuing
KEYWORDS: *education objectives; French; modern language studies*

9/0446

Department of Education, Keele, Staffordshire ST5 5BG
0782 621111
Toy, K. Mr; *Supervisor*: Wringe, C. Dr
Educational management, teacher evaluation and teacher autonomy
Abstract: This is principally a conceptual and library study. Theories of educational management and teacher evaluation are to be explored in relation to a concept of teacher autonomy. Historical and current expectations and practice will be examined in the light of available documentary evidence, and a small number of exemplary case studies may be undertaken.
Status: Individual research
Date of Research: 1986 - continuing
KEYWORDS: *management in education; teacher evaluation; teacher role*

9/0447

Department of Education, Keele, Staffordshire ST5 5BG
0782 621111
Gleeson, D. Prof.; Carlen, P. Dr; Wardough, J. Mr
Law, education and social control: the case of non-school attendance
Abstract: This study looks at the processing of non-school attendance in relation to inter-agency links: education, law, social and welfare services.
Status: Sponsored project
Source of Grant: Economic and Social Research Council £65,000
Date of Research: 1988 - continuing
KEYWORDS: *attendance; compulsory education; dropouts; law enforcement; social services; truancy*

9/0448

Department of Education, Keele, Staffordshire ST5 5BG
0782 621111
Kim, J. Mr; *Supervisor*: Wringe, C. Dr
Well-being and education
Abstract: This is a philosophical study examining the concept of well-being as an educational aim. Various conceptions of well-being will be examined, a distinction established between material welfare and a broader conception of well-being, and the links between this conception of well-being and education explored.
Status: Individual research
Date of Research: 1991 - continuing
KEYWORDS: *educational objectives; educational philosophy; quality of life; well being*

9/0449

Department of Education, Keele, Staffordshire ST5 5BG
0782 621111
Parkhouse, P. Mr; *Supervisor*: Parkhouse, P. Mr
Undergraduate physicists' and post-graduate scientists' (undergoing teacher training) understanding of the nature of science
Abstract: The current research is concerned with students' understanding of the nature of science. It is in two principle parts: one concerned with undergraduate physicists and the other with post-graduate science students undergoing a course of training for teaching at Keele University. Some of the post-graduate science students will be followed during their teaching practice to see if their teaching exemplifies their beliefs and whether the researcher is able to influence this by heightening their awareness through prolonged contact with them. The approach is ethnographic and the stimulus of a free-response questionnaire followed by recorded interviews elucidating their responses has been adopted. In addition both samples have to interact with specially prepared practical materials designed to reveal further their philosophical standpoints.
Status: Individual research
Date of Research: 1991 - continuing
KEYWORDS: *comprehension; philosophy of science; science education; scientific concepts; student attitudes*

9/0450

Department of Education, Keele, Staffordshire ST5 5BG
0782 621111
Miller, D. Mr
Curriculum development in mathematics: using and applying mathematics
Abstract: The aims of this research are to extend the breadth of the secondary school mathematics curriculum, within the context of the National Curriculum, with particular reference to the use and application of mathematics, and to influence and enrich mathematics teachers' current methodologies. The nature of the research is to provide teachers of mathematics with new, or unfamiliar, activities and contexts for using and applying mathematics. These activities and contexts include mathematics as it is used by different cultures, topics from the history of mathematics, cross-curricular material and micro-computer and calculator applications. The results will be detailed in appropriate journals, the materials wil be published in a suitable format.
Published Material: MILLER, D.J. (1990). Activity Maths, Level 5. Ormskirk: Causeway Press Ltd.; MILLER, D.J. (1990). Activity Maths, Level 5, Teachers' Book. Ormskirk: Causeway Press Ltd.; MILLER, D.J. (1990) Micromathematics, Levels 5 and 6. Ormskirk: Causeway Press Ltd.; MILLER, D.J. (1990). Micromathematics, Levels 5 and 6, Teachers' Book. Ormskirk: Causeway Press Ltd.; A full list of publications is available from the researcher.
Status: Individual research
Date of Research: 1989 - continuing
KEYWORDS: *curriculum development; information technology; mathematics education; secondary education*

9/0451

Department of Education, Keele, Staffordshire ST5 5BG
0782 621111
McLean, M. Mrs; *Supervisor*: Gleeson, D. Prof.
Local evaluation of Technical and Vocational Education Initiative (TVEI), TVEI-Related Inservice Training (TRIST) and Grant Related INSET (GRIST)

Abstract: The study looks at the background and development of Technical and Vocational Education Initiative (TVEI) and TVEI-Related Inservice Training (TRIST) in local institutions. The research adopts an action oriented approach to evaluation, involving formative methods of reporting. Reports will be sent to the schools and colleges involved.

Published Material: GLEESON, D. (1988). TVEI and secondary education. Buckingham: Open University Press.; GLEESON, D. (1989). The paradox of training: making progress out of crisis. Buckingham: Open University Press.
Status: Sponsored project
Source of Grant: Staffordshire LEA; Training, Enterprise & Education Directorate £221,000
Date of Research: 1985 - continuing
KEYWORDS: inservice teacher education; technical education; vocational education

9/0452
Department of Psychology, Keele, Staffordshire ST5 5BG
0782 621111
Afzalnia, M. Mr; *Supervisor:* Hartley, J. Prof.
Reading, listening and television viewing: a study in children's cognition
Abstract: This research is concerned with the relationships between children's television viewing and their school performance with an emphasis on their reading, listening and viewing comprehension skills. Seventy eight 9-10 year olds were selected from a local school to take part. Tests of reading, intelligence and listening skills, together with questionnaires, were used to collect information about the children's abilities and their parents' and teachers' attitudes towards their reading and listening habits. While the results of the test studies supported the assumption that predicted that children's general reading and listening skills would relate to their viewing comprehension, the obtained data did not produce much support for the hypothesis that assumed a positive relationship between children's sensitivity to the audio channel of television and their verbal receptive achievements. The assumption that there would be a positive relationship between children's background variables and their reading, listening and viewing skills was mostly supported. However, the data indicated that some variables (such as library membership) were more important than the others. It was found that children with low achievements in reading and listening also had some difficulty with their overall cognition which was shown in their difficulty in general learning.
Published Material: AFZALNIA, M.R. (1993). 'Television literacy and young children's promotion of mental health'. In: TRENT, D. (Ed). Promotion of mental health, Aldershot: Avebury.; A full list of proposed publications is available from the researcher.
Status: Sponsored project
Source of Grant: Government of Iran
Date of Research: 1988 - continuing
KEYWORDS: academic achievement; cognitive ability; listening skills; reading achievement; television research; television viewing

9/0453
Department of Psychology, Keele, Staffordshire ST5 5BG
0782 621111
Hartley, J. Prof.
Designing instructional text
Abstract: This research focuses on the design of instructional text – mainly in the form of printed materials – which enables the reader to do or to understand something. The research covers three areas: (1) the layout of such materials; (2) the language of such materials; and (3) the use of structural devices which enable people to find their way about a piece of text. Work with layout stresses the importance of using the 'white-space' systematically in order to convey the underlying structure of text. Work with language suggests the importance of simpler wording. Work with 'access structures' indicates how devices such as headings and summaries can aid recall. Recently the research has shifted its focus of interest from work with printed text to work with Braille, audio-taped instruction, and electronic text.
Published Material: HARTLEY, J. (1989). 'Text design and the setting up of Braille', Information Design Journal, Vol 5, pp.183-190.; HARTLEY, J. (1990). 'Textbook design: current status and future directions', International Journal of Educational Research, Vol 14, pp.533-541.; HARTLEY, J. (1990). 'Author, printer, reader, listener: four sources of confusion when listening to tabular/diagrammatic information', British Journal of Visual Impairment, Vol VIII, pp.51-53.; HARTLEY, J. (1991). 'Psychology, writing and compu-

ters', Visible Language, Vol 25, pp.339-375.; HARTLEY, S. (1992). 'The layout of computer-based text' In: SASSOON, R. (Ed). Computers and Typology. Oxford: Intellect Books.
Status: Individual research
Date of Research: 1970 - continuing
KEYWORDS: educational materials; educational media; textbooks

9/0454
Department of Psychology, Keele, Staffordshire ST5 5BG
0782 621111
Seale, J. Mrs; Newberry-Tarrier, S. Mrs; Topping, M. Mr; *Supervisor:* Hegarty, J. Dr
Computer applications to special education
Abstract: The aim of the research is to support users of microcomputers in special education, particularly those who work with adults who have severe learning difficulties. The work combines research, development of software and hardware devices, consultancy and staff training. There are three major research projects: (1) Staff development – a detailed study of 11 centres using micros has revealed the dimensions of effective management of the computer as an educational resource. The research has produced a management profile (AMMASE) which can be used to identify weaknesses and strengths in management and create goals; (2) Expert Systems Project – detailed observational research of adults with a mental handicap whilst shopping for groceries has produced a specification for a computer aid which will help them produce their own shopping lists based on the grocery stocks normally required for their weekly needs. The software is now written for a hand-held microcomputer with integral touch screen and printer which allows clients who cannot read or write to input the current grocery stocks and thus create a shopping list (which is graphical). Evaluation of the system is in progress; (3) A robotic device to allow people to eat unassisted has been developed. This low cost device is now in use and is being evaluated.
Published Material: COLLINS, R. (1989). 'Computers and special education for adults'. In: HARTLEY, J. & BRANTHWAITE, J.A. (Eds). The Applied Psychologist. Buckingham: Open University Press.; HEGARTY, J.R. (1991). Into the 1990s: the Present and Future of Microcomputers for People with Learning Difficulties. Market Drayton: Change Publications.
Status: Sponsored project
Source of Grant: Various public and charitable sources
Date of Research: 1985 - continuing
KEYWORDS: computer system design; computer uses in education; severe learning difficulties; special educational needs

9/0455
Department of Psychology, Keele, Staffordshire ST5 5BG
0782 621111
Trueman, M. Mr
Attitudes towards computers
Abstract: A series of four studies has been carried out using the Lloyd and Gressard (1984) Computer Attitude Scale to measure computer anxiety, computer liking and computer confidence. A study of undergraduate students showed that males had more experience in using computers and liked computers more than females did. However, there were no sex differences in computer anxiety or computer confidence. A second study of undergraduates found that males had more experience of using computers, liked computers more and were more confident with computers than females in the study. This study also showed a correlation between higher neuroticism scores and found that males had more experience with computers and were more likely to have access to a computer than females were. Males were more confident about using computers and they liked computers more than females. The final study looked at the relationship between androgeny (as assessed by the Personal Attributes Questionnaire, Spence & Helmreich, 1978) and the Computer Attitude Scale in a sample of 4th form school children. There were no sex differences in computer anxiety, computer liking or computer confidence. However, androgynous individuals had higher computer liking scores than masculine, feminine or undifferentiated individuals. Also, there were a series of significant sex and androgeny interactions in which androgenous males and masculine females were less anxious, liked computers more and were more confident about computers than the other groups.
Published Material: TRUEMAN, M. (1989). 'Attitudes towards computers', Paper presented to the 5th Annual Wolverhampton Polytechnic Educational Research Conference. Ibiza: San Antonio.; TRUEMAN, M. (1990). 'The effects of gender and computer experi-

ence on attitudes towards computers', CORE (Collected Original Resources in Education), Vol 14, No 3. (Fr. B01 on No 1 of 9 microfiches).
Status: Individual research
Date of Research: 1985 - continuing
KEYWORDS: *attitudes; computer literacy; computers; sex differences*

9/0456
Department of Psychology, Keele, Staffordshire ST5 5BG
0782 621111
Loumidis, K. Mr; *Supervisor:* Hill, A. Dr
An evaluation study of the efficacy of 'Social Problem Solving Training', with people who have learning difficulties, living in residential and community settings
Abstract: 'Social Problem Solving Training' has been used with a variety of clinical and non-clinical populations. With learning difficulties, research has mainly focused on the mildly handicapped group living in the community, or in residential settings. Much of the work has had rather narrow objectives, e.g. to enhance the decision making of mothers with learning difficulties, to enhance dating skills and public transportation skills. The present study attempts to extend previous research by adapting 'Social Problem Solving Training' to give a more generic training, relevant to the needs of moderately handicapped people. In Part 1 of the study, adults with learning difficulties living in the community as well as in a residential hospital, will be assessed to establish baseline measures of intellectual functioning, degree of psychological distress and ability to solve hypothetical but personally relevant problems. The second part of the research will consist of a period of six months training in social problem solving with one 75-90 minutes session each week. In the third part, the effects of training will be assessed by comparing performance on the problem solving test, used to establish baseline performance. Generalisation of training will also be evaluated on two parallel sets of new problems. Pre-post measures of dependent variables will be compared using 2 x 2 ANOVA (community/residential x Time os assessment). Qualitative analyses of individual cases will also be carried out.
Published Material: LOUMIDIS, K.S. (1991). 'Can "Social Problem Solving Training" help people with a learning difficulty?', Proceedings of the First Annual Conference on the Promotion of Mental Health, September. Avebury: Gower Publications.
Status: Individual research
Date of Research: 1990 - continuing
KEYWORDS: *moderate learning difficulties; problem solving; severe learning difficulties; social skills; special educational needs*

Kingston University

9/0457
Faculty of Education, Kingston Hill Centre, Kingston Hill, Kingston upon Thames, Surrey KT2 7LB
081 549 1141
Jones, B. Mr; *Supervisor:* Pope, M. Prof.
An action project designed to promote the development of mentors in the context of initial teacher training (ITT) teaching practice
Abstract: A quantitative research project designed to illuminate and promote staff development in the context of largely school-based initial teacher training. The sample is relatively small, but the quantitative methods of research have generated a great deal of relevant information. The research is based on enabling practitioners to reflect on this practice, with use made of interviews, video-taping, practical counselling sessions, case studies of particular school instances and leading to collaborative staff development. This research will also look at links with inservice education of teachers (INSET) provision, again of a collaborative nature.
Status: Individual research
Date of Research: 1987-1992
KEYWORDS: *mentors; preservice teacher education; staff development; student teacher supervisors; teaching practice*

Lancaster University

9/0458
Department of Educational Research, Cartmel College, Bailrigg, Lancaster LA1 4YW
0524 65201
Simco, N. Mr; *Supervisor:* Smith, L. Dr
Initial teacher training and professional development within dimensions of classroom activity ambiguity
Abstract: The research seeks to illuminate aspects of the professional development of students undergoing initial teacher training. In particular it aims to richly describe classrooms where students are operating and to draw from this description common strands of professional progress made by beginning teachers. The study has, as a central focus, the development made along two dimensions of 'ambiguity', namely the degree of activity openness enabled and the degree of teacher clarity in delivering activity. In this respect activity will be described in four 'cells': activity which is open and clear; activity which is closed and clear; activity which is open and vague; activity which is closed and vague. The empirical work has an ecological approach, allowing issues to emerge for semi-structured observation and pre- and post-activity interviews with student teachers and children. In essence it is a longitudinal study which focuses on the professional progress of four students during teaching practices at various times in their training. These case studies represent the first stage of the research. This stage attempts to be purely descriptive. From this description a second prescriptive stage is likely to emerge.
Status: Individual research
Date of Research: 1990 - continuing
KEYWORDS: *ambiguity; class activities; preservice teacher education; student teachers; teaching practice; teaching styles*

9/0459
Department of Educational Research, Cartmel College, Bailrigg, Lancaster LA1 4YW
0524 65201
Summerfield, P. Dr
Gender, training and employment: an historical analysis 1939-50
Abstract: This is a study of the relationships between the training and employment of women during the Second World War and the immediate post-war period. The central research question is whether wartime training altered the position of women in the labour market on either a temporary or a permanent basis. In pursuit of answers the research scrutinizes the formulation and outcomes of training and employment policy in the period 1939-50.
Published Material: SUMMERFIELD, P. (1989). 'What women learned from the second world war', History of Education, Vol 18, No 3, pp.213-230, September.
Status: Sponsored project
Source of Grant: Economic and Social Research Council £43,000
Date of Research: 1990-1992
KEYWORDS: *educational history; training; women's education; women's employment*

9/0460
Department of Educational Research, Cartmel College, Bailrigg, Lancaster LA1 4YW
0524 65201
Rimmershaw, R. Dr
Collaborative writing
Abstract: This is a study of the collaborative writing practices of writers in the academic community. The main focus is on why they are involved, how they manage the collaboration, and how they deal with issues of identity and power in collaborating. The sample comprises 20 academic writers from eight disciplines, and from undergraduate to professional status. The main source of data is in-depth interviews. Additional sources used are observation and tape-recordings of collaborations in progress, and written reports by collaborators on the production of specific pieces of writing.
Published Material: RIMMERSHAW, R.E. 'Collaborative writing practices and writing support technologies'. In: SHARPLES, M. (Ed). Computers and Writing: Issues and Implementations. Dordrecht: Kluwer.
Status: Individual research
Date of Research: 1990 - continuing
KEYWORDS: *authors; cooperation; writing – composition*

9/0461

Department of Educational Research, Cartmel College,
Bailrigg, Lancaster LA1 4YW
0524 65201
Rimmershaw, R. Dr

Reading and writing in student learning

Abstract: This research into students' reading and writing development is in two phases. In the first phase undergraduate students worked with the researcher to reflect on and analyse their own reading and writing development before and during their courses at Lancaster University. In the second phase a cohort of 16 non-traditional students were followed through the three years of their degree programme. The methods used include individual interviews, group discussions and deconstruction of particular reading and writing tasks as the students perform them.

Published Material: BENSON, N., GURNEY, S., HARRISON, J. & RIMMERSHAW, R.E. 'The place of academic writing in the whole-life writing experiences of three university students'. In: HAMILTON, M., BARTON, D. & IVANIC, R. (Eds). Worlds of Literacy. Clevedon: Multilingual Matters. (in press).

Status: Individual research

Date of Research: 1989 - continuing

KEYWORDS: *critical reading; reading; student development; study skills; writing – composition; writing skills*

9/0462

Department of Educational Research, Cartmel College,
Bailrigg, Lancaster LA1 4YW
0524 65201
Serafingos, J. Mr; *Supervisor:* Rogers, C. Dr

Teachers planning and evaluation of mathematics in Greek high schools

Abstract: This project is an examination of the ways in which a sample of Greek mathematics teachers think about their subject and their teaching, and how these understandings influence the kinds of experiences that are selected and presented to children in the mathematics curriculum. This is of particular interest in Greek education because of the high emphasis that is placed upon high school teachers' subject degree studies and the lack of any significant professional training for high school teaching.

Status: Sponsored project

Source of Grant: Greek Ministry of Education scholarship

Date of Research: 1988-1991

KEYWORDS: *Greece; mathematics education; mathematics teachers; teacher education*

9/0463

Department of Educational Research, Cartmel College,
Bailrigg, Lancaster LA1 4YW
0524 65201
New, S. Ms; *Supervisor:* Summerfield, P. Dr; Mason, J. Dr

Preparation for life: TVEI and equal opportunities (gender)

Abstract: From its inception, the Technical and Vocational Education Initiative (TVEI) included, as a central objective, a commitment to the promotion of equal opportunities for boys and girls within pilot schemes. Using a triangulated case study approach, this research seeks to explore, within a theoretical framework informed by feminist research and theory on gender and education, the development, implementation and impact of TVEI equal opportunities policy and practice in one local education authority, from the dual perspectives of: (a) policymakers (both at local authority and school level); and (b) the young people involved in the second year of the pilot scheme. With regard to the former perspective, methods have included the analysis of archive documentation and interviews with key local authority personnel, and with regard to the latter, the analysis of careers service destinations data, questionnaire data and data from in-depth interviews, conducted at various stages up to two-and-a-half years after leaving school. In particular, the research seeks to understand the nature of the underlying philosophy/philosophies reflected in the equal opportunities developments of the LEA in question, and the impact this has had on the young people involved, and the implications of this for the promotion of equal opportunities work within a feminist framework.

Published Material: NEW, S.J. (1990). The destinations of 1989 leavers from the five TVEI pilot schools. (Working Paper). City of Salford Education Department (14-19 Development Unit).; NEW, S.J. (1990). The Salford school leavers survey: a report based on the experiences of 1989 leavers from the five TVEI pilot schools. (Work-

ing Paper). City of Salford Education Department (14-19 Development Unit).

Status: Individual research

Date of Research: 1990 - continuing

KEYWORDS: *equal education; gender equality; technical education; transition education; vocational education*

9/0464

Department of Educational Research, Cartmel College,
Bailrigg, Lancaster LA1 4YW
0524 65201
Skelding, A. Ms; *Supervisor:* Smith, L. Dr

Interactive science in the primary school

Abstract: The project aims to evaluate an interactive, 'hands-on' approach to teaching science and technology in a primary school. Systematic classroom observation and interviews are being used to examine teachers' roles in this teaching approach, and to assess children's acquisition of scientific concepts and skills, and to consider the role of language and mathematics in their learning.

Status: Individual research

Date of Research: 1988-1991

KEYWORDS: *learning activities; practical science; primary education; science education; teaching methods; technology education*

9/0465

Department of Educational Research, Cartmel College,
Bailrigg, Lancaster LA1 4YW
0524 65201
Fulton, O. Prof.

Government intervention and policy change in higher education: a comparative study. Stage 1

Abstract: This is a large scale comparative study (up to 11 'Organisation for Economic Co-operation and Development' countries) of the intended and unintended effects of government intervention in policy-making and implementation for higher education. It focuses particularly on issues such as diversification or integration of higher education in a context of expanding numbers and contracting resources during the 1980s. The first stage is a review of broad policy developments in each country, contributed by a local 'expert'. Further empirical investigations may follow.

Published Material: FULTON, O. (1991). 'Slouching towards a mass system: society, government and institutions in the United Kingdom', Higher Education, Vol 21, No 4, pp.589-606.

Status: Sponsored project

Source of Grant: Ministry of Education, Finland

Date of Research: 1990-1991

KEYWORDS: *comparative education; educational finance; educational policy; government role; higher education; student numbers*

9/0466

Department of Educational Research, Cartmel College,
Bailrigg, Lancaster LA1 4YW
0524 65201
Fulton, O. Prof.

Enterprise in higher education: evaluation

Abstract: This is a rolling evaluation of enterprise in higher education at Lancaster University. The first year investigated organisational and implementation issues, using interviews with staff. The second year focused on student experiences, using interviews with students. The third year looked at institutional diffusion and impact using staff and student interviews and student questionnaires.

Status: Sponsored project

Source of Grant: Training, Enterprise and Education Directorate £35,000

Date of Research: 1988 - continuing

KEYWORDS: *enterprise education; higher education; programme evaluation; work-education relationship*

9/0467

Department of Educational Research, Cartmel College,
Bailrigg, Lancaster LA1 4YW
0524 65201
Knight, P. Dr

Assessment of National Curriculum History Key Stages 1-3

Abstract: The English National Curriculum makes history a mandatory part of the curriculum for children in Key Stages 1-4 (ages 6-16).

However, earlier research shows that this alone is an innovation in primary schooling. Moreover, the curriculum is to be assessment-led. Yet, not only is there little tradition of this sort of assessment in Key Stages 1 and 2 (ages 6-11) but it is not endemic in Key Stage 3 (ages 12-14). Lastly, there are doubts about the validity of the domain-specific developmental sequence underpinning both assessment and the curriculum. This study builds on earlier, funded work. Two inter-related approaches will be taken: (1) with the aid of advisers, teachers and children, methods of teacher assessment which match National Curriculum requirements for history and which are compatible with the exigencies of classroom life will be devised, tested, refined and propagated; (2) using the data gained from the above and from clinical interviewing, a developmental account of children's historical reasoning will be offered. Results from the research will be presented in two forms: (1) detailed 'rich' guidelines for teachers; (2) a model of development.
Published Material: KNIGHT, P.T. (1991). 'Teaching as exposure: the case of good practice in junior school history', British Educational Research Journal, Vol 17, No 2, pp.129-140.
Status: Individual research
Date of Research: 1990 - continuing
KEYWORDS: history studies; National Curriculum; primary education; school-based assessment

9/0468

Department of Educational Research, Cartmel College, Bailrigg, Lancaster LA1 4YW
0524 65201
Knight, P. Dr

Degree specialism and pedagogic understanding in primary PGCE courses
Abstract: The question is whether students who enter primary Postgraduate Certificate in Education (PGCE) courses with history or geography degrees show any greater grasp of the pedagogy of those subjects either at the start of the course, or at the end of it. The hypothesis is that the subject teaching methods element of the PGCEs will not make a difference, and that differences apparent on entry will be reproduced on exit. Students in three institutions were given questionnaires about geography and history – the subjects and their pedagogy – on entry to the course, and will do the same questionnaires on completion. In addition, during the course they undertake a planning exercise and an evaluation exercise, in both of which they are required to apply their grasp of primary geography and primary history to lifelike teaching problems. Reports will be published separately for geography and history and will be written by the colleagues in the institutions concerned. Lancaster University is co-ordinating the project.
Status: Individual research
Date of Research: 1991-1992
KEYWORDS: degrees – academic; main subjects; Postgraduate Certificate in Education; preservice teacher education

9/0469

Department of Educational Research, Cartmel College, Bailrigg, Lancaster LA1 4YW
0524 65201
Knight, P. Dr

A comparative study of outcomes and process in English higher education
Abstract: This is a comparative study of the outcomes of higher education institutions and universities. Although there has been plentiful research into student learning in higher education, and consequent recommendations for effective teaching, it does not readily allow explanation of the performance of public sector institutions in the 1980s. In a decade where student expenditure has remained below that of the university sector (allowing for research funding), when public sector student numbers have burgeoned, and when staff-student ratios have become less favourable, the number and proportion of 2:1 and 1st class degrees have also grown on a sector-wide basis as compared to universities. The study attempts to find out why this should be. The focus is upon academic departments teaching the same subject. The usual forms of input and process data are to be collected, but close attention is being given also to the structure of courses; to observation of teaching; and to the assessment of student performance leading to degree classification. The working hypothesis is that there are general, distinct differences in the teaching/learning processes in the two sectors (university:public).
Status: Individual research

Date of Research: 1991 - continuing
KEYWORDS: college effectiveness; higher education; outcomes of education; universities and colleges

9/0470

Department of Educational Research, Cartmel College, Bailrigg, Lancaster LA1 4YW
0524 65201
Goodyear, P. Dr

JITOL: Just In Time Open Learning
Abstract: JITOL aims to explore the use of electronic communications networks and multimedia computer conferencing in order to support continuing professional development and upating by skilled workers distributed throughout Europe. The lead partner in the project is NeuropeLab (in Archamps, France). Other partners include Logica, DEC, Credit Agricole, Dida*el and the universities of Lisbon and Namur.
Published Material: LEWIS, R., GOODYEAR, P. & BODER, A. (1992). Just In Time Open Learning: a DELTA project outline. Archamps, France: NeuropeLab. (Occasional Paper 92/1) (obtainable from Dr Goodyear at Lancaster University)
Status: Sponsored project
Source of Grant: European Community DELTA Programme £453,600
Date of Research: 1992 - continuing
KEYWORDS: communications; distance education; networks; open education; teleconferencing

9/0471

Department of Educational Research, Cartmel College, Bailrigg, Lancaster LA1 4YW
0524 65201
Goodyear, P. Dr; *Supervisor:* Goodyear, P. Dr

TOSKA: Tools and Methods for a Sophisticated Knowledge Based Authoring Facility
Abstract: The main objectives of the TOSKA project are: (1) to define a generic framework for knowledge-based support of authoring interactive learning environments; and (2) to contribute to the standardization of an authoring methodology. The authoring framework must be able to support authors in building a wide variety of interactive learning systems (ranging from simple simulation systems to individualized tutorial instruction) in different domains. In its first phase the project has been searching for the generic components of instructional systems, domain representations, instructional methods and learner characteristics. Further, based on these generic components, it has developed some initial prototypes and methods to control the knowledge-based authoring process. In its second phase, the project is evaluating the applicability of the generic components and applying them in two selected test domains. The first concerns teaching the maintenance of aeroplane components; the second is training users in the use of a software package.
Published Material: GOODYEAR, P. (Ed). (1991). 'Research on teaching and the design of intelligent tutoring systems', Chapter 1. In: Teaching Knowledge and Intelligent Tutoring. New Jersey: Ablex, Norwood.; JOHNSON, R. & GOODYEAR, P. (1990). 'Knowledge-based authoring of adaptive courseware', Paper for the 2nd European Congress on Artificial Intelligence and Training, Lille, France, September.; GOODYEAR, P. & JOHNSON, R. (1990). 'Knowledge-based authoring of knowledge-based courseware', Proceedings of the 7th International Conference on Technology and Education, Vol 1, pp.379-381, Brussels, March.; GOODYEAR, P. (1989). 'Development of learning technology at the European level', Educational and Training Technology International, Vol 26, No 4, pp.335-341.
Status: Sponsored project
Source of Grant: European Community DELTA Programme £115,000
Date of Research: 1989-1991
KEYWORDS: artificial intelligence; authoring aids – programming; computer-assisted learning; computer software

9/0472

Department of Educational Research, Cartmel College, Bailrigg, Lancaster LA1 4YW
0524 65201
Goodyear, P. Dr; *Supervisor:* Goodyear, P. Dr

IRLME: Interactive Resources for Small and Medium Sized Enterprises
Abstract: The goal of this project is to produce an interactive video

(IV) about the uses of interactive video for training in small and medium sized enterprises (SMEs). The project involves research into methods of designing IV materials for use in SMEs in several European countries.

Status: Sponsored project
Source of Grant: European Community COMETT Programme £170,212
Date of Research: 1990-1992
KEYWORDS: computer-assisted learning; interactive video

9/0473
Department of Educational Research, Cartmel College, Bailrigg, Lancaster LA1 4YW
0524 65201
Goodyear, P. Dr
RIE: design and evaluation of an interactive videodisc for small and medium sized enterprises
Abstract: The goal of this project is to create and evaluate an interactive videodisc (IV) whose subject matter is the application of IV for training and information services in small and medium sized enterprises (SMEs). The project is led by the University of Barcelona. The design of the disc entailed the development of new techniques for modelling decision-making situations. Production is expected to be complete by early 1992. Field trials will be conducted in Summer 1992 in Spain, United Kingdom and Portugal.
Status: Sponsored project
Source of Grant: European Community COMETT Programme £20,000
Date of Research: 1990-1992
KEYWORDS: computer-assisted design; computer-assisted learning; interactive video; simulation

9/0474
Department of Educational Research, Cartmel College, Bailrigg, Lancaster LA1 4YW
0524 65201
Johnson, R. Mr; Goodyear, P. Dr
DISCOURSE: Design & Interactive Specification of Courseware
Abstract: The goal of DISCOURSE is to build a set of computer-based tools to help the producers of computer-based learning materials work through the early stages of courseware design. Tools will be built to help with representing subject matter, teaching strategies and characteristics of target learners. Courseware designers will be able to work with a variety of presentational possibilities, including multimedia simulations. The project builds on earlier work in the EC DELTA projects TOSKA and Simulate. The lead partner for DISCOURSE is Dornier (part of Deutsche Aerospace).
Status: Sponsored project
Source of Grant: European Community DELTA Programme £256,900
Date of Research: 1992 - continuing
KEYWORDS: artificial intelligence; computer-assisted learning; educational materials; material design

9/0475
Department of Educational Research, Cartmel College, Bailrigg, Lancaster LA1 4YW
0524 65201
Goodyear, P. Dr; Self, J. Dr; *Supervisor:* Goodyear, P. Dr; Self, J. Dr
SIMULATE: Simulation Authoring Tools Environment
Abstract: The general topic of SIMULATE is learning and instruction with computer simulations and even more specifically, authoring for learning and instruction with computer simulations. Computer simulations are seen as a vehicle for acquiring knowledge and skills in an active way, by providing the learner an exploratory environment. In this respect computer simulations used in an educational environment are different from general courseware, because they are not aimed at substituting the individual, experienced, teacher, but offer new teaching opportunities. The starting point of the project is the observation that in order to be effective, simulations require the presence of an instructor to monitor the performance of the student and to provide support, both directive and non-directive. For open-learning situations this would mean embedding the simulation into an adaptive learning environment, capable of functioning in the above respects as a human tutor. The SIMULATE sub-project will deliver require-

ments and (global) specifications for an authoring environment (also) called SIMULATE (SIMULation Authoring Tools Environment), that can be used to create simulations embedded in an intelligent learning environment. In this document a simulation with such an environment will be called an ISLE (Intelligent Simulation Learning Environment).
Published Material: GOODYEAR, P. & TAIT, K. (1990). 'Learning with computer based simulations: tutoring and student modelling requirements for an intelligent learning advisor'. In: CARRETERO, M. et al (Eds). Learning and Instruction. Oxford: Pergamon Press.; GOODYEAR, P. (1990). 'The provision of tutorial support for learning with computer-based simulations'. In: DE CORTE, E. (Ed). Computer-based Learning Environments and Problem Solving. Belgium: Springer Verlag.; GOODYEAR, P., RONTELTAP, T. & VAN KOUWEN, A. (1990). 'Intelligent support for simulation-based learning: tutoring at the discussion level', paper presented at the 3rd European Seminar on Intelligent Tutoring Systems, December, Denmark, Aarhus.; GOODYEAR, P. (1989). 'Development of learning technology at the European level', Educational and Training Technology International, Vol 26, No 4, pp.335-341.
Status: Sponsored project
Date of Research: 1989-1991
KEYWORDS: artificial intelligence; authoring aids – programming; computer-assisted learning; human-computer interaction; simulation

9/0476
Department of Educational Research, Cartmel College, Bailrigg, Lancaster LA1 4YW
0524 65201
Smith, L. Dr
Critical assessment: Jean Piaget
Abstract: The aim of this collection is to survey, over the period 1950-1990, Piagetian commentary and criticism. The collection is in four volumes, each of which deals with a series of case-studies relevant to central issues in this Piagetian critique. The four volumes are: (1) understanding and Intelligence; (2) children's thinking; (3) education and society; (4) intellectual development. Each volume includes an integral guide to the selected papers. A general introduction (in Volume 1) and a concluding assessment (in Volume 4) are also provided. The papers have been selected with two features in mind. First, the issues in each volume have included contributions dealing with replication, elaboration, application and evaluation of Piaget's work at both empirical and theoretical levels. Second, mindful of the competing appraisals of Piaget's work, contributions have been selected with due attention to the successive dialogues which have been characteristic of the Piagetian critique over this period. Piaget's work continues to attract the attention of developmentalists. There is every expectation that this will continue in the 1990s. This is not merely because Piaget's questions are fundamentally interesting to those with a concern for developmental theory, it is also because his work is still a fertile intellectual resource both which provide contributions that go towards answering these questions and which are suggestive in opening up novel answers for other developmentalists. Piagetian research is a vast and expanding body of interdisciplinary writings. Those who are daunted by the prospect of thinking about Piaget's problems often turn to this research in their search for clarification and enlightenment. In fact, Piagetian research makes more, not less, demands on developmentalists.
Published Material: SMITH, L. (Ed.). (1992). Critical Assessment: Jean Piaget. London: Routledge.
Status: Individual research
Date of Research: 1988-1991
KEYWORDS: developmental psychology; education history; educational theories; intellectual development; intelligence; Piagetian theory

9/0477
Department of Educational Research, Cartmel College, Bailrigg, Lancaster LA1 4YW
0524 65201
Rogers, C. Dr; *Supervisor:* Rogers, C. Dr; Galloway, D. Prof.
Learned helplessness and self-worth motivation in children with special educational needs
Abstract: The project aims to identify: (1) the prevalence of the motivational styles of mastery orientation, self-worth motive and learned helplessness in pupils in two secondary schools and their feeder primary schools; (2) the degree to which the distribution of stlyes varies in children with special needs contrasted to whole populations; (3) changes in prevalence of style over time in a longi-

tudinal sample; (4) changes in prevalence across year groups with cross-sectional samples; (5) differences between curriculum areas with regard to the prevalence of motivational styles; and (6) to examine the degree to which factors associated with school (e.g. school attended, teacher) influence the prevalence of each style. Theoretical developments by Weiner, Nicholls and Covington provide a general background to the research. The sample consists of all children in the final year of 12 primary schools who are followed into years seven and eight in two secondary schools. Further cross-sectional samples are obtained with pupils in years nine and eleven in the secondary schools. Information about motivational style is obtained from analysis of children's performance on curriculum related tasks in mathematics and English. Additional information is obtained from questionnaires completed by pupils and teachers. Pupil attainment data is used to identify children with special needs and also to allow comparisons between motivational style and achievement levels. A sub-sample of children have been interviewed. Data analysis has recently commenced. Initial results suggest increases in maladaptive motivational styles consequent upon transfer to secondary schools, and differences in proportion of pupils showing maladaptive styles as a function of the curriculum subject.
Status: Sponsored project
Source of Grant: Economic and Social Research Council £84,280
Date of Research: 1991 - continuing
KEYWORDS: *helplessness; motivation; self-esteem; special educational needs*

9/0478
Department of Educational Research, Cartmel College,
Bailrigg, Lancaster LA1 4YW
0524 65201
McCulloch, G. Prof.
Tripartism and education in 20th century Britain
Abstract: This research project is designed to explore the tripartite distinctions in educational provision in 20th century Britain, and how they have been reconstructed and developed in the final decades of the century. The theme of 'education for leadership' originally associated with the 19th century public school has been one focus of the research. The attempts to promote a 'respectable' form of technical education, for example through the post-war secondary technical schools, has provided another. Lastly the tradition of working class schooling seen in the central schools and secondary modern schools is an important theme for further research. Continuities and shifts in emphasis underlying policy documents such as Hadow in the 1920s, Spens in the 1930s, Norwood in the 1940s, and Crowther in the 1950s. The relationships between these and the educational policies of the 1980s-90s are another aspect of the research project.
Published Material: McCULLOCH, G. (1989). The secondary technical school: a usable past? London: Falmer Press.; McCULLOCH, G. (1991). Philosophers and kings: education for leadership in modern England. Cambridge: Cambridge University Press.
Status: Individual research
Date of Research: 1987 - continuing
KEYWORDS: *educational administration; educational history; educational policy; public education; secondary education; tripartite system*

9/0479
Department of Educational Research, Cartmel College,
Bailrigg, Lancaster LA1 4YW
0524 65201
Tomlinson, S. Prof.
Alternatives in education – an analysis of past and present educational policies and ideologies and suggested alternatives for the future
Abstract: The research will develop a critical analysis of educational policies from 1944 to 1988, with a focus on the failures of the 'left' and the influence of the 'right' in terms of ideology. The working out of the Education Act 1988 in terms of policy and practice will be examined and suggestions for alternative educational policies based on particular values will be put forward. A study will be made of European education systems, particularly Germany, and the possibility of a future European education system explored.
Status: Sponsored project
Source of Grant: Leverhulme Trust £20,400
Date of Research: 1990-1992
KEYWORDS: *comparative education; educational history; educational policy*

9/0480
Department of Educational Research, Cartmel College,
Bailrigg, Lancaster LA1 4YW
0524 65201
Jackson, C. Ms; *Supervisor:* Rogers, C. Dr
Is the sex-type of an individual an influencing factor in teacher-pupil interaction and motivational style amongst school children?
Abstract: Evidence demonstrating sex-differences in motivational style and teacher-pupil interaction is now well documented. The aim of this research is to consider the importance of sex-type (masculine, feminine, androgynous or undifferentiated, as defined by the BEM Sex Role Inventory, 1978), on these two areas. Is sex-type a more useful and predictive concept than biological sex? The tests developed by Craske (1988) are the intended tool to identify motivational style amongst samples of secondary school children in the two key areas of mathematics and English. The BEM Sex-Role Inventory is selected to identify sex-type. Teacher perceptions of the sex-type of children may be identified using a short pupil rating scale completed by the teacher.
Status: Individual research
Date of Research: 1991 - continuing
KEYWORDS: *motivation; sex differences; sexual identity; teacher-pupil relationship*

9/0481
Department of Educational Research, Cartmel College,
Bailrigg, Lancaster LA1 4YW
0524 65201
Armstrong, D. Mr; *Supervisor:* Galloway, D. Prof.
The assessment and statementing of children with emotional and behavioural difficulties: child and parent perspectives
Abstract: A sample of 29 children, who were being assessed under the Education Act 1981 because of emotional and behavioural difficulties, was identified for an in depth case study of the assessment procedures. The research focused in particular on the perspectives of the children and their parents. The research had 3 aims: (1) to examine the perspectives of children and their parents on the procedures for assessing special educational needs; (2) to describe and provide a theoretical account of the concept of emotional and behavioural difficulties informed by the perspectives of children and their parents; (3) to describe and provide a theoretical analysis of sources of conflict and agreement between clients and professionals and to consider the implications of these for conceptualisations of the client-professional relationship.
Published Material: ARMSTRONG, D., GALLOWAY, D. & TOMLINSON, S. (1991). 'Decision-making in psychologists' professional interviews', Educational Psychology in Practice, Vol 7, No 2, pp.82-87.; ARMSTRONG, D. & GALLOWAY, D. (1992). 'On being a client: conflicting persectives on assessment'. In: BOOTH, T., SWANN, W., MASTERSON, M. & POTTS, P. (Eds). Policies for diversity in education. London: Routledge/Open University.; ARMSTRONG, D. & GALLOWAY, D. 'Who is the child psychologist's client? Responsibilities and options for psychologists in educational settings', Association for Child Psychology and Psychiatry Newsletter. (forthcoming).; Details of proposed publications are available from the researcher.
Status: Individual research
Date of Research: 1989 - continuing
KEYWORDS: *behavioural disorders; emotional disturbances; special educational needs; statements – special educational needs*

9/0482
Department of Educational Research, Cartmel Colleege,
Bailrigg, Lancaster LA1 4YW
0524 65201
McCulloch, G. Prof.; *Supervisor:* McCulloch, G. Prof.
Education and the working class: history, theory, policy and practice
Abstract: The project seeks to identify and explore a tradition of working class secondary education in modern Britain. It will assess its origins, its character, its wider influence, and its longer-term significance. The working hypothesis is that this tradition has been related to different forms of educational provision that have been developed over the past century, especially in the higher grade schools, the central schools, and the secondary modern schools. The aim is to study the curriculum, pedagogy, pupils, examinations and class relationships that developed in each of these types of schools,

as well as changing policies and attitudes towards them. The underlying continuities are related to policy and provision especially in secondary education but also at other levels of educational provision in the 1990s, to examine how far the forms, assumptions and relationships that underlay these earlier types of provision have survived to play a part in our current outlooks and methods.
Status: Sponsored project
Source of Grant: Leverhulme Trust £42,400
Date of Research: 1992 - continuing
KEYWORDS: *educational history; educational policy; educational principles; school systems; secondary education; secondary modern schools; tripartite system; working class*

9/0483
Department of Educational Research, Cartmel College, Bailrigg, Lancaster LA1 4YW
0524 65201
Proctor, J. Ms; *Supervisor:* Gray, H. Dr
The management of politically, or financially expedient change in a college of further education
Abstract: The research concerns the management of change within a college of further education. It focuses particularly on the processes of change which result from policies adopted primarily as a political or financial expedient. The research draws on varied case study materials spanning the period from 1975 to 1990. It is possible to make a comparison between two distinct leadership styles and two distinct management structures. These materials are related to minutes of Local Authority committees to deepen the perspective of explanations of events. The case study is also contrasted with the management of non-consensus policies in the National Health Service and with other case studies of change in further education. The study argues that in a period of accelerated change the 'integrative' model of policy information is insufficient to explain the complexity of the change process. The study emphasises the subjective responses of college members to policies which are imposed because of decisions taken outwith the college, but posits that although these responses are related to personal experience they are to an extent consensual and predictable since they also relate to the 'climate' of the college, to the expected behaviour of the executive and to common human responses when dealing with stress. The study is illustrated by references to attempts to implement particular policies, including equal opportunity policies as they relate to racial minorities and to women, and the development of open learning.
Published Material: PROCTOR, J. (1990). 'Literature review'. In: The assessment of management competences. CNAA, BTEC, Department of Employment (Training).; POWNEY, J., PROCTOR, J. & CROWCROFT, C. (1991). 'Opening up the debate'. In: Assessing Management Competence, final report. CNAA, BTEC, Department of Employment (Training).; PROCTOR, J. & POWNEY, J. (1991). 'The standard of qualification in management education: unresolved questions', Higher Education Review, Vol 23, No 3.; PROCTOR, J. (1991). 'Managers working for patients: using competences in management development', NHSTD.; PROCTOR, J. & JACKSON, C. (1992). 'Women managers in the NHS: a celebration of success', Department of Health, NHSME, Women's Unit.
Status: Individual research
Date of Research: 1988-1992
KEYWORDS: *change strategies; colleges of further education; educational administration; educational change; management in education*

9/0484
Department of Educational Research, Cartmel College, Bailrigg, Lancaster LA1 4YW
0524 65201
Ding, D. Mr; Supervisor: Fulton, O. Prof.
Enterprising higher education: links between higher education institutions and industrial, commercial sectors
Abstract: As a comparative study, this research focuses on mapping out the main trends over the past decade of higher education institutionsl (HEIs) links with industrial and commercial sectors in Britain and China, examining the rationales and attempting to find appropriate models for each. Through interviews with a selective sample of personnel numbering nearly 60 in HEIs in both countries; together with documentation review, this qualitative study illustrates a diversified picture of the present links respectively, where some interesting similarities are found. Meanwhile, differences of the links are also paid attention and probed, as obvious gaps remain between the two nations' fundamental social structures as well as educational systems.

In sum, the current linkage at all levels would, against resistance, continue to exist since there is a growing recognition that this link is not only a channel eventually generating funds for the much needed HEI pool, particularly in a time when its main, central funding sources are dwindling in real terms, but also a vitality which animates higher education progress. However, at present the links have formulated a challenge in both HE frameworks, since its behaviours are generally alien, unfamiliar to many, and still on a trial base. This controversy has inevitably confronted traditional ethos long established in higher education. Currently found issues show that unless some all-round strategies and policies are available and in effect, the links for some HEIs would cause quality problems and put the health of those linking institutions in jeopardy.
Status: Sponsored project
Source of Grant: Overseas research studentship; Lancaster University studentship
Date of Research: 1989 - continuing
KEYWORDS: *enterprise education; higher education institutions; industry higher education relationship*

9/0485
Department of Educational Research, Cartmel College, Bailrigg, Lancaster LA1 4YW
0524 65201
Nwaokolo, P. Mr; *Supervisor:* Saunders, M. Dr
Public construction of the status of teachers and teaching in Nigeria with special interest in vocational teachers: a case study of the Delta and Edo States of Nigeria
Abstract: This study arose following complaints as evidenced in the literature about poor public image and poor status of teachers in Nigeria. Its aim is to ascertain the extent of the problem, explore its nature and why it exists, with a view to proffering suggestions for the solution of the problem. The enquiry was carried out as a case study of the Edo and Delta States of Nigeria between January 1991 and September 1992. A total of 171 teachers, student-teachers, educational administrators, business and public administrators, professionals, clerks/artisans and typical village peasant farmers were interviewed in 9 major towns of Edo and Delta States. A questionnaire was also administered on 150 subjects, mainly to teachers and student-teachers. Its principal aim was to locate the teacher and the teaching profession on an occupational prestige ladder. Secondly, it aimed at identifying the social standing of the vocational teacher among colleagues in the same secondary school system. Data on the subject matter was also generated through documents, and more unobtrusive means such as monitoring radio commentaries and casual discussion with members of the public. The data is now being analysed but it is already clear that the poor status of teachers in Nigeria is traceable to unattractive conditions of service such as poor pay; salary irregularity; the unhelpful attitude of civil servants implementing policies that favour teachers; poor working environment; presence of a large number of unqualified teachers in the system; poor promotion, denial of and/or delayed fringe-benefits; and non-professionalisation of teaching. Other factors which are a consequence of the earlier ones include poor teacher dedication to duty and unimpressive appearance and attitude that portray teaching as synonymous with poverty.
Status: Sponsored project
Source of Grant: European Community
Date of Research: 1990 - continuing
KEYWORDS: *Nigeria; professional recognition; status need; teacher attitudes; teachers; teaching profession*

9/0486
Department of Educational Research, Cartmel College, Bailrigg, Lancaster LA1 4YW
0524 65201
Konting, M. Mr; *Supervisor:* Knight, P. Dr
Study of teacher effectiveness in the Malaysian secondary school
Abstract: Despite voluminous research findings in the literature on teacher effectiveness, its contribution, particularly from the theoretical and practical aspects is still being debated. This research is undertaken with the assumptions that teachers make a difference and that true knowledge of teaching is achieved by practice and experience in the classroom. The objectives of the study are to: (a) identify and determine the constructs of teacher effectiveness; (b) examine and describe the effective teacher's teaching; and (c) study the planning and implementation of the teacher training programme, particularly on how the programme takes into account the construct

of teacher effectiveness. A total of 41 effective lower secondary school teachers, nominated by educational authorities, who teach National Language (12 teachers), English (13 teachers), and Mathematics (16 teachers) are asked, through open-ended questionnaire and interview, to identify and to list the characteristics of an effective teacher, and to explain why such a characteristic is important for the teacher to be an effective teacher. They are also asked about what they do and do not do in teaching, and why. Classroom teaching of the subjects is also observed using a systematic classroom observation schedule. The results of the study indicate that there exists peculiar characteristics of effective teacher and specific effective teacher's teaching styles.

Status: Sponsored project
Source of Grant: Universiti Pertanian, Malaysia £2,400
Date of Research: 1991 - continuing
KEYWORDS: Malaysia; secondary school teachers; teacher behaviour; teacher effectiveness; teaching styles

9/0487
> Department of Educational Research, Cartmel College,
> Bailrigg, Lancaster LA1 4YW
> 0524 65201
> Bray, R. Mr; *Supervisor:* Fulton, O. Prof.

An evaluation of career development courses in higher education
Abstract: There is evidence of a significant growth in careers education provision in higher education in recent years. Contributory causes may include: transfer from the experiences of secondary and further education (e.g. Technical and Vocational Education Initiative); influence of the Enterprise in Higher Education project with its focus on transferable personal skills; and policy responses to graduate unemployment. This research aims to identify the reasons for such growth, the nature of the provision and likely future trends. The research will involve two stages. Stage 1 involves a questionnaire to all United Kingdom institutions of higher education investigating extent of careers education content and aims. Stage 2 uses Stage 1 results to select a sample (6-10) of institutions for in depth follow up: interviews with management, teaching staff and students concerning course aims, content and outcomes.

Status: Individual research
Date of Research: 1991 - continuing
KEYWORDS: career education; higher education; vocational guidance

9/0488
> Department of Educational Research, Cartmel College,
> Bailrigg, Lancaster LA1 4YW
> 0524 65201
> Fulton, O. Prof.; *Supervisor:* Fulton, O. Prof.

Mature students perceptions and performance of polytechnic degree courses
Abstract: Because of the increasing number of places available, coupled with the drop in birth rate more mature students enter higher education. However, they often face difficulties such as poor educational background and a more complex personal background. Such difficulties have been studied but not acted upon because mature students have been seen as an homogenous group and their problems considered accordingly. Although research has shown that mature students' examination results compare favourably with traditional entry students, the researcher believes that they could perform better and, equally importantly, could enjoy their courses more if their particular needs were considered. Using a broadly phenomenological perspective, the researcher contends that within polytechnics many mature students do not get the type of education that best fits their needs, needs which have been created by their past experiences. By studying different types of courses, with their contrasting styles and philosophies of teaching, in relation to categories of mature students we may better understand their needs. The research will involve statistically analysing questionnaires from around 600 mature degree students. Students' perceptions of higher education courses and the teaching styles used will be examined, and these perceptions related to their social and academic backgrounds and degree classification in order to establish any relationship between them. The findings will be used to assess through modelling the strength of the relationships between the various elements of the research, and thus gain an overview of the effects of specific types of courses on categories of mature students.

Status: Sponsored project
Source of Grant: Economic and Social Research Council
Date of Research: 1991 - continuing

KEYWORDS: academic achievement; educational experience; higher education; mature students; student attitudes

9/0489
> Department of Educational Research, Centre for the Study of
> Education and Training, Cartmel College, Bailrigg,
> Lancaster LA1 4YW
> 0524 65201
> Saunders, M. Dr; Fuller, A. Ms; Lobley, D. Mr; *Supervisor:*
> Fuller, A. Ms; Saunders, M. Dr

Employees' attitudes to learning at work
Abstract: This research has been commissioned by an international drinks company. The company is going through a period of rapid change following a take-over in the late eighties. Senior managers are reviewing all aspects of the business including human resource development. As a consequence, the Centre for the Study of Education and Training was asked to provide independent research on employees' attitudes to training and learning and work as well as to qualifications. Surveys and case studies have been conducted and the findings reported in a series of confidential documents. The researchers are hoping to publish their findings on completion of the work.

Status: Sponsored project
Source of Grant: United Distillers £110,000
Date of Research: 1990-1992
KEYWORDS: employee attitudes; on the job training; training; work-education relationship

9/0490
> Department of Educational Research, Centre for the Study of
> Education and Training, Cartmel College, Bailrigg,
> Lancaster LA1 4YW
> 0524 65201
> Helsby, G. Ms; Saunders, M. Dr

Lancaster Technical and Vocational Education Initiative evaluation programme
Abstract: The focus of the work has varied over the lifetime of the project, being based upon a consortium of 15 local education authorities (LEAs) under Technical and Vocational Education Initiative (TVEI) pilot, and a consortium of seven LEAs under TVEI extension. During TVEI pilot the researchers investigated the effect of TVEI upon students, teachers and institutions. This work included widescale student surveys amongst some 7,000 TVEI and non-TVEI students, as well as qualitative inquiry. Areas of particular interest included profiling, work experience, technology, cross-curriculum developments and teaching and learning strategies. During TVEI extension the focus was particularly upon the use of teacher-generated performance indicators as a route into self-evaluation. More recently the researchers have undertaken an investigation of the TVEI effect, including its impact upon whole institutional working and its influence upon change.

Published Material: A complete list of publications is available from the researcher
Status: Sponsored project
Source of Grant: LEAs Consortium; Employment Department/(MSC/Training Agency)
Date of Research: 1984 - continuing
KEYWORDS: programme evaluation; technical education; vocational education

9/0491
> Department of Educational Research, Centre for the Study of
> Education and Training, Cartmel College, Bailrigg,
> Lancaster LA1 4YW
> 0524 65201
> Davies, P. Mr; McHugh, G. Mrs

Career guidance in Avon: encouraging collaboration
Abstract: The aim of the study was to obtain a clear understanding of the expectations and needs of guidance users so that careers guidance provision in Avon is made more appropriate and effective. The research was undertaken on the basis of 300 questionnaires completed by students, 100 individual interviews and eight group interviews. The report for Avon Training and Enterprise Council concluded that although guidance users were satisfied with the guidance provision, greater collaboration and networking by guidance providers would enhance the overall provision of careers guidance.

Status: Sponsored project

Source of Grant: Avon Training and Enterprise Council £14,500
Date of Research: 1991-1991
KEYWORDS: career counselling; careers service; vocational guidance

9/0492
     Department of Educational Research, Centre for the Study of
     Education and Training, Cartmel College, Bailrigg,
     Lancaster LA1 4YW
     0524 65201
     Davies, P. Mr
Career guidance in Birmingham: a preliminary study
Abstract: The aim of the study was to map the career guidance
provision for young people in schools and colleges in Birmingham
and to identify the principal providers. Of particular importance was
the investigation of the potential for partnership agreements to be
drawn up between the main guidance providers. The research was
based on a study of documentary evidence and interviews with key
personnel. It was concluded that the partnership approach offered
considerable scope for the improvement of careers guidance in
schools and colleges. A report was produced for Birmingham Training and Education Council.
Status: Sponsored project
Source of Grant: Birmingham Training and Enterprise Council £4,800
Date of Research: 1991-1992
KEYWORDS: career counselling; careers service; vocational guidance

9/0493
     Department of Educational Research, Centre for the Study of
     Education and Training, Cartmel College, Bailrigg,
     Lancaster LA1 4YW
     0524 65201
     Machell, J. Ms; *Supervisor:* Saunders, M. Dr
**The reconstruction and transfer of learning: teaching for
effective learning in higher education**
Abstract: 'Transfer of learning' is a much used but misused phrase.
'Transfer' represents a facile, inflexible and surface approach to
learning which has limited use value. In contrast 'reconstructing
learning' – applying previous learning creatively in new contexts –
offers far more potential benefits and it is this ability, rather than
simple transfer, which instructional strategies should aim to develop.
The research will: (1) identify the key differences between transfer
and reconstruction; (2) establish connections between current educational concerns and reconstruction; (3) examine key theories of
learning which contribute to an understanding of reconstruction; (4)
explore the ways in which teaching in higher education facilitate
reconstruction; (5) discuss the implications of reconstructions for
teaching methods in higher education.
Status: Individual research
Date of Research: 1989 - continuing
KEYWORDS: higher education; prior learning; transfer of learning

9/0494
     Department of Educational Research, Centre for the Study of
     Education and Training, Cartmel College, Bailrigg,
     Lancaster LA1 4YW
     0524 65201
     Frank, F. Ms; *Supervisor:* Hamilton, M. Dr
Adult learning at work
Abstract: The aims of this project are to chart the contemporary
process of workplace literacy schemes, making the process more
viable and aiding its growth. Three main case studies with other minor
ones are being used plus a sample of 100 telephone interviews with
employers in the North West, in small and large sized companies.
The case studies will include interviews with students, union representatives, management and college staff involved at each site. Questionnaires are also being circulated to groups of students and group
discussions with students and union representatives have been organised. Loosely structured interviews will lead to qualitative data.
Telephone interviews will be carried out with the organisation personnel responsible for training, to ascertain the companies' attitudes
to workplace basic education training. Results and conclusions of the
research will be presented in a way which is accessible to employers
and trades unions and which will set out practical ways in which these
groups can proceed to set up workplace basic education schemes. A
longer report will be produced for the Leverhulme Trust.
Status: Sponsored project

Source of Grant: Leverhulme Trust £31,300
Date of Research: 1991-1992
KEYWORDS: adult basic education; adult literacy; works schools

9/0495
     Department of Educational Research, Centre for the Study of
     Education and Training, Cartmel College, Bailrigg,
     Lancaster LA1 4YW
     0524 65201
     Saunders, M. Dr; Machell, J. Ms; Lewis, R. Prof.
**The MEDA project (Methodologie d'Evaluation des
Didacticiels pour les Adultes)**
Abstract: MEDA is a collaborative European Community funded
project, involving participants from France, Belgium, Germany, Italy
and the United Kingdom which began in 1987. Stage 1 of the project
involved surveys of users of training courseware evaluation
throughout Europe. Stage 2 of MEDA had as its objective the
development of a generic evaluation tool for computer-based training
courseware. The team have now developed both a text-based and
software version of the MEDA tool. Stage 3 involved disseminating
the MEDA tool throughout Europe.
Published Material: The MEDA evaluation tool. (in press)
Status: Sponsored project
Source of Grant: European Community EUROTECNET Programme
Date of Research: 1987-1991
KEYWORDS: computer-assisted learning; educational material
evaluation; educational materials; educational software; training

9/0496
     Department of Educational Research, Centre for the Study of
     Education and Training, Cartmel College, Bailrigg,
     Lancaster LA1 4YW
     0524 65201
     McHugh, G. Mrs; Fuller, A. Ms; *Supervisor:* Saunders, M. Dr
**Individual motivation and take-up of National Vocational
Qualifications in the South West**
Abstract: This project aims to: (i) identify key factors which influence
and motivate individuals to pursue and obtain National Vocational
Qualifications (NVQs); (ii) to help Training and Enterprise Councils
(TECs) identify ways of increasing take-up of NVQs.
Status: Sponsored project
Source of Grant: Training, Enterprise and Education Directorate
£2,500
Date of Research: 1992-1992
KEYWORDS: employment qualifications; industry-education rela-
tionship; N ational Vocational Qualifications; student recruitment;
Training and Enterprise Councils; vocational education

9/0497
     Department of Educational Research, Centre for the Study of
     Education and Training, Cartmel College, Bailrigg,
     Lancaster LA1 4YW
     0524 65201
     McHugh, G. Mrs; *Supervisor:* Saunders, M. Dr
Evaluation of the Lancashire Licensed Teachers Scheme
Abstract: This is a brief evaluation of the Lancashire Licensed
Teachers Scheme which has been jointly delivered by Lancashire
Local Education Authority and the two collaborating colleges of
education, which has been running since September 1991.
Status: Sponsored project
Source of Grant: Lancashire Local Education Authority £37,000
Date of Research: 1992 - continuing
KEYWORDS: licensed teachers; preservice teacher education; pro-
gramme evaluation; teachers qualifications; teaching profession

9/0498
     Department of Educational Research, Centre for Women's
     Studies, Cartmel College, Bailrigg, Lancaster LA1 4YW
     0524 65201
     Tinkler, P. Dr
Young women and leisure, 1920-1950
Abstract: This research has two aims. First, it explores the structural
and ideological context within which young women's leisure was
situated in terms of the social and economic conditions in which girls
grew up and the influences which young women were exposed to
through the family, schooling, paid work, formal leisure provision,

media and popular culture. Second, it aims to uncover the actual leisure practices of young women during the period 1920-50. The research is structured in two parts reflecting these dual aims. The first part of this research addresses the social, economic and ideological context of young women's leisure activity. It draws upon a range of sources including official documentation, academic and popular literature; census material and Board/Ministry of Education statistics; a range of data relating to the conditions of life of young women including that pertaining to schooling, paid work, housing and home conditions, health, courtship and sexuality. Three main themes structure this part of the research – access to leisure, the temporal dimensions of leisure, and the question of suitable leisure activity. The second part of the research explores young women's experience and understanding of leisure using oral history sources as well as autobiographies, diaries, contemporary studies and material from the Mass Observation Archive (Sussex University).
Status: Sponsored project
Source of Grant: British Academy
Date of Research: 1990 - continuing
KEYWORDS: *girls; leisure time; recreational activities; women's studies*

9/0499
Department of Educational Research, Cartmel College, Bailrigg, Lancaster LA1 4YW
0524 65201
Reading University, Department of Education Studies and Management, Bulmershe Court, Woodlands Avenue, Earley, Reading RG6 1HY
0734 875123
Deem, R. Prof.; Brehony, K. Dr
Reforming school governing bodies: a sociological investigation
Abstract: School governing bodies in England and Wales were reshaped in the autumn of 1988 as a result of the 1986 (No 2) Education Act, with greater parental representation and more co-opted governors (including those from the business community). The 1986 Act and the 1988 Education Act have also given governors more power over schools than previously. The project is an in depth study of ten school governing bodies (four primary and six secondary) in two local education authorities. A pilot study ran from October 1988 to July 1992. The research has monitored what coping strategies governing bodies are using to deal with the tasks and responsibilities given to them by the new educational legislation and has also focused on the identification of power relations (including gender and race/ethnicity), decision making processes and networks of influence operating in the eight governing bodies. The project also, in addition, seeks to discover whether co-opted governors and parent governors (widely described as 'consumer') come to predominate over those sometimes termed 'producer' governors (teacher and local education authority representative) and headteachers. The work has been done through observation of formal, informal and sub-committee meetings, questionnaires and interviews.
Published Material: BREHONY, K.J.B. (1990). 'Neither rhyme nor reason – primary schooling and the National Curriculum'. In: FLUDE, M. & HAMMER, M. (Eds). The 1988 Education Act. London: Falmer Press.; DEEM, R. (1990). 'The reform of school governing bodies – the power of the consumer over the producer?'. In: FLUDE, M. & HAMMER, M. (Eds). The 1988 Education Act. London: Falmer Press.; DEEM, R. & BREHONY, K.J.B. (1990). 'The long and the short of it', Times Educational Supplement, 13 July.; HEMMINGS, S. (1990). 'Determined to see it through', Times Educational Supplement, 21 July.
Status: Sponsored project
Source of Grant: Economic and Social Research Council £56,720
Date of Research: 1990 - continuing
KEYWORDS: *local management of schools; parent participation; participative decision making; school-based management; school governing bodies; school governors*

9/0500
Department of Linguistics and Modern English Language, Cartmel College, Bailrigg, Lancaster LA1 4YW
0524 65201
Barton, D. Dr; Hamilton, M. Dr
Literacy in the community
Abstract: This project will investigate the role of literacy in adult life in contemporary Britain, by means of ethnographic interviews and observation. It will document the everyday practical uses of literacy in the household and in the community and examine how they interface with school and work. The aim is to extend the view of literacy which currently informs educational practice at all levels and to contribute to the debate on levels of literacy in our society. The focus will be on literacy 'practices' or 'events' and on exploring the social meanings of literacy to the people involved.
Published Material: A series of working papers are available on request from the researcher.
Status: Sponsored project
Source of Grant: Economic and Social Research Council £54,000
Date of Research: 1989-1991
KEYWORDS: *educational objectives; life skills; literacy*

Leeds Metropolitan University

9/0501
Department of Education, Faculty of Cultural and Education Studies, Beckett Park, Leeds LS6 3QS
0532 832600
Abou El-Khir, M. Mr; *Supervisor:* Perkin, R. Dr; Long, J. Mr; Duffield, B. Mr
The use of resources in the development of learning through drama in education in primary schools
Abstract: The study seeks to examine the assertion that the use of theatre resources (such as lighting, costume, properties, sound effects etc.) enhances the symbolic fictitious world created in educational drama sessions thereby influencing learning outcomes. A localised survey followed by selective interviews will provide data relating to the attitudes of primary teachers to the assertion. The assertion itself will be tested through action research and participant observation, culminating in a case study of drama practice with a particular class of primary children.
Status: Sponsored project
Source of Grant: Egyptian Education Bureau
Date of Research: 1990 - continuing
KEYWORDS: *drama education; dramatics; learning processes; primary education; theatre arts*

Leeds University

9/0502
Adult Education Centre, 37 Harrow Road, Middlesbrough, Cleveland TS5 5NT
0642 814987
Durham University, Department of Adult and Continuing Education, 32 Old Elvet, Durham DH1 3HN
091 374 3724
Dodd, J. Mr; *Supervisor:* Taylor, R. Prof.; Williamson, W. Dr
Accelerated access to higher education from science and technology based industries
Abstract: The project arose from discussions of adult education provision in the Teesside area involving the departments concerned at Durham and Leeds universities. The aim is to facilitate entry into undergraduate courses by staff from the science and technology based industries, in conjunction with ICI, British Steel and Tioxide (UK). Admissions tutors in the relevant departments of both universities were consulted individually on their attitudes towards, and experience of, mature students having non-standard entry qualifications. Whilst they were favourably-disposed towards such students, concern was expressed that although most satisfied the general Matriculation requirement they did not necessarily meet specific entry requirements for individual courses, and that there was a general weakness in mathematics. A survey of technicians on Teesside and in Leeds produced 360 returns of a questionnaire which showed that more than half were interested in proceeding into higher education and most of these had at least the minimum educational qualifications to do so, but the vast majority wished to do so on a part-time basis. A detailed investigation of the nature of mathematical provision at sub-degree level, including the running of two short courses on Teesside, produced two levels of mathematics acceptable to tutors. These were incorporated into a modular access programme including biology, chemistry and physics, a suitable selection from which was

agreed by tutors as qualifying for admission. Forty students are now following the programme in Leeds or Middlesbrough. An Apel procedure is being developed to identify suitable candidates for entry with advanced standing.

Status: Sponsored project
Source of Grant: Training, Enterprise and Education Directorate £120,000
Date of Research: 1990-1992
KEYWORDS: *Access programmes; access to education; higher education; industry-higher education relationship; mature students; technician education*

9/0503
Centre for Studies in Science & Mathematics in Education, Leeds LS2 9JT
0532 431751
Jagger, J. Mrs; *Supervisor:* Orton, A. Dr
Students' understanding of acceleration as a vector in the context of mechanics
Abstract: This research aims to investigate the growth in students' understanding of acceleration as rate of change in velocity (as distinct from rate of change of speed) in the context of mechanics. Pupils' understanding was investigated by means of questionnaires administered to them three times during their A-level mathematics course. A questionnaire was also given to first year Honours mathematics undergraduates. The sample involved included: 120 lower sixth formers who had elected to study mathematics at A-level; 120 upper sixth formers who were studying mathematics at A-level; 60 first year Honours mathematics undergraduates. The school pupils were taken from three comprehensive schools in the north of England. About 40 of them have been followed through from lower sixth to upper sixth including an extra questionnaire in March.
Published Material: JAGGER, J.M. (1985). 'Introducing mechanics – a response', Mathematics in School, Vol 14, No 1, pp.24-26.; JAGGER, J.M. (1985). 'A review of the research into the learning of mathematics'. In: ORTON, A. (Ed). Studies in mechanics learning. Leeds University.; JAGGER, J.M. (1987). 'Students' understanding of acceleration', Mathematics in School, Vol 16, No 4, pp.24-25.
Status: Individual research
Date of Research: 1985-1992
KEYWORDS: *acceleration – physics; comprehension; higher education; mathematics education; mechanics – physics; secondary education*

9/0504
Centre for Studies in Science and Mathematics Education, Leeds LS2 9JT
0532 334675
Leach, J. Mr; *Supervisor:* Driver, R. Prof.; Scott, P. Mr; Wood-Robinson, C. Mr
Conceptual progression in science
Abstract: This research project has been commissioned by the National Curriculum Council to undertake research into the progression of children's conceptual understanding in attainment target 2 (AT2) of the National Curriculum, The Variety of Life. This attainment target focuses upon classification of living things, the cycling of matter, flows of energy and interdependency in ecosystems. Data will be collected, across the 5-16 age range at eight different sampling ages, using interview, paper and pencil and direct classroom techniques. These various approaches are designed to ascertain children's understanding of key ideas such as photosynthesis, respiration and decay at the different ages. The final report of the project will contain information about the progression in children's understandings relating to key ideas in this area. A review of existing research literature will be included and information about current approaches to teaching in this area will also be provided. A booklet for the use of teachers will be prepared and a package of inservice training material will also be produced.
Published Material: LEACH, J. (1990). 'Progression in children's understanding from age 5-16 around AT2 in the Science National Curriculum: The Variety of Life'. Paper presented to the British Educational Research Association, Roehampton Institute, September 1990. Derby: British Educational Research Association.
Status: Sponsored project
Source of Grant: National Curriculum Council £78,478
Date of Research: 1990-1991
KEYWORDS: *concept formation; National Curriculum; science education*

9/0505
Centre for Studies in Science and Mathematics Education, Leeds LS2 9JT
0532 431751
Bassett, J. Mr; *Supervisor:* Wain, G. Mr
Key Stage 1 of the National Curriculum in Mathematics as it relates to infant schools in Huddersfield
Abstract: This research study will investigate the mathematics curriculum of 70 schools engaged in Key Stage 1 of the National Curriculum in Huddersfield. It will cover the background to the setting up of the National Curriculum and the philosophy which underpins it. It will involve looking at infant/first school models of the curriculum and, in particular, the mathematics curriculum and to relate these to the National Curriculum. The content of Key Stage 1 of the National Curriculum will be analysed and compared with the pre National Curriculum mathematics curriculum. Similarly the assessment component will be analysed in terms of assessment theory and pre National Curriculum assessment procedures in school. The influence of the Standard Assessment Tasks of school internal curriculum assessments and approaches to teaching methods will be ascertained. The results of the first unreported Standard Assessment Tasks and the first reported Standard Assessment Tasks will be analysed in terms of what they mean in themselves and the affect on schools. The effects of the National Curriculum on the content of the mathematics curriculum in schools, internal assessment, and approaches to mathematics teaching will be assessed by means of a teacher questionnaire. This will be sent to all teachers involved in Key Stage 1 in 70 Huddersfield schools. A separate questionnaire will be sent to mathematics co-ordinators in the same schools. Selective interviews in a sample of the schools will be used to support the questionnaires. The questionnaires cover teacher opinions on effectiveness of National Curriculum INSET (Inservice Education of Teachers), areas where further training is needed, areas in which teachers feel confident/lacking confidence and resource needs to implement National Curriculum Mathematics.
Status: Individual research
Date of Research: 1989 - continuing
KEYWORDS: *assessment; first schools; infant schools; mathematics curriculum; mathematics teachers; standard assessment tasks*

9/0506
Centre for Studies in Science and Mathematics Education, Leeds LS2 9JT
0532 431751
Hargreaves, S. Mr; *Supervisor:* Wain, G. Mr; Beard, R. Dr
Cohesive ties in children's use of language in relation to the teaching of mathematics
Abstract: A cohesive tie is defined as a semantic relation between items of a text, or between an item of a text and some feature of a broader context to which the textual item is perceived to be related. Cohesive ties may be recognised in all forms of text, including mathematics text and spoken or written discourse. Natural language communication is 'fuzzy'; that is characterised by probablistic structures and operations which are not fully delimited. Computer operations are taken to be logical, even when inputs and outputs are in the form of natural language signs or symbols, and therefore 'unfuzzy'. Observations and video-recordings were made of children in pairs discussing with a view to problem solving an interactive mathematical computer-based game. The main purpose of the empirical work was to seek evidence to support a view that children's use of language is characteristic of particular stages or states of learning; and that their use of language, as learning progresses, becomes increasingly characteristic of a competent or expert user. As natural language is 'fuzzy' there are problems in attempting any analysis of its manifestations if this is not to rely on purely formal definitions such as those of a dictionary. Therefore it was necessary to develop a systematic model which was somewhat removed from natural language description. Recorded discussions were analysed into categories of cohesive ties and this data subjected to cluster analysis and represented as hierarchical trees. An independent narrow measure of children's competence and efficiency in achieving the object of play was also used. The recordings contained material which suggested, possibly, that children were responding differently to their task by reasons of variations in their past experience, their knowledge, mood and intention. Something of the influence of such matters was revealed more clearly by the clustering technique adopted suggesting that it may be an effective means of representing effects of non-observable entities. The method of analysis and modelling would seem to have useful application as a bridging technique between views held on the basis

of general psychological or epistemological theory and records of performance based upon individual observation. The empirical study was seen upon analysis to reveal patterns of association in meaning which have implications for producers and users of educational software. Perhaps the form of modelling adopted and developed would be useful, with appropriate modifications, in exploring children's responses to methods and materials adopted by schools in their efforts to implement the National Curriculum.
Status: Individual research
Date of Research: 1985-1992
KEYWORDS: child language; computer uses in education; language of instruction; mathematics education

9/0507
Department of Adult Continuing Education, Leeds LS2 9JT
0532 431751
Chase, M. Dr; Donajgrodzki, A. Dr; Harrison, B. Mr;
Murphy, B. Ms
Evaluating rural adult learning
Abstract: This project aims to evaluate the educational content and delivery of 'non-educational' agencies in rural areas. It provides an assessment of mature learning activity in rural areas: how adults learn, where, for what purposes and to what effect. It highlights current good practice at the interface of non-formal and statutory continuing education provision.
Status: Sponsored project
Source of Grant: Universities Funding Council £35,900
Date of Research: 1990-1991
KEYWORDS: adult education; continuing education; evaluation; mature students; nonformal education; rural areas

9/0508
Department of Adult Continuing Education, Leeds LS2 9JT
0532 431751
Payne, J. Dr; *Supervisor:* Ward, K. Mr; Forrester, K. Mr
The Leeds adult learners at work project
Abstract: The aims of the project are to study work-based learning to: (1) identify existing schemes and facilities by which employers cater for the continuing general education and training of their employees; (2) determine the factors that affect the success of such schemes; (3) explore the theoretical issues emerging which relate to adult learning at the workplace; (4) examine the policy issues relating to the development of lifelong learning; and (5) make international comparisons. In practical terms this will involve: gathering information about existing schemes; visiting existing schemes, together with interested individuals and organisations; and selecting a number of schemes in different kinds of enterprise for more detailed evaluation. Newsletters, journal articles and a final report will be produced.
Status: Sponsored project
Source of Grant: Universities Funding Council
Date of Research: 1991 - continuing
KEYWORDS: adult education; labour force development; works schools

9/0509
Department of Adult Continuing Education, Leeds LS2 9JT
0532 431751
Taylor, R. Prof.
Continuing education practice in Canada and the United Kingdom: a case study of Calgary and Leeds Universities
Abstract: Continuing education provision in Canada and the United Kingdom operates on different models. This research analyzes assumptions, priorities, models, financing, curriculum approaches and outcomes in the two countries, using case study material for Calgary and Leeds.
Status: Sponsored project
Source of Grant: Alberta/Leeds Exchange Scheme £1,800
Date of Research: 1988-1992
KEYWORDS: adult education; Canada; comparative education; continuing education

9/0510
Department of Adult Continuing Education, Leeds LS2 9JT
0532 431751
Taylor, R. Prof.; Steele, G. Dr

An examination of the inter-relationship between the development of adult education, Gandhian philosophy, the Congress Party, and the legacy of the British Raj, in India between 1935 and 1955, and an analysis of subsequent developments in adult education in the period up to the 1980s
Abstract: This project concerns the influence of British cultural values, practices and structures on the development of adult education in India from the 1930s to the 1980s. British cultural legacy was not homogenous, as with the industrial British society from which it sprang, its imperial strands were diverse and often conflicting. A major theme of the study will be to disentangle these various elements and to match them up both to the empirical development of adult education structures in India, and to the political dimensions of British culture in the UK. An essential concern will be the relationship between Gandhian philosophy and adult education development. Linked to this will be a study of the educational dimension to the emerging Congress Party as the dominant political force in India before, during and after Indian independence.
Status: Sponsored project
Source of Grant: Universities Funding Council £42,000
Date of Research: 1989-1992
KEYWORDS: adult education; educational history; India

9/0511
Department of Adult Continuing Education, Leeds LS2 9JT
0532 431751
Gardiner, J. Ms; *Supervisor:* Taylor, R. Prof.
Widening access to human resources disciplines: developing opportunities for ethnic minority students at the University of Leeds
Abstract: The project is part of a national collaborative action research project on widening access to higher education. The aims are to: (1) evaluate strategies for pre-degree and degree course curriculum change in the social sciences and humanities which enhance access to degree programmes for black/ethnic minority mature students; (2) gather evidence on and evaluate the experiences of non-traditional students from different ethnic backgrounds on access and degree coures; (3) analyse the results of ethnic monitoring of applications, offers and acceptances for undergraduate places at the University of Leeds; and (4) disseminate the project results. Methods used include: (1) participant observation of curriculum development processes; (2) content analysis of structured interviews; and (3) statistical analysis of ethnic monitoring and course outcomes data.
Status: Sponsored project
Source of Grant: Department of Employment via Focus Educational Consultancy £17,882
Date of Research: 1991-1992
KEYWORDS: access to education; black students; equal education; ethnic groups; higher education; mature students

9/0512
Department of Adult Continuing Education, Leeds LS2 9JT
0532 431751
Steele, G. Dr; *Supervisor:* Titmus, C. Prof.
The export of the British extramural model to Africa 1945-60
Abstract: The aim is to describe and analyse the development of British extramural education in Africa during the immediate pre-independence and post-independence period. The research examines the role of education within British colonial policy under the Labour government and especially the parts played by the Fabian Colonial Bureau and the Colonial Secretary Creech-Jones; the original initiative of the University of Oxford Delegacy and its secretary Thomas Hodgkin; the relationship of the initial courses to African nationalist movements; the establishment of African university adult education departments; the role of Sidney Raybould and other leading British adult educationists in Africa; the subsequent Africanisation of university extramural departments; the roles of American and European influences in countering the British model; the comparison with 'mass education' and the origins of 'community development'. The intention is to conclude with some firm observations on the nature of cultural borrowing. Sources of material used are mostly archival including universities in Britain and Africa and the Public Records Office, but interviews and correspondence with exponents will add significant detail.
Published Material: STEELE, T. 'Metropolitan extensions: a comparison of two moments in the export of British University Adult Education, Europe 1890-1910 and Africa 1945-1955'. In: MAR-RIOTT, J.S.M. & HAKE, B. (Eds). (1992). Leeds Studies in the

Education of Adults, Proceedings of the Leiden Conference of Intercultural Adult Education.
Status: Sponsored project
Source of Grant: Universities Funding Council
Date of Research: 1990-1992
KEYWORDS: adult education; Africa; colonialism; educational history; extension education

9/0513
Department of Adult Continuing Education, Leeds LS2 9JT
0532 431751
Steele, G. Dr; *Supervisor:* Marriott, J. Prof.
The international reception of British university extension 1885-1925
Abstract: The aim is to discover the extent of the influence of British 'university extension'. The research will examine and analyse the wide variety of adult educational practices in Europe which appeared during the 1890s which were called 'university extension' and attempts to assess their relationship to the British model. Sources of the research are primarily archival, including reports of international conferences published in Britain and France, reports in British and American university extension journals, collections of papers and memoirs. A chronology of the development of university extension in Europe (excluding Germany) will be attempted, this will try to create a typology of occurrences. The research will also isolate and describe significant features of the development including the objectives of university extension, the role of radical and liberal university lecturers, the international networking and solidarising of schoolteachers as a profession, the relation of adult education to national and workers' movements, scientific and objective education and the nature of cultural borrowing.
Published Material: STEELE, T. (1992). 'Metropolitan extensions: a comparison of two moments in the export of British University Adult Education, Europe 1890-1910 and Africa 1945-1955'. In: MARRIOTT, J.S.M. & HAKE, B. (Eds). (1992). Leeds Studies in the Education of Adults, Proceedings of the Leiden Conference of Intercultural Adult Education.
Status: Sponsored project
Source of Grant: Universities Funding Council
Date of Research: 1990-1992
KEYWORDS: adult education; comparative education; educational history; extension education

9/0514
Department of Adult Continuing Education, Study of Continuing Education Unit, Leeds LS2 9JT
0532 431751
Malcolm, J. Ms
A study of the relationship between intentions and outcomes of policy initiatives related to women's education and training
Abstract: This study will investigate the relationship between government policy initiatives and the provision and outcomes of continuing education aimed mainly at women. It will attempt to establish whether the outcomes of, e.g. access courses, employment training and 'positive action' courses run over the last 15 years are in accordance with their publicly espoused purposes. The strategies adopted in such initiatives will be critically examined in terms of their roots in the policy process, their rationale and the consequences for women students and for educational institutions. The study will analyse the link, if it exists, between educational programmes directed at women and longer-term changes in their social and economic position as a group.
Status: Individual research
Date of Research: 1991 - continuing
KEYWORDS: Access programmes; continuing education; educational benefits; educational objectives; women's education

9/0515
Department of Continuing Professional Education, Leeds LS2 9NG
0532 431751
Todd, F. Dr; Tovey, P. Dr; *Supervisor:* Todd, F. Dr
Quality assurance in continuing professional education
Abstract: United Kingdom universities offer programmes of continuing professional education for a wide range of professional groups. The clientele for continuing professional education (CPE) includes professional institutions, employers and individual professionals. A substantial proportion of such programmes comprises short, intensive courses which are not credit-rated and which are planned and held outside existing university course monitoring mechanisms. In the context of an increasing interest in quality assurance procedures (including the setting up of the Committee of Vice-Chancellors and Principals' academic audit unit) this project will explore the quality assurance mechanisms that are or could be used in (primarily university-based) CPE provision. The research will explore current practice in this field by universities. It will examine quality assurance procedures used in other sectors (e.g. the construction industry, social services and health care) and will assess the applicability of such methods and concepts (e.g. the use of British Standard 5750) to university-based CPE. Data will be collected through questionnaires to all university CPE providers, to a sample of academic departments which provide CPE independently and to certain professional institutions, employers, and clients. Interviews will be used to follow up key issues in greater depth. Consultancy advice will be taken on quality assurance procedures outside higher education. The aims will be to produce recommendations on good practice and the results of the research will be discussed through workshops and/or conferences as well as through papers and publications.
Status: Sponsored project
Source of Grant: Universities Funding Council £36,570
Date of Research: 1990-1992
KEYWORDS: course evaluation; professional continuing education; quality assurance; quality control

9/0516
Department of Continuing Professional Education, Leeds LS2 9JT
0532 431751
Todd, F. Dr; Neale, P. Mrs
United Kingdom professions and the European challenge
Abstract: This research arises out of the European Community Directive on rights of establishment which was implemented from 1991, together with the various sectoral directives already in force. Professional groups in the United Kingdom are faced with the need to develop new policies, practices and requirements in regard to Europe. These formal and public moves are being made in the context of changing attitudes toward the Directive, and complex developments in cross-national working relations between partner professional institutions and their members. This is a three year, real-time study of British professionals, their employers and their institutions in a period of change. It is examining the extent and nature of the links being established with other professional organisations within the European Community to analyse developing policies and practices towards Europe and how these might be affected by cross-national working relations. An assessment will be made of the implications for continuing professional education. The first phase of this project has been a comprehensive study of the 77 professional institutions whose members are affected by the First General Directive on the Mutual Recognition of Qualifications. The response rate to this recently completed exercise has been 70%. The second phase will involve a series of case studies of selected professional institutions and particular issues raised by the professions' response to Europe. The preliminary computer data analysis suggests that the advent of the Single European Market is not as significant as one might have predicted for all the professions surveyed. Many have taken an international stand on their professional activities on behalf of their members for a substantial number of years. Nonetheless, professional institutions are aware of the opportunities and problems that may arise for their practitioners in the next few years and they are becoming increasingly active on behalf of their members, and of the public they serve.
Status: Sponsored project
Source of Grant: Universities Funding Council £75,491
Date of Research: 1990 - continuing
KEYWORDS: European Community; professional associations; professional continuing education; qualifications; Single European Market

9/0517
School of Education, Leeds LS2 9JT
0532 333210
Marriott, J. Prof.
Hudson Shaw and the university extension movement
Abstract: This research is a biography of G.W. Hudson Shaw. Although Shaw was always acknowledged as one of the greatest figures of the Oxford Extension Movement, he has not received serious biographical attention. The study will set the record right about his

origins, his early life and personal/family circumstances. It will treat him as the eiptome of the Oxford Extension Movement, and examine the origins and character of his educational beliefs and commitments. Leading sub-themes will be: use of the ideas of John Ruskin; the attitude to working-class education and the effects of a changing political climate; relations to the early Workers' Educational Association (WEA); his position as an ordained clergyman of the Church of England; his relationship to Maude Royden, feminist and advocate of female ordination. The method of research is conventionally historical and biographical.
Published Material: MARRIOTT, J.S. (1985). 'Shaw, George William Hudson 1859-1944'. In: THOMAS, J.E. & ELSEY, B. (Eds). International biography of Adult Education. Nottingham University.
Status: Individual research
Date of Research: 1988 - continuing
KEYWORDS: adult education; biographies; educational history; extension education; universities; working class

9/0518
   School of Education, Leeds LS2 9JT
   0532 333210
   Marriott, J. Prof.
University extension and national education
Abstract: This research is a policy and organisational study of the university extension system (1873-1914) which argues that the movement cannot be adequately understood in terms of the later concept of 'adult education'. The aspirations and efforts of extension are presented in the context of changing attitudes towards secondary, technical and higher education, and in the light of its aims of becoming a recognised element within 'national education'. Also emphasised is the implicit shaping of policy by the internal organisational problems of the movement. Sub-themes include: the search for financial aid from the State; the relation to technical instruction; the relation to secondary education and the training of teachers; involvement in local institutes for higher education; historical application of organisation theory. The method used is historical; the analysis draws additionally on the sociology of organisations.
Published Material: MARRIOTT, J.S. (1981). 'State Aid', Studies in Adult Education, No 13.; MARRIOTT, J.S. (1981). 'The University Extension movement and the education of teachers', History of Education, No 10.; MARRIOTT, J.S. (1983). 'The whisky money and the University Extension movement', Journal of Educational Administration and History, No 15.; MARRIOTT, J.S. (1981). A backstairs to a degree. Leeds: Leeds University.
Status: Individual research
Date of Research: 1988 - continuing
KEYWORDS: adult education; educational history; educational policy; extension education; working class

9/0519
   School of Education, Leeds LS2 9JT
   0532 431751
   Chambers, G. Mr; *Supervisor:* Sugden, D. Dr;
   Tomlinson, P. Dr
The demotivated pupil in the modern language classroom – a comparative study
Abstract: The National Curriculum heralds the implementation of the 'Language for All' policy, introduced in some schools in the course of the 1980s. Of great concern to teachers is how to cater for the disaffected or demotivated pupil. It is generally felt that German pupils are more motivated to learn English than British pupils are to learn German. Popular reasons for this include English as the language of the business world and pop-culture. How much of this is fact and how much myth? The purpose of the study is to investigate the problem of demotivation in foreign language learners in Leeds and Kiel. The study will look at similar groups of 13-14 year olds in terms of ability and background in similar schools in Leeds and Kiel. This age range has been chosed as it is at this stage that demotivation commonly and significantly manifests itself. Surveys and subsequent interviews with pupils and teachers will try to identify the causes of demotivation and the strategies used to counter it. The study will examine several questions: 1) the effect on motivation of the attitude to language learning brought from home and friends; the influence of the media; the influence of the teacher and teaching methods; the influence of pupil perception of need; the influence of the language learning environment; 2) how teachers identify demotivated pupils; 3) how teachers deal with demotivated pupils.
Status: Individual research

Date of Research: 1991 - continuing
KEYWORDS: language attitudes; language teachers; learning motivation; modern language studies

9/0520
   School of Education, Leeds LS2 9JT
   0532 431751
   Finer, A. Mr; *Supervisor:* Child, D. Prof.
The effect of a thinking skills programme on the development of selected performance measures in prelingual deaf students
Abstract: The aim of the present investigation is to utilize a course for deaf students that provides a conceptual framework which underpins the many curricula changes taking place in schools. The course consists of a series of visually based discussion tasks which highlight and develop many essential cross-curricular pupil resources. The course addresses a range of overlapping cognitive, linguistic, personal and social issues, all of which are relevant to the specific needs of deaf students. Samples of prelingual deaf students attending resourced mainstream schools will be used at primary and secondary levels. Assessment will be made of intellectual abilities, reading comprehension, social functioning, problem solving ability and educational measures similar to proposed standard attainment tasks in the context of the National Curriculum. Subjects will follow a programme over the period of an academic year and rate and amount of improvement will be measured and comparisons made with control groups. Four schools will be used with experimental and control groups totalling 60 in each at both primary and secondary level. Stepwise regression analysis will be used to identify predictor variables for a number of criterion measures, prior to the use of multiple analysis of co-variance. Teacher and educational interpreter effects will be examined on the development of the criterion measures.
Published Material: FINER, A.R. (1990). 'The effectiveness of a thinking skills programme on the educational attainment of secondary age deaf students'. Proceedings of the 17th International Congress on Education of the Deaf, in Rochester, New York. National Technical Institute for the Deaf.
Status: Individual research
Date of Research: 1989 - continuing
KEYWORDS: course evaluation; curriculum development; deafness; interdisciplinary approach; special educational needs; thinking skills

9/0521
   School of Education, Leeds LS2 9JT
   0532 431751
   Roper, T. Mr; *Supervisor:* Orton, A. Dr
The historical development of selected principles in mechanics and the relationship with growth of understanding in students
Abstract: The development of the principles of mechanics throughout history has been slow and faltering. The same can be said about the growth of understanding of these principles in students. The study aims to investigate the relationship between the historical development and the growth of understanding.
Status: Individual research
Date of Research: 1989 - continuing
KEYWORDS: comprehension; mechanics – physics; student development

9/0522
   School of Education, Leeds LS2 9JT
   0532 431751
   de Medeiros, C. Mrs; *Supervisor:* Orton, A. Dr
An investigation into errors made in attempts to solve mathematical problems
Abstract: The study aims to investigate teacher perceptions of pupils' errors in elementary arithmetic with a view to developing teacher training techniques which will enable teachers to improve their teaching methods. Selected groups of young pupils have been tested using simple problems and their errors have been classified by teachers in training, in a preparatory study aimed at clarifying the issues and problems. A further study of pupils' problem solving has yielded data which is currently being analyzed.
Status: Sponsored project
Source of Grant: Brazilian Government
Date of Research: 1988-1992
KEYWORDS: arithmetic; mathematical ability; mathematics education; problem solving; teacher education; teaching methods

9/0523

School of Education, Leeds LS2 9JT
0532 431751
McAuley, J. Mr; *Supervisor:* Orton, A. Dr
Cognitive style and learning mathematics
Abstract: The implications of cognitive styles such as field dependence and field independence in learning mathematics have not been widely investigated. This study aims to focus on such styles and the implications in learning matrices. It is expected that pupils will be assessed and classified on a field dependence/field independence spectrum and the effects of different teaching styles will be measured.
Status: Individual research
Date of Research: 1989 - continuing
KEYWORDS: cognitive processes; cognitive style; field dependence/independence; learning; mathematics; teaching styles

9/0524

School of Education, Leeds LS2 9JT
0532 431751
Child, D. Prof.; Baker, R. Mr
Survey of communication practices in schools for the hearing impaired in the United Kingdom
Abstract: In 1987 a survey was carried out with a number of schools for the hearing impaired in England and Scotland using a total communication approach. When the findings were circulated, suggestions were made by several headteachers for a further study to explore in more detail the ways in which different modes of communication are used, demand for resource materials, training of staff and parents in communication skills and the roles of deaf people in the schools. It has subsequently been suggested that a new survey be carried out to establish exactly what range of approaches are used throughout all the schools at the present time. A questionnaire was designed which asks for communication approaches in use, in order to provide a base of information for planning for future needs. At the same time, it goes more deeply into aspects of practices in schools using a total communication approach, in response to the requests already made by headteachers. The questionnaire has now been circulated and a 100% return obtained. The data are in the process of being analyzed. The findings will be circulated to all participants.
Status: Sponsored project
Source of Grant: Northern Counties School for the Deaf £4,000
Date of Research: 1990-1992
KEYWORDS: communication skills; deafness; hearing impairments; hearing therapy; special schools; total communication

9/0525

School of Education, Leeds LS2 9JT
0532 431751
Lewis, I. Mr; *Supervisor:* Jenkins, E. Mr; Donnelly, J. Dr
A study of technological capability as manifest in secondary school pupils' project work
Abstract: The study is an exploration of 'the technology project' with particular attention being given to its origination, development and closure. An attempt is made to establish the criteria used by pupils in, for example, choosing one solution/design criteria in preference to another, evaluating/apraising their project as it develops. The work is based on an ethnographic study of pupils in classes in five Sheffield schools. A sample size of about 10 pupils is likely to be involved.
Status: Sponsored project
Source of Grant: Leeds University: School of Education; Sheffield Local Education Authority
Date of Research: 1989-1991
KEYWORDS: ability; projects – learning activities; pupil projects; secondary education; technology education

9/0526

School of Education, Leeds LS2 9JT
0532 431751
Snape, J. Mr; *Supervisor:* Child, D. Prof.
Stress on college lecturers working in the North East of England and its possible effects on student learning
Abstract: This study presents the findings of research into aspects of stress among lecturers working in colleges of further education in the North East of England. The empirical work was carried out over one academic year with 130 lecturers and 213 of their students, all chosen at random, participating in the study. Seven instruments were used, namely: a 'stress' questionnaire; two types of logs, and a personality questionnaire for lecturers; and one 'annoyance' questionnaire and two types of logs for students. The study set out to address the broad question of whether stress among college lecturers affected the teaching process and, in turn, the students' learning. The data highlighted that there were three broad problem areas or sources of stress for the lecturers: the teaching process; relationships; and other factors. These were further divided into the categories: resources; teaching; environment; students; staff; management; aspects external to the college; and administration. The effects of these stressors on the lecturers were demonstrated in feelings and actions which affected the role as a teacher, both inside and outside the classroom. Statistical analysis of all the responses revealed that similar stressors, and sources of annoyance, occurred throughout the academic year in all the colleges sampled. The lecturers with the most class-contact were found to have lower levels of self-esteem and higher levels of anxiety. This aspect was demonstrated particularly by female respondents, and those new to teaching. There were indications that the teaching process and students' learning were negatively affected by lecturers' stress, as perceived either directly or indirectly, by both students and lecturers. It was the potential learning experience that was seen to be most at risk.
Status: Individual research
Date of Research: 1986-1991
KEYWORDS: colleges of further education; stress – psychological; teacher behaviour; teacher-student relationship

9/0527

School of Education, Leeds LS2 9JT
0532 431751
Henry, M. Mr; *Supervisor:* Jenkins, E. Mr; Sharp, P. Dr
Technical education, 1880-1914, with particular reference to the printing trade
Abstract: The study uses a range of primary sources to examine the origins, nature and development of technical education for the printing industry from 1880 to 1914. The study is placed in the broader context of the technical education movement and addresses the questions concerned with the politics of curriculum design and innovation in the area of vocational education. It also examines the relationship between employers and employees and evaluates the effect of technical education classes upon the education and training of printers.
Published Material: HENRY, M. (1987). 'The nineteenth-century printing apprenticeship: elements of change'. In: MYERS, R. & HARRIS, M. (Eds). Aspects of printing from 1600. Headington: Oxford Polytechnic Press.
Status: Individual research
Date of Research: 1986-1992
KEYWORDS: educational history; printing; technical education; vocational education

9/0528

School of Education, Leeds LS2 9JT
0532 431751
Moncur, D. Mr; *Supervisor:* Orton, A. Dr
Students' understanding of literal algebraic equations and formulae
Abstract: This research has been devised to compare the ability of pupils and students to solve numerical and literal equations in order to analyse why many learners find the step from numerical to literal so difficult. A preliminary study based on group testing was carried out using pupils from four schools in different parts of Britain. In some schools the literal equations were placed before the numerical. The main part of the research is based on individual interviews with a large sample of pupils, and transcription of this data is currently taking place.
Status: Individual research
Date of Research: 1987 - continuing
KEYWORDS: algebra; cognitive processes; comprehension; mathematical formulas; mathematics education

9/0529

School of Education, Overseas Education Unit, Leeds LS2 9JT
0532 431751
Coleman, H. Mr
Language learning in large classes research project
Abstract: The project is primarily concerned with the learning and

teaching of English as a second language or foreign language in the context of large classes. It has four aims: to develop links with individuals and institutions concerned with large classes (LCs); to organize meetings and other events for the purpose of discussing current research; to undertake and promote research into specific aspects of language learning and teaching in LCs; and to develop and maintain a bibliography. A series of project reports is now being published, and more reports will appear in the future. Colloquia have been organized in Chicago (1988), Warwick (1989), San Antonio (1989), Dublin (1990), San Francisco (1990), New York (1991) and Exeter (1991). A Specialist Conference was organised in Karachi, Pakistan, in 1991. The specific issues being investigated include the following: (1) the aetiology of large classes, the definition of a 'large class', patterns of teacher and learner behaviour in large classes, teachers' perceptions of large classes, learners' perceptions of large classes, and approaches to the management of large classes; (2) relationship between class size and language acquisition, and teachers' and learners' strategies in large classes.
Published Material: A complete list of publications is available from the researchers.
Status: Sponsored project
Source of Grant: The British Council £1,500; The Bell Educational Trust £300; The Centre for British Teachers £500
Date of Research: 1986 - continuing
KEYWORDS: class size; English – second language; second language learning; second language teaching

9/0530
School of Education, Leeds LS2 9JT
0532 431751
Coles, J. Mrs; *Supervisor:* Marriott, J. Prof.
The idea of 'university extension' across the English-speaking world, 1867-1914
Abstract: The project continues an earlier Leverhulme-funded enquiry into the intercultural links between adult education in England and Germany since the late 19th century. Earlier research revealed the brief but significant influence of the English idea of 'university extension' (a form of adult education) in Germany and Austria. It also became clear that a more substantial 'export' of this idea was to other parts of the English-speaking world. The new project is investigating the export of university extension philosophy and method to the United States, as evidenced in the work of the American Society for the Extension of University Teaching (Philadelphia) and the new University of Chicago. The influence of the American Chautauqua system (a form of summer school) on English adult education will also be studied. The export of university extension to British Empire countries (primarily Australasia, but also Canada and Cape Colony) will also be investigated.
Status: Sponsored project
Source of Grant: Leverhulme Trust £18,750
Date of Research: 1991 - continuing
KEYWORDS: adult education; comparative education; educational history; extension education

9/0531
School of Education, Leeds LS2 9JT
0532 431751
Zachos, I. Mr; *Supervisor:* Orton, A. Dr
Problem solving in geometry in Greek schools
Abstract: The solution of Euclidean geometry problems is difficult for pupils in Greek schools, as it has always been for all pupils where Euclidean geometry has been taught. The aim is to produce a new scheme for teaching the subject, based on worked examples but theoretically underpinned by recent research on the writing of geometry proofs. Matched control and experimental groups will be used, the matching being carried out by using van Hiele levels and a specially constructed test. Pupils in Greek schools will be taught and tested in groups, with a large sample also having individual interviews.
Status: Individual research
Date of Research: 1990 - continuing
KEYWORDS: geometry education; Greece; mathematics education; problem solving

9/0532
School of Education, Leeds LS2 9JT
0532 431751
Bradford & Ilkley Community College, Great Horton Road,

Bradford BD1 1AY
0274 753166
Robinson, P. Mr; *Supervisor:* Marriott, J. Prof.
Attitudes towards 'economic course' provision in the public further education sector
Abstract: During the 1980s the further education (FE) sector has come under increasing pressure to operate within the context of a 'New Right Market Economy'. The purpose of this research is to enquire into and collect information about people's perceptions of how economic course provision within FE can be developed more effectively. Given a context of increasing competitiveness from other public and private agencies, the research aims to examine the attitudes of staff in terms of their willingness to embrace this current entrepreneurial philosophy, as well as to further consider present management and administrative structures in order to assess the degree to which these existing structures may hinder or facilitate flexible responses to commercial demands. The research has an ethnographic base and will aim to interview respondents from four sample areas: college managers and administrators; college staff academic and technical, other local training providers; and industrial managers. An initial pilot project took place within Bradford & Ilkley Community College during the academic year 1989/90 and five subsequent research projects were developed during the following 18 months.
Status: Sponsored project
Source of Grant: Bradford & Ilkley Community College £4,800
Date of Research: 1989 - continuing
KEYWORDS: course evaluation; economics education relationship; educational administration; educational economics; entrepreneurship; further education

9/0533
School of Education, Nurse Selection Project, Leeds LS2 9JT
0532 431751
Child, D. Prof.; Borrill, C. Dr; Ciechanowski, A. Ms; Michaud, A. Mrs
Nurse selection project – United Kingdom Central Council for Nursing, Midwifery and Health Visiting (UKCC)
Abstract: The project is concentrating on two main research areas: monitoring the career choices of adolescents and a validation study of the DC test series, an alternative entry route into nurse training. The study of young people's career choices is cross-sectional and longitudinal and is exploring how and why they become interested in nursing as a career, and why it is they change their minds. The insights from this work will be used to make recommendations about how to encourage and keep young people interested in nursing. A sample of 648 school pupils and college students in three regions of England are being followed over a period of four to five years using questionnaires and a subsample of 20% interviewed each year. The validation study of the DC test series is following the progress of 629 entrants to nurse training. The performance of 315 students who entered training with five O-levels or more is being compared with 314 who passed a DC test to enter. Further research has been carried out on the test, such as a study of the effect of age on performance and the effect of practice and coaching on performance. The project also carries out short term research at the request of the funding bodies.
Published Material: CHILD, D. et al (1988). Selection for nurse training; making decisions. Leeds: University of Leeds Press.; BORRILL, C.S. (1988). 'Cultivating an interest in nursing', Nursing Times, pp.44-45, December 14th.; BORRILL, C.S. (1989). 'Nursing an ambition', Nursing Times, Vol 85, No 34, pp.30-32.; CHILD, D. et al (1990). Taking the DC test – a guide for candidates. Leeds: University of Leeds Press.
Status: Sponsored project
Source of Grant: United Kingdom Central Council for Nursing, Midwifery and Health; Visiting; Department of Health £300,000
Date of Research: 1987-1992
KEYWORDS: career choice; nurse education; nursing; qualifications; recruitment; selection; student motivation

9/0534
School of Education, Leeds LS2 9JT
0532 431751
Universitat Tubingen, Institut fur Erziehungswissenschaft II, FRG-7400 Tubingen, Germany Marriott, J. Prof.; Coles, J. Mrs; Fretloh-Thomas, S. Dr
Intercultural influence in adult/popular education: England and Germany 1890-1955

Abstract: The overall project involves a historical investigation of the intercultural 'reception' of ideas and institutional forms in the field of adult education. The present phase deals with reciprocal Anglo-German contacts at the periods: (1) 1890-1914 – emphasis on German interest in the university extension and settlement movements; (2) 1918-1933 – structure and effects of international contact with special reference to pacifism, women's and workers' education; (3) 1945-1955 – 'German educational reconstruction' and the contribution of English adult education and adult educators.
Published Material: MARRIOTT, S. (1987). 'Un role sociale pour les universites? Reactions francaises au mouvement d'extension des universites en Angleterre dans les annees 1890'. In: UEBER-SCHLAG, G. & MULLER, F. (Eds). Education Populaire. Presses Universitaires de Lille.; MARRIOTT, S. (1992). Germany and the World Association for Adult Education, 1919-1946. (In press.)
Status: Sponsored project
Source of Grant: Leverhulme Trust £10,600
Date of Research: 1988-1991
KEYWORDS: *adult education; comparative education; educational history; extension education; intercultural communication; labour education; university*

Leicester University

9/0535

Department of Psychology, University Road, Leicester
LE1 7RH
0533 522522
Gillett, R. Dr
Sample size determination in replication attempts
Abstract: A replication attempt is a study undertaken to establish whether an earlier finding represents a genuine effect. Sample size determination can prove difficult if the theory motivating the original experiment is insufficiently precise to provide strong predictions about the expected magnitude of the experimental effect. A method is being developed to determine sample size in a replication attempt when there is uncertainty about the magnitude of the experimental effect. The method uses information provided by the original study to construct a distribution of probable effect sizes. The sample size to be employed in a replication attempt is that which supplies an expected power of the desired amount over the distribution of probable effect sizes.
Published Material: GILLETT, R. (1986). 'Sample size determination in replication attempts: the standard normal Z test', British Journal of Mathematical and Statistical Psychology, Vol 39, No 2, pp.190-207.
Status: Individual research
Date of Research: 1983 - continuing
KEYWORDS: *research methodology; sample size*

9/0536

Department of Psychology, University Road, Leicester
LE1 7RH
0533 522522
Gillett, R. Dr
Matching: an exact test procedure
Abstract: Studies using the matching paradigm aim to establish whether a one-to-one pairing of objects or people from two groups contains more pairing of a particular kind than expected under the null hypothesis. By applying the combinatorial technique of Rook methodology, a flexible and general framework for constructing exact tests in the matching paradigm is being developed. Among the practical benefits of the approach are: (a) a more sensitive test of individual matching performance; (b) the assessment of broad agreement when raters are uncertain; and (c) a solution to the problem of infeasible pairings.
Published Material: GILLETT, R. (1985). 'The matching paradigm: an exact test procedure', Psychological Bulletin, Vol 97, No 1, pp.106-118.; GILLETT, R. (1985). 'Nominal scale response agreement and rater uncertainty', British Journal of Mathematical and Statistical Psychology, Vol 38, No 1, pp.58-66.; GILLETT, R. (1985). 'Allowing for infeasible pairings in the matching paradigm', Psychometrika, Vol 50, No 3, pp.265-274.
Status: Individual research
Date of Research: 1983 - continuing

KEYWORDS: *models; predictive validity; probability; statistical inference*

9/0537

Department of Psychology, University Road, Leicester
LE1 7RH
0533 522522
Annett, M. Dr
Phonological and visuospatial processing at the left and right of the laterality distribution
Abstract: The right shift (RS) theory of handedness has led to the hypothesis that there are specific risks for cognitive processing, associated with the rs-- and rs++ genotypes. The genotypes cannot be identified directly, but are more frequent at the left and right of the continuum of right minus left (R-L) hand skill. Those at the left are at risk because they lack something which assists the growth of speech in the left hemisphere. Those at the right are at risk because they carry a double dose of a factor which appears to work by handicapping the right hemisphere. Annett and Manning (1990) have shown that reading ability varies with laterality in normal school children such that children at both extremes are likely to be poorer readers than those in the centre. The purpose of the research is to show that a double dissociation between people specifically at risk for phonological and visuospatial processing is associated with the left and right of the R-L hand skill distribution; and that this dissociation is relevant to subtypes of dyslexia. Among poorer readers, error patterns associated with 'phonological' versus 'surface' or 'dyseidetic' dyslexias could be more prevalent at the left and the right of the laterality distribution respectively.
Published Material: ANNETT, M. & MANNING, M. (1990). 'Reading and a balanced polymorphism for laterality and ability', Journal of Child Psychology and Psychiatry, Vol 31, No 4, pp.511-529.; ANNETT, M. (1992). 'Phonological processing and right minus left hand skill', Quarterly Journal of Experimental Psychology, No44, pp.33-46.; ANNETT, M. (1991). 'Reading upside down and mirror text in groups differing for right minus left hand skill', European Journal of Cognitive Psychology, No 3, pp.363-377.
Status: Sponsored project
Source of Grant: Wellcome Trust £50,545
Date of Research: 1991 - continuing
KEYWORDS: *brain hemisphere functions; dyslexia; handedness; lateral dominance; reading difficulties; visual perception*

9/0538

Department of Psychology, University Road, Leicester
LE1 7RH
0533 522522
Sluckin, A. Mrs; Foreman, N. Dr; Herbert, M. Prof.
The aetiology and treatment of selective mutism (children who do not talk in school)
Abstract: This research analyses the phenomenon of the child who does not talk in school despite having age-appropriate speech at home. Data on 25 such cases, including details of home background, exposure to more than one language, age at referral and number of school terms spent mute, has been accumulated. The research also involves scrutinisation of the treatment programmes to which children were exposed, in particular the extent to which behavioural treatment methods were incorporated. Statistical analysis revealed that those children having made little progress at follow-up were those having a clinical psychopathology in the immediate family (often maternal depression), and those having been given standard remedial programmes in school without a behavioural component. The results suggest that a subgroup of selective mute children can be identified that is likely to persist in selectivity of speaking, and that would benefit from the early application of treatment methods having a behavioural content. Current research is aimed at extending the data to a larger sample, analysing more closely the quality of speech shown by selective mute children in the home environment, and assessing quality of speech in the school environment on recovery. It is hoped to develop procedures for assessing the possible role of behavioural inhibition in the aetiology of the condition. The work may have import for the testing of children who are reluctant to speak under National Curriculum arrangements.
Published Material: SLUCKIN, A., FOREMAN, N. & HERBERT, M. Behavioural treatment programmes and selectivity of speaking at follow-up in a sample of twenty-five selective mutes. Australian Psychologist. (in press).
Status: Individual research

Date of Research: 1975 - continuing
KEYWORDS: behaviour problems; elective mutism; inhibition; psychopathology

9/0539

Department of Psychology, University Road, Leicester LE1 7RH
0533 522522
Foreman, N. Dr; Supervisor: Foreman, N. Dr
The development of spatial awareness in children with physical handicaps, particularly those integrated in mainstream schools

Abstract: Children's spatial awareness has been tested using a variety of paradigms, and the development of cognitive mapping skills charted across the preschool and primary school age-range. Using search tasks with groups of 10-20 infants, it has been shown that spatial awareness develops especially rapidly between 2 and 5 years (Foreman et al, 1984), and that reference memory develops in advance of working memory for visited places (Foreman, Warry & Murray, 1990). The research has also found, in groups of 30-40 able-bodied children, that independent spatial choice is necessary for the development of spatial awareness (Foreman, Foreman et al, 1990). In disabled children integrated in mainstream schools (N=10) it was found that mobility status determined accuracy in using cognitive spatial representations of the classroom and school campus compared with a matched control group (Foreman et al, 1989; Foreman & Gell, 1990). This work was carried out collaboratively between the Psychology Department of Leicester University and the Advisory Service for Physically Impaired Pupils in Mainstream Schools, based at Westbrook Special School, Long Eaton, Derbyshire. Current research is extending the earlier work, investigating whether locomotion in space and/or spatial choice in able-bodied pupils specifically affects working or reference components of spatial memory, and whether spatial skill relates to other areas of intellectual development such as reading, mathematical or technical ability. The research attempts to develop desk-top procedures and computerised tasks which measure spatial development. This will enable schools to identify spatial disabilities and offer appropriate remedial help. Within special education, the researchers are currently exploring the use of 'virtual reality' computerised environments as a possible means of remediating spatial difficulties in more severely disabled pupils, and in relating spatial difficulties to particular forms of cerebral dysfunction.
Published Material: FOREMAN, N., ARBER, M. & SAVAGE, J. (1984). 'Spatial memory in preschool infants', Developmental Psychobiology, Vol 17, pp.129-137.; FOREMAN, N., FOREMAN, D., CUMMINGS, A. & OWNES, S. (1990). 'Locomotion, active choice, and spatial memory in children', Journal of General Psychology, Vol 117, pp.215-232.; FOREMAN, N. & BERRYMAN, M. (1990). 'Kids in space (Access, Mobility and Motability Section)', Special Children, No 35, pp.20-21.; FOREMAN, N., ORENCAS, C., NICHOLAS, E., MORTON, P. & GELL, M. (1989). 'Spatial awareness in seven to 11-year-old physically handicapped children in mainstream schools', European Journal of Special Needs Education, Vol 4, No 3, pp.171-180.
Status: Individual research
Date of Research: 1983 - continuing
KEYWORDS: cognitive processes; mainstreaming; spatial abiity; special educational needs

9/0540

Department of Psychology, University Road, Leicester LE1 7RH
0533 522522
Colley, A. Dr; Supervisor: Colley, A. Dr; Hargreaves, D. Dr
Gender differences in educational computing in the humanities
Abstract: Although Information Technology (IT) has become an important part of education at all levels, there is clear evidence that girls receive less benefit from IT. Research shows that boys are more interested in computers, and that they use them more at home and at school. Computers are widely used in the male-dominated areas of science and technology but they are now making a significant impact in the arts, in subject areas which traditionally have attracted girls. This project uses a large scale survey method (N=1,500) to investigate secondary school boys' and girls' interest in, attitudes towards and use of IT in English and music in which new technologies are increasingly being used. Previous research has found that girls are likely to perform better in science and technology subjects in single-

sex schools, where they do not feel in competition with their male peers. A comparison will therefore be made between pupils in co-educational and single sex schools. Gender stereotyping has prevented many girls from developing an interest in science and technology. The project will provide valuable information which can be used to ensure that girls do not miss out on technological advancements in the humanities.
Status: Sponsored project
Source of Grant: Leverhulme Trust £41,593.12
Date of Research: 1991 - continuing
KEYWORDS: computer uses in education; gender equality; humanities; information technology; sex differences

9/0541

School of Education, University Road, Leicester LE1 7RH
0533 522522
Fogelman, K. Prof.; Reeder, D. Dr; Crook, D. Mr
Processes and outcomes of the introduction of comprehensive schools in England and Wales
Abstract: This research looks at the processes and outcomes of the introduction of comprehensive schools in England and Wales. Ten representative authorities are being studied and Duke University, North Carolina (collaborating in the project) are working on data gathered by the National Child Development Study.
Status: Sponsored project
Source of Grant: Spenser Foundation
Date of Research: 1991-1992
KEYWORDS: comprehensive schools; educational change; educational history; secondary education

9/0542

School of Education, University Road, Leicester LE1 7RH
0533 522522
Hilliam, S. Miss; Supervisor: Sutton, J. Mr
The evaluation of school-initiated INSET in selected junior schools: teacher and headteacher perspectives
Abstract: Although much has been written in general terms about evaluation, very little is known about teachers' concepts of inservice teacher education (INSET) evaluation. Particularly in view of the increasing and direct involvement of headteachers and teachers in the management and delivery of INSET, research into this area is of considerable significance. This research will examine the concepts of evaluation of junior school headteachers and teachers and relate these findings to school-initiated INSET and teacher development. Two groups of fifteen schools will be randomly selected in two local education authorities (North Yorkshire and Leeds). The design of the research involves questionnaires to the headteacher and two colleagues plus interviews with the headteacher and a member of staff. Observations and documentation will be incorporated in the triangulation of the findings.
Status: Sponsored project
Source of Grant: Leeds City Council
Date of Research: 1989-1992
KEYWORDS: inservice teacher education; junior schools; programme evaluation; school-based inservice education; teacher attitudes; teacher development

9/0543

School of Education, University Road, Leicester LE1 7RH
0533 522522
Gerard, M. Mr; Supervisor: Fogelman, K. Prof.; Merry, R. Dr
Evaluation of multisensory rooms in the education of children with profound and multiple learning difficulties
Abstract: Many schools for children with severe learning difficulties (SLD) have invested time, floor space, staffing and money for the purchase of equipment in constructing 'multisensory rooms'. The intention of the project is to find out the size of the investment made, the nature of the rooms, the equipment installed, the level of use, the client population and the teachers' evaluations of their installations in a number of areas such as development of visual skills, development of fine and gross motor skills, and general multisensory stimulation. Analysis of the 75 responses (out of 100 sent to SLD schools in the English Midlands) to the questionnaire, alongside interviews with teachers and manufacturers of the specialist equipment and analysis of questionnaires submitted to peripatetic teachers for the visually impaired should help to answer some of the issues outlined above. At the same time some consideration is given to the theoretical

justifications that are advanced for undertaking multisensory room work.
Status: Sponsored project
Source of Grant: Leicestershire County Council
Date of Research: 1980-1992
KEYWORDS: *multisensory rooms; severe learning difficulties; special educational needs; special schools*

9/0544
    School of Education, University Centre, Barrack Road, Northampton NN2 6AF
    0604 36369
    Fogelman, K. Prof.; Edwards, J. Mrs
Citizenship project
Abstract: A centre established to investigate the teaching of citizenship, particularly in the National Curriculum. An annotated bibliography, inservice teacher education (INSET) work, teacher training and case studies are all in hand. A book is planned and market research will be undertaken.
Status: Sponsored project
Source of Grant: Barclaycard; ESSO
Date of Research: 1991 - continuing
KEYWORDS: *citizenship education; National Curriculum*

9/0545
    School of Education, University Road, Leicester LE1 7RH
    0533 522522
    Dobson, N. Mr; *Supervisor:* Aplin, R. Mr; Wortley, A. Mrs
The use of outdoor pursuits in schools in England and France
Abstract: Outdoor pursuits have grown greatly in importance in the educational programme of school children in England and France since World War Two. In 1951 the first local authority residential outdoor pursuits centre in England and Wales was opened, and the first class of elementary school children was taken to the Alps for a month of half-time skiing and half-time normal lessons. After a slow start the number of children being taken, through the education authorities of both countries, to experience outdoor pursuits, has expanded enormously. This study will attempt to describe this movement and to discover what value the authorities, parents, teachers and children ascribe to outdoor pursuit activities.
Status: Individual research
Date of Research: 1991 - continuing
KEYWORDS: *activities; comparative education; France; outdoor pursuits; physical education*

9/0546
    School of Education, University Road, Leicester LE1 7RH
    0533 522522
    Everton, C. Mr
16-19 mathematics support materials project
Abstract: To research and produce support materials for teachers using 16-19 mathematics. The end product is to be a set of three booklets. Trialling of the booklets will be carried out by asking pertinent questions and building up a set of answer data.
Status: Sponsored project
Source of Grant: Trustees of the School Mathematics Project
Date of Research: 1991-1992
KEYWORDS: *educational materials; mathematics education; sixteen to nineteen education*

9/0547
    School of Education, University Road, Leicester LE1 7RH
    0533 522522
    Tomley, D. Mr
Individual action plan project
Abstract: The project aims to introduce the process of Action Planning within the PGCE (Postgraduate Certificate of Education) courses at Leicester University. The project will follow the PGCE students who secure posts locally for two years, to see how individual action planning is built upon during their induction period.
Status: Sponsored project
Source of Grant: Training, Enterprise & Education Directorate
Date of Research: 1991 - continuing
KEYWORDS: *planning; Postgraduate Certificate in Education; teacher education*

9/0548
    School of Education, University Road, Leicester LE1 7RH
    0533 522522
    Yazigy, A. Miss; *Supervisor:* Cortazzi, M. Mr
Reading and schema theory
Abstract: The aim of the research is to help students at primary levels, learning English as a second language, to be good readers (i.e. with a high level of comprehension) using the schema theory.
Status: Sponsored project
Source of Grant: Christian Aid
Date of Research: 1989-1991
KEYWORDS: *English – second language; reading comprehension; schemata – cognition; teaching methods*

9/0549
    School of Education, University Road, Leicester LE1 7RH
    0533 522522
    Akkoyunlu, B. Miss; *Supervisor:* Ball, D. Mr
The use of microcomputers in British schools, the implications for their use in Turkish schools and the improvement of computer assisted learning in Turkish schools
Abstract: Computer assisted instruction is a new area for study and practice in Turkey. Research studies are very limited and qualified personnel are scarce. Utilisation of computers has a relatively long history, in some countries such as England, the USA, Japan and Holland, and there is a considerable amount of experience and accumulated knowledge in the use of computers for education. By reviewing research studies and investigating practices and the present status of computer assisted instruction in the other countries the study aims to achieve the following objectives: (1) to draw relevant lessons of experience for Turkish computer assisted instruction practices in order to establish a sound ground for implementation and development; (2) to suggest procedures and methods which will fit the Turkish educational system for the development of the use of microcomputers for instruction; (3) to provide criteria and a frame of reference for evaluating the practices of computer assisted instruction in Turkey. The data will be gathered in two ways: (1) by reviewing and analysing the literature on computer assisted instruction and by drawing implications for the Turkish case; (2) by conducting some case studies in which different approaches are utilised for the implementation of computer assisted or computer based instruction. For data collection, an observation list, questionnaires and interview techniques will be employed. The full design of the study will be completed by collaborative and co-operative work with related members of the School of Education at Leicester University.
Status: Sponsored project
Source of Grant: Hacettepe University
Date of Research: 1985-1991
KEYWORDS: *comparative education; computer-assisted learning; computer uses in education; Turkey*

9/0550
    School of Education, University Road, Leicester LE1 7RH
    0533 522522
    Galton, M. Prof.; Fogelman, K. Prof.; Hargreaves, L. Dr; Cavendish, S. Dr
Rural schools curriculum enhancement national evaluation (S.C.E.N.E.) project
Abstract: The rural S.C.E.N.E. (Schools Curriculum Enhancement National Evaluation) project is evaluating 14 pilot projects using education support grants (ESG) to extend the range or improve the quality of the curriculum in rural primary schools. The various local authority pilot projects have used a range of strategies to achieve this, e.g. the use of clustering of schools to share resources and inservice provision, the employment of coordinators and advisory teachers with varying duties and the provision of transport to bring children from small schools together into larger peer groupings. The grants were provided for three to five years. Six case studies of schools in local education authorities which used similar strategies are being conducted. The data collection includes interviews; questionnaires to ESG and non-ESG schools; classroom observation of children's' activities and projective activities for children. Major themes which are emerging include the history of school cooperation within areas and the effectiveness of 'working alongside' as an inservice method.
Status: Sponsored project
Source of Grant: Department of Education and Science £90,000
Date of Research: 1988-1991

KEYWORDS: *cooperative programmes; curriculum enrichment; primary schools; rural areas; rural schools; shared resources and services*

9/0551

School of Education, University Road, Leicester LE1 7RH
0533 522522
Brown, M. Mrs; *Supervisor:* Wright, C. Dr;
Fogelman, K. Prof.
Multicultural education: images at primary level
Abstract: Is concern about minority pupils a worthy matter or are there more pressing problems in education? What does multicultural education mean in terms of actual school practice? Who is referred to when we use the term 'ethnic minority'? In this study an observational research will be conducted, with the aim of analysing attitudes and views of teachers and pupils of given primary schools. Three types of schools will be researched and formal and informal interviews with individuals and groups of teachers and pupils will be conducted. Records and reports will also be assessed in order to discover views on multicultural education and to ascertain if school experiences of ethnic minority pupils in the various schools are similar. It will also be decided whether the internal system of the schools and their teaching methods have differential effects on the pupils of ethnic minority. The three different types of school examined are: (a) large primary schools in inner city areas (Birmingham and London) where there exists a high percentage of pupils from ethnic minority backgrounds. In these schools multicultural educational techniques are used to an extreme to cater for 'supposed needs' especially in the area of language development; (b) primary schools in developing towns (Northampton and Cambridge) where pupils of multiethnic backgrounds attend on a smaller scale, and multicultural teaching methods and practices are incorporated in the curriculum successfully; (c) rural primary schools where heads and teachers alike believe that multicultural education is not needed in their school as no pupils of multiethnic backgrounds attend and they find multicultural education baffling, misleading and foreign. The study prompts questions in relation to the degree of multicultural awareness and practices observed in schools.
Status: Sponsored project
Source of Grant: Overstone Park Kindergarten & Preparatory School
Date of Research: 1988 - continuing
KEYWORDS: *ethnic groups; multicultural education; multiethnic education; primary schools*

9/0552

School of Education, University Centre, Barrack Road, Northampton NN2 6AF
0604 36369
Drane, J. Mrs; *Supervisor:* Lofthouse, M. Dr
The changing role of secondary headteachers
Abstract: This research focuses upon the changing role of secondary headteachers following the Education Reform Act (1988). The main area of interest is the centralisation v decentralisation conflict within recent legislation and the effect this has had on the role of the headteacher. Questions of interest are: (1) headteachers and governors – their working relationship; (2) headteachers or chief executives; (3) headteachers and power/authority – enhanced or diminished; and (4) headteachers and their senior management teams – real or imagined team work.
Status: Individual research
Date of Research: 1990 - continuing
KEYWORDS: *administrator role; educational change; headteachers; role conflict; school-based management; secondary schools; teacher role*

Liverpool John Moores University

9/0553

School of Education and Community Studies, I.M. Marsh Campus, Barkhill Road, Liverpool L17 6BD
051 724 2321
Blackmore, M. Dr; Clemson, D. Mr

Initial teacher education and the new technology
Abstract: This project has four main elements: (1) an evaluation of the explicit information technology inputs on all initial teacher training (ITT) courses in this institution; (2) an audit of current implicit use of information technology across all routes and areas of the ITT courses; (3) assessment of the status quo in schools in the region; and (4) suggestions for an institutional staff development programme.
Status: Sponsored project
Source of Grant: National Council for Educational Technology £11,000
Date of Research: 1990-1992
KEYWORDS: *computer uses in education; information technology; preservice teacher education*

9/0554

School of Education and Community Studies, I.M. Marsh Campus, Barkhill Road, Liverpool L17 6BD
051 724 2321
Thomson, S. Ms
Technical and Vocational Education Initiative
Abstract: The main themes of this project examining the Technical and Vocational Education Initiative include: (1) active learning strategies; (2) profiling and Records of Achievement; (3) information technology and the curriculum; and (4) links between education and the world of work.
Status: Sponsored project
Source of Grant: Training Agency £100,000
Date of Research: 1989-1991
KEYWORDS: *technical education; vocational education; work education relationship*

9/0555

School of Education and Community Studies, I.M. Marsh Campus, Barkhill Road, Liverpool L17 6BD
051 724 2321
Clemson, D. Mr
Models of the primary teacher in use in primary B. Ed. courses
Abstract: The education and training of teachers is currently of central concern to both trainers and national governments. The inception of accreditation demands through the Council for the Accreditation of Teacher Education (CATE) has caused widespread re-organisation of teacher education courses. The focus of this research activity is the Primary B. Ed. (Council for National Academic Awards (CNAA) validated courses only) and the ways in which course writers depict the model of the primary teacher which underpins their course. Possible tensions between desired models and externally provided, or approved, models will be explored. Data will be assembled from course documents, CATE criteria, and other formal/official groups and publications.
Status: Sponsored project
Source of Grant: Liverpool Polytechnic £6,750
Date of Research: 1990-1991
KEYWORDS: *B. Ed. degrees; course content; curriculum design; education courses; educational policy; preservice teacher education*

9/0556

School of Information Science and Technology, Tithebarn Street, Liverpool L2 2ER
051 207 3581
Chandler, H. Mrs; *Supervisor:* Bakewell, K. Prof.;
McGarry, K. Dr
Use of official European Community information sources in schools and colleges
Abstract: At a time of increasing emphasis by the Department of Education and Science on the importance of the development of curricula and syllabuses for post-16 age groups to reflect the requirements of business and industry with the approach of the Single European Market in 1992, educational establishments are experiencing financial constraints imposed by Local Management of Schools and the implementation of the Community Charge, and the attendant difficulties in provision of additional resource materials to meet the demands of new courses. Merseyside is particularly affected by such problems. It is, however, an area which has a unique advantage in hosting the one regional European Depository Library in the United Kingdom which is accessible to the general public. This research proposes to: (1) investigate both the extent to which national syllabuses reflect the European dimension and the extent to which support

resources have already been developed; (2) evaluate these resources for identified post-16 student groups; and (3) concurrently, investigate the use, means and problems of access to official European Community information in various educational establishments on Merseyside. The hypothesis is that problems of access obtain. If this is proven, the research would proceed to investigate types of learning programmes/packages which could meet local requirements, and, based primarily on the European Depository Library collection, develop and test such programmes using both quantitative and qualitative methodologies on student groups from collaborating establishments. Consequent on this would be the assessment, modifications and re-evaluation of processes and products. Potential outcomes of the research would be an educational product or products supporting post-16 courses in Merseyside, but with the potential for development on a broader scale; and the furtherance of the commitment of Liverpool John Moores University's (previously Liverpool Polytechnic) to Service to the Community in contributing to the regional good through direct partnership of its staff with the public sector.
Status: Individual research
Date of Research: 1991 - continuing
KEYWORDS: *curriculum; European studies; industry-education relationship; international educational exchange; international studies; sixteen to nineteen education*

Liverpool University

9/0557
Department of Education, PO Box 147, Liverpool L69 3BX
051 794 2000
Beattie, N. Dr
The Freinet Movement in its international context
Abstract: The aim is to explore the Freinet Movement, which has been central to most 'progressive' developments in French education, over the period 1920 to the present day and to describe and discuss its cross-national impact. This has been considerable in some areas (e.g. Italy post-1945, Portugal post-1974) and nil in others (e.g. United Kingdom). By placing a very broad movement of opinion and practice in its cultural and historical context, this long-term enquiry should produce some clarification of elusive culture-bound ideas such as 'progressive' and 'international' dissemination.
Status: Individual research
Date of Research: 1987 - continuing
KEYWORDS: *comparative education; educational history; educational theories; progressive education*

9/0558
Department of Education, PO Box 147, Liverpool L69 3BX
051 794 2000
Harrop, S. Mrs
History of the University of Liverpool 1981-1991
Abstract: This project is to update and extend Thomas Kelly's History of Liverpool University 1981 to 1991, (KELLY, T. (1981). For advancement of learning. Liverpool: Liverpool University Press). The research will be based on documentary sources and oral evidence from past and present staff and students.
Status: Sponsored project
Source of Grant: Liverpool University
Date of Research: 1989-1991
KEYWORDS: *educational history; universities*

9/0559
Department of Education, PO Box 147, Liverpool L69 3BX
051 794 2000
Meakin, D. Mr
Philosophy of the curriculum with particular reference to moral, religious, physical education and personal and social education
Abstract: This research has been within the area of the philosophy of the curriculum with particular reference to moral, religious, aesthetic and physical education. It has mainly been concerned with three questions: (i) how these kinds of education are to be characterised; (ii) how, if at all, they might be justified; (iii) whether any general criteria can be established for including subjects and activities in the school curriculum.

Published Material: MEAKIN, D.C. (1983). 'On the justification of physical education', Momentum, Vol 8, No 3, pp.10-17.; MEAKIN, D.C. (1986). 'The moral status of competition: an issue of concern to physical educators', Journal of Philosophy of Education, Vol 20, No 1, pp.59-67.; MEAKIN, D.C. (1988). 'The justification of religious education reconsidered', British Journal of Religious Education, Vol 10, No 2, pp.92-96.; MEAKIN, D.C. (1989). 'Personal, social and moral education and religious education: the need for conceptual clarity', British Journal of Religious Education, Vol 11, No 1, pp.15-21.; MEAKIN, D.C. (1990). 'How physical education can contribute to personal and social education', Physical Education Review, Vol 13, No 2, pp.108-119. A full list of publications is available from the researcher.
Status: Individual research
Date of Research: 1973 - continuing
KEYWORDS: *curriculum development; education philosophy; individual development; moral education; physical education; religious education*

9/0560
Department of Education, PO Box 147, Liverpool L69 3BX
051 794 2000
Martland, J. Mr; Stewart, R. Mr; Walsh, S. Ms; *Supervisor:* Martland, J. Mr
Developing navigational skills in young children
Abstract: Many geographical skills are taught to primary children but the learning fails when children use large scale maps to plot route and to travel to a location. The research studied the natural behaviours of 300 children, aged 7-11 years, as they followed two routes across a uniform square grid of lines. The routes were of increasing complexity and involved turns of 180 degrees. The ability to keep the map orientated to the terrain, and to update one's position on the map, were major problems for the young. An analysis of the errors showed that children attempted to locate their route by using finger pointing to retrace their journey. Children below the age of 8 tended to locate their current position on the map, equivalent to saying 'I am here', but then moved randomly. Following the initial research, 30 children aged 7+ years were introduced to the concept of orientation via landmarks and features and by using a compass. Two new routes were planned acrosss the grid layout. The results showed that children who used the compass maintained orientation and completed the task whereas children who became disorientated using the landmark strategy resorted to trial and error route finding. The landmark and compass strategies were also applied to a sample of 120 children and the results reinforced the finding that they use the compass to maintain orientation with greater facility than using landmarks. The research has examined how the concepts and skill related to direction, for example, bearings can be taught. 148 children, aged 11, were taught to use a compass to take bearings from a map and apply them to the terrain. 50 per cent received a skill based, rote learning approach and 50 per cent received additional input highlighting the concept of a bearing. This approach was termed relational. In individual tests, in unfamiliar terrain, the relational group performed significantly better than the rote group in practical and applied situations.
Published Material: WALSH, S.E., MARTLAND, J.R. & STEWART, R.R. (1991). 'The map orientation skills of young children – a preliminary investigation', Scientific Journal of Orienteering, Vol 7, No 1/2, pp.90-103.; MARTLAND, J.R., STEWART, R.R. & WALSH, S.E. (1991). 'How do we teach our young orienteers to use the compass more effectively?' Scientific Journal of Orienteering, Vol 7, No 1/2, pp.104-114.; STEWART, R.R., MARTLAND, J.R. & WALSH, S.E. (1991). 'Personal and social dimensions of developing orienteering and self-navigation in primary schools: a turn for the better?', Social Science Teacher, Vol 20, No 3, pp.95-96.; WALSH, S.E. & MARTLAND, J.R. (1993). 'The orientation and navigational skills of young children: an application of two intervention strategies', Journal of Navigation, (forthcoming).; MARTLAND, J.R., STEWART, R.R. & WALSH, S.E. (1991). Second Annual Report, 1990/91, 'Developing navigational skills with young children', Sport Science Education Programme, National Coaching Foundation. A full list of publications is available from the researcher.
Status: Sponsored project
Source of Grant: Sports Council/National Coaching Foundation £54,000
Date of Research: 1989 - continuing
KEYWORDS: *geography education; mathematics education; navigation; orientation; orienteering; outdoor pursuits; primary education*

9/0561

Department of Education, PO Box 147, Liverpool L69 3BX
051 794 2000
Marsden, W. Mr

A headteacher dynasty: illuminating the history of education in England and Wales from the 1840s to the 1930s through the biographies of three generations of one teaching family

Abstract: In the course of previous educational history research, it became apparent that a large amount of, albeit widely scattered, archive material is available on a notable headteacher dynasty, the Adams family. The intention is to undertake a longitudinal study of this family, following through three generations of educational experience from the 1840s to the 1930s, a critical hundred years in the history of education in England and Wales. The range of institutions with which the family, at least six members of which were headteachers, was involved covers: training; a National Society School; several British and Foreign Schools and training colleges; a works school; London Board schools; two universities; army education; 20th century 'Central' secondary schools; and a private school, in a wide range of geographical settings. The study will explore continuity and change in education in England and Wales; a range of educational trends and theories as applied in particular cases; and shifting social contexts and values as they interacted in various rural but mostly urban settings within the period under review.
Published Material: MARSDEN, W.E. (1990). Educating the respectable; a study of Fleet Road Board School, Hampstead, 1879-1903. London: The Woburn Press.
Status: Sponsored project
Source of Grant: Liverpool University Research Fund
Date of Research: 1990 - continuing
KEYWORDS: educational history; headteachers

9/0562

Department of Education, PO Box 147, Liverpool L69 3BX
051 794 2000
Ferguson, S. Mr

School/Industry Compacts: the translation of an American model to England

Abstract: The Boston Compact has been used as a model for school/industry compacts in the United Kingdom which have been promoted by government, industry and local authorities since late 1987. This research builds upon first-hand knowledge of the original Boston Compact to make comments upon the applicability of this American model to the English education setting.
Status: Individual research
Date of Research: 1988 - continuing
KEYWORDS: comparative education; industry-education relationship; United States of America; work-education relationship

9/0563

Department of Education, PO Box 147, Liverpool L69 3BX
051 794 2000
Taylor, I. Mr; *Supervisor:* Harlen, W. Prof.; Derricott, R. Mr

Evaluation of the programme of appraisal of teaching in the veterinary faculty at Liverpool University

Abstract: A programme for evaluating teaching in the Faculty of Veterinary Science at Liverpool University was introduced in 1988. Two members of the Department of Education submitted a proposal to evaluate this innovation. The evaluation of the appraisal of teaching focuses on both the processes and the products of appraisal. Data are collected about the operation of teaching appraisal from students, academic staff and from 'official peers' who observe teaching.
Status: Sponsored project
Source of Grant: Liverpool University £50,000; Universities Funding Council £25,000
Date of Research: 1988-1991
KEYWORDS: teaching effectiveness; veterinary medicine

9/0564

Department of Education, PO Box 147, Liverpool L69 3BX
051 794 2000
Hall, J. Ms; *Supervisor:* Hamilton, D. Prof.

Investigation of the effects of different Inservice Education of Teachers (INSET) experiences on teachers' understanding and perception of their role in teaching science at the elementary level (in US schools)

Abstract: Twenty-four elementary school teachers in Vermont, USA, were involved in an extensive summer workshop run by primary science specialists from England in 1987. Eighteen have continued follow-up work consisting of a 13-week series of meetings. Inservice work has been directed at enabling teachers to encourage children's use of process skills in science activities. Teachers' understanding of these skills and their role in learning has been monitored during the course. Some instruments have also been used with teachers involved in a conventional inservice course in elementary science in the USA and with a group of teachers in England, for comparison.
Status: Individual research
Date of Research: 1988-1992
KEYWORDS: elementary schools; inservice teacher education; primary education; process education; science education; skill development; United States of America

9/0565

Department of Education, PO Box 147, Liverpool L69 3BX
051 794 2000
Doubler, S. Ms; *Supervisor:* Harlen, W. Prof.

Science teaching: supporting effective teacher change

Abstract: This research is linked with the Science Teaching Action Research (STAR) Project which focuses on promoting effective learning and teaching of science in the primary school. This work is concerned more specifically with teachers and their experiences during the STAR Project. The main questions addressed by the study are: (1) Does thinking and practice change as a result of project efforts? (2) What are the significant factors in producing or inhibiting change? The study is being conducted in the Boston, Massachusetts area, and involves 10 teachers from six school districts. The key factors in identifying members of the study group were interest; involvement in process-based science; and three years participation in the STAR Project. The impact of intervention with teachers is determined by taking into consideration teachers' work situations, education, experience, thinking and current practice. As well as identifying changes within the entire study group, a case study of each teacher identifies individual change and its related causes. Information has been collected through the use of two STAR Project research instruments, as well as other instruments designed specifically for this study. A questionnaire was used to collect baseline data about each teacher's work situation and background. Information about practice and the teacher's perception of change was gathered through interviews, surveys, formal student observations and documentation of teacher comments and writing over three consecutive years.
Status: Individual research
Date of Research: 1987-1991
KEYWORDS: primary education; science education; science teachers; teacher role; United States of America

9/0566

Department of Education, Centre for Research in Primary Science & Technology, PO Box 147, Liverpool L69 3BX
051 794 3270
McGuigan, L. Ms; Ewart, M. Ms; Boyes, E. Dr; Johnston, K. Ms; Petrie, I. Mr; *Supervisor:* Russell, T. Mr; Qualter, A. Dr

Evaluation of implementation of science key stages 1-3

Abstract: The project is evaluating the implementation of science in the National Curriculum at key stages 1, 2 and 3. In particular missing, deferred or overlooked areas of the curriculum – issues relating to conceptual progression and issues relating to meeting the needs of children of all abilities and achievements including those with special educational needs. The programme will collect information on a national basis in England. More intensive and qualitative work will be conducted in collaborative work with schools in a core sample having more restricted distribution.
Status: Sponsored project
Source of Grant: National Curriculum Council
Date of Research: 1991 - continuing
KEYWORDS: evaluation; National Curriculum; science education

9/0567

Department of Education, Centre for Research in Primary Science & Technology, PO Box 147, Liverpool L69 3BX
051 794 3270
Russell, T. Mr; Qualter, A. Dr

Evaluation of the implementation of science in the National Curriculum

Abstract: The evaluation rests on a number of issues which have been

raised by Her Majesty's Inspectorate, the National Curriculum Council, and by others. There are three main ones: (1) coverage; (2) progression; and (3) differentiation. In relation to coverage, it has been observed that teachers are to some extent failing to cover certain aspects of the National Curriculum in science; they may be overlooking them; or they may be deferring them. The reasons why this is the case are being explored with a focus on planning for teaching science. The second study, on progression, involves a consideration of the match between the levels in the National Curriculum intended to represent progression in learning, and the order in which pupils develop their understanding in science. The third issue involves the study of the appropriateness of the order for less able and more able and talented pupils. A mixture of individual interviews of teachers and pupils, national questionnaire, group interviews and classroom observation is used in meeting the not inconsiderable challenges of this project.
Status: Sponsored project
Source of Grant: National Curriculum Council £345,000
Date of Research: 1991 - continuing
KEYWORDS: *curriculum development; National Curriculum; science education*

9/0568
Department of Education, Centre for Research in Primary Science & Technology, PO Box 147, Liverpool L69 3BX
051 794 2000
London University, King's College, Centre for Educational Studies, Cornwall House Annexe, Waterloo Road, London SE1 3TY
071 836 5454
Russell, T. Mr; Osborne, J. Mr; Longden, K. Mr; McGuire, L. Ms; Bell, D. Dr; Wadsworth, P. Mrs; *Supervisor:* Harlen, W. Prof.; Black, P. Prof.

Primary science processes and concept exploration project (Primary SPACE Project)
Abstract: The Primary SPACE (Science Processes and Concept Exploration) project is an action research project which aims to explore the ideas primary school children hold in the science concept areas of: changes in materials; evaporation/condensation; electricity; growth; forces and their effect on movement; light; living things and their adaptation to their environment; and sound. Information is being collected by teachers and researchers through interview, discussion and analysis of children's written work and drawings. This information is then being used as a starting point for trying to influence the formation and development of children's ideas through application of process skills during classroom work. The study involves forty two classes in schools within London, Knowsley and Lancashire local education authorities, and covers the entire primary age range. The research is being continued into all areas of the National curriculum in Science and used as a basis for curriculum material development.
Published Material: HARLEN, W. (1987). What is going on in SPACE. University of Liverpool: Centre for Research in Primary Science and Technology.; WATT, D. (1987). 'Primary SPACE project phase one: an exploration of children's specific ideas', Primary Science Review, No 4, pp.27-28, Summer.; Research reports entitled 'Growth', 'Light', 'Evaporation and Condensation', 'Sound' and 'Materials' are available from Liverpool University Press.
Status: Sponsored project
Source of Grant: Nuffield Foundation 1987-1989; Nuffield-Chelsea Curriculum Trust 1989-1991
Date of Research: 1987-1991
KEYWORDS: *primary education; science education; scientific education*

9/0569
Department of Psychology, PO Box 147, Liverpool L69 3BX
051 794 2000
Faber, D. Mrs; *Supervisor:* Lovie, A. Dr

Binet's work and achievement: the first intelligence scales of 1905
Abstract: The area of this research is the history of psychology. Although Binet is recognised as the pioneer of intelligence testing and his influence has been very great, the genesis of his scales is often misrepresented. The researcher's aim is to explain the achievement of Alfred Binet (1857-1911) with reference to his Intelligence Scales of 1905, the first 'true' tests of intelligence. The research involves identifying Binet's changing conceptions of intelligence and its developmental aspects, and tracing the origins of the test items in his experimental work in the 20 years preceding 1905. This also necessi-

tates an examination of Binet's view of psychology as a science, his conception of a psychological experiment and the nature and role of introspections. The social and cultural contexts are important contributing factors to Binet's achievement, and are explained with reference to testing in other countries. In France, political forces and an immediate educational problem led to the Minister of Education's decision to have Paris school children tested or screened for ineducability. Binet's work, particularly that in association with the 'Sociate Libre pour L'Etude Psychologique de l'Enfant', was known by the authorities in 1904. The commission was entrusted to Binet; his earlier work and later collaboration with Simon resulted in the finally produced Scales of 1905, amply justifying their trust in the psychological work of Binet.
Status: Individual research
Date of Research: 1988 - continuing
KEYWORDS: *educational history; France; intelligence tests; psychological testing; psychology*

9/0570
Department of Sociology, PO Box 147, Liverpool L69 3BX
051 794 2000
Roberts, K. Mr; Strivens, J. Ms; Derricott, R. Mr

16-19 Initiative: Liverpool
Abstract: Random samples, totalling 1,600, of 15 and 17 year old cohorts from Liverpool schools were surveyed by questionnaire in 3 successive sweeps. Interview surveys with sub-samples were also conducted. The aim was to identify different career trajectories from education into the labour market, and to relate their career paths to economic and political socialisation, the development of social representation, social attributions, self-concepts and efficacy.
Status: Sponsored project
Source of Grant: Economic and Social Research Council £74,000
Date of Research: 1986-1991
KEYWORDS: *career choice; cohort analysis; school leavers; school to work transition; youth employment*

London Borough of Wandsworth

9/0571
Education Department, Professional Centre, Franciscan Road, Tooting, London SW17 8HE
081 682 3759
Strand, S. Dr; *Supervisor:* Strand, S. Dr

Baseline assessment at age 4+
Abstract: Wandsworth LEA (local education authority) is instigating a baseline assessment for every pupil starting full-time education in a reception class in a Wandsworth school. The aims of the assessment are: (i) to provide structured materials to support teachers in identifying children with problems in their first term of school; (ii) to identify children for further diagnostic assessment or referral to LEA support agencies (e.g. Integrated Support Service, Educational Psychology Service); (iii) to act as a baseline against which to evaluate the child's progress at the end of National Curriculum Key Stage 1. Baseline will consist of two elements: (i) a teacher completed checklist giving detailed background information on the child, and an assessment of the child's social and emotional development, motor skills, attainment in oral language, early reading and writing, mathematics and science; (ii) a shortened form on the Linguistic Awareness for Reading Readiness (LARR) Test. Both assessments will be completed by the classroom teacher during the course of the child's first term in school. A borough-wide pilot involving over 2,000 pupils in 63 schools started in Autumn term 1992. The LEA will evaluate the reliability and concurrent validity of baseline in an interim report in 1993. This will include investigating the relationship between pupil attainment and gender, home language(s), ethnic group, family size, birth order and age (summer born). The final report, evaluating the predictive validity of baseline, will be compiled when the cohort have completed their Key Stage 1 assessment in 1994.
Published Material: Copies of Baseline materials are available from the researcher.
Status: Sponsored project
Source of Grant: Wandsworth Local Education Authority £10,000
Date of Research: 1991 - continuing
KEYWORDS: *assessment; pupil development; pupil evaluation; reception classes; school entrance age; screening tests*

London University

9/0572

Birkbeck College, Department of Psychology, Malet Street, London WC1E 7HX
071 580 6622
Van der Lely, H. Dr
A psycholinguistic investigation into the underlying cause of specific language impairment in children
Abstract: Specific language impaired (SLI) children suffer from language disorder in the absence of any other impairments. The underlying nature and cause of this disorder, affecting an estimated 500,000 children, is still poorly understood. This research proposes a hypothesis about the underlying deficit in SLI children based on the findings from expression and comprehension. The extent of the hypothesised 'domain specific' language deficit will be tested by investigating grammatical, general linguistic and non-linguistic (domain neutral) representations. This will give a better understanding of SLI children and of the mechanisms of language acquisition in general.
Published Material: VAN DER LELY, H.K.J. & DEWART, H. (1986). 'Sentence comprehension strategies in specifically language impaired children', British Journal of Disorders of Communication, No 21, pp.291-306.; VAN DER LELY, H.K.J. & DEWART, H. (1987). 'How do specifically language impaired children understand sentences?', Proceedings from the First International Symposium for Specific Speech and Language Disorders in Children, London: Association for All Speech Impaired Children (AFASIC).; VAN DER LELY, H.K.J. & HARRIS, M. (1990). 'Specifically language impaired children's comprehension of reversible sentences', Journal of Speech and Hearing Disorders, Vol 55, No 1, pp.101-117.
Status: Sponsored project
Source of Grant: British Academy £64,000
Date of Research: 1991 - continuing
KEYWORDS: language acquisition; language handicaps; learning disabilities; psycholinguistics

9/0573

Goldmsiths' College, Faculty of Education, Lewisham Way, New Cross, London SE14 6NW
081 692 7171
Hurst, V. Mrs; *Supervisor:* Kelly, A. Prof.
Teachers' strategies of self evaluation
Abstract: The project aims to gain an insight into classroom processes of evaluation and curriculum development. It is an ethnographic investigation through case studies of two infant classrooms, a group of initial teacher education (ITE) students on teaching practice, ITE students on college-based courses, collaborative work with a museum education department plus two nursery centres for the purpose of comparison.
Status: Individual research
Date of Research: 1986-1992
KEYWORDS: classroom observation techniques; evaluation methods; self evaluation – individuals; student teacher education; teacher effectiveness; teacher evaluation

9/0574

Goldsmith's College, Art Psychotherapy Unit, Lewisham Way, New Cross, London SE14 6NW
081 692 7171
Sussex University, Faculty of Social Sciences, Sussex House, Falmer, Brighton BN1 9RH
0273 606755
Gilroy, A. Ms; *Supervisor:* Smith, P. Dr
Art therapists and their art
Abstract: This research outlines the processes of career choice and occupational development of art therapists, focusing on their own art practice and the varying influences upon it, from early childhood through to the present. The study is survey based, using questionnaires and supplemented by interviews. Two consecutive academic years of postgraduate art therapy students (44) and art teacher students (38), and 217 practising art therapists were the respondents. A route is traced from art therapy and art teacher students' interest in art, through to entry into postgraduate education. Although the two groups were found to have much in common with each other, the art therapy students were distinguished by stressful experiences during their childhoods and early adult lives. Art therapy students learning in experiential groups was seen to promote increases in self awareness and spontaneity in art, as well as a more honest engagement with personal imagery. It is demonstrated that most art therapists continue with some form of art, although its frequency diminishes upon entry into the profession. The nature of art therapists' art is seen to vary and the influence of clinical practice may be positive or negative, but the activity itself remains of critical importance in their lives. That their own art enables art therapists to sustain a sense of personal and professional well being implies that art therapists should not neglect their art practice, and that art therapy educators should pay attention to students' art practice during their professional education.
Published Material: GILROY, A.J. (1989). 'On occasionally being able to paint', Inscape, pp.2-9, Spring.
Status: Sponsored project
Source of Grant: Goldsmith's College £250
Date of Research: 1983-1991
KEYWORDS: art expression; art therapy; career choice; career development

9/0575

Goldsmiths' College, Department of Continuing and Community Education, Lewisham Way, New Cross, London SE14 6NW
081 692 7171
Clyne, P. Mr; *Supervisor:* Coben, D. Ms
Professional development of adult educators in south east London
Abstract: This project seeks to research the need for professional development of adult educators in south east London. This will be done through consultation with other providers of adult and continuing education in a range of settings including the new local education authorities, health authorities, social services and others. The aim will be to develop the curriculum and appropriate accreditation and transferability and to begin to provide short courses.
Status: Sponsored project
Source of Grant: Universities Funding Coucil £15,000
Date of Research: 1991 - continuing
KEYWORDS: adult education teachers; adult educators; professional development

9/0576

Goldsmiths' College, Department of Continuing and Community Education, Lewisham Way, New Cross, London SE14 6NW
081 692 7171
O'Rourke, R. Ms; *Supervisor:* Mace, J. Ms
Student publishing in adult literacy
Abstract: Adult literacy in the UK adopted a practice (from the mid 1970s) of publishing reading material written by literacy students themselves. There has been some evidence to show that: a) this practice gave new confidence both to the student authors and to their readers; and b) it is a practice which since the late 1980s appears to be in decline. The study aims to establish the rationale, extent, and educational effects of the practice of publishing writing by adult literacy students in this country and to examine the staff development implications of these. It is a national study which will consist of: a) a literature search (both of theoretical work on writing development, and of the publications which have resulted from student writing); b) visits and interviews with tutors and students at a sample of 20 centres across the UK; c) a postal questionnaire of 200+ tutors and organisers in literacy programmes; d) interviews/group events with up to 6 groups of 12 students each; e) a national consultative conference on the draft report.
Status: Sponsored project
Source of Grant: Leverhulme Trust £26,000
Date of Research: 1991-1992
KEYWORDS: adult literacy; writing for publication; writing improvement

9/0577

Goldsmiths' College, Department of Continuing and Community Education, Lewisham Way, New Cross, London SE14 6NW
081 692 7171
Gibbs, L. Ms
Professional development of private music teachers

Abstract: It is likely that private music teachers exert the most extensive influence upon musical life and development in this country and yet we know very little of their activities beyond casual anecdotal evidence. (A PRIVATE music teacher is anyone teaching music on a SELF-EMPLOYED basis, whether in a studio, at home, or under the aegis of an educational agency or institution). In the absence of any research in the area, the project has the general aim of gaining an impression of the scope and state of private music teaching, and a more specific aim of looking at the professional development of training, if any, of individual private music teachers. A comprehensive questionnaire has been circulated nationally which addresses the issues of: teaching experience, preparation for teaching, musical training and education, current musical activities, perceived effectiveness of preparation for teaching, certification, and teacher training priorities. From the collected information, 50 questionnaire respondents are selected for interview so that a qualitative picture of the data can be drawn. One specific task of the data is to relate preparation/training for teaching or lack of it to perceived teaching effectiveness.
Published Material: GIBBS, L. (1990). 'Private lives', Music Teacher, Vol 69, No 8, pp.11-12.; GIBBS, L. (1990). 'How good are private music teachers', Journal of the Incorporated Society of Musicians, Vol 53, No 3, pp.78.; GIBBS, L. (1991). 'Research into the professional development and training of private music teachers', Journal of the European Piano Teachers Association, Vol 12, No 36, pp.36.
Status: Sponsored project
Source of Grant: Universities Funding Council £20,000
Date of Research: 1991-1992
KEYWORDS: *music teachers; professional development; professional training; teacher education*

9/0578
Goldsmiths' College, Department of Continuing and Community Education, New Cross, London SE14 6NW
081 692 7171
Adams, T. Ms; Grandison, S. Ms; *Supervisor:* Adams, T. Ms
Investigation into what factors pre-dispose students to seek counselling with special reference to: subject bias, special categories of college entry and history of mental instability
Abstract: Data collected by Goldsmiths' Counselling Service over the last three years profiles a number of factors which the case-load presents. With regard to strategies of resourcing and academic pastoral support the data moves beyond an equation of student numbers and counselling hours. Relevant factors so far identified are that subject bias can appear to influence student stability; that special categories of students (e.g. mature) can cause considerable stress on the counselling provision; and that aspects of the psychological backgrounds of vulnerable students can lead to the service responding to problems that are reactivated through study. In order to address then the essential responsibilities of the Counselling Service provision the present study aims to evaluate students' specific needs by investigating what factors pre-dispose students to seek counselling. By appropriating the preliminary data, special reference is given in the study to subject bias, categories of college entry and history of mental instability. Research on student counselling services has been largely conducted by practising counsellors upon their own services. Such relatively small-scale research has resulted in a dearth of comparative studies across services. The present study is a comparative study made of the case-loads of counselling services in three institutions in the first instance. On identifying the small sample of services, students' specific needs are accessed by means of a semi-structured interview schedule, through which a base of information evolves and from which the final field work questions can be structured. The design of the pilot questionnaires will incorporate attitudes to and expectations of the counselling service, i.e. how the perception of student counselling consumerism affect the service provision. As a pilot study this research initiative will be broadened in scope at a national level.
Status: Sponsored project
Source of Grant: London University: Goldsmiths' College £1,900.
Date of Research: 1991-1992
KEYWORDS: *counselling services; higher education; pastoral care – education; student counselling; student needs*

9/0579
Goldsmiths' College, Department of Continuing and Community Education, Lewisham Way, New Cross, London

SE14 6NW
081 692 7171
Kent University, Canterbury CT2 7NZ
0227 764000
Coben, D. Ms; *Supervisor:* McLellan, D. Prof.
Radical heroes: Gramsci, Freire and the liberal tradition in adult education
Abstract: In the 1970s and 1980s many radical adult educators in Britain turned to the work of Antonio Gramsci and Paulo Freire for theoretical insights to support new initiatives in the education of adults in the wake of the Russell Report. The thesis considers the significance of the work of Gramsci and Freire on the development of theories of adult education in Britain in the period following the publication of the Russell Report. The thesis begins by charting the origins of the dominant tradition in British adult education, the Liberal Tradition, in the nineteenth century, starting with an analysis of the struggle for education and for emancipation by working class groupings. This is contrasted with the development of liberal adult education in the twentieth century with its emphasis on education for leisure as opposed to vocational education and an analysis of the origins and development of radical critiques of adult education in the period 1973-1990. Gramsci's writing on hegemony and the nature of education in a revolutionary process is considered, as is the development of Freire's analysis of the transformative role of adult education in liberating the oppressed. The relationship between Gramsci, Freire and the Liberal Tradition is explored, and the thesis looks at ways in which Gramsci and Freire have been used as 'Radical Heroes' in radical critiques and developments of the Liberal Tradition.
Status: Individual research
Date of Research: 1985-1992
KEYWORDS: *adult education; educational history; educational theories*

9/0580
Goldsmiths' College, Faculty of Education, Lewisham Way, New Cross, London SE14 6NW
081 692 7171
Hurst, V. Mrs; Blenkin, G. Ms
Monitoring and evaluation in workplace nurseries
Abstract: The project aims to gain an insight into the evaluation procedures used by workplace nurseries, in particular the role of the 'outsider'. Ethnographic action research, based on two nursery centres, will investigate how staff may be supported in the monitoring and evaluation of their practice.
Status: Sponsored project
Source of Grant: London University: Goldsmiths' College £3,700
Date of Research: 1990 - continuing
KEYWORDS: *employer supported day care; evaluation methods; institutional evaluation; self evaluation – groups*

9/0581
Goldsmiths' College, Faculty of Education, Lewisham Way, New Cross, London SE14 6NW
081 692 7171
Matthews, B Mr; Thumpston, G. Ms
Collaborative learning and equal opportunities
Abstract: There has been an increasing emphasis on collaborative learning in all aspects of education. Within the National Curriculum, evaluation of pupils discussing and taking part in group work is now statutory. In particular, recent research projects have shown how important the discussion of ideas is to children learning about science and other subjects. The action research is to find ways of: studying interactions; finding strategies that will enable pupils to be aware of their interactions; finding strategies that will enable pupils to change the ways they discuss; encouraging greater learning of all pupils; encouraging girls and boys to see each other as full people, rather than to relate to each other through stereotypes; encouraging pupils from all ethnic backgrounds to see each other as full people, rather than to relate to each other through stereotypes. The project is focused on all curriculum areas in primary and secondary schools, but will also apply to adults. As it is an action research project set in the classroom it is possible that local education authorities will be interested.
Status: Sponsored project
Source of Grant: Goldsmiths' College Internal Grant £2,800
Date of Research: 1991 - continuing
KEYWORDS: *discussion; group work; interaction; intergroup education; learning activities*

9/0582

Goldsmiths' College, Faculty of Education, Lewisham Way, New Cross, London SE14 6NW
081 692 7171
Patterson, J. Mr; Kimbell, R. Mr; Baird, T. Mr; Compton, J. Ms; Farrell, A. Ms; O'Hagan, P. Mr

Standard Assessment Tasks in design and technology and information technology at Key Stage 3 of the National Curriculum

Abstract: The aim of the research is twofold. Firstly, to generate, test and evaluate teaching and learning materials that are a valid and reliable means of assessing the capability of 14 year olds in design and technology (D&T). Secondly, to generate, test and evaluate models of INSET (inservice teacher education) required to achieve suitably reliable assessment. The design and technology schedule will involve a trial in 1990 of 3,000 pupils; a First Pilot in 1991 of 15,000 pupils and a principal pilot in 1992 of 15,000 pupils. The Information Technology Schedule will involve a trial in 1990 of 500 pupils, and informal pilot in 1991 of 2,500 pupils and a pilot in 1992 of 15,000 pupils. The INSET schedule will involve approximately 175 teachers in 1990, approximately 500 teachers in 1991 and approximately 500 teachers in 1992. After each trial and pilot, a full report is to be written for the Schools Examination and Assessment Council. This covers the appropriateness of the assessment materials and INSET and includes statistical data support for any recommendations that are made.

Status: Sponsored project
Source of Grant: School Examinations and Assessment Council £1,900,000
Date of Research: 1989-1992
KEYWORDS: *design education; information technology; inservice teacher education; National Curriculum; standard assessment tasks; technology education*

9/0583

Goldsmiths' College, Faculty of Education, Lewisham Way, New Cross, London SE14 6NW
081 692 7171
Kimbell, R. Prof.; Stables, K. Ms; Patterson, J. Mr; Wheeler, A. Mr; *Supervisor:* Kelly, A. Prof.; Kimbell, R. Prof.

Assessment of Performance Unit in design and technology: aimed at monitoring the performance of 15 year old pupils in design and technology

Abstract: The Assessment of Performance Unit was established in 1975 with the prime task of surveying and monitoring levels of achievement in schools. Progressively the concern became to understand why pupils performed in the ways they did; teasing out learning blocks and helping teachers to enhance the learning of their pupils. The Design and Technology Project set out to: (a) identify those aspects of an understanding of both design and technology most likely to be reflected in primary and secondary schools; (b) to consider when and where abilities in design and technology appear in the school curriculum; (c) to suggest how those aspects of pupils' development might be assessed; (d) develop a test of capability; (e) administer to 2% of a 15 year old cohort in England, Wales and Northern Ireland (1988-89); and (f) analyse data and report on strengths/weaknesses in relation to a variety of background variables. The sample used was 10,000 – 2% of all 15 year old pupils from schools throughout the United Kingdom. A pilot survey (1887-88) was made using short term (90 minute) pencil/paper activities to establish the viability of the test design and the form of the main survey activities. Information was gathered from schools on curriculum matters. The main survey (1988-89) consisted of: case records of extended activity (on GCSE project); short term (90 minute pencil/paper activities; extended half day modelling activities involving real materials and allowing collaboration between pupils; and collection of data on schools and pupils.

Published Material: Learning through design and technology: the APU model, Leaflet No 1. School Examination and Assessment Council, 1990.; The assessment of performance in design and technology: final report. School Examination and Assessment Council, 1991.
Status: Sponsored project
Source of Grant: School Examinations and Assessment Council £979,923
Date of Research: 1985-1991
KEYWORDS: *achievement; assessment; craft design technology; design education; technology education*

9/0584

Goldsmiths' College, Faculty of Education, Lewisham Way, New Cross, London SE14 6NW
081 692 7171
London University, Institute of Education, Department of English and Media Studies, 20 Bedford Way, London W21H OAL
071 580 1122
Gregory, E. Ms; *Supervisor:* Spencer, M. Mrs

The significance of boundary negotiation between teachers and children from 'non-school-oriented backgrounds' in early school reading lessons

Abstract: The study originates in inservice work with teachers aiming to foster links with the families of children experiencing difficulty in learning to read in school. It aims to investigate the reasons behind the very different early reading progress of children from 'non-school-oriented backgrounds'. The sample studied are a group of reception-aged children of mixed social, cultural and linguistic background, their parents or caregivers and their teachers during the children's first eighteen months in school. Ethnographic and ethnomethodological approaches are being used. The project aims to find reasons explaining the different progress of children from 'non-school-oriented' backgrounds and in teacher-child interaction during early reading lessons. Analyses so far point to a differential tuition which is taking place during individual 'shared reading' lessons and examine the form this takes.

Published Material: GREGORY, E. (1989). 'Do English eat octopus?: teacher and child negotiate reading in the multilingual classroom', English in Education, Vol 23, No 3, pp.13-20, Autumn.
Status: Individual research
Date of Research: 1985-1992
KEYWORDS: *early reading; home-school relationship; reading achievement; social background; teacher-pupil relationship*

9/0585

Imperial College of Science, Technology and Medicine, Humanities Programme, Mechanical Engineering Building, Exhibition Road, London SW7 3BX
071 589 5111
Hughes, J. Mr; *Supervisor:* Goodlad, S. Dr

Tutoring from colleges to schools

Abstract: The aim of the project is to promote peer tutoring schemes, similar to Imperial College's 'Pimlico Connection', around the United Kingdom. This is when volunteer students from further or higher education act as tutors in local primary and secondary schools often in science, mathematics and technology lessons. The professional teacher uses them as an extra, and valuable, teaching resource. The student tutors provide positive role models to the school pupils and in doing so it is hoped to increase the aspiration for them to stay on in education and training beyond age 16. Students acquire communication, organisational and problem-solving skills as well as self-confidence. Student tutoring involves volunteer students going into local primary and secondary schools on a sustained and systematic basis. From the original Pimlico Connection Scheme the number has risen to 96 similar projects.

Published Material: GOODLAD, S. & HIRST, B. (1989). Peer tutoring: a guide to learning by teaching. London: Kogan Page.; GOODLAD, S. & HIRST, B. (1990). Explorations in peer tutoring. Oxford: Blackwell.; HUGHES, J.C. (1992). Tutoring: students as tutors in school. London: BP Educational Service.; HUGHES, J.C. (1991) (Ed). Tutoring Resource Pack. London: BP Educational Service.
Status: Sponsored project
Source of Grant: British Petroleum (BP) Aiming for a College Education Initiative £300,000
Date of Research: 1990 - continuing
KEYWORDS: *mathematics education; peer influence; peer teaching; science education; student volunteers; technology education*

9/0586

Imperial College of Science, Technology and Medicine, St Mary's Hospital Medical School, Norfolk Place, Paddington, London W2 1PG
071 723 1252
McManus, I. Dr; Richards, P. Prof.; Vincent, C. Mr

Three longitudinal studies of medical student selection

Abstract: This project is an assessment of the process of medical student selection at five medical schools, for admission in October 1981 with follow-up of the entrants between October 1981 and

October 1986
Status: Sponsored project
Source of Grant: Leverhulme Trust
Date of Research: 1990 - continuing
KEYWORDS: admission criteria; medical schools; medical students; selective admission

9/0587
Institute of Education, 20 Bedford Way, London WC1H 0AL
071 580 1122
Dyer, D. Mr; Lines, D. Mr
Cambridge Business Studies Project
Abstract: This project has six objectives: (1) to foster the development of business education courses at 16+ and 18+ level, giving advice and support to teachers; (2) to develop and disseminate teachers aids and materials primarily of value for 16+ and 18+ courses; (3) to develop inservice training courses for intending teachers and others wishing to extend their expertise; (4) to liaise with examining bodies and others for appropriate curriculum development, to foster dialogue between teachers and others interested in business education; (5) to liaise with business and industry; and (6) to monitor work and interpret and report as required.
Published Material: DYER, D.M. & CHAMBERS, I. (1987). Business Studies: an introduction. Harlow: Longman.; WHITEHEAD, D. & DYER, D.H. (1991). New developments in economics and business education: handbook for teachers. London: Kogan Page.; A list of teaching materials and syllabuses is available from the researchers.
Status: Sponsored project
Source of Grant: Cambridge Business Studies Trust
Date of Research: 1967 - continuing
KEYWORDS: business education; curriculum development; inservice teacher education

9/0588
Institute of Education, 20 Bedford Way, London WC1H 0AL
071 580 1122
Dee, L. Mrs
Assessment of students with disabilities or learning difficulties
Abstract: An investigation into current assessment procedures used by colleges of further education (FE) to identify the learning support needs of young people and adults with disabilities or learning difficulties, with a view to producing guidelines for good practice.
Status: Sponsored project
Source of Grant: Further Education Unit £20,000
Date of Research: 1992 - continuing
KEYWORDS: assessment; colleges of further education; diagnostic assessment; disabilities; further education; moderate learning difficulties; special educational needs

9/0589
Institute of Education, 20 Bedford Way, London WC1H 0AL
071 580 1122
Dee, L. Mrs
Funding for special educational needs – post school provision
Abstract: This is a survey of funding arrangements and unit costs in three local authorities in order to establish costs for students with disabilities and learning difficulties in colleges of further education (FE) and adult education. Recommendations on interim and long term funding arrangements will be made.
Published Material: DEE, L. (1992). 'The funding and costing of provision for learners with learning difficulties or disabilities in colleges and adult education institutes'. FEU Report 725.
Status: Sponsored project
Source of Grant: Further Education Unit £16,735
Date of Research: 1992-1992
KEYWORDS: access to education; adult education; educational finance; further education; local education authorities; special educational needs

9/0590
Institute of Education, Centre for Multicultural Education, 20 Bedford Way, London WC1H 0AL
071 580 1122
Hicks, D. Dr; *Supervisor:* Gundara, J. Dr
Global futures project
Abstract: If we are concerned about fully educating young people for the 21st century, what sort of preparation do they need and how will the National Curriculum provide it? To make sense of life in the 1990s contemporary trends and events need to be set in a context which is both globally and future orientated. This project focuses on the entitlement of pupils to preparation for responsible and active citizenship as future adult members of a global community. It arises out of, and builds on, much of the innovative work carried out in world studies during the last decade. In particular, it will help both teachers and pupils to: (a) explore current concerns about the state of the planet; (b) clarify their choice of preferred futures at scales from the personal to the global; (c) envision alternative futures which are both just and ecologically sustainable; (d) develop their own personal and political skills; (e) exercise their rights responsibly as active citizens in the local and global community. The project will be of interest to primary and secondary teachers concerned, for example, with English, science, design and technology, geography or R.E., and cross-curricular issues such as personal and social education, environmental education and citizenship. It will provide both appropriate INSET programmes and also work with schools to produce relevant resource materials for teachers and pupils.
Published Material: HICKS, D. (1991). 'Exploring alternative futures: a teacher's interim guide', Global Futures Project, University of London, Institute of Education; HICKS, D. (1991). 'Preparing for the millennium: reflections on the need for futures education', Futures, Vol 23, No 6.
Status: Sponsored project
Source of Grant: Worldwide Fund for Nature £100,365
Date of Research: 1989-1992
KEYWORDS: citizenship education; conservation – environment; environmental education; futures – of society; global approach; world studies

9/0591
Institute of Education, Consortium for Assessment and Testing in Schools, 20 Bedford Way, London WC1H 0AL
071 580 1122
Furlong, J. Prof.
Consortium for assessment and testing in schools – key stage 3, English
Abstract: The Consortium for Assessment and Testing in Schools (CATS) was formed in January 1989 to develop Standard Assessment Tasks for the National Curriculum at key stage 1. The Consortium comprises the Institute, the University of London Examinations and Assessment Council and Hodder & Stoughton Publishers. To develop Standard Assessment Tasks for pupils at the end of key stage 3 (age 14), the Consortium was joined by two other schools of the University: Goldsmiths' College and King's College. The assessments enable teachers, students and parents to know whether the attainment targets specified for the subjects of the National Curriculum have now been met.
Status: Sponsored project
Source of Grant: School Examinations and Assessment Council £1,567,000
Date of Research: 1989-1992
KEYWORDS: assessment; English studies; National Curriculum; standard assessment tasks

9/0592
Institute of Education, Department of Child Development and Primary Education, 20 Bedford Way, London WC1H 0AL
071 580 1122
Moore, T. Prof.; *Supervisor:* Hindley, C. Prof.
Data analysis of the longitudinal research project: changes in general ability, personality, attitudes, values etc. of normal children from infancy to adolescence
Abstract: The research began in 1949 as a collaborative project between the Institute of Education and Department of Child Health at London University. There is thus a parallel research under Professor J.M. Tanner on the physical development of the same subjects. As representative a sample as possible of the London West Central 1 area was recruited from 1949 to 1952. 223 subjects were recruited, and 186 were in the sample at 18 months. For many purposes the researchers have around 110 subjects with records complete enough for general use up to 14 years; and 84 plus, up to 17 years. Subjects were seen at 8 days, 6 weeks, 3, 6, 9, 12 and 18 months, and then annually from 2 to 18 years. The aim was to obtain reasonably comprehensive information, which includes: (1) regular interviews with mothers about their child's behaviour and parental methods; (2)

testing of abilities, personality, etc; (3) assessment of interests, attitudes, personal values; and (4) interviews with adolescent subjects. Data on social and family background have been obtained throughout. The researchers interests have been: (i) comparison of child-rearing methods and early locomotion across collaborating European samples; (ii) infant sleep and the effects of anoxia at birth; (iii) effects of daily substitute care; (iv) stability and change in IQs and personality using individual curve fitting in addition to correlations etc; (v) factors influencing development – family, social, life events, school etc; and (vi) children's views of themselves or school, of their future and their correspondence with outcome.
Published Material: A full list of publications is available from the researchers.
Status: Sponsored project
Source of Grant: Leverhulme Trust £60,250
Date of Research: 1949 - continuing
KEYWORDS: ability; child development; developmental continuity; longitudinal studies; personality development

9/0593
Institute of Education, Department of Child Development and Primary Education, 20 Bedford Way, London WC1H OAL
071 580 1122
St James-Roberts, I. Dr; Sing, G. Mrs; Papakyriakopoulos, C. Mr
Emotional and behavioural problems in reception class children
Abstract: The first aim has been to develop instruments which enable reception class teachers to assess emotional and behavioural problems in their pupils. Contextually appropriate, reliable and valid procedures have been developed. The researchers are now studying factors in children, families and classroom contexts which lead to such problems.
Status: Sponsored project
Source of Grant: Association of Commonwealth Universities; London University Central Research Fund
Date of Research: 1989-1992
KEYWORDS: behaviour problems; emotional problems; reception classes; young children

9/0594
Institute of Education, Department of Curriculum Studies, 20 Bedford Way, London WC1H OAL
071 580 1122
Simons, H. Dr; Maw, J. Miss
Soviet/British curriculum development project
Abstract: The purpose of this action research project is to examine ways in which teachers handle ethnocentrism in their teaching, focusing initially on the teaching of history. Working with a small group of schools, the research will document the strategies teachers employ in the teaching of history, encouraging teachers to conduct self-monitoring of their teaching strategies and jointly analyse the results. Classroom observation will be the major approach, supplemented by interviews with teachers and pupils and analysis of tapes, transcripts and observations of classroom practice. The project is part of a broader Soviet/British Curriculum Development Project sponsored collaboratively with colleagues from the Academy of Pedagogical Science in the USSR. The early part of the project involved an analysis of the image of each other's society in history textbooks at GCSE level. This current project takes up the crucial issue of how texts and teaching materials are mediated in the classroom.
Status: Sponsored project
Source of Grant: Joseph Rowntree Charitable Foundation; Joseph Rowntree Social Service Trust; Elizabeth & Barrows Cadbury Foundation; Westcroft Trust £43,900
Date of Research: 1989-1991
KEYWORDS: cross cultural studies; ethnic studies; ethnocentrism; history; teacher attitudes; teaching methods; USSR

9/0595
Institute of Education, Department of Curriculum Studies, 20 Bedford Way, London WC1H 0AL
071 580 1122
Bradley, G. Ms; Green, W. Ms
London Plan (London Record of Achievement)
Abstract: The aims of the project are to develop the formative processes of individual action planning through case studies across a
range of programmes in further education and with managing agents and employers, involving students of different ages and abilities.
Status: Sponsored project
Source of Grant: Training, Enterprise and Education Directorate £151,576
Date of Research: 1990-1992
KEYWORDS: further education; planning; planning education

9/0596
Institute of Education, Department of Curriculum Studies, 20 Bedford Way, London WC1H 0AL
071 580 1122
Lawton, D. Prof.
National Council for Vocational Qualifications (NCVQ) Fellowship
Abstract: This four year project is to examine impact and take-up of the new framework for National Vocational Qualifications (NVQs); it examines and supports the technical processes required to develop and implement NVQs as well as providing a critique of policy and strategy formation in vocational qualifications in the United Kingdom.
Status: Sponsored project
Source of Grant: National Council for Vocational Qualifications £216,669
Date of Research: 1990 - continuing
KEYWORDS: National Vocational Qualifications; qualifications; vocational education

9/0597
Institute of Education, Department of Curriculum Studies, 20 Bedford Way, London WC1H 0AL
071 580 1122
Greenwich University, Avery Hill Campus, Bexley Road, Eltham, London SE9 2PQ
081 316 8000
Harland, L. Ms; *Supervisor:* Gipps, C. Dr
Supporting teachers, supporting children with special educational needs: an exploration of the partnership between class teachers and support teachers
Abstract: The role of the support teacher is changing extensively. It is assumed that the move from withdrawing children with special educational needs from the classroom, towards working within the classroom, with the accompanying need to advise/consult the class teacher, has resulted in a qualitative improvement of educational provisions for these children. Questions are proposed which will explore the nature of the partnership between support teacher and class teachers. It is intended to uncover some of the tensions which accompany the work of the support teacher. So far there has been little evaluation of any possible improvement in educational provision for children with special educational needs which may have been accounted for by support teacher/class teacher collaboration.
Status: Individual research
Date of Research: 1986 - continuing
KEYWORDS: special educational needs; support teachers; teachers

9/0598
Institute of Education, Department of Economics, Geography and Business Education, 20 Bedford Way, London WC1H OAL
071 580 1122
University College of Swansea, Singleton Park, Swansea SA2 8PP
0792 205678
Thomas, L. Dr; Williams, M. Prof.
Teacher Training for Economic Awareness: Welsh extension
Abstract: The Economic Awareness Teacher Training Programme (EcATT) aims to promote and monitor the development and implementation of economic awareness programmes in schools, colleges and LEAs (local education authorities). This project aims to extend the EcATT network to University College, Swansea.
Published Material: JEPHCOTE, M. (1992). 'Understanding economics or economics understanding? A case study for developing economics understanding as a pupil curriculum entitlement'. In: BLOOMER, G., BROOKES, K. & JEPHCOTE, M. 'Putting the economics in EIU'. EATE Research Report No 4, October, 1992.; JEPHCOTE, M. & HENDLEY, D. (1992). 'Design and technology and economic awareness', A guide to economic awareness in the

National Curriculum 1992.
Status: Sponsored project
Source of Grant: Esmee Fairbairn Charitable Trust £45,000
Date of Research: 1990-1992
KEYWORDS: curriculum development; economics education; enterprise education; teacher education; Wales

9/0599

Institute of Education, Department of Economics, Geography and Business Education, 20 Bedford Way, London
WC1H 0AL
071 580 1122
Manchester University, School of Education, Oxford Road, Manchester M13 9PL
061 275 3437
Thomas, L. Dr; Hodkinson, S. Mr
Teacher Training for Economic Awareness
Abstract: The Economic Awareness Teacher Training Programme (EcATT) which began in 1986 is a response to calls for the introduction of economic awareness programmes into schools and colleges. The initiative is based upon a partnership between the Department of Education and Science, the Department of Trade & Industry, teacher training institutions, local education authorities and industrial and commercial organisations. British Petroleum, Banking Information Service, the Department of Trade & Industry, Unilever and the Esmee Fairbairn Trust Fund have provided funds to allow the appointment of academic and administrative staff. Initially, the Institute of Education and the University of Manchester will take responsibility for coordinating the programme, which will include: the development, piloting and evaluation of training programmes, schemes of work and training materials; the establishment of a forum to help local education authorities to identify their training needs and to devise strategies to meet these needs; promoting and supporting the development of teacher groups of advisers, coordinators and advisory teachers across local education authority boundaries as well as the development of links between training institutions, local education authorities and industry and commerce; the extension of the initiative to institutions in other areas of the country.
Published Material: DUNHILL, R. (1990). 'Three of a kind? a review of three LEA publications on Economic Awareness', Economic Awareness, Vol 2, No 2.; JOHNSON, C. & CLARKE, P. (1990). 'Coal: an economic awareness lesson in humanities', Economic Awareness, Vol 2, No 3, pp.15-19.; DAVIES, P. (1990). 'Industrial change – a lower school geography lesson', Economic Awareness, Vol 2, No 3, pp.20-22.; THOMAS, L. & WOOD, K. et al (1991). 'What is slavery anyway? – the economic awareness implications of work on a theme in history', Economic Awareness, Vol 3, No 2.; HODKINSON, S. (1991). 'Modern foreign languages and economic awareness: a comment', Economic Awareness, Vol 4, No 1, pp.7-9. A full list of publications is available from the researcher.
Status: Sponsored project
Source of Grant: Department of Trade & Industry; Banking Information Service; British Petroleum; Unilever £643,000
Date of Research: 1986 - continuing
KEYWORDS: curriculum development; economics education; enterprise education; teacher education

9/0600

Institute of Education, Department of Economics, Geography and Business Education, 20 Bedford Way, London
WC1H 0AL
071 580 1122
Naish, M. Mr; Young, M. Dr
The Technical and Vocational Education Initiative in initial teacher training
Abstract: The Technical and Vocational Education Inititative (TVEI) in the Initial Teacher Training (ITT) project is funded by the Training Enterprise & Education Directorate as a pilot project to consider the implications of TVEI for ITT. The focus is on staff development and, through that, course development. The project is sponsoring a number of mini research projects which are being undertaken by Postgraduate Certificate in Education (PGCE) staff and will feed into proposals for course development. These proposals will be trialled and evaluated in order to ascertain their viability for implementation in the course.
Status: Sponsored project
Source of Grant: Training, Enterprise & Education Directorate £161,274
Date of Research: 1989-1992

KEYWORDS: Postgraduate Certificate in Education; preservice teacher education; technical education curriculum; vocational education

9/0601

Institute of Education, Department of Economics, Geography and Business Education, 20 Bedford Way, London
WC1H 0AL
071 580 1122
Thomas, L. Dr
Economics education 16-19 project
Abstract: An Economics Association project, it aims to stimulate and coordinate a fundamental review of the nature of economics thinking in response to the last decade's shift in the basic concerns of the discipline: by focusing on the full range of classroom contexts at 16-19, to help teachers to investigate the implications of this review for teaching, learning and assessment strategies; and developing and publishing reports, materials and resources to provide access for other teachers to the expertise which will eventually be required by all.
Published Material: THOMAS, L. (1991). 'Project Briefing No 1 June 1991', Economics, Vol XXVII, Part 2, No 114, Summer.; THOMAS, L. (1991). 'Project Briefing No 2 November 1991', Economics, Vol XXVII, Part 4, No 116, Winter.; THOMAS, L. (1992). 'The Economics Education 16-19 Project: setting the scene', Economics, Vol XXVIII, Part 2, No 118, Summer.; THOMAS, L. (1992). 'Working Paper No 1', Economics Association.; THOMAS, L. (1992). 'Economics Education 16-19 Project', Newsletter No 1, Oxford: Heinemann.
Status: Sponsored project
Source of Grant: Economics Association £27,000
Date of Research: 1991 - continuing
KEYWORDS: curriculum development; economics education; sixteen to nineteen education

9/0602

Institute of Education, Department of Economics, Geography and Business Education, 20 Bedford Way, London
WC1H 0AL
071 580 1122
Lines, D. Mr
Economics and business studies education
Abstract: To provide a comprehensive 16-19 curriculum package in economics and business studies, including teaching and learning aids and a post-16 assessment vehicle.
Status: Sponsored project
Source of Grant: Nuffield Foundation £110,157
Date of Research: 1991 - continuing
KEYWORDS: business education; curriculum development; economics education; sixteen to nineteen education

9/0603

Institute of Education, Department of Educational Psychology and Special Educational Needs, 20 Bedford Way, London WC1H 0AL
071 580 1122
Haines, C. Dr
Effect of perceptuo-motor difficulty on early handwriting speech and reading
Abstract: In an earlier study, children entering school routinely completed neurodevelopmental tasks in the entrant school medical examination. To study the effect of difficulties with these on later school activities in and around the classroom, teachers completed a questionnaire in final year infant and first year junior classes, and children copied a sentence from the blackboard. Some four thousand children were involved. Now the geometric shapes copied at school entry, and the sentence copied from the blackboard are being assessed in greater detail to test the effect of perceptuo-motor difficulties on early handwriting skills.
Published Material: HAINES, C. (1992). 'Young children's difficulty with capital letters', Handwriting Review, pp.44-54.
Status: Sponsored project
Source of Grant: Nuffield Foundation £2,560
Date of Research: 1992 - continuing
KEYWORDS: handwriting; motor development; perceptual motor coordination; reading; speech

9/0604

Institute of Education, Department of Educational
Psychology and Special Educational Needs, 20 Bedford
Way, London WC1H OAL
071 580 1122
Henderson, S. Dr; Dubowitz, L. Dr

Motor and perceptual competence in prematurely born children
Abstract: The focus of this study, which is being carried out jointly with the Royal Postgraduate Medical School, is on children who were born prematurely, both with and without brain damage. The study has two distinct objectives: the first is to investigate the progress of these children in school; the second is to investigate the specific perceptual and motor difficulties which many of the children experience.
Status: Sponsored project
Source of Grant: Medical Research Council £87,326; Nuffield Foundation £ 5,000
Date of Research: 1989 - continuing
KEYWORDS: child development; motor development; neurological impairments; perceptual handicaps; premature infants; special educational needs

9/0605

Institute of Education, Department of Educational
Psychology and Special Educational Needs, 20 Bedford
Way, London WC1H OAL
071 580 1122
Blatchford, P. Dr; Ireson, J. Dr; Francis, H. Prof.

Teaching of reading in primary schools
Abstract: Much of the present debate on the teaching of reading is based on false information about what is happening in schools and what approaches are effective. The basic aim of this project, therefore, is to describe current practice in a sample of schools in three local education authorities. There will be 60 schools in all, 20 in each authority, and they will be chosen to include children from a range of backgrounds, and schools with a range of approaches to reading. A range of research techniques will be used, including interviews with teachers and heads and classroom observations. One main aim is to develop a methodology capable of providing a reliable and comprehensive account of different components involved in the teaching of reading. This will provide the basis for a follow up study which would seek to evaluate different approaches.
Status: Sponsored project
Source of Grant: Esmee Fairbairn Charitable Trust £40,000
Date of Research: 1991-1992
KEYWORDS: primary education; primary schools; reading strategies; reading teaching; teacher effectiveness; teaching methods

9/0606

Institute of Education, Department of Educational
Psychology and Special Educational Needs, 20 Bedford
Way, London WC1H OAL
071 580 1122
Wedell, K. Prof.; Norwich, B. Dr; Lunt, I. Ms; Evans, J. Mrs

Clusters project
Abstract: The project will describe the functioning of the cluster from an organisational point of view and look at the impact of the cluster organisation on special educational needs provision. Clusters of schools will be visited in four LEAs (local education authorities) and interviews of headteachers, teachers, educational psychologists (EPs) and other LEA personnel will be carried out.
Status: Sponsored project
Source of Grant: Economic and Social Research Council £46,760
Date of Research: 1991 - continuing
KEYWORDS: cluster grouping; educational cooperation; special educational needs; special schools

9/0607

Institute of Education, Department of Educational
Psychology and Special Educational Needs, 20 Bedford
Way, London WC1H OAL
071 580 1122
Henderson, S. Dr

A new look at perceptuo-motor disorders in cerebral palsied children
Abstract: The focus of the project is on children who find it difficult to negotiate their way around in the environment i.e. children who cannot judge the size of doorways, who cannot perceive distances accurately etc. Such children are handicapped in a school setting because they need so much help from others with their wheelchairs, in PE lessons, on the way to school etc. The aim of the study will be to try to establish what causes these problems – lack of motor experience, visual disorders such as squints which lead to absence of stereopsis and types of brain disorder will be investigated.
Status: Sponsored project
Source of Grant: Spastics Society £29,683
Date of Research: 1991 - continuing
KEYWORDS: Cerebral Palsy; disabilities; motor reactions; perceptual handicaps; perceptual motor coordination; special educational needs

9/0608

Institute of Education, Department of Educational
Psychology and Special Educational Needs, 20 Bedford
Way, London WC1H OAL
071 580 1122
Cowan, R. Dr

Children's development of number competence
Abstract: The research aims to develop an accurate account of how children's understanding of number develop from 4 to 7 years. Studies have been conducted to refine tasks used to assess children's understandings of number and procedures such as counting and sharing, to determine the causes of children's conconserving responses, to explore whether children with severe language disorders show a qualitatively different pattern of development, and to identify what experiences make children more likely to count.
Published Material: COWAN, R. (1991). 'The same number'. In: DURKIN, K. & SHIRE, B. (Eds). Language in mathematical education: research and practice. Milton Keynes: Open University.; A full list of publications is available from the researcher.
Status: Individual research
Date of Research: 1974 - continuing
KEYWORDS: arithmetic; cognitive development; number concepts; numbers; numeracy; primary education

9/0609

Institute of Education, Department of Educational
Psychology and Special Educational Needs, 20 Bedford
Way, London WC1H OAL
071 580 1122
Cowan, R. Dr

Primary school children's understanding of heat and temperature
Abstract: Assessment of Performance Unit surveys suggest that few 11-year-olds understand much about heat and temperature and how to measure them. Studies have been conducted to assess children's knowledge of temperature phenomena in connection with daily life, i.e. body temperature, ice cream and swimming pools. In addition, 9-11-year-olds have been interviewed to assess their understanding of the two common temperature scales. Children between 7 and 12 have been tested on verbal and numerical versions of temperature prediction tasks. The researchers found confusion over temperature was common even when no reference to numerical temperatures was made.
Published Material: COWAN, R. & SUTCLIFFE, N. (1991). 'What children's temperature predictions reveal of their understanding of temperature', British Journal of Educational Psychology', Vol 61, Part 3, pp.300-309.
Status: Individual research
Date of Research: 1987 - continuing
KEYWORDS: cognitive development; comprehension; heat; primary education; science education; temperature

9/0610

Institute of Education, Department of Educational
Psychology and Special Educational Needs, 20 Bedford
Way, London WC1H 0AL
071 580 1122
Adult Literacy and Basic Skills Unit, 229/231 High Holborn,
London WC1V 7DA
071 405 4017
Kambouri, M. Dr; *Supervisor:* Francis, H. Prof.; Brain, S. Mr

Drop out and progression in adult basic skills provision

Abstract: The main thrust of this report is a postal questionnaire sent to a sample of 1,500 former students plus limited interviews, together with a questionnaire to organising tutors, in a minimum of six local education authorities (LEA) areas. The data will be analysed using SSPX; and the data collected and final report published by Adult Literacy and Basic Skills Unit (ALBSU) in May 1993.
Status: Sponsored project
Source of Grant: Department for Education £49,943; Adult Literacy and Basic Skills Unit £9,900
Date of Research: 1992 - continuing
KEYWORDS: *achievement; adult basic education; adult dropouts; basic skills; dropout research*

9/0611

Institute of Education, Department of Educational Psychology and Special Educational Needs, 20 Bedford Way, London WC1H 0AL
071 580 1122
Worrall, N. Dr
Teacher-pupil relationships in the primary classroom
Abstract: This is continuing research being carried out with colleagues and research students. The sample size of a given study varies from 30 to 100. Methods have been mainly questionnaires/rating scales, increasingly supplemented by interviews. Topics explored range from child autonomy through differential curricular experiences and the development of mutual regard between children and teachers.
Published Material: INGRAM, J. & WORRALL, N. (1987). 'The negotiating classroom', Early Child Development and Care, Vol 28, pp.401-415.; WORRALL, N. & TSARNA, H. (1987). 'Teachers' reported practices towards boys and girls in science and languages', British Journal of Educational Psychology, Vol 57, pp.300-312.; WORRALL, N., WORRALL, C. & MELDRUM, C. (1988). 'Children's reciprocations of teacher evaluations', British Journal of Educational Psychology, Vol 58, pp.78-88.; THIRKELL, B. & WORRALL, N. (1989). 'Differential ethnic bias in Asian and white children', Educational Research, Vol 31, pp.181-188.; INGRAM, J. & WORRALL, N. (1992). 'Children's self-allocation and use of classroom curricular time', British Journal of Educational Psychology, Vol 62, No 1, pp.45-55.
Status: Individual research
Date of Research: 1987 - continuing
KEYWORDS: *primary school pupils; primary school teachers; primary schools; teacher-pupil relationship*

9/0612

Institute of Education, Department of Educational Psychology and Special Educational Needs, 20 Bedford Way, London WC1H 0AL
071 580 1122
May, D. Mr; *Supervisor:* Worrall, N. Dr
School stress
Abstract: The research uses focused interviews of some 100 secondary school teachers. Teachers are taken through a systematic hierarchical analysis of their 'life space' so to identify major and minor stress episodes. These episodes are analyzed for the effective, cognitive and bodily manifestations, before, during and after the episode. In addition, teachers' offered constructs and comparisons are incorporated into the analysis. Rather than aggregate across teachers, autoregressive response modelling is used to build a model of stress and coping patterns for each teacher. As a second stage, communality across teacher models can thus be examined, with a view to developing a more general picture of teacher stress-coping patterns in secondary schools.
Published Material: WORRALL, N. & MAY, D. (1988). 'Towards a person-in-situation model of teacher stress', British Journal of Educational Psychology, Vol 59, Part 2, pp.174-186.
Status: Sponsored project
Source of Grant: Nuffield Foundation
Date of Research: 1987-1992
KEYWORDS: *secondary school teachers; stress – psychological; stress management; stress variables*

9/0613

Institute of Education, Department of Educational Psychology and Special Educational Needs, 20 Bedford Way, London WC1H 0AL
071 580 1122
Earp, P. Ms; *Supervisor:* Ware, J. Dr; Norwich, B. Dr
Social interactions around microcomputers between children with severe learning difficulties
Abstract: It is known that pupils working with a microcomputer not only interact with the micro but also with each other. Pupils with severe learning difficulties are also known to interact more with each other when adults take a less dominant role. The study has already investigated the extent to which children with severe learning difficulties spontaneously interact when using a micro without the presence of an adult. An alternating treatments design was used to compare the effectiveness of the two conditions: computer and non-computer activities for improving the social interaction of two children with severe learning difficulties. The computer condition reliably increased the task-relevant social responses of both children, whereas the non-computer condition increased responses although many of these are non-task relevant. Subsequent experiments have developed ideas based on the original studies, these have continued to use quasi-experimental designs.
Status: Individual research
Date of Research: 1987-1992
KEYWORDS: *computer uses in education; human-computer interaction; interaction; severe learning difficulties; special educational needs*

9/0614

Institute of Education, Department of Educational Psychology and Special Educational Needs, 20 Bedford Way, London WC1H 0AL
071 580 1122
O'Connor, N. Dr; Hermelin, B. Dr
Memory, intelligence and talent
Abstract: This is a Medical Research Council developmental psychology project. The proposed experiments address questions concerning the nature of the specific talents found among idiots-savants and gifted normal children. One question is the degree to which the cognitive strategies used by such talented people are intelligence independent. A second is the nature of the impressive memory which seems to underlie their frequently surprising performance. Experiments will test whether this memory is predominantly rote or organized and, if the latter, whether organized 'semantically' or according to some 'syntactic' system as for logic or mathematics. In addition, the possible relevance of non-cognitive variables such as obsessive preoccupations will be assessed.
Published Material: HERMELIN, B. & O'CONNOR, N. (1985). 'Logico-affective states and non-verbal language'. In: SCHOPLER, E. & MESIBOV, G. (Eds). Communication Problems in Autism. New York: Plenum Publishing Company.; SLOBODA, J., HERMELIN, B. & O'CONNOR, N. (1985). 'An exceptional musical memory', Music Perception, Vol 3, No 2, pp.155-170.; HERMELIN, B. & O'CONNOR, N. (1986). 'Spatial representations in mathematically and artistically gifted children', British Journal of Educational Psychology, Vol 56, pp.150-157.; HERMELIN, B. & O'CONNOR, N. (1986). 'Idiot-savant calendrical calculators: rules and regularities', Psychological Medicine, Vol 16, pp.885-893.
Status: Sponsored project
Source of Grant: Medical Research Council £71,757
Date of Research: 1987-1991
KEYWORDS: *cognitive ability; cognitive development; exceptional child research; exceptional persons; gifted; intelligence; memory; mental retardation*

9/0615

Institute of Education, Department of Educational Psychology and Special Educational Needs, 20 Bedford Way, London WC1H 0AL
071 580 1122
Naish, M. Mr; Watkins, C. Mr
Support of mentors in the classroom
Abstract: The Institute of Education Post Graduate Certificate of Education (PGCE) is developing an area based approach to teacher education, involving school teachers in initial teacher education. Linked teachers in the schools require training and support. This project will isolate their needs, develop training and support and evaluate processes and outcomes.
Status: Sponsored project
Source of Grant: Paul Hamlyn Foundation £13,500

Date of Research: 1991-1992
KEYWORDS: mentors; preservice teacher education; student teacher supervisors; teacher training

9/0616

Institute of Education, Department of Educational Psychology and Special Educational Needs, 20 Bedford Way, London WC1H 0AL
071 580 1122
Francis, H. Prof.; Abell, S. Mrs
Effectiveness of different kinds of literacy provision
Abstract: Three main types of provision were identified in eight participating local education authorities (LEAs). Each was examined for evidence of student satisfaction and benefit and for student, staffing, organisation and teaching factors which influenced student experience and outcomes. Little evidence emerged which differentiated clearly between styles, but overall a number of issues were identified which must be taken into account in evaluating provision in order to improve it.
Published Material: ABELL, S. (1992). Effective approaches in adult literacy: research into evaluating the effectiveness of different styles of provision in adult literacy. London: ALBSU.
Status: Sponsored project
Source of Grant: Adult Literacy & Basic Skills Unit £71,864
Date of Research: 1989-1991
KEYWORDS: adult basic education; adult literacy; programme effectiveness

9/0617

Institute of Education, Department of Educational Psychology and Special Educational Needs, 20 Bedford Way, London WC1H 0AL
071 580 1122
Henderson, S. Dr
Pencils with triangular barrels
Abstract: The objective of this project was to evaluate the effectiveness of a triangular shaped pencil as a beginner's writing implement. Both the writing and pencil grip was be examined in 100 5-6 year olds. A technical report has been produced for Berol.
Status: Sponsored project
Source of Grant: Berol Ltd £2,489
Date of Research: 1990-1991
KEYWORDS: educational materials; handwriting

9/0618

Institute of Education, Department of Educational Psychology and Special Educational Needs, 20 Bedford Way, London WC1H 0AL
071 580 1122
Wedell, K. Prof.; Lunt, I. Ms; Norwich, B. Dr; Evans, J. Ms
Clusters Project (Extension)
Abstract: This is an extension of the Clusters Project funded by the Economic and Social Research Council.
Status: Sponsored project
Source of Grant: Waldburg Foundation £20,000
Date of Research: 1993 - continuing
KEYWORDS: cluster grouping; educational cooperation; special educational need; special schools

9/0619

Institute of Education, Department of Educational Psychology and Special Educational Needs, 20 Bedford Way, London WC1H 0AL
071 580 1122
Wedell, K. Prof.; Norwich, B. Dr
Developing policy in the field of special educational needs for the 1990s
Abstract: The preparation and publication of policy papers on special educational needs provision.
Status: Sponsored project
Source of Grant: B & G Cadbury Trust; Economic and Social Research Council
Date of Research: 1992 - continuing
KEYWORDS: educational policy; special educational needs

9/0620

Institute of Education, Department of English and Media Studies, 20 Bedford Way, London WC1H 0AL
071 580 1122
Cox, C. Ms; *Supervisor:* Burgess, A. Dr
The interrelationship of verbal and visual narrative: its importance as a teaching tool
Abstract: This project aims to make better use of visual materials to improve writing techniques across the ability range. Following a review of the existing literature, an analysis of a cartoon story drawn by three year eight pupils on an expressive arts course was carried out. The use of illustration with narrative and its role in early reading was also analysed. Work has also been carried out with mixed ability multi-ethnic groups.
Status: Individual research
Date of Research: 1984-1992
KEYWORDS: teaching methods; verbal learning; visual aids; visual learning; writing skills

9/0621

Institute of Education, Department of English and Media Studies, 20 Bedford Way, London WC1H 0AL
071 580 1122
Furlong, J. Prof.; Stubbs, M. Prof.
Development of Standard Assessment Tasks at the end of Key Stage 3 in the National Curriculum for English
Abstract: The work requires the development of (Standard Assessment Tasks) for English. Standard Assessment Tasks will be constructed to include written and oral work, so that a pupil's performance can be set against any of the 10 levels associated with the National Curriculum attainment targets. Trialling in selected local education authorities will be carried out in 1989-90, a pilot exercise on a broader sample in 1991, and a full scale unreported assessment in Summer 1992.
Status: Sponsored project
Source of Grant: School Examinations and Assessment Council £1,883,000
Date of Research: 1989-1992
KEYWORDS: assessment; English studies; National Curriculum; standard assessment tasks

9/0622

Institute of Education, Department of English and Media Studies, 20 Bedford Way, London WC1H 0AL
071 580 1122
Buckingham, D. Mr
Development of television literacy
Abstract: This research will investigate the development of children's competencies as television viewers between the ages of seven and twelve. The research will be primarily qualitative, and will concentrate particularly on the ways in which interpretations of the medium are established and negotiated in small group talk. It will also focus on the role of social class, gender and ethnic background in determining children's understanding and use of the medium. A core sample of ninety children will be interviewed both individually and in small groups on a total of eight occasions over an 18 month period. Additional interviews will be held with their teachers and parents and control groups will be used at appropriate stages. Interviews will be transcribed and analysed using techniques derived from social semiotics and discourse analysis. Particular aspects of study will include the development of children's conceptions of television genres and narrative forms: their judgements about its representations of the social world and its degrees of realism; and their understanding of the processes of television production. The project aims to provide an analysis of children's understanding of television which will enable broadcasters and educationalists to respond constructively to public concern about the 'effects' of the medium. In particular, it is hoped that the research will inform the development of media education within the National Curriculum.
Published Material: BUCKINGHAM, D. (1991). 'What are words worth? Interpreting children's talk about television', Cultural Studies, Vol 5, No 2.; BUCKINGHAM, D. (1992). 'Media education: the limits of a discourse', Journal of Curriculum Studies, Vol 24, No 4, pp.297-313.; BUCKINGHAM, D. (1993). Children talking television: the making of television literacy. London: Falmer Press.; BUCKINGHAM, D. (1993). 'Boys' talk: television and masculinity'. In: BUCKINGHAM, D. (Ed). Reading audiences: young people and the media. Manchester: Manchester University Press.

(forthcoming).; MOSS, G. (1991). 'Children and television: gendered readings', Women: an international Cultural Review, Vol 2.
Status: Sponsored project
Source of Grant: Economic and Social Research Council £103,410
Date of Research: 1989-1991
KEYWORDS: *comprehension; television; television viewing; visual literacy*

9/0623
Institute of Education, Department of English and Media Studies, 20 Bedford Way, London WC1H 0AL
071 580 1122
College of the Bahamas, PO Box No 8843, Nassau, Bahamas
Wright, L. Mrs; *Supervisor:* McLeod, A. Mr
An analysis of the sociolinguistics of the Creole-standard continuum and its relationship to education in a selected sample of secondary schools in Jamaica
Abstract: This research involves 530 Grade 9 pupils aged 15+ and 54 Grade 9 teachers and the purpose of the present investigation is to: (1) determine and describe the nature of the sociolinguistic situation in a selected sample of Jamaican secondary schools by focusing on: (a) the attitudes of pupils and their teachers to Jamaican Creole and Standard English; (b) pupils' perceptions of the role and status of both languages; (c) pupils' experience of, and their reactions to, criticism of Creole use at home and in school; (d) linguistic focusing and patterns of language use; (e) language variability evidenced by specimens of pupils' writing; (2) explore in some depth critical issues arising out of (1) above, e.g. the mesolect, or interlanguage; (3) assess the training levels and linguistic expertise of teachers in relation to national language goals set for this secondary sector; (4) criticize the gap between the rhetoric of avowed national goals and the realities of Grade 9 classrooms; and (5) make recommendations for language and linguistic training for teacher education, and in so doing, challenge traditionally held assumptions about language teaching and teacher education.
Status: Individual research
Date of Research: 1983-1991
KEYWORDS: *dialect studies; Jamaican Creole; language policy; language role; language usage; native speakers; secondary schools; sociolinguistics*

9/0624
Institute of Education, Department of English and Media Studies, 20 Bedford Way, London WC1H 0AL
071 580 1122
University of California, School of Education, Centre for the Study of Writing, Berkeley, CA 94720, USA
McLeod, A. Mr; Freedman, S. Dr; *Supervisor:* McLeod, A. Mr; Freedman, S. Dr
Writing exchange across the Atlantic: a study of secondary school students' writing, exchanged with peers in London and the Bay Area, California
Abstract: Following a survey of the teaching of writing in the USA and the UK, an exchange of secondary school student writing (age 12-15) was arranged between five classes in California and five classes in the London area in 1986/87, the hypothesis being that an actual peer audience for student writing over a period of a whole school year would reveal changes in the quality, interest and commitment of the student writers. The 10 classroom teachers evaluated the outcome in the first instance. The principal researchers collaborated on a report 'Comparing the teaching and learning of writing in the United States and the United Kingdom: audience exchange', which has now been presented to the Office for Educational Research and Instruction, Washington DC.
Status: Sponsored project
Source of Grant: US National Writing Project
Date of Research: 1986-1992
KEYWORDS: *comparative education; peer evaluation; secondary schools; United States of America; writing – composition; writing skills; writing teaching*

9/0625
Institute of Education, Department of English and Media Studies, 20 Bedford Way, London WC1H 0AL
071 580 1122
West Sussex Institute of Higher Education, Bishop Otter College, College Lane, Chichester PO19 4PE
0243 787911
Brider, J. Mr; *Supervisor:* Spencer, M. Mrs
The non-teacher directed peer-group classroom talk of nine-year olds
Abstract: Observations and tape-recordings will be made of peer group non-teacher directed talk in an opportunity sample of classrooms of nine-year olds in the context of whole class and group teaching strategies. Analysis will be carried out using various historical methodologies of analysis of transcripts to isolate talk which others have ignored.
Status: Sponsored project
Source of Grant: West Sussex Institute of Higher Education
Date of Research: 1984-1992
KEYWORDS: *classroom communication; group discussion; nondirective methods; peer groups; primary school pupils*

9/0626
Institute of Education, Department of History, Humanities and Philosophy, 20 Bedford Way, London WC1H 0AL
071 580 1122
Dickinson, A. Mr; Kent, A. Mr
Humanities and information technology (Extension)
Abstract: The project aims to support teachers' groups in history, humanities and geography who wish to explore ways in which information technology can be effectively used. It also aims to encourage collaboration between local education authorities and initial teacher training institutions and dissemination of good practice at local, regional and national levels.
Published Material: NCET. Interpretations of women 1890-1914 – The Suffragettes. NCET/Longman, 1992.; NCET. Trading people. NCET/Longman. 1992.; NCET. A day in the life of a National Park. NCET/Longman, 1990.; NCET. Weather and people. NCET/Longman. 1990.
Status: Sponsored project
Source of Grant: National Council for Educational Technology £70,000
Date of Research: 1990-1992
KEYWORDS: *computer uses in education; geography; history; humanities; information technology*

9/0627
Institute of Education, Department of History, Humanities and Philosophy, 20 Bedford Way, London WC1H 0AL
071 580 1122
Dickinson, A. Mr; Lee, P. Mr
Concepts of history and teaching approaches at National Curriculum Key Stages 2 & 3
Abstract: The project is concerned with the teaching and learning of history in National Curriculum key stages 2 and 3, and falls into three phases. In phase 1 the development of children's understandings of the concepts of evidence and explanation in history will be investigated. Phase 2 will seek to categorise teaching approaches according to their attention to progression in childrens' ideas. Phase 3 will explore relationships between teaching approaches and learning outcomes.
Status: Sponsored project
Source of Grant: Economic and Social Research Council £71,127
Date of Research: 1991 - continuing
KEYWORDS: *history; history studies; National Curriculum; teaching methods*

9/0628
Institute of Education, Department of History, Humanities and Philosophy, 20 Bedford Way, London WC1H 0AL
071 580 1122
Silto, W. Mr; *Supervisor:* Gordon, P. Prof.
The origins, development and failure of the Day Continuation School Movement in England and Wales
Abstract: This research deals with the background behind the rise of Continuation Schools following the First World War. The importance of the 1918 Education Act and the Oxford school of idealist philosophers are described. The development and failure of the movement are traced in examination of local records of the seven LEAs which implemented Day Continuation Schools: this will also involve a study of Public Record Office files in order to ascertain the views of the Board of Education as well as the political papers of the main supporters of the movement and other interest groups.

Status: Individual research
Date of Research: 1990 - continuing
KEYWORDS: adult education; continuing education; educational history

9/0629

Institute of Education, Department of History, Humanities and Philosophy, 20 Bedford Way, London WC1H 0AL
071 580 1122
Lee, P. Mr; Supervisor: Gordon, P. Prof.

Some aspects of historical understanding

Abstract: The research undertakes an analysis of concepts involved in the idea of historical understanding (rationality, intentionality, practical inference) and of related ideas (imagination, empathy, sympathy, identification, intuition, fellow-feelings, tolerance). An attempt is made to show that imagination (as supposal) is criterial to understanding in history. There is a discussion of major accounts of historical explanation (covering-law, explanation by rationale, narrativist and Marxist accounts). The relation between explanation, understanding and interpretation in history is examined, with particular attention to notions of meaning and significance. The second part of the research is concerned to argue some implications of the earlier analysis for children's thinking and, in particular, the development of their ideas (explicit and tacit) about the nature and status of history (i.e. the ideas in question are second-order as opposed to substantive). Possible consequences for teaching will also be discussed. Previous work is examined, both from wider psychological research and from the more specific research undertaken within education, bearing directly upon children's abilities and thinking in history. The argument will draw upon empirical investigations performed by the author and by research projects in which he has been involved. It is anticipated that these will provide evidence bearing on children's ideas at all ages between 7 years and 19 years.
Status: Individual research
Date of Research: 1977 - continuing
KEYWORDS: comprehension; explanation; historiography; history; imagination

9/0630

Institute of Education, Department of History, Humanities and Philosophy, 20 Bedford Way, London WC1H 0AL
071 580 1122
Dickinson, A. Mr; Supervisor: Gordon, P. Prof.

Children's thinking and understanding in history with special reference to the role of computer assisted learning (CAL)

Abstract: The main aims of the research are to investigate further, children's conceptions of evidence and enquiry and to explore aspects of the contribution that computers can make to pupils' thinking and understanding in history (in particular their reflexive thinking, substantive understanding and notions of historical evidence and enquiry). A key principle underlying the work is that research into the learning and teaching of history requires analysis of the conceptual base of the discipline and empirical investigation of children's thinking and ideas (both explicit and tacit understandings). The work involves the use of video-recording techniques pioneered by the History Department at the Institute of Education with the aim of revealing the processes of children's thinking in history, pupils' strategies for making sense of the past and their understandings (explicit and tacit) of specific historical concepts (second order and substantive).
Status: Individual research
Date of Research: 1967 - continuing
KEYWORDS: comprehension; computer-assisted learning; computer uses in education; history; thinking skills

9/0631

Institute of Education, Department of History, Humanities and Philosophy, 20 Bedford Way, London WC1H 0AL
071 580 1122
Gomersall, M. Dr; Supervisor: Aldrich, R. Dr

The elementary education of females in England 1800-1870 with particular reference to the lives and work of girls and women in industrial Lancashire and rural Norfolk and Suffolk

Abstract: The study explores the education and schooling of girls from the lower socioeconomic ranks in the period between 1800 and 1870, with particular attention to the experiences of girls in the industrial regions of Lancashire and the agricultural districts of Norfolk and Suffolk. It aims both to reconstruct an area of the past hitherto 'hidden from history', and also to investigate critically the causes and consequences of girls' schooling and broader educational experiences through exploration of the wider socioeconomic and cultural contexts in which that education was located. The study thus includes areas and issues beyond those conventionally explored in histories of education. It examines changes and continuities in the lives and work of women, and links these to the purposes and practices of female elementary schooling and the informal educational experiences of girls in the industrial and rural communities of the two regions. It is organised in two main sections, focusing firstly on responses to changing economic and social conditions before the 1830s, then moving to an examination of the contributory influences which led to the 'reformism and respectability' of the post 1850 period. Tensions and ambiguities are noted throughout, in relation to shifts and variations in the concept of the 'good' working-class wife and mother, and between the expressed ideals of elementary schooling and the realities of schooling provision and practices. Similarities and differences in the nature and quality of educational experiences across and within the selected regions are also noted, and it is through these dimensions that the key determinants of girls' educational experiences are clarified. The study then concludes with an assessment of the relative importance of schooling in the lives and work of women in the two regions, in an evaluation of the many educative influences which shaped their lives.
Published Material: GOMERSALL, M. (1988). 'Ideals and realities: the education of working-class girls 1800-1870', History of Education, Vol 17, No 1.; GOMERSALL, M. (1989). 'Women's work and education in Lancashire 1800-1870; a response to Keith Flett', History of Education, Vol 18, No 2.
Status: Individual research
Date of Research: 1983-1991
KEYWORDS: educational benefits; educational history; elementary education; social history; socioeconomic influences; women's education; working class

9/0632

Institute of Education, Department of History, Humanities and Philosophy, 20 Bedford Way, London WC1H 0AL
071 580 1122
Bedford College of Higher Education, Polhill Avenue, Bedford MK41 9EA
0234 351671
Smart, G. Mr; Supervisor: Aldrich, R. Dr

The training and education of Froebelian teachers in England and Wales, 1889-1926

Abstract: The research is concerned with the dissemination of child-centred theories and methods of education of young children in England and Wales between 1889 and 1926. The work is an investigation of the contribution of the Froebel movement to this process through the training and education of kindergarten teachers under the auspices of the National Froebel Union, whose previously unpublished archives form the basis of the source material. It considers the nature of the institutions concerned, the curricula followed by the students and the relationship between the Froebel movement and the maintained system.
Published Material: SMART, R. (1985). 'The diffusion of Froebelian ideas and methods in England, 1882-1914', Historia Infantiae (Budapest), Vol 2, pp.29-48.
Status: Individual research
Date of Research: 1984-1992
KEYWORDS: educational history; educational theories; Froebel schools; kindergarten; preschool teachers; teacher education

9/0633

Institute of Education, Department of History, Humanities and Philosophy, 20 Bedford Way, London WC1H 0AL
071 580 1122
Ministry of Defence, Directorate of Army Education, Court Road, Eltham, London SE9 5NR
071 854 2242
Smith, E. Lt.Col; Supervisor: Gordon, P. Prof.

The army schoolmaster and the development of elementary education in the Army 1812-1920

Abstract: This dissertation deals with a number of aspects of the Army Schoolmaster from the origins of Army education in 1812 until the establishment of the Royal Army Education Corps in 1920. It is concerned with the Army Schoolmasters training in the early times:

the impact of educational reforms of the Gleig era, i.e. post 1846 and the service; the curriculum and examination for adult and children's schools; informal education; inspection of Army schools; the Army Schoolmaster's status and conditions of service; and the First World War and its impact on the nature of Army education.
Status: Sponsored project
Source of Grant: Ministry of Defence
Date of Research: 1986-1992
KEYWORDS: *armed forces education; educational history; elementary education; teachers*

9/0634

Institute of Education, Department of History, Humanities and Psychology, 20 Bedford Way, London WC1H 0AL
071 580 1122
Lee, P. Mr
Cambridge history project
Abstract: Two A and AS level projects, developing new history course for the 16-19 age range. The projects include a radical assessment package. The courses are designed to follow GCSE in terms of progression, clear objectives, encouragement of active learning, and to overcome problems of content-coherence in concept/ability-led courses. Option 1 (People, Power and Politics) has been apprpoved by School Examinations and Assessment Council (SEAC), Option 2 (Technology and Society) has restricted approval from SEAC. This stage of the project follows an earlier one which ran from September 1988 to September 1991.
Published Material: LEE, P.J. (joint author) (1988). 'Depth study, module 2, Exploring Intentions, Actions and Events', Trial materials, Option 1 People, Power and Politics. Stanley Thornes.; LEE, P.J. (joint author) (1989). 'Depth study, module 3, Understanding the Past', Trial materials, Option 1 People, Power and Politics. Stanley Thornes.
Status: Sponsored project
Source of Grant: Essex Local Education Authority; University of Cambridge Local; Examinations Syndicate £9,650
Date of Research: 1991-1992
KEYWORDS: *A level examinations; A level examinations – AS; curriculum development; history; history studies*

9/0635

Institute of Education, Department of International & Comparative Education, 20 Bedford Way, London WC1H 0AL
071 580 1122
Singh, A. Mr; *Supervisor:* Little, A. Prof.
Cultural bases of educational forms: an inquiry into the learning patterns of the 40 primary school children in an Indian village
Abstract: The proposed research intends to examine a case of a very high incidence of absenteeism, stagnation and wastage in primary education among the tribal people in India (the Dhebar Commission, All India Educational Survey 1986). The study explores a case of contradiction prevailing between primary schooling and domestic routines especially in rural areas. For example, tribal children from the very beginning assume economic roles under parental guidance in the domestic settings. But the process of transmission of knowledge and skills in primary schools to the children is not effective as shown in their apathetic attitudes towards their school work. The case in question is the domestic learning of raising silkworms and the classroom learning about them in a peasant village of Singhbhum, India. These issues need to be examined in the light of larger theoretical questions such as: why are some educational forms more effective than others? what is the connection between children's learning and their current and emergent occupational roles? and how cultural discontinuities between two educational experiences affect the educational performance of a child and a community at large? To analyse the case, the researcher proposes to use the Theory of Activity based on the sociocultural approach as developed by Vygotsky and his disciples. This approach has a large following in current educational research, especially in examining the role of cultural mediation in the current and emergent educational practices. The research proposed is a case study of the Ho tribe in the peasant village of Singhbhum, where silk farming is the main subsidiary occupation. Intensive fieldwork will include: making full length direct observation of learning activities of raising silkworms; taking in-depth interviews of parents, teachers and children in the village; and making a scientific content analysis of the textbooks taught in primary schools. The research aims to make a critical analysis of the discontinuity between

primary schooling and domestic routines (especially silk making) in the light of theoretical premises and the empirical evidence gathered which together will provide a meaningful insight into the problem of a very high incidence of absenteeism, stagnation and wastage among the Ho tribe in India.
Status: Individual research
Date of Research: 1989-1992
KEYWORDS: *attendance; India; learning motivation; primary education; socioeconomic background*

9/0636

Institute of Education, Department of International & Comparative Education, 20 Bedford Way, London WC1H 0AL
071 580 1122
Aishiding, H. Mrs; *Supervisor:* Little, A. Prof.
Access to higher education in Xinjiang Uyghur Autonomous Region, China, 1949-1987
Abstract: Despite tremendous achievements in the quantitative expansion of education, there have been problems of equality in higher education for the various ethnic groups in the Uyghur Autonomous Region of Xinjiang (UARX). This study is aimed at examining some of these problems which are concomitant with the expansion since the revolution. According to various definitions in the international literature, equality in higher education refers to a wide range of issues such as equal access to the system, which includes equal provision of facilities, equal participation in the system or the probability of survival and equal attainment throughout the system. In other words, equality of output or in the performance of the applicants and equal opportunity which applies to the value of education in its achieving equal access to jobs, income, political power and social networks. All of these can vary in their effects for citizens in the different regions, e.g. urban and rural: for men and women; for the different ethnic groups; for the different socioeconomic groups and for the physically healthy and the disabled. This study confines itself to the equality of access to higher education for Han-Chinese and non-Han people (refers to Uyghurs, Kazaks, Kirghiz, Hui, Mongols, Sibo, etc.) in UARX between 1949 and 1987.
Status: Individual research
Date of Research: 1987-1991
KEYWORDS: *access to education; China; higher education*

9/0637

Institute of Education, Department of Mathematics, Statistics and Computing, 20 Bedford Way, London WC1H 0AL
071 580 1122
Goldstein, H. Prof.
Extending multilevel models
Abstract: This project extends the work of the earlier projects entitled 'Developing the use of multilevel models' and 'Developing and disseminating multilevel models'. The three aims of the current project are: 1) to disseminate knowledge of multilevel modelling to the social science research community through conferences, seminars and training sessions in the use of statistical software developed for this form of analysis; 2) to extend existing methodology, especially in the area of time series and linear structural relations models; and 3) to study the practical application of the models to real data sets, especially with a view to increasing robustness and developing data diagnostic procedures. Work is in progress in many domains including: improving the operational efficiency of the 'Iterative Generalised Least Squares' (IGLS) algorithm used in fitting multilevel models; developing the theory of multilevel analysis with latent variables; comparing various methods for treating missing data in multilevel analysis; developing loglinear, time series and survival multilevel models.
Published Material: GOLDSTEIN, H. (1987). Multilevel models in educational and social research. London: Griffin.; GOLDSTEIN, H. & McDONALD, R.P. (1988). 'A general model for the analysis of multilevel data', Psychometrika, No 53, pp.455-467.; GOLDSTEIN, H. (1989). 'Models for multilevel response with an application to growth curves'. In: BOCK, R.D. (Ed). Multilevel analysis of educational data. New York: Academic Press.; GOLDSTEIN, H. (1989). 'Restricted (unbiased) iterative generalised least squares estimation', Biometrika, Vol, 76, No 3, pp.622-623.
Status: Sponsored project
Source of Grant: Economic and Social Research Council £177,770
Date of Research: 1990 - continuing
KEYWORDS: *models; research tools; statistical analysis*

9/0638

Institute of Education, Department of Mathematics, Statistics and Computing, 20 Bedford Way, London WC1H OAL
071 580 1122
Sutherland, R. Dr

Gap between arithmetical and algebraic thinking

Abstract: The aim of this research project is to develop understanding of what is meant by arithmetical and algebraic approaches to problem solving. The underlying assumption being investigated is that certain computer-based experiences can help pupils bridge the gap between arithmetical and algebraic thinking. Longitudinal studies of pupils (ranging in age from 10 to 16) will be carried out in the classroom with some pupils being studied across the primary/secondary school divide.

Published Material: SUTHERLAND, R. (1991). 'Some unanswered research questions on the teaching and learning of Algebra', For the Learning of Mathematics, Vol 11, No 3.; SUTHERLAND, R. 'Thinking algebraically: pupil models developed in Logo and Spreadsheet Environment'. In: LEMUT, E. (Ed). Cognitive models and intelligent environments for learning programming. NATO ASI series F. (in press).; SUTHERLAND, R. Connecting theory and practice: results from the teaching of Logo, Educational Studies for Mathematics. (in press).; SUTHERLAND, R. Consciousness of the unknown: symbolising mathematical experience, For the Learning of Mathematics. (in press).

Status: Sponsored project
Source of Grant: Economic and Social Research Council £47,570
Date of Research: 1990-1992
KEYWORDS: *algebra; arithmetic; computer uses in education; mathematics education; problem solving*

9/0639

Institute of Education, Department of Mathematics, Statistics and Computing, 20 Bedford Way, London WC1H OAL
071 580 1122
Hoyles, C. Prof.; Tagg, W. Dr; Stevenson, I. Mr; Hassell, D. Mr

Computer based modelling across the curriculum

Abstract: The aim of the project is to develop materials to support the use of the computer as a tool for modelling in the following subjects: mathematics, business studies, science and geography. A major objective will be to use modelling with teachers in order to develop curriculum materials for classroom use. The intention is to use generic software (rather than content-specific software) which can be adapted for use across the curriculum, in order to enhance pupil and teacher understanding of the modelling process as it is relevant to different knowledge domains, and in order that pupils themselves can create and interpret their own models.

Status: Sponsored project
Source of Grant: Training, Enterprise & Education Directorate £112,254
Date of Research: 1989-1992
KEYWORDS: *computer software; computer uses in education; models*

9/0640

Institute of Education, Department of Mathematics, Statistics and Computing, 20 Bedford Way, London WC1H OAL
071 580 1122
Wolf, A. Dr

Measurement and accreditation of broad skills

Abstract: Over a three-year period the project will examine the types of assessment – both written and practical – which are most effective in predicting retention of skills, and ability to generalise to other more or less closely related areas. The work will be carried out with students (aged 16-20, and adult) who are nearing completion of vocational training courses. It will build upon previous research including a large study completed for the Training Agency (now Training, Enterprise and Education Directorate – TEED) by the Institute of Education. TEED has a strong interest in the current project, because of its implications for the development of assessment procedures for National Vocational Qualifications (NVQs), and for the design and regulation of training schemes receiving government funding. The policy implications of the research will therefore be of major concern to the team throughout the project. The study will be longitudinal and will relate to: current mastery; success, at time of mastery, in generalising to related tasks; measured retention of skills at a later date; and success in generalising to related tasks at a later date. The use of definitions and measures of 'mastery' is central to the project, reflecting the criterion-referenced nature of current reforms in vocational standards and testing.

Status: Sponsored project
Source of Grant: Training, Enterprise and Education Directorate £197,000
Date of Research: 1990 - continuing
KEYWORDS: *assessment; job skills; mastery tests; retention – psychology; vocational education*

9/0641

Institute of Education, Department of Mathematics, Statistics and Computing, 20 Bedford Way, London WC1H OAL
071 580 1122
Goldstein, H. Prof.

Multilevel modelling for New York Project

Abstract: The purpose of this project is to provide software support and professional advice to the New York Central Board of Education in a multilevel longitudinal analysis of test scores.

Status: Sponsored project
Source of Grant: New York City Public Schools £9,474
Date of Research: 1990-1992
KEYWORDS: *computer software; models; research tools; statistical analysis; United States of America*

9/0642

Institute of Education, Department of Mathematics, Statistics and Computing, 20 Bedford Way, London WC1H OAL
071 580 1122
Sutherland, R. Dr

Algebraic processes and the role of symbolism

Abstract: A seminar group is aiming to coordinate and synthesise the United Kingdom work on algebraic thinking in school mathematics. By working together the group aims to produce a set of clear questions and working hypotheses for future research collaboration with European colleagues.

Status: Sponsored project
Source of Grant: Economic and Social Research Council £4,950
Date of Research: 1992 - continuing
KEYWORDS: *algebra; mathematics education; symbols – mathematics*

9/0643

Institute of Education, Department of Mathematics, Statistics and Computing, 20 Bedford Way, London WC1H 0AL
071 580 1122
Sussex University, Institute of Continuing & Professional Education, Sussex House, Falmer, Brighton BN1 9RH
0273 606755
Hoyles, C. Prof.; Healy, S. Ms; Pozzi, S. Mr; Eraut, M. Prof.; Petch, R. Ms

Group work with computers

Abstract: Because of the scarcity of computers, pupils using them frequently work in groups. However, the potential of groupwork is rarely exploited, and collaborative learning in such groups happens more by chance than design. There are some compelling theoretical reasons for believing that groupwork has considerable potential for the enhancement of learning. Psychologists believe that for some learning goals and tasks, groupwork is likely to be more effective than individual learning. This project will seek to provide guidance to teachers seeking to gain the maximum benefit from the use of computers. It will focus on seven questions: (1) For what types of learning goal is groupwork with computers most appropriate? (2) What is its potential contribution to the curriculum? (3) How can computer and non-computer based tasks be designed which facilitate groupwork? (4) Is it possible to identify criteria for task design, group management and their interrelationships, for effective groupwork to be established? (5) What kinds of group are best for achieving particular goals? (6) How can such groupwork best be prepared for, implemented and evaluated? (7) Is training in collaborative groupwork a significant advantage?

Published Material: ERAUT, M. & HOYLES, C. (1988). Groupwork with computers, ESRC Occasional Paper: INTER/3/88. University of Lancaster, Department of Psychology.; ERAUT, M. & HOYLES, C. (1989). 'Groupwork with computers', Journal of Computer Assisted Learning, Vol 5, No 1, pp.12-24.; HOYLES, C., HEALY, L. & POZZI, S. (1992). Groupwork with computers: final report to the ESRC, July.; HOYLES, C., HEALY, L. & POZZI, S. (1991). 'Computer-based group as vehicles for learning mathematics'. In: Proceedings of the Fifteenth International Conference for the Psychology of Mathematics Education, Vol 11, pp.9165-9172, Italy.

Status: Sponsored project
Source of Grant: Economic and Social Research Council £136,090
Date of Research: 1988-1992
KEYWORDS: computer uses in education; group work; teaching methods

9/0644

Institute of Education, Department of Music Education, 20 Bedford Way, London WC1H OAL
071 580 1122
Pacey, F. Ms; *Supervisor:* Swanwick, K. Prof.

The effect of varied practice in instrumental teaching

Abstract: The main research question is the applicability of Schmidt's focusing on the variable practice hypothesis which is that in learning a motor skill, many different ways of practising that skill are more efficient than repeating one way many times. Work has included background reading on the psychology of learning, on what the literature has to offer on musical ability in the aural sense as well as the expressive sense, on what constitutes a good learner, and the learning theories that preceded Schimdt's (1975) theory. The Leeds String Teaching Department has carried out field studies to discover whether variable practice is indeed useful in the real world. The first study, which aimed to help pupils learn to vary volume by using quicker and slower strokes of the bow, seemed to show positive results. The second study was concerned with achieving the asked for-tempo and third small study was carried out by one teacher in the area of intonation.
Status: Sponsored project
Source of Grant: Leeds City Council
Date of Research: 1988-1992
KEYWORDS: music education; music techniques; musical instruments; psychomotor activity

9/0645

Institute of Education, Department of Music Education, 20 Bedford Way, London WC1H OAL
071 580 1122
Derbyshire College of Higher Education, Kedleston Road, Derby DE3 1GB
0332 47181
Hodges, R. Mr; *Supervisor:* Swanwick, K. Prof.

Childrens' perception of pitch relationships

Abstract: This study examines the perceptual and cognitive structures that children employ when listening to music. A number of chronometric studies use reaction time to attempt to identify developmental aspects of a schema theory of hierarchical music processing. A chronometrically measured forced-choice paired-comparisons experimental paradigm was used to test childrens' discrimination of same and different semitones presented dichotically by a computer-driven closed environment in context-free and various contextual presentations. The results suggest that the maturation of children between the ages of six to twelve find increasing ease in both context-free and contextual presentation in exhibiting fewer errors and decreasing reaction times with increasing age. No significant difference in mean reaction time for correct responses between the conditions of same and different suggest that the processing required for the mental translation of auditory stimuli into a verbal response is the same for both conditions. It is proposed that the observed differences in reaction time responses serve as a measure of the internalisation of cognitive structures such as tonality and responses may therefore be classified according to a perceptual hierarchy.
Status: Sponsored project
Source of Grant: Derbyshire College of Higher Education
Date of Research: 1986-1992
KEYWORDS: applied music; computer uses in education; music education; perception

9/0646

Institute of Education, Department of Policy Studies, 20 Bedford Way, London WC1N ONU
071 612 6423
Ouston, J. Dr; *Supervisor:* Ouston, J. Dr

Management development centre: follow-up study

Abstract: A follow-up interview-based study of 22 participants in management development centre programmes, which explores the knowledge, skills and qualities needed by education managers and how these are acquired.

Status: Sponsored project
Source of Grant: Baring Foundation £4,000
Date of Research: 1992-1992
KEYWORDS: management development; management in education

9/0647

Institute of Education, Department of Policy Studies, 20 Bedford Way, London WC1H 0AL
071 580 1122
Williams, G. Prof.; Loder, C. Ms

Study of independent further and higher education

Abstract: The Centre for Higher Education Studies is undertaking a survey of independent further and higher education in Great Britain in order to provide information on: (1) number and type of institutions; (2) number and characteristics of students (including age, sex, mode of study and domicile); (3) range of courses offered; (4) number and range of qualifications obtained by students; and (5) sources of financial support for students (e.g. grants under PICKUP, sponsorship by employers, mandatory and discretionary awards from local education authorities and training vouchers).
Status: Sponsored project
Source of Grant: Department of Education and Science £79,075
Date of Research: 1991 - continuing
KEYWORDS: further education; higher education; independent colleges; private education; private universities

9/0648

Institute of Education, Department of Policy Studies,
20 Bedford Way, London WC1H 0AL
071 580 1122
Williams, G. Prof.; Loder, C. Ms

Review of United Kingdom social science resources

Abstract: An examination of the sources, and distribution by institution, subject of research, and type of research, of United Kingdom social science research expenditure during 1988/89.
Published Material: LODER, C. (1992). Support for Social Science Research: setting the scene. ESRC (forthcoming).
Status: Sponsored project
Source of Grant: Economic and Social Research Council £24,283
Date of Research: 1990-1991
KEYWORDS: financial support; research opportunities; social science research; social sciences

9/0649

Institute of Education, Department of Policy Studies,
20 Bedford Way, London WC1H 0AL
071 580 1122
Williams, G. Prof.

Identifying and developing a quality ethos for teaching in higher education

Abstract: The primary aim of the project is to increase understanding of quality in higher education teaching by a systematic series of surveys of students, academics, administrators and employers of graduates.
Status: Sponsored project
Source of Grant: Leverhulme Trust £137,879
Date of Research: 1991 - continuing
KEYWORDS: educational quality; higher education; teacher effectiveness

9/0650

Institute of Education, Department of Policy Studies,
20 Bedford Way, London WC1H 0AL
071 580 1122
Howell, D. Dr

Committee of Vice Chancellors and Principals of the UK: a study of its development and role

Abstract: A study of the Committee of Vice Chancellors and Principals of the UK (CVCP) from a political science perspective, concentrating on its current role in the higher education policy making process and its relationship with other organisations involved therein.
Status: Sponsored project
Source of Grant: Nuffield Foundation £2,860
Date of Research: 1991 - continuing
KEYWORDS: advisory committees; higher education; policy formation; politics education relationship; universities

9/0651

Institute of Education, Department of Policy Studies, Centre for Higher Education Studies, 20 Bedford Way, London WC1H OAL
071 580 1122
Williams, G. Prof.; Loder, C. Ms

Review of UK Social Science Research (Extension)

Abstract: The study provides the first detailed analysis of the financial backers of the United Kingdoms's social science research base. The Centre for Higher Education Studies surveyed research institutions throughout the UK to identify which organisations are supporting what kinds of research.

Published Material: LODER, C. (1992). 'Support for Social Science research: setting the scene', CHES Policy series in association wtih ESRC.; LODER, C. (1992). 'Support for Social Science research: examining the eighties', CHES Policy series.; LODER, C. (1992). 'Support for Social Science research: focus on funders', CHES Policy series.; LODER, C. & FRY, H. (1992). 'Who supports Social Science research?'. In: VINCENT, J. (Ed). Critics and customers: the control of social policy research. Aldershot: Gower Publishing.

Status: Sponsored project
Source of Grant: Economic and Social Research Council £24,941
Date of Research: 1991-1992
KEYWORDS: *financial support; grants; research opportunities; social science research*

9/0652

Institute of Education, Department of Policy Studies, Centre for Higher Education Studies, 20 Bedford Way, London WC1H 0AL
071 580 1122
Woodhall, M. Ms; Mace, J. Mr; Loder, C. Ms; *Supervisor:* Williams, G. Prof.

Monitoring and evaluation of new funding mechanisms in higher education

Abstract: The Education Reform Act (1988) brought about radical changes in the method of funding on the basis of contracts, rather than grants. The principal aims of the research will be to: (1) examine the rationale for alternative models of funding higher education within the general framework of contractual responsibility by institutions to their funding bodies; (2) evaluate the operation and effects of funding arrangements prior to 1988 which contain contractual obligations between higher education institutions and funding bodies; (3) propose ways of monitoring the effects of new funding mechanisms, including identifying the data requirements for measurement of output or institutional performance; (4) monitor the introduction of the new funding arrangements, in order to provide a basis for the full-scale evauation of the system, once it is fully operational. Broadly, this stage of the project will involve three activities: (a) discussions with Finance Officers and other senior administrators in universities, colleges and polytechnics to identify categories of activities subject to contractual arrangements; (b) a postal questionnaire to all higher education institutions seeking information on the extent of the activities identified and the institutional responses to them; (c) the selection of a limited number of examples, probably about 25, which would be the subject of detailed case studies to examine the educational and other implications of different funding mechanisms.

Status: Sponsored project
Source of Grant: Department of Education and Science £17,806
Date of Research: 1988-1991
KEYWORDS: *contracts; educational finance; financial support; higher education*

9/0653

Institute of Education, Department of Policy Studies, Centre for Post Sixteen Education, 20 Bedford Way, London WC1H 0AL
071 580 1122
Young, M. Dr

Unqualified school leaver

Abstract: The project involved an extensive literature review of research and evaluation of policy initiatives in this country in the last decade as well as a section on comparative studies of participation in post compulsory education in France and Germany. Its outcome was a report that included a number of proposals for how future research might be linked more closely both to policy evaluation as well as a greater awareness of the aspirations and needs of young people.

Published Material: MORTIMORE, J. (1992). 'The unqualified school leaver'. In: YOUNG, M. (Ed). Post 16 Education Centre Report No 8.

Status: Sponsored project
Source of Grant: British Gas £7,500
Date of Research: 1991-1991
KEYWORDS: *comparative education; qualifications; school leavers; school to work transition; sixteen to nineteen education*

9/0654

Institute of Education, Department of Policy Studies, Health and Education Research Unit, 20 Bedford Way, London WC1H OAL
071 580 1122
Warwick, I. Mr; *Supervisor:* Aggleton, P. Dr; Whitty, G. Prof.

Health Education Authority HIV/AIDS and homeless young people project

Abstract: This is a project to identify the Human Immunodeficiency Virus/Acquired Immune Deficiency Syndrome (HIV/AIDS) health education needs of young homeless people. Via a programme of national consultations involving workers from the statutory and non-statutory sectors, it will seek to access perspectives on the HIV/AIDS health education needs of young people who are homeless and rootless.

Status: Sponsored project
Source of Grant: Health Education Authority
Date of Research: 1990 - continuing
KEYWORDS: *Acquired Immune Deficiency Syndrome; health education; homeless people*

9/0655

Institute of Education, Department of Policy Studies, Health and Education Research Unit, 20 Bedford Way, London WC1H OAL
071 580 1122
Aggleton, P. Dr; Whitty, G. Prof.

South East Thames regional HIV education and training evaluation project

Abstract: This is a project to evaluate the implementation of the South East Thames Regional Human Immunodeficiency Virus (HIV) Education and Training Strategy at district level. It will seek to identify via interviews with Human Immunodeficiency Virus/Acquired Immune Deficiency Syndrome (HIV/AIDS) prevention coordinators, trainers, training providers, workers in relevant non-statutory agencies and other key informants. The aims of the project are to discover (1) awareness of South East Thames Regional HIV Education and Training Strategy; (2) perceptions of its appropriateness and inclusiveness in meeting the HIV/AIDS training needs of relevant health authority personnel; (3) perceptions of the effectiveness and inclusiveness of this strategy in meeting the needs of clients and carers, for appropriate priorities for future HIV education and training; (4) appropriate ways in which the South East Thames Regional Health Authority might promote and support such work; and (5) appropriate strategies by which such education and training might be monitored and evaluated on an ongoing basis.

Status: Sponsored project
Source of Grant: South East Thames Regional Health Authority £15,865
Date of Research: 1991 - continuing
KEYWORDS: *Acquired Immune Deficiency Syndrome; evaluation; health education; training*

9/0656

Institute of Education, Department of Policy Studies, Health and Education Research Unit, 20 Bedford Way, London WC1H OAL
071 580 1122
Aggleton, P. Dr

Learning about AIDS project

Abstract: The Learning about AIDS (Acquired Immune Deficiency Syndrome) is an initiative to develop, produce and disseminate participatory training resources for use in local authorities, health authorities and voluntary organisations. Two training packages have already been produced and disseminated widely across England. In excess of 2,000 Human Immunodeficiency Virus/Acquired Immune Deficiency Syndrome (HIV/AIDS) workers have participated in one to two day training workshops using Learning about AIDS materials. These workshops have been externally evaluated by a consultant

attached to the project. A third phase of development activity is currently underway which will result in the publication of a second edition of the existing Learning about AIDS training resource.
Published Material: HOMANS, H., AGGLETON, P.J. & WARWICK, I. (1987). 'Learning about AIDS' – Interim Materials. Horsham: AVERT.; AGGLETON, P.J., HOMANS, H., MOJSA, J., WATSON, S. & WATNEY, S. (1989). AIDS: Scientific and Social Issues. Edinburgh: Churchill Livingstone.; AGGLETON, P.J., HOMANS, H., MOJSA, J., WATSON, S. & WATNEY, S. (1989). Learning about AIDS. Edinburgh: Churchill Livingstone.
Status: Sponsored project
Source of Grant: Health Education Authority £500,000
Date of Research: 1986-1991
KEYWORDS: Acquired Immune Deficiency Syndrome; educational materials; health education

9/0657

Institute of Education, Department of Policy Studies, Health and Education Research Unit, 20 Bedford Way, London WC1H OAL
071 580 1122
Aggleton, P. Dr; Whittaker, M. Mr
The Health Education Authority HIV/AIDS local evaluation initiative
Abstract: The Health Education Authority HIV/AIDS (Human Immunodeficiency Virus/Acquired Immune Deficiency Syndrome) Local Evaluation Support Initiative is a project to support and guide local HIV/AIDS workers in the monitoring and evaluation of HIV/AIDS health promotion activities. The project has developed a range of resources including a training manual for local HIV/AIDS workers, an edited collection of papers offering case studies in local monitoring and evaluation, and an HIV/AIDS and Sexual Health Programme Paper reporting on findings from a survey of HIV/AIDS monitoring and evaluation in practice. A national dissemination programme across England to alert local HIV/AIDS workers to the existence of the training resource will shortly commence, organised on a regional basis. The programme will offer workers the opportunity to examine comparative, survey and ethnographic styles of evaluation, and to consider the appropriateness of each of these techniques for work with which they are involved.
Published Material: MOODY, D., AGGLETON, P.J., KAPILA, M., PYE, M. & YOUNG, A. (1991). 'Monitoring and evaluating local HIV/AIDS health promotion: a review of theory and practice, HIV/AIDS and Sexual Health Programme Paper 11', London: Health Education Authority.; AGGLETON, P.J., YOUNG, A., MOODY, D., KAPILA, M. & PYE, M. (1991). HIV/AIDS health promotion – does it work? London: Health Education Authority.; AGGLETON, P.J., MOODY, D. & YOUNG, A. (1992). Evaluating local HIV/AIDS health promotion. London: Health Education Authority.
Status: Sponsored project
Source of Grant: Health Education Authority £240,000
Date of Research: 1990 - continuing
KEYWORDS: Acquired Immune Deficiency Syndrome; educational materials; evaluation; health personnel

9/0658

Institute of Education, Department of Policy Studies, Health and Education Research Unit, 20 Bedford Way, London WC1H OAL
071 580 1122
Walker, R. Ms; *Supervisor:* Aggleton, P. Dr
AIDS Education and Research Trust (AVERT) HIV/AIDS and nursing project
Abstract: This is a project to examine the interface between professional, scientific and biomedical understandings of Human Immunodeficiency Virus/Acquired Immune Deficiency Syndrome (HIV/AIDS) and nurses' awareness, attitudes, beliefs and anxieties about HIV disease. It is broadly exploratory in nature. Data will be collected by means of semi-structured small group interviews so as to identify respondents' recurrent concerns, beliefs and anxieties. Fieldwork will be carried out in six colleges of nursing involving student nurses in their first and final year of training. Two of these colleges will be linked to hospitals and/or community settings in which there is considerable experience of care for people with HIV/AIDS. Two will be institutions without such links, and two will be colleges with intermediate levels of experience.
Status: Sponsored project

Source of Grant: AVERT (AIDS Education and Research Trust) £39,000
Date of Research: 1991-1992
KEYWORDS: Acquired Immune Deficiency Syndrome; nurse education

9/0659

Institute of Education, Department of Policy Studies, Health and Education Research Unit, 20 Bedford Way, London WC1H OAL
071 580 1122
Sheffield University, Division of Education, 388 Glossop Road, Sheffield S10 2TN
0742 768555
Cambridge University, Department of Education, The Old Schools, Trinity Lane, Cambridge CB2 1TN
0223 337733
Whitty, G. Prof.; Furlong, J. Prof.; Barton, L. Prof.; Miles, S. Ms; *Supervisor:* Whitty, G. Prof.
Modes of teacher education: towards a basis for comparison
Abstract: This project is designed to provide a sharper focus to current policy debates about the future of teacher education. Using a national survey of all courses of initial training in England and Wales, and a detailed study of a sample of 50 courses across a variety of routes to Qualified Teacher Status (QTS). The project will provide an up-to-date database on the nature and costs of different approaches to teacher education and the models of professionalism that they seek to engender.
Published Material: WHITTY, G. et al (1992). 'Initial teacher education in England and Wales', Cambridge Journal of Education, Vol 22, No 3, pp.293-306.; BARRETT, E. et al (1992). 'New routes to Qualified Teacher Status', Cambridge Journal of Education, Vol 22, No 3, pp.323-335.
Status: Sponsored project
Source of Grant: Economic and Social Research Council £41,580
Date of Research: 1991-1992
KEYWORDS: education courses; preservice teacher education; professional education

9/0660

Institute of Education, Department of Policy Studies, Health and Education Research Unit, 20 Bedford Way, London WC1H OAL
071 580 1122
Whitty, G. Prof.; Furlong, J. Prof.; Barton, L. Prof.; Miles, S. Ms; *Supervisor:* Whitty, G. Prof.
Changing modes of professionalism? A case study of teacher education in transition
Abstract: This project will build upon the earlier Modes of Teacher Education Project. Using baseline data from that project, it will explore the nature and impact of current changes in initial teacher education in England and Wales. The study will focus on the experience, outcomes and costs of teacher training in the new modes required by government policy. It will also consider how far the new approaches foster new conceptions of professionalism and professionality.
Status: Sponsored project
Source of Grant: Economic and Social Research Council £94,910
Date of Research: 1993 - continuing
KEYWORDS: preservice teacher education; professional recognition; teaching profession

9/0661

Institute of Education, Department of Policy Studies, Health and Education Research Unit, 20 Bedford Way, London WC1H OAL
071 580 1122
Whitty, G. Prof.; Aggleton, P. Dr; *Supervisor:* Whitty, G. Prof.
AVERT AIDS: working with young people project
Abstract: This project extends earlier work which researched the Human Immunodeficiency Virus/Acquired Immune Deficiency Syndrome (HIV/AIDS) training needs of adults who work with young people in youth service settings. A number of needs were identified. These ranged from information on social and medical issues to ways in which young people may be helped to learn about HIV infection and AIDS. The findings were disseminated via a resource for youth workers. The current project aims to develop the work to include the needs of teachers in secondary schools. It will : (1) research the needs

of teachers in relation to classroom-based activity on HIV and AIDS; (2) compare these needs with those of workers in youth service settings; (3) identify ways in which teachers might best support and enable pupils in learning about the medical and social issues associated with HIV and AIDS. The projects findings will be disseminated via an updated resource package which emphasises participatory training within a clearly defined equal opportunities framework.
Published Material: AGGLETON P. et al (1990). AIDS: working with young people. Horsham: AVERT. (Second edition (in press) 1993).
Status: Sponsored project
Source of Grant: AIDS Education and Research Trust (AVERT) £38,299
Date of Research: 1992 - continuing
KEYWORDS: Acquired Immune Deficiency Syndrome; health education; secondary schools

9/0662
Institute of Education, Department of Policy Studies, Health and Education Research Unit, 20 Bedford Way, London WC1H OAL
071 580 1122
Whitty, G. Prof.; Aggleton, P. Dr; *Supervisor:* Whitty, G. Prof.
Learning about AIDS Project (continuation)
Abstract: This project aims to update earlier research on the training needs of adults who educate other adults about Human Immunodeficiency Virus (HIV) infection and Acquired Immune Deficiency Syndrome (AIDS). A series of national consultative meetings identified that adult HIV/AIDS trainers have had the following concerns: (1) relevant scientific and medical issues on HIV and AIDS should continue to be clarified; (2) psychological dimensions of HIV/AIDS should be explored; (3) there should be a greater attention to 'newer issues' in HIV/AIDS works (such as children and HIV); and (4) monitoring and evaluation, pre-course planning and post-course action should be further examined. A series of interactive focus groups will be held across the country so that the above issues might be explored in greater detail. Attention will be focused on the need to develop accessible and relevant information as well as on the ways trainers might be supported in their work. Resource materials will be produced which will help trainers conduct effective HIV/AIDS education.
Status: Sponsored project
Source of Grant: Health Education Authority £177,318
Date of Research: 1992 - continuing
KEYWORDS: Acquired Immune Deficiency Syndrome; educational materials; health education

9/0663
Institute of Education, Department of Policy Studies, Health and Education Research Unit, 20 Bedford Way, London WC1H OAL
071 580 1122
Whitty, G. Prof.
AIDS Education and Research Trust (AVERT) HIV/AIDS and Nursing project
Abstract: Following Phase I of this project (a qualitative study of student nurses' lay beliefs of Human Immunodeficiency and Acquired Immune Deficiency Syndrome (HIV and AIDS) conducted between September 1991 and September 1992) Phase II will: (1) Produce and disseminate policy recommendations detailing how HIV/AIDS might best be addressed on Project 2000 courses; (2) Provide curriculum guidance for lecturers, nurse tutors and clinical teachers on how HIV/AIDS might best be addressed on Project 2000 courses and in allied clinical practice; (3) Produce a booklet of information and guidance for student nurses.
Status: Sponsored project
Source of Grant: AIDS Education and Research Trust (AVERT) £58,042
Date of Research: 1992 - continuing
KEYWORDS: Acquired Immune Deficiency Syndrome; nurse education; nurses; sexually transmitted diseases

9/0664
Institute of Education, Department of Policy Studies, 20 Bedford Way, London WC1H OAL
071 580 1122
Loughborough University of Technology, Department of

Education, Loughborough LE11 3TU
0509 263171
Saran, R. Dr; Busher, H. Mr
Teachers' morale and teachers' conditions of service
Abstract: The purpose of this research is to explore the impact of recent legislation on teachers. Methods used include interviews in different local education authorities (LEAs) at primary and secondary school level, and at LEA level, through the periods 1987/88 and 1990/91. Conclusions reached are that: teachers are demoralised; the management style of headteachers makes a difference; the paradoxes of power, not least that trade union power, has been strengthened at institutional level whilst being weakened at national level.
Published Material: BUSHER, H. & SARAN, R. (1992). Teachers' conditions of employment: a study in the politics of school management. London: Kogan Page.
Status: Sponsored project
Source of Grant: Leverhulme Trust
Date of Research: 1988-1992
KEYWORDS: educational change; educational legislation; teacher attitudes; teacher employment benefits; teacher morale

9/0665
Institute of Education, Department of Policy Studies, Social Science Research Unit, 20 Bedford Way, London WC1H OAL
071 580 1122
Mayall, B. Dr
Health care of primary school children
Abstract: The project will study the perspectives of parents, teachers and children themselves on the division of labour and responsibility between children and adults for child health care.
Published Material: MAYALL, B. (1991). 'The health care of primary school children', Report to the Nuffield Foundation.
Status: Sponsored project
Source of Grant: Nuffield Foundation £2,850
Date of Research: 1991-1991
KEYWORDS: health; primary health care; primary school pupils

9/0666
Institute of Education, Department of Science Education, 20 Bedford Way, London WC1H OAL
071 580 1122
Ogborn, J. Prof.
Iconic model maker
Abstract: To develop a novel object-oriented computer modelling facility for early secondary and late primary use. The program is an extension of the concept of a cell automaton. Pupils and teachers can specify rules for how objects and backgrounds behave: movement, interaction, appearance; disappearance and change. These facilities make it possible to generate models from very simple games up to diffusion, crystal growth and ecological interactions.
Published Material: OGBORN, J. (1990). 'A future for modelling in science education', Journal of Computer Assisted Learning, Vol 6, No 2, pp.103-112.; OGBORN, J. (1990). 'Modellizzazione con l'elaboratore: possibilita e prospettive', La Fisica nella Scuola, Anno XXIII, No 2, pp.32-43.; OGBORN, J. (1991). 'Modelacao com o computador: possibilidades e perspectivas'. In: TEODORO V.D., FREITAS, J.C. (Eds). (1991). Educacao e computadores, Lisbon, Portugal: Ministerio da Educacao.
Status: Sponsored project
Source of Grant: National Council for Educational Technology £50,700
Date of Research: 1990-1992
KEYWORDS: computer software; computers; icons; models; science education

9/0667
Institute of Education, Department of Science Education, 20 Bedford Way, London WC1H OAL
071 580 1122
Ogborn, J. Prof.; Hawkins, A. Mrs
Exploratory Data Analysis (extension)
Abstract: In many areas of the school curriculum students come across quantitative data – in the form of tables, graphs, charts and so on. They are also confronted by data in newspapers and on television, and by arguments based on such data. This project is a small-scale experiment aimed at teaching ways of understanding and looking

critically at such data. The material produced will be aimed primarily at the 16-18 age range, but much of it will also be appropriate at GCSE level. Exploratory Data Analysis (EDA) may be used in a wide range of curriculum areas, and the materials will cover not only the concepts and techniques of EDA but also its applications in different subjects. It is hoped that students will gain greater confidence in the handling of quantitative data, and will be able to formulate and criticize arguments based on such data. They should develop skills of analysing and presenting data to the best effect.

Published Material: BOOHAN, R. & OGBORN, J. (1991). Making Sense of Data. Harlow: Longman.; OGBORN, J. (1991). 'Making sense of data: Ein Projekt zur Entwicklung von Materialien zur Explorative Datenanalyse im Schulunterricht', Der Mathematikunterricht, Special issue, Explorative Daenanalyse im Mathematikunterricht, Journal 37, Heft 6, pp.54-63, November.

Status: Sponsored project
Source of Grant: Nuffield Foundation £27,609
Date of Research: 1990-1991
KEYWORDS: curriculum development; data analysis; statistical analysis; statistical data

9/0668
Institute of Education, 20 Bedford Way, London WC1H 0AL
071 580 1122
Sussex University, Institute of Continuing Education, Sussex House, Falmer, Brighton BN1 9RH
0273 606755
Glasgow University, Department of Education, 8 University Gardens, Glasgow G12 8QQ
041 339 8855
Wolf, A. Dr; Drake, P. Ms; Eraut, M. Prof.; Holroyd, C. Mr; Dunn, W. Mr; *Supervisor:* Wolf, A. Dr

National standards for training and development within masters programmes

Abstract: A new structure of qualifications is being put in place to encourage employers and employees to raise standards of performance in the workplace. The qualifications are called National and Scottish Vocational Qualifications (NVQs and SVQs). The qualifications are based on standards of competence which are being set by Lead Bodies. National Standards for Training and Development were published by the Training and Development Lead Body, first in January 1991, then in revised form in March 1992. These National Standards are intended to cover all work roles that have a training and development content. The whole shift towards competence-based qualifications means there is a need for standards to which the assessors of competence must work: these are included. The National Standards have a number of uses: as a basis for job descriptions; to identify training needs; to develop training programmes; as a basis for assessment; as benchmarks for development; and to form vocational qualifications. The Lead Body has defined the key purpose of training as 'to develop human potential to assist organisations and individuals to achieve their objectives'. Given this broad definition, it is clear that National Standards can be applied to the work of teachers in schools and to the work of lecturers in colleges and universities. The extent to which they will be applied, and the rate of the application, is currently unpredictable. A research study has been funded by the Department of Employment to explore the delivery of the National Standards for Training and Development within Masters degree programmes. The project involves the Universities of London, Sussex and Glasgow. The three institutions involved have had distinct plans and priorities: however, the project was conceived as a consortium activity and each site has learned from the others. The first stage of the project has these aims: (1) To examine the feasibility of incorporating the National Standards for Training and Development within Masters Degrees; (2) To determine appropriate methods for achieving such incorporation; (3) To secure approval for, and then to prepare for the implementation of, pilot programmes; and (4) To integrate the parallel work of the three participating institutions, both internally and with other relevant developments.

Published Material: Four papers are available on request from the researchers.; Paper 1. Recognition of TDLB key roles by M.Ed. students (November 1991).; Paper 2. Staff views on basic issues (November 1991).; Paper 3. Recognition of TDLB units and elements by M.Ed. students (September 1992).

Status: Sponsored project
Source of Grant: Department for Education
Date of Research: 1991 - continuing
KEYWORDS: competency-based education; higher education; Masters courses; National Vocational Qualifications; qualifications; standards

9/0669
Institute of Education, The Directorate, 20 Bedford Way, London WC1H 0AL
071 580 1122
Mortimore, P. Prof.; Mortimore, J. Mrs

Innovative uses of non-teaching staff in primary and secondary schools

Abstract: The efficient and cost-effective use of trained staff is crucial to any enterprise. The implementation of the Education Reform Act (1988) is likely to have resulted in a re-examination of the traditional roles of both teaching and non-teaching staff. The research aims to identify examples of innovatory uses of non-teaching staff, to draw up a typology of staffing models and to estimate cost benefits (and disbenefits) of different models.

Published Material: MORTIMORE, P. & MORTIMORE, J. et al. (1992). The innovative uses of non-teaching staff in primary and secondary schools project. London: DFE/Institute of Education.

Status: Sponsored project
Source of Grant: Department of Education and Science £60,000
Date of Research: 1991-1992
KEYWORDS: administration; paraprofessional personnel; school personnel; staff utilisation; support staff; teacher aides

9/0670
Institute of Education, The Directorate, 20 Bedford Way, London WC1H 0AL
071 580 1122
Mortimore, P. Prof.; MacGilchrist, B. Mrs; Savage, J. Ms; Beresford, C. Mr

Impact of school development plans in primary schools

Abstract: School development plans provide a mechanism to link the planning of improvements with the financial and staff development planning of the school as a whole. This project aims to investigate whether these plans – and the process of planning – are having positive impacts. Schools in contrasting areas make up the sample. A mixture of research methods has been chosen for this three year study.

Published Material: MORTIMORE, P., MacGILCHRIST, B., SAVAGE, J. & BERESFORD, C. 'School development planning: does it make a difference?', Special issue of International Journal of Educational Research (forthcoming).; BERESFORD, C., MORTIMORE, P., MacGILCHIRST, B. & SAVAGE, J. (1992). 'School development planning in the U.K.', Unicorn, Vol 18, No 2, pp.12-16.

Status: Sponsored project
Source of Grant: Economic and Social Research Council £85,120
Date of Research: 1991 - continuing
KEYWORDS: development plans; educational administration; planning; primary schools

9/0671
Institute of Education, Thomas Coram Research Unit, 41 Brunswick Square, London WC1N 1AZ
071 580 1122
Caplan, M. Dr; McGurk, H. Prof.

Quality of daycare provision in the United Kingdom

Abstract: The goal of this project is to develop instruments and procedures that can contribute to the monitoring, evaluation, and enhancement of the quality of centre and family based (childminding) childcare settings.

Status: Sponsored project
Source of Grant: Department of Health £209,716
Date of Research: 1992 - continuing
KEYWORDS: child caregivers; child minding; day care; day care centres; preschool children; quality control

9/0672
Institute of Education, Thomas Coram Research Unit, 41 Brunswick Square, London WC1N 1AZ
071 278 2424
Lloyd, E. Ms; Statham, J. Ms; *Supervisor:* Moss, P. Dr; Melhuish, E. Dr

Playgroups' study

Abstract: The first stage of this project examines the pattern of preschool provision nationally, looking especially at the role of playgroups within it, and at the relationship between playgroups and other under-fives services. Some of the data for this stage comes from an analysis of national statistics, but the main component is a study

of 25 local authorities in England, or roughly a quarter of the total. Each area has been visited, and key workers in the Education Department, Social Services Department, and the Preschool Playgroups Association (PPA) interviewed. The second stage is a detailed study of playgroups in contrasting areas, both rural and urban. Approximately 20 playgroups will be selected in each area, taken from the local authority register so as not to confine the sample to PPA members. This stage is based on interviews with around 200 mothers and on interviews with playgroup leaders, covering such issues as resources, training, parental involvement, methods of management, and liaison with the local authority. It is also intended during this stage to do some exploratory work on children's experiences in different playgroups, using observational methods.
Published Material: LLOYD, E. et al (1989). 'A review of research on playgroups', Early Child Development and Care, Vol 43, pp.77-99, March.
Status: Sponsored project
Source of Grant: Department of Health £229,000
Date of Research: 1987-1991
KEYWORDS: *playgroups; preschool children; preschool education*

9/0673
Institute of Education, Thomas Coram Research Unit, 41 Brunswick Square, London WC1N 1AZ
071 580 1122
Hennessy, E. Dr; Martin, S. Ms; *Supervisor:* Melhuish, E. Dr; Moss, P. Dr
Day care and later development
Abstract: The day care project, which finished in 1988, was concerned with single and dual-career families over the first three years of the child's life. The current project is a follow-up of these families, which aims to answer substantial questions about the usage and effects of day care, and also parental employment over the subsequent three years. The children in the study are now attending primary school, and the implications of this for dual-career families are being examined. The project also considers the implications of different types of early day care experience for the child's socio-emotional and cognitive development at the age of six. The project staff are visiting 243 families remaining in the day care project when the children are six years old. The mothers are to be interviewed, particularly about child care and employment histories over the last three years. The children's cognitive development is assessed using standardised psychometric measure, their socio-emotional development by questionnaires which are completed by the mother and class teacher.
Published Material: BRANNEN, J. & MOSS, P. (1988). New mothers at work: employment and childcare. London: Unwin.
Status: Sponsored project
Source of Grant: Department of Health £86,123
Date of Research: 1988-1991
KEYWORDS: *child development; cognitive development; day care; emotional development; mothers; preschool children; social development; women's employment*

9/0674
Institute of Education, Thomas Coram Research Unit, 41 Brunswick Square, London WC1N 1AZ
071 580 1122
Back, L. Mr; *Supervisor:* Tizard, B. Prof.; Phoenix, A. Ms
Social identity in adolescence
Abstract: This project is concerned with the social identities of young Londoners. The researchers aim to describe the range of social groups they feel they belong to, the strength of the affiliation they feel towards each group, and what they see as the important characteristics of each group. It is also intended to describe which of these identities are most central in their lives. The social identities in which the researchers are particuarly interested are the neighbourhood, church, gender, social class, ethnic group and nationality. Interest is also being shown in the extent to which young people in schools of different ethnic composition have developed multiracial friendships, and the extent to which their skin colour is an important organising identity in their lives. In relation to this, the researchers aim to explore their attitude to, and experience of, racial discrimination, and the extent to which their attitudes and coping strategies have been influenced by families and friends.
Published Material: TIZARD, B. & PHOENIX, A. (1989). 'Black identity and transracial adoption', New Community, Vol 15, No 3, pp.427-437.
Status: Sponsored project

Source of Grant: Department of Health £157,309
Date of Research: 1988-1992
KEYWORDS: *adolescents; ethnic groups; identity; racial identification; racial integration; social background; social class; social environment*

9/0675
Institute of Education, Thomas Coram Research Unit, 41 Brunswick Square, London WC1N 1AZ
071 580 1122
Plewis, I. Mr
Changes in the classroom experience of Inner London pupils
Abstract: The focus of this project is on infant schools, and on measuring changes in pupils' experiences in them following the changes introduced by the Education Reform Act. Comparisons will be made with data obtained at the Thomas Coram Research Unit (TCRU) in 1984/85. The project will concentrate on how much time pupils spend on different parts of the curriculum, and how much of the mathematics curriculum they experience. It will also look at classroom organisation in terms of how pupils are grouped for mathematics and how this varies over time. As well as looking at changes in pupils' experiences at a time of considerable change in the educational system, the project will contribute to the development of theory about factors influencing children's learning, and to the development of statistical methods for the analysis of longitudinal data sets in educational research.
Status: Sponsored project
Source of Grant: Economic and Social Research Council £76,250
Date of Research: 1992 - continuing
KEYWORDS: *classroom management; curriculum research; Education Reform Act 1988; educational change; educational experience; infant schools; learning*

9/0676
Institute of Education, Thomas Coram Research Unit, 41 Brunswick Square, London WC1N 1AZ
071 580 1122
Petrie, P. Dr
Out of school services survey and evaluation
Abstract: Twelve case studies of playschemes, using a consultative approach with providers and staff, followed by a survey of 100 schemes looking at objectives and their realisation; organisation and resources.
Status: Sponsored project
Source of Grant: Department of Health £181,827
Date of Research: 1990 - continuing
KEYWORDS: *child caregivers; community services; play; play centres; recreational activities*

9/0677
King's College, Centre for Education Studies, Cornwall House Annexe, Waterloo Road, London SE1 3TY
071 836 5454
Weller, B. Mr; *Supervisor:* Brown, M. Prof.; Davies, B. Prof.
The effects of the introduction of the GCSE on the work of a group of mathematics teachers: an ethnographic study
Abstract: The thesis forms a study of the effect of public examinations on the teaching of mathematics, with a particular focus on the way developments in mathematics education have been advanced or hindered by the presence of the public examination system. The research took the form of an ethnographic study of a mathematics department in a comprehensive upper school (13-18 year old pupils) over a period of four years. The department was observed closely during this period as the General Certificate of Secondary Education (GCSE) examination in mathematics was introduced. The thesis makes a contribution to knowledge on the way departments function in secondary schools, the effect of external constraints on the work of teachers in classrooms, and on the whole process of teacher development in general.
Status: Individual research
Date of Research: 1986-1991
KEYWORDS: *examinations; General Certificate of Secondary Education; mathematics education; mathematics teachers*

9/0678
King's College, 552 King's Road, London SW10 0UA
071 836 5454

Bliss, J. Dr; Ogborn, J. Prof.; Martinand, J-L. Prof.;
Jensen, J. Prof.
The Esprit project
Abstract: The aim of the research programme is to provide the specifications for explanation facilities intelligible to children within intelligent learning environments. The project was conceived in order to explore ways of closing the gap between recent research in cognitive science and education which construes explanation as a constructive act, and explanation as currently implemented in expert and knowledge based systems. The design of the study is fourfold: (1) to focus on children's and teachers' explanations for a given domain; (2) to examine the issues involved in implementing such explanations within an information technology learning environment; (3) to evaluate the acceptability of prototype explanation systems to children using microworld and simulation software; and (4) to specify the final prototype explanation systems. The working group will fund individual research proposals submitted within these relevant areas. The outcomes will have both theoretical and practical significance. It will be possible to describe the explanations that satisfy children within a given domain and to compare these to those of the expert/teacher. Simultaneously, it will be possible to provide an analysis of the formal and practical problems of implementing explanation systems where explanations match both need and understanding.
Status: Sponsored project
Source of Grant: European Community
Date of Research: 1989-1992
KEYWORDS: computer uses in education; expert systems; explanation

9/0679
King's College, Centre for Educational Studies, Cornwall House Annexe, Waterloo Road, London SE1 3TY
071 836 5454
Southampton University, Faculty of Educational Studies, Highfield, Southampton SO9 5NH
0703 595000
Hill, F. Ms; Turner, G. Mr; *Supervisor:* Hill, F. Ms
HIV/AIDS education within further education and tertiary colleges
Abstract: This is a case study extension of a survey of Human-Immuno Virus/Acquired Immune Deficiency Syndrome (HIV/AIDS) Education in further education colleges and tertiary colleges catering for the 16-19 age range. The case studies have been selected to highlight good practice. Six colleges have been selected in order to describe and evaluate a range of different approaches to HIV/AIDS education. The case studies focus on: (a) the nature of college policies on HIV/AIDS, staff workshops, training and links with outside agencies; and (b) the effectiveness of a range of educational strategies, from lectures and tutorials to drama and student union activities. The latter is explored principally through group interviews with students in each college. Methods also include interviews with relevant staff, observation of appropriate activities and collection of materials. A report will be produced to highlight effective approaches to HIV/AIDS education which can be disseminated nationally.
Status: Sponsored project
Source of Grant: Health Education Authority £40,000
Date of Research: 1991-1991
KEYWORDS: Acquired Immune Deficiency Syndrome; colleges of further education; health education; sexually transmitted diseases; tertiary colleges

9/0680
King's College, 552 King's Road, London SW10 0UA
071 836 5454
London University, Institute of Education, 20 Bedford Way, London WC1H 0AL
071 580 1122
Bliss, J. Dr; Ogborn, J. Prof.
Tools for exploratory learning programme
Abstract: The aim of this research is to examine whether or not computer tools facilitate different types of reasoning in two different modes of learning. Exploratory learning is defined as the learning that occurs when children use software tools containing representations or models of a specific domain. Expressive learning occurs when children are given the facility to represent their own ideas about the domain. Preliminaries will be a teaching session for familiarisation with the computer, followed by a session to teach the children how to use the relevant software. The main study will be composed of a preliminary interview to record pupils' spontaneous reasoning in the

domain area. Children will be then set an extended task in which they will use the software followed by a final interview to examine their reasoning. The tasks will be designed to call on reasoning in one of the three areas: quantitative; semi-quantitative; and qualitative. The rationale of tasks will be to create 'what if' situations, that is to ask children to explore or express alternatives to reach a specific goal. Approximately 2,000 children will be sampled in the course of the study. These children will be in the age range 11 to 14 years from middle or secondary schools. During the study the children will work in same sex friendship pairs on one specific task, using one particular software tool. The interviews will be transcribed, as will any conversation between the children. These transcriptions together with observational data will form the basis of the data to be analyzed. The data will be qualitatively analyzed using systemic networks.
Published Material: BLISS, J. & OGBORN, J. (1989). 'Tools for exploratory learning', Journal of Computer Assisted Learning, Vol 5, No 1, pp.37-50.; OGBORN, J. (1989). 'Computational modelling: a link between mathematics and other subjects'. In: BLUM, W. et al.; Modelling, applications and applied problem solving. Hemel Hempstead: Horwood (Ellis).; MILLER, R., OGBORN, J., TURNER, J., BRIGGS, J.H. & BROUGH, D.R. (1990). 'Towards a tool to support semi-quantitative modelling', Proceedings of International Conference on Advanced Research on Computers in Education, July 1990. Tokyo: Gakashuin University.
Status: Sponsored project
Source of Grant: Economic and Social Research Council £82,940
Date of Research: 1988-1991
KEYWORDS: computer software; computer uses in education; discovery learning; models

9/0681
London School of Economics and Political Science, Centre for Educational Research, Houghton Street, London WC2A 2AE
071 405 7686
Varlaam, A. Mr; Walker, A. Mr; *Supervisor:* Nuttall, D. Prof.
Teacher training and teacher recruitment in the inner city
Abstract: The research consists of four parts: (1) a questionnaire survey of a sample of about 600 final year Bachelor of Education (B. Ed.) and Postgraduate Certificate in Education (PGCE) students selected from a cross-section of training institutions, supplemented by group interviews in four institutions; (2) group discussions at six training institutions with first year B. Ed. students and PGCE students early in their year of study, to investigate whether their views are more malleable; (3) an identification of the local education authorities that were the first destination of students acquiring Qualified Teacher Status (QTS) in 1988 and 1989, possibly supplemented by an analysis of the home addresses, by institution and of applicants successfully entering a B. Ed. or a PGCE course in 1991; and (4) a questionnaire survey of a sample of about 300 teachers in their first three years of service, supplemented by group interviews.
Status: Sponsored project
Source of Grant: Department of Education and Science £42,300
Date of Research: 1991-1991
KEYWORDS: departments of education; inner city; preservice teacher education; probationary teachers; teacher appointment; teacher distribution

9/0682
London School of Economics and Political Science, Department of Geography, Houghton Street, London WC2A 2AE
071 405 7686
Bennett, R. Prof.; Wicks, P. Dr; *Supervisor:* Bennett, R. Prof.
Education-Business Partnerships (EBPs): targets and stocktake
Abstract: The objective of the report is to provide a stocktake of the current development of Education-Business Partnerships (EBPs). This has the purpose of acting like a 'church tower appeal' in that a visual impression is to be given of the current level of development in EBPs in different local education authorities (LEAs). The purpose of the stocktake is to provide a measure of the current development of EBPs against which future evolution and progress can be judged. It is intended that this will encourage existing effective EBPs whilst setting clear targets for the LEAs which have not yet developed full EBPs, and that further assessments will be made annually to stimulate the development of EBPs. The analysis assesses the progress in development of EBPs against a five level classification.
Published Material: BENNETT, R.J. (1991). Education-Business

Partnerships. London: Confederation of British Industry.; BEN-NETT, R.J., MCCOSHAN, A. & SELLGREN, J. (1989). 'The organisation of Business/Education links: further findings from the CBI Schools Questionnaire'. (Department of Geography Research Papers). London: London University.
Status: Sponsored project
Source of Grant: Shell UK; Confederation of British Industry £14,000
Date of Research: 1988 - continuing
KEYWORDS: *industry-education relationship; local education authorities; school to work transition; vocational education*

9/0683

University College London, Department of Psychology, Gower Street, London WC1E 6BT
071 636 8000
National Hospitals' College of Speech Sciences, Chandler House, 2 Wakefield Street, London WC1N 1PG
071 837 0113
Snowling, M. Dr; Goulandris, N. Dr
Developmental analysis of dyslexia in childhood
Abstract: The development of 24 dyslexic children (reading at the 6, 7 and 8 year levels) is being closely monitored, and compared with a control gorup of average readers. Experimental investigations have included qualitative comparisons of their literacy skills and phonological processing abilities. The consistency of their reading has been investigated to explore the status of the lexical reading system of the dyslexic and normal readers. Preliminary evidence suggests that the dyslexics are less consistent in their reading behaviour even when processing familiar words.
Published Material: SNOWLING, M., HULME, C. & GOULANDRIS, N. (1990). 'Phonological coding in deficits in dyslexia'. In: HALES, G. (Ed). Meeting points in dyslexia. Proceedings of the First International Conference of the British Dyslexia Association. Reading: British Dyslexia Association, pp.93-97.; GOULANDRIS, N. & SNOWLING, M. 'Visual memory deficits: a plausible explanation for reading failure?' Cognitive Neuropsychology, (in press).; HULME, C. & SNOWLING, M. 'Deficits in output phonology cause developmental phonological dyslexia, Mind and Language, (in press).
Status: Sponsored project
Source of Grant: Medical Research Council £65,000
Date of Research: 1989 - continuing
KEYWORDS: *dyslexia; language handicaps; reading difficulties*

9/0684

University College London, Department of Psychology, Gower Street, London WC1E 6BT
071 387 7050
Watford General Hospital, Shrodells Wing, Vicarage Road, Watford WD1 8HB
0923 244366
Millar, W. Dr; Weir, C. Dr
An investigation of the relationship between perinatal risk factors and contingency learning and attentive behaviour in later infancy
Abstract: The research examines the relationship between specific major categories of perinatal risk and cognitive functioning in later infancy. Attentional and contingency analysis behaviours are examined in relation to several medical risk factors because of their potential central nervous system (CNS) involvement: prematurity; the effects of oxygenation/respiratory problems. Three groups of infants are established on the basis of clinical data and objective brain imaging data: (i) infants who revealed a normal brain scan and who at term were neurologically normal, i.e. no discernable CNS involvement; (ii) infants whose scan analysis revealed discrete but non-threatening injury; and (iii) infants whose scan revealed more complex and extensive injury. Behavioural measures on two attention/learning tasks obtained from 6-12 month old infants who previously experienced the categories of perinatal risk in order to examine the effects of early CNS related risk/damage to later cognitive functioning. The findings are expected to be relevant to early educative interventive strategies for basic skills acquisition in early infancy and early childhood.
Status: Individual research
Date of Research: 1985 - continuing
KEYWORDS: *attention; cognitive development; early experience; infant behaviour; learning; neurological impairments*

Loughborough University of Technology

9/0685

Department of Computer Studies, Loughborough LE11 3TU
0509 263171
Fish, J. Mr; *Supervisor:* Scrivener, S. Dr
Cognitive model for the design of sketching systems
Abstract: A model is proposed for the mental representation of artists' sketches. Evidence is presented to support the theory that artists' sketches are hybrid images consisting of visible precept and a cognitive component of a superimposed mental image. It is further argued that sketches amplify the mind's ability to generate imagery from long term memory by facilitating translation between descriptive and depictive modes of representation. The model is used to suggest new improved computer software packages parts of which it is hoped to implement. The implication of the model for the way in which drawing is taught and the future use of sketching systems in education is analysed.
Published Material: FISH, J.C.H. & SCRIVENER, S. (1990). 'Amplifying the mind's eye: sketching and visual cognition', Leonardo, Vol 23, No 1.
Status: Individual research
Date of Research: 1983 - continuing
KEYWORDS: *computer-assisted design; computer graphics; drawing*

9/0686

Department of Education, Loughborough LE11 3TU
0509 263171
Busher, H. Mr
Managing staff development in schools
Abstract: The research has sought to explore: 1) how teachers have responded to the 1987 conditions of service, through the use of semi-structured interviews; and 2) how the professional development necessary to help teachers meet these new conditions is being organised. Questionnaires and document searches are also being used.
Published Material: BUSHER, H.C. (1990). 'Managing compulsory INSET under teachers' new conditions of service', Educational Management & Administration, Vol 18, No 3, pp.39-45.; BUSHER, H.C. (1992). 'Towards a systematic management of professional staff development in schools'. In: WALLACE, G. (Ed). (1992) Local Management of schools: research and experience. BERA dialogs No 6. Multilingual Matters.; BUSHER, H.C. & SARAN, R. (1992). Teachers and their conditions of employment: a study in the politics of schools. London: Kogan Page.
Status: Individual research
Date of Research: 1989-1991
KEYWORDS: *professional development; staff development; teacher employment*

9/0687

Department of Education, Loughborough LE11 3TU
0509 263171
Tyler, K. Mr
Experiential learning in initial teacher education
Abstract: This is an investigation into experiential learning in teacher education. The work will focus on the development of interpersonal skills within an experiential workshop setting with primary Post Graduate Certificate of Education (PGCE) students, and the relevance of such an approach to the students' overall preparation for teaching in a primary school.
Status: Individual research
Date of Research: 1990 - continuing
KEYWORDS: *experiential learning; interpersonal competence; learning experience; preservice teacher education; student teachers; workshops*

9/0688

Department of Education, Loughborough LE11 3TU
0509 263171
Reid, I. Prof.; Wild, P. Dr; Blease, D. Mr; Busher, H. Mr; Zanker, N. Mr; *Supervisor:* Reid, I. Prof.
Leicestershire Technical and Vocational Education Initiative Extension evaluation project

Abstract: This project sets out to draw conclusions on the effectiveness of the Technical and Vocational Education Initiative Extension scheme (TVEI (E)) in promoting a change of pedagogy and content in the 14-18 curriculum. This evaluation is expected to provide valuable information collected from schools, teachers, pupils and parents through illustrative case accounts and analysis of numerical returns of students: (1) uptake on pre-vocational/vocational courses; and (2) involvement in areas such as flexible learning, information technology, residential/work experience and records of achievement. A sample size of 69 schools and colleges covers the whole local education authority, surveyed initially by questionnaire and followed up through semi-structured interviews.
Status: Sponsored project
Source of Grant: Leicestershire County Council £19,674
Date of Research: 1991-1992
KEYWORDS: *programme evaluation; technical education; vocational education*

9/0689
Department of Education, Loughborough LE11 3TU
0509 263171
Reid, I. Prof.; Blease, D. Mr; Wild, P. Dr; Busher, H. Mr; *Supervisor:* Reid, I. Prof.
Leicestershire Technical and Vocational Education Initiative Extension evaluation consultancy
Abstract: This project provides consultancy for institutions in the final year of the Technical and Vocational Education Initiative Extension (TVEI (E)) in order to sustain and develop their monitoring and evaluation programmes. The consultancy programme is based on a supporting cascade model involving skills acquisition and dissemination. Fourteen institutions are actively involved.
Status: Sponsored project
Source of Grant: Leicestershire County Council £19,875
Date of Research: 1991-1992
KEYWORDS: *education consultants; monitoring; programme evaluation; technical education; vocational education*

9/0690
Department of Education, Loughborough LE11 3TU
0509 263171
Reid, I. Prof.; *Supervisor:* Reid, I. Prof.
The development and application of sociospatial indices
Abstract: This project looks at the use of commercially based post code applications to school populations to allow for comparisons, and the construction and application of the derived scale of social advantage/social deprivation to school and pupil performance.
Status: Sponsored project
Source of Grant: Bradford Metropolitan Council, Directorate of Education
Date of Research: 1990 - continuing
KEYWORDS: *academic achievement; performance factors; scaling; school effectiveness; social environment; socioeconomic influences*

9/0691
Department of Education, Loughborough LE11 3TU
0509 263171
Demaine, J. Dr
Citizenship and education
Abstract: A study of the concept of citizenship in the context of the National Curriculum requirement for teaching in schools.
Status: Individual research
Date of Research: 1991 - continuing
KEYWORDS: *citizenship education; National Curriculum*

9/0692
Department of Education, Loughborough LE11 3TU
0509 263171
Busher, H. Mr
The politics of working in secondary schools
Abstract: This research aims to look at the interaction between individuals and institutions (between individuals and groups of individuals in institutions) when implementing and negotiating changes in secondary schools. The research is small scale and has been carried out ethnographically. It has explored the different interpretations that participants give to the same events. It has focused on time periods when people were most likely to notice dysfunctions between personal views of education and institutionally sustained views of education. The study has focused on six main participants, on how they perceived their work in their schools and how their colleagues perceived them working. The research has made use of tape-recorded semi-structured interviews, of classroom observation, and of enriched interviews (using video-recordings of teacher activity to trigger discussion). Some 30 interviews in all were conducted during the course of one academic year. Tentative conclusions are that school organisations can be adequately described using a political systems model and that the management of schools is an intensely political process rather than a mechanistically rational one.
Status: Individual research
Date of Research: 1987-1992
KEYWORDS: *educational change; institutional administration; interaction; school organisation; secondary schools; teacher-administrator relationship; teacher attitudes*

9/0693
Department of Education, Loughborough LE11 3TU
0509 263171
Demaine, J. Dr
Student evaluation of teaching in higher education in the UK
Abstract: An investigation into student evaluation of teaching in higher education in the United Kingdom.
Status: Individual research
Date of Research: 1991 - continuing
KEYWORDS: *higher education; student evaluation of teacher performance; teacher effectiveness*

9/0694
Department of Education, Loughborough LE11 3TU
0509 263171
Demaine, J. Dr
Local Management of Schools
Abstract: A study of the effects of Local Management of Schools (LMS) on a select group of schools in England.
Status: Individual research
Date of Research: 1991 - continuing
KEYWORDS: *educational administration; educational change; local management of schools; school-based management*

9/0695
Department of Education, Loughborough LE11 3TU
0509 263171
Demaine, J. Dr
Socio-political attitudes of teacher trainers in the United Kingdom
Abstract: An investigation into the sociopolitical attitudes of teacher trainers in the United Kingdom.
Status: Individual research
Date of Research: 1991 - continuing
KEYWORDS: *political attitudes; social attitudes; teacher attitudes; teacher education; teacher educators*

9/0696
Department of Education, Loughborough LE11 3TU
0509 263171
El-Laithy, S. Mrs; *Supervisor:* Smedley, D. Mr
Curriculum development and evaluation of Teaching English as a Second Language (TESOL) courses at foundation level in the United Arab Emirates
Abstract: The research will evaluate the effectiveness of the present curriculum for teaching English as a second language at foundation level in the six colleges of higher education in the the United Arab Emirates, and indicate what further developments might be appropriate. The methods used include questionnaires to students, staff and administrators, follow-up interviews of a selected sample, and documentary analysis.
Status: Individual research
Date of Research: 1991 - continuing
KEYWORDS: *Arab states; English – second language; higher education*

9/0697
Department of Education, Loughborough LE11 3TU

0509 263171
Wild, P. Dr; *Supervisor:* Wild, P. Dr; Richardson, S. Mr
Evaluation of information technology systems used to support administration in schools
Abstract: A consequence of the Education Reform Act 1988 (ERA) is the need for information technology (IT) systems to support the Local Management of Schools (LMS). It is well known from research in the commercial and industrial sectors that the success rate for the implementation of such systems is as low as 20%. If the IT systems being installed in schools are to achieve their potential in helping to administer, or, more importantly, manage the working of the school then it is essential that some evaluation of the systems is carried out. A methodology developed at the Human Sciences and Advanced Technology (HUSAT) Research Institute at Loughborough University, called the User Acceptance Audit, is being modified for the school environment. A detailed task analysis is required of the management and administration within the schools so that the evaluation tool developed by HUSAT can be made context sensitive. The final outcome should be an 'evaluation package' which could be used by local education authorities and/or individual schools to assess the potential barriers to successful implementation.
Published Material: WILD, P., SCIVIER, J.E. & RICHARDSON, S.J. (1992). 'Evaluating information technology-supported Local Management of Schools: the User Acceptability Audit', Education Management and Administration, Vol 20, No1, pp.40-48.
Status: Individual research
Date of Research: 1989 - continuing
KEYWORDS: computer uses in education; educational administration; information technology; local management of schools; management systems; school-based management

9/0698
    Department of Education, Loughborough LE11 3TU
    0509 263171
    Wild, P. Dr; Simmons, C. Mr
A study of the information technology skills used by teachers in the first two years in the profession: comparison of these skills with the information technology content of Post Graduate Certificate of Education courses
Abstract: During 1989-90 a questionnaire survey was used to evaluate the effects of the Post Graduate Certificate of Education courses on students' development of the use of information technology skills in teaching. The questionnaires were used at the start and end of their courses. It will now be very useful to follow a sample of the students through their first two years of teaching to assess the impact of the teacher training course on the use of information technology (IT) within schools. The results of this survey will provide a useful contribution to the present debate on the models of IT coverage within teacher education and their relevance to the first years of teaching. It will also provide some preliminary evidence concerning the extent of IT use within the developing National Curriculum which could form the basis for further research in this area. The research will be carried out by questionnaire and follow up visits to a sample of schools in the United Kingdom. Results will be disseminated through the Information Technology in Teacher Education Group, which is an active 'grass roots' body supporting IT developments in teacher education, as well as the relevant journals.
Published Material: WILD, P. & HODGKINSON, K. (1990). 'Providing information technology competency in primary and secondary initial teacher training', Proceedings of the Third National Conference in Design and Technology Education and Research', Loughborough University.; SIMMONS, C. & WILD, P. (1991). 'Student teachers learning to learn through IT', Educational Research, Vol 33, No 3, pp.163-173.; SIMMONS, C. & WILD, P. (1991). 'New forms of student teacher learning', Educational Review, Vol 44, No 2, pp.31-40.; WILD, P. (1992). 'Information technology in teacher training and early years of teaching', 9th International Conference on Technology and Education, March.
Status: Sponsored project
Source of Grant: Loughborough University £1,000
Date of Research: 1990-1992
KEYWORDS: information technology; preservice teacher education; probationary teachers

9/0699
    Department of Education, Loughborough LE11 3TU
    0509 263171
    Thomas, J. Mr
History of educational psychology in Britain with special reference to university departments of education
Abstract: This project includes the development of bibliographies on individual psychologists of education and case studies of individual university departments of education. It involves the use of primary and secondary historical services. The long term aim is a monograph on the history of educational psychology in Britain, including its clinical practice.
Published Material: THOMAS, J.B. (1982). 'J.A. Green, educational psychology and the Journal of Experimental Pedagogy', History of Education Society Bulletin, No 29, pp.41-45.
Status: Individual research
Date of Research: 1982 - continuing
KEYWORDS: educational history; educational psychology; teacher education

9/0700
    Department of Education, Loughborough LE11 3TU
    0509 263171
    Thomas, J. Mr
Studies of teacher education in the Victorian day training college
Abstract: The project aims to describe and analyse the work of education departments in universities from 1890 to 1918. It consists of case studies of individual institutions, biographical studies and investigations of related areas, for example, the development of the academic study of education and the greater opportunities for the professional education of women.
Published Material: THOMAS, J.B. (1986). 'Amos Henderson and the Nottingham Day Training College', Journal of Educational Administration and History, Vol 18, No 2, pp.24-33.; THOMAS, J.B. (1986). 'University College, London, and the training of teachers', History of Education Society Bulletin, Vol 37, pp.44-49.; THOMAS, J.B. (1986). 'Students, staff and curriculum in a day training college (Cardiff)', Collected Original Resources in Education, Vol 10, No 3, Fiche 1 A04.; THOMAS, J.B. (1988). 'University College, Bristol: pioneering teacher training for women', History of Education, Vol. 17, No 1, pp.55-70.; THOMAS, J.B. (Ed). (1990). British universities and teacher education: a century of change. London: Falmer Press.
Status: Individual research
Date of Research: 1978 - continuing
KEYWORDS: educational history; preservice teacher education

9/0701
    Department of Education, Loughborough LE11 3TU
    0509 263171
    Hinton, R. Mr; Wild, G. Dr
Communication problems of blind students in higher education
Abstract: As a result of its experience in producing tactile diagrams, the department has in recent years been asked to help several blind students in higher education who are pursuing courses with a high content of visually orientated material. It has become apparent that not only are more blind students seeking to study courses which have an inherent visual content but also that courses which have in the past had a predominantly verbal structure are now making increasing use of visual resources. Resources which make it possible for a blind student to access visually orientated course work may exist but they are not always easily available or may require further development. Many existing students still struggle to obtain good quality resources and some students are refused entry to the courses of their choice partly because suitable resources are not available. The present study is making detailed case studies of ten individual students pursuing a wide variety of courses with a significant visual content. Through maintaining contact with the students and their teaching and support staff over at least one complete academic year it sets out to: (1) identify academic subjects where such problems occur; (2) locate the causes of the problems; (3) develop more effective teaching resources where necessary; and (4) provide for any necessary staff advice.
Status: Sponsored project
Source of Grant: Leverhulme Trust £16,450
Date of Research: 1990-1991
KEYWORDS: blindness; communication problems; higher education; nonverbal communication; special educational needs; visual impairments

9/0702
    Department of Education, Loughborough LE11 3TU
    0509 263171

Demaine, J. Dr
Labour's education policy
Abstract: A study of the Labour Party's education policy in the recent past and for the future.
Published Material: DEMAINE, J. (1992). 'Labour's education policy', British Journal of Educational Studies, Vol 40 (forthcoming).
Status: Individual research
Date of Research: 1991 - continuing
KEYWORDS: educational policy; politics education relationship

9/0703
Department of Education, Loughborough LE11 3TU
0509 263171
Demaine, J. Dr
Problems with right wing education policy
Abstract: The research examines right wing arguments on educational provision, including the notion of a voucher scheme and the introduction of elements of a 'free market' into public sector education. It examines right wing argument on 'gradualism' as a means of securing educational reform. The research examines arguments put forward by the Right on the idea of a General Teaching Council, on the teacher labour market, and on the status of teachers.
Published Material: DEMAINE, J. (1988). 'Teachers' work, curriculum and the New Right', British Journal of Sociology of Education, Vol 9, No 3, pp.247-264.; DEMAINE, J. (1989). 'Privatisation by stealth: New Right Education Policy', ACE (Advisory Centre for Education) Bulletin, No 28, Advisory Centre for Education, pp.5-7.; DEMAINE, J. (1989). 'A General Teaching Council and the status of teachers', ACE (Advisory Centre for Education) Bulletin, No 32, Advisory Centre for Education, pp.3-5.; DEMAINE, J. (1990). 'The reform of secondary education'. In: HINDNESS, B. (Ed). Reactions to the Right. London: Routledge.
Status: Individual research
Date of Research: 1987-1992
KEYWORDS: educational change; educational policy; educational vouchers; politics education relationship

9/0704
Department of Education, Loughborough LE11 3TU
0509 263171
Shepherd, D. Ms; Ayres, D. Mr
Survey of HIV/AIDS education in secondary schools in the East Midlands to discover its curriculum organization, incidence and teaching strategies, the problems and INSET needs of teachers and the impact of the National Curriculum
Abstract: This research will involve a survey of 150 headteachers and health education coordinators to discover their teaching and curriculum problems, needs and organization in HIV/AIDS (Human Immunodeficiency Virus/Acquired Immune Deficiency Syndrome), particularly in the context of DES Circular 11/87, 'Sex Education and National Curriculum Health Education' Cross Curricular Theme. Methodology will be structured questionnaires with respondents providing basic data for subsequent analysis and report.
Status: Individual research
Date of Research: 1989 - continuing
KEYWORDS: Acquired Immune Deficiency Syndrome; health education; sex education

9/0705
Department of Education, Loughborough LE11 3TU
0509 263171
Demaine, J. Dr
Racism and multicultural education
Abstract: The research examines the arguments surrounding the notions of multicultural and antiracist education with particular reference to the pedagogic practice. The research is also concerned with the ways in which terms and categories are deployed in analyses, and discussion of differences in educational achievement between social groups whose identity is usually specified in terms of 'race' or 'ethnicity'.
Published Material: DEMAINE, J. & KADOWALA, D. (1988). 'Multicultural and antiracist education: the unnecessary divide', Curriculum, Vol 9, No 2, pp.99-102.; DEMAINE, J. (1989). 'Race, categorisation and educational achievement', British Journal of Sociology of Education, Vol 10, No 2, pp.195-214.
Status: Individual research
Date of Research: 1988 - continuing

KEYWORDS: antiracism education; ethnic groups; multicultural education

9/0706
Department of Education, Loughborough LE11 3TU
0509 263171
Simmons, C. Mr
School education and young people in Saudi Arabia
Abstract: This project compares the results of two surveys, the main aim of which was to portray what young people think, feel and believe about important aspects of their lives, using as evidence own written statements. The subjects comprised 89 Saudi Arabian and 107 English adolescents aged between 13-15 years. The open-ended questionnaire comprised 10 prompts designed to elicit responses concerning ideals and least ideals, most and least preferred companions, use of solitude, summun bonum, most and least desired outcomes to life and nascent philosophies. Two methods of analysis were used: first, references to dominant themes were totalled; second, responses were assigned to six categories according to the dominant values expressed from materialistic to altruistic. Significant differences were found in the dominant themes and between the values expressed by the two samples. Most marked were the pervasive religious values in the Saudi Arabian sample and the absence of these in the English sample.
Status: Individual research
Date of Research: 1991 - continuing
KEYWORDS: comparative education; cross cultural studies; educational attitudes; pupil attitudes; Saudi Arabia

9/0707
Department of Education, Loughborough LE11 3TU
0509 263171
Simmons, C. Mr
School education and young people in Japan
Abstract: This project compares the results of two surveys, the main aim of which was to portray what young people think, feel and believe about important aspects of their lives, using as evidence their own written statements. The subjects comprised 820 fifteen-year-olds in six schools in England in 1981 and 283 fourteen-year-olds at two schools in Japan in 1986. The open-ended questionnaire comprised 10 prompts designed to elicit responses concerning ideals and least ideals, most and least preferred companions, use of solitude, summum bonum, most and least desired outcomes to life and nascent philosophies. Two methods of analysis were used: first, references to dominant themes were totalled; second, responses were assigned to six categories according to the dominant values expressed from materialistic to altruistic. Similarities but also significant differences were found in the dominant themes and significant differences were also apparent between the values expressed by the two samples. Most marked was the tendency for the Japanese sample to place a higher valuation on education than the English but to express less regard for their parents and family.
Published Material: SIMMONS, C.V. (1987). Some comparisons between English and Japanese young people: a report on two surveys. Research Report 15. Tokyo: National Institute for Educational Research.; SIMMONS, C.V. & WADE, W. (1988). 'Contrasting attitudes to education in England and Japan', Educational Research, Vol 30, No 2, pp.146-152.
Status: Sponsored project
Source of Grant: Loughborough University Academic Initiative Fund £5,000
Date of Research: 1987-1991
KEYWORDS: comparative education; cross cultural studies; educational attitudes; Japan; pupil attitudes

9/0708
Department of Education, Loughborough LE11 3TU
0509 263171
Litawski, R. Mrs; *Supervisor:* Thomas, J. Mr
The role of the female deputy headteachers: an investigation into the role and profiles of female deputy headteachers in co-educational comprehensive schools in one local education authority
Abstract: This research examines sexual discrimination and/or role differentiation in comprehensive schools using a theory of micropolitics of the school, use of survey, case studies, and structured interview methodology.

Status: Individual research
Date of Research: 1988-1992
KEYWORDS: *deputy headteachers; equal opportunity – jobs; sex discrimination; sex role; women*

9/0709
Department of Education, Loughborough LE11 3TU
0509 263171
Todd, N. Mr; *Supervisor:* Hinton, R. Dr
The integration of visually impaired students in further education
Abstract: This research includes a survey by questionnaire of a large number of mainstream further education colleges in the Midlands to ascertain the numbers of visually impaired students studying in them. Further questionnaires to individual students seek to examine the reasons for the students' choice of course and college and the quality of support they receive to allow comparison with the quality of support which college staff 'believe' they are providing. Recommendations will be made for improving the provision for visually impaired students in the future.
Status: Individual research
Date of Research: 1988 - continuing
KEYWORDS: *further education; mainstreaming; special educational needs; visual impairments*

9/0710
Department of Education, Loughborough LE11 3TU
0509 263171
Smith, A. Mr; *Supervisor:* Thomas, J. Mr
The psychological treatment of emotionally and behaviourally disordered children within a special school setting: a conceptual, experimental and survey analysis
Abstract: After reviewing the residential treatment of emotionally and behaviourally disturbed children, the author surveys present provision and therapy in a national sample of schools and homes, and concludes with an analysis and evaluation of family therapy in a case study of one such school.
Status: Individual research
Date of Research: 1987-1991
KEYWORDS: *behaviour disorders; emotional disturbances; special educational needs; special schools*

9/0711
Department of Education, Loughborough LE11 3TU
0509 263171
Hough, J. Prof.; *Supervisor:* Hough, J. Prof.
Cost-benefit analysis in education
Abstract: The research surveys educational cost-benefit analysis with particlar reference to third world countries. The project covers the definition and development of cost benefit analysis (CBA), methodology of CBA alternative approaches, comparison with other techniques in educational planning and extensive surveys of CBA results both in developed and in third world countries. The research focuses particularly on problems relating to concepts, data, assumptions, methodology and interpretation of CBA results. Finally, the project will suggest ways in which CBA studies can become more practical and implementable.
Status: Sponsored project
Source of Grant: Overseas Development Administration (British Government) £11,688
Date of Research: 1991-1992
KEYWORDS: *cost effectiveness; developing countries; educational economics; educational finance; efficiency*

9/0712
Department of Education, Loughborough LE11 3TU
0509 263171
Hough, R. Prof.; *Supervisor:* Hough, R. Prof.
The education system in England and Wales
Abstract: This research is surveying developments in the education system in England and Wales with emphasis on changes since the Education Reform Act 1988. The research includes: the Department of Education and Science; local education authorities; the Education Reform Act 1988; the comprehensive school; the private sector of education; the education of the 16-19 age group and the further education sector; and higher education. In each case the project studys recent changes, especially those stemming directly from the Educa-

tion Reform Act and considers the effects and consequences.
Published Material: HOUGH, J.R. (1991). The education system in England and Wales: a synopsis. Papers in Education Series. Loughborough University of Technology, Department of Education.
Status: Sponsored project
Source of Grant: Loughborough University of Technology: Department of Education
Date of Research: 1991-1992
KEYWORDS: *Education Reform Act 1988; educational change; educational development; educational planning; educational policy; government role; local education authorities*

9/0713
Department of Education, Loughborough LE11 3TU
0509 263171
Hough, J. Prof.; *Supervisor:* Hough, J. Prof.
Financial management in education
Abstract: The project surveys financial management in education with particlar reference to third world countries. Topics included are: characteristics of financial management; how developed are current financial management systems?; cash management; budgeting and budget practices; school site budgeting; project budgeting; zero based budgeting; control of costs; accounting and double entry book-keeping; and planning, programming, budgeting, evaluation assessments (PPBES).
Status: Sponsored project
Source of Grant: UNESCO
Date of Research: 1990-1992
KEYWORDS: *comparative analysis; developing countries; educational administration; educational finance; financial policy*

9/0714
Department of Education, Loughborough LE11 3TU
0509 263171
Rovira-Garza, N. Miss; *Supervisor:* Hinton, R. Dr
Factors influencing the successful integration of children with Down's Syndrome in mainstream education
Abstract: A study of the factors influencing successful integration of children with Down's Syndrome into mainstream classes, and in particular the influence of the teacher's attitude to the child and the quality and appropriateness of the pedagogic strategies.
Status: Sponsored project
Source of Grant: National Mental Health Foundation
Date of Research: 1991 - continuing
KEYWORDS: *Down's Syndrome; mainstreaming; special educational needs*

9/0715
Department of Education, Loughborough LE11 3TU
0509 263171
King Saud University, The College of Education, Riyadh, Saudi Arabia Al Rawat, H. Dr; *Supervisor:* Simmons, C. Mr
An open university for women in Saudi Arabia: problems and prospects
Abstract: This study investigates the prospects of setting up an open university for women in Saudi Arabia against the background of the problems which Saudi women face in pursuing higher education. A review is given of the development of modern public education for women since its beginning in 1960, with emphasis on the more recent development of higher education for women. The position of women in Islam and in contemporary Saudi society is examined as this has influenced their access to higher education. Three open universities in the United Kingdom, Thailand and Pakistan are described (the latter in an Islamic country). A questionnaire was devised in order to gather data on attitudes to the setting up of an open university for women in Saudi Arabia, on perceptions of its feasibility, and on possible obstacles to its foundation. The questionnaire also included a section on the most suitable model for an open university for women in Saudi Arabia. The questionnaire was distributed in government bodies and higher educational establishments in Saudi Arabia to policy makers, academics and female students. An analysis of the data reveals a very positive response to the setting up of an open university for women in Saudi Arabia. Respondents, however, demonstrated a realistic awareness of the problems of gaining public acceptance for a new type of higher education in a time of restrictions on government spending. Finally, on the basis of the findings a proposal is being made for the setting up of an open university for women in Saudi Arabia.

Published Material: AL RAWAT, H.S. & SIMMONS, C.V. (1991). 'The education of women in Saudi Arabia', Comparative Education, Vol 27, No 3, pp.287-295.
Status: Individual research
Date of Research: 1986-1990
KEYWORDS: distance education; open universities; Saudi Arabia; women's education

9/0716

Department of Education, Loughborough LE11 3TU
0509 263171
Leeds University, School of Education, Leeds LS2 9JT
0532 324527
Reid, I. Prof.; Wiegand, P. Mr

An investigation into the social and educational impact of project work in GCSE

Abstract: This is an investigation into project work in General Certificate of Secondary Education (GCSE) subjects. The first stage involves the analysis of questionnaires completed by some 400 pupils who completed GCSEs in the summer of 1990. The second stage involves parents and teachers. The thrust of the investigation is to review the impact of project work on pupils and the extent to which factors of social background and gender affect attitudes and performance. It will also look at the overall demands and level of coordination of such coursework by level of ability and subject choice.
Status: Sponsored project
Source of Grant: Leeds University: School of Education £1,500
Date of Research: 1990-1991
KEYWORDS: coursework; General Certificate of Secondary Education; projects – learning activities; pupil experience; pupil projects; sex differences; social influences

9/0717

Department of Education, Loughborough LE11 3TU
0509 263171
London University, King's College, Centre for Educational Studies, Cornwall House Annexe, Waterloo Road, London SE1 3TY
071 836 5454
Nolder, R. Ms; Supervisor: Johnson, D. Prof.

Bringing teachers to the centre of the stage: a study of secondary school teachers' responses to curriculum change in mathematics

Abstract: The research aims to examine the ways in which teachers respond to changes in classroom practice demanded of them in the course of radical curriculum change in mathematics. The fieldwork was carried out from 1985 to 1988 when various changes were being introduced into the secondary methematics curriculum largely in connection with the new examination at 16 plus, the General Certificate of Secondary Education. The research falls into the category of interpretivist research. It focuses on teachers in two mathematics departments (N=8, of 12 in the two schools). Qualitative research methods are used; the main research strategy is participant observation. Data have been collected in the form of field notes, documentation and audiotapes of interviews. A network which represents a set of 11 interrelated concepts associated with professional change (including competence, confidence, control and constraints on professional practice) has been developed from the data. This network has served as an analytic tool, firstly to monitor professional change for two case study subjects and secondly to identify commonalities and differences in responses to change among teachers in the study. From these analyses an empirically based model of the process of accelerated professional development associated with radical change has been developed. The model comprises five stages: anticipation, immersion, coping, consolidation, and extension.
Published Material: NOLDER, R.B. (1988). 'Responding to change'. In: PIMM, D. (Ed). Mathematics, Teachers and Children. London: Hodder and Stoughton.; NOLDER, R.B. & TYTHERLEIGH, B. (1990). 'R2MC: a springboard to curriculum change', British Journal of Inservice Education, Vol 16, No 1, pp.14-22.; NOLDER, R.B. (1990). 'Accommodating curriculum change in mathematics: teachers' dilemmas', Proceedings of the 14th Annual Conference of the International Group for the Psychology of Mathematical Education, Oaxtepec, Mexico, Vol 1, pp.167-174.
Status: Individual research
Date of Research: 1985-1991
KEYWORDS: curriculum development; educational change; mathematics curriculum; secondary school teachers; teacher attitudes

9/0718

Department of Education, Loughborough LE11 3TU
0509 263171
Warwick University, Department of Science Education, Coventry CV4 7AL
0203 523523
Melrose, J. Miss; Supervisor: Schwarzenberger, R. Prof.

An exploration into the notion of levels of attainment in mathematics

Abstract: This research is a comparison of young children and older low-attainers in their thinking about mathematics topics including subtraction and three dimensional visualisation. The methods employed are principally individual interviews with the children together with reflections from their teachers.
Status: Individual research
Date of Research: 1989 - continuing
KEYWORDS: low achievement; mathematics achievement; mathematics education

Lowestoft College

9/0719

St Peter's Street, Lowestoft, Suffolk NR32 2NB
0502 583521
Stainsby, R. Mr; Snook, C. Mr; Supervisor: Neville, C. Miss

Marketing PICKUP in Europe

Abstract: Lowestoft College has developed considerable expertise in fibre optics over a period of four years. With Professional, Industrial and Commercial Updating (PICKUP) backing, a conference has been held and a certificated short course programme has been developed which has been supported by local and national firms dealing in fibre optics. The College perceives that there is a market available on the European mainland for its courses. The aims of the project are: to identify fibre optic training and certification currently available in West Germany and Holland; to examine the level of expertise in English language of the target population; to carry out a survey of the pricing of similar short course provision in these countries; to look at course delivery in site, in conjunction with equipment suppliers and training establishments; and to prepare a model for further education colleges for marketing PICKUP courses in Europe. Methods used to establish contacts and links in West Germany and Holland will include correspondence, telephone and visits. The outcomes of the project will be to establish a network of firms in West Germany and Holland for the marketing of the short course programme; to provide a coordinated set of information on equivalence of providers and certification, awareness and response to 1992, a year plan of trade fairs and exhibitions and a dossier of support available to UK colleges and firms wishing to benefit from the College's experience. A report will provide the model for marketing PICKUP courses in Europe.
Status: Sponsored project
Source of Grant: Further Education Unit
Date of Research: 1990-1991
KEYWORDS: courses; industrial training; market research; marketing; technical education; telecommunications

Manchester Metropolitan University

9/0720

Department of Hotel, Catering and Tourism Management, Hollings Faculty, Old Hall Lane, Manchester M14 6HR
061 247 2000
Keele University, Department of Education, Keele, Staffordshire ST5 5BG
0782 621111
Ineson, E. Mrs; Supervisor: Kempa, R. Prof.

Study of factors affecting students' success and dropout rates in hotel management courses

Abstract: Students' success in hotel management courses is frequently judged by employers in terms of a range of qualities other than academic ones. The research aims at identifying these non-academic

qualities and, thereafter, will focus on the extent to which their development can be predicted before or at the commencement of students' courses. Central to the study is the administration of personality and related inventories to students on hotel management training courses. Data obtained in this way will be supplemented by information from interviews.
Status: Individual research
Date of Research: 1986 - continuing
KEYWORDS: *assessment; dropout characteristics; hotel and catering education; hotel management education; success*

Manchester University

9/0721
Hester Adrian Research Centre, Oxford Road, Manchester M13 9PL
061 275 3340
Emerson, E. Mr; Cooper, J. Ms
Evaluation of quality and costs of services to people with multiple sensory impairments and severe learning difficulties provided by SENSE in the Midlands
Abstract: The project will examine the quality and costs of services provided by the residential further education facility operated by SENSE (The National Deaf-Blind and Rubella Association) in the Midlands. Comparisons will be made between a group of 18 current students and a matched waiting list control group with regards to: the range and costs of services received; nature of teacher-student interaction; nature of student activity; student participation in community activities.
Status: Sponsored project
Source of Grant: Department of Health £64,000
Date of Research: 1990-1992
KEYWORDS: *deaf-blind; further education; institutional evaluation; residential institutions; severe learning difficulties; special educational needs*

9/0722
Hester Adrian Research Centre, Oxford Road, Manchester M13 9PL
061 275 3340
Emerson, E. Mr; Howard, D. Ms
An investigation into the schedule control of stereotyped and self-injurious behaviours in young people with severe learning difficulties
Abstract: The project is examining whether stereotyped behaviours shown by children and young people with severe learning difficulties may occur as 'side-effects' of teaching procedures based upon the systematic use of positive reinforcers. The project involves the observation of rates of stereotyped and self-injurious behaviours shown by six young people in classroom settings and a number of experimental settings in which the scheduling of reinforcers is manipulated.
Status: Sponsored project
Source of Grant: Medical Research Council £18,000
Date of Research: 1990-1991
KEYWORDS: *behaviour disorders; self destructive behaviour; self mutilation; severe learning difficulties; special educational needs*

9/0723
School of Education, Oxford Road, Manchester M13 9PL
061 275 2000
Almajid, A. Mr; *Supervisor:* Reid, D. Dr
The use of microcomputers in Saudi secondary schools
Abstract: The use of microcomputers in Saudi secondary schools is ineffectual. Problems centre around the software, which is not Arabized and therefore causes difficulty, around the Saudi information technology (IT) curriculum. This is program-focused. The thesis argues the case for an applications based strategy.
Status: Individual research
Date of Research: 1989-1991
KEYWORDS: *Arab states; computer uses in education; educational software; microcomputers*

9/0724
School of Education, Oxford Road, Manchester M13 9PL
061 275 2000
Reid, D. Dr
Comparative issues in science curriculum: USA & UK
Abstract: Large amounts of currency have been spent on developing the science curriculum in both the USA & UK. In the USA the science curriculum has remained intransigent whilst in the UK a number of successful innovations have taken place since the late 1980s. Why, when the social and economic pressures for change have been the same in both countries, has one country been relatively successful and the other not? It is argued that the structure of the American High School is not conducive to collegiality and teacher empowerment. It is the highly developed department structure, with the head of department as mentorial, which has facilitated science curriculum innovation in the UK.
Status: Individual research
Date of Research: 1990-1992
KEYWORDS: *comparative education; curriculum development; science curriculum*

9/0725
School of Education, Oxford Road, Manchester M13 9PL
061 275 2000
Reid, D. Dr
Picture-text interaction in children's learning of science
Abstract: The Picture Superiority Effect (PSE) is ambiguous. What are the variables which contribute to it? The investigations are data driven and school based to optimise ecological validity. Typically between 100 and 200, 13-14 year old children are given memory recall tasks of science comprehension. Use of microcomputers has shown that PSE is enhanced when the material to be learned is present redundantly in both picture and text, the learning task is memory based, the structure of the picture is optimised in terms of those perceptual elements known to direct or attract attention and the learner is trained how to use pictures in relation to the text.
Published Material: A full list of publications is available from the researcher.
Status: Individual research
Date of Research: 1985 - continuing
KEYWORDS: *memory; pictorial stimuli; science education; visual learning*

9/0726
School of Education, Oxford Road, Manchester M13 9PL
061 275 2000
Braund, C. Mr; *Supervisor:* Hoy, C. Dr
Management cultures within primary schools
Abstract: The aim of this study is to illuminate concepts of culture within primary schools, in relation to their management. It will involve a wide ranging review of literature and industrial comparatives, extended by empirical techniques used to verify and/or clarify school cultures.
Status: Sponsored project
Source of Grant: Crewe & Alsager College of Higher Education
Date of Research: 1989 - continuing
KEYWORDS: *educational administration; educational environment; management in education; primary schools*

9/0727
School of Education, Centre for Adult and Higher Education, Oxford Road, Manchester M13 9PL
061 275 2000
Turner, J. Prof.; *Supervisor:* Carmen, R. Dr
Rural social development: education, literacy and organisation in the Third World
Abstract: After the previous four decades (since World War II) of economic development with directive, top-down strategies and non-directive efforts known under 'community development' and 'integrated rural development', we are now in the 1980s and 1990s, entering the era of self-directed, autonomous development. The very term 'autonomy' does not figure on current development and education library indexes, therefore there is an urgent need for compilation and research.
Status: Individual research
Date of Research: 1989-1992
KEYWORDS: *community development; developing countries; development education; economic development; rural development*

9/0728

School of Education, Centre for Adult and Higher Education, Oxford Road, Manchester M13 9PL
061 275 2000
Boreham, N. Dr

Cognitive components of experience in professional diagnosis and decision making, with implications for professional education

Abstract: Task analyses are being carried out of diagnosis and decision making in selected professions. Using protocol analysis techniques, computable models of the cognitive processes involved are being constructed. Comparisons between experts and novices are being made, and the results are being used to suggest improvements in current professional education and training.

Published Material: BOREHAM, N.C. (1989). 'Modelling medical decision making under uncertainty', British Journal of Educational Psychology, Vol 59, Part 2, pp.187-199.; BOREHAM, N.C. (1987). 'Causal attributions by sensing and intuitive types during diagnostic problem solving', Instructional Science, Vol 16, pp.123-136.

Status: Individual research
Date of Research: 1987 - continuing
KEYWORDS: cognitive processes; decision making; professional education

9/0729

School of Education, Centre for Adult and Higher Education, Oxford Road, Manchester M13 9PL
061 275 2000
Boreham, N. Dr

Cognitive components of expertise in professional judgement, with reference to factors influencing acquisition of the relevant cognitive skills

Abstract: The aim of this research is to analyse the knowledge and cognitive skills underpinning professional judgement, and to derive implications for higher education and continuing professional education. The fields encompassed include medical decision making, personnel management, fault finding and educational psychology. The methodology includes task analysis, skills analysis, cognitive simulation, expert-novice comparisons and learning experiments. The results point to the cognitive processes and structures crucial to cognitive skill acquisition, and lead to recommendations about teaching and learning.

Published Material: BOREHAM, N.C., FOSTER, R.W. & MAWER, G.E. (1989). 'The phenytoin game: its effect on decision skills', Simulation and Games, Vol 20, pp.292-299.; BOREHAM, N.C. (1989). 'Modelling medical decision making under uncertainty', British Journal of Educational Psychology, Vol 59, Part 2, pp.187-199.; BOREHAM, N.C. (1988). 'Models of diagnosis and their implications for adult professional education', Studies in the Education of Adults, Vol 20, pp.95-108.; BOREHAM, N.C. (1987). 'Causal attribution by sensing and intuitive types during diagnostic problem solving', Instructional Science, Vol 16, pp.123-136.

Status: Individual research
Date of Research: 1980 - continuing
KEYWORDS: cognitive processes; decision making; professional autonomy

9/0730

School of Education, Centre for Audiology, Education of the Deaf and Speech Pathology, Oxford Road, Manchester M13 9PL
061 275 2000
Lynas, W. Dr; *Supervisor:* Lynas, W. Dr

The educational management of children with Usher Syndrome

Abstract: The aim of the research is to develop sound principles for the educational management of children with Usher Syndrome. Diagnosed children and young people are observed in a variety of educational settings – special school for the deaf, unit, mainstream class, further education college and special provisions for deaf pupils/students with deteriorating vision are noted. The data collected include material from informal interviews with teaching staff and from the Usher pupils themselves. So far, 15 Usher children/young people have been observed.

Published Material: LYNAS, W. (1991). 'Deaf children with Usher Syndrome', Journal of British Association of Teachers of the Deaf, Vol 15, No 2, pp.33-39.; LYNAS, W. (1991). The educational management of children with Usher Syndrome. London: SENSE.

Status: Sponsored project
Source of Grant: National Deaf-Blind and Rubella Association (SENSE)

Date of Research: 1989 - continuing
KEYWORDS: deafness; hearing impairments; special education; special educational needs

9/0731

School of Education, Centre for Audiology, Education of the Deaf and Speech Pathology, Oxford Road, Manchester M13 9PL
061 275 2000
Aplin, D. Dr

Psychological assessment of cochlear implantees

Abstract: A cochlear implant has important psychological implications for recipients and usually has a major impact on the lives of implantees and their families. There have been relatively few reports of psychological assessment of patients from cochlear implant projects world-wide. Psychological assessment has formed an integral part of the Manchester multi-channel cochlear implant programme. Subjects are seen in order to assess their psychological suitability pre-implant and the progress of implantees is reviewed at regular intervals post-implant. Cognitive, educational, personality, anxiety and depression assessments are carried out. The aim of the research is to assess and monitor intellectual and personality profiles of implantees and to evaluate the psychosocial benefits of implantation. Investigation of the possible psychological predictors of audiological outcome for implantees will also be carried out. The subjects will be all cochlear implantees in the Manchester programme. Up to December 1991 29 adults (of whom three are deaf and blind) and two children (aged nine years) have been implanted with multi-channel devices. As the project is on-going, the numbers in the research will continue to increase (with 12 adults per year and a smaller number of children being implanted). In the adult programme subjects have ranged in age from 14 to 80.

Status: Individual research
Date of Research: 1989 - continuing
KEYWORDS: communication aids – for disabled; deafness; hearing aids; hearing impairments; psychological evaluation

9/0732

School of Education, Centre for Educational Guidance and Special Needs, Oxford Road, Manchester M13 9PL
061 275 2000
Conti-Ramsden, G. Dr; Donlan, C. Mr

The National Curriculum and language disorders

Abstract: The project intends to study Year 2 language disordered children who receive educational provision in the Greater Manchester area. The project aims to observe current practice and study the relationship between children's profiles and curricular opportunities.

Status: Sponsored project
Source of Grant: Education and Science Research Council £10,000
Date of Research: 1990-1991
KEYWORDS: communication disorders; National Curriculum; special educational needs; speech handicaps

9/0733

School of Education, Centre for Educational Guidance and Special Needs, Oxford Road, Manchester M13 9PL
061 275 2000
Farrell, P. Mr

The assessment of children with emotional and behaviour difficulties (EBD)

Abstract: This is a case study using qualitative research methods, 16 cases in all. Professionals, parents and children were interviewed from receipt of referral until the conclusion. The main areas of the research are to look at the decision making processes which affect the assessment and intervention of children's referral as having emotional and behavioural difficulties.

Status: Sponsored project
Source of Grant: Manchester University Research Support Fund £7,800
Date of Research: 1991-1992
KEYWORDS: behaviour disorders; child psychiatry; diagnostic assessment; emotional disturbances; special educational needs

9/0734

School of Education, Centre for Educational Guidance and Special Needs, Oxford Road, Manchester M13 9PL

061 275 2000
Farrell, P. Mr
Development of revised training materials for teaching people with severe learning difficulties – Education of the Developmentally Young (EDY)
Abstract: Evaluative research projects will assess the effectiveness of the revised training course in improving trainees' skills and knowledge and to see whether these techniques can be successfully applied in the classroom.
Published Material: 'Teaching people with severe learning difficulties', EDY Trainee's Workbook. Manchester University Press, 1992.; 'Teaching people with severe learning difficulties', EDY Instructor's Handbook. Manchester University Press, 1992.
Status: Sponsored project
Source of Grant: Manchester University Press £10,000
Date of Research: 1990-1992
KEYWORDS: behaviour modification; severe learning difficulties; special educational needs; training

9/0735
School of Education, Centre for Educational Guidance and Special Needs, Oxford Road, Manchester M13 9PL
061 275 2000
Mittler, P. Prof.; *Supervisor:* Mittler, P. Prof.; Farrell, P. Mr; Boreham, N. Dr
Meeting the needs of children with emotional and behavioural disorders
Abstract: This project aims to investigate decision making processes in the assessment of children referred as having emotional and behavioural difficulties. Structured interviews are conducted with referring teachers, educational psychologists, parents and the pupils themselves. The aim is to match decisions made against a hypothetical decision making model. Additional questionnaire research on larger samples will be conducted on: (1) assessment techniques used by particular groups, e.g. educational psychologists; (2) the perceptions of children who are placed in schools and units for children who have emotional and behavioural problems; (3) the range of provision which is currently offered in local authorities in England and Wales.
Status: Sponsored project
Source of Grant: Manchester University Research Support Fund £23,000
Date of Research: 1991-1991
KEYWORDS: behaviour disorders; child psychiatry; diagnostic assessment; emotional disturbances; special educational needs; special schools

9/0736
School of Education, Centre for Educational Guidance and Special Needs, Oxford Road, Manchester M13 9PL
061 275 2000
Mittler, P. Prof.; *Supervisor:* Mittler, P. Prof.
Access to the National Curriculum for pupils with severe and complex learning difficulties
Abstract: Starting with the 'broad, balanced and relevant' curriculum of the Education Reform Act 1988, in depth studies have been carried out with the aim of demonstrating ways in which programmes of study and cross-curricular elements can be integrated with core and foundation subjects to meet the individual needs of children with severe and complex learning difficulties. Statements of attainment for the core subjects have been broken down for Key Stage 1 of the National Curriculum.
Published Material: FAGG, S., AHERNE, P., SKELTON, S. & THORBURN, A. (1990). Entitlement for all in practice: towards a broad, balanced and relevant curriculum for pupils with severe and complex learning difficulties in the 1990s. London: Fulton.; FAGG, S. & SKELTON, S. (1990). Science for All. London: Fulton.; AHERNE, P. & THORBURN, A. (1990). Mathematics for all: an interactive approach within level 1. London: Fulton.; AHERNE, P. & THORBURN, A. (1990). Communication for all: a cross-curricular skill involving interactions between speaker and listener. London: Fulton.; MOUNT, H. & ACKERMAN, D. (1991). Technology for all. London: Fulton.
Status: Sponsored project
Source of Grant: Manchester Education Committee (secondments)
Date of Research: 1989 - continuing
KEYWORDS: curriculum development; National Curriculum; severe learning difficulties; special educational needs

9/0737
School of Education, Centre for Educational Guidance and Special Needs, Oxford Road, Manchester M13 9PL
061 275 2000
Pumfrey, P. Prof.; *Supervisor:* Pumfrey, P. Prof.
The concerns of young people
Abstract: This research concerns the psychosocial development of young persons aged from 11 to 18 years. The aim is to plot the changing concerns of males and females in relation to personal, educational and vocational issues. This is seen as a first step whereby young people can be helped to address their concerns in a variety of educational settings. Data are being collected from a variety of educational establishments using a specially devised checklist covering 15 major aspects of psychosocial development. In the present phase of the study, the current version of the Concerns Checklist is deliberately lengthy. To date, checklists from 3,000 pupils have been obtained. This database is being further extended.
Status: Individual research
Date of Research: 1990 - continuing
KEYWORDS: adolescent attitudes; adolescent development; adolescents; educational attitudes; interests; personality development; social development; vocational interests

9/0738
School of Education, Centre for Educational Guidance and Special Needs, Oxford Road, Manchester M13 9PL
061 275 2000
Piotrowski, J. Mrs; *Supervisor:* Pumfrey, P. Prof.
Integration and responsibility for learning in mainstream primary schools
Abstract: This study is set within the theoretical framework of social learning theory. It comprises a cross-sectional study of about four hundred 6-11 year old boys and girls. Hypotheses concerning the relationships between the independent variables (year group, sex and special educational needs) and the dependent variables (locus of control, belief, self-concept and attendance) will be tested. The study will examine the implications of the results for integration policies and practices in mainstream primary schools.
Status: Individual research
Date of Research: 1991 - continuing
KEYWORDS: locus of control; mainstreaming; primary schools; self-esteem; socialisation; special educational needs

9/0739
School of Education, Centre for Educational Guidance and Special Needs, Oxford Road, Manchester M13 9PL
061 275 2000
Lewis, J. Ms; *Supervisor:* Pumfrey, P. Prof.
Children's reading comprehension: self-image, attainments and attitudes. A cross-cultural study
Abstract: This cross-cultural study is designed to identify changes in pupils' reading comprehension attainments and to consider these in relation to pupils' self-concepts as learners and their attitudes to reading. Samples of about 1,200 pupils will be tested in both Kingston/St Andrews in Jamaica and in an urban local education authority in the north-west of England. Each sample will comprise three year groups with average ages of 9, 11 and 13 years.
Status: Sponsored project
Source of Grant: World Council of Churches; University of Manchester Bursory ORS Award Scheme
Date of Research: 1990-1992
KEYWORDS: comparative education; pupil attitudes; reading achievement; reading comprehension

9/0740
School of Education, Centre for Educational Guidance and Special Needs, Oxford Road, Manchester M13 9PL
061 275 2000
Pumfrey, P. Prof.; Reason, R. Mrs; *Supervisor:* Pumfrey, P. Prof.; Reason, R. Mrs
Specific learning difficulties (dyslexia): challenges and responses
Abstract: This is a national enquiry mounted in 1988 by the Division of Educational and Child Psychology of the British Psychological Society. A team of nine qualified and experienced educational psychologists from eight local education authorities were involved under the co-ordination of Professor Pumfrey and Mrs Reason, the authors

of the final report. The inquiry had two main aims: (1) to provide a wide-ranging account of current theory and research with regard to specific learning difficulties; and (2) to investigate relevant educational and policies and practices. The historical context was reviewed and key theoretical and practical issues considered. A comprehensive review of psychological, psychoeducational and psychomedical theory and research was undertaken. Relevant educational policies and practices were surveyed covering: (a) policies of local education authorities; (b) practices of educational psychologists; and (c) policies of examination boards on dispensations for pupils deemed to have specific learning difficulties. The views of a wide range of voluntary bodies and professional organisations were sought in relation to the concept of specific learning difficulties, identification and assessment, prevention, teaching methods and the provision of resources.
Published Material: PUMFREY, P.D. & REASON, R. (1991). Specific learning difficulties (dyslexia): challenges and responses. Windsor: NFER-Nelson.; PUMFREY, P.D. (1991). 'Introduction: purposes, context and scope of a National Enquiry', Abstracts of the Annual Conference of the British Psychological Society, pp.12, April.; PUMFREY, P.D. (1991). 'Identifying and alleviating specific learning difficulties (dyslexia): Issues and implications for LEA's, professionals and parents', Educational Psychology in Practice, Vol 6, No 4, pp.222-228.; PUMFREY, P.D. & REASON, R. (1989). 'A national enquiry 1989. specific learning difficulties (dyslexia): challenges, responses and recommendations, further details', Division of Educational and Child Psychology Newsletter, No 33, pp.14-16.
Status: Sponsored project
Source of Grant: Division of Educational and Child Psychology of the British; Psychological Society £1,000
Date of Research: 1988-1991
KEYWORDS: dyslexia; learning disabilities; special educational needs

9/0741

School of Education, Centre for Educational Guidance and Special Needs, Oxford Road, Manchester M13 9PL
061 275 2000
Conti-Ramsden, G. Dr
Contingency and breakdown: interactions with language disordered children
Abstract: In this research the linguistic environment of severely language disordered children will be studied. Mother and child; father and child; and sibling interactions will be video-recorded at home, transcribed and analysed. The study aims to identify conversational breakdown in dyadic interaction. The study will ask if fathers experience more conversational breakdown than mothers do with their language disordered child; and what is the possible effect of language impairment on sibling interaction.
Status: Sponsored project
Source of Grant: March of Dimes Birth Defect Foundation, USA £2,394
Date of Research: 1990-1992
KEYWORDS: communication disorders; parent child relationship; sibling relationship; speech handicaps; verbal communication

9/0742

School of Education, Centre for Educational Guidance and Special Needs, Oxford Road, Manchester M13 9PL
061 275 2000
Stockport Metropolitan Borough Council, Education Division, Schools' Psychological Service, Stopford House, Stockport, Cheshire SK1 3XE
061 480 4949
Elliott, C. Dr; Pumfrey, P. Prof.; *Supervisor:* Elliott, C. Dr; Pumfrey, P. Prof.; Tyler, S. Dr
Reading standards in a local education authority: 1976-1991
Abstract: The aim of the research was to identify a representative sample of pupils in National Curriculum Year 3 in a local education authority and to see whether reading standards had changed over a 15 year period. A comparison with American pupils was also undertaken. The relationship between objective test scores and AT2 Reading, as measured by Standard Assessment Tasks at Key Stage 1 was also examined. The pupils were tested on the British Ability Scales Word Reading Test and the Differential Ability Scales; the former was standardised in the United Kingdom in 1976 and the latter in the United States of America in 1989. In addition, information on the pupils' scores on National Curriculum (NC) English Attainment

Target (AT) 2 Reading obtained in the Summer term, 1991, was collected. The sample was selected from all the primary schools in a local education authority. Twelve schools and 209 pupils were involved. The sample of schools selected was based on the proportion of pupils in receipt of free school meals. The tests (BAS & DAS) were administered individually with order of administration and pupil sex counterbalanced. The results include the means and ranges on both BAS and DAS word reading tests and on the Standard Assessment Test AT2 Reading for the total sample, and for children at each of the four levels of reading attainment recorded on the basis of the NC English Standard Assessment Task. The relationship between the three sets of reading tests scores are considered. The results suggest that, in this particular LEA, standards of word reading have not changed significantly since 1976. The sample of pupils did not score as highly as American pupils on the DAS word reading test. An important finding was the high range of both BAS and DAS word reading scores associated with each of the four levels of reading attainment represented by Key Stage 1 Standard Assessment Tasks reading assessments.
Status: Individual research
Date of Research: 1991-1992
KEYWORDS: ability tests; reading achievement; reading tests

9/0743

School of Education, Centre for Educational Guidance and Special Needs, Oxford Road, Manchester M13 9PL
061 275 2000
University of Victoria, Faculty of Education, Victoria V8W 3N4, British Columbia, Canada
Pumfrey, P. Prof.; Ward, J. Prof.; *Supervisor:* Pumfrey, P. Prof.; Ward, J. Prof.
Term of birth and special educational placement: the impact of assessment procedures in a local education authority
Abstract: One source of unplanned systematic bias in the selection of pupils for special educational placement has been the tendence for children born in the final term of the school year to be over-represented among those designated mildly retarded or as having moderate learning difficulties, and educated in special schools. The issue of selection bias relates to a more general problem area in education, the so-called 'relative-age' effect. The present study was undertaken to ascertain whether a relative-age bias is currently evident in children in segregated special education placement and, if it exists, whether it is confined to particular groups. Of particular interest in this study are comparisons with the earlier data obtained in the same local education authority before the implementation of the Education Act 1981 in April, 1983. Data were obtained concerning 1,192 pupils attending 14 special schools in a local education authority. Analyses by 'term of birth' and 'age group' were carried out. At each age level no significant association between term of birth and the expected frequencies was identified. A comparison between term of birth and frequency of special educational placement in 1974 and the present study at three age levels was also carried out. In 1974 the association differed markedly with the expected theoretical frequencies. In the current data, no significant association was identified. The importance of the use of monthly age allowances in the selection procedures is identified as an important factor in this change in pattern over time.
Published Material: PUMFREY, P.D. & WARD, J. (1991). 'Term of birth and special educational placement: the impact of assessment procedures in an LEA', Research in Education, No 46, pp.61-71, November.
Status: Individual research
Date of Research: 1989-1991
KEYWORDS: age grade placement; age groups; birth; pupil placement; special educational needs; special schools

9/0744

School of Education, Centre for Ethnic Studies, Oxford Road, Manchester M13 9PL
061 275 2000
Canterbury Christchurch College of Higher Education, North Holmes Road, Canterbury CT1 1QU
0227 767700
Verma, G. Prof.; Zec, P. Mr
Inter-ethnic relationships in secondary schools
Abstract: Among issues highlighted by the Swann Report (Education for All, HMSO, 1985) was the state of inter-ethnic relationships in schools and the potential impact of school policy and practice on such relationships. The project is investigating the nature of pupil relation-

ships in nine multiethnic schools through the use of surveys, observation and interviews with pupils and staff. The factors influencing these relationships (including school policy and practices) will be assessed and compared.
Status: Sponsored project
Source of Grant: Leverhulme Trust £78,000
Date of Research: 1990-1992
KEYWORDS: cultural interrelationships; ethnic groups; ethnic relations; multiculturalism; school policy; secondary schools

9/0745

School of Education, Centre for Formative Assessment Studies, Oxford Road, Manchester M13 9PL
061 275 2000
Owen, P. Dr; *Supervisor:* Christie, T. Mr
An investigation into the calibration of GCSE grades and National Curriculum levels of attainment at Key Stage 3/4
Abstract: The study was commissioned by the Northern Examinations Association (NEA) as a response to published guidance by the Schools Examinations and Assessment Council (SEAC) on the assessment of Key Stage 4 attainment through GCSE, and the pronouncement by the Secretary of State for Education and Science that examining bodies assessing performance of students at age 16 should be responsible for auditing the standards of pupils at age 14. The development and trial of the assessment material lead to the conclusion that: (1) external examination papers can be designed around statements of attainment (SoA) while retaining the integrity of the subject as a whole; (2) overlapping differentiated papers covering three National Curriculum profile components levels within bands as a viable structure; (3) assessment material suitable for students of the same chronological age but at widely differing levels of attainment can be devised following a set structure and relating to a single theme; (4) mark schemes can be constructed around SoA according to formula and recontextualised for different examining occasions; and (5) there is need for further investigation into calibration focusing on steps from strand to attainment target (AT) and AT to subject score. Data from all levels of specifity are currently being analysed to inform calibration rules.
Status: Sponsored project
Source of Grant: Northern Examinations Association £6,000
Date of Research: 1992-1992
KEYWORDS: assessment; examinations; General Certificate of Secondary Education; moderation – marking; standard assessment tasks

9/0746

School of Education, Centre for Formative Assessment Studies, Oxford Road, Manchester M13 9PL
061 275 2000
Owen, P. Dr; *Supervisor:* Christie, T. Mr
Formative assessments of reading
Abstract: The aim of this research is to develop procedures for the implementation of formative assessments of reading in the classroom and to design and evaluate the effectiveness of Inservice Education of Teachers (INSET) provision for monitoring reading standards. A literacy audit is made to: (i) describe the print environment to which children in Years 1-6 are exposed; and (ii) establish the degree of teachers' awareness of text types and 'readability' levels. This is followed by a survey of the range and type of reading purposes provided for children to inform current practice in relation to task setting. The results of the first phase are: (1) the beginnings of an acquisitions policy for schools; (2) an experimental set of guidelines for text selection; (3) an outline INSET programme for local education authority (LEA) intervention. The second phase of the research involves the development of internal (school) and external (LEA) procedures for monitoring reading performance. This involves the moderation of text selection and task definition within and across schools and the standardisation of teachers' judgements of levels of achievement. The sample is 30 schools (infant, junior and middle) with 15 operating as a lead group and 15 as a follow-up group. Experience with the lead group is encapsulated in trial INSET materials/activities for the follow-up group. The outcome is a long-term rolling programme for LEA based INSET on the teaching and assessment of reading.
Status: Sponsored project
Source of Grant: Leeds Local Education Authority (Phase One) £20,000
Date of Research: 1990-1992

KEYWORDS: assessment; inservice teacher education; reading achievement; school-based assessment

9/0747

School of Education, Centre for Formative Assessment Studies, Oxford Road, Manchester M13 9PL
061 275 2000
Harrison, I. Mr; Dean, D. Mr; *Supervisor:* Christie, T. Mr
Evaluation of National Curriculum Assessment at Key Stage 1 Technology
Abstract: The major aim of the evaluation is to provide evidence to form the basis of an examination of National Curriculum Assessment (NCA) in Technology and to provide formative feedback to the Schools Examination and Assessment Council, the Standard Assessment Tasks development agency, local education authority trainers and moderators on the interpretation of NCA results.
Status: Sponsored project
Source of Grant: School Examinations and Assessment Council £210,000
Date of Research: 1991-1992
KEYWORDS: assessment; National Curriculum; standard assessment tasks; technology education

9/0748

School of Education, Centre for Formative Assessment Studies, Oxford Road, Manchester M13 9PL
061 275 2000
Peers, I. Dr; *Supervisor:* Peers, I. Dr; Ray, R. Dr
The headteachers' role in the implementation of National Curriculum
Abstract: Beginning with a pilot group of three headteachers, a log was kept to establish how a headteacher's time is spent. The activities were coded and time spent on National Curriculum was established. Other headteachers are now being recruited into the project. Fifteen headteachers took part in a structured interview as part of a needs analysis exercise. The role of the headteacher as facilitator of National Curriculum implementation will be defined with a view to producing a report and training materials.
Status: Sponsored project
Source of Grant: Council for Educational Technology £30,000
Date of Research: 1991-1992
KEYWORDS: curriculum development; headteachers; national curriculum; school organisation

9/0749

School of Education, Centre for Formative Assessment Studies, Oxford Road, Manchester M13 9PL
061 275 2000
Owen, P. Dr; *Supervisor:* Christie, T. Mr; Owen, P. Dr
Formative assessment of reading in the primary classroom: the Leeds Reading Project
Abstract: The aim of the Leeds Reading Project is to assist schools to develop procedures for the implementation of formative assessments of reading in the classroom and to design a framework for the development by schools of a guidance manual for monitoring reading standards. The sample comprised 30 schools (infant, junior and middle) with 15 operating as a lead group and 15 as a follow-up group. Experience with the lead group is encapsulated in trial Inservice Education of Teachers (INSET) materials/activities for the follow-up group. The outcome is a long-term rolling programme for local education authority based INSET on the teaching and assessment of reading. A literacy audit was conducted to: (1) describe the print environment to which children in Years 1-6 are exposed; and (2) establish the degree of teachers' awareness of text types and 'readability' levels. This was followed by a classification of the range and type of reading purposes provided for children and an analysis of reading difficulties to inform current practice in relation to task setting and instructional method. Case studies tracking the progress of individual children in relation to types of texts, reading purposes and intervention strategies are currently being undertaken.
Status: Sponsored project
Source of Grant: Leeds Local Education Authority £5,000
Date of Research: 1990-1992
KEYWORDS: assessment; formative evaluation; primary schools; reading; reading achievement; school-based assessment

9/0750

School of Education, Centre for Formative Assessment Studies, Oxford Road, Manchester M13 9PL
061 275 2000
Owen, P. Dr; *Supervisor:* Christie, T. Mr

The hermeneutics of assessment: text interpretation and the assessment of writing

Abstract: The proposition is that the legitimacy of assessment practices can be established only by redefining validity in terms of the methods used to systematise formal procedures of interpretation. The focus of the research is the assessment of writing, with particular reference to the examining procedures pertaining to formative, progressive and criterion-referenced assessments such as those used in the Joint Matriculation Board's scheme of Staged Assessments In Literacy (SAIL). The assessment of writing is taken to be part of a more general process of criticism. Consideration is given to the methodology of criticism from the perspective of different schools of thought in literary theory. Hermeneutics, the study of the effects of signification, is taken to be of central importance in seeking to verify criterion-referenced assessments of writing. Taking the perspective that threats to validity derive from a lack of clarity in interpretative procedures and a failure to establish the legitimacy of readings of texts, it is argued that the quality of writing assessment schemes should be judged on the basis of the appropriacy of the inferential strategies and attributional reasoning used by the reader in relation to the structure of the text. Parallels are thereby drawn between the examining process and the reading process; both being represented as acts of interpretation governed by expectations about genre.

Status: Individual research
Date of Research: 1987-1991
KEYWORDS: critical reading; literary criticism; text structure

9/0751

School of Education, Centre for Formative Assessment Studies, Oxford Road, Manchester M13 9PL
061 275 2000
Boyle, W. Mr; Davies, P. Mr; *Supervisor:* Christie, T. Mr

Development of Key Stage 1 Geography Standard Assessment Tasks

Abstract: The Standard Assessment Tasks are to be developed as manageable for use by teachers and pupils, using resources normally available in primary schools. They are not extended curricular activities but used to provide valid and reliable assessments of pupils against the first four levels of attainment in each of the attainment targets for National Curriculum Geography. They will also enable teachers to identify pupils at the end of Key Stage 1 who are working towards level 1. Trialling of developmental Geography Task material will utilise Postgraduate Certificate of Education/B.Ed. students at three centres – Manchester University, Crewe and Alsager, Bangor Normal College – with more formalised Standard Assessment Tasks trialling in English and Welsh local education authorities during January, May and September 1992.

Status: Sponsored project
Source of Grant: School Examinations and Assessment Council £250,000
Date of Research: 1991-1992
KEYWORDS: assessment; geography education; National Curriculum; standard assessment tasks

9/0752

School of Education, Centre for Formative Assessment Studies, Oxford Road, Manchester M13 9PL
061 275 2000
Harrison, I. Mr; *Supervisor:* Christie, T. Mr

Developing formative teacher assessment – as an example of the management of educational innovations

Abstract: The national assessment system has been designed to serve several functions. It will be formative, summative, evaluative, informative, and helpful in promoting teachers' professional development. The basic proposition of this thesis, (and the major forms of the research) is that strategies to manage the required changes in teachers' assessment practices need to be developed. The 'change' literature, especially that relating to school effectiveness, identifies monitoring pupil progress as one characteristic of effective primary school organisation. However, further analysis of this body of literature reveals the apparent dichotomy between school effectiveness and improvement movements – the critical issue being the focus upon schools as organisations, or upon individuals. The empirical studies address this issue in order to provide evidence to support the development of strategies to promote teachers' formative assessment practice.

Status: Individual research
Date of Research: 1984-1991
KEYWORDS: educational change; formative evaluation; teacher evaluation

9/0753

School of Education, Centre for Physical Education, Oxford Road, Manchester M13 9PL
061 275 2000
Sanderson, P. Dr; *Supervisor:* Murray, C. Dr

Factors influencing attitudes of secondary school pupils to aesthetic aspects of sport and dance

Abstract: The development of aesthetic awareness is stated regularly in the physical education (PE) literature as a major objective, yet little research is available concerning its achievement. Attitude research could provide relevant information. This study investigates the relative influence of age, sex, social class, school type, pupils' and their families' interests in arts and sports. Attitude scales were developed in a pilot study, incorporated into a questionnaire along with measures of the independent variables, and administered to 1,668 pupils, aged between 11 and 16 supplied by 19 schools throughout England. Analyses of variance were employed to ascertain the effect of age, sex, social class and school type, and multiple regression analyses for the influences of pupils' and their families' interests in arts and sports. Results show: no effect of age or attitude; the impact of the sex factor is complex; generally more favourable attitudes are displayed by those from higher social classes, but for ballet, only for girls; family and pupil interests promote positive attitudes but on all scales but two, the influence is small; specialist arts education promotes positive attitudes only for girls towards ballet; extensive sports experience does not apparently promote positive attitudes.

Published Material: SANDERSON, P. (1986). 'Factors influencing attitudes of secondary school pupils towards aesthetic aspects of sport and dance. Dance: the study of dance and the place of dance in society', Proceedings of the VIIIth Commonwealth and International Conference on Sport, Physical Education, Dance, Recreation and Health. Glasgow. London: E. & F.N. Spon. pp.137-143.; SANDERSON, P. (1988). 'A methodology for measuring attitudes to dance', Proceedings of the CORD Conference, Canada, Toronto, pp.161-167.; SANDERSON, P. (1989). 'Secondary school pupils' attitudes to dance', Proceedings of the DACI Conference, London, Roehampton Institute, pp.244-251.

Status: Individual research
Date of Research: 1984-1991
KEYWORDS: aesthetic values; dance; physical education; pupil attitudes; sports

9/0754

School of Education, Centre for Physical Education, Oxford Road, Manchester M13 9PL
061 275 2000
Carroll, R. Mr

Assessment and examinations in physical education

Abstract: Since the 1970s there has been a movement in schools into physical education examinations, first with Certificate of Secondary Education (CSE), later General Certificate of Secondary Education (GCSE) and A-levels. There has also been a similar movement by the further education sector into vocational qualifications such as City and Guilds and BTEC, and physical education has widened into the leisure industries. In addition there have been developments such as Records of Achievement (ROA) and the National Curriculum. The aim of the research has been to monitor such developments. The research has taken the form of a number of small projects and has been accumulative rather than one major project. This information has been collected from all the examination boards on statistics and structure, and from teachers and pupils on the functioning of examinations and assessment methods. Examples of Records of Achievement have also been collected, and questionnaires and interviews carried out. The findings show the dramatic take-up of examinations in physical education. These statistics are continually updated and published. Analysis of GCSE and National Curriculum has been made to show the changes which will have to be undertaken in these examinations.

Published Material: CARROLL, R. (1990). 'Examinations and assessment in physical education'. In: ARMSTRONG, N. (Ed). New Directions in Physical Education. Human Kinetics, pp.137-160.; CARROLL, R. (1990). 'The twain shall meet: GCSE and the National Curriculum', British Journal of Physical Education, Vol 21, No 3,

pp.29-32.; CARROLL, R. & JEPSON, J. (1991). 'ROA versus reports: what the pupils say', British Journal of Physical Education, Vol 22, No 2, pp.19-22.
Status: Individual research
Date of Research: 1986 - continuing
KEYWORDS: assessment; examinations; physical education

9/0755
School of Education, Centre for Physical Education, Oxford Road, Manchester M13 9PL
061 275 2000
Papaioannou, A. Mr; *Supervisor:* MacDonald, A. Mr
Students' motivation in physical education classes perceived to have different goal perspectives
Abstract: Based on recent theories of achievement motivation (Nicholls, 1989; Dweck, 1988) a questionnaire was developed in order to reveal physical education (PE) classes with different achievement orientations. Both exploratory and confirmatory factor analytic results deriving from three studies (in which were involved more than 2,000 students in 80 PE classes) revealed a solution of two learning and three performance oriented factors with good internal consistency. The hypothesized relationships among these five factors and several self-related constructs as well as perceptions of classes' environments were established, suggesting validity for each scale of the questionnaire. Further, only the learning-oriented factors were positive predictors of intrinsic motivation, interest in the lesson, perceived usefulness of the lesson, attitudes towards exercise and intentions for involvement and effort expenditure in the class. Moreover, teachers' differential behaviour towards high and low achievers was negatively related with learning orientation but positively related with performance orientation. In addition, when learning orientation was salient in the class, both high and low perceived competence students were more willing to cooperate with either high or low athletic ability peers and low perceived competence students were less anxious to play with high achievers. In the first two studies both between and within classes, differences were observed regarding perceptions of classes' goals. Results from the third study (394 students in 16 PE classes) revealed that the teacher, the particular class, students' personal orientations in sport, attitudes towards the specific teacher, and attitudes towards PE teachers in general, were significant predictors of perceptions of classes' goals. In a fourth study, eight PE classes were observed revealing that high learning-oriented classes were characterized by an emphasis on teaching issues of technique and students' skill practice, students' cognitive involvement, less game and less students' off-task behaviour. More teachers' orders/directions and students' unpredictable behaviours were recorded in high than in low performance oriented classes. All the results suggest that in order to increase motivation and achievement and to maintain equality in the PE classes, a learning orientation should be adopted. Suggestions for the creation of a learning-oriented climate in the class are offered.
Status: Individual research
Date of Research: 1990-1992
KEYWORDS: achievement; motivation; orientation; physical education

9/0756
School of Education, Oxford Road, Manchester M13 9PL
061 275 2000
Cranfield Institute of Technology, School of Management, Cranfield, Bedfordshire MK45 4DT
0234 751122
Fletcher, C. Dr; Ruddock, R. Mr
Exploring the concept of 'formation' in adult learning
Abstract: The aim of the research is to establish the use of the term 'formation' in Anglophone educational discourse. The sense proposed is an extension of its general usage in European languages towards recognition of self-formation and learning in social systems, drawing upon the understandings of inter-actionism and critical sociology, with illustrations from life histories and observations in schools, adult and health education. A four-process model with a working diagram has been evolved, i.e. formation — deformation — reformation — transformation.
Published Material: FLETCHER, C. & RUDDOCK, R. (1986). 'Key concepts for an alternative approach to adult education', Convergence, Vol XIX, No 2.; RUDDOCK, R. (1980). 'Beyond Vocational Education', International Conference Report, Nottingham University.
Status: Individual research

Date of Research: 1985-1991
KEYWORDS: adult learning; andragogy; attitude formation

9/0757
School of Education, English Language Teaching Unit, Oxford Road, Manchester M13 9PL
061 275 2000
O'Brien, T. Ms; *Supervisor:* Jordan, R. Mr
A comparison of linguistic performance in continuous assessment and unseen examination writing at undergraduate level
Abstract: The research aims to discover whether there is any basis to students' intuitive feeling that their linguistic performance deteriorates in examination conditions. Continuous assessment essays and examination questions written on the same areas and within a very short space of time of each other are being analysed in ignorance of the grades already awarded. Scope is limited to undergraduates in the Department of Psychology, writing in four special subject areas. The results of the analysis of linguistic performance up to and including discourse level, will eventually be compared with the grades that have been awarded.
Published Material: O'BRIEN, T. (1987). 'Writing for continuous assessment or examinations: a comparison of style'. In: Proceedings of the Selmous Conference, 1985. ELT Docs. Oxford: Pergamon Press.; O'BRIEN, T. (1987). 'Predictive items in student writing'. In: Written language (published papers of the Annual Conference of the British Association of Applied Linguistics, Reading University, 1986). London: CILT/BAAL.
Status: Individual research
Date of Research: 1982-1992
KEYWORDS: examinations; linguistic performance; undergraduate students; writing – composition; writing evaluation

9/0758
School of Education, Oxford Road, Manchester M13 9PL
061 275 2000
London University, Institute of Education, 20 Bedford Way, London WC1H 0AL
071 580 1122
Hodkinson, S. Mr; Thomas, L. Dr
The Economic Awareness Teacher Training Programme (EcATT)
Abstract: The Economic Awareness Teacher Training Programme (EcATT) aims to promote and monitor the development and implementation of economic awareness programmes in schools, colleges and local education authorities (LEAs).
Published Material: HODKINSON, S.R. & THOMAS, L.M. (Eds). (1988). 'What is economic awareness?', Economic Awareness Journal, Vol 1, No 1, pp.5-11, September.
Status: Sponsored project
Source of Grant: BP £30,000; Banking Info Serv £30,000; DTI £107,000; Unilever £10,000; Esmee Fairbairn Charit Trust £33,300; Univ Grants Comm £60,000
Date of Research: 1986 - continuing
KEYWORDS: curriculum development; economics education; enterprise education; teacher education

9/0759
School of Education, Oxford Road, Manchester M13 9PL
061 275 2000
Universiti Sains Malaysia, Pusat Pongajian, Ilmu Pendidikan, 11800 Nimden, Penang, Malaysia
Ahmed, S. Mr; *Supervisor:* Reid, D. Dr
Teacher appraisal in Malaysia: towards a strategy
Abstract: Current trends in Malaysian secondary education are towards a national system of teacher appraisal. What has Malaysia to learn from the British model, and what features of the Malaysian teacher population demand special attention? A survey of 1,200 teachers in Malaysia is being used to determine the attitudes and opinions of secondary school teachers to appraisal. A strategy for appraisal will be developed on the basis of the survey.
Status: Individual research
Date of Research: 1989 - continuing
KEYWORDS: Malaysians; secondary schools; teacher evaluation

Medical Research Council

9/0760
> Cognitive Development Unit, 17 Gordon Street, London
> WC1H OAL
> 071 387 4692
> Das Gupta, P. Dr

The development of causal reasoning
Abstract: The main focus of this research has been the development of causal understanding in the preschool years. The relationship between intelligence and causal reasoning has been explored with particular attention to causal inferences made by children with learning difficulties and autism. Although children with learning difficulties solve causal reasoning tasks correctly, they show considerable delay. This is also true of the autistic sample. Normal 4-year-olds are significantly better at causal reasoning tasks than children with learning difficulties whose mental age is below 5 years. The major thrust of the research has been on exploring the way preschool children make causal inferences. An attempt has been made to distinguish knowledge from inference and one strand of the research explores how knowledge of familiar transformations may be accessed to make appropriate inferences. Variations of the task and how these improve inferences have also been explored.
Published Material: DAS GUPTA, P. & BRYANT, P. (1989). 'Young childrens' causal inferences', Child Development, Vol 60, pp.1138-1146.
Status: Sponsored project
Source of Grant: Medical Research Council
Date of Research: 1988-1992
KEYWORDS: cognitive development; learning disabilities; preschool children

MENCAP National Centre

9/0761
> 123 Golden Lane, London EC1Y ORT
> 071 454 0454
> Further Education Unit, Spring Gardens, Citadel Place,
> Tinworth Street, London SE11 5EH
> 071 962 1280
> Griffiths, M. Mr; *Supervisor:* Hood, P. Ms

Post-school learning opportunities for people with profound intellectual and multiple impairments
Abstract: The aim of the project is to identify existing practice and the current perceptions of learning opportunities for adults with profound intellectual impairment who are likely to have multiple disabilities and to produce a curriculum framework for these learners. The project will use the following methods: (a) a nationwide survey by questionnaire; (b) selection from the above and otherwise by a multi-disciplinary working group who will: (1) identify core learning experiences; (2) generate a curriculum framework; (3) produce and test learning material.
Status: Sponsored project
Source of Grant: Department of Health £12,500; Further Education Unit £ 12,500
Date of Research: 1991 - continuing
KEYWORDS: access to education; adult basic education; adult learning; intelligence differences; multiple disabilities; severe learning difficulties

National Children's Bureau

9/0762
> 8 Wakley Street, London EC1V 7QE
> 071 278 9441
> Ames, J. Ms; *Supervisor:* Berridge, D. Dr

A study of the long-term foster care of children and young people with severe learning difficulties
Abstract: Barnardo's has been closely involved in establishing schemes to enable young people with a range of problems to live with families. This research programme focuses on the work of one such scheme, the Professional Fostering Project, based in Barnardo's north-west division in Liverpool. This project establishes and supports foster placements for around 70 young people with severe learning disabilities. Given the complex dynamics of foster-care placements, the general question addressed in the research is: how can Barnardo's fostering project staff secure and sustain successful foster placements for children and young people with severe learning disabilities? In addition to a broad evaluation of the current work of the fostering project, two aspects of the work are being examined in detail: 1) the experiences and feelings of the natural children of foster carers about sharing their homes with young people fostered through the project; 2) the impact of placing a second child from the project upon the life of a household.
Status: Sponsored project
Source of Grant: Barnardo's
Date of Research: 1990-1992
KEYWORDS: disabilities; foster care; foster children; foster family; severe learning difficulties; voluntary agencies

9/0763
> 8 Wakley Street, London EC1V 7QE
> 071 278 9441
> Grimshaw, R. Dr; *Supervisor:* Berridge, D. Dr

A comparative, evaluative study of residential special schools for children with emotional and behavioural difficulties
Abstract: This is an 18 month research study to investigate the processes by which children are defined as having emotional and behavioural difficulties (EBD) and being in need of residential experience. This will be approached with particular regard to the overlap between education and social service responsibilities. The work will analyze the treatment methods, social and educational functioning and impact on children of a sample of EBD residential schools. This will be located within the context of what is known to be good practice in residential child care. The researcher will be observing the schools for significant periods, noting daily activities and interviewing adults and pupils.
Status: Sponsored project
Source of Grant: The Nuffield Foundation £75,000; The Healey Group and the National Children's Home
Date of Research: 1991-1992
KEYWORDS: behaviour disorders; emotional disturbances; special educational needs; special schools

National Foundation for Educational Research

9/0764
> The Mere, Upton Park, Slough, Berkshire SL1 2DQ
> 0753 574123
> NFER Northern Office, Langwith College, University of
> York, Haslington, York YO1 5DD
> 0904 430000
> Harland, J. Dr; Kinder, K. Ms; *Supervisor:* Bradley, J. Dr

Patterns of local education authority inservice education and training of teachers (INSET) organisation
Abstract: Recent changes in inservice education and training of teachers (INSET) funding arrangements have resulted in local education authorities (LEAs) adopting a wide range of strategies for the planning and delivery of professional development activities. The proposed research would mapped the major types and patterns of LEA INSET organisation with the intent of developing guidelines on good practice. A national survey of INSET coordinators was followed by case study work in five LEAs exhibiting different types of INSET policy and practice. The views of LEA and school staff was sought on the benefits, problems and effectiveness of the varying approaches to INSET. A report on the project will be produced in 1993.
Status: Sponsored project
Source of Grant: National Foundation for Educational Research £64,000
Date of Research: 1991 - continuing
KEYWORDS: educational administration; inservice teacher education; Local Education Authorities

9/0765

The Mere, Upton Park, Slough SL1 2DQ

0753 574123

Smith, P. Dr; Drysdale, D. Dr; Lindley, P. Dr

The initial assessment of youth trainees with special needs: improving access to National Vocational Qualifications (NVQs) at level 1

Abstract: The project provided a 'module' or source document to assist Surrey Managing Agents in conducting the initial assessment of youth trainees with special needs (particularly Special Needs B, i.e. these with moderate learning difficulties). The module covered the range of assessments which might be needed and how to use the results of these in selecting appropriate NVQ Level 1 training opportunities in Surrey for such trainees. A survey of NVQ Level 1 provision in the Surrey area (including the nature of courses, entry requirements, etc.) was carried out. Potential assessment devices were reviewed for their suitability with this trainee group. The information drawn from these sources was then documented in a form which is practical for use by Managing Agents.

Status: Sponsored project

Source of Grant: Surrey Training and Enterprise Council

Date of Research: 1991-1991

KEYWORDS: assessment; moderate learning difficulties; National Vocational Qualifications; special educational needs; trainees; youth opportunities

9/0766

The Mere, Upton Park, Slough SL1 2DQ

0753 574123

Jones, G. Mrs; Richardson, J. Mrs; *Supervisor:* Whetton, C. Mr

Key stage 1 non-mandatory standard assessment tasks

Abstract: Standard assessment tasks have been developed to assess pupils' attainment in National Curriculum history at key stage 1. Collectively, they will help teachers to make their end-of-key stage assessments of pupils in the three attainment targets for history. There will be no statutory requirement for schools to use the standard assessment task(s). Separate standard assessment task(s) have been developed for England and Wales, and Welsh standard assessment task(s) are both English and Welsh medium. The standard assessment task(s) are simple, straightforward and manageable for use by teachers and pupils, using resources normally available in primary schools. They provide valid and reliable assessment of pupils against levels 1-3 of each attainment target, and are appropriate for use with the widest possible ability range of pupils, including those with special educational needs. The duration of the contract was from 1st October 1991 until 31st December 1992. In the first phase of development, informal trials took place in 20 schools in England and Wales and standard assessment task materials were produced cooperatively with teachers. In the second phase from January to March 1992 materials were formally trialled in a further 60 schools in England and Wales. Standard assessment task materials will be available for use in schools from early 1993.

Status: Sponsored project

Source of Grant: School Examinations and Assessment Council £213,286

Date of Research: 1991-1992

KEYWORDS: attainment tests; history studies; National Curriculum; primary education; standard assessment tasks

9/0767

The Mere, Upton Park, Slough SL1 2DQ

0753 574123

Harris, S. Mrs; *Supervisor:* Whetton, C. Mr

Information technology: software in primary schools

Abstract: Information technology (IT) capability is one of the attainment targets of Technology in the National Curriculum. Within the non-statutory guidance provided by the National Curriculum Council, five strands of information technology capability are identified: Communicating information; handling information; modelling; measurement and control; and applications and effects. The first four strands are related to types of software, the fifth is not. The research aims to investigate the range of software in use in primary schools to support the first four strands of IT capability. In addition, the following areas will be investigated: the provision of hardware within schools; sources used by schools to obtain software; and the range of support services offered by local education authorities (LEAs). Data will be collected from the following sources: a) interviews with a small number of LEA IT advisers; b) a questionnaire survey of all LEA IT advisers in England and Wales; c) a questionnaire survey of a sample of 400 schools within the primary sector in England and Wales.

Published Material: A report detailing the projects findings, is available from NFER.

Status: Sponsored project

Source of Grant: National Foundation for Educational Research £25,000

Date of Research: 1991-1992

KEYWORDS: computer software; information technology; local education authorities; National Curriculum; primary schools; technology education

9/0768

The Mere, Upton Park, Slough SL1 2DQ

0753 574123

Smith, P. Dr; *Supervisor:* Whetton, C. Mr

Development of a spatial ability handbook

Abstract: This project was developed as a response to the belief that the education process does not currently attract sufficient attention to the development and use of spatial skills. It aims to produce a handbook for those educators who want to develop the spatial thinking and capitalise on the spatial strengths of their pupils, but who are not sure how best to do so. The handbook will be in two parts. The first will describe the necessary background ideas in a non-technical way and will also include guidance on self-assessment and the role of parents and the home environment in developing spatial skills. The second part will include a wide range of teaching ideas and resource information, divided into four sections dealing with spatial memory, spatial thinking skills, spatial skills within specific subject areas and spatial presentation/study techniques. Some of the sub-sections within Part II will be written by external consultants.

Published Material: SMITH, P. & TRAYNELIS, J.F. (1991). 'Keeping memory in shape', Physics Education, Vol 26, No 5, pp.262.

Status: Sponsored project

Source of Grant: Macfarlane Smith Bequest £45,502

Date of Research: 1991 - continuing

KEYWORDS: memory; perceptual development; spatial ability

9/0769

The Mere, Upton Park, Slough SL1 2DQ

0753 574123

Maychell, K. Ms; *Supervisor:* Bradley, J. Dr; Maychell, K. Ms

Evaluation and monitoring at local education authority level

Abstract: Local education authorities (LEAs) have a statutory duty to inspect schools. The Department of Education and Science require LEAs to define their policy for inspection, including details of procedures, reporting and roles of LEA personnel. School development plans, classroom observation, performance indicators, and the use of information technology to assist analysis and reporting all have a place within the national picture, along with school self-evaluation by heads and teachers. The research has three main aims: 1) to gather detailed information on the operation of a range of LEA monitoring and evaluation strategies; 2) to carry out a national survey of LEAs and schools that would provide useful information when developing evaluation and monitoring strategies; 3) to provide practical information and guidance to assist LEAs in the future development of good practice in this area of their work. The first phase of the research involves case study investigation in six LEAs. These reflect the range of strategies currently being used or planned by LEAs. Each case study involves interviews with headteachers and LEA officers as well as examination of LEA and school documentation. The second phase comprises two questionnaire surveys – one to all LEAs and the other to a representative sample of 500 schools. The purpose of these is to provide a national picture on all aspects of policy and practice with regard to inspection, evaluation and monitoring and to describe the successes, problems and issues emerging for LEAs and schools. A final report will be produced at the end of the project.

Status: Sponsored project

Source of Grant: National Foundation for Educational Research

Date of Research: 1991 - continuing

KEYWORDS: evaluation; inspection; local education authorities; monitoring; schools

9/0770

The Mere, Upton Park, Slough SL1 2DQ

0753 574123

Sizmur, S. Mr; Harris, S. Mrs; *Supervisor:* Ruddock, G. Dr
Primary science assessments
Abstract: Assessment materials for 'Science Assessment Modules'
were developed to assist teachers to make teacher assessment of
science for pupils work at key stages 1 and 2 of the National
Curriculum. They include worksheets and practical tasks, and cover
all of the new statements of attainment in science at levels 1 to 5.
They were published in December 1992 by NFER/Nelson.
Status: Sponsored project
Source of Grant: NFER/Nelson; Thomas Nelson U.K. Ltd
Date of Research: 1989-1992
*KEYWORDS: assessment; National Curriculum; primary education;
science education*

9/0771
The Mere, Upton Park, Slough SL1 2DQ
0753 574123
Smith, P. Dr; *Supervisor:* Whetton, C. Mr
The analysis and use of spatial ability in educational contexts
Abstract: This project has developed two paper and pencil tests of
spatial memory, suitable for use as educational and psychological
research tools. One uses a drawing response and is scored for correctness of shapes and proportions. The other uses multiple choice then
shape-arranging on a grid and is scored for correctness of shape,
position and orientation. An experimental computerised test, which
runs on IBM compatibles, has also been developed. Evidence has
been gathered to support the U.S. research literature which suggests
that spatial memory is the key component of spatial ability. Differential validity studies have been carried out with the paper and pencil
tests by testing large samples of 8, 12 and 16 year olds, then comparing their scores with performance measures in various school subjects. The tests are being prepared for publication by the NFER as
research tools.
Published Material: SMITH, P. (1991). 'Spatial Ability', Topic, 5.
Status: Sponsored project
Source of Grant: MacFarlane Smith Bequest
Date of Research: 1989 - continuing
KEYWORDS: assessment; memory; spatial ability

9/0772
The Mere, Upton Park, Slough SL1 2DQ
0753 574123
Sainsbury, M. Dr; Christophers, U. Mrs; Ashby, J. Mr;
Clarke, J. Mrs; *Supervisor:* Whetton, C. Mr
**Development of standard assessment tasks for pupils at the
end of the first key stage of the National Curriculum**
Abstract: A consortium consisting of NFER, Bishop Grosseteste
College, NFER-Nelson and two local education authorities developed standard assessment tasks and associated INSET (Inservice
Education and Training of Teachers) material. The standard assessment tasks provided valid, reliable assessments of attainment targets
in mathematics, English (or Welsh) language and science, appropriate to seven year-olds. Issues such as the production of evidence for
moderation, bias, special educational needs and the assessment of low
and high achieving children were all addressed. INSET material was
developed in order to ensure that national assessment and standard
assessment tasks were fully understood. The project was extended to
cover the production of standard assessment tasks for the first two
years of full national assessment (1991, 1992) and evaluations of its
use in both these years.
Status: Sponsored project
Source of Grant: School Examinations and Assessment Council
Date of Research: 1989-1992
*KEYWORDS: assessment; attainment tests; educational testing; in-
service teacher education; primary education; standard assessment
tasks*

9/0773
The Mere, Upton Park, Slough SL1 2DQ
0753 574123
Jamison, J. Mr; Froud, K. Ms; *Supervisor:* Stoney, S. Dr
**Evaluation of the Health Education Authority's 'My Body'
Integration Project**
Abstract: The My Body Project is a Health Education Authority
project designed for use in primary schools, and aims to teach pupils
about the workings of the human body and to enable them to explore
issues related to health education and to develop decision-making

skills. The aim of the evaluation is to assess the impact of the My
Body Project and identify a range of good practice at each level of
delivery of the project material. A range of qualitative research
methods will be employed within a broad case-study structure. Data
will be collected from 6 local authorities and 24 schools (4 within
each). Within each of the case-study authorities, one school will be
selected as a key school in which more detailed work will be undertaken. The My Body Project Team will be observed as they provide
training and support. A final report will be submitted to the Health
Education Authority which documents the main evaluation findings
and identifies models and instances of good practice.
Status: Sponsored project
Source of Grant: Health Education Authority £23,279
Date of Research: 1992-1992
KEYWORDS: health education; human body; primary education

9/0774
The Mere, Upton Park, Slough SL1 2DQ
0753 574123
Macneil, M. Dr; *Supervisor:* Stoney, S. Dr
The Gaelic Language Development Project
Abstract: As part of an expanding research programme, the Gaelic
College (SMO) commissioned an investigation into the methods and
effectiveness of school-based Gaelic language development, with the
aims of identifying good practice and strategies for enhancing the
current level of effectiveness. The scope of the research covers the
development of Gaelic within both first and second language frameworks, and as a medium for the delivery of the curriculum in the
primary and secondary sectors. Three surveys are planned to cover:
(1) all Scottish secondary schools which teach Gaelic as first and/or
second language; (2) all Scottish primary schools which teach Gaelic
as first and/or second language; and (3) all Gaelic medium and
bilingual medium units. Additional information will be obtained from
case-study work, currently underway in a sample of the kinds of
schools described above. This element of the research will focus on
teaching methods, resources, and the needs of children in the Gaelic
and bilingual units, and be undertaken primarily through classroom
observation and detailed interviews with key personnel.
Status: Sponsored project
Source of Grant: The Gaelic Medium College of Further Education
in conjunction with the Scottish Inter-Authority Standing Group for
Gaelic £ 19,743
Date of Research: 1992-1992
*KEYWORDS: bilingualism; Celtic languages; Gaelic; language
maintenance; language of instruction; mother tongue; second languages*

9/0775
The Mere, Upton Park, Slough SL1 2DQ
0753 574123
Tomlins, B. Dr; *Supervisor:* Stoney, S. Dr
Reorganising further education: the tertiary option
Abstract: Since the first tertiary college was established at Exeter in
1970, demographic changes and constraints on local authority spending have encouraged other authorities to consider reorganising educational provision for 16-19 year olds along tertiary lines, and there
are now more than 70 tertiary colleges. Much of the literature on
tertiary systems is based on personal accounts of tertiary reorganisation and provision. The project seeks to provide a broad based and
objective assessment of the tertiary option. It aims to explore the
variety of approaches to tertiary reorganisation to be found in different local authorities and to provide a fund of data and set of guidelines
on the management of tertiary systems. Interviews have been conducted with senior local education authority officers and college
principals in fifteen tertiary authorities, and more detailed case study
work carried out in seven authorities. Approaches and experiences in
all other tertiary and non-tertiary authorities are being explored by
means of questionnaires. A literature review and final report of the
project have now been published.
Published Material: TOMLINS, B. & MILES, J. (1991). Reorganising post-16 education: the tertiary option. Slough: NFER
Status: Sponsored project
Source of Grant: National Foundation for Educational Research
£129,000
Date of Research: 1990-1991
*KEYWORDS: further education; sixteen to nineteen education; ter-
tiary colleges; tertiary education*

9/0776

The Mere, Upton Park, Slough SL1 2DQ
0753 574123
Taylor, M. Miss; Bagley, C. Dr; *Supervisor:* Stoney, S. Dr

Multicultural education after ERA: concerns and challenges for the 1990s

Abstract: The values underpinning the Education Reform Act 1988 (ERA) and the structures and targets set by the implementation of the National Curriculum and Local Management of Schools (LMS) have raised new issues and challenges in the realisation of equal opportunities in the translation of multicultural antiracist policies into practice. This project has sought to be diagnostic and responsive by establishing current concerns among local education authorities (LEAs) and identifying promising developmental strategies in relation to institutional, training and curricular issues. The research has had three phases: a national questionnaire, interviews, and thematic case studies. Initially the project identified LEA concerns, constraints and challenges for multicultural antiracist education in post-ERA developments. As a result, five themes formed the focus of subsequent research: (1) the implementation of Section 11 changes; (2) Training and Enterprise Councils (TECs) and the Ethnic Minority Grant; (3) equal opportunities in governor training; (4) the issues of cultural diversity in Religious Education and the Standing Advisory Councils on Religious Education (SACREs); and (5) managing quality and equality – the permeation of multicultural antiracist education in school inspections. Research dissemination has occurred during the project and included ongoing publications, seminars, conference presentations and talks to various audiences.
Published Material: TAYLOR, M.J. (1992). Multicultural Antiracist Education After ERA: Concerns, Constraints and Challences. NFER.; TAYLOR, M.J. (1992). Equality after ERA? NFER.; BAGLEY, C.A. (1992). Back to the Future: Section 11 of the Local Government Act 1966: Local Education Authorities and Multicultural/Antiracist Education. NFER.; BAGLEY, C.A. (1993). An Enterprising Initiative? Training and Enterprising Councils and the Ethnic Minority Grant. NFER.; Publications on Equal Opportunities in governor training; Race, culture and ethnic diversity in inspection; and an overview of the project are due in Spring/Summer 1993.
Status: Sponsored project
Source of Grant: National Foundation for Educational Research £154,649
Date of Research: 1991 - continuing
KEYWORDS: *antiracism education; Education Reform Act 1988; educational planning; equal education; local education authorities; multicultural education*

9/0777

The Mere, Upton Park, Slough SL1 2DQ
0753 574123
Sims, D. Mr; *Supervisor:* Stoney, S. Dr

Evaluation of the Construction Industry Training Board's curriculum centre initiative

Abstract: The Construction Industry Training Board (CITB) is establishing up to 50 Curriculum Centres around the country with the aim of: (1) establishing 'construction' as a genuine context for cross-curricular learning; (2) providing practical facilities which will simulate real-work situations; and (3) providing a platform for a continuing dialogue between education and industry. The National Foundation for Educational Research is providing advice and devising materials for the self-evaluation of the initiative by the CITB and the Centres themselves. It will also conduct periodic evaluative reviews of the self-evaluation outputs and of data collected independently by the Foundation. The evaluation is proceeding in a series of phases. A preliminary phase (when a self-evaluation strategy and materials were devised) was completed in August 1991. The first phase of the main evaluation was completed in February 1992 and resulted in a report, published by the CITB, on the progress and outcomes of the initiative to date. During the remainder of 1992 further work (Phase 2) was conducted and resulted in an evaluation up-date report, a report on the employers' contribution to the initiative and an evaluation handbook. During Phase 3, in 1993, a series of evaluation workshops are being organised in order to disseminate the evaluation findings and to promote local self-evaluation.
Status: Sponsored project
Source of Grant: Construction Industry Training Board £10,680
Date of Research: 1991 - continuing
KEYWORDS: *construction – process; construction industry; cross curricular approach; industry-education relationship; vocational education*

9/0778

The Mere, Upton Park, Slough SL1 2DQ
0753 574123
Tomlins, B. Dr; Harris, S. Mrs; *Supervisor:* Stoney, S. Dr

Evaluation of English Nature's School Grants Scheme

Abstract: Nature areas in the school grounds can assist in the teaching of required knowledge, skills and understanding and cultivate desirable attitudes towards the natural environment and living things. They can be used as a resource for aspects of science and geography in the National Curriculum. The Nature Conservancy Council (NCC) now English Nature (EN) has since 1985, awarded grants to assist schools in the setting up of nature areas. The aims of the research project are to: (1) assess the extent to which grant-aided nature areas have raised both the quality of environmental education and children's levels of awareness of conservation issues; (2) investigate how far the School Grants Scheme has stimulated interest in the creation of nature areas; (3) examine the range of strategies employed by schools for the management of nature areas; (4) investigate the range and extent of support provided to schools for nature areas by local education authorities (LEAs); (5) assess the extent to which educational institutions are aware of the School Grants Scheme and whether the activities of other organisations are seen to be in competition; and (6) investigate cost/benefit relationships in schools where grants have been awarded. Questionnaires have been circulated to 750 schools which have applied to English Nature for a grant and 400 schools which have not, both samples including primary and secondary schools. A separate questionnaire has been sent to all LEA Advisers with responsibility for environmental education. The research also includes 40 school visits, 20 of these constituting case-studies.
Status: Sponsored project
Source of Grant: English Nature £35,035
Date of Research: 1991-1992
KEYWORDS: *educational facilities; environmental education; gardens; grants; natural resources; physical environment*

9/0779

The Mere, Upton Park, Slough SL1 2DQ
0753 574123
Macneil, M. Dr; *Supervisor:* Stoney, S. Dr

Evaluation of the licensed teacher route to Qualified Teacher Status

Abstract: The evaluation of the new licensed teacher route to Qualified Teacher Status (QTS) has aimed to provide a detailed overview of the structure and operation of this route and to monitor its effects and implications at local education authority (LEA), training institution and school level. The evaluation has been conducted mainly through case-study and survey methods, with some background documentary analysis. Three surveys have been conducted during 1991, designed to investigate the experience of schools in implementing this route, with questionnaires for licensed teachers, their headteachers, and mentors. A further two surveys conducted in 1992, were designed to explore the roles of local education authorities and institutions of higher education (IHEs). The case-study work has focused on interviews with the key personnel involved in the training of licensed teachers, within a wide representation of different ways of implementing the licensed teachers route. A final report was presented to the Department for Education in Autumn 1992 and dissemination opportunities are being considered.
Status: Sponsored project
Source of Grant: Department for Education £116,866
Date of Research: 1990-1992
KEYWORDS: *licensed teachers; mentors; programme evaluation; school-based inservice education; student teachers; teacher education*

9/0780

The Mere, Upton Park, Slough SL1 2DQ
0753 574123
Maychell, K. Ms; *Supervisor:* Bradley, J. Dr

Multi-professional support for young adults with special needs

Abstract: The need for cooperation among various services involved in supporting young people with special needs has long been recognised. Yet relatively few examples may be cited of cooperative action to meet the needs of these young people in their transition from school or college to adult life. The study aimed to: (1) identify relevant models of inter-professional working; (2) ascertain how they relate to desired objectives in terms of supporting young people as they progress from school or college to continuing education and training;

and (3) highlight the lessons for practice elsewhere. It also aimed to make an assessment of the type of training that would facilitate the introduction and development of cooperative working relationships. The first phase involved identifying those local authorities where cooperative working was being planned or already in existence in order to gain information on their development and operation. On the basis of the information gathered, a number of initiatives were selected for detailed investigation in phase two, involving extended field visits to each location. The final report documents the range of initiatives studied, analyses these for their relevance to the practice of cooperative working in other locations, and provides information to guide future policy and practice.

Published Material: MAYCHELL, K. & BRADLEY, J. (1991). Preparing for partnership: multi-agency support for special needs. Slough: NFER.

Status: Sponsored project

Source of Grant: National Foundation for Educational Research £78,000

Date of Research: 1988-1991

KEYWORDS: school leavers; services; special educational needs; transition education; youth

9/0781

The Mere, Upton Park, Slough SL1 2DQ
0753 574123
Fletcher-Campbell, F. Miss; *Supervisor:* Bradley, J. Dr

Local education authority policy and practices in supporting special education in provision in schools

Abstract: The research aims to: (1) document and analyse local education authorities (LEAs) current policies for special educational needs (SEN); (2) examine the nature of special support as policy is realised in practice; (3) identify Inservice Education of Teachers (INSET) needs and provision; (4) investigate the effect of the Education Reform Act 1988 on SEN provision; and (5) consider the ways in which LEAs monitor and evaluate their SEN provision. In the initial phase, all LEAs in England and Wales were invited to submit any documentation relating to SEN. In the second phase, a small number of LEAs are being studied in depth . Issues being focused on are: structure and management of support services; assessment; monitoring and evaluation; INSET and resourcing. The final report will be published in 1993.

Status: Sponsored project

Source of Grant: National Foundation for Educational Research £150,000

Date of Research: 1990-1992

KEYWORDS: educational planning; educational policy; educational practices; local education authorities; special educational needs

9/0782

The Mere, Upton Park, Slough SL1 2DQ
0753 574123
Earley, P. Mr; Harland, J. Dr; Kinder, K. Ms; *Supervisor:* Earley, P. Mr

The role of the local education authority in the professional development of new teachers

Abstract: Awareness of the potentially powerful role of local education authorities (LEAs) and schools in programmes of professional development for new teachers has been heightened following the introduction of the new training routes to Qualified Teacher Status (QTS), the proposed changes in the nature and content of initial teacher training courses and the abolition of probation. A growing number of LEAs and schools are offering induction and training programmes designed to ensure the continuing development of the professional skills and competencies currently required of new teachers, not least in the delivery of the National Curriculum. This 18-month study is employing both survey and case study research methods to investigate the role of the LEAs in the extension of initial training. It intends to analyse the professional development programmes offered to new teachers and seek perceptions of the range of professionals involved on their effects and outcomes. The main aim of the research is to contribute to the improvement of the quality of support offered to new teachers. More specifically, the research has three aims: (i) to gather a broad base of information from all LEAs on their structures and procedures for training and supporting new teachers; (ii) to collect more detailed information from selected authorities and schools on professional development programmes in practice; and (iii) to ascertain the perceptions of a wide range of providers and practitioners on the benefits, problems and overall

effectiveness of the various approaches to the induction and development of new teachers. The research will begin with a series of exploratory interviews in several LEAs to gather initial perspectives from key training personnel on the main issues relating to the induction and professional development of new teachers. The material collected from these interviews, complemented by the findings from recent research studies, will be used to develop a questionnaire which will be sent to each authority. An interim report based on the questionnaire findings will be available by autumn 1992. In the next phase of the research, interviews will be held with LEA personnel to clarify and expand upon the questionnaire data. About six LEAs will then be chosen for case study investigation. In each case study location, interviews will be held with relevant LEA personnel and all documentation relating to the professional development of new teachers will be collected. A sample of schools will be selected to represent the primary and secondary sectors as well as grant-maintained schools within each LEA. The work in the schools will involve interviews with headteachers, INSET coordinators, staff with responsibility for the guidance and support of new teachers, and the new teachers themselves. It will, of course, be important to ensure that teachers following different routes to QTS are included in the sample. The particular emphasis during the case study phase will be on collecting more detailed information on the content and delivery of training and support programmes in the selected LEAs and schools, whilst also focusing on emerging issues. A final report, drawing on both the survey and case study evidence will be produced at the end of the project.

Published Material: EARLEY, P. (1992). Beyond initial teacher training: induction and the role of the LEA. Slough: NFER.

Status: Sponsored project

Source of Grant: National Foundation for Educational Research £135,000

Date of Research: 1992 - continuing

KEYWORDS: local education authorities; preservice teacher education; probationary teachers; teacher development; teacher education; teacher induction

9/0783

The Mere, Upton Park, Slough SL1 2DQ
0753 574123
Sainsbury, M. Dr; Ashby, J. Mr; Sizmur, S. Mr;
Christophers, U. Mrs; Clarke, J. Mrs; *Supervisor:*
Whetton, C. Mr

Development of standard assessment tasks in the core subjects for pupils at the end of the first key stage of the National Curriculum for 1993

Abstract: A consortium led by the National Foundation for Educational Research (NFER) developed standard assessment tasks to provide valid, reliable assessments of attainment targets in English (or Welsh), mathematics and science, appropriate to seven-year-olds. Issues such as classroom manageability, comparability of judgements, bias, special educational needs and low and high achieving children were all addressed. The project led to the production of standard assessment tasks for use at key stage 1 in 1993, the third year of operation of National Curriculum assessment.

Status: Sponsored project

Source of Grant: School Examinations and Assessment Council

Date of Research: 1992-1992

KEYWORDS: assessment; English studies; mathematics achievement; National Curriculum; primary education; science education; standard assessment tasks; Welsh studies

9/0784

The Mere, Upton Park, Slough SL1 2DQ
0753 574123
Whetton, C. Mr; White, J. Ms; *Supervisor:* Whetton, C. Mr; White, J. Ms

Standard tests in English for pupils at the end of the second key stages of the National Curriculum in 1994, 1995, 1996

Abstract: The purpose of this work is to provide assessments of individual pupils' attainments in National Currciulum English at the end of key stage 2 (Year 6, typical age of pupils, 11 years). The assessments will be made in relation to the attainment targets English 2 (reading), English 3, 4 and 5 (writing, spelling and handwriting) in the statutory curriculum order for English. It is envisaged that the tests will be predominantly written and timed. Developmental work leading up to the first full test of year 6 pupils in England and Wales in 1994 includes a pre-test carried out in December 1992 in about 70 schools. A range of materials and approaches were tried in the pre-test, from which a selection will be made for use in a national 2% pilot to be undertaken in May 1993. In advance of the pilot, the sponsoring agency, the School Examinations and Assessment Council, will be hosting several regional conferences to familiarise participating schools and teachers with the procedures to be adopted in the pilot test. During the initial developmental stage of the work, the research team at the National Foundation for Educational Research worked intensively with teacher consultants, acting as material writers. Members of this panel will reconvene in successive stages of the project to revise and adapt material. Draft materials are scrutinised by an internally appointed vetting panel, while the work as a whole is under regular supervision by the committees of the School Examinations and Assessment Council

Status: Sponsored project
Source of Grant: School Examinations and Assessment Council
Date of Research: 1992 - continuing
KEYWORDS: *assessment; English studies; National Curriculum; reading achievement; standard assessment tasks; writing skills*

9/0785

The Mere, Upton Park, Slough SL1 2DQ
0753 574123
Sainsbury, M. Dr; Ashby, J. Mr; Sizmur, S. Mr; Hargreaves, E. Ms; Evans, M. Ms; *Supervisor:* Whetton, C. Mr
Development of standard assessment tasks in mathematics and science for pupils at the end of the first key stage of the National Curriculum for 1994-1996
Abstract: A research team at the National Foundation for Educational Research (NFER) is developing standard assessment tasks in mathematics and science for pupils at the end of the first key stage of the National Curriculum. The tasks will provide valid, reliable assessments of attainment targets and be appropriate to seven-year-old children. Issues such as classroom manageability, comparability of judgements, bias and special educational needs will all be addressed. The tasks for each year will be monitored in operation and a commentary produced. The project will lead to the production of assessment materials to be used nationally in 1994, 1995 and 1996.
Status: Sponsored project
Source of Grant: School Examinations and Assessment Council
Date of Research: 1992 - continuing
KEYWORDS: *assessment; mathematics achievement; National Curriculum; primary education; science education; standard assessment tasks*

9/0786

The Mere, Upton Park, Slough SL1 2DQ
0753 574123
Smith, P. Dr; *Supervisor:* Whetton, C. Mr
Standardisation of the LARR short-form test
Abstract: The project has standardised a new version of the Canadian 'Linguistic Awareness in Reading Readiness (LARR) test' for use with British children at the start of formal schooling. The new version, 'The LARR short-form', will be published by NFER-Nelson. The standardisation involved administering the test to nearly 500 nursery children and over 2,300 children in reception classes in schools throughout England and Wales during October 1992. The test was found to be too demanding for the nursery children but appropriate for the reception sample. Norms were created for the age range from 4 years 0 months to 5 years 3 months. The results, together with administration instructions and guidance on interpreting the test scores, were written for the test manual. In parallel with the national standardisation, the test was also given to all reception age pupils in Wandsworth schools as part of the Local Education Authorities baseline assessment. The National Foundation for Educational Research (NFER) then carried out a local standardisation for Wandsworth.
Published Material: 'LARR Short-Form', (1993). NFER-Nelson. (in press).
Status: Sponsored project
Source of Grant: NFER-Nelson; Wandsworth Local Education Authority
Date of Research: 1992 - continuing
KEYWORDS: *infant school pupils; nursery school pupils; reading; reading readiness; reception classes; tests*

9/0787

The Mere, Upton Park, Slough SL1 2DQ
0753 574123
Hagues, N. Mr; Courtenay, D. Ms
Item bank testing
Abstract: An item bank is a large collection of pre-trialled questions, a small proportion of which can be selected to construct a test to the user's specification and to a pre-determined level of difficulty. Because these tests are custom-made, the test is unique and hence a very high level of security can be guaranteed. The National Foundation for Educational Research maintains item banks in verbal reasoning, non-verbal reasoning, mathematics and English, and these have been used in recent years with pupils aged 8 to 14 for attainment testing, monitoring, screening and selection.
Date of Research: 1983 - continuing
KEYWORDS: *assessment; item banks; screening tests; test items; test selection; tests*

9/0788

The Mere, Upton Park, Slough SL1 2DQ
0753 574123
Dickson, P. Mr; Lee, B. Ms; *Supervisor:* Dickson, P. Mr
Local education authority support for continuity and progression in the 5-16 curriculum
Abstract: The introduction of the National Curriculum and associated assessment has provided a new context for the activities which have been traditionally undertaken to ensure curriculum continuity, within school and on transfer between school phases. The research aims to investigate continuity from two different perspectives: the support provided by local education authorities (LEAs) and the measures taken at school level. Through the use of six case studies, based on 'families' of schools, and a questionnaire survey of LEAs, information will be sought on: (1) strategies for promoting continuity in different LEA contexts; (2) collaboration and arrangements for transfer between school phases; and (3) methods used for promoting continuity within schools and subject areas. The findings of the research will be disseminated through workshops for participants and a project report.
Status: Sponsored project
Source of Grant: National Foundation for Educational Research £129,359
Date of Research: 1992 - continuing
KEYWORDS: *curriculum development; developmental continuity; local education authorities; National Curriculum; primary secondary education*

9/0789

The Mere, Upton Park, Slough SL1 2DQ
0753 574123
Foxman, D. Mr; Mason, K. Mr; *Supervisor:* Foxman, D. Mr; Mason, K. Mr
Teacher assessment in the National Curriculum core subjects: Mathematics, Science and English
Abstract: In September 1989, following the Education Reform Act 1988, The National Curriculum was introduced in the core subjects of mathematics, science and English in all schools in England and Wales for the the cohort of pupils in year 1. A year later saw the implementation of the National Curriculum in the core subjects in year 3; the first year of Key Stage 2. National Curriculum assessment arrangements include teacher assessment (TA) based on pupils' classroom work over the course of each key stage, as well as statutory national assessments. Over the next two or three years, teachers of pupils at Key Stage 2 will be required to address a number of issues in their assessment practices, and to form and implement appropriate school policy. The broad aims of this project are to study the various facets of teacher assessment in the three National Curriculum core subjects, as carried out by teachers in Key Stage 1 and 2 classrooms, and to identify good practice. The particular aims are to: (1) investigate if and how teachers use cross-curricular or topic work to make assessments in more than one subject; (2) determine the purposes to which teachers put the results of their assessments; (3) examine the range of procedures for recording pupil attainment; and (4) make recommendations on the professional development of teachers in teacher assessment practices, and the role of the local education authority (LEA) in this regard. After an initial phase spent reviewing LEA and national documents on assessment, and contacting LEAs and primary schools, the project is to be carried out through a number of case studies of teachers. The case studies, which will take place

during the school year 1992/93, will involve the observation of the classroom work of teachers of years, 1, 2, 3, and 4. A final report, to be written toward the end of the project, will point up good practice in teacher assessment, and make recommendations on the professional development of teachers in this area. A programme of dissemination will take place toward the end of the project within the LEAs participating in the research.
Status: Sponsored project
Source of Grant: National Foundation for Educational Research £120,000
Date of Research: 1992 - continuing
KEYWORDS: assessment; core curriculum; English studies; mathematics education; National Curriculum; science education

9/0790
The Mere, Upton Park, Slough SL1 2DQ
0753 574123
Sharp, C. Miss; Baginsky, M. Mrs; Maychell, K. Ms; Walton, I. Ms; *Supervisor:* Bradley, J. Dr; Sharp, C. Miss
An evaluation of educational materials on HIV and AIDS for nurses
Abstract: Human Immuno Virus/Acquired Immune Deficiency Syndrome (HIV/AIDS) presents major challenges to nurses and nurse educators. This reserch is aiming to evaluate the educational materials currently available and to discover the needs for new information presented in different formats. Methods include a mapping exercise (carried out by Anglia Polytechnic University (formerly Anglia Polytechnic)), a literature review, and interviews with nursing staff, students, nurse teachers and representatives from regional health authorities in six English regions.
Status: Sponsored project
Source of Grant: Department of Health
Date of Research: 1992-1992
KEYWORDS: Acquired Immune Deficiency Syndrome; educational materials; information needs; nurse education; nurses

9/0791
The Mere, Upton Park, Slough SL1 2DQ
0753 574123
Stoney, S. Dr; Saunders, L. Ms; Morris, M. Ms; *Supervisor:* Stoney, S. Dr; Saunders, L. Ms
National evaluation of Compacts
Abstract: The Compacts initiative, funded by the Department of Employment from 1988, has the main aim of raising the attainment of young people in education, training and work by guaranteeing a job with training for all young people aged 14 and over who meet their personal goals. Each Compact is a contract between employers, schools, colleges, training providers and young people, where each party makes a commitment to achieve agreed goals such as: (a) schools, colleges and training providers work with young people to improve levels of achievement; (b) young people make a commitment to attend school regularly and to complete their course work on time and to the best of their ability; (c) employers agree to provide jobs with training, or training leading to a job, for young people who achieve their goals. There are currently over 50 Compacts in existence based in Urban Programme Authority areas in England and priority areas in Scotland and Wales. The National Foundation for Educational Research (NFER) has been commissioned by the Department of Employment to carry out a national evaluation in England and Wales, the overall aim of which is to establish whether the Compacts initiative is being effective in meeting its stated objectives with respect to students, schools and employers. The evaluation will take place over the period 1990-1994 and has a nation-wide focus. Although individual schemes are not being evaluated, most Compacts are being asked to provide information for the study in some way by assisting with one or more of the following: (a) an annual questionnaire to key decision-makers (Compact directors and Compact school staff), to collect factual information on the management and performance of Compacts; (b) a series of questionnaires to key participants (Compact students, parents, employers and training providers) to gather a range of viewpoints of the programme's impact; (c) questionnaires to students participating in Compacts during the four years to look at the longer-term outcomes of the programme for young people's decisions, qualifications and destinations; (d) questionnaires to non-Compact students and schools to provide comparisons. Additionally, 'case studies' in four contrasting travel to work areas are under way which will identify key issues and collect in depth data concerning the operational effectiveness of Compacts in differ-

ent kinds of labour markets. Annual reports will be produced with an overview report in 1994.
Published Material: MORRIS, M., SAUNDERS, L. & SCHAGEN, I. (1992). The impact of Compact 1991 together with a summary. Sheffield: Department of Employment.; SAUNDERS, L., MORRIS, M. & FROUD, K. (1992). 'Compact: the contributions and views of employers. Sheffield: Department of Employment.; MORRIS, M., SCHAGEN, I. & STRADLING, B. (1992). 'Compact' 'Technical Report 1991', Sheffield: Department of Employment.; SAUNDERS, L. & MORRIS, M. et al (1992). Motivating young people for success in the inner cities. Sheffield: Department of Employment.
Status: Sponsored project
Source of Grant: Department of Employment £447,633
Date of Research: 1990 - continuing
KEYWORDS: cooperative education; school to work transition; vocational education; work education relationship

9/0792
The Mere, Upton Park, Slough SL1 2DQ
0753 574123
Foxman, D. Mr; *Supervisor:* Burstall, C. Dr
Second International Assessment of Educational Progress (IAEP2)
Abstract: In this research the National Foundation for Educational Research (NFER) acted as the agency for the participation of England and Wales in a second International Assessment of Educational Progress (IAEP) coordinated by the Centre for the Assessment of Educational Progress in the United States. The first IAEP, of 13 year-olds in mathematics and science in 6 countries (12 educational systems), was carried out in February 1988. The aim of reporting within a year was successfully achieved at both international and national levels early in 1989. The reports aroused a good deal of interest and about 20 countries participated in the second assessment. In IAEP2 a second age group, 9 year-olds, was involved. There were also some questions on geography and an exploratory administration of practical items in mathematics and science for 13 year-olds. (England did not take part in the geography test.) Three international reports were published: one on the written tests of mathematics; a second on the written tests of science; and the third on the results of the practical assessment. A national report on the findings in England was produced by the NFER.
Status: Sponsored project
Source of Grant: Department of Education and Science £22,500
Date of Research: 1989-1992
KEYWORDS: academic achievement; assessment; geography education; international educational exchange; mathematics education; science education

9/0793
The Mere, Upton Park, Slough SL1 2DQ
0753 574123
Jamison, J. Mr; *Supervisor:* Stradling, R. Dr
Survey of health education policies in schools for the Health Education Authority
Abstract: Over the last decade there has been a growing recognition of the strategic and influential role which schools can play in the health education of the population and, as a result, a wide range of centrally funded initiatives has been implemented. A growing number of schools now have health education coordinators and written health education policies. The research aims to evaluate the range, form and quality of written health education policies in schools, investigate the impact of policy on the organisation of the curriculum and classroom practice in schools, review the processes of policy implementation, and identify examples of good practice. A questionnaire will be sent to a sample of 900 schools in England, stratified to ensure adequate representation of different types of school and different regions and education authorities. From the responses, a selection will be made of 100 schools for more intensive qualitative research. A final report will be submitted to the Health Education Authority documenting the main findings and identifying examples of good practice suitable for adoption by other schools.
Status: Sponsored project
Source of Grant: Health Education Authority
Date of Research: 1992-1992
KEYWORDS: health education; school policy; sex education

9/0794

The Mere, Upton Park, Slough SL1 2DQ
0753 574123
Jamison, J. Mr; *Supervisor:* Stradling, R. Dr

Developing European awareness: the role of local education authorities and schools in the 1990s

Abstract: As part of the preparation for the creation of a single European Market by the end of 1992, the Council of the European Community passed a resolution in May 1988 aimed at promoting and strengthening the European dimension at all levels of education. Although a growing number of local education authorities (LEAs) and schools are now taking steps to incorporate the European dimension, research evidence on established practice and new developments is still limited. The purpose of the evaluation therefore is to update and extend the database on LEA and school-based initiatives on European Awareness, and to evaluate the impact of established LEA programmes on school practice. In addition, the project will determine how LEAs are supporting these activities. Finally, the project will identify successful practices and establish which initiatives are appropriate to different educational phases, ability ranges and school contexts. Methods employed will include a survey of all LEAs in England and Wales by questionnaire, concerning their policy documents and initiatives on European Awareness, and a national survey of primary and secondary schools regarding the incorporation of European Awareness into the curriculum. These will be accompanied by case study research in schools in selected LEAs. The research team plans to produce a written report on activities at LEA level and a handbook for schools and advisory staff with supporting materials which could be used for staff development.
Status: Sponsored project
Source of Grant: National Foundation for Educational Research £100,000
Date of Research: 1993 - continuing
KEYWORDS: *curriculum development; European community; European studies; local educational authorities*

9/0795

The Mere, Upton Park, Slough SL1 2DQ
0753 574123
Sims, D. Mr; Harland, J. Dr; Tomlins, B. Dr; Twitchin, R. Mr; *Supervisor:* Stoney, S. Dr

Evaluation of the second year of the Training Credits pilot: three case studies

Abstract: This evaluation sought to explore any changes in attitudes, culture and practice amongst young people, school staff, careers staff, employers and training providers which may have occurred as a result of the introduction of the Training Credits (TC) pilot and since the first round of evaluations. The project has focused on the extent to which the original aims of the Training Credits pilots have been achieved, how much progress has been made in overcoming difficulties identified from the first-year evaluations and making practical recommendations to assist in the further development of the pilots. The three case studies employed the following research methods: postal questionnaires; telephone and face-to-face interviews; and group discussions. Key groups of people targeted in each area and the number in each questionnaire sample were as follows: Year 11 students (200), Year 12 students (50), young people (200 TC-users; up to 50 non-TC users) and training providers (25). Interviews were conducted with up to 20 operational personnel such as Training and Enterprise Councils (TECs), local education authority (LEA) and Careers Service staff and 100 employers (50 TC-users; 50 non-TC users). Broadly, findings indicate that TECs are making strenuous efforts to promote the Training Credits pilot but are finding that outcomes and impact are being seriously constrained by the current recession. The main outcomes from the project will be three case-study reports and one overall national report.
Status: Sponsored project
Source of Grant: Department of Employment £87,064
Date of Research: 1992 - continuing
KEYWORDS: *credits; school to work transition; training; Training and Enterprise Councils; vocational education; vocational guidance*

9/0796

The Mere, Upton Park, Slough SL1 2DQ
0753 574123
Tomlins, B. Dr; *Supervisor:* Stoney, S. Dr

Environmental education: a directory and review of research

Abstract: There is currently a widespread and diverse research community in the field of environmental education research but little in the way of formal networking to aid communication between groups. This project aims to collate a directory of members of the research community listing basic information such as name, address and area of interest/activity. This would facilitate communication and a more coordinated approach to the development of research in environmental education. A form will be devised to collect this information and will be circulated to all relevant institutions. A review of existing and, as far as possible, ongoing environmental education research will be conducted in order to identify the main themes and findings. Gaps in the research would also be highlighted. The directory and review will initially cover the United Kingdom but could be expanded to include a representative range of European institutions. It will focus on research involving the teaching of 5-18 year-olds and will be produced in a format which facilitates updating. A directory and review of environmental education research in the United Kingdom will be produced.
Status: Sponsored project
Source of Grant: National Foundation for Educational Research £10,770
Date of Research: 1993 - continuing
KEYWORDS: *directories; educational research; environmental education*

9/0797

The Mere, Upton Park, Slough SL1 2DQ
0753 574123
Christophers, U. Mrs; *Supervisor:* Stoney, S. Dr; Whetton, C. Mr

Developing tools to measure the outcomes of guidance

Abstract: The aim of the project is to produce valid and reliable instruments for measuring the outcomes of vocational or careers guidance. Vocational guidance is increasingly seen as a requirement in a range of effective employment strategies. Guidance is one of a number of services offered through Training and Enterprise Councils and subject to systematic evaluation. Currently, methods of evaluating guidance rely on measures of customer satisfaction and/or numbers of clients seen. The new instruments are intended to provide alternative and more objective measures. The present-day theoretical formulation of careers guidance provided the starting point for this new approach. The process of guidance involves assisting clients themselves to achieve as good a match as may be possible between their interests and skills and their job aspirations, bearing in mind the opportunities open to them. An additional aim is to foster the transition skills which will stand clients in good stead in their job search now and at other times in their lives. Four areas, therefore, are frequently addressed in guidance: Opportunity Awareness; Self Awareness; Decision Making Skills; and Transition Skills. The new instrument probes the extent to which learning in these areas has occurred and how well this persists. A national trial involving 1,500 clients has been undertaken and clients will be followed up after two weeks and after three months to discover how the guidance affected their job search and employment status. An additional aim of the project is to produce a diagnostic tool, which, when used during guidance, will assist workers in pinpointing a client's particular areas of difficulty. It is likely that the instrument devised will be published. However, this will not be certain for some time. The title of the new instrument is the Measure of Guidance Outcomes (MGO).
Status: Sponsored project
Source of Grant: Department of Employment £77,933
Date of Research: 1992 - continuing
KEYWORDS: *career counselling; evaluation methods; guidance objectives; measurement techniques; vocational guidance*

9/0798

The Mere, Upton Park, Slough SL1 2DQ
0753 574123
Taylor, M. Miss; *Supervisor:* Stoney, S. Dr

Values education in Europe

Abstract: This project, the first collaborative exercise of the Consortium of Institutes of Development and Research in Education in Europe/Values Education in Europe Programme (CIDREE/VEEP), has been commissioned by United Nations Educational Scientific and Cultural Organisation (UNESCO). It has three parts: (1) To provide guidelines for Values Education in Europe (this work is being undertaken by Ian Barr, Chair of CIDREE/VEEP at the Scottish Consultative Council on the Curriculum, Dundee, Scotland); (2) To provide an annotated bibliography on Values Education in Europe from

1985-1992; (3) To provide an overview of the state of the art in Values Education in Europe (2) and (3) are being coordinated and undertaken by National Foundation for Educational Research (NFER). The objectives of the project are to coordinate and facilitate the exchange of information and to build a foundation for undertaking further collaborative projects on a European scale. Almost 30 countries are participating in the bibliography (up to 20 entries per country) and survey. Values Education has different emphases and scope in the education systems of Europe and the overview will seek to establish common ground, and review historical and ideological backgrounds, aims and objectives, aspects of provision, theoretical influences, current concerns, teacher training, teaching methods, curriculum development research and evaluation and aspects of informal education relating to Values Education. There are likely to be three publications, corresponding to the three aspects of the project: guidelines, annotated bibliography and overview of state of the art. These were launched by UNESCO at an international conference in Norway in September 1993.
Status: Sponsored project
Source of Grant: UNESCO £4,500; CIDREE £1,000; National Foundation for Educational Research £2,770
Date of Research: 1992 - continuing
KEYWORDS: Europe; international educational exchange; values education

9/0799
   The Mere, Upton Park, Slough SL1 2DQ
   0753 574123
   Stradling, R. Dr; Schagen, I. Dr; Saunders, L. Ms;
   Supervisor: Stradling, R. Dr
Quantitative analysis for self-evaluation by schools
Abstract: This project will pilot test a self-evaluation package for schools which will help them to make use of the data they have to collect for the Department for Education for school management and evaluation purposes. The package will include access to a multilevel model which will be more sensitive than league tables of results. It will have a value-added element using tests and teacher assessments of student intake, and guidance to school managers on how to interpret the information.
Status: Sponsored project
Source of Grant: National Foundation for Educational Research £21,000
Date of Research: 1993 - continuing
KEYWORDS: institutional evaluation; measurement technique; model; performance indicators; self evaluation – groups

9/0800
   The Mere, Upton Park, Slough SL1 2DQ
   0753 574123
   Brunel University, Department of Education and Design, Runnymede Campus, Cooper's Hill Lane, Egham TW20 OJZ
   0784 431341
   Ruddock, G. Dr; Harris, D. Prof.; Tomlins, B. Dr; Brooks, G. Dr; Putman, K. Mr; *Supervisor:* Whetton, C. Mr; Foxman, D. Mr
Evaluation of National Curriculum Assessment at Key Stage Three in mathematics, science, English and technology
Abstract: The project will evaluate the first nationwide National Curriculum assessment of fourteen year olds in science and mathematics in 1992, and in English and technology in 1993. The results of these will be surveyed and the procedures used will be evaluated. The focus of evaluation is the validity and reliability of the results. Three elements make up the study: a statistical survey of results; case studies of schools' management of the assessment process; and review of the assessment materials used.
Published Material: RUDDOCK, G., TOMLINS, B. et al. Teacher assessment in mathematics and science at key stage 3. London: SEAC.
Status: Sponsored project
Source of Grant: School Examinations and Assessment Council £569,000
Date of Research: 1991 - continuing
KEYWORDS: assessment; English studies; evaluation; mathematics education; National Curriculum; science education; secondary education; technology education

9/0801
   Welsh Office, 39 St James Crescent, Abertawe, Swansea SA1 6DR
   0792 459800
   Powell, R. Mr; Lewis, G. Mr; Jones, Ll. Ms; Lewis, T. Mr
Development of standard assessment tasks in Welsh for key stage 3 of the National Curriculum
Abstract: This is an extension of the original contract for Welsh key stage 3 standard assessment tasks which ran from July 1989 to August 1991. The requirement is for the creation of standard assessment tasks to assess the range of attainment from Level 1 to Level 10 on both the Welsh and Welsh Second Language programmes contained in the Statutory Orders. Following pilots in 1991 and 1992 the first statutory assessment will be held in 1993. The standard assessment tasks comprise a long task for assessment of oracy and reading through oral response to be administrated in the classroom over three months, and written tests for assessment of writing and reading through written response.
Status: Sponsored project
Source of Grant: School Examinations and Assessment Council £700,000
Date of Research: 1991 - continuing
KEYWORDS: assessment; attainment tests; National Curriculum; standard assessment tasks; Welsh studies

National Institute for Careers Education and Counselling

9/0802
   Sheraton House, Castle Park, Cambridge CB3 OAX
   0223 460277
   Watts, A. Mr; Hawthorn, R. Ms; *Supervisor:* Watts, A. Mr
Occupational profiles of vocational counsellors
Abstract: This is one of a series of studies of various occupations, designed to build into a European Directory of Occupational Profiles. Its objectives are to: 1) identify the main occupational groups involved in education and/or careers guidance work with young people and/or adults; 2) analyse the main tasks carried out by each of them; and 3) examine the training provided for them.
Published Material: WATTS, A.G. (1992). Occupational profiles of vocational counsellors in the European Community: a Synthesis Report, Berlin: CEDEFOP.; HAWTHORN, R. & BUTCHER, V. (1992). Guidance workers in the UK: their work and training, Cambridge: CRAC/Hobsons.
Status: Sponsored project
Source of Grant: European Centre for the Development of Vocational Training; (CEDEFOP) £49,000
Date of Research: 1991-1992
KEYWORDS: career counselling; careers teachers; occupations; teaching profession; training; vocational education teachers; vocational guidance

9/0803
   Sheraton House, Castle Park, Cambridge CB3 OAX
   0223 460277
   Watts, A. Mr; Hawthorn, R. Ms
Guidance aspects of the Enterprise in Higher Education programme
Abstract: The aim of the project is to examine ways in which institutions involved in the Training, Enterprise and Education Division's EHE (Enterprise in Higher Education) programme can help students to establish linkages between the competencies and skills they are developing and their possible futures. The project is preparing case studies of examples of existing practice in five institutions, feeding back the case studies to the institutions concerned in ways which will be likely to foster further development work, and disseminating examples of good or interesting practice to other institutions involved in the EHE initiative. The case studies will be made available in published form as part of a document including recommendations for policy and guidelines for practice.
Published Material: WATTS, A.G. & HAWTHORN, R. (1992). Careers educationa and the curriculum in higher education, Cambridge: CRAC/Hobsons.
Status: Sponsored project

Source of Grant: National Institute for Careers Education and Counselleng
Date of Research: 1990-1992
KEYWORDS: *career choice; career counselling; career development; enterprise education; higher education; vocational guidance; work education relationship*

9/0804

Sheraton House, Castle Park, Cambridge CB3 0AX
0223 460277
Policy Studies Institute, 100 Park Village Street, London
NW1 3SR
071 387 2171
Killeen, J. Mr; White, M. Mr; *Supervisor:* Watts, A. Mr
Reviewing the economic benefits of careers guidance
Abstract: The project aims to develop conceptual models for evaluating the economic benefits of careers guidance, and to review the existing research literature on the effects of careers guidance in the light of these models.
Published Material: KILLEEN, J., WHITE, M. & WATTS, G. (1992). The economic value of careers guidance, London: Policy Studies Institute.; 'Economic benefits of careers guidance', (1992). NICEC Briefing. Cambridge: NICEC.
Status: Sponsored project
Source of Grant: Department of Employment £15,960
Date of Research: 1991-1991
KEYWORDS: *career counselling; cost effectiveness; evaluation; vocational guidance*

Nene College

9/0805

Faculty of Education, Health and Science, Moulton Park,
Northampton NN2 7AL
0604 715000
Silcock, P. Dr
Monitoring the implementation of the National Curriculum in primary schools
Abstract: The research aims to evaluate changes brought about in schools by the National Curriculum from the point of view of practitioners. The method of investigation used so far comprises an in-depth open-ended interview of a headteacher and at least one class teacher, in each school visited, involved with implementing and assessing pupils within the English National Curriculum. The only constraint set is that both positive and negative evaluates have to be elicited: i.e. practitioners are required, in so far as they are able, to describe the positive benefits accruing to the school through the introduction of the National Curriculum and any drawbacks they have discovered. This approach allows an interviewer to focus on changes occurring at the time of interview, since an important feature of the National Curriculum is its ongoing revision and development. A small number of schools are sampled, representing a cross section of primary schools within a single county. The outcome of the research is the publication of related articles. This is ongoing research. The project for 1991-1992 includes a case study of a school implementing change. The researcher will work with the staff of the school and investigate through observation, informal discussion, and interview.
Published Material: SILCOCK, P.J. (1990). 'Implementing the National Curriculum': some teachers' dilemmas', Education 3-13, Vol 18, No 3, pp.3-10.; SILCOCK, P.J. (1992). 'The reflective practitioner in the year of the SAT', Education 3-13, Vol 20, No 1, pp.3-9.; SILCOCK, P.J. (1992). 'Primary school teacher-time and the National Curriculum: managing the impossible?', British Journal of Education Studies, Vol XXXX, No 2, pp.163-173.
Status: Individual research
Date of Research: 1990 - continuing
KEYWORDS: *educational change; National Curriculum; primary schools*

9/0806

Faculty of Education, Health and Science, Moulton Park,
Northampton NN2 7AL
0604 715000

Warwick University, Faculty of Educational Studies,
Coventry CV4 7AL
0203 523523
Duncan, D. Ms; *Supervisor:* Burgess, R. Prof.
Mature women entrants to teaching: an analysis of the process of adjustment to the student role in the four year B. Ed. course
Abstract: The research study has two distinct aims: (1) To investigate mature candidates' previous career and work experiences and the factors leading to a decision to pursue a career in the teaching profession; (2) To identify the problems, resource needs and learning needs of mature students in the first year of the B. Ed. course. A case study approach will be used to chart the socialisation process of 26 mature women into the student role in the first year of the B. Ed. course (1991-92). The research will be conducted using mainly qualitative research methods. Much of the data will be gathered via tape recorded interviews using a 'structured conversation' approach. Interviews will be conducted at key points of their first year (before entry; once in each of the three terms; and at the end of the post-examination period of the first year) in order to identify the changes which have occurred in their behaviour, and in their perceptions of the student role in the first year of a teacher training course.
Status: Individual research
Date of Research: 1989 - continuing
KEYWORDS: *mature students; preservice teacher education; student behaviour; student teacher attitudes; student teachers; women's education*

New College Durham

9/0807

Department of Education and Administration, Neville's
Cross Centre, Darlington Road, Neville's Cross, Durham
DH1 4SY
091 384 7325
Beverton, S. Dr
Teachers' perceptions of oracy and information technology project
Abstract: The aim of the research is to investigate teachers' perceptions of oracy and information technology (IT) in a number of local authorities. These two subject areas, although separate in themselves, were chosen because of two common factors: (1) both are 'new' in the sense of having acquired new status in the National Curriculum with little historical background as subjects *per se*; (2) the National Curriculum demands that all teachers address these themes. The research aims to survey a wide range of perceptions to reflect the current position of oracy and IT in the curriculum in primary and secondary schools. A questionnaire has been designed and developed to be used in a pilot survey. Appropriate modifications will then be made before the questionnaire is distributed to schools in a number of local authorities. It is envisaged that a variety of perceptions in both areas will be revealed and that these might have implications for classroom practice. After analysis, the questionnaires will be followed up by more in-depth studies of particular teachers and schools, with the intention of revealing the nature of the relationship between perceptions and practice. The results will determine the current status of oracy and IT in terms of perceptions and practice. The dissemination of these results will inform and assist teachers' practice and also enable authorities to plan inservice education of teachers (INSET) courses appropriately.
Status: Sponsored project
Source of Grant: New College Durham
Date of Research: 1990 - continuing
KEYWORDS: *information technology; National Curriculum; oracy; teacher attitudes*

University of Wales College of Cardiff

9/0808

School of Education, Senghennydd Road, Cardiff CF2 4AG
0222 874000

Nicosia General Hospital, School of Nursing, Nicosia,
Cyprus Antoniou, M. Miss; *Supervisor:* Nolan, R. Dr
The implications for nursing education in Cyprus commensurate with joining the European Community: a problem study
Abstract: The research aims to explore the changes required for nursing education in Cyprus commensurate with the EC directive re: nursing to be implemented in 1993. The study will compare nurse education in Cyprus with the changes in the United Kingdom in the implementation of Project 2000 and the need to conform to the EC directives as Cyprus has applied to join the European Community.
Status: Individual research
Date of Research: 1991 - continuing
KEYWORDS: *change; Cyprus; nurse education*

North Cheshire College

9/0809
Padgate Campus, Fearnhead Lane, Warrington WA2 0DB
0925 814343
Lancaster University, Department of Management Learning, Cartmel College, Bailrigg LA1 4YW
0524 65201
Lloyd, P. Mr; *Supervisor:* Davies, J. Mrs
Assessment of work experience in relation to management learning
Abstract: The aim of this research is to investigate and evaluate the validity of supervised work experience as a degree course component that: (1) Enables students to acquire knowledge and skills; (2) Enables students to complement the college based learning prior to the placement period; (3) Enables students to develop appropriate and meaningful learning strategies following work experience periods; (4) Facilitates course development through 'wash back' on existing learning programmes; (5) Promotes staff development in terms of updating current practices within the industrial/commercial environment; (6) Enhances host awareness and sympathy towards participation in supervised work experience programmes; (7) Accurately assesses student development and performance in terms of: (a) personal/social skills; and (b) academic/cognitive skills. A further aim is to test the above through a process of primary and secondary research into short- and long-term supervised work experience programmes in several institutions offering a range of vocational related courses. It also aims to establish the theoretical concepts via primary and secondary sources of the notions underpinning: (1) experiential learning; (2) education and training; (3) teaching and learning methods; (4) assessment and profiling; and (5) competence and competition.
Status: Individual research
Date of Research: 1991 - continuing
KEYWORDS: *industry-higher education relationship; management studies; placement; work experience*

9/0810
Padgate Campus, Fearnhead Lane, Warrington WA2 0DB
0925 814343
Manchester University, School of Education, Oxford Road, Manchester M13 9PL
061 275 2000
Walters, M. Mrs; *Supervisor:* Nichol, B. Mr
To investigate whether there is a difference in the support/counselling provision needed for the mature student compared to younger students
Abstract: Mature students, by re-entering education, have already made major choices. These choices may have been influenced or precipitated by major life incidents, some traumatic, e.g. redundancy, divorce, bereavement, failure or loss. Students have tremendous commitment to making a success of their venture; they may or may not, however, have come to terms with their changing circumstances, self-image, aspirations and present role. Their positive drive and energy, therefore, may be dissipated by their underlying problems, which sometimes have to be addressed and resolved to enable their energy to be recharged and channelled into academic work. The objective of the research is to investigate whether there is a difference in the support/counselling provision needed for the mature student compared to younger students. The methods used will, on the whole, be qualitative rather than quantitative. It will involve in-depth inter-
views of students and of student counsellors and careers advisors; and case studies which may be journalistic, quantitative or evaluative. Surveys will be carried out on: students' problems; students' evaluation of student services; and student services, including counsellors and careers advisors.
Status: Individual research
Date of Research: 1991 - continuing
KEYWORDS: *counselling services; higher education; mature students; student counselling*

North East Wales Institute of Higher Education

9/0811
Clwyd Centre for Educational Development and Research, Cartrefle, Cefn Road, Wrexham, Clwyd LL13 9NE
0978 290390
Bowen-Surtees, M. Mrs; Robertson, C. Mrs; Thomas, G. Mrs
Evaluating a programme for the teaching and learning of Welsh as a second language in year one and two infants
Abstract: As today's children are growing up in a multicultural society and as Britain is increasingly recognising its place within Europe, there is a developing awareness of second language teaching. This research has been carried out in Wales as, for many years, learning a second language has been a feature of Welsh education even in the infant sector. As a result many approaches and materials have been produced. The television programme 'Parablu' is one such approach, developed by Harlech Television and introduced into the primary schools of Clwyd with local education authority support in 1990. This project has been undertaken to evaluate the effectiveness of this programme and to extract from our observations and research findings, principles of good practice in second language learning.
Published Material: A detailed report is available from Clwyd Centre for Educational Development and Research.
Status: Sponsored project
Source of Grant: Clwyd Centre for Educational Development and Research
Date of Research: 1991-1992
KEYWORDS: *educational television; infant school education; programme evaluation; second language learning; Welsh*

Northern College of Education

9/0812
Aberdeen Campus, Hilton Place, Aberdeen AB9 1FA
0224 283615
Northcroft, D. Dr; *Supervisor:* Lloyd, J. Dr; Peacock, C. Mr
The teaching of English in Scottish secondary schools 1940-1990: a study of change and development
Abstract: This study follows the progress of a key school subject towards its slow, partial fulfilment of the 1940s aspiration for equality of educational opportunity within the post-war reconstruction of Scottish Society. Its focus is on 'English' at both the level of public pronouncement and of day-to-day classroom experience – and on the intricate interactions between these two worlds. Therefore, in addition to analysis of official documentation and school materials, the personal testimony of twenty long-serving participants, practitioners as well as policy makers, is woven into the account. Two factors have helped to elucidate this history: 1) the centralised, uniform nature of the Scottish system; 2) the post-war inheritance of two articulated but competing models of English: a) the initially dominant Scottish Education Department supported academic syllabus built on knowledge inculcation, national examination and institutional division into 'junior' and 'senior' secondary curricula as against; b) the progressivist alternative of 'the full and harmonious development of the individual' to be sought in 'omnibus' schools. Superficially, 1940-1990 may be viewed as the gradual, orderly movement towards Standard Grade English as a consensual acceptance of the progressivist version, a process facilitated by an opening up of decision making into a partnership between SOED (Scottish Office Education Department) and the profession through such bodies as the Consultative

Council and a devolved examination board. A detailed investigation of actual practice shows a more ambiguous curricular reality in which pragmatic management and deeply embedded assumptions sustain a contradictory adherence to didactic methodology and rigid assessment procedure. The Scottish experience suggests that curricular change is a necessarily problematic process whose promotion depends upon a sensitive appreciation of its complex rhythms. In Scotland this means using the traditional authority of the centre to establish clear frameworks and appropriate assessment targets within and against which the individual teacher is freed to work out a matching pedagogy and to take control of in-course evaluations. Above all, the educational innovator must be alert to the power of historical inheritance in the construction of classroom practice.
Status: Sponsored project
Source of Grant: Northern College
Date of Research: 1986-1991
KEYWORDS: *curriculum research; educational history; English; Scotland*

Nottingham University

9/0813
Department of Adult Education, 14-22 Shakespeare Street, Nottingham NG1 4FJ
0602 515151
Sherman, I. Mr; Naylor, M. Mrs; Green, P. Ms; Vanaman, J. Ms; *Supervisor:* Jotham, R. Dr
The logistics of provision of vocational training in information technology for adult students with physical and sensory disabilities
Abstract: The aim is to establish and evaluate a model for the delivery of information technology (IT) training to disabled adults by direct experimentation. A key feature of the arrangement is that training operates in parallel with a workshop managed by disabled people with IT skills. The methodology involves regular consultation between staff, trainers and associated practitioners. The group of disabled people involved numbers approximately 70.
Published Material: A list of publications is available from the researchers.
Status: Sponsored project
Source of Grant: Nottingham Task Force; European Social Fund; Nottinghamshire County Council
Date of Research: 1988 - continuing
KEYWORDS: *adult vocational education; adults; computer literacy; disabilities; information technology; sheltered workshops; special educational needs; training centres*

9/0814
Department of Adult Education, 14-22 Shakespeare Street, Nottingham NG1 4FJ
0602 515151
Wood, G. Mr; *Supervisor:* Jotham, R. Dr; Dolan, T. Mr
Information technology and the learning needs of emotionally and behaviourally disturbed children
Abstract: The research will test the hypothesis that the learning inhibiting behaviours (classroom conformity, task orientation, acceptance of authority, peer relationships, emotional control, self worth, self responsibility and problem solving) emitted by the emotionally disturbed child can be significantly reduced by the use of computer assisted learning/information technology (CAL/IT), providing the opportunity for a significant improvement in learning. It will be be necessary to: (1) measure and record the child's learning inhibiting behaviours in the presence and absence of CAL/IT; (2) measure and record the child's attainments and progress in the presence and absence of CAL/IT; and (3) ascertain reasons for this progress/lack of progress in terms of: (a) the child's academic abilities; (b) personality and attitude to CAL/IT; (c) the presentation model of the learning task; and (d) the learning environment of the hardware.
Status: Individual research
Date of Research: 1988-1992
KEYWORDS: *behaviour disorders; computer-assisted learning; computer uses in education; emotional disturbances; information technology; moderate learning difficulties; special educational needs*

9/0815
Department of Adult Education, 14-22 Shakespeare Street, Nottingham NG1 4FJ
0602 515151
Wood, A. Mr; *Supervisor:* Jotham, R. Dr
The role of information technology in the education of socially handicapped children
Abstract: Particular topics in numeracy and literacy areas are taught to groups of children in a special school for maladjusted children in formats which: (a) do not use information technology (IT); and (b) use IT extensively. Observers, who are normally present in classes, record characteristics such as attention span systematically for individual children in order to establish primary data for comparison.
Status: Individual research
Date of Research: 1989 - continuing
KEYWORDS: *behaviour disorders; computer uses in education; information technology; special educational needs; special school*

9/0816
Department of Adult Education, 14-22 Shakespeare Street, Nottingham NG1 4FJ
0602 515151
Leicester, D. Mr; Busby, M. Mrs; Green, P. Ms; *Supervisor:* Jotham, R. Dr
The use of information technology in adult basic education of students with physical and sensory handicaps
Abstract: Against a backcloth of computer courses for disabled adults in the University Adult Centre at Nottingham University, students whose educational needs lie primarily in the area of adult basic education, are worked with individually and/or in very small groups. Various teaching methods and materials are compared and contrasted, but the principle methodology is regular review of students' progress with tutors and Centre staff. The group of students under study numbers approximately 50.
Published Material: A complete list of publications is available from the researchers.
Status: Sponsored project
Source of Grant: Leverhulme Trust; Nottinghamshire County Council; Lincolnshire County Council; Derbyshire County Council
Date of Research: 1987 - continuing
KEYWORDS: *adult basic education; adults; computer literacy; disabilities; information technology; special educational needs*

9/0817
Department of Adult Education, 14-22 Shakespeare Street, Nottingham NG1 4FJ
0602 515151
Green, P. Ms; Naylor, M. Mrs; Lamerton, P. Mrs; Quinton, E. Mrs; *Supervisor:* Jotham, R. Dr
The logistics of provision of courses in information technology for adult students with physical and sensory disabilities
Abstract: Centres with good disabled access have been equipped with computers and software for the provision of computer courses for disabled students and mixed groups of disabled and able-bodied students. As well as continually reviewing the logistics of such provision, including the need for special hardware aids, student progress is monitored and compared with progress of able-bodied adults attending similar computer courses at other centres. The number of disabled students involved in this educational programme is approximately 300.
Published Material: A list of publications is available from the researchers.
Status: Sponsored project
Source of Grant: Leverhulme Trust; Nottinghamshire County Council; Lincolnshire County Council; Derbyshire County Council
Date of Research: 1985 - continuing
KEYWORDS: *adults; computer literacy; disabilities; information technology; special educational needs; training centres*

9/0818
Department of Adult Education, 14-22 Shakespeare Street, Nottingham NG1 4FJ
0602 515151
Jones, D. Dr; *Supervisor:* Jones, D. Dr; Stephens, M. Prof.
Adult education in the United Kingdom and China
Abstract: Working with colleagues at Shandung Teachers University,

it is intended to carry out a comparative study of adult education in the United Kingdom and China which will examine: (a) theories and philosophies of adult education; (b) organisation and structure of adult education; (c) aims and purposes of adult education; (d) target groups; (e) institutions for adult education; (f) teaching methods; (g) developments and trends in adult education.
Status: Individual research
Date of Research: 1992 - continuing
KEYWORDS: *adult education; China; comparative education*

9/0819
    Department of Adult Education, 14-22 Shakespeare Street, Nottingham NG1 4FJ
    0602 515151
    Ali, R. Mr; *Supervisor:* Wallis, J. Dr; Allman, P. Dr
Policy and practice in community education: a study of the youth service and ethnic minority girls and young women in Peterborough
Abstract: The research centres on studies of social and cultural issues among young Asians with a view to identifying patterns of conflict, continuity and change in their emerging value systems. The information is being gathered via: a questionnaire completed by over 100 adolescents; in depth interviews with over 50 of these respondents and their parents; group discussions with young people; informal discussions with Asian community leaders, youth workers, teachers etc; and participant observation. The findings are aimed at eliciting the circumstances, experiences and views of young people of Asian ethnic origin in an inner city area. Where necessary the questions are translated into Asian languages or dialects. A small number of representative case studies will be drawn up to illustrate the various forms of conflict revealed by the research. The use of a computerised database programme will be incorporated into the system for collecting and recording data.
Status: Individual research
Date of Research: 1988-1992
KEYWORDS: *Asians; community education; ethnic groups; women's education; youth service*

9/0820
    Department of Adult Education, 14-22 Shakespeare Street, Nottingham NG1 4FJ
    0602 515151
    Shorthouse, R. Mr; *Supervisor:* Lawson, K. Dr; Allman, P. Dr
Defining the role of metaphor in adult learning and development
Abstract: The purpose of this research is to demonstrate, by means of a linguistic philosophical analysis, the central role of metaphor in adult learning, within the context of the diverse contemporary phenomena of post-modernism with particular regard to the epistemological issue in education.
Status: Individual research
Date of Research: 1986-1992
KEYWORDS: *adult learning; linguistics; metaphors*

9/0821
    Department of Adult Education, 14-22 Shakespeare Street, Nottingham NG1 4FJ
    0602 515151
    Wallis, J. Dr
The curricular impact of the Teachers into Industry Project
Abstract: The research addresses the recent initiative in the social policy directed at creating closer links between education and the economy. The research is based upon interviews with teachers in one county. The sample will be drawn from all teachers who have taken part in the scheme. The sample size is approximately 50. The findings should reveal examples of 'good' practice for dissemination in the field and that the degree to which components of a 'hidden' curriculum are being constructed.
Status: Sponsored project
Source of Grant: Nottingham University £600
Date of Research: 1991-1992
KEYWORDS: *economics-education relationship; industry; industry education relationship; teachers*

9/0822
    Department of Adult Education, 14-22 Shakespeare Street, Nottingham NG1 4FJ
    0602 515151
    Yang, K-T. Mr; *Supervisor:* Jones, D. Dr; Stephens, M. Prof.
Analysis of the adult education problem in Taiwan, Republic of China: a comparative study of adult education between Taiwan and England and its implications in Taiwan
Abstract: This is a comparative study of university adult education in the United Kingdom and China. Questionnaires and semi-structured interviews will be used to collect data on attitudes towards univeristy adult education. All departments of adult education in the United Kingdom will be contacted and a selection in China.
Status: Sponsored project
Source of Grant: Government of Taiwan
Date of Research: 1991 - continuing
KEYWORDS: *adult education; comparative education; Taiwan; United Kingdom; universities*

9/0823
    Department of Adult Education, 14-22 Shakespeare Street, Nottingham NG1 4FJ
    0602 515151
    Stephens, M. Prof.; *Supervisor:* Daines, J. Dr; Graham, B. Mr
Leadership training in Chinese adult education
Abstract: The Department of Adult Education at Nottingham University is helping to establish China's first institute of research and training in adult education at Jinan. Three members of staff have been seconded to Nottingham from Jinan for three years to train for leadership roles in Chinese adult education. They will read for Ph.D. degrees in adult education, review policy and practice throughout the United Kingdom, and the programme will be assessed in the final year of the research funding. This project is part of an interconnecting programme of initiatives.
Status: Sponsored project
Source of Grant: Leverhulme Trust £70,000
Date of Research: 1988 - continuing
KEYWORDS: *adult education; China; leadership*

9/0824
    Department of Adult Education, 14-22 Shakespeare Street, Nottingham NG1 4FJ
    0602 515151
    Sherman, I. Mr; Barnes, K. Mr; *Supervisor:* Jotham, R. Dr
The potential of computer-mediated-communication for developing social and educational opportunities for adults with physical and sensory difficulties
Abstract: The aim is to establish a communication network for training and related activities between disabled centres and individual users in the East Midlands with links through the Joint Academic Network and the Packet Switch system to researchers, practitioners and other disabled people in the United Kingdom and worldwide. The efficient use of the network will be evaluated by monitoring traffic and by consultation with disabled users and professionals working with them.
Published Material: A list of publications is available from the researchers.
Status: Sponsored project
Source of Grant: Leverhulme Trust £55,000; Universities Funding Council £10,400
Date of Research: 1989 - continuing
KEYWORDS: *communications; computer networks; disabilities; training; wide area networks*

9/0825
    Department of Adult Education, 14-22 Shakespeare Street, Nottingham NG1 4FJ
    0602 515151
    Elsdon, K. Prof.; Stewart, S. Mrs; Reynolds, J. Dr
Educational impact of voluntary organisations
Abstract: The project aims to investigate the learning effects of local voluntary organisations on their members as individuals, and through them on their catchment population. An intensive study is planned of a representative sample of about 25 organisations chosen to take account of factors such as purpose, activities, size, ethnicity, geographical area, sex and age range of members. Each study will rest on the organisations's records and structured interviews and ques-

tionnaires administered individually or in groups as appropriate. Independent sources of evidence in the community will also be tapped. The individual case studies will be published on completion and will form the basis of evidence on which the final report will rest; together they will also form a thesaurus of good practice. The analysis and interpretation of the case studies will be used to arrive at any general principles and practical applications.
Published Material: ELSDON, K.T. (1991). Adult learning in voluntary organisations: Vol 1: case studies 1 and 2. Nottingham: University of Nottingham, Department of Adult Education.; ELSDON, K.T. (1991). Voluntary organisations and the White Paper. In: Educational Centres Association Annual Report 1991.; ELSDON, K.T. (1992). Voluntary organisations, learning and democracy. Adult Education and Development; February.
Status: Sponsored project
Source of Grant: Universities Funding Council £18,900
Date of Research: 1990 - continuing
KEYWORDS: adult education; community; individual development; social change; voluntary agencies

9/0826
　　　Department of Adult Education, 14-22 Shakespeare Street, Nottingham NG1 4FJ
　　　0602 515151
　　　Jotham, R. Dr; Ellis, M. Mrs
Aspects of educational practice in the physical sciences and information technology
Abstract: The aim of this project is to evaluate, comment upon and improve educational practice in science and information technology. The methodology involves direct experimentation work with student groups, followed by discussion with students and tutors. The research also includes extensive studies of statistical information on the extent, diversity and logistics of provision of adult education in this general area.
Published Material: A list of publications is available from the researchers.
Status: Individual research
Date of Research: 1970 - continuing
KEYWORDS: adult education; educational practices; higher education; information technology; physical sciences; science education

9/0827
　　　Department of Adult Education, 14-22 Shakespeare Street, Nottingham NG1 4FJ
　　　0602 515151
　　　Thomas, J. Prof.
Investigation of the relationship between education, politics, language and religion in Wales
Abstract: This is an intellectual analysis of the relationships between language, religion, politics and nationalism in Wales. It seeks to show that that the alleged aims of nationalism are counterproductive to the best aims and interests of Wales. It shows the tension between nationalism and internationalism which characterises Welsh history.
Status: Sponsored project
Source of Grant: Nottingham University £12,000
Date of Research: 1990-1992
KEYWORDS: history; mother tongue; nationalism; politics; religion; Wales; Welsh

9/0828
　　　Department of Adult Education, 14-22 Shakespeare Street, Nottingham NG1 4FJ
　　　0602 515151
　　　Henson, C. Rev.; *Supervisor:* Mackie, K. Dr; Parsons, W. Dr
The space within an interdisciplinary study of voluntary groups engaging with AIDS and HIV
Abstract: The aim of the research is to discover a model for adult education based on voluntary groups engaging with Acquired Immune Deficiency Syndrome (AIDS) and Human-Immunodeficiency Syndrome (HIV) and to understand the ethical and theological implications of this model. The research will include interviews with selected voluntary groups and a comparative study of educational philosophies.
Status: Individual research
Date of Research: 1989 - continuing
KEYWORDS: Acquired Immune Deficiency Syndrome; adult education; ethics; sexually transmitted diseases; voluntary agencies

9/0829
　　　Department of Adult Education, 14-22 Shakespeare Street, Nottingham NG1 4FJ
　　　0602 515151
　　　Cox, D. Mr; Hannah, J. Dr
Beyond training – adult education in the workplace
Abstract: The project will undertake an investigation of the demand for adult education opportunities within a sample of the working population of the East Midlands. A questionnaire will be distributed to establish the dimensions of need amongst a sample of employees in the region.
Status: Sponsored project
Source of Grant: National Westminster Bank Research Fund £4,150
Date of Research: 1990-1992
KEYWORDS: adult education; works schools

9/0830
　　　Department of Adult Education, 14-22 Shakespeare Street, Nottingham NG1 4FJ
　　　0602 515151
　　　Cox, D. Mr
The mass media and the social construction of memory
Abstract: The research will explore the ways in which many parts of people's memories are socially derived and will especially focus on those parts that are dependent on vicarious experience, learned about via the mass media (although the research will not ignore the importance of inter-personal vicarious experience). Using a case study approach, the research will attempt to locate mass media influence in an historicised context. This is necessary because of: (a) the way we interpret present events will be affected by what we remember from the past; and (b) how we remember events from the past will be qualified by how new events are reported. As what we remember will also be filtered through the ideological positions of different people, then socially constructed memory has also to be seen in terms of ideological memory. The case studies chosen for the research will examine the reporting of various types of industrial relations issues in national daily newspapers, but will not use conventional content analysis techniques alone. There will be an attempt to refine other qualitative measures. The research will also consider issues in the education of adults, especially how students' memory resources can be channelled, and how they have to be critically questioned and interpreted, rather than being simply accepted as evidence.
Status: Individual research
Date of Research: 1988 - continuing
KEYWORDS: adult learning; mass media; memory

9/0831
　　　Department of Adult Education, 14-22 Shakespeare Street, Nottingham NG1 4FJ
　　　0602 515151
　　　Sutton, I. Dr
The value of field residential courses in the teaching of earth sciences
Abstract: The research is intended to investigate the value of field studies in the teaching of adults in the area of earth sciences. The study involves the investigation of the way field activities can be integrated into the teaching of earth sciences to adults with special reference to teaching methods, and day, weekend, longer residential and foreign study tours. The value of pre-course preparation for the field study is an important aspect of the research.
Status: Individual research
Date of Research: 1986 - continuing
KEYWORDS: adult education; adult learning; earth science; field studies; field studies centres; study abroad

9/0832
　　　Department of Adult Education, 14-22 Shakespeare Street, Nottingham NG1 4FJ
　　　0602 515151
　　　Daines, J. Dr; Graham, B. Mr
Look after yourself tutor training
Abstract: The aim is to: (a) evaluate tutor training; (b) advise and consult on subsequent training and allied activities; and (c) develop a training strategy
Published Material: DAINES, J. & GRAHAM, B. (1989). LAY report: innovations and outcomes 1978-1986. Nottingham: University of Nottingham, Department of Adult Education.; DAINES, J. &

GRAHAM, B. (1989). Adult learning; adult teaching: a manual. Nottingham: University of Nottingham, Department of Adult Education.
Status: Sponsored project
Source of Grant: Health Education Authority £120,000
Date of Research: 1982-1992
KEYWORDS: *health education; teacher education; training; tutors*

9/0833
> Department of Adult Education, 14-22 Shakespeare Street, Nottingham NG1 4FJ
> 0602 515151
> Associacao Portuguesa de Paralisia Cerebral, Rua Delfim Maia, 4300 Porto, Portugal
> Jotham, R. Dr; Da Cunha, A. Sr; *Supervisor:* Jotham, R. Dr

Comparative study of information technology training for disabled people in Britain and Portugal
Abstract: A Portugese researcher will spend two months in the United Kingdom gathering information on the training of disabled people in information technology. This will be followed by gathering comparative data in Portugal and the results will be collated to generate a report which will be published in both English and Portugese.
Status: Sponsored project
Source of Grant: Gulbenkian Foundation £5,000
Date of Research: 1991 - continuing
KEYWORDS: *adult vocational education; comparative education; disabilities; information technology; Portugal; special educational needs; training; United Kingdom*

9/0834
> Department of Adult Education, Centre for Research into the Education of Adults, 14-22 Shakespeare Street, Nottingham NG1 4FJ
> 0602 515151
> Kai, J. Ms; *Supervisor:* Morgan, W. Mr; Stephens, M. Prof.

The role of foreign experts in the development of Chinese universities
Abstract: The aims of this project are to: (1) evaluate the work that foreign experts have done in Chinese universities since 1978 when China adopted the open door policy; (2) measure the benefits of these undertakings for China's educational reform; and (3) assess the effect of recent policital changes.
Status: Sponsored project
Source of Grant: British Council; Nottingham University Scholarship
Date of Research: 1988-1992
KEYWORDS: *China; education consultants; educational change; educational development; universities*

9/0835
> Department of Adult Education, Centre for Research into the Education of Adults, 14-22 Shakespeare Street, Nottingham NG1 4FJ
> 0602 515151
> Bridge, H. Ms; Salt, H. Ms; *Supervisor:* Morgan, W. Mr; Davies, J. Mr; Dale, M. Dr

Access and delivery in continuing educational training: a survey of contemporary literature
Abstract: The aim of this research has been to produce a report and a select annotated bibliography to support the work of those with an interest in access and delivery in continuing education and training. A broad definition is taken to mean learning and training opportunites taken up after compulsory education has been completed. The research identifies literature, assesses its relevance and accessibility and reviews its content. It focuses on material relating to the United Kingdom, published since 1985, dealing with the 18-55 age group.
Status: Sponsored project
Source of Grant: Department of Employment £56,000
Date of Research: 1992-1992
KEYWORDS: *access to education; adult education; adult vocational education; continuing education; literature reviews; training*

9/0836
> Department of Adult Education, Centre for Research into the Education of Adults, 14-22 Shakespeare Street, Nottingham NG1 4FJ
> 0602 515151

McCarthy, J. Mr; *Supervisor:* Morgan, W. Mr; Bayliss, F. Prof.

Adult employment training in Nottinghamshire: case studies
Abstract: Shortcomings in training are at the core of the National Skills and Training debate. What are the causes of these shortcomings? This enquiry attempts to answer this question and to indicate how firms local to the Nottinghamshire area seek to overcome them. Semi-structured interviews are undertaken with key providers and consumers of training. These are accompanied by a series of case studies, both of major employers and of small to medium sized industries.
Published Material: McCARTHY, J., MORGAN, W.J. & BAYLISS, F.J. (1992). Adult employment training in Nottinghamshire. Nottingham: University of Nottingham, Department of Adult Education.
Status: Sponsored project
Source of Grant: National Westminster Bank Research Fund £18,000; Department of Employment £20,000
Date of Research: 1990 - continuing
KEYWORDS: *adult vocational education; employment; job skills; job training; work-education relationship*

9/0837
> Department of Adult Education, Centre for Research into the Education of Adults, 14-22 Shakespeare Street, Nottingham NG1 4FJ
> 0602 515151
> Bo, J. Mr; *Supervisor:* Morgan, W. Mr; Muckle, J. Dr

An evaluation of current British policy concerning postgraduate overseas students
Abstract: The research is a study of overseas student issues from a host country perspective. It focuses on the 'managing' of the growth of incoming postgraduate students and on the extent to which the needs and obligations perceived and accepted by the policy making machinery shape the experience of students. The costs and benefits to the host country are considered in both immediate and longer terms.
Status: Sponsored project
Source of Grant: Overseas Research Studentship; British Council
Date of Research: 1990 - continuing
KEYWORDS: *educational policy; graduate study; higher education; overseas students*

9/0838
> Department of Adult Education, Centre for Research into the Education of Adults, 14-22 Shakespeare Street, Nottingham NG1 4FJ
> 0602 515151
> Morgan, W. Mr

Adult employment training in four regions (East Midlands, South Wales, Bremen, and Baden Wurttemberg)
Abstract: The research concentrates upon: (i) the changing continuing education needs of the regions; (ii) the impact of the 1992 single market; and (iii) the possibility of a European model emerging from British-German experience.
Status: Sponsored project
Source of Grant: Universities Funding Council £55,000
Date of Research: 1990 - continuing
KEYWORDS: *adult education; comparative education; continuing education; European Community; Germany; United Kingdom; vocational education*

9/0839
> Department of Adult Education, Centre for Research into the Education of Adults, 14-22 Shakespeare Street, Nottingham NG1 4FJ
> 0602 515151
> Morgan, W. Mr

Political education, voluntary associations and civil society in state socialist countries
Abstract: The research seeks to identify and analyse the relationship of adult political education and voluntary associations to the emergence of civil society in state socialist countries. The key concepts will be defined theoretically and examined empirically through a series of related historical and sociological studies.
Published Material: MORGAN, W.P. (1989). 'Homo-Sovieticus – political education and civil society in the Soviet Union'. In: MORGAN, W.P. (Ed). Proceedings of the Standing Conference of Univer-

sity Teachings and Research into the Education of Adults. Nottingham.; MORGAN, W.P. (1989). 'Workers adult education in the Soviet Union', Bulletin of the International Congress of University Adult Education, Vol 2, No 1, Spring 1989.
Status: Sponsored project
Source of Grant: British Council; Beatrice Webb Trust
Date of Research: 1989 - continuing
KEYWORDS: adult education; citizenship education; political influences; social change; socialist countries; voluntary agencies

9/0840
Department of Adult Education, Centre for Research into the Education of Adults, 14-22 Shakespeare Street, Nottingham NG1 4FJ
0602 515151
Thompson, E. Mrs; *Supervisor:* Morgan, W. Mr;
Stock, A. Prof.
An international information and resources collection in adult education and training
Abstract: The aim of the research project is to establish an international information and bibliographical resources collection on adult education and training which will be of value to researchers engaged in international and comparative studies. The project involves the establishment of a database and production of a bibliography on comparative adult education and training.
Status: Sponsored project
Source of Grant: Universities Funding Council £15,000
Date of Research: 1990 - continuing
KEYWORDS: adult; adult education; comparative education; continuing education; databases; vocational education

9/0841
Department of Adult Education, Centre for Research into the Education of Adults, 14-22 Shakespeare Street, Nottingham NG1 4FJ
0602 515151
Bin, L. Ms; *Supervisor:* Morgan, W. Mr; Lawson, K. Dr
A comparison of the main concepts in the philosophy of education used in Britain and China
Abstract: The main concepts used in the philosophy of education in Britain and China will be defined, analysed and compared, with a view to establishing both universals and those that are bound within a cultural context.
Status: Individual research
Date of Research: 1989-1992
KEYWORDS: China; comparative education; cultural differences; educational philosophy; United Kingdom

9/0842
Department of Adult Education, Centre for Research into the Education of Adults, 14-22 Shakespeare Street, Nottingham NG1 4FJ
0602 515151
Wong, K. Mr; *Supervisor:* Morgan, W. Mr; Shipstone, D. Dr
Evaluation of the process of curriculum design of technical and vocational education in Hong Kong
Abstract: An evaluation of the process of curriculum design in technical and vocational education in Hong Kong will be undertaken. Special reference will be made to the interaction between education, training, employment and economic outcomes. It is also intended to identify present and likely difficulties, and to suggest ways of linking technical and vocational education with the general education system in order to ensure an adequate supply of competent technical personnel for the 1990s and beyond 1997.
Status: Individual research
Date of Research: 1989 - continuing
KEYWORDS: curriculum evaluation; economics-education relationship; Hong Kong; technical education; training; vocational education; work-education relationship

9/0843
Department of Adult Education, Centre for the Research into the Education of Adults, 14-22 Shakespeare Street, Nottingham NG1 4FJ
0602 515151
Ling, J. Ms; Jiangling, J. Mr; *Supervisor:* Morgan, W. Mr

An investigation into the present situation and problems of English language learning of adult Chinese immigrants in Nottingham and London
Abstract: The proposed study will concentrate on the adult Chinese immigrants in London and Nottingham. Professionals and students will be excluded. The study aims at a thorough assessment of the actual level of English proficiency, the social, cultural or linguistic constraints that inhibit their English learning, the effects of their language disadvantage and the English second language (ESL) provisions that are available to them, with their effectiveness.
Status: Sponsored project
Source of Grant: Nuffield Foundation
Date of Research: 1992-1992
KEYWORDS: Chinese; English – second language; ethnic groups; immigrants; language proficiency; second language learning

9/0844
Department of Adult Education, 14-22 Shakespeare Street, Nottingham NG1 4FJ
0602 515151
Derby Tertiary College, Wilmorton Campus, Wilmorton, Derby DE2 8UG
0332 73012
Cooper, A. Mr; *Supervisor:* Jotham, R. Dr
Establishing access to the tertiary curriculum for adults with special educational needs
Abstract: The purpose of the project is to evaluate the effectiveness of an educational support centre for special needs students located within a college of further education. Methodology involves regular consultation with the Centre staff, students and management staff.
Status: Individual research
Date of Research: 1987-1992
KEYWORDS: access to education; adult education; further education; special educational needs; support services; tertiary education

9/0845
Department of Adult Education, 14-22 Shakespeare Street, Nottingham NG1 4FJ
0602 515151
East Midlands Arts, Mountfields House, Forest Road, Loughborough LE11 3HU
0509 218292
Anderson, L. Ms; *Supervisor:* Preston, P. Mr; Hicks, D. Ms
Writers' workshop leaders project
Abstract: The aim of the project is to investigate the training needs of leaders of writers' workshops in a variety of adult education and community contexts. In the first phase the project worker will visit groups and interview both leaders and group members, (this phase will be carried out in those geographical areas common to East Midlands Arts and the Extra-Mural Region of the University of Nottingham). Out of this investigation will arise an interim report and the preparation of a training programme. The second phase will involve the coordination, monitoring and evaluation of a training programme. The final phase will comprise the compilation of a training resource pack and the preparation of a final report.
Status: Sponsored project
Source of Grant: Arts Council of Great Britain £5,000; Gulbenkian Foundation £3,000; East Midlands Arts £3,000; Nottinghamshire County Council £1,500
Date of Research: 1992-1992
KEYWORDS: adult education; authors; community education; leadership training; writing – composition

9/0846
Department of Adult Education, 14-22 Shakespeare Street, Nottingham NG4 4FJ
0602 515151
University of British Columbia, 5597 Iona Drive, Vancouver, Canada Riddell, B. Ms; *Supervisor:* Daines, J. Dr; Graham, B. Mr
Staff development in higher education
Abstract: This research is aimed at addressing the issue of teacher versus learner centred approaches to teaching/instruction. The research uses participants in 'instructor training' workshops as subjects. Using a case study method, it will seek to establish the antecedents and ongoing effects of training, experience and self-reflection upon teaching approaches. In particular it will seek to identify changes in

values, attitudes and beliefs of participants towards more learner-centred approaches to university teaching.
Status: Individual research
Date of Research: 1990 - continuing
KEYWORDS: learner-centred methods; staff development; teaching process; universities; university teaching

9/0847

Department of Adult Education, 14-22 Shakespeare Street, Nottingham NG1 4FJ
0602 515151
University of East Anglia, School of Education, Norwich NR4 7TJ
0603 56161
South Bank University, 103 Borough Road, London SE1 OAA
071 928 8989
Griffiths, M. Dr; McBride, R. Dr; Weiner, G. Ms
Equal opportunities and social justice
Abstract: This is a theoretical and philosophical examination of the central concepts and their relationship to teacher development in the 1990s. The work as a whole will include an investigation of the concept of justice and social justice, to inequality with reference to race, class, sexuality, etc. Key themes will include: the importance of focusing on both individuals and groups as a unit of analysis; the significance of metaphors of balance and harmony and their possible inappropriateness in a dynamic society; changing meanings of the notion of justice across time and place. These themes will be used to illuminate evidence about inequalities in modern British society. The implications for policy will be drawn out and formulated in terms of an education agenda for the 1990s.
Status: Individual research
Date of Research: 1990-1991
KEYWORDS: educational policy; equal education; justice; opportunities; social attitudes

9/0848

Department of Psychology, University Park, Nottingham NG7 2RD
0602 515151
Underwood, G. Prof.
Cognitive processes in reading and spelling
Abstract: The aim of the project is to identify the cognitive processes which enable us to read and spell – those processes through which written information must be transformed by the competent reader to reach understanding. Dependent measures of reading speed and accuracy are observed as a function of controlled variables. Measures are also used to observe eye movements. Experiments have been performed on skilled adult readers, young readers and latter with reading difficulties. Recognition of isolated words and the comprehension of coherent text have been investigated. The role of attention in recognition concerning isolated words has been studied and also the role of alternative processing routes (graphemic/phonological) by manipulating the orthographic regularity of the words presented. The role of regularity in spelling has also been investigated. Findings suggest that for children of 10+ and adults, attention is not essential for isolated word recognition but is for measuring of sentences. Good and poor readers do not differ in their ability to recognise the meanings of isolated words so much as in their ability to use the meanings after recognition. Individual differences in reading ability are more associated with post-recognition processes such as those involved in the use of working memory than with initial encoding. One of the researcher's interests is in the patterns of eye movements (saccades, regressive saccades and fixation durations) made by skilled readers who are comprehending sentences, with specific interest in the cognitive mechanisms of eye guidance. Computer-based learning support with classroom computers is currently being investigated. The questions being asked here are: how can computers be used to enhance the cognitive processes involved in reading and spelling?; and what uses can teachers make of classroom computers with children of different ability background?
Published Material: A list of publications is available from the researchers on request.
Status: Sponsored project
Source of Grant: Medical Research Council; Science and Engineering Research Council
Date of Research: 1979 - continuing
KEYWORDS: cognitive processes; computer-assisted reading; reading comprehension; reading skills; spelling; word recognition

9/0849

Department of Psychology, Blind Mobility Research Unit, University Park, Nottingham NG7 2RD
0602 515151
Dodds, A. Dr; Doyle, A. Dr; Beggs, W. Dr; Flannigan, H. Ms; Ng, B. Ms; *Supervisor:* Howarth, C. Prof.
The mobility of blind and visually impaired persons
Abstract: The unit publishes its work in the national and international journals. Principal interests are investigation of the assessment of visual handicap and how trainers are taught to teach mobility of visually impaired people. A scale of adjustment is being developed.
Published Material: BEGGS, W.D.A. (1991). 'The psychological correlates of walking speed in the visually impaired', Ergonomics, Vol 34, No 1, pp.91-102.; BEGGS, W.D.A. (1990). 'Goal setting in sport'. In: GRAHAM-JONES, J. & HARDY. L. (Eds). Stress and performance in sport. Chichester: John Wiley & Sons.; DODDS, A.G. (1991). 'Psychological assessment and the rehabilitation process', New Beacon, LXXV (885), pp.101-106.; DODDS, A.G. (1991). 'The psychology of rehabilitation', British Journal of Visual Impairment, Vol 9, No 2, pp.38-40.; DODDS, A.G., BAILEY, P., PEARSON, A. & YATES, L. (1991). 'Psychological factors in acquired visual impairment: the development of a scale of adjustment', Journal of Visual Impairment and Blindess, Vol 85, No 7, pp.306-310. A full list of publications is available from the Blind Mobility Research Unit.
Status: Sponsored project
Source of Grant: Department of Health £186,000
Date of Research: 1960 - continuing
KEYWORDS: assessment; blindness; mobility aids; partial vision; special educational needs; travel training; visual impairments; visually handicapped

9/0850

School of Education, University Park, Nottingham NG7 2RD
0602 515151
Thompson, W. Mr; *Supervisor:* Sands, M. Dr
The role of a change agent in the introduction of a new curriculum in technical teacher training
Abstract: The research stems from involvement as a consultant on a large project in an overseas country. This was to introduce a new teacher training curriculum into four faculties of technical/vocational teacher training, based upon common, core subjects/modules, that would apply in all faculties. It involved major structural and equipment refurbishment and the provision of new equipment. The basic method is the use of case studies based upon observation as a full participator. Curriculum documents, discussion papers, questionnaires, minutes of meetings, project documents, will be used as the database. Major themes to be considered will be the management of the project, role of consultancy and individual consultants, working methods of consultants, development of curriculum, development of faculty management resources and facilities. Comparison will be made with published accounts of other similar projects undertaken in overseas countries. From this an hypotheses about the role of change agents in similar situations will be generated.
Status: Individual research
Date of Research: 1990 - continuing
KEYWORDS: change agents; curriculum development; preservice teacher education; technical education; vocational education

9/0851

School of Education, University Park, Nottingham NG7 2RD
0602 515151
Goody, J. Mr; *Supervisor:* Shipstone, D. Dr; Selkirk, K. Dr
Technology for all: educational models for effective implementation
Abstract: Design and technology activity is cross-curricular. This, and its relatively recent appearance in schools' curricula, has made consensus and clarity concerning its nature difficult to achieve and the introduction of the National Curriculum has led to new interpretations. The study aims to establish a coherent theoretical framework to support the development of technology within the curriculum and to clarify the nature of technology and its role in education past, present and future. The problems to be addressed are: (1) defining technology; (2) describing the nature of technology; (3) investigation of the role of human values in technology education; (4) identifying fundamental aims and objectives; (5) developing a descriptive model to demonstrate the central ideas of technological activity; (6) determining current organisational structures; (7) identifying the princi-

ples of learning and teaching technology; (8) developing models for implementing 1-7 above; (9) critique of the National Curriculum Orders in relation to 1-8 above; (10) issues relating to assessment and evaluation. The methodology will include literature surveys; structured interviews, e.g. with practitioners working with students in the 5-18 age range; classroom observation and case studies.
Status: Individual research
Date of Research: 1990 - continuing
KEYWORDS: *curriculum development; design education; National Curriculum; technology education*

9/0852
School of Education, University Park, Nottingham NG7 2RD
0602 515151
Whyte, G. Mr; *Supervisor:* Bennett, S. Mr; Shipstone, D. Dr
The enterprising college
Abstract: The aims of this research project are to: (1) propose an overall definition of the terms 'enterprise' and 'enterprising' and to identify the characteristics associated with enterprising people and their characteristics; (2) identify good practice in the techniques used by employers to develop an enterprising work force; (3) evolve a series of training events to enable managers to apply these techniques within further education and evaluate both the effectiveness of these techniques and the methods of importing them; (4) develop a mechanism for introducing enteprise approaches into the work of students and evaluate the effectiveness of these approaches; and (5) make recommendations for further applications of enterprise approaches within further education. This research requires the integration of academic disciplines in that it combines approaches to both educational research and to management development in the field of enterprise. The methodology falls into three distinct phases: (1) review of the literature; (2) project activity; and (3) evaluation.
Status: Individual research
Date of Research: 1991 - continuing
KEYWORDS: *enterprise education; further education; work-education relationship*

9/0853
School of Education, University Park, Nottingham NG7 2RD
0602 515151
Griffiths, M. Dr
Self esteem and educational practice
Abstract: This is a philosophical examination, which draws on psychological and feminist sources. The research considers the central concepts of achievement and belonging and their role in fostering self esteem. Current influential theories emphasise the dependence of self esteem on personal achievement, though others focus on belonging. The internal and mutual coherence of the two are being investigated. The theories are being considered in the light of philosophical theories of personal identity, and of feminist theories of identity politics. The implications for educational practice will be drawn out, with special reference to equal opportunities.
Status: Individual research
Date of Research: 1990-1991
KEYWORDS: *achievement; educational practices; equal education; personality; self concept; self-esteem*

9/0854
School of Education, University Park, Nottingham NG7 2RD
0602 515151
Bakioglu, A. Mrs; *Supervisor:* Day, C. Prof.; Adey, K. Dr
The Principal's role in innovation in schools
Abstract: This study attempts to answer the following questions: (1) do headteachers experience some career stages during the time they are in post; (2) what difficulties does each stage have; (3) how do these stages influence the development of their professional life. A questionnaire was developed to investigate three aspects of headteachers' role, i.e. internal, external, staff and staffing issues. Each category was divided into two sections: (a) questions related to change and innovation; and (b) questions related to administrative matters. A Likert Scale was used which contained five levels of difficulty ranging from very serious to not a problem. Of the three hundred and five surveys sent to the secondary school headteachers in Nottinghamshire, Derbyshire, Lincolnshire and Leicestershire, one hundred and ninety-six were returned (overall response rate of 64.2%). The most significant items related to previous headteachers'

actions, with less experienced headteachers having greater difficulty with this issue. Headteachers with 4-8 years of experience seem to be the most successful and feel least difficulty in internal issues, although headteachers with 1-3 years and over 8 years of experience have great problems. In order to investigate further, a semi-structured interview schedule was designed, and all data received illustrated on tables and charts.
Status: Sponsored project
Source of Grant: Republic of Turkey, per annum £7,000
Date of Research: 1989-1992
KEYWORDS: *career development; careers; headteachers; teaching profession*

9/0855
School of Education, University Park, Nottingham NG7 2RD
0602 515151
Masterman, L. Dr
Critical responses to recent developments in advertising and marketing
Abstract: This research will attempt to: (1) describe the most up-to-date techniques used in marketing, especially via the mass media, e.g. product placement, industrial political marketing, public relations, manufacture and privatisation of information; (2) explore the central issues and questions raised by these developments, especially in relation to work in schools (traditionally, teachers of English and media studies have taught about advertising as it is more narrowly defined); (3) provide materials for use in schools – especially at General Certificate of Education (GCSE) and A level in media studies.
Published Material: MASTERMAN, L. (1980). Teaching about television. London: Macmillan.; MASTERMAN, L. (1985). Television mythologies. London: Routledge.; MASTERMAN, L. (1985). Teaching the media. London: Routledge. (formerly Comedia).
Status: Individual research
Date of Research: 1989-1992
KEYWORDS: *advertising; marketing; mass media; media studies*

9/0856
School of Education, University Park, Nottingham NG7 2RD
0602 515151
Shipstone, D. Dr
The Technical and Vocational Education Initiative (TVEI) in initial teacher training
Abstract: This research and development project has a substantial staff development component and focuses upon the changes that have taken place within education in the 14-18 age range through the impetus provided by the Technical and Vocational Education Initiative (TVEI). Many School of Education lecturers engage in research studies within 5 broad themes: new technology learning; personal and social education, guidance and profiling; industry links and work experience; and equal opportunities. Publications will take the form of workshop materials and case studies to be used on initial and inservice training courses; research papers and monographs dealing with aspects of education which have been particularly influenced by TVEI.
Status: Sponsored project
Source of Grant: Training Agency £100,000
Date of Research: 1989-1991
KEYWORDS: *inservice teacher education; preservice teacher education; technical education; vocational education*

9/0857
School of Education, University Park, Nottingham NG7 2RD
0602 515151
Parker-Jenkins, M. Dr
What is the experience of Muslim girls in a Muslim school in Britain?: An ethnographic study with proposals for change
Abstract: Muslims comprise the third largest religious group in Britain today, after Roman Catholics and Anglicans. Whilst multiracial, multicultural and multilingual in nature, they are united by the faith dimension of their lives. The powerful revival of Islamic Fundamentalism of late has deeply affected the thinking of Muslim minority groups in the West. The education system has been criticised by Muslims, who see an incompatibility between values taught at home and those at school. The objective of this research is therefore to make a study of Muslim education as offered by a selected Muslim girls' independent school and to accumulate new and timely infor-

mation. Other research aims are to examine the cognitive basis of Islamic education and the selection of knowledge. The research methodology is predominantly ethnographic with an in depth study of a girls Muslim school and shorter studies of five other Muslim schools for comparative analysis. Following the traditions of ethnography, the research aims to examine the experience of Muslim girls in a Muslim school. Furthermore, proposals for change will be explored, outlining areas concerning the educational needs of Muslim children within the maintained school system. The study involves 6 Muslim and 6 non-Muslim schools and is conducted by a small team of researchers comprising both Muslims and non-Muslims. A report will be published profiling educational provision within a Muslim school with recommendations for the maintained school system.
Published Material: PARKER-JENKINS, M. (1990). 'Why Muslim needs won't disappear', New Era in Education, Vol 71, No 1, pp.14-16.
Status: Sponsored project
Source of Grant: Economic and Social Research Council £14,500
Date of Research: 1993 - continuing
KEYWORDS: *Islamic education; Muslims; religion and education; religious cultural groups; women's education*

9/0858

School of Education, University Park, Nottingham NG7 2RD
0602 515151
Parker-Jenkins, M. Dr
What do Muslim children need from the education system?
Abstract: This case study of the Muslim Girls' High School, by Leicester will provide an insight into an unexplored area which has recently provoked educational debate here and abroad: the lack of understanding between the State educational system and the Muslim community. Adopting an ethnographic approach, the aim of the study is to examine educational provision in non-maintained Muslim schools and to consider the extent to which the maintained school sector is able to accommodate Muslim needs. The two year project will comprise of four stages of work. Firstly, initial research of the Muslim Girls' High School, Leicester, visits to other Muslim schools in Britain to provide comparative analysis, and in-depth interviewing of interested parties; educationalists; clergy; academics; and community leaders. Finally, the production of a report, study guide and articles for publication, offering practical solutions to the problems of educating Muslim children within State schools and in accordance with parents' religious convictions. The education system is presently being criticised by 'Muslims' who see an incompatibility between values taught at home and those at school. Although voluntary aided status may be granted to Muslim schools in the future, there will still be a large element of Muslim children who remain in regular maintained schools. Accommodating their educational needs will continue to be a pressing concern for educationalists and this research will provide a direct contribution to knowledge in the field of cultural diversity.
Published Material: PARKER-JENKINS, M. (1990). 'Muslin needs won't disappear', New Era in Education, Vol 17, No 1.; PARKER-JENKINS, M. (1990). 'Muslim educational needs', Multicultural Education Journal, (U.S.A.), Vol 8, No 2.; PARKER-JENKINS, M. (1990). 'Multiculturalism in British schools: lessons for Canada', Canadian School Executive', Vol 10, No 5.; PARKER-JENKINS, M. (1991). 'Muslim matters: exploring the educational needs of the Muslim child', New Community, Vol 17, No 4.
Status: Sponsored project
Source of Grant: Nottingham University Administered Funding Body £5,048
Date of Research: 1991 - continuing
KEYWORDS: *Islamic education; Muslims; religion and education; religious cultural groups; women's education*

9/0859

School of Education, University Park, Nottingham NG7 2RD
0602 515151
Day, C. Dr; Ellis, C. Mr; Sutton, I. Dr
Investigating the effectiveness of continuing education
Abstract: Much research has focused upon developing continuing education provision in adult education, inservice training for teachers and industrial and professional training. The aim of this research is to examine critically these theories in practice, and to evaluate both independently and through comparison their effectiveness in terms of client/consumer expectations, relevance of

course provision to client need and its effects on professional and institutional growth.
Status: Sponsored project
Source of Grant: Universities Funding Council £59,840
Date of Research: 1991 - continuing
KEYWORDS: *adult education; continuing education; industrial training; inservice teacher education; professional training; vocational education*

9/0860

School of Education, University Park, Nottingham NG7 2RD
0602 515151
Harrison, B. Mrs; *Supervisor:* Parsons, W. Dr; Hay, J. Dr
The interface of feminism, education and the Church: a study of power
Abstract: This research looks at definitions of power and at what are regarded as the structures of authority in the Church of England. A case has been made for the existence of patriarchy but little can be found on the mechanisms by which it works. This research proposes to look further into the theory of the management of complex organisations, and will involve working with a group from a church congregation on the language used for the experience of God. The management language used by church bureaucrats will also be studied. The researcher also may work with a group from another parish. Study sessions for clergy on inclusive language and the liturgy, have been conducted, and the aim is to provide material for a deanery synod to work with.
Status: Individual research
Date of Research: 1990 - continuing
KEYWORDS: *church and education; feminism; language usage; power structure; Protestant churches*

9/0861

School of Education, Centre for the Study of Human Relations, University Park, Nottingham NG7 2RD
0602 515151
Hall, E. Dr; Hall, C. Mrs
Outcomes of experiential learning
Abstract: This is an ongoing project which examines the outcomes of experiential interpersonal skills training programmes which have been developed over the years at the Centre for the Study of Human Relations at the University of Nottingham. A series of studies have been conducted, partly associated with four Ph.D. students. All of the evaluations have involved experienced teachers who attended six-day residential courses or extended award bearing courses to gain an M.Ed. or an Advanced Diploma. Data has been collected before, during and up to three years after the courses. Data was collected using standardised questionnaires, interviews, diaries of critical incidents, outcomes of goal setting, learning journals and data collected during experiential exercises during the courses. A consistent pattern has emerged over several studies. The participants reported significant changes in both their personal and professional lives. These changes involved reports of reductions in stress, a greater sense of control over one's life and a shift to a more humanistic approach to discipline issues. These changes involved relationships with both students and colleagues. There was also a strong 'Sleeper effect' in several of the studies in which a significant improvement was obtained at the end of the course, followed by a much more substantial increase one year later.
Published Material: HALL, E., WOODHOUSE, D.A. & WOOSTER, A.D. (1984). 'An evaluation of inservice courses in human relations', British Journal of Inservice Education, Vol 11, No 1, pp.55-60.; WOODHOUSE, D.A., HALL, E. & WOOSTER, A.D. (1985). 'Taking control of stress in teaching'', British Journal of Educational Psychology, Vol 55, Part 2, pp.119-123.; HALL, E. & HALL, C.A. (1988). Human relations in education. London: Routledge.; HALL, E., HALL, C.A. & LEECH, A. (1990). A scripted fantasy in the classroom. London: Routledge.
Status: Sponsored project
Source of Grant: Nottingham University: School of Education £4,000; Universities Funding Council £4,000; Enterprise in Higher Education £7,500
Date of Research: 1974 - continuing
KEYWORDS: *experiential learning; interpersonal competence; locus of control; outcomes of education; stress – psychological; student experience; teacher education*

9/0862
School of Social Studies, University Park, Nottingham
NG7 2RD
0602 515151
Evetts, J. Dr
Gender and headship: career contexts and strategies
Abstract: This is a study of how details of individuals' life histories and career biographies can contribute to educational and sociological understanding about teachers' careers and about gender differences in career building. Using career history interviews from a sample of twenty headteachers, ten men and ten women, from two Midlands educational authorities, the research has considered what were the external structural conditions and the characteristics of the labour market for constructing careers in teaching. The research has also considred what strategies men and women have devised to manage and negotiate such contexts. The researcher has argued that one can demonstrate that career histories illustrate both structural conditions, in particular labour markets and the strategies of individuals' developing careers.
Published Material: EVETTS, J. (1991). 'The experience of secondary headship selection: continuity and change', Educational Studies, Vol 17, No 3, pp.285-294.; EVETTS, J. (1992). 'When promotion ladders seem to end: the career concerns of secondary headteachers', British Journal of Sociology of Education, Vol 13, No 1, pp.37-49; A complete list of publications is available from the researcher.
Status: Individual research
Date of Research: 1990-1992
KEYWORDS: career development; headteachers; sex differences; teaching profession

Open University

9/0863
Walton Hall, Milton Keynes MK7 6AA
0908 274066
Tyler, S. Ms; *Supervisor:* Light, P. Prof.
Spatial cognition: childrens' pictorial representations
Abstract: Modern accounts of childrens' drawings still take intellectual/visual realism (or elaborations) as their focal point. The current research treats drawing as problem-solving, with solutions determined/constrained by factors such as lack of particular spatial concepts. However, Piaget's accounts of the child's construction of representational space, and his premise of perception in 2D are not accepted. Thus in the first experiments, which focused on inconsistencies in response when children are requested to draw an array in which one object is partly hidden by another, the dimensions of the objects were systematically varied (2D/3D). Results showed that children aged 4-7 years are sensitive to object dimensions. When 2D equivalents of 3D objects are used children are less likely to segregate either outlines or 2D cutouts when drawing or arranging materials on paper, than when the objects are 3D. They are able to arrange 2D materials so that one is partially hidden, provided the arrangement is made 'in space' so that many gaps can be left to represent object depth. They can also match arrays, using identical materials. The findings show that childrens' difficulties are confined to the 2D drawing surface, and that they have no problems with understanding simple spatial relationships, with allowing objects to be partially hidden, or with viewpoint. Other findings showed that children will treat 3D objects as 2D provided object depth is not an essential feature (as it is in spheres, cones etc.). A current experiment is investigating whether partial occlusion can be facilitated by triggering what may be schemas for drawing familiar objects – schemas that may be 2D in concept.
Status: Sponsored project
Source of Grant: Economic and Social Research Council £21,000
Date of Research: 1990 - continuing
KEYWORDS: cognitive ability; depth perception; drawing; problem solving; spatial ability; visual perception

9/0864
Walton Hall, Milton Keynes MK7 6AA
0908 274066
Levacic, R. Ms; Marren, E. Mr
The effects of the 1988 Education Act's formula funding of schools
Abstract: The study addresses two key questions, the first at local education authority (LEA) level and the second at school level: (1) How does formula funding affect the budgets which different types of schools receive compared to the previous 'historic' or 'traditional' method of funding?; and (2) how do schools respond to changes in the level and character of their funding? The project is assessing the extent to which official intentions of the Local Management of Schools (LMS) legislation that schools should be better able to allocate resources efficiently and according to educational priorities are being fulfilled. A case study approach is used. One county LEA is studied and within that eleven schools have been selected to represent pairs of schools 'winning' and 'losing' in relation to changes in their budgets due to formula funding and to cover the different phases. The methods used are: (1) collection and analysis of documents from LEA and schools on budget data and decisions relating to the allocation of finance; (2) statistical analysis of numerical data on financial and related resource variables; (3) interviews with teachers, school and LEA finance officers and governors; (4) observation of meetings – the latter almost entirely in schools.
Published Material: LEVACIC, R. (1992). 'Management of schools: aims, scope and impact', Educational Management and Administration, Vol 20, No 1, pp.16-29.
Status: Sponsored project
Source of Grant: Economic and Social Research Council £32,000
Date of Research: 1990-1991
KEYWORDS: Education Reform Act 1988; educational finance; local management of schools; school-based management

9/0865
Walton Hall, Milton Keynes MK7 6AA
0908 274066
Woods, P. Mr; *Supervisor:* Mackay, H. Dr; Cosin, B. Mr
Consumerist perspectives on education
Abstract: A study of the development of institutionalised forms of home-school links with particular reference to parent governors. These links are contextualised in notions of consumerism, which is considered in terms of its displacing the hitherto dominant approaches to the area of labourism and socialism.
Status: Individual research
Date of Research: 1985 - continuing
KEYWORDS: governing bodies; parent participation; parent-school relationship

9/0866
Institute of Educational Technology, Walton Hall, Milton Keynes MK7 6AA
0908 274066
Chambers, E. Ms; Durbridge, N. Ms
Distance education and the humanities
Abstract: This is an investigation of all aspects of adult students' encounters with distance courses in the Humanities. To date most research has been done into beginning students (i.e. those taking an interdisciplinary Foundation course) and those studying philosophy and music. The research covers: students' expectations of and attitudes to studying; students' acquisition of study skills; the particular problems facing students new to the study of philosophy (and, in 1992, literature, art history, music and history). The methods used are: survey questionnaires, large and small samples; interviews; small samples; institutional data (e.g. drop out, examination pass rates etc.).
Published Material: CHAMBERS, E.A. (1984). 'A project component in architectural history'. In: HENDERSON, E. & NATHENSON, M. (Eds). Independent learning in higher education. Englewood Cliffs, New Jersey: Prentice-Hall Inc.; CHAMBERS, E.A. & DURBRIDGE, N. (1987). 'Preparing for the examination', A102 An Arts Foundation Course, Units 31-32. Milton Keynes: Open University Press.; CHAMBERS, E.A. (1992). 'Workload and the quality of student learning', Studies in Higher Education, (in press).; CHAMBERS, E.A. (1991). 'Improving Foundation Level study at the Open University through Evaluation of student experience'. In: Proceedings of the CNAA Conference 'Academic Quality Assurance'. London: CNAA.
Status: Sponsored project
Source of Grant: Open University
Date of Research: 1975 - continuing
KEYWORDS: adult students; distance education; humanities; mature students; open universities; student attitudes

9/0867

Institute of Educational Technology, Walton Hall, Milton Keynes MK7 6AA
0908 274066
Kirkup, G. Ms; Kirkwood, A. Mr; Jones, A. Dr
An evaluation of home computers in adult distance education
Abstract: An investigation of the effects of compulsory use of a personal computer students studying particular courses in the undergraduate programme of the Open University. Students were sampled during their studies in 1988, 1989, 1990 and 1991. Issues of interest include: access and availability of equipment; costs; the effect of introducing home based computing on study habits; content difficulty; and the impact on family of computer in home. Teaching staff are also researched to discover the effects on contact with students and teaching load. Research methods include: survey questionnaires at points in the year; interviews; and self-completion journals.
Published Material: KIRKWOOD, A. & KIRKUP, G. (1991). 'Access to computing for home-based students', Studies in Higher Education, Vol 16, No 3.; KIRKUP, G. (1991). 'Computer conferencing and gender', Computers in Adult Education and Training, Vol 2, No 2.; JONES, A., KIRKUP, G., KIRKWOOD, A. & MASON, R. (1992). Providing computing for distance learners: a strategy for home use', Computers and Education, No 18, pp.1-3.; KIRKUP, G., JONES, A. & KIRKWOOD, A. (1992). Personal computers for distance learning. London: Paul Chapman.
Status: Sponsored project
Source of Grant: Open University
Date of Research: 1988 - continuing
KEYWORDS: *computer uses in education; distance education; microcomputers; open universities*

9/0868

Institute of Educational Technology, Walton Hall, Milton Keynes MK7 6AA
0908 274066
Womphrey, R. Mr; Calder, J. Dr
Annual survey of new Open University courses
Abstract: Each year the Open University surveys its students in order to acquaint the University with the reactions of students to course materials and services. Being a distance-teaching institution the self-completion questionnaires are mailed to the students. A survey of all undergraduate courses in first presentation is carried out at the end of the courses. The samples vary from 200 – 800 undergraduates who all receive a mailed self-completion survey report form, followed by two reminders. The survey results assist the allocation of resources to courses, and the improvement of the design of courses.
Status: Sponsored project
Source of Grant: Open University
Date of Research: 1991-1992
KEYWORDS: *course evaluation; distance education; open universities; student attitudes; surveys*

9/0869

Institute of Educational Technology, Walton Hall, Milton Keynes MK7 6AA
0908 274066
Lefrere, P. Dr
The trainers' workbench
Abstract: The project aims at a partial codification, for proof of concept purposes, of open learning expertise, with a view to developing rule-based systems. A prototype system will provide on-the-job help with the design and evaluation of learning materials, including computer-assisted learning.
Status: Individual research
Date of Research: 1990 - continuing
KEYWORDS: *computer-assisted learning; educational materials; educational media; open education*

9/0870

Institute of Educational Technology, Walton Hall, Milton Keynes MK7 6AA
0908 274066
Fitzgerald, D. Mr; *Supervisor:* Morgan, A. Dr
Qualitative thinking in tertiary education
Abstract: This research looks at approaches to teaching and consequent learning outcomes in tertiary education students, to investigate what techniques might be implemented in order to develop students' independence in thinking. The background work centres on research which suggests three fundamental approaches to learning (surface, strategic, deep) used by students. It will examine how it may be possible to aspire towards deep learning, i.e. how might critical thinking be instantiated into the learning process. How to think rather than what to know is the underlying rationale.
Status: Sponsored project
Source of Grant: Open University, per annum £5,000
Date of Research: 1991 - continuing
KEYWORDS: *learning processes; learning strategies; teaching methods; tertiary education*

9/0871

Institute of Educational Technology, Walton Hall, Milton Keynes MK7 6AA
0908 274066
Vincent, T. Dr; Child, D. Mr
Alternatives to print for visually impaired students
Abstract: This research will be to see whether improved access to textual material could be provided to visually disabled students through use of new information technology. This project concerns investigation of three formats for material which could be produced easily with the aid of new technology. They are enlarged print, braille and synthetic speech. The final result will be sets of guidelines relating to each of these possibilities indicating how best they can be exploited. This research has included an investigation into the use of compact disc technology (CD-ROM) together with hypertext retrieval systems and synthetic speech environments to give interactive access to text on an electronic form.
Status: Sponsored project
Source of Grant: The Mercers' Company; Clothworkers' Foundation, jointly £9,500
Date of Research: 1989-1991
KEYWORDS: *blindness; braille; human-computer interaction; information technology; magnification methods; speech synthesisers; tactile adaptation; visual impairments*

9/0872

Institute of Educational Technology, Walton Hall, Milton Keynes MK7 6AA
0908 274066
Jones, A. Dr; Petre, M. Dr
Investigating effective reasoning models for students: what courses provide and what students concoct
Abstract: This research has two main aims: to investigate elements that contribute to the formation of mental models by novice users and to evaluate metaphors by which models are suggested. A further aim is to consider practical issues for designing instructional material for independent study. A pilot project will investigate instructional elements that contribute to the formation of mental models by novice users. Particular questions include: (1) Is there a generaliseable set of initial information that obstructs learning if it is absent or encourages learning if it is offered at the outset?; (2) Do the principle metaphors work; where do they break down, when and in what circumstances do users reject them? Practical issues for designing instructional material for independent study include the question of how people actually use the resources provided and when does the time it takes to become minimally competent with a system become prohibitive? The pilot study takes the form of a case study of a practical element of an Open University course. The domain is learning a computer application.
Status: Individual research
Date of Research: 1992 - continuing
KEYWORDS: *computers; educational materials; metaphors; reasoning*

9/0873

Institute of Educational Technology, Walton Hall, Milton Keynes MK7 6AA
0908 274066
Vincent, T. Dr
Study of the IBM screen reader for blind students in distance education
Abstract: The study seeks to establish how the IBM PS/2 computer and Screen Reader can be used to meet the needs of blind Open University students studying from home for those activities where

writing is an essential component of the course-related activities; such as assignment and essay writing. Three students are involved: two who are following Arts or Social Studies courses and have little or no computer literacy; one who will be following a computing, mathematics, science or technology course where a degree of computer literacy might be expected. In each case, the students will have their individual needs assessed; and a programme of induction training arranged (using or supplementing training material provided with the Screen Reader) to provide the necessary skills in using the Screen Reader. Further advice and training will be provided to meet specific needs and applications. The evaluation will focus on how quickly and easily a student can progress to independence in the various writing activities associated with distance education. Progress towards independence in using the Screen Reader and application software will be closely monitored. In particular, the relationship to the level of support (advice and training) provided.
Status: Sponsored project
Source of Grant: IBM £24,000; Open University Development Fund £8,000
Date of Research: 1989-1991
KEYWORDS: *blindness; computer system design; computer uses in education; distance education; human-computer interaction; special educational needs; speech synthesisers; visual impairments*

9/0874

Institute of Educational Technology, Walton Hall, Milton Keynes MK7 6AA
0908 274066
Hawkridge, D. Prof.; Vincent, T. Dr
How do computers best help children and adults to overcome learning difficulties?
Abstract: This project reports and evaluates recent United Kingdom experience of using computers in schools and colleges to aid children and adults with learning difficulties caused by a wide range of physical, sensory and psychological disabilities, in their study of the curriculum. Fieldwork was carried out by selected teachers, advisory teachers, further education coordinators and adult educators, working under the principal researchers' direction. Each person selected was asked to compile a critical account of recent experience, particularly the best current practice, in his or her institution or district. Chapters were written by the principal researchers incorporating material from the fieldwork accounts, and sent to the fieldworkers for comment. Additional chapters were written by the principal researchers to provide context and a broad view of the state of the art, together with commentary. The study's main audience is likely to be those engaged in helping children and adults with learning difficulties: parents; policy-makers; administrators; principals; advisory teachers; advisors and teachers; staff and students in teacher training institutions. It will also be of interest to some adult students with learning difficulties.
Published Material: HAWKRIDGE, D. & VINCENT, T. (1992). Learning difficulties and computers: access to the curriculum. London: Jessica Kingsley Publishers.
Status: Sponsored project
Source of Grant: Nuffield Foundation £5,000
Date of Research: 1990-1991
KEYWORDS: *computer uses in education; moderate learning difficulties; special educational needs*

9/0875

Institute of Educational Technology, Walton Hall, Milton Keynes MK7 6AA
0908 274066
Zand, H. Dr; Burt, G. Mr
Affect and learning mathematics
Abstract: Learners of mathematics experience a variety of emotions such as anxiety, raised/lowered self image, depression, elation, etc. In this project, the researchers have been studying the emotional experiences of mathematics learners and their influence on their ability to learn. The researchers are also interested in questions such as: how affects exert their influence and the implications for teaching mathematics; how affects influence memory and mathematical insight.
Published Material: ZAND, H. & BURT, G.J. (1989). 'Social and emotional aspects learning mathematics', Educational and Training Technology International, Vol 26, No 1.
Status: Individual research
Date of Research: 1986 - continuing

KEYWORDS: *affective behaviour; emotional response; mathematics; student behaviour*

9/0876

Institute of Educational Technology, Walton Hall, Milton Keynes MK7 6AA
0908 274066
Burt, G. Mr
The curriculum as culture and ideology
Abstract: According to the common-sense view, education is about indiviudal people 'learning' ideas and skills. It is an apolitical activity, which meets the needs of individuals and of society as a whole. The aim of the curriculum as culture and ideology project is to challenge this view. Education is not about people learning ideas and skills; it is about cultural ideas and practices taking possession of people. Education then is simply one of a number of arenas in which different culutres and ideologies with differential powers seek to promote themselves, and hence come into conflict. Cultures seek to promote themselves in every sphere of society. Hence cultures demand education about every social sphere. The aim of the research project is to study educational provision with a view to identifying the cultural and ideological promotions involved. Currently under study are the arenas of educational technology, educational computing, mathematics and technology education, management education and community education. Teaching materials in these areas involve cultural and ideological promotion relating to issues of gender, class, ethnicity, individualism, technicism and militarism. Proposals for how education might be redesigned to take account of this critique are also being developed.
Published Material: BURT, G.J. (1989). 'Social forces and school computing', British Journal of Educational Technology, Vol 20, No 2, pp.140-141.; BURT, G.J. (1989). 'Computers in schools as culture and ideology', International Council for Distance Education Bulletin, Vol 20, pp.19-24.; BURT, G.J. (1989). 'Beyond educational technology: the new discipline of cultural and ideological technology', Research in Distance Education, Vol 1, No 3, pp.9-11.; BURT, G.J. (1989). 'The message behind the medium', Information Technology and Learning, December, pp.55-56.; BURT, G.J. (1991). 'Culture and ideology in the training literature', Educational Technology and Training International, Vol 28, No 3, pp.229-237. A full list of publications is available from the researcher.
Status: Individual research
Date of Research: 1988 - continuing
KEYWORDS: *cultural influences; curriculum; educational philosophy; ideology*

9/0877

Institute of Educational Technology, Walton Hall, Milton Keynes MK7 6AA
0908 274066
Mason, R. Dr; Kaye, A. Mr
Computer conferencing in distance education
Abstract: The Open University pioneered the use of computer conferencing in mass distance education on its Information Technology course in 1988. The University is now looking to rewrite that course and to offer it to students throughout Europe. Computer conferencing will form a major component of the course, both as a medium for supporting students and as a means of presenting and maintaining the course. Through a series of pilot schemes and other small applications, the researchers are refining the use of this medium as a tool for distance education. Some of the areas under investigation are: (1) its integration with other media; (2) its use over ISDN links; (3) its use as a tool for collaborative writing of course material with other institutions; and (4) its application to training and continuing education. The focus of research by Open University Ph.D. students includes: discourse analysis of conferencing interactions; and critical mass for successful conference interactions. The researchers are also investigating the design of conferencing systems and front ends to provide low cost, easy to use access for home-based students throughout Europe.
Published Material: MASON, R. & KAYE, A.R. (Eds). (1989). Mindweave: communication, computers and distance education. Oxford: Pergamon Press.; MASON, R. (1989). 'The use of computer networks in education and training', Report No OL87. Moorfoot, Sheffield: Training Agency.; KAYE, A.R. (Ed.) (1992). Collaborative learning through computer conferencing. Heidelberg: Springer-Verlag.
Status: Sponsored project

Source of Grant: Training, Enterprise and Education Directorate; Economic and Social Research Council – studentships; European Community DELTA projects
Date of Research: 1990 - continuing
KEYWORDS: distance education; international educational exchange; open universities; teleconferencing

9/0878

Institute of Educational Technology, Walton Hall Milton Keynes MK7 6AA
0908 274066
Burt, G. Mr

Strategic management and development in educational organisation

Abstract: There is a growing attention to 'management' in educational organisations. However it is important that fashionable management ideas should not be accepted uncritically. The project studies the strategic process at the Open University noting the presence of structural and political dimensions. Special attention is given to studying the values and ethics dimensions.

Status: Individual research
Date of Research: 1990 - continuing
KEYWORDS: educational planning; management in education; university administration

9/0879

Institute of Educational Technology, Walton Hall, Milton Keynes MK7 6AA
0908 274066
Vincent, T. Dr; Supervisor: Vincent, T. Dr

CD-ROM as a curriculum delivery medium for blind and partially sighted learners

Abstract: The potential for using CD-ROM has been explored within the Open University to provide blind students with access to course material and related books. A project funded by the Department for Education takes access to curriculum materials a step further and, by providing speech output and large character interfaces to existing CD-ROM applications, enables learners to control the search for information as well as to read it. The process of identifying and using relevant material is required by most areas of the National Curriculum. Providing access to CD-ROM publications offers a chance for this to be carried out independently. Four schools and one college are involved in the project, covering a wide range of age and ability. Similar workstations are used in each location which are based on an IBM compatible PC with CD-ROM drive, and enabling devices and software to produce large screen print and/or speech output. Each location has chosen a number of CD-ROMs (such as Times/Sunday Times/ and Grolier Encyclopaedia) that are relevant to the curriculum. Enabling software has been prepared for each CD-ROM, and training has been provided for teachers both in terms of the functionality of the hardware and software, as well as the most important aspect of how this technology can give new or enhanced access to the curriculum.

Published Material: HAWKRIDGE, D. & VINCENT, T. (1992). Learning difficulties and computers: access to the curriculum. London: Jessica Kingsley Publishers.
Status: Sponsored project
Source of Grant: Department for Education £40,000; Open University £ 17,000; Fund for Blind and Partially Sighted £10,000
Date of Research: 1991 - continuing
KEYWORDS: blindness; computer uses in education; optical data discs; special educational needs; speech synthesisers; visual impairments

9/0880

Institute of Educational Technology, Walton Hall, Milton Keynes MK7 6AA
0908 274066
Whalley, P. Dr; Moar, M. Mr

Classroom based multimedia authoring tools

Abstract: The proposed project is concerned with children's use of the dynamic representations made possible by the newly available multimedia tools. With the micros affordable by schools, it is now possible to capture high quality colour images, sound, and short video clips. The purpose of this project is to develop an authoring tool for integrating these components which will be accessible to young children with a wide range of abilities, and to indicate ways in which it could enhance their work. Considerable success has already been achieved in the classroom with a prototype of the proposed system. The researchers intend to further refine the software to better incorporate video, and to provide detailed documentation as to how the various components of a dynamic document can be created, manipulated and finally assembled together. Technology, even if it is freely available, is of no use if it can not be integrated into classroom practice. The selection, organisation and presentation of learned materials is seen as a valuable part of current educational practice in British classrooms. Documenting how our software environment, together with paper based planning tools, can enable and extend these activities is seen as an important part of the project. Examples of completed projects on topics such as the 'rain cycle' and 'digestion' will be included, both in their final state and in the form of separate image and sound components.

Published Material: MOAR, M. (1992). 'The construction of dynamic documents by children', Proceedings of the East-West conference on emerging computer technologies in education, Moscow, April 1992.
Status: Sponsored project
Source of Grant: National Council for Educational Technology £10,000; Stirling Microsystems – equipment loan
Date of Research: 1992 - continuing
KEYWORDS: animation; authoring aids – programming; computer-assisted learning; computer uses in education; multimedia approach

9/0881

Institute of Educational Technology, Walton Hall, Milton Keynes MK7 6AA
0908 274066
Whalley, P. Dr; Williams, D. Dr

A 'virtual' microscope

Abstract: This project is concerned with developing a 'virtual' microscope which allows the student to choose, manipulate and examine rock samples on the computer screen. Embedding the 'virtual' microscope within a general multimedia database will provide the student with a powerful tool for enquiry and learning. The primary problems that the researchers intend to tackle are pedagogic not technical – what does or does not aid student learning in the summer school environment, and how may computer-based materials be integrated with the other media being used. An important part of the project will be the developmental testing of the materials at Open University summer schools with the general aim of finding the right balance between questioning and support for the student. An immediate use of the materials will be to enrich the experience of the less mobile students attending these summer schools. Whilst other students go out collecting samples 'in the field', these students will be able to make detailed analyses of equivalent rock samples and consequently be able to make greater contributions to group discussions. A simple extension of the project on the lines of the well known 'Eco-Disc' project would allow the student to 'move' around computer based images and video clips of the hill or quarry and choose from where they would like a 'sample' to be taken. This would obviously empower disabled students to undertake courses and projects from which they would otherwise be blocked.

Status: Sponsored project
Source of Grant: Open University: Institute of Educational Technology £ 60,300
Date of Research: 1993 - continuing
KEYWORDS: computer-assisted learning; earth science; educational equipment; microscopes; simulation; special educational needs

9/0882

Institute of Educational Technology, Walton Hall, Milton Keynes MK7 6AA
0908 274066
Whalley, P. Dr

An alternative metaphor for teaching control technology

Abstract: Control technology is viewed as a good way to provide practical experience of programmable systems that are familiar to children such as sliding doors, level crossings etc. Teachers using this technology usually also have the higher level goals of encouraging 'systems thinking' and general problem solving skills. Using a computer in this way to control physical micro-worlds cannnnn be an interesting and powerful educational experience. Unfortunately there is often a gulf between these aims and what happens in the classroom. The higher order goals are frequently lost in the struggle to cope with

the presently available control technology environments. The project represents an attempt to create a graphic object-orientated control language for children. The underlying nature of environments like HyperTechnic is quite different from their procedural equivalents, and is in several ways intuitively more comprehensible. For example conditionals and loop-control are implicit in the way that the objects operate and do not have to be explicitly taught. The micro-worlds that the children are to explore and control are made up of plastic and cardboard models, rather than the purely screen-based, and hence necessarily more abstract, micro-worlds that are often provided for children. The immediate practical goal of this research is to evaluate to what extent the level of description and explanatory metaphors used to describe control technology problems affects children's understanding of them. A longer term aim is to foster understanding of how children comprehend the deeper conceptual problems underlying this form of task.
Published Material: WHALLEY, P. (1990). 'HyperTechnic – a graphic object-orientated control language'. Presented at the Seventh International Conference on Technology and Education, Brussels, March 1990.; WHALLEY, P. (1991). 'Level of description as a factor in children's interactions with computers'. Presented at the Fourth European Conference for Research on Learning and Instruction (EARLI), Turku, Finland, August 1991.; WHALLEY, P. (1992). 'An alternative metaphor for teaching control technology'. Proceedings of the East-West Conference on Emerging Computer Technologies in Education, Moscow, April 1992.; WHALLEY, P. (1993). 'Making control technology work in one classroom', British Journal of Educational Technology (in press).
Status: Individual research
Date of Research: 1990 - continuing
KEYWORDS: computer simulation; computer uses in education; control technology; logo; models

9/0883
    Institute of Educational Technology, Walton Hall, Milton Keynes MK7 6AA
    0908 274066
    Moar, M. Mr; *Supervisor:* Whalley, P. Dr
The construction of dynamic documents by children
Abstract: Project work seeks to encourage the pupils' freedom to investigate a subject. It requires the selection, organisation and presentation of learned materials and as such is seen as a valuable part of current educational practice in British classrooms. Typically, the end product of a project is a document consisting of text together with appropriate graphics. It is now possible however to produce dynamic computer-based documents in the classroom, which incorporate moving images, text and sound. The thesis explores this possibility by looking briefly at the cognitive effects of producing media in an educational context and considering the representational qualities of such dynamic documents. The development of a methodology for dynamic document use based on conventional classroom practice is described, and suggestions for future research are made.
Published Material: MOAR, M. (1992). 'The construction of dynamic documents by children'. In: Proceedings of the East-West Conference on Emerging Computer Technologies for Education, Moscow, April 1992.
Status: Sponsored project
Source of Grant: Economic and Social Research Council
Date of Research: 1989 - continuing
KEYWORDS: animation; computer uses in education; pupil projects

9/0884
    Institute of Educational Technology, Walton Hall, Milton Keynes MK7 6AA
    0908 274066
    Issroff, K. Ms; *Supervisor:* Scanlon, E. Dr; Jones, A. Dr
Motivation and collaboration in computer-assisted learning of chemistry
Abstract: This research aims to investigate the motivation of secondary school students learning from computers in different learning situations. Motivation appears to change when students use computers for learning, especially when working collaboratively. In order to investigate the nature of this different motivation, quantitative and qualitative motivational indices can be measured. Quantitative indices refer to the students behaviours during learning, while qualitative indices refer to their feelings and attitudes towards the learning. Studies of cooperative learning at the computer have focused pre-

dominantly on the cognitive aspects of the interaction and results have not been conclusive. By investigating the psychological environment which surrounds the computer, it may be possible to explain some aspects of the cooperative learning process. The main study involves 15 individuals and 30 pairs learning chemistry from a computer. There is pre- and post-testing of both cognitive and motivational factors and the sesssions are video-taped for quantitative motivational indices. It is hoped that the results of this research will provide guidelines for designers of educational software, and educators in setting up effective computer-assisted learning situations and help us to understand the processes which occur when students work at the computer in different learning situations.
Published Material: ISSROFF, K. (1992). Cooperative computer-assisted learning. CITE Report No 173. Milton Keynes: Open University; Institute of Educational Technology.; ISSROFF, K. (1992). Motivation and computer-assisted learning. CITE Report No 174. Milton Keynes: Open University; Institute of Educational Technology.
Status: Sponsored project
Source of Grant: Economic and Social Research Council
Date of Research: 1991 - continuing
KEYWORDS: computer-assisted learning; computers in education; co-operative learning; human-computer interaction; learning processes

9/0885
    Institute of Educational Technology, Walton Hall, Milton Keynes MK7 6AA
    0908 274066
    Queen Mary and Westfield College, Mile End Road, London E1 4NS
    081 980 4811
    Bornat, R. Prof.; Reeves, S. Dr; O'Shea, T. Prof.
Cognitive skills in formal reasoning about programs
Abstract: The aim of the research is to test the hypothesis that with appropriate support, in particular with mechanical aids for symbolic calculation, a very much larger proportion of students can be made competent in formal techniques of reasoning about programs. In the Spring of 1991 and during the course of the academic year 1991 to 1992 a number of empirical studies were undertaken to assess the difficulties which students encounter in learning formal methods of reasoning. Information was obtained from 'diary' records kept by a selection of students. Exchanges on those electronic bulletin boards related to the programming course were noted and an informal electronic link was established between first year computer science students at Queen Mary & Westfield College (QMW) and investigators at the Open University (OU). Sets of data based on answers, given by students, to questions on their backgrounds, their motivations for studying computer science and their expectations of the course were combined with video and audio interviews of them discussing their work. The results of these empirical studies have been used as feedback to researchers at QMW. During this period, the project members at QMW have investigated what graphical tools are currently available to help students learn formal reasoning methods and have designed and developed their own computer-based tools. A series of empirical studies are being undertaken from 1992 to 1993, during which students will be observed using the graphical tools developed in the first phase of the project. These studies will serve as the basis of an evaluation of the help such tools afford to students and will contribute to the further refinement of the tools themselves.
Published Material: FUNG, P. & O'SHEA, T. 'Formal reasoning as a culture shock for computer science students'. In: Development in the Teaching of Computer Science'. Proceedings of Conference at University of Kent, Canterbury, April, 1992, pp.26-34.; FUNG, P & O'SHEA, T. 'Fear of formal reasoning'. In: Proceedings of the Fifth Psychology of Programming Workshop, Paris, 1992, December, pp.207-236.
Status: Sponsored project
Source of Grant: Economic and Social Research Council; Science and Engineering Research Council; Medical Research Council
Date of Research: 1991 - continuing
KEYWORDS: cognitive development; computer programming; reasoning

9/0886
    School of Education, Walton Hall, Milton Keynes MK7 6AA
    0908 274066
    Bancroft, D. Dr
Temporal inference research project

Abstract: It is arguably the case that much human reasoning and problem solving rests on an understanding of the temporal interrelations between events. Early and effective development of temporal understanding may then make a considerable contribution to wider cognitive skills. There has been a considerable amount of European laboratory based research investigation of the development of childrens' understanding of time. One outcome is the suggestion that the coordination of temporal concepts is problematic for children until late in childhood since it depends on considerable cognitive sophistication. Another possibility is that young children are capable of dealing with temporal concepts when not obstructed by 'interfering' factors. There is also evidence from the psycholinguistic tradition which suggests that children use the language of 'time' effectively from a very early age. The aim of the project is to investigate childrens' ability to reason about, and manipulate the concepts of Order and Duration in order to resolve some of the theoretical issues and to identify means of encouraging the development of temporal reasoning. Children aged between 4 and 7 years are presented with temporal problems on a microcomputer. Children have either mouse or concept keyboard control of the computer, thus allowing a behavioural indication of comprehension. Results to date indicate that, although not all temporal problems are of equal complexity, children of this age are capable of producing sophisticated solutions and that this ability can be developed and promoted.
Status: Sponsored project
Source of Grant: Open University
Date of Research: 1987 - continuing
KEYWORDS: *cognitive development; reasoning; temporal integration; time perspective*

9/0887

School of Education, Walton Hall, Milton Keynes MK7 6AA
0908 274066
Edwards, R. Dr
Educational responses to adult employment
Abstract: The aim of this research is to critically examine the policies and practices which produce and respond to adult unemployment in contemporary society and the role of education and training discourse and programmes in overcoming and/or reproducing adult unemployment. This is pursued through desk research and interviews with policy makers, practitioners and participants in the field. Conclusions are always provisional, dependent on the changing constellation of policy and practice.
Published Material: EDWARDS, R. (1991). 'The Canadian jobs strategy', Unemployment Bulletin, Autumn, pp.8-13.; EDWARDS, R. (1991). 'The inevitable future? post-Fordism and open learning', Open Learning, Vol 6, No 2, pp.36-43.; EDWARDS, R. (1991). 'Guidance and unemployment in Canada', Adults Learning, Vol 2, No 10, pp.279-282.; EDWARDS, R. 'Winners and losers: the education and training of adults'. In: RAGGATT, P. & UNWIN, L. (Eds). Change and intervention: vocational education and training. London: Falmer Press.
Status: Sponsored project
Source of Grant: Canadian High Commission £1,800
Date of Research: 1990 - continuing
KEYWORDS: *adult vocational education; employment patterns; training; unemployment*

9/0888

School of Education, Walton Hall, Milton Keynes MK7 6AA
0908 274066
Light, P. Prof.
Social interaction and cognitive development in school aged children
Abstract: An extensive programme of research (mostly in the form of small experimental projects) has addressed social aspects of children's cognitive development. Topics have encompassed social perspective taking, spatial perspective taking and drawing, conservation and logical reasoning. Current work is focused on the role of pragmatic schemes in deductive reasoning and the role of peer interaction in problem-solving, using computers.
Published Material: LIGHT, P. & PERRET-CLERMONG, A.N. (1989). 'Social context effects in reasoning and testing'. In: GELLATLY, A. et al (Eds). Cognition and social worlds. Oxford: Clarendon Press.; LIGHT, P. & BLAYE, A. (1990). 'Computer-based learning: the social dimensions'. In: FOOT, H.C., MORGAN, M.J. & SHUTE, R.H. (Eds). Children helping children. Chichester: John Wiley & Sons Ltd.; LIGHT, P., GIROTTO, V. & LEGRENZI, P.

(1990). 'Children's reasoning on conditional promises and permissions', Cognitive Development, No 5, pp.369-383.
Status: Sponsored project
Source of Grant: Economic and Social Resarch Council; Foundation Fyssen (Paris); Open University; Leverhulme Trust
Date of Research: 1979 - continuing
KEYWORDS: *cognitive development; interaction; peer groups; reasoning*

9/0889

School of Education, Walton Hall, Milton Keynes MK7 6AA
0908 274066
Thomas, G. Rev.; *Supervisor:* Levacic, R. Ms
The Framework for Local Management of Schools: a study of local education authorities' approved Local Management of Schools schemes
Abstract: This is a survey of Local Management of Schools schemes approved by the Department of Education and Science (DES) for implementation in 1990/91, and is supplemented by data from Section 42 financial statements. The study analyses 82 schemes for England and Wales from a total of 103. The aspects of schemes surveyed are: (1) the extent of delegation of management responsibilities to schools; (2) age-weighted element of the formula; (3) other elements; (4) financial regulations; (5) monitoring and evaluation. It includes detailed statistical tables reproducing the data base of financial and formula variables for all the authorities surveyed. An additional aspect of the study investigated the changes to local education authorities original local management of schools submissions required by the DES before the schemes were finally approved .
Published Material: THOMAS, G. (1991). The framework for local management of schools: a study of local education authorities' approved local management of schools schemes. Milton Keynes: Open University.; THOMAS, G. & LEVACIC, R. (1991). 'Centralising in order to decentralise? DES scrutiny and approval of LMS schemes', Journal of Educational Policy, Vol 6, No 4, pp.401-416.
Status: Sponsored project
Source of Grant: Open University
Date of Research: 1990-1991
KEYWORDS: *educational administration; educational planning; local education authorities; local management of schools; school-based management*

9/0890

School of Education, Walton Hall, Milton Keynes MK7 6AA
0908 274066
Bristol University, Senate House, Bristol BS8 1TH
0272 303030
Austin, J. Mr; *Supervisor:* Bell, R. Dr; Low-Beer, A. Dr
The Preparatory School experience 1918-1940
Abstract: This is an historical study of the nature of preparatory school experience for boys and staff in the period between the wars. It will involve oral history methods as well as analysis of school magazines, autobiographies and other literary sources.
Status: Individual research
Date of Research: 1991 - continuing
KEYWORDS: *boys; educational history; preparatory schools*

9/0891

School of Education, Walton Hall, Milton Keynes MK7 6AA
0908 274066
Glasgow University, Department of Adult and Continuing Education, 8 University Gardens, Glasgow G12 8QQ
041 339 8855
Small, N. Mr; *Supervisor:* Bell, R. Dr; Brown, L. Prof.
The role of education for citizenship with reference to Zambia
Abstract: The research explores the informal area of education from which, and by which, adults develop a sense of identity at a national level. More positive is the idea and work of 'nation building' which can also arise from educational provision. The context is 'what counts as citizenship in States formed in the last century in former British colonial territories in east and central Africa?'. This offers a comparative background to the main focus on Zambia. Zambia was administered by a chartered company for about a quarter of a century; was the responsibility of the British Colonial Office for forty years as Northern Rhodesia; and has been an independent State in the Commonwealth for a quarter of a century. In that last period, it has faced particular external difficulties, reflecting circumstances in

Southern Rhodesia (now Zimbabwe); and from its position economically with regard to South Africa. Internally, copper mining has been the major supplier of exports and of foreign exchange; but a decline in demand and a fall in price have seriously affected the robustness of the economy to finance the expansion of desired infrastructure, and social, health and educational development. The researcher hopes to review the role of education among adults, and indicate if and how it contributes to a commitment of a sense of identity with the State; and whether the adult as citizen is a concept that is consciously pursued by agencies formal and informal.

Status: Individual research
Date of Research: 1985 - continuing
KEYWORDS: *citizenship; citizenship education; identity; nationalism; role of education; Zambia*

9/0892

School of Education, Walton Hall, Milton Keynes MK7 6AA
0908 274066
Sheffield University, Division of Education, 388 Glossop Road, Sheffield S10 2TN
0742 768555
Levacic, R. Ms; Jesson, D. Mr
Resourcing Sheffield schools
Abstract: The project is constructing a school funding formula which meets the requirements of the Education Reform Act 1988 and which is based on a needs assessment for educating pupils aged 3-18 at schools with different characteristics. A major source of evidence for constructing the model is a survey of current patterns of resource use in Sheffield Education Authority's 32 secondary schools, 191 primary schools and 6 colleges. This will be supplemented by professional assessment of resource requirements to construct an activity led resourcing model to provide age-weightings for the funding formula.
Status: Sponsored project
Source of Grant: Sheffield Education Authority £30,000
Date of Research: 1991-1992
KEYWORDS: *educational finance; educational planning; financial support; local education authorities; local management of schools; school-based management*

9/0893

Chorlton House, 70 Manchester Road, Chorlton-cum-Hardy, Manchester M21 1PQ
061 861 9823
Underley Hall School, Kirkby Lonsdale, Carnforth LA6 2HE
0524 271206
Litt, L. Dr; Pain, J. Dr
Asessment of handwriting and its relationship to spelling and reading in six and a half to seven and a half year old children
Abstract: The research arises from the development of a dictation test for use with top infant (six and a half to seven and a half year old) children. Data (total scores) is available for several thousand children. From these, a sub-sample of some 500 scripts is being analysed in detail so that comparisons may be made between handwriting characteristics and attainments in spelling and reading. Anomalies identified in these comparisons will be investigated on an individual basis to identify causal factors.
Status: Individual research
Date of Research: 1991 - continuing
KEYWORDS: *handwriting; infant school pupils; reading; spelling; writing skills*

Oxford University

9/0894

University Offices, Wellington Square, Oxford OX1 2JD
0865 270000
Harrison, B. Dr; Howarth, J. Mrs; Greenstein, D. Dr; Curthoys, M. Dr; Pottle, M. Dr
The origins and destinations of Oxford University students and teachers 1900-1979
Abstract: The project has aimed at systematically recording and analysing data relating to the origins and destinations of students and dons at the university of Oxford in the twentieth century. The work on students has focused on a 10% sample of those who matriculated between 1900 and 1979. It has involved the collection and computerisation of data relating: to pre-Oxford schooling and origins (father's occupation and address, place and date of birth, etc.); to university career – date and college of matriculation, performance in finals, scholarships won, degrees attained; and to post-Oxford career – location and nature of job, and career progression. The work on dons has focused on specific years – 1912, 1937, 1957 and 1976 and has recorded, though not computerised, data on undergraduate career, college membership and, where possible, career progression. The sample involved in the work on students, defined as junior members, has been randomly selected from the 133,000 who matriculated inbetween 1900-1979; it represents approximately 10% of the junior membership in the years in question. Data has been collected by two methods – traditional 'record search' involving scrutiny of published sources such as Who's who, College and school registers, etc. and a postal survey questionnaire to those who matriculated after 1929. The research into the careers of Oxford dons has relied on the use of published sources, including those issued by the university. The sample has been comprehensive within the years specified, and an attempt has been made to include all teachers at the university, and not just those whose college membership and teaching commitment justified the description of 'don'.
Status: Sponsored project
Source of Grant: Leverhulme Trust; Economic and Social Research Council; Oxford University
Date of Research: 1988-1991
KEYWORDS: *academic staff; careers; degrees – academic; educational history; outcomes of education; socioeconomic background; university students*

9/0895

Department of Applied Social Studies and Social Research, Barnett House, Wellington Square, Oxford OX1 2ER
0865 270325
Aldgate, P. Dr; Heath, A. Dr; *Supervisor:* Aldgate, P. Dr; Heath, A. Dr
The educational progress of children in care
Abstract: This research has identified factors contributing to the educational success or difficulties of middle school-aged children in long-term foster care. To this end the researchers studied the school-aged children in foster care in one local authority, together with their parents and carers over a period of three years. The educational attainment of these children in reading ability, mathematics and vocabulary was compared with a contrast group of children of the same age and from similar backgrounds who were living with their own families, known to Social Services Departments, and who were receiving social work help (usually under Section 1 of the 1980 Child Care Act). A combination of longitudinal and cross-sectional research design was used. Children's educational progress was charted over three years. Both groups of children were low achievers by national standards. Factors influencing the foster children's attainment included their early histories, and the stability of the current foster home. Contact with families of origin had no effect on children's achievement or behaviour. There was an interaction between children's behaviour and their educational attainment. Social workers place educational attainment low on their agenda of activities in relation to children in foster care.
Published Material: HEATH, A.F., COLTON, M. & ALDGATE, J. (1989). 'The education of children in and out of care', British Journal of Social Work, No 19, pp.447-460.; ALDGATE, J. (1990). 'Foster children at school: success or failure?' Adoption and Fostering, Vol 14, No 4, pp.38-49.; COLTON, M., ALDGATE, J. & HEATH, A.F.(1991). 'Behavioural problems among children in and out of care', Social Sciences Review, Vol 2, No 3, pp.177-191.
Status: Sponsored project
Source of Grant: Economic and Social Research Council £56,830
Date of Research: 1987-1991
KEYWORDS: *academic achievement; academic failure; child welfare; family environment; foster children; home-school relationship; low achievement; social services*

9/0896

Department of Educational Studies, 15 Norham Gardens, Oxford OX2 6PY
0865 274024
Haggarty, L. Ms; *Supervisor:* McIntyre, D. Mr

Investigating a framework for mathematics teacher education: an action research study
Abstract: The aim of the research was to set up and investigate a model of school based initial teacher education, working as university tutor in partnership with mathematics mentors in schools. The setting up and testing of the model was done within a framework of action research and the first cycle of the research was concerned with establishing a partnership with school supervisors acting as mentors; and also designing and testing a mathematics curriculum programme which satisfied the principles of the Internship Scheme, being implemented at Oxford University. Results from this work suggested that the hypothetical solution had gone according to plan. However, it was discovered that mentors had not been able to implement two fairly fundamental aspects of the model, so in the second cycle of the research, attention was focused on the mentors, in an attempt to discover how each approached their agreed role. Content analysis was used as a major research method in order to determine the nature of conversations between mentors and interns (students) in schools. Results suggested that whilst mentors were taking many of the agreed actions, they were also interpreting their roles in quite different ways. The third cycle of the research focused on the mathematics interns and, taking an ethnographic approach, asked what and how interns learn within the model of teacher education. Whilst many of the findings are consistent with those in the research literature, this research identifies important issues about both school-based models of teacher education and beginning teachers' learning.
Published Material: DAVIES, C. & HAGGARTY, L. (1989). 'Learning to teach'. In: BENTON, P. (Ed). Internship: integration and partnership in initial teacher training. London: Gulbenkian Foundation.; HAGGARTY, L. (1988). 'Investigating a new framework for mathematics teacher education: an action research study', Conference paper in the proceedings of the British Society for the Research into Learning Mathematics.; BACHHOUSE, J.K. & HAGGARTY, L. (1988). 'An 'Internship' approach to the initial training of mathematics teachers', a paper presented at ICME in Budapest.; HAGGARTY, L. (1988). 'PGCE: a new approach', Mathematics Teaching, No 124, pp.42-43, September.
Status: Individual research
Date of Research: 1985-1992
KEYWORDS: mathematics teachers; mentors; preservice teacher education; professional tutors; student teachers; supervision

Paisley College

9/0897
High Street, Paisley PA1 2BE
041 848 3000
Connor, S. Mrs; *Supervisor:* Young, A. Prof.; Wylie, J. Mr
Organising academic-industry liaison: theory and evidence
Abstract: The main aim of this research is an attempt to determine the most effective strategies and forms of organisation which academic institutions should adopt to facilitate and encourage liaison with industry, commerce and the public sector. Empirical work relating to the organisation forms and strategies operating in higher education institutions has been completed. This involved surveys (by personal interview) of the perceptions of over 400 academics and members of senior management groups in 11 central institutions throughout Scotland. These interviews were conducted by a team led by the researcher who was also responsible for the survey design. Preliminary results of the research suggest that a system of delegated control, together with guidelines for liaison activities, contribute towards the instigation, maintenance and extension of liaison activities in Scottish Central Institutions. At this stage an analysis of the empirical study data and at the theoretical level will be carried out and an attempt will be made to construct and test models of 'best practice' of college-industry liaison.
Published Material: CONNOR, S., WYLIE, J. & YOUNG, A. (1986). 'Academic-industry liaison in the United Kingdom: economic perspectives', Higher Education, Vol 5, No 5, pp.407-420.; CONNOR, S. & WYLIE, J. (1985). 'Post-experience vocational education: an investigation of its role in linking colleges, universities and business', Scottish Journal of Adult Education, Vol 7, No 2.; CONNOR, S. & WYLIE, J. (1986). 'Driving a hard bargain', Times Higher Education Supplement, 4.7.86.
Status: Individual research
Date of Research: 1985-1991

KEYWORDS: cooperative programmes; industry-higher education relationship

Plymouth University

9/0898
Enterprise Unit, 92 Cobourg Street, Plymouth PL4 8AA
0752 232376
Davies, J. Mr
Mentors in education and training
Abstract: Mentors were introduced into Plymouth University's inservice Certificate in Education course in 1985 as a means of providing a link between the students' course of study and their place of work. As mentors have come to take an increasingly important role in education and training, so a need for mentor training has been identified. In order to design coherent training programmes, it is essential to have a clear view of the roles of both mentors and proteges. Through the literature, this research aims to clarify and identify established roles, to create a typology, and to suggest training programmes appropriate to the different roles.
Status: Sponsored project
Source of Grant: Plymouth University: Rolle Faculty of Education £750; Plymouth University: Enterprise in Higher Education £750
Date of Research: 1991 - continuing
KEYWORDS: inservice teacher education; mentors; training

9/0899
Department of Mathematics and Statistics, Centre for Teaching Mathematics, Drake Circus, Plymouth PL4 8AA
0752 600600
May, W. Ms; *Supervisor:* Berry, J. Prof.; Mosley, P. Mrs
The effects of maturation on pupils participation and achievement in mathematics
Abstract: The purpose of this research is to investigate if there are gender differences related to maturation and the participation and achievement of pupils in mathematics, particularly of associated absences and any related, psychological or physical factors.
Status: Individual research
Date of Research: 1992 - continuing
KEYWORDS: individual development; mathematics achievement; mathematics education; pupil participation; sex difference

9/0900
Department of Psychology, Drake Circus, Plymouth PL4 8AA
0752 600600
Newstead, S. Prof.; Franklyn-Stokes, A. Dr
Academic dishonesty in students
Abstract: The purpose of the present project is to investigate the nature, frequency and causes of various forms of cheating behaviour. A general purpose questionnaire has been developed which has so far been given to staff and students at one 'new' and one 'old' university. The results indicate that staff underestimate the frequency of cheating compared to students, and this is especially marked with coursework. Staff also rated most types of cheating behaviour as more serious than did students, but there were exceptions to this, notably cheating in group projects. Among the students, there were also interesting differences between mature students and others, with mature students responding more like staff. Follow-up research will investigate self-reported frequency of cheating, the motives and causes of cheating, and cheating in other educational contexts.
Published Material: NEWSTEAD, S.E. & FRANKLYN-STOKES, A. (1993). 'Staff and student perceptions of the frequency and gravity of cheating behaviours'. Paper presented at the Annual Conference of the British Psychological Society, Blackpool, April.
Status: Individual research
Date of Research: 1992 - continuing
KEYWORDS: cheating; discipline problems; higher education; plagiarism; student behaviour

9/0901
Rolle Faculty of Education, Douglas Avenue, Exmouth EX8 2AT

0395 255309
Holt, D. Dr
The Centre for the Study of the Arts in Primary Education (CENSAPE): development of resource collections of examples of good practice in primary arts education
Abstract: The centre is an initiative of the expressive arts section of the Rolle Faculty of Education at Polytechnic South West (now Plymouth University). As well as drawing on the resources of this institution, The Centre for the Study of the Arts in Primary Education (CENSAPE) also works closely with schools and local education authorities (LEAs) in the South West of England. The principal concerns of the centre are to collect and disseminate examples of good practice in primary arts education and to undertake associated programmes of research and publication. The current phase of the project is directed towards the establishment of a series of resource collections containing annotated examples of good primary practice in the areas of visual art, drama, dance and music, and with the development of a loan system to make such material available to schools, teachers and others with an interest in primary arts education. When this work is complete, CENSAPE will continue to pursue a variety of projects concerned with research and publication in this area of the curriculum.
Published Material: HOLT, D.A. (1990). 'CENSAPE: Centre for the Study of the Arts in Primary Education', NFAE Journal, No 6, pp.18-19.
Status: Sponsored project
Source of Grant: Caloustie Gulbenkian Foundation £15,000
Date of Research: 1990-1992
KEYWORDS: art; art activities; art education; dance; drama; music; primary education

9/0902

Rolle Faculty of Education, Douglas Avenue, Exmouth
EX8 2AT
0395 255309
Mackenzie, R. Mr; *Supervisor:* Hannan, A. Dr; Taylor, G. Dr
Educating teachers to be intellectuals: a study of an attempt to enable preservice primary teachers to develop as critically reflective practitioners
Abstract: The concept of the reflective practitioner has been explored and extended in a critical direction, and the investigation has been both conceptual and empirical. The case for teachers to act as transformative intellectuals rather than State technicians has been argued within the context of a period of cultural and legislative change in society and in relation to primary school practices developed beyond the ideological polarisations of the past period. The empirical part of the investigation is based on an attempt to incorporate the concept of teachers as intellectuals in a B. Ed. Educational Studies course component entitled 'Teachers and Children of the Future'. The course aims to support emerging teachers in developing a personal philosophy of education within collegial frameworks so that contemporary challenges should not swamp them personally or professionally. Action research has been used to investigate the aims, content, pedagogy and outcomes of the course which 80 B. Ed. students have now completed. A smaller group of ex-students, now Newly Qualified Teachers (NQTs), are assisting a follow through into the first year of teaching: the aspiration is to compare and contrast the conceptual and empirical positions of the course with the experienced realities of being an NQT in the 1990s.
Published Material: MACKENZIE, R. (1993). The Cox Views of English and Primary Practice in the 1990s. English in Education (in press).
Status: Sponsored project
Source of Grant: Plymouth University: Rolle Faculty of Education £4,657.50
Date of Research: 1990 - continuing
KEYWORDS: intellectuals; preservice teacher education; probationary teachers; professional development; teacher role; teaching profession

9/0903

Rolle Faculty of Education, Douglas Avenue, Exmouth
EX8 2AT
0395 255309
Graham, J. Mr
An investigation into the feasibility of presenting mathematics in the same form to pupils within National Curriculum key stages 2, 3 and 4

Abstract: Circular No. 17/91 (DES, 1991) states that 'Teachers are required to teach with a view to pupils achieving levels of attainment within the ranges specified for that key stage'. The aim of the research is to ascertain how realistic it is to present pupils in different key stages with common 'teaching materials' aimed at giving them opportunities to achieve common levels of attainment. It is envisaged that four different teaching 'units' will be employed and four different 'clusters' of schools will be sought comprising the following types: (a) primary – pupils aged 10/11, and middle – pupils aged 11 (key stage 2); (b) lower secondary – pupils aged 14 (key stage 3); (c) upper secondary – pupils aged 16 (key stage 4). In total, 16 groups/classes will be approached. The research will include a quantitative analysis of the effectiveness of the teaching materials used, using a two-way analysis of variance linked to a Latin square design.
Status: Sponsored project
Source of Grant: Plymouth University: Rolle Faculty of Education £2,546.50
Date of Research: 1993 - continuing
KEYWORDS: assessment; educational materials; mathematics achievement; mathematics education; National Curriculum

9/0904

Rolle Faculty of Education, Douglas Avenue, Exmouth
EX8 2AT
0395 255309
Fisher, R. Mrs; *Supervisor:* Taylor, G. Dr; Clibbens, J. Dr; Hannan, A. Dr
A study of the role and practice of the teacher of reading at National Curriculum key stage 1
Abstract: The study aims to examine the decisions made by teachers of early reading as demonstrated by their responses to children. A pilot study examined the role of the teacher in four Reception/Year One classes and considered the relationship between what the teacher did to teach reading and what the children learned. This has led to a further study using video of infant teachers in the classroom. Teachers will be videoed in their interactions with children in relation to literacy. They will then be interviewed about their thinking at the time of interaction. This aims to develop an understanding of the cognitive processes involved in the spontaneous decisions related to the teaching of reading made by teachers in the classroom.
Published Material: FISHER, R. (1992). Early Literacy and the Teacher. London: Hodder and Stoughton.; FISHER, R. (1993). 'Starting to read', Reading, Vol 27, No 1, Spring (in press).
Status: Individual research
Date of Research: 1991 - continuing
KEYWORDS: beginning reading; infant school education; reading teaching; teacher-pupil relationship; teaching methods

9/0905

Rolle Faculty of Education, Douglas Avenue, Exmouth
EX8 2AT
0395 255309
Clark, V. Ms; *Supervisor:* Halstead, M. Dr; Hannan, A. Dr
How does bereavement affect spiritual and moral thinking in children?
Abstract: The general principles established in the first section of the Education Reform Act 1988 (ERA) ensure that the education received 'promotes the spiritual, moral (and) cultural...development of pupils at school and of society'. Such developments, however, may be affected by personal rather than educational circumstances – such as the loss by death of a significant person in the child's life. Despite steady increase in research into the effects of bereavement in the adult population, less has been written about bereaved children's reactions and, in particular, of the links that may exist with spiritual and/or moral development. The aim of this research is: (a) to review the literature concerning spiritual, moral (and religious) development and bereavement reactions and to identify common themes, particularly regarding children; (b) to analyse the responses obtained through interviews and questionnaires from children, adolescents and adults concerning their thinking and behaviour following childhood/adolescent bereavement; and (c) to indicate what the implications of these findings are for the implementation of ERA. Respondents, who will be contacted through schools, colleges, bereavement counselling groups and national networks, will provide information through taped interviews and questionnaires, thus providing both breadth and depth of response. It is anticipated that some correlation between childhood bereavement and spiritual and/or moral thinking/development will appear, despite variations in its

frequency and intensity and in individual awareness of it. Adults are likely to provide a longer term perspective of their development in this respect; children and adolescents, information as to how their educational life is/was affected by bereavement.
Status: Individual research
Date of Research: 1993 - continuing
KEYWORDS: adolescent development; bereavement; child development; death; moral development; religious attitudes

9/0906
Rolle Faculty of Education, Douglas Avenue, Exmouth
EX82AT
0395 255309
Leedham, W. Mr; *Supervisor:* Hannan, A. Dr; Halstead, M. Dr; Hayes, D. Mr
Expanding horizons: multicultural and international education in the South West of England
Abstract: The research examines one aspect of the relationship between a system of state education and the society which supports and funds it. The United Kingdom is a multicultural and multiracial society, one of many such societies in a diverse and changing world, but the National Curriculum introduced recently makes few specific references to this broader picture. Much will be left to the initiative of individual schools and teachers. The research looks at the effects of greater centralisation on the one hand, and the need for state schools to provide an education appropriate for all pupils on the other. It focuses on examples of good practice in multicultural and international education in what is mainly a 'white' area (the South West of England) and asks – is a more centralised curriculum necessarily a more relevant one, as the legislators claim?
Status: Sponsored project
Source of Grant: Polytechnics and Colleges Funding Council £19,000
Date of Research: 1992 - continuing
KEYWORDS: centralisation; educational practices; international education; multicultural education; National Curriculum

9/0907
Rolle Faculty of Education, Douglas Avenue, Exmouth
EX8 2AT
0395 255309
Silver, H. Prof.
Good schools, effective schools: judgements and their history
Abstract: A study of the development of research interests in effective schools and school differences in the 1970s-1980s, in the United States and Britain, in a historical context. The investigation covers perceptions of what has constituted a good school, who has had the power to define what is good, and the criteria that have been used for different kinds of schooling. It considers the difference between 19th and earlier 20th century judgements about the quality of schooling and the research-based interest in effective schools after the decline in confidence in the outcomes of schooling in the late 1960s and early 1970s. It looks at the implementation of effective schools criteria in individual American states and in Congressional legislation in 1988. The study will also examine alternatives to school reform based on the effective schools research – in the US essential and accelerated schools and forms of restructuring, and in the UK government-sponsored approaches to curricula and assessment. The study is mainly document-based, except for visits to Connecticut, Rhode Island and Washington DC to visit administrators and schools.
Published Material: SILVER, H. (1991). 'Poverty and effective schools', Journal of Education Policy, Vol 6, No 3, pp.271-285.; SILVER, H. (1991). Educational research and the policy environment: the case of 'effective schools', *liber amoricum* for H. Remak, Indiana University.
Status: Individual research
Date of Research: 1989 - continuing
KEYWORDS: comparative education; educational history; educational quality; school effectiveness; United States of America

9/0908
Rolle Faculty of Education, Douglas Avenue, Exmouth
EX8 2AT
0395 255309
Hayes, D. Mr; *Supervisor:* Hannan, A. Dr; Holt, D. Dr; Howarth, S. Mr
Decision-making and school policy: a case study of a primary school at a time of rapid change

Abstract: The case-study focuses upon the decision-making process within a combined first and middle school in the South West of England. It aims to provide a perspective on the involvement of staff and governors in the process in the light of the rapidly changing circumstances created through government education legislation. Data have been gained during 1991 and 1992 through non-participant observation at staff meetings and governors' meetings, through formal and informal discussions with staff, and through familiarity with school management structures and procedures. Data analysis indicates that the rapidity of change has placed a considerable strain upon the headteacher and staff, jeopardising the carefully designed management system established within the school, and creating insufficient opportunity for reflection upon, implementation, and subsequent amendment of decisions taken. The extent of teacher participation has varied according to the priority given to an issue by the staff and their beliefs about the genuineness of the consultation process. The need to act swiftly has sometimes obliged the headteacher to pre-empt full staff consultation by presenting, in consultation with governors and senior staff, a limited range of options or a single alternative, thereby undermining her preference for joint decision-making and collegial relations among staff.
Status: Sponsored project
Source of Grant: Plymouth University: Rolle Faculty of Education
Date of Research: 1991 - continuing
KEYWORDS: change strategies; educational administration; educational change; primary schools; school-based management; school organisation; staff-school relationship

9/0909
Rolle Faculty of Education, Douglas Avenue, Exmouth
EX8 2AT
0395 255309
Warham, S. Mrs
How do primary school teachers teach? An investigation into what the use of language by primary school teachers can tell us about their teaching strategies
Abstract: This research for publication is based on 40 case studies of teachers working in their classrooms. Based on the assumption that communication is crucial to the process of teaching, it examines the communication strategies of different teachers working in their classrooms, and attempts to discover what the communication skills of teachers can tell us about how primary school teachers teach. An attempt is made to reconstruct the ways in which different teachers control and create learning experiences for their pupils. The research finds that teachers set up different identities and power relationships with their pupils, and perform acts of hegemony. The differences in acts of hegemony are examined, and exploration of other aspects of teachers' work attempts to expose something of the complex power context in which teachers perform their professional activities, and how this affects their teaching. The research finally concludes that in order to carry out their professional activities teachers need to be professionally literate.
Status: Sponsored project
Source of Grant: Plymouth University: Rolle Faculty of Education: 940
Date of Research: 1990-1992
KEYWORDS: classroom communication; primary school teachers; teacher behaviour; teacher-pupil relationship; teaching methods

9/0910
Rolle Faculty of Education, Douglas Avenue, Exmouth
EX8 2AT
0395 255309
Mason, P. Mr; *Supervisor:* Hannan, A. Dr; Essex, S. Dr
The Learn to Travel School's Project
Abstract: This research has three aims: (1) To examine the claims made for introducing travel and tourism into the primary school curriculum. The research explores arguments about the importance of knowledge of travel and tourism in primary schools; and the use of travel and tourism as a vehicle for developing values and attitudes and acquiring skills; (2) To undertake action research in curriculum development in these areas by the design and implementation of a 'Learn to Travel School's Project'. This is an attempt to test, in practice, the ideas of the first aim. The researcher, with a group of teachers in Devon, will design, produce, implement and evaluate curriculum resources for the 'Learn to Travel School's Project'; (3) To evaluate the impact of this contribution to primary school children's education, in relation to the first aim. This will involve the use

of questionnaire surveys with children; and interviews with children and teachers.

Published Material: MASON, P. (1992). Learn to travel: activities in travel and tourism for primary schools. Godalming: Worldwide Fund for Nature UK.

Status: Individual research

Date of Research: 1990 - continuing

KEYWORDS: *curriculum development; primary education; tourism; travel*

9/0911

Rolle Faculty of Education, Douglas Avenue, Exmouth
EX8 2AT
0395 255309
Dyer, A. Mr

Re-storying the landscape

Abstract: An environmental education project aimed at using all of the arts in the interpretation and discovery of the natural world. Children are encouraged to rediscover some of the stories about particular or nearby landscapes, or invent new ones. The experimental phase of the project took place at Killerton Park near Exeter in Devon, with a group of children taking part in a 'Dragon Quest'. Twenty-eight children met with the organisers every other Saturday and came together for regular weekend camps. The results are being written up and will be published in a handbook for teachers, leaders and parents.

Status: Sponsored project

Source of Grant: National Trust/Plymouth University: Rolle Faculty of Education £; 1,039

Date of Research: 1990-1992

KEYWORDS: *environmental education; field studies; geographic location; local studies; story telling*

9/0912

Rolle Faculty of Education, Douglas Avenue, Exmouth
EX8 2AT
0395 265344
Open University, School of Education, Walton Hall, Milton Keynes MK7 6AA
0908 274066
Cambridge University, Newnham College, Cambridge CB3 9DF
0223 335700
Parker, D. Mr; *Supervisor:* Bell, R. Dr; Sutherland, G. Dr

Elementary education, society and politics in Hertfordshire 1918-1939

Abstract: This research follows a Master of Philosophy thesis entitled 'The impact of the First World War upon elementary education in Hertfordshire'. Both studies examine the provision of elementary education locally in the light of national thought and trends. The primary research mainly involved source material in the Hertfordshire Record Office (County Council papers, parish files and school files), the Public Record Office (Board of Education files), the British Library, Colindale (county newspapers and national journals), the Census Office, private collections and local museums. Oral evidence was taken from local residents. The PhD thesis will analyse the impact of new rapid residential and industrial development upon local society and public affairs, and the effect of national economic and political thought and trends upon education. The factors influencing curriculum change will be highlighted, in particular to shed light upon the growing vocational aspect of education for older elementary children (not least the attention given to technical and rural education in the county), the equivocal attitude towards the role of the central schools and the concern to determine an 'appropriate' expansion of secondary education. The impact of the three Hadow reports, especially that of 1926, will be examined, with its major implication for local reorganisation, parental attitudes, school meals, transport, the future of Dual Control and the role of the denominational schools. Research has been undertaken into the county's attempts to identify and provide for children suspected of mental deficiency and backwardness, and into the ambivalent attitudes towards the education of elementary schoolchildren after the age of eleven.

Status: Sponsored project

Source of Grant: Hertfordshire County Council: 1988-1989 £6,000

Date of Research: 1988-1992

KEYWORDS: *educational history; educational legislation; educational theories; educational trends; elementary education; politics education relationship; socioeconomic influences*

9/0913

Rolle Faculty of Education, Douglas Avenue, Exmouth
EX8 2AT
0395 255309
University College of Swansea, Department of Education, Hendrefoilan, Swansea SA2 7NB
0792 201231
Cashmore, C. Mrs; *Supervisor:* Hannan, A. Dr; Halstead, J. Dr; Furlong, J. Prof.

School-based teacher training: a comparative case study of an Articled Teacher course and a one-year Post Graduate Certificate in Education (PGCE) course

Abstract: The aim of the study is to consider recent moves to develop school-based teacher training and in particular to carry out a comparative case study of the Articled Teacher course and a more traditional one-year Post Graduate Certificate of Education (PGCE) course based at Rolle Faculty of Education, University of Plymouth, concentrating on the 1991 intake. The study will be an evaluation based on the 'illuminative' approach using participant observation, questionnaires and interviews. There are 12 Articled Teachers and 75 students on the one-year course, of which 12 will be studied in detail.

Status: Individual research

Date of Research: 1991 - continuing

KEYWORDS: *articled teachers; Postgraduate Certificate in Education; preservice teacher education; student teachers; teacher education*

9/0914

Rolle Faculty of Education, Douglas Avenue, Exmouth
EX8 2AT
0395 255309
University of the West of England at Bristol, Coldharbour Lane, Frenchay, Bristol BS16 1QY
0272 656261
Payne, G. Mrs; *Supervisor:* Hannan, A. Dr; Silver, H. Prof.; Menter, I. Mr

Competence-based teacher training for the primary years: a comparative approach

Abstract: The aim of the investigation is, generally, to contribute to our understanding of the management of change in initial teacher education. The specific aims are to: (1) analyse proposals over the past 10 years to change primary teacher training with particular reference to moves to introduce a competence-based approach; (2) undertake a national survey of how such change has been managed; (3) investigate in depth the experiences of a number of institutions selected to illustrate the range of responses; and (4) undertake a comparative study of two institutions in the process of adaptation. This research will focus on the management of change in initial teacher training (ITT) for the primary years, in particular on proposals for introducing competence-based training. Development of the research will be through a number of stages: (1) an analysis of the wide range of proposals over the past 10 years to change primary teacher training; (2) a national questionnaire survey of ITT providers (postal questionnaire to the 94 institutions offering ITT courses); (3) follow-up interviews with a selection of institutions; and (4) a comparative case study of the experience of change in two institutions.

Status: Individual research

Date of Research: 1992 - continuing

KEYWORDS: *competency-based teacher education; preservice teacher education*

Reading University

9/0915

Department of Arts and Humanities in Education, Bulmershe Court, Woodlands Avenue, Earley, Reading RG6 1HY
0734 875123
Pegg, L. Mrs; *Supervisor:* Kemp, A. Dr

National programme of training for primary school music consultants

Abstract: The purpose of the project is to provide a programme of inservice training for primary school music teachers who wish to develop consultancy skills. This training is offered on a national basis, organised in various locations throughout the country, and consists of four-week phased courses of the kind held at the University of Reading Music Education Centre since 1982. These courses offer teachers an updated view of recent developments in the primary music curriculum and training in the processes of consultancy work amongst colleagues. They also offer conferences for primary head-teachers within their structure. A second important facet of the project will be the development of regional groups of music consultants to encourage on-going professional interchange and aftercare.

Published Material: SMITH, J. (1987). Music consultancy in Berkshire primary schools. Reading: Royal County of Berkshire Music Department.; KEMP, A.E. (1988). 'Towards national adoption of music consultancy in primary schools'. In: BARTON, M. & STEWART, A. (Eds). British Music Education Year Book 1988/89. London: Rhinehold.; KEMP, A.E. & WOOTTON-FREEMAN, S. (1988). 'New tasks for music in primary schools and teacher training', International Journal of Music Education, No 11, pp.21-24.; PEGG, L.J. (1992). 'If music is for all pupils then it must be for all teachers', Early Education, No 7, pp.8.; KEMP, A.E. (1993). 'School within communities; are music opportunities being missed?'. In: KEMP, A.E. & PEGG, L.J. Consultancy Matters. Reading: Reading University.
Status: Sponsored project
Source of Grant: Music Industries Association £75,000; Caloustie Gulbenkian Foundation £15,000
Date of Research: 1988 - continuing
KEYWORDS: *consultants; inservice teacher education; music education; music teachers; primary school teachers*

9/0916

Department of Arts and Humanities in Education, Bulmershe Court, Woodlands Avenue, Earley, Reading RG6 1HY
0734 875123
Drever, M. Mrs; *Supervisor:* Richards, B. Dr
Teaching English in a multilingual classroom
Abstract: The research has two aims: (1) to carry out a survey of strategies used by class teachers in the teaching of the English language in a multilingual context; i.e. in a class composed of pupils from more than one linguistic home background, including English mother tongue; and (2) to suggest strategies which might benefit all pupils in attaining a competent level of English performance in order to cope with more sophisticated and subject specific language, semantically and structurally, as they move up the curriculum. The research will use classroom observation, interviews and questionnaires.
Status: Individual research
Date of Research: 1990 - continuing
KEYWORDS: *English; minority groups; multilingualism; teaching methods*

9/0917

Department of Arts and Humanities in Education, Bulmershe Court, Woodlands Avenue, Earley, Reading RG6 1HY
0734 875123
Middleton, R. Mr; *Supervisor:* Richards, B. Dr;
Lockwood, M. Dr
Teaching non-fiction in the secondary school
Abstract: This research will examine the question of why teachers use non-fiction. Is it for language development, reading and writing cross-fertilisation, or for helping pupils refine their knowledge of the world and themselves? What kinds of linguistic, intellectual and cultural demands do non-fiction texts make on pupils? Is non-fiction literature taught in the same way as fiction literature or does the case for using non-fiction rest partly on its difference from fiction? What kinds of teaching strategies are appropriate and is a specialist critical vocabulary necessary? Research methodology will include case studies/surveys of practice, lesson observation and interviewing of teachers and pupils and a survey of pupils' voluntary non-fiction reading. This will involve the cooperation of Berkshire's education library service and possible contributions of linguistic and literary theory.
Status: Individual research
Date of Research: 1990 - continuing
KEYWORDS: *English studies; literature studies; non-fiction; secondary education*

9/0918

Department of Arts and Humanities in Education, Bulmershe Court, Woodlands Avenue, Earley, Reading RG6 1HY
0734 875123
Kempe, A. Mr; *Supervisor:* Weller, M. Mr
Drama and special needs
Abstract: The research syndicate will be made up of three teachers in a special school, (the Avenue School, Reading), two university lecturers and a small number of Postgraduate Certificate of Education (PGCE) drama students. The project will aim to find ways of enabling young people with a variety of special educational needs to engage with drama as an expressive and performing art. The practical work will be trialled with one group of 11 to 12 year olds with moderate learning difficulties and one group of 15 to 17 year olds with various physical and learning difficulties. A report documenting all of the practical project and referring it to the available theory in the field will be produced.
Published Material: KEMPE, A. (1991). 'Learning both ways', British Journal of Special Education, Vol 18, No 4, pp.137-139.
Status: Sponsored project
Source of Grant: Technical and Vocational Education Initiative (TVEI) syndicate £1,500
Date of Research: 1990-1991
KEYWORDS: *drama; special educational needs*

9/0919

Department of Arts and Humanities in Education, Bulmershe Court, Woodlands Avenue, Earley, Reading RG6 1HY
0734 875123
Hall, J. Mr; *Supervisor:* Adelman, C. Prof.
The development, implementation and evaluation of a model of practice in art and design teacher education
Abstract: This is a longitudinal study of a sample of beginning teachers of art and design, following them through a one year postgraduate course of initial teacher education and into their first teaching appointments. The research will investigate the effectiveness of the Post Graduate Certificate of Education (PGCE) Art and Design Course at Reading University, and the processes through which beginning teachers learn to teach and go on to develop and improve their practice.
Published Material: HALL, J. (1991). 'The roles of practising teachers and university lecturers in the initial training of teachers of art and design', Journal of Art and Design Education, Vol 10, No 3, pp.317-327.
Status: Individual research
Date of Research: 1991 - continuing
KEYWORDS: *art; design; Postgraduate Certificate of Education; preservice teacher education; probationary teachers; programme effectiveness; student teachers*

9/0920

Department of Arts and Humanities in Education, Bulmershe Court, Woodlands Avenue, Earley, Reading RG6 1HY
0734 875123
Lee, F-J Mr; *Supervisor:* Straughan, R. Dr
Emotivism, prescriptivism and moral education
Abstract: The traditional Chinese moral education model places emphasis on authoritarian discipline dealing with heteronomy in behaviour training and doctrines of specific items, therefore less concern is placed on the education of moral autonomy and the capacities of making moral judgements. However, in view of the rapid changes in social structure and diversified value-judgement concepts of today, moral rules based solely on heteronomy are insufficient. On the other hand, the meta-ethics developed by the western world aim to clarify and justify the supporting claims beneath the traditional ethical theories, emphasising the analysis of moral languages and concepts, and investigating the logical frameworks of moral reasoning and decisions. This would contribute to the establishment of a rational and feasible theory in moral education. Since prescriptivism advocated by R.M. Hare and emotivism proposed by C.L. Stevenson play leading roles, this study attempts to investigate and compare them and to interpret their implications on moral education, such as decision of educational aims, selection of teaching contents, planning of curriculum organisation, methodology of moral education, and so on. The objectives to be achieved in this research are as follows: (1) to deal with the philosophical background of meta-ethics; (2) to investigate the theory of emotivism and elaborate its implications on moral education; (3) to investigate the theory of prescriptivism and elaborate its implications on moral education; (4) to compare and criticise the two theories, their limits and applicabilities; (5) to discuss Confucianism and its implication on moral education in Taiwan; and (6) to propose the recommendable ways to improve the theory and practice of moral education according to the

research results. This study will deal with the philosophical background of emotivism and prescriptivism through historical approach, and will apply theoretical analysis to elucidate them.
Status: Individual research
Date of Research: 1991 - continuing
KEYWORDS: *educational philosophy; moral education; Taiwan*

9/0921
> Department of Arts and Humanities in Education, Bulmershe Court, Woodlands Avenue, Earley, Reading RG6 1HY
> 0734 875123
> Cox, G. Dr; *Supervisor:* Kemp, A. Dr; Straughan, R. Dr

The right place of music in education: a history of music education in England 1870-1927 with particular reference to the role of Her Majesty's Inspectorate (HMI)
Abstract: The study focuses on the music curriculum during a period in which there was a steady advance away from the often irksome and uncongenial traditions associated with the revised code towards the cultivation of taste rather than the acquirement of technical proficiency. This broadening of scope was symbolized in the change of nomenclature in 1927 – from 'singing' to 'music'. The central concerns of the study include: the significance of Her Majesty's Inspectorate as agents of curriculum change; the original contributions to the development of music and education; notions of intrinsic and extrinsic values in music education. The study is organised in three parts: (1) John Hullah and the decline of music in schools 1872-1883; (2) the utilitarian era of Stainer 1883-1901; (3) the liberalisation of the music curriculum and the contribution of Arthur Somervell 1901-1927. The research draws upon a considerable amount of unpublished materials, oral evidence, and texts of the period. It provides a detailed study of curriculum change and conflict which should lead to a greater knowledge of the process involved in 'becoming a subject'.
Status: Individual research
Date of Research: 1988-1992
KEYWORDS: *educational history; inspectors – of schools; music curriculum; music education*

9/0922
> Department of Arts and Humanities in Education, Bulmershe Court, Woodlands Avenue, Earley, Reading RG6 1HY
> 0734 875123
> Wells, C. Mr; *Supervisor:* Kemp, A. Dr; Hopper, G. Mrs

The effects of information technology on the sequencing and development of concept acquisition, particularly in open ended, creative situations
Abstract: A preliminary study has been completed over a period of one year in a primary school with very good access to computer facilities. Work in creative areas, particularly in creative writing and in art, was monitored throughout the year – both with and without the use of the computer. Children from ages 5 to 11 were involved, though more detailed observations were made of a group of thirty, 9 to 10 year olds. This data, once analysed, will enable the focusing of particular sequencing and developmental trends in the main research.
Status: Individual research
Date of Research: 1990 - continuing
KEYWORDS: *computer uses in education; concept formation; creative development; learning processes*

9/0923
> Department of Arts and Humanities in Education, Bulmershe Court, Woodlands Avenue, Earley, Reading RG6 1HY
> 0734 875123
> Theale Green School, Bath Road, Reading RG7 5DA
> 0734 302741
> Kempe, A. Mr; Holroyd, R. Mr

Drama in the English National Curriculum
Abstract: The end product of the research will be two books for use in top primary/lower secondary classrooms. A pupil book will contain a range of resources on three separate topics. Literature, visual material, realia and research or creative tasks will be bound together by a linking narrative for each of the three topics. An accompanying teacher's book will outline how each individual resource may be used as part of an enactive learning programme and suggest various strategies by which the resources may be combined into dramatic structures. Within the whole project, there will be opportunities to meet the stated attainment targets of English in the National Curriculum document and some reference will also be made to the history, science, and craft, design and technology (CDT) documents. Most of the material is being trialled at a comprehensive school in Reading. Other elements are being used on Inservice Education of Teachers (INSET) courses and a programme of primary school sessions. The final publications will hopefully provide the basis for a more extensive and refined publishing programme aimed at meeting the needs of the National Curriculum without destroying current good practice.
Published Material: KEMPE, A. & HOLROYD, R. (1986). 'Team teaching: cheap relief for a taxing problem', 2D Vol 6, No 1, pp.60-71.; KEMPE, A. (1992). 'Enthusiastic beginners'. Drama, Vol 1, No 1, pp.13-16.
Status: Individual research
Date of Research: 1988 - continuing
KEYWORDS: *drama education; educational materials; English studies curriculum; National Curriculum*

9/0924
> Department of Education Studies and Management, Bulmershe Court, Woodlands Avenue, Earley, Reading RG6 1HY
> 0734 875123
> Bedford College of Higher Education, Cauldwell Street, Bedford MK24 9AH
> 0234 345151
> Keiner, J. Ms; Grugeon, A. Mrs

Evaluation of the National Oracy Project
Abstract: The National Oracy Project was established to promote good practice in oral work across the curriculum and to develop appropriate modes of assessment for pupils aged 3 to 18 years. This evaluation of the National Oracy Project aims to explore the extent to which the Project's work fulfils its stated aims. A case study approach has been adopted, drawing on a selection of seven local authority consortia of teacher-based groups involved in the Project, in conjunction with studies of the National Project Team; its relationship with National Curriculum Council and other national educational policy bodies; and publications an other data emerging from the project. Methods used include analysis of published material and other documents; field visits and interviews; and participant observation. Results and conclusions will be published in a final report.
Status: Sponsored project
Source of Grant: National Curriculum Council £22,000
Date of Research: 1990 - continuing
KEYWORDS: *oracy; oral language; programme evaluation; speech communication*

9/0925
> Department of Linguistic Science, Whiteknights, Reading RG6 2AH
> 0734 875123
> Kerswill, P. Dr; Williams, A. Dr

A new dialect in a new city: childrens' and adults' speech in Milton Keynes
Abstract: The research aims to examine the processes behind the formation of a new dialect in a city where the majority of the population originates from different parts of the country and to enquire how children develop 'sociolinguistic competence' – awareness of different accents and dialects in their community, and of their use. A range of sociolinguistic methods are used in the study of 48 children aged 4, 8 and 12.
Published Material: KERSWILL, P. & WILLIAMS, A. (1992). 'Some principles of dialect contact: evidence from the New Town of Milton Keynes'. In: WARBURTON, I. & INGHAM, R. (Eds). Working Papers 1992. Reading University, Department of Linguistic Science.
Status: Sponsored project
Source of Grant: Economic and Social Research Council £51,550
Date of Research: 1990 - continuing
KEYWORDS: *dialect studies; language variation; sociolinguistics*

9/0926
> Department of Linguistic Science, Whiteknights, Reading RG6 2AH
> 0734 875123
> Fletcher, P. Prof.; Ingham, R. Dr; *Supervisor:* Fletcher, P. Prof.

Syntactic input and the acquisition of the verb lexicon
Abstract: This research examines the relation between syntax and the

lexical properties of verbs in children's acquisition of English as a first language. It is a hypothesis-based experimental study whose variables are motivated by recently published work in linguistic theory and language acquisition. It is expected that the results of this project will offer improved understanding of the relations between children's syntax and their lexical representations for verbs, on the one hand, and between adult syntax and children's lexical acquisition on the other.

Status: Sponsored project
Source of Grant: Economic and Social Research Council £40,000
Date of Research: 1990-1992
KEYWORDS: language acquisition; syntax; verbs; vocabulary development

9/0927
   Department of Psychology, Whiteknights, Reading RG6 2AH
   0734 875123
   Henry, L. Dr; Norman, T. Miss; *Supervisor:* Henry, L. Dr
The development of visual memory strategies in children
Abstract: The aim of this research was to chart the development of verbal memory strategies in children. Previous research suggested that children progress from visual to verbal strategies of memory coding with age. However, this claim has not been adequately tested. The first stage of the present research has been to test this claim with a wide age range (5, 7, 9, and 11 year olds). Children recalled sequences of pictures which were either visually similar (they looked the same) or phonemically similar (they sounded the same). Recall for these types of pictures was contrasted with recall for control pictures which were neither visually nor phonemically similar. The results showed that all age groups were poorer at remembering phonemically similar pictures, suggesting that they all used verbal memory strategies. There was very little evidence for the use of visual memory strategies in any group. Further work with 4 year olds found that they did not appear to use any distinct strategy for remembering pictures. These findings conflicted with previous research which showed that five year olds used visual coding, and ongoing research is testing the competing claim of various hypotheses concerning the development of picture memory in children.
Status: Sponsored project
Source of Grant: Reading University Endowment £21,000
Date of Research: 1990 - continuing
KEYWORDS: child development; memorisation; phonemics; pictorial stimuli; verbal development; visual learning

9/0928
   Department of Science and Technology Education, Bulmershe Court, Woodlands Avenue, Earley, Reading RG6 1HY
   0734 875123
   Harries, D. Mr
The attitudes and confidence of primary school teachers regarding mathematics education
Abstract: Many people have a suspicious and wary attitude to mathematics, viewing it as a highly abstract and difficult subject to master, even though they make effective use of 'everyday' mathematics. Some primary teachers who are not mathematics specialists exhibit these attitudes, and appear to have high anxiety levels regarding their own mathematical abilities. This can lead to a sterile teaching approach, whereas the National Curriculum requires a variety of approaches in the teaching of mathematics, including practical and investigative work. This study is intended to provide more precise information about attitudes to mathematics amongst primary school teachers, and the nature of any problems that may arise. Such information can be used to inform Inservice Education of Teachers (INSET) planning and development. Initially a questionnaire survey of a local sample of teachers will be carried out. Further in-depth work will be undertaken through selected individual interviews.
Status: Sponsored project
Source of Grant: Universities Funding Council £12,200
Date of Research: 1991 - continuing
KEYWORDS: inservice teacher education; mathematics; primary school teachers; teacher attitudes

9/0929
   Faculty of Education & Community Studies, Bulmershe Court, Woodlands Avenue, Earley, Reading RG6 1HY
   0734 875123

Goodwyn, A. Mr
The relationship between the use and understanding of narrative structures and general language development
Abstract: The project will investigate the links between children's general language competence and their ability to comprehend and use narrative structures. This will involve the study of children's reading and writing habits and the pedagogical implications for the way narratives are used in schools. The project will be chiefly of interest to teachers of language in primary schools and to teachers of English in secondary schools. In the early stages research will involve small scale studies of narrative work with children at primary and secondary level. These early studies will be used as the basis for more detailed work with a small number of children, mainly at secondary level. It is hoped that the study will produce results that can help teachers and children to improve both their work with language and on narrative. Particular areas would include: the suitability of stories for specific age groups or development groups; the appropriateness of certain forms of narrative structure for particular age groups; the identification of staging points in pupils' development; the development of pedagogical strategies for improving children's engagement with narratives; identifying relationships between children's reading level and writing level; children's comprehension of visual narratives and their relationships to other forms.
Status: Individual research
Date of Research: 1989-1992
KEYWORDS: language skills; narration; reading comprehension; story telling; writing skills

9/0930
   Faculty of Education and Community Studies, Bulmershe Court, Woodlands Avenue, Earley, Reading RG6 1HY
   0734 875123
   Dawkins, J. Mr; *Supervisor:* Fidler, B. Dr
Local management of secondary schools in Berkshire - an evaluation
Abstract: The aim of this research is to monitor and evaluate the implementation of Local Management of Schools (LMS) in secondary schools in Berkshire to assess over the initial period if the quality of education in those schools has been enhanced by the provision of LMS. The researcher will aim to: (i) keep abreast of, and include current research in terms of a developing national perspective of the implementation of LMS; (ii) to detail within Berkshire the changes planned within the Local Education Authority as direct result of delegated budgets in secondary schools; (iii) evaluate (by means of a detailed case study of 3 secondary schools) the LMS pilot scheme; (iv) evaluate 3 further (non-pilot) schools as case studies; and (v) conclude whether the quality of education has been enhanced by the provision of LMS. Research will be carried out through questionnaires and follow up interviews of LEA officers and governors, teachers and administrators from at least six secondary schools.
Status: Sponsored project
Source of Grant: Berkshire Local Education Authority £450
Date of Research: 1989 - continuing
KEYWORDS: educational change; evaluation; local management of schools; school-based management; secondary schools

9/0931
   Faculty of Education and Community Studies, Bulmershe Court, Woodlands Avenue, Earley, Reading RG6 1HY
   0734 875123
   Colinvaux, D. Ms; *Supervisor:* Gilbert, J. Prof.; Pope, M. Prof.
Theories and conceptions of change: a study in science education
Abstract: The thesis investigates people's understanding of change. Change is seen to be important within the context of science education. It is recognised that individuals have conceptions of change in relation to everyday theorising as well as in the public domain. Research studies in science education that investigate the learner's perspective are discussed and the implications of theories and conceptions of change for science education are addressed. The two dimensions, social/personal and formal/everyday life provide a framework for the study. The theoretical perspective underpinning the thesis is that of constructivism, and the methodological framework devised is consistent with this philosophical base. The fieldwork involved the use of questionnaires and interviews. An innovative instrument allowing participants to make comments about photographs in terms of the presence or absence of change was devised. The sample was drawn from 7 year olds, secondary school

children, from university students, and adults in Brazil. The results provide information regarding participants' views of change, non-change, and their judgements regarding the nature of change. Several dimensions are identified. There is particular emphasis on the time dimension and how the various participants conceive the process of change on the basis of their understanding of the time dimension. Both qualitative and quantitative data will be presented and case studies drawing together several aspects of an individual's conceptions of change.
Status: Sponsored project
Source of Grant: CPNQ – Brazil
Date of Research: 1988-1992
KEYWORDS: *change; concept formation; science education*

9/0932

Faculty of Education and Community Studies, Bulmershe Court, Woodlands Avenue, Earley, Reading RG6 1HY
0734 875123
Sellers, M. Mrs; Palmer, B. Prof.; *Supervisor:* Palmer, B. Prof.

The integration of deaf and partially hearing children in Berkshire schools

Abstract: Largely as a result of legislation such as the 1976 and 1981 Education Acts, 'special needs' children, including 90% of those with a hearing disability, are now taught 'wherever possible' in ordinary schools. What is uncertain is how well hearing impaired children are faring, especially since the 1988 Education Reform Act with its introduction of the National Curriculum and Local Management of Schools, and with possible changes in local education authority (LEA) 'statementing' practices. This project is designed as a pilot for a larger multinational study. Its aims are to: (a) establish a database which will list all children with a hearing disability in Berkshire schools and partially hearing units, together with relevant details such as their audiometric profile; the communication support and resources available to each individual child; and the children of Berkshire residents at schools for the deaf outside the county; (b) review 'statements' and the 'statementing' process in principle and in practice; (c) conduct case studies in which the progress of a sample number children will be explored in depth; (d) identify specific research questions and strategies for the major study. The survey will be carried out by reference to published data and Berkshire LEA documentation; interviews with children, parents and teachers in relation to the case studies; and interviews with LEA staff involved in 'statementing' and with a sample of professional staff submitting advice. It is intended that the results of this intitial survey will be publised in different forms in educational journals and in more popular specialist publications for deaf people. The survey will act as the basis for an application for European funding for the major project.
Status: Sponsored project
Source of Grant: Reading University Research Endowment Fund £24,000
Date of Research: 1991-1992
KEYWORDS: *access to education; deafness; disabilities; hearing impairments; mainstreaming; special educational needs*

9/0933

Faculty of Education and Community Studies, Bulmershe Court, Woodlands Avenue, Earley, Reading RG6 1HY
0734 875123
Fletcher-Campbell, F. Miss; *Supervisor:* Straughan, R. Dr

The caring school

Abstract: Most schools claim to be caring institutions but it is not clear as to how this claim should be interpreted. The research analyses accounts in the literature and as given by a small sample of secondary headteachers. A philosophical analysis of the concept of the caring school is then undertaken before practical recommendations for schools' policy and practice are made.
Status: Individual research
Date of Research: 1988 - continuing
KEYWORDS: *educational environment; educational philosophy; pastoral care – education; pupil-school relationship; pupil welfare*

9/0934

Faculty of Education and Community Studies, Bulmershe Court, Woodlands Avenue, Earley, Reading RG6 1HY
0734 875123

Spear, M. Dr; Singh, A. Dr; *Supervisor:* Singh, A. Dr

A local authority based demonstration trial of 'good practice' in road safety education

Abstract: The primary aim of the project is to develop, implement and evaluate policies of 'good practice' in road safety education for children aged 5-16. The initial phase of the project is being spent developing guidelines for the management and coordination of road safety education both at local authority and at school level in collaboration with educational advisers, teachers, road safety officers, health education officers and the police; and in conducting a pilot trial in one local authority. During the second phase of the research, the revised policy document will be implemented through inservice training in all the primary and secondary schools (about 130 schools) within the selected areas of the two trial authorities. The third phase of the research will be concerned with monitoring the implemented programmes closely in 20 primary and 10 secondary schools in order to assess the impact on educational outcomes over a given period of time, for example in pupils' knowledge, skills, attitudes, behaviour and future intentions regarding road safety. The research design will be quasi-experimental. The input, process and evaluation data will be obtained through visits, interviews, questionnaires, telephone calls, observation of lessons and unobtrusive observation of actual behaviour on the roads. The cost effectiveness of programmes including measures of changes in casualty rate will also be assessed. The final phase of the research will comprise feedback to the participants, dissemination of the findings and the production of a report designed to assist local authorities and schools in implementing such policy(ies) effectively and economically.
Status: Sponsored project
Source of Grant: Department of Transport: Transport and Road Research Laboratory £407,303
Date of Research: 1988 - continuing
KEYWORDS: *safety education; traffic safety*

9/0935

Faculty of Education and Community Studies, Bulmershe Court, Woodlands Avenue, Earley, Reading RG6 1HY
0734 875123
Loban, S. Mr; *Supervisor:* Edwards, V. Dr

The language learning experiences of Somalis and Eritreans in Britain and Italy

Abstract: This is an investigation into the language learning of refugees in Europe. Somalis and Eritreans were chosen for this project as both Somalia and Eritrea were colonised by both Britain and Italy. The research will focus on the language learning needs of Somalis and Eritreans in Europe, and will address the following issues: (1) does language education meet needs; (2) attitudes towards bilingual education; (3) curriculum development and delivery; and (4) teaching methods. The research will include: participant observation; open-ended semi-structured interviews; and study of policy documents. Fieldwork will take place in a college of further education in London and comparable institutions in Rome and Perugia, Italy.
Status: Individual research
Date of Research: 1991 - continuing
KEYWORDS: *bilingualism; refugees; second language learning*

9/0936

Faculty of Education and Community Studies, Bulmershe Court, Woodlands Avenue, Earley, Reading RG6 1HY
0734 875123
Redfern, A. Mrs; Edwards, V. Dr

Policy and practice in multicultural education in Canada and Great Britain

Abstract: This is a comparative analysis of British and Canadian multicultural education policies and practices. In particular the study will look at: (1) policy development which is responsive to the needs of a multilingual, multicultural school population; (2) strategies for providing language support for children in the process of acquiring English; and (3) the planning and management of multicultural, multilingual classroom resources. The research will be a mixture of observation of classroom practices; interviews with teachers, principals and policy-makers and administrators; and analysis of published policy papers. The sample consisted of the principals and staff of two elementary and two high schools, and the trustees, superintendants and other administrators of a board of education. Staff at York University and the Ontario Institute for Studies in Education were also involved.
Status: Sponsored project

Source of Grant: Canadian Government: Department of External
Affairs £ 5,500
Date of Research: 1990-1991
KEYWORDS: *comparative education; educational policy; English–
second language; multicultural education; multilingualism*

9/0937
>Faculty of Education and Community Studies, Bulmershe
>Court, Earley, Reading RG6 1HY
>0734 875123
>Kempe, A. Mr

The uses of playscripts in the secondary school curriculum
Abstract: The research will involve collating the responses to a
questionnaire sent to a sample of English and Drama departments in
secondary schools around the country. The questionnaire will ascertain the range and type of playscripts held in stock and the appeal of
newly advertised titles. Furthermore, the research will try to gauge
recent shifts in trends regarding the use of playscripts as either a
stimulus for creative drama work or as a means of delivering the
National Curriculum Orders for English at key stage 3. It is envisaged
that articles reporting the research will be submitted to national
English and Drama publications.
Status: Individual research
Date of Research: 1993 - continuing
KEYWORDS: *drama education; English studies curriculum; Na-
tional Curriculum; scripts; secondary education*

9/0938
>Faculty of Education and Community Studies, Centre for
>Education Management, Bulmershe Court, Woodlands
>Avenue, Earley, Reading RG6 1HY
>0734 875123
>Simpson, T. Mr; *Supervisor:* Fidler, B. Dr

**Pressure on primary headteachers during and following the
implementation of Local Management of Schools**
Abstract: The investigation focuses on pressures on primary headteachers in Berkshire during the historically significant early stages of
the receipt of delegated budget management (Local Management of
Schools) by their schools. Research is by questionnaire, interview
and diary completion. Perceptives of: (a) pressure; (b) role change;
(c) Type 'A'/'B' behaviour characteristics; (d) psychoneurotic states
(using the Middlesex Hospital questionnaire) and time management
skills are being assessed while a small pilot group has carried out a
heart rate monitoring exercise, the results of which have been
measured against a diary of daily work based activity. Results so far
suggest that the major source of pressure on the respondents relates
to a perception of lack of time to achieve their objectives and that
their major predicted pressure (as forecast prior to the receipt of LMS)
was the 'need to read and absorb an increasing flow of papers,
documents etc'. Over the first year of LMS, respondents (in 1989 and
1990) noted a modification of role toward that of 'Communicator and
Budget Manager'. Psychoneurotic scores were compared with
general population norms and the results of previous headteacher
findings, with the largest representative group that surveyed in April
1991, females scored similarly to the general population and males
compared closely with previous primary headteacher scores. Continuing research is examining more closely the relationship between
pressure and management of time.
Status: Sponsored project
Source of Grant: Berkshire County Council grant and self funding
Date of Research: 1989-1992
KEYWORDS: *change; headteachers; local management of schools;
primary schools; role conflict; stress variables; time management*

9/0939
>Faculty of Education and Community Studies, Bulmershe
>Court, Woodlands Avenue, Earley, Reading RG6 1HY
>0734 875123
>Council for Environmental Education, Reading University,
>Faculty of Education and Community Studies, National
>Environmental Resource Base, London Road, Reading RG1 5AQ
>0734 756061
>Dorian, C. Dr; *Supervisor:* Gayford, C. Dr

**Planning review and profiling in environmental education in
the school curriculum**
Abstract: This project involves monitoring the ways in which schools
are delivering environmental education in the National Curriculum.

Models for achieving integration of cross-curricular elements in the
whole curriculum will be investigated and approaches to profiling
pupils performance developed. Training materials suitable for pro-
viding appropriate Inservice Education of Teachers (INSET) will be
produced.
Status: Sponsored project
Source of Grant: World Wide Fund for Nature; National Westminster
Bank £ 60,000
Date of Research: 1991-1992
KEYWORDS: *curriculum development; environmental education;
National Curriculum*

9/0940
>Faculty of Education and Community Studies, Department of
>Arts and Humanities, Bulmershe Court, Woodlands Avenue,
>Earley, Reading RG6 1HY
>0734 875123
>Gathumbi, A. Mrs; *Supervisor:* Richards, B. Dr;
>Goodwyn, A. Mr

**Verbal discourse events and teaching styles of English
language teachers in Kenyan secondary schools**
Abstract: Kenyan English language teachers undergo pre-service and
inservice training in the country's teacher training institutions, but
there has not been any follow-up to find out what exactly goes on in
the classrooms and the methods teachers use; therefore the effectiveness of the teacher training programmes is not known. Important as
it is, classroom interaction research has been overlooked in Kenya.
This is ironical bearing in mind that in recent years, claims have been
made that standards of English are falling. It is important therefore
that much more should be known about English language teaching
in Kenya since it is the official language and the medium of instruction. The aims of this research are to: (1) reveal the practised teaching
styles and the cognitive level of questions used by a sample of English
language teachers in Kenya through the study of teacher-pupil interaction; (2) compare the teaching styles of inservice and non-inservice
English language teachers; and (3) make recommendations for
teacher training programmes, curriculum development, inspectorate
and educational planning sectors. The target population for this study
will comprise 12 English language teachers from public and private
schools and also Form 3 students. The sample will be selected from
a rural and an urban district. There will be a pilot study before the
main study. This will enable the researcher to become familiar with
data collection procedures and to make adjustments where necessary.
The methods to be used are: unstructured observation notes; video
and audio recording of teacher-pupil discourse; and a teachers'
questionnaire.
Status: Sponsored project
Source of Grant: International Development Research Centre £31,200
Date of Research: 1991 - continuing
KEYWORDS: *English studies; English studies teachers; Kenya;
teaching styles*

9/0941
>Faculty of Education and Community Studies, Department of
>Arts and Humanities in Education, Bulmershe Court,
>Woodlands Avenue, Earley, Reading RG1 1HY
>0734 875123
>Free University, Van der Boechorststraat 1, 1081 BT
>Amsterdam
>020 5489111
>Straughan, R. Dr; Spiecker, B. Prof.

Freedom and indoctrination in education
Abstract: Freedom and indoctrination are topics that have long dominated pedagogical and educational discourse in Europe and North
America. On the national level, there have always been considerable
differences in the way these topics are discussed. Now that the inner
borders of the European countries are disappearing, supra-national
structures will gradually change pedagogical ideologies and the
demands on national, educational systems and institutions. As a
result, freedom and indoctrination will become even more topical
subjects for debate. The book, published as a result of the research,
contains contributions from European and North American educationists.
Published Material: STRAUGHAN, R.R. & SPIECKER, B. (Eds).
(1991). Freedom and indoctrination in education: international perspectives. London: Cassell.
Status: Individual research
Date of Research: 1988-1992

KEYWORDS: *educational philosophy; indoctrination; intellectual freedom*

9/0942
> Reading and Language Information Centre, Bulmershe
> Court, Woodlands Avenue, Earley, Reading RG6 1HY
> 0734 875123
> Abbas, S. Mrs

Access to Information on Multicultural Education Resources (AIMER)
Abstract: AIMER is a database project which offers students, teachers, advisers and others information on multicultural antiracist teaching materials. In recent years there has been a proliferation of booklets, packs and other resources produced within local education authorities (LEAs) and other organisations. AIMER acts as a clearing house for materials of this kind. In addition to a postal inquiry service, it publishes resource lists on a wide range of topics which are updated on an annual basis. It is possible either to buy individual resource lists or the whole set at a substantial discount in the form of a single volume, 'Photocopiable resources to support the multicultural dimension of the National Curriculum'. A publications list is available on request. 01 17
Date of Research: 1987 - continuing
KEYWORDS: databases; multicultural education; resource materials

Robert Gordon University

9/0943
> School of Librarianship and Information Studies, Hilton
> Place, Aberdeen AB9 1FR
> 0224 283837
> Johnson, I. Mr; Hannabuss, C. Mr; Wildgoose, D. Mr

A review of management education for librarians
Abstract: The review arises out of recent general interest in the extent and quality of management education and training, and particular concern about the nature of management training for librarians. The aim of the study is to investigate the need for the provision of management education for mid-career professional librarians in all types of library and concentrates on middle and senior management levels. The objectives are: (1) to identify management competencies and skills necessary at different career levels, relating these to exisiting and likely future job needs; (2) review existing provision – examining what is available and what can be provided by external agencies, e.g. NBA, DMS programmes, Local Government Unit, Industrial Society etc; (3) study the profession's perceptions of provision, and the pattern of uptake; (4) identify gaps in existing provision; (5) make recommendations as to future provision, and propose a development plan. A review of existing and planned courses in Scottish institutions leading to management qualifications, and short courses in Scotland in management topics was undertaken. In addition a survey of provision of short courses in management for librarians was undertaken. The enquiry also elicited the profession's perception of provision and the pattern of uptake, information on resources available for staff development, and the relative priorities attached to management development.
Status: Sponsored project
Source of Grant: Library and Information Services Committee (Scotland) £ 6,500
Date of Research: 1990-1991
KEYWORDS: librarians; management development

9/0944
> School of Librarianship and Information Studies, Hilton
> Place, Aberdeen AB9 1FR
> 0224 283837
> Robertson, J. Miss; *Supervisor:* Williams, D. Dr

The application of computer aided learning to the development of information skills in further education
Abstract: The project seeks to examine the way in which further education (FE) students explore and utilise sources of information. The intial test group are National Diploma in Business Studies students at Telford College, Edinburgh and subsequently the students of similar courses in other Scottish FE colleges. A Hypertext system has been developed to guide students through information searches,

and to log individual student's use of the system. These logs will be analysed to evaluate learning patterns.
Status: Individual research
Date of Research: 1990 - continuing
KEYWORDS: computer-assisted learning; further education of students; hypertext; information seeking; information sources

9/0945
> School of Librarianship and Information Studies, Hilton
> Place, Aberdeen AB9 1FR
> 0224 283837
> Heriot-Watt University, Institute of Computer-Based
> Learning, Riccarton Campus, Currie, Edinburgh EH14 4AS
> 031 449 5111
> Hannabuss, C. Mr; *Supervisor:* McAleese, R. Dr

Knowledge representation and information exchange in instruction
Abstract: This research aims to investigate knowledge representation in the context of knowledge paradigms and conceptual frameworks. It examines ways in which experts and novices know and come to know management concepts, and induce and undergo meta-positional change through the representation of canonical knowledge in idio-syncratic ways, epistemic and axiological, explicit and assumptive.
Published Material: HANNABUSS, C.S. (1987). 'Negotiating meaning', Education Today, Vol 37, No 1, pp. 13-22.; HANNABUSS, C.S. (1987). Knowledge management. Bradford: MCB University Press.; HANNABUSS, C.S. (1987). 'Collaborating over meanings in management', Personnel Review, Vol 16, No 5, pp.34-39.; HANNABUSS, C.S. (1988). 'Knowledge paradigms and change', International Journal of Sociology and Social Change, Vol 8, No 1, pp.23-31.
Status: Individual research
Date of Research: 1986-1992
KEYWORDS: comprehension; epistemics; management theories; models

Roehampton Institute

9/0946
> Digby Stuart College, Roehampton Lane, London SW15 5PU
> 081 876 8273
> Pinsent, P. Ms

Antiracism and children's literature
Abstract: This investigation into racism/antiracism in children's literature is based on a belief in the influence of literature in the formation of attitudes, and a conviction that children should not be provided with sub-standard writing simply because the attitudes displayed in it are acceptable. Those writers who incorporate positive attitudes towards equality within quality children's books need discovering and supporting. The research includes personal reading and the evaluation of fiction; the findings may be published.
Published Material: PINSENT, P. (1990). 'Anti-racism and children's literature', The School Librarian, Vol 38, No 2, pp.45-50, May.
Status: Individual research
Date of Research: 1989 - continuing
KEYWORDS: antiracism education; children's literature; fiction; racial attitudes

9/0947
> Digby Stuart College, Roehampton Lane, London SW15 5PU
> 081 876 8273
> Payne, M. Ms

Teaching art appreciation in the nursery school
Abstract: The research considered the response of nursery school children to art appreciation when it was introduced into their curriculum. It explains how art appreciation was integrated into an intercurriculum approach and 'taught' through activities that are a 'normal' part of a nursery school day such as mime, movement, telling stories, expressing feelings, games and puzzles. This work stemmed from a question as to whether appreciation is a means to learning and if young children develop in confidence and visual understanding as their awareness grows about the world of art 'outside the classroom'. The research aimed to discover: how nursery school 3 and 4 year olds

could be engaged in the activity; if their involvement could be sustained; which works of art attracted their interest; and whether the activity could be a vehicle for building positive attitudes with regard to multicultural issues. With such questions in mind a programme of activities in the sample school (Eastwood Nursery School, Aubyn Square, London SW15) and at the Tate Gallery was planned. The research has included 2 exhibitions: (1) Eastwood Nursery School at the Tate Gallery, an educational display of text and visual material detailing the educational value of the visit. Exhibited at the Tate Gallery from September to December 1989; (2) Art Appreciation in a Multicultural Nursery School, an educational display – text and visuals. Exhibited at Spencer Park Teachers' Centre (ILEA), Summer 1989. Although the research is ongoing the findings suggest that critical appreciation of paintings and sculptures allows for reflective and physical participation, cognitive growth, observation, the development of vocabulary and can lead to children responding sensitively to stylistic similarities and being able to make cross references between paintings.
Published Material: PAYNE, M. (1989). 'Under fives at the Tate Gallery', Nursery World, Vol 89, No 3178.; PAYNE, M. (1990). 'Teaching art appreciation in the nursery school: its relevance for 3 and 4 year olds', Early Child Development and Care, Vol 61, pp.93-106.
Status: Individual research
Date of Research: 1989 - continuing
KEYWORDS: *aesthetic education; art activities; art appreciation; nursery school education*

9/0948

Digby Stuart College, Mathematics Division, Roehampton Lane, London SW15 5PU
081 876 8273
Laboratoire LSDZ-IMAG, BP53X 38041 Grenoble Cedex, France
Institut fur Didaktik der Mathematik, Universitat Bielefeld, Postfach 8640, D-4800 Bielefeld 1, Germany Rogers, L. Mr
Cabri geometry
Abstract: Cabri geometry is a software package created by French mathematics educators at Grenoble, France. The package provides the student with a set of tools for the dynamic investigation of plane geometry. Research to date in France and Germany has considered the didactic applications of the material. The aim of the pilot project is to assess the suitability and potential for its use in England.
Published Material: MASON, J. (1991). 'Pythagores in Cabri Geometre', Micromath, Vol 7, No 2, pp.15-17.
Date of Research: 1991-1991
KEYWORDS: *computer uses in education; educational software; geometry; mathematics education*

Royal Association for Disability and Rehabilitation (RADAR)

9/0949

25 Mortimer Street, London W1N 8AB
071 637 5400
Simpson, P. Mr
The employment of disabled teaching staff
Abstract: This research aims to update a previous Royal Association for Disability and Rehabilitation (RADAR) survey which interviewed disabled members of the teaching profession. This national quantitative survey assesses data provided by 51 local education authorities in the United Kingdom on their recruitment, retention policies, and practices regarding disabled teachers. The postal questionnaire will provide information on: the numbers of disabled teachers employed in the primary, secondary and tertiary sectors; support services for disabled staff (including newly disabled people); facilities provided and measures taken to recruit disabled staff.
Status: Sponsored project
Source of Grant: Royal Association for Disability and Rehabilitation – RADAR
Date of Research: 1990-1992
KEYWORDS: *disabilities; employment practices; equal opportunity – jobs; teacher employment; teacher recruitment*

Ruskin College

9/0950

Ruskin Hall, Old Headington, Oxford OX3 9BZ
0865 63437
Bryant, R. Mr; Noble, M. Mr
Financial circumstances of adult/mature students
Abstract: This is a long-term evaluation of the financial circumstances of adult students at Ruskin College, with particular reference to students on the CQSW/Social Work course. The research aims to: (1) monitor the financial difficulties experienced by mature/adult students; (2) compile data on how financial problems impact upon recruitment and the course work of students; and (3) evaluate the impact of the student loans scheme on students at Ruskin.
Published Material: BRYANT, R. & NOBLE, M. (1988). Reflections on Social Work Education. Oxford: Ruskin College.; BRYANT, R. & NOBLE, M. (1989). Education on a Shoestring. Oxford: Ruskin College.
Status: Individual research
Date of Research: 1986 - continuing
KEYWORDS: *adult students; financial problems; mature students; student costs; student financial aid; student loans; student recruitment*

9/0951

Ruskin Hall, Old Headington, Oxford OX3 9BZ
0865 63437
William Temple Foundation, Manchester
061 275 6534
Bryant, R. Mr; Addy, T. Rev.
Communities in crisis: an adult education and resource programme for local groups and community leaders
Abstract: The project has two aims: (1) to provide local activists/volunteers with the opportunity to reflect on their experiences and share ideas across different localities, towns and regions. The programme seeks to link groups in the north-west with groups in the southern regions; (2) undertake project based learning which: (a) will be of value to the participants, (e.g. confidence, writing skills etc.); and (b) will yield socially useful knowledge for local groups, e.g. data for jobs and applications. Research and evaluation is concerned with: (a) recording the organisation of the programme; (b) monitoring the experiences of the participants; (c) evaluating the use of the project material by local groups.
Published Material: ADDY, T. & BRYANT, R. et al. (1985). Communities in crisis. Ruskin College/William Temple Foundation.; BRYANT, R. (1989). Learning from experience: project work with community groups. Ruskin College/William Temple Foundation.
Status: Sponsored project
Source of Grant: Ruskin College; William Temple Foundation
Date of Research: 1983 - continuing
KEYWORDS: *adult education; community education; community programmes; group experience; groups; intergroup relations*

Scottish Council for Research in Education

9/0952

15 St John Street, Edinburgh EH8 8JR
031 557 2944
Black, H. Mr; Turner, E. Mrs; Devine, M. Mrs; Schlapp, U. Ms
A diagnostic resource for technology
Abstract: The outcome of the project was a diagnostic resource which can be used in classroom assessment by teachers of technology within a range of subject areas across the curriculum. The assessment instruments result from collaborative work with practising teachers and relate to central and fundamental aspects of technology learning. They are appropriate for use in standard grade courses, short courses, National Certificate modules and General Certificate of Secondary Education.
Published Material: TURNER, E., BLACK, H. & DEVINE, M. (1989). Technology in home economics. Edinburgh: SCRE/SARSU.; TURNER, E., BLACK, H. & DEVINE, M. (1990). 'Technology: an

annotated bibliography'. Edinburgh: SCRE/SARSU.
Status: Sponsored project
Source of Grant: Training, Enterprise and Education Directorate
Date of Research: 1989-1991
KEYWORDS: *assessment; school-based assessment; technology education*

9/0953

15 St John Street, Edinburgh EH8 8JR
031 557 2944
Black, H. Mr; Hall, J. Dr; Martin, S. Dr

Advanced courses development programme

Abstract: The main aim of the project is to evaluate the Advanced Courses Development Programme with regard to its overall effectiveness. It will examine the actual process of developing the Higher National units used in advanced courses and will also concern the product of this process, and the actual units and courses themselves. Each of these two concerns will focus on aspects such as criteria for good practice, strengths and weaknesses, and articulation with other qualifications.
Status: Sponsored project
Source of Grant: Scottish Office Education Department £46,758
Date of Research: 1990-1991
KEYWORDS: *curriculum development; higher grade examinations; modular courses; qualifications; Scotland*

9/0954

15 St John Street, Edinburgh EH8 8JR
031 557 2944
Black, H. Mr; Malcolm, H. Ms; Blair, A. Ms; Latta, J. Ms; Zaklukiewicz, S. Mr; *Supervisor:* Black, H. Mr

Teaching and learning strategies in the extension of TVEI in Scotland

Abstract: This research seeks to evaluate the changes in and impact of teaching and learning strategies in the Technical and Vocational Education Initiative (TVEI) extension in Scotland. Five questions will be addressed: (1) What strategies for teaching, learning and assessment are used in schools and colleges to deliver TVEI in selected areas of the curriculum, and how effectively is assessment integrated with teaching and learning?; (2) What claims are made for these teaching, learning and assessment strategies, particularly in relation to their preparing young people for adult and working life?; (3) To what extent are these strategies supportive of the aspiration of TVEI?; (4) What impact do they have on student achievements which will be of value to them in adult and working life, both in terms of formal qualifications and other characteristics?; (5) How does 'what is taught' and 'how it is taught' articulate with other aspects of the management of the curriculum in Scottish education? The research will identify examples of interesting and effective practice in five Round Two and Round Three TVEI projects through a series of related stages leading through progressive focusing to a small set of case studies. There are five stages. Stages 1 and 2 will provide an overview of practice, Stage 1 through a documentary analysis and Stage 2 through interviews with key individuals. Stage 3 will involve a questionnaire analysis of the nature and extent of practice identified in the first two stages. Stage 4 will comprise visits to and interviews with the key staff of a short list of possible units for case study. Stage 5 will provide the most substantial set of data through intensive case studies of practice using interviews, observation of classroom and other relevant work, and questionnaires.
Published Material: BLACK, H.D. et al. (1991). 'Staff development in teaching and learning'. SCRE Project Report 27.; BLACK, H.D. et al. (1991). 'Teaching and learning in an 'Education for Life' Programme'. SCRE Project Report 29.; BLACK, H.D. et al. (1991). 'Teaching and learning staff development'. SCRE Project Report 30.; BLACK, H.D. et al. (1991). 'The spread of resource-based learning methods'. SCRE Project Report 32; BLACK, H.D. et al. (1991). 'Changing teaching, changing learning'. SCRE/Employment Department. A full list of publications is available from the Researcher.
Status: Sponsored project
Source of Grant: Training, Enterprise and Education Directorate £152,153
Date of Research: 1989-1991
KEYWORDS: *learning strategies; programme evaluation; Scotland; teaching methods; technical education; vocational education*

9/0955

15 St John Street, Edinburgh EH8 8JR
031 557 2944
Black, H. Mr; Devine, M. Mrs; Fenwick, N. Ms; Gray, D. Mr; Mingard, S. Dr; *Supervisor:* Black, H, Mr

Schools Assessment Research and Support Unit (SARSU)

Abstract: The Schools Assessment Research and Support Unit (SARSU) carries out a rolling programme of action research and exploratory studies in assessment. It also encourages the dissemination of research findings and provides a support service for local authorities' inservice staff development programmes in assessment.
Published Material: BLACK, H.D., DEVINE, M., TURNER, E. & HARRISON, C. (1988). Standard Grade Assessment: a support package for schools. Edinburgh: SCRE/SARSU in collaboration with the Scottish Education Department.; BLACK, H.D. & DEVINE, M. (1988). Mathematics checkpoint 7: assessment materials for primary 7 pupils. Edinburgh: SCRE/SARSU.; TURNER, E., BLACK, H.D., HALL, J. & DEVINE, M. (1989). Technology in Home Economics. Edinbugh: SCRE/SARSU.; BLACK, H.D., DEVINE, M. & TURNER, E. (1989). Aspects of assessment: a primary perspective. Edinburgh SCRE/SARSU.; TURNER, E., BLACK, H.D. & DEVINE, M. (1990). Technology: an annotated bibliography. Edinburgh: SCRE/SARSU. A full list of publications is available from the researcher.
Status: Sponsored project
Source of Grant: Local authorities; Scottish Council for Research in Education; Scottish Office Education Department
Date of Research: 1983 - continuing
KEYWORDS: *action research; assessment; educational research; school-based assessment*

9/0956

15 St John Street, Edinburgh EH8 8JR
031 557 2944
Munn, P. Mrs; Johnstone, M. Mrs; Chalmers, V. Mrs; *Supervisor:* Munn, P. Mrs

Discipline in Scottish schools

Abstract: The main focus of this research into classroom and whole-school discipline was on 'effective discipline' in a range of different contexts. Case studies of primary and secondary schools were supplemented by surveys on secondary teachers' and headteachers' views on discipline.
Published Material: MUNN, P., JOHNSTONE, M. & HOLLIGAN, C. (1990). 'Pupils' perceptions of 'effective disciplinarians'', British Educational Research Journal, Vol 16, No 2, pp.191-198.; JOHNSTONE, M. & MUNN, P. 'Discipline in Scottish secondary schools: a survey'. SCRE Research Report Series No 35, Edinburgh: Scottish Council for Research in Education.
Status: Sponsored project
Source of Grant: Scottish Office Education Department £119,877
Date of Research: 1987-1991
KEYWORDS: *classroom discipline; classroom management; discipline; discipline policy; primary schools; pupil behaviour; Scotland; secondary schools*

9/0957

15 St John Street, Edinburgh EH8 8JR
031 557 2944
Munn, P. Mrs; Holroyd, C. Mr; *Supervisor:* Munn, P. Mrs

Investigating in the social subjects

Abstract: An exploration of the demands which 'investigations' at Standard Grade make on staff and pupils. The research aims at the identification of good practice in terms of school administration, teaching and learning.
Published Material: HOLROYD, C. (1992). 'Investigating in the social subjects', SCRE Research Report Series, No 34. Edinburgh: Scottish Council for Research in Education.; HOLROYD, C. (1992). 'Investigating in the social subjects', SCRE Spotlights Series, No 35. Edinburgh: Scottish Council for Research in Education.
Status: Sponsored project
Source of Grant: Scottish Office Education Department £5,000
Date of Research: 1991-1991
KEYWORDS: *examinations; investigations; learning activities; Scotland; social studies; standard grade examinations*

9/0958
15 St John Street, Edinburgh EH8 8JR
031 557 2944
Black, H. Mr; Devine, M. Ms; Hall, J. Dr; Martin, S. Dr;
Supervisor: Black, H. Mr
Achievements and competence of Standard Grades 3-6
Abstract: The research aims to describe: the actual language and mathematics competence of pupils gaining grades 3, 4, 5 and 6 in Standard Grade English and Mathematics; and the competence shown in school work by pupils failing to achieve at least grade 6 in Standard Grade English and Mathematics. It will also identify changes in grade-related criteria which might lead to improvements in the teaching of basic competence in language and mathematics.
Status: Sponsored project
Source of Grant: Scottish Office Education Department £39,904
Date of Research: 1991-1992
KEYWORDS: competence; English studies; linguistic competence; mathematics achievement; mathematics education; Scotland; secondary education; standard grade examinations

9/0959
15 St John Street, Edinburgh EH8 8JR
031 557 2944
Munn, P. Mrs; MacDonald, C. Mrs; Lowden, K. Mr
The needs of mature entrants in higher and further education
Abstract: The research focuses on the identification and effectiveness of innovative approaches in supporting the needs of mature entrants in higher and further education and on ways of attracting potential adult returners back into education and training. It builds on previous work in these areas, concentrating on case study approaches in higher and further education institutions to complement our larger scale survey work. The case studies have concentrated on areas where there has traditionally been difficulty in attracting mature students, i.e. engineering, electronics, mathematics and sciences. A telephone survey of potential returners has supplemented the case study work.
Published Material: MUNN, P., MACDONALD, C. & LOWDEN, K. (1992). 'Helping adult students cope: mature students on science, mathematics and engineering courses', SCRE Research Report Series, No 39. Edinburgh: Scottish Council for Research in Education.
Status: Sponsored project
Source of Grant: Scottish Office Education Department £61,969
Date of Research: 1990-1991
KEYWORDS: further education; higher education; mature students; student needs; student recruitment

9/0960
15 St John Street, Edinburgh EH8 8JR 931 557 2944 Munn, P. Mrs; Johnstone, M. Mrs; Lowden, K. Mr; *Supervisor:* Munn, P. Mrs
Scottish Wider Access Programme study
Abstract: This project complements the Leverhulme Access study by focusing on a survey of 100 Access students. It will identify any problems which Access students experience in their courses and in transition to higher education and will explore the effective ways of dealing with them and identify measures to increase the success rates of Access students.
Status: Sponsored project
Source of Grant: Scottish Office Education Department
Date of Research: 1991-1992
KEYWORDS: Access programmes; access to education; adult students; higher education; mature students

9/0961
15 St John Street, Edinburgh EH8 8JR
031 557 2944
Munn, P. Mrs
Returners to teaching
Abstract: The research aims to explore the factors affecting the career choice of different groups of non-practising teachers and to assess whether there are practical measures to encourage these groups to return to teaching. Stage One of the research consisted of face-to-face interviews with over 40 teachers about the factors affecting their non-return. Stage Two involved telephone interviews with 500 non-practising teachers using the information from the first stage to construct a telephone interview schedule.
Published Material: ROBINSON, R., MUNN, P. & MACDONALD, C. (1992). 'Once a teacher always a teacher? Encouraging return to

teaching', SCRE Research Report Series, No 36. Edinburgh: Scottish Council for Research in Education
Status: Sponsored project
Source of Grant: Scottish Office Education Department £36,659
Date of Research: 1989-1991
KEYWORDS: career choice; teacher employment; teacher recruitment; teacher supply and demand; teaching profession

9/0962
15 St John Street, Edinburgh EH8 8JR
031 557 2944
Munn, P. Mrs; Allan, J. Ms; *Supervisor:* Munn, P. Mrs
An evaluation of area learning support teams and observation of cooperative teaching
Abstract: The project, based in Dumfries and Galloway, has two distinctive strands. The first of these evaluated the effectiveness of a new initiative for learning support provision. The second phase focuses on cooperative teaching strategies for meeting the needs of pupils with learning difficulties.
Published Material: ALLAN, J. (1992). 'Providing learning support through area teams', SCRE Spotlights Series, No 34, Edinburgh: Scottish Council for Research in Education.; ALLAN, J. & MUNN, P. (1992). 'Teaming-up: area teams for learning support', SCRE Research Report Series, No 38, Edinburgh: Scottish Council for Research in Education.
Status: Sponsored project
Source of Grant: Scottish Office Education Department £6,250; Dumfries and Galloway Region £6,250
Date of Research: 1990-1991
KEYWORDS: learning disabilities; special educational needs; support services; team teaching

9/0963
15 St John Street, Edinburgh EH8 8JR
031 557 2944
Thorpe, G. Mr; Pollard, J. Mr; Whitcombe, D. Mr; Bichard, A. Dr; *Supervisor:* Thorpe, G. Mr
Central Support Unit: the Assessment of Achievement Programme
Abstract: The Central Support Unit (CSU) has been funded by the Scottish Office Education Department to provide the technical support and infra-structure for its Assessment of Achievement Programme (AAP). The AAP is a systematic programme, designed to monitor pupil attainment. Individual teams with knowledge and expertise in the particular subject under study are established to have responsibility for the content-specific part of the projects. The CSU provides technical support to all projects across the subject spectrum. This support includes: advice on experimental design; sampling; liaison with schools; collation, distribution and collection of test materials; computing the desired analyses and advising on the statistics of these. Part of the general support of the AAP will incorporate the development and continuous updating of a set of guidelines for AAP projects. These guidelines will assist the project teams in the efficient design of their assessment programmes, will offer a repertoire of analytic approaches designed to enable the teams to extract different kinds of information from their data, and will make practical suggestions which will help to overcome anticipated difficulties.
Published Material: 'Noticeboard' – a newsletter for schools and Feedback booklets covering the 1989 science and 1990 mathematics surveys are available from the Scottish Council for Research in Education.
Status: Sponsored project
Source of Grant: Scottish Office Education Department
Date of Research: 1987 - continuing
KEYWORDS: academic achievement; achievement rating; assessment; educational research

9/0964
15 St John Street, Edinburgh EH8 8JR
031 557 2944
Black, H. Mr; Hall, J. Dr; Martin, S. Dr; *Supervisor:* Black, H. Mr
Dealing with knowledge in the Museums Sector Standards: an evaluation of an approach using carefully chosen examples
Abstract: This research is an investigation of the best ways in which to describe the knowledge base which underpins standards within the Department of Employment's Standards Programme. Using 'exam-

ples' of typically competent performance within the Museums Sector, the project will seek to: (1) explore the potential of an 'examples' approach to knowledge clarification; (2) describe and evaluate the process by which standards developers might use such an approach; and (3) investigate the extent to which industry experts feel it is likely that sound assessments would result if the existing draft standards statements, supported by examples of knowledge, were all that were available to them.
Status: Sponsored project
Source of Grant: Department of Employment £13,861
Date of Research: 1991-1992
KEYWORDS: *competence; job performance; knowledge level; museums; standards; vocational education*

9/0965
15 St John Street, Edinburgh EH8 8JR
031 557 2944
Munn, P. Mrs; Allan, J. Ms; *Supervisor:* Munn, P. Mrs
Parents' views on values in education
Abstract: This project aims to: explore methods of eliciting parents' views about values; investigate how parents perceive values in education; and investigate parents' views on whether values should be explicitly transmitted by teachers and if so what these values should be.
Status: Sponsored project
Source of Grant: Gordon Cook Foundation £5,150
Date of Research: 1992-1992
KEYWORDS: *parent attitudes; values; values education*

9/0966
15 St John Street, Edinburgh EH8 8JR
031 557 2944
Munn, P. Mrs; Johnstone, M. Mrs; Edwards, L. Ms; Wake, R. Ms; *Supervisor:* Munn, P. Mrs
Anti-bullying strategies
Abstract: The aim of this research is to develop a package of ideas and information based on current research in Britain and in Scandinavia on the good practice of experienced teachers. The finished package will contain: a booklet outlining points to consider and steps to take; case-studies for teacher discussion; action plans for management/staff consideration and lists of information on resource and curricular materials.
Published Material: MUNN, P., JOHNSTONE, M. & EDWARDS, L. (1992). Action against bullying: a support pack for schools. Edinburgh: Scottish Council for Research in Education.
Status: Sponsored project
Source of Grant: Scottish Office Education Department £18,700
Date of Research: 1991-1991
KEYWORDS: *bullying; comparative education; discipline policy; discipline problems; material development*

9/0967
15 St John Street, Edinburgh EH8 8JR
031 557 2944
Munn, P. Mrs; Johnstone, M. Mrs; *Supervisor:* Munn, P. Mrs
Study of mature entrants to teaching
Abstract: The overall aim of the research is to address the question: why are there not more mature student entrants to secondary teaching and what could be done to attract more mature entrants to teaching? This question will be addressed by collecting evidence through three separate surveys of: (1) mature secondary teaching students at colleges of education, at Stirling University, and on Scottish Wider Access Programme (SWAP) secondary teaching courses; (2) a sample of final year mature students in higher education; and (3) mature people who enquired about secondary teaching but did not apply.
Status: Sponsored project
Source of Grant: Scottish Office Education Department £35,162
Date of Research: 1991-1992
KEYWORDS: *mature students; preservice teacher education; secondary school teachers; student recruitment; student teacher attitudes; student teachers*

9/0968
15 St John Street, Edinburgh EH8 8JR
031 557 2944

Munn, P. Mrs; Robinson, R. Ms; Johnstone, M. Mrs; *Supervisor:* Munn, P. Mrs
The effectiveness of Access courses
Abstract: The aim of this project is to assess the effectiveness of science and social science Access courses in preparing adults for degree level study. The research will provide a greater understanding of the strengths and weaknesses of Access courses, as well as recommendations for good practice both in Access courses themselves and in higher education responsiveness to Access students.
Status: Sponsored project
Source of Grant: Leverhulme Trust £90,000
Date of Research: 1991 - continuing
KEYWORDS: *Access programmes; access to education; adult students; higher education; mature students; programme evaluation; science education; social sciences*

9/0969
15 St John Street, Edinburgh EH8 8JR
031 557 2944
Munn, P. Mrs; Blair, A. Ms; Lowden, K. Mr; Powney, J. Ms; McPake, J. Ms; Arney, N. Mr; *Supervisor:* Munn, P. Mrs
Adult education: provision, guidance and progression
Abstract: The research will be carried out in four studies. It will provide a broad based national picture of opportunities for progression and of guidance while enabling more detailed information on adults' experiences and on the operation of particular systems to be collected. The four studies are: (1) case studies of adults' experiences of guidance, provision and progression, Scottish Council for Research in Education (SCRE) and Scottish Community Education Council (SCEC); (2) a survey of opportunities for progression, focusing particularly on inter-sector links and on links between formal and informal services, together with in depth analysis of opportunities for progression within one region; (3) a survey of guidance provision together with in depth analysis of a small number of new initiatives and an assessment of user experience (SCRE); and (4) a special study of adults in schools, investigating the opinions of adults and of the schools about the advantages of this form of provision (SCRE).
Status: Sponsored project
Source of Grant: Scottish Office Education Department £149,671
Date of Research: 1991 - continuing
KEYWORDS: *access to education; adult education; adult students; community education; educational guidance; mature students; student attitudes*

9/0970
15 St John Street, Edinburgh EH8 8JR
031 557 2944
Harlen, W. Prof.; *Supervisor:* Harlen, W. Prof.
5-14 Development Programme: coordination of the evaluation of its implementation
Abstract: The work of coordinating the planning of the 5-14 education projects began in February 1991. The coordinated programme will cover all aspects of the new developments in the curriculum, assessment, use of test materials and reporting to parents as these are implemented during the next few years.
Status: Sponsored project
Source of Grant: Scottish Office Education Department £17,500
Date of Research: 1991 - continuing
KEYWORDS: *curriculum development; primary secondary education; programme evaluation*

9/0971
15 St John Street, Edinburgh EH8 8JR
031 557 2944
Munn, P. Mrs; Arney, N. Mr; Holroyd, C. Mr; *Supervisor:* Munn, P. Mrs
Provision and take-up of School Board training
Abstract: The research concentrates on four main areas: (1) Board members' views on the information and training available to them; (2) their preferences for particular forms of training; (3) the factors affecting the take-up and selection of forms of training provision; (4) gaps in available provision. The research design combines depth with breadth and is in three strands. Strand One consists of a telephone survey of 100 Boards. Strand Two involves case studies of 15 Boards. Strand Three involves a survey of 1,000 Board members.
Published Material: MUNN, P., ARNEY, N. & HOLROYD, C. (1990). 'The provision and take-up of School Board Information and

Training: a summary', SCRE Spotlights Series, No 29, Edinburgh: Scottish Council for Research in Education.
Status: Sponsored project
Source of Grant: Scottish Office Education Department £62,792
Date of Research: 1990-1991
KEYWORDS: *parent control; school-based management; school boards – Scotland; school governing bodies*

9/0972
> 15 St John Street, Edinburgh EH8 8JR
> 031 557 2944
> Munn, P. Mrs; Allan, J. Ms; *Supervisor:* Munn, P. Mrs

OECD integration project: pupils with special educational needs
Abstract: A number of case studies of the integration policies and practice of schools in the UK will be undertaken as the UK contribution to Phase II of the OECD/CERI project 'Integration in the school'. The project's concern is with resourcing, access to the National Curriculum and the role of the special school. SCRE has been subcontracted to undertake the Scottish case study.
Status: Sponsored project
Source of Grant: National Foundation for Educational Research; Organisation for Economic Cooperation and Development (OECD) £8,000
Date of Research: 1991-1991
KEYWORDS: *equal education; mainstreaming; Scotland; special educational needs; special school*

9/0973
> 15 St John Street, Edinburgh EH8 8JR
> 031 557 2944
> Black, H. Mr; Malcolm, H. Ms

Evaluation of the Lothian Region Technical and Vocational Education Initiative (TVEI) Extension
Abstract: The team provides an ongoing evaluation service to Lothian's Technical and Vocational Education Initiative (TVEI) Extension project – contact with the project being sustained through membership of the TVEI Evaluation Group. Evaluative studies and other services are negotiated throughout the lifetime of the evaluation. Three identified to date are: the project's school/college week; mechanisms for neighbourhood management group activity and ideas sharing; and curriculum auditing.
Status: Sponsored project
Source of Grant: Lothian Region
Date of Research: 1989 - continuing
KEYWORDS: *programme evaluation; technical education; vocational education*

9/0974
> 15 St John Street, Edinburgh EH8 8JR
> 031 557 2944
> Powney, J. Ms; Harlen, W. Prof.; Martin, S. Dr;
> Holroyd, C. Mr; *Supervisor:* Powney, J. Ms

Follow-up study on the initial training of newly qualified teachers – a feasibility study
Abstract: This study, initiated by the Council for the Accreditation of Teacher Education, and financed by the Department of Education and Science (DES) will focus on the match between initial teacher training and the requirements of the first posts held by newly qualified teachers. Evidence will be sought about current practices in Northern Ireland, Wales and England of tracking students from their initial teacher training through their early professional experience and how such information could or does provide feedback to their initial training institutions. Informants will include newly qualified teachers and staff from initial teacher training institutions, local education authorities/Library Boards and schools. From the evidence collected by questionnaire and interview in the initial stage of the project, the research team will draft a framework for a possible national scheme to follow up initial teacher training. This framework will be the basis for a series of discussions with small groups exploring the feasibility, desirability, nature, content and cost of a possible national scheme. In this consultative exercise, the discussion groups will involve representatives from Northern Ireland, Wales and England drawn from the same categories of informants as the first stage of the project. The outcome of the study will be recommendations to the DES on the feasibility of a national scheme for initial training institutions to appraise their effectiveness by tracking their newly qualified teachers as they begin their careers.

Status: Sponsored project
Source of Grant: Department of Education and Science £34,888
Date of Research: 1991-1992
KEYWORDS: *curriculum; preservice teacher education; probationary teachers; programme evaluation; student teachers; teacher education; teaching experience*

9/0975
> 15 St John Street, Edinburgh EH8 8JR
> 031 557 2944
> South Bank University, 103 Borough Road, London SE1 0AA
> 071 928 8989
> Powney, J. Ms; Weiner, G. Miss; McPake, J. Ms;
> *Supervisor:* Powney, J. Ms

Equitable staffing policies in further and higher education
Abstract: This project will explore the strategies deployed by further and higher educational institutions committed to developing and implementing equitable staff policies and practices. Further it will disseminate examples of good practice for information to other institutions. The specific aims of the project are to: (1) develop understanding of the policies and practices which enhance the promotion of under-represented groups, e.g. female and black and ethnic minority staff in educational institutions; (2) encourage wider implementation and evaluation of such policies and practices; (3) develop understanding of processes of change by drawing together theoretical and empirical work in the fields of equal opportunities and the study of organisations; and (4) contribute to understanding and utilisation of evaluative case-study methodologies.
Status: Sponsored project
Source of Grant: Economic and Social Research Council £36,930
Date of Research: 1991 - continuing
KEYWORDS: *academic staff; academic staff promotion; employment opportunities; equal opportunities – jobs; further education; higher education*

Sheffield University

9/0976
> Department of Psychology, Sheffield S10 2TN
> 0742 768555
> Banks, M. Dr; Roker, D. Ms

Socialisation of elites
Abstract: The aim of this project is to assess the effects of private education on occupational aspirations and attitudes. The researchers carried out a secondary analysis of the Youthscan data base which consists of the 1970 birth cohort of 15,000 births.
Status: Sponsored project
Source of Grant: Economic and Social Research Council
Date of Research: 1990-1992
KEYWORDS: *occupational aspiration; private education; work attitudes*

9/0977
> Department of Psychology, Medical Research Council, Sheffield S10 2TN
> 0742 768555
> Banks, H. Dr; Parkinson, B. Dr

Work socialisation of youth (WOSY): a cross-national study
Abstract: This is a collaborative cross-national research approach that seeks to describe and explain work role development of youth in ten countries, through a common theoretical and methodological framework. A minimum of two samples are drawn in each country, representing jobs selected to emphasise work with either 'data' or 'things'. The samples will comprise 200 young people beginning jobs with information systems such as word processors, and 200 machine operators in manufacturing companies. Interviews will be carried out on three occasions: within six months of starting the job or training scheme, nine to twelve months later, and two years after the first interview. Interviews will gather information about education, early career, and job characteristics. Motivational variables include employment commitment, job attitudes, and information about the personal meanings of work. Young people's perceptions of the personal impact on their job and their colleagues and the match between prior

expectations and later circumstances, will also be assessed. In addition several indices of career advancement and satisfaction will be obtained. The aim is to determine individual, organisational and societal factors which underlie successful entry into the labour market. Changes across time will be identified, and these will be examined in relation to previously gathered data. Cross-national comparisons will permit evaluation of characteristic educational and training arrangements within each country.
Status: Sponsored project
Source of Grant: Medical Research Council
Date of Research: 1988-1992
KEYWORDS: *cross cultural studies; job satisfaction; motivation; school to work transition; socialisation; vocational adjustment; work attitudes; youth employment*

9/0978
Department of Psychology, Sheffield S10 2TN
0742 768555
Smith, P. Prof.; Laver, R. Ms; Cowie, H. Dr
Prejudice, isolation and bullying: intervention in ethnically mixed classes
Abstract: Research has shown that racial prejudice, social isolation and bullying are far from uncommon during the middle school period. The first aim of the project is to document the extent and interrelationship of these problems on a large sample of classes. At present, for example, it is not known whether racial prejudice and bullying are related, and if so, whether in some cases the former may be a cause of the latter. In a previous, one year Economic and Social Research Council (ESRC) funded project, the research team found that prejudice could be ameliorated to some extent, and liking of peers increased, in classes where teachers were trained in and used cooperative group work (CGW). The central feature of this approach is the opportunity to learn through the expression and exploration of diverse ideas and the cooperative solution of problems, in groups formed across ethnic and gender barriers. In the present project, the CGW curriculum will be refined and more focused in some respects, based on previous experience. The second aim of the project is that it should provide a more definitive test of the efficacy of this form of school-based intervention program. The extent to which the preliminary results from the one year project can be replicated will be assessed on a larger sample and over a longer time period. Periodic assessments, both quantitative and qualitative, will be made of the nature of social relationships in the participating classes.
Published Material: BOULTON, M.J. & SMITH, P.K. (1991). 'Bullying and withdrawn children'. In: VARMA, V.P. (Ed). Truants from life: theory and therapy. London: David Fulton.; COWIE, H., BOULTON, M.J. & SMITH, P.K. (1992). 'Bullying: pupil relationships'. In: JONES, N. & JONES, E.B. (Eds). Learning to behave: curriculum and whole school management approaches to discipline. London: Kogan Page.
Status: Sponsored project
Source of Grant: Economic and Social Research Council £82,496
Date of Research: 1990 - continuing
KEYWORDS: *bullying; cooperation; ethnic relations; intergroup relations; intervention; middle school education; pupil behaviour; social isolation*

9/0979
Department of Psychology, Sheffield S10 2TN
0742 768555
Beer, A. Prof.; Smith, P. Prof.; Higgins, C. Ms; Sheat, L. Ms; *Supervisor:* Smith, P. Prof.; Beer, A. Prof.
The impact of pupil participation in playground design on pupil satisfaction with playtime and the incidence of bullying in school playgrounds
Abstract: Bullying has been found to be a pervasive as well as distressing phenomenon in many schools. Some 20% of pupils report some degree of involvement in bullying over the previous term (Smith, 1991). Much of this bullying takes place in the playground, during lunch hour or mid-morning break. A team of researchers at Sheffield University are currently examining both the incidence of bullying in a sample of some 24 junior/middle and secondary schools, and ways of intervening to reduce the extent of the problem. Various kinds of intervention will be negotiated with the schools, and to some extent resourced for them. These interventions will either be based on existing expertise, or in some cases developed by the research team. Work in playgrounds is one important intervention in this package, and one which is proving a popular option amongst the

schools involved. The main research project (funded by the DES) is planning to concentrate on producing a useful training course/materials for lunchtime supervisory assistants, who are often inadequately prepared or trained for the task of supervising large numbers of children, distinguishing bullying from more playful activities, and knowing how to respond appropriately. The other main aspect of playground intervention is the design of the playground, facilities, and pupil involvement in these aspects of the playground environment. An attractive playground which allows a variety of activities of interest to children – when combined with informed supervision – is less likely to be a breeding ground for bullying. The Department of Psychology at Sheffield University is collaborating with the Department of Landscape Architecture to work on playground design and pupil participation. In the latter department, students usually carry out a small project in playgrounds, and a variety of methods and game formats have been devised to involve pupils in this activity. The projects themselves are small scale (lasting about a week) but the methods will be used on a larger scale, over a six-month period, to assist four schools which are seriously interested in involving their pupils in designing/changing/improving playground facilities. The design process will proceed in stages, culminating in a joint presentation of short-listed designs in February 1992. The second phase of the project will be involved in assisting the implementation of these designs, and monitoring their impact, on behaviour in the playground generally and bully/victim problems in particular.
Status: Sponsored project
Source of Grant: Gulbenkian Foundation £87,000
Date of Research: 1991-1992
KEYWORDS: *bullying; discipline problems; playgrounds; pupil behaviour; pupil participation; recreational activities*

9/0980
Department of Psychology, Sheffield S10 2TN
0742 768555
Smith, P. Prof.; Sharp, S. Ms; Ahmad, Y. Ms; Boulton, M. Dr; Cowie, H. Dr; Thomson, D. Dr; *Supervisor:* Smith, P. Prof.
The DFE Sheffield Bullying Project: a follow up survey on bully/victim problems in one local education authority with monitoring and evaluation of the actions and interventions taken as a result of the survey
Abstract: The Department for Education (DFE) Sheffield Bullying Project aims to identify through evaluation, ways in which schools can effectively tackle the problem of bullying. The project follows on from a survey which took place in November 1990 which monitored the nature and extent of bullying in 24 Sheffield schools (number of pupils = 6,758). 23 of these schools, (16 primary, 7 secondary) wished to continue with the intervention project. All of the schools have at a minimum developed a whole school anti-bullying policy which clarifies for staff, pupils and parents what bullying is and what can be done about it. Other interventions have also been explored. These include: strategies for tackling bullying through the curriculum; strategies for working directly with bullies and victims; and strategies for enhancing the playground environment. Data gathered through regular monitoring, pupil and staff interviews and observation will be combined with information gathered from a follow-up survey in November 1992 to indicate how successful schools have been in reducing levels of bullying, and which interventions work best.
Published Material: SHARP, S. & SMITH, P.K. (1991). 'Bullying in UK schools: the DES Sheffield Bullying Project', Early Child Development Care, No 77, pp.47-55.; COWIE, H. & SHARP, S. (1992). 'Students themselves tackle the problem of bullying', Pastoral Care, December.; SHARP, S. & SMITH, P.K. 'Tackling bullying in the Sheffield Project'. In: TATTUM, D. (Ed). Understanding and managing bullying. London: Heinemann, (in press).; COWIE, H., SHARP, S. & SMITH, P.K. (1992). 'Tackling bullying in schools: the method of common concern', BPS Education Section Review, No 16, pp.55-57.
Status: Sponsored project
Source of Grant: Department for Education £173,972
Date of Research: 1991 - continuing
KEYWORDS: *antisocial behaviour; behaviour problems; bullying; discipline; discipline policy; pupil behaviour*

9/0981
Department of Psychology, Sheffield S10 2TN
0742 768555
Smith, P. Prof.; Thompson, D. Dr; Whitney, I. Ms;

Supervisor: Smith, P. Prof.; Thompson, D. Dr
Assessing and interviewing in problems of bullying with pupils with special needs
Abstract: This project examined whether certain categories of statemented children with special educational needs (SENs) were more, or less likely to be involved in bully/victim problems at school. At total of 186 children from 8 schools were interviewed. The 3 junior/middle schools had integrated resource units for children with, moderate learning difficulties, mild learning difficulties and hearing impairments and for the 5 secondary schools the units were for children with hearing impairments, moderate learning difficulties, SENs physically handicapped and visual impairments. 93 children with SENs and 93 mainstream children matched for age, ethnicity and gender were interviewed. A member of staff was also interviewed about the children with SENs. The interviews were semi-structured, designed to explore both the child's and the teacher's perception of their relationships with peers, their feelings about the school, and whether or not they were involved in bullying or being bullied. These interviews took place in between October and December 1991, and were repeated between May and July 1992. During this year, planned interventions designed to reduce bullying problems had taken place within these schools (via a DFE funded project), so these second interviews focused on how these interventions affected the child, as well as whether any involvement in bully/victim problems had been reduced. The main findings were that children with SENs were bullied more than mainstream (MS) children and had fewer friends in school. Teachers tended to underestimate how often children with SENs were being bullied. The number of children with SENs being bullied and bullying others had decreased over time and most children perceived that bullying had got better in their schools; these changes seemed attributable to effects of intervention rather than age *per se.*
Published Material: WHITNEY, I., NABUZOKA, D. & SMITH, P.K. (1992). 'Bullying in schools: mainstream and special needs', Support for Learning, No 7, pp.3-7.; NABUZOKA, D., WHITNEY, I., SMITH, P.K. & THOMPSON, D.A. 'Bullying and children with special needs in schools'. In: TATTUM, D. (Ed). Understanding and managing bullying. London: Heinemann, (in press).
Status: Sponsored project
Source of Grant: Economic and Social Research Council £25,150
Date of Research: 1991-1992
KEYWORDS: *bullying; discipline; intervention; mainstreaming; special educational needs*

9/0982
Department of Psychology, Sheffield S10 2TN
0742 768555
Higgins, C. Ms; Sheat, L. Ms; *Supervisor:* Smith, P. Prof.;
Beer, A. Prof.
The impact of pupil participation on playground design and school bullying
Abstract: Four junior schools took part in this project. Initially students and staff from the Department of Landscape at Sheffield University worked with the pupils and staff of the schools, finding out which activities were done to which areas of the existing playgrounds, good and bad features, and then, with a series of games and exercises, what kind of playground they would like to have. Following this, a design brief was prepared for each school playground, together with applications for funding and implementation. These design briefs aimed towards a more diversified and challenging playground environment, which might reduce opportunities and incentives for bullying (a problem all these schools were working on). During the second part of the project the school commenced implementing aspects of the design briefs. Feedback was obtained from both pupils and staff concerning: (a) satisfaction about changes in the playground; and (b) levels of bullying.
Published Material: SHARP, S. & SMITH, P.K. Making changes to playtime. Topic 1993. (in press).
Status: Sponsored project
Source of Grant: Caloustie Gulbenkian Foundation (UK) £7,000
Date of Research: 1991-1992
KEYWORDS: *bullying; discipline problems; playgrounds; pupil attitudes; pupil behaviour; pupil participation; recreational activities*

9/0983
Department of Psychology, Sheffield S10 2TN
0742 768555
Smith, P. Dr; Binney, V. Ms; Bowers, L. Ms; *Supervisor:*
Smith, P. Dr; Binney, V. Ms

Family background factors characteristic of victims and bullies in middle childhood
Abstract: Prevalence studies on bullying have emphasised the extent and severity of bully/victim problems in schools, with about 1 in 6 children in South Yorkshire secondary and middle schools reporting being bullied, and 1 in 12 pupils admitting to taking part in such bullying. The immediate and long term consequences for both bullies and victims is of great concern. At extremes a victim may take his or her life to escape torment, and bullying has been associated with later violent crime and alcohol abuse. The role of family factors is thought to be crucial to the full understanding of the origins and maintenance of bully/victim relations in childhood and adolescence although little evidence exists to implicate a causal relationship between the two. The proposed investigation will aim to locate the structural and psychodynamic family factors thought to be characteristic of bullies and victims, as perceived by the children themselves. A sample pool of 170, 9-10 year old children will be used, from which after peer and teacher nominations, 20 children often proposed as bullies, 20 children often nominated as victims, and 20 controls will be selected for further data collection. This will measure the childrens' perceptions of family relations. This procedure will make use of the Family Relations Test, a modified version of the Parental Bonding Instrument, a modified version of the Separation Anxiety Test, and the FAST family sculpt test. Differences between the subject groups will be analysed and the data will be examined for possible sub-groups of bullies and victims.
Status: Sponsored project
Source of Grant: Medical Research Council £13,000
Date of Research: 1990-1991
KEYWORDS: *antisocial behaviour; bullying; family environment; family influence; pupil behaviour*

9/0984
Department of Psychology, Sheffield S10 2TN
0742 768555
Tapton Mount School for the Blind, 20 Manchester Road,
Sheffield S10 5DG
0742 667151
Spencer, C. Dr; Blades, M. Dr; Ungar, S. Mr
Evaluation of mobility education for young blind children
Abstract: The researchers' previous work on the education for mobility of the visually handicapped has included: (1) development of spatial concepts; (2) the hierarchy of skills underlying successful mobility; (3) the evaluation of experimental programmes to improve aspects of training; and (4) the evaluation of tactile maps in learning a novel area. One such project – on the parental approach to independence and mobility skills for children prior to school – has led the researchers to embark upon the present project, which will study children through the years prior to entry to blind school, and their first few years of formal mobility training within the school. Research will be conducted in conjunction with Tapton Mount, the special school for the visually handicapped in Yorkshire and surrounding counties. The aim is to plan and test mobility training programmes designed to develop the child's techniques for: (1) acquiring and storing knowledge of spatial layout; (2) updating one's position within a locale; and (3) applying systems of spatial concepts to plan routes.
Published Material: BLADES, M. & SPENCER, C. (1990). 'The development of 3-6 year olds' map using ability: the relative importance of landmarks and map alignment', Journal of Genetic Psychology, No 151, pp.181-194.; MORSLEY, K., SPENCER, C. & BAYBUTT, K. (1991). ' Is there any relationship between a child's body image and spatial skills?', British Journal of Visual Impairment, No 9, pp.41-43.; MORSLEY, K., SPENCER, C. & BAYBUTT, K. (1991). 'Two techniques for encouraging movement and exploration in the visually impaired child', British Journal of Visual Impairment, No 9, pp.75-78.; PIKE, E. (1991). 'Children's reactions to Nomad, an audio-tactile graphic processor', British Journal of Visual Impairment, No 9, pp.105-107.; SPENCER, C., MORSLEY, K., UNGAR, S., PIKE, E. & BLADES, M. (1992). 'Developing the blind child's cognition of the environment: the role of direct experience and map given experience', Geoforum, No 23, pp.191-197.
Status: Sponsored project
Source of Grant: Economic and Social Research Council
Date of Research: 1990 - continuing
KEYWORDS: *blindness; mobility aids; visual impairments; visually handicapped mobility*

9/0985
Division of Education, 388 Glossop Road, Sheffield S10 2TN
0742 768555
Wellington, J. Dr
Information technology in education and employment
Abstract: This research carries on from the previous research project
'Skills for the Future'. The research has arisen from the increase in
the use of microcomputers in both education and industry. In consequence, greater attention has been paid to the need for specific
'information technology skills' – skills which need to be taught in
schools, colleges and training schemes to meet the needs of industry.
This project draws on interviews with a sample of employers, questionnaire responses, in depth interviews and case studies. By also
considering previous research in the area, the project gives a detailed
investigation into present provision, aims, and policy in training
related to 'IT' (Information Technology) and discusses how this
provision relates to employers' needs and requirements. The final
publication gives a clear and accessible overview of the connection
between IT and industry's needs.
Published Material: WELLINGTON, J.J. (1989). Education for
employment: the place of information technology. Windsor: NFER-
Nelson.
Status: Sponsored project
Source of Grant: Training Agency – 1986 only £31,000; Universities
Funding Council
Date of Research: 1986-1992
KEYWORDS: *industry-education relationship; information technol-
ogy; microcomputers; skill development*

9/0986
Division of Education, 388 Glossop Road, Sheffield S10 2TN
0742 768555
Pullin, R. Mr; Poppleton, P. Dr
Change in teacher education: an Anglo-Soviet study
Abstract: The content, process and organisation of initial teacher
education is now a key item on the government's agenda for change
following the debate on teaching quality and the legislative changes
in the Education Reform Act 1988. These will seek to bring about
greater centralised control of the teaching profession, and ultimately,
greater uniformity in preparation for it. The first stage of this exploratory study is to seek the views of those most concerned: teachers,
employers and administrators on the impact on initial teacher education of the Education Reform Act and other changes that have affected
schools. The ultimate aim is a more comprehensive study that will
assess the nature and direction of desired change and lead to a
programme for its implementation. This study runs parallel to a
similar one being conducted by colleagues in the USSR as part of a
collaborative research agreement between the University of Sheffield
and the Academy of Pedagogical Sciences, Moscow, USSR. Soviet
teacher education has also been under pressure to change, though in
opposit directions, from total centralisation to relative autonomy.
Both studies will enable the researchers to draw up a number of
priority statements which represent a wide range of views and which
can then be put to larger representative groups of 'consumers' in each
country.
Status: Sponsored project
Source of Grant: Sheffield University: Division of Education £3,000;
The British Council £1,280
Date of Research: 1991-1992
KEYWORDS: *comparative education; Education Reform Act 1988;
educational change; preservice teacher education; teaching profes-
sion; USSR*

9/0987
Division of Education, 388 Glossop Road, Sheffield S10 2TN
0742 768555
Hannon, P. Dr
Working with parents to promote early literacy development
Abstract: The project is the United Kingdom's contribution to the
European Communities' Action Research Programme on the Prevention and Combatting of Illiteracy and is linked to 16 others in the
member states. It aims to develop methods of working with parents
of preschool children to promote literacy development in the early
stages. The focus is on children's learning at home, but both home-
based and school-based methods are being explored through a set of
14 case studies of families. The project team has adopted an emergent
literacy perspective and has attempted to share it with parents, some
in distinctly disadvantaged circumstances. The outcomes will be

descriptions of methods to be shared with other workers, and a
qualitative evaluation of their feasibility and impact which may lead
to future experimental studies.
Published Material: HANNON, P. (1990). 'Parental involvement in
preschool literacy development'. In: WRAY, D. (Ed). Emerging
partnerships: current research in language and literacy. BERA (British Educational Research Association) Dialogues in Education, 4.
Clevedon, Avon: Multilingual Matters.; WEINBERGER, J., HAN-
NON, P. & NUTBROWN, C. (1990). 'Ways of working with parents
to promote early literacy development'. USDE (University of Sheffield, Division of Education) Papers in Education', 14. Sheffield:
University of Sheffield, Division of Education.; HANNON, P.,
WEINBERGER, J. & NUTBROWN, C. (1991). 'A study of work
with parents to promote early literacy development', Research Papers
in Education, Vol 6, No 2, pp.77-97.; NUTBROWN, C., HANNON,
P. & WEINBERGER, J. (1991). 'Training teachers to work with
parents to promote early literacy development', International Journal
of Early Childhood, Vo, 23, No 2, pp.1-10.
Status: Sponsored project
Source of Grant: European Commission; Department of Education
and Science
Date of Research: 1988-1991
KEYWORDS: *early childhood education; early reading; literacy;
parent participation; preschool education*

9/0988
Division of Education, 388 Glossop Road, Sheffield S10 2TN
0742 768555
Gray, J. Prof.; Jesson, D. Mr; Booker, J. Mrs
Performance indicators project
Abstract: More than one in ten of the country's local education
authorities (LEAs) have requested specific help in the areas of
shaping and implementing policy initiatives, particularly in the area
of the evaluation of pupil and school performance. In one LEA a
thorough review of secondary school examination performance has
been undertaken, whilst elsewhere advisers and inspectors have
sought assistance in developing comprehensive indicators of institutional performance. An increasing number of professional bodies
(such as the the National Association of Inspectors and Advisers and
the Association of Metropolitan Authorities) have turned to the group
for advice and assistance.
Published Material: GRAY, J. & JESSON, D. (1990). 'The negotiation and construction of performance indicators, some principles,
proposals and problems', Evaluation and Research in Education, Vol
4, No 2, pp.93-108.; GRAY, J., JESSON, D. & SIMS, N. (1990).
'Estimating differences in the examination performances of secondary schools in six LEAs: a multilevel approach to school effectiveness', Oxford Review of Education, Vol 16, No 2, pp.137-158.;
GRAY, J. (1990). 'Performance indicators and the social organisation of evaluation: some proposals for change'. In: FITZ-GIBBON,
C.T. (Ed). Performance indicators. Clevedon: Multilingual Matters
for British Educational Research Association.
Status: Sponsored project
Source of Grant: Local Education Authorities £16,000
Date of Research: 1989-1992
KEYWORDS: *educational quality; examination results; local educa-
tion authority; performance indicators; school effectiveness*

9/0989
Division of Education, 388 Glossop Road, Sheffield S10 2TN
0742 768555
Gillborn, D. Dr; Rudduck, J. Prof.; Nixon, J. Dr
Positive approaches to discipline in inner city schools
Abstract: Inner city schools are likely, for a number of familiar
reasons, to present the greatest challenge to the building and sustaining of a supportive and orderly environment for working. Carefully
contextualised accounts of good practice in schools which have
different pasts, localities, characters and problems, can powerfully
demonstrate the possibilities that are open to all schools staffs. It is
now more than a decade since Her Majesty's Inspectors (HMI)
published 'Ten good schools', (HMI (1977)). Ten good schools: a
secondary school inquiry: a discussion paper by some members of
HM Inspectorate of Schools. Great Britain: Department of Education
and Science. In the United States of America, Lightfoot's 'The good
high school', (LIGHTFOOT, S.L. (1983). The good high school:
portraits of character and culture. New York: Basic) has made a
considerable impact on people's perceptions of schools and their
achievements. This study will build on these models by using detailed

studies of six inner city schools to identify and explore what HMI have called 'The complex and difficult task of achieving and maintaining high standards of behaviour and discipline'.

Status: Sponsored project
Source of Grant: Department of Education and Science £44,755
Date of Research: 1990-1991
KEYWORDS: *discipline; educational quality; inner city; pupil behaviour; school effectiveness; urban schools*

9/0990
>   Division of Education, 388 Glossop Road, Sheffield S10 2TN
>   0742 768555
>   Rudduck, J. Prof.; Harris, S. Dr

Making your way through secondary school: pupils' experiences of teaching and learning
Abstract: The project is one of a number of parallel research studies funded as part of the initiative 'Innovation and change in education: the quality of teaching and learning'. The broad aims of the research are to: (1) collect contextualised information about pupils' experiences of teaching and learning as they move through their final years of secondary schooling; (2) contribute to knowledge and understanding of the ways in which pupils perceive, make sense of and respond to the teaching and learning opportunities that their school provides. The specific aim is to examine pupils experiences of and reactions to teaching and learning in relation to the concept of 'school career'. The research is being conducted in a single comprehensive school in three separate local education authorities (LEAs). It is developmental, using a longitudinal, interview based design and concentrates on one cohort of pupils in each school, who were 12 years old at the start of the research and will be 16 years at the end. The data is contextualised through information gathered in interviews with teachers, observation and the analysis of school records and documents. Fieldwork already undertaken over four terms has included: interviews with headteachers and members of senior management teams; interviews with the form tutor, subject teachers and pupils within the target classes; and interviews with the nominated school contact person. The researchers have also attended key events (e.g. parents' evenings) which affect their target group.
Published Material: HARRIS, S. & RUDDUCK, J. (1993). 'Establishing the seriousness of learning in the early years of secondary schooling', British Journal of Educational Psychology, (in press).
Status: Sponsored project
Source of Grant: Economic and Social Research Council £80,890
Date of Research: 1991 - continuing
KEYWORDS: *learning experience; pupil attitudes; pupil school relationship; school effectiveness; secondary education; secondary school pupils; teaching process*

9/0991
>   Division of Education, 388 Glossop Road, Sheffield S10 2TN
>   0742 768555
>   Social and Community Planning Research, 35 Northampton Square, London EC1V OAX
>   071 250 1866
>   Gray, J. Prof.; Jesson, D. Mr; Courtenay, G. Ms; Hedges, B. Mr

Pathways 16-19: the youth cohort study of England and Wales
Abstract: The Youth Cohort Study is a collaborative project researched by Sheffield University, Division of Education and Social and Community Planning Research. The project is surveying nationally representative samples from five cohorts of young people in England and Wales. Each respondent is contacted on three occasions, at ages 16+ and 18+ years, by means of a postal questionnaire. Data from the surveys will provide a comprehensive framework of information to illuminate the processes of transition from school to work. The intention is that those responsible for policy on education, training and employment provision for young people over 16 years of age will have, for the first time, a common database to inform aspects of their decision-making and planning. A basic concern of the study is to learn more about the 'routes' young people take through the framework of 16-19 provision. At the same time, another major aim of the monitoring exercise is to produce detailed data which are sufficiently flexible, not merely to test hypotheses formulated at the outset of the project, but to address a range of issues and questions which may occur as the project proceeds. The study will, for example, enable the evaluation of: (1) the various routes for transition from school to further education, training and employment; (2) the relevance of education and qualifications to subsequent train-

ing and occupations (and progress within these occupations); and (3) the extent and nature of training and its usefulness across a variety of job types.
Published Material: A full list of publications is available from the researchers.
Status: Sponsored project
Source of Grant: Training Agency; Department of Education and Science; Department of Employment, jointly £1,000,000
Date of Research: 1985-1992
KEYWORDS: *cohort analysis; further education; school leavers; school to work transition; sixteen to nineteen education; vocational education; youth; youth employment*

9/0992
>   Division of Education, 388 Glossop Road, Sheffield S10 2TN
>   0742 768555
>   York University, Department of Economics and Related Studies, York YO1 5DD
>   0904 430000
>   Jesson, D. Mr; Mayston, D. Prof.

Developing models of educational accountability
Abstract: The research attempts to model the ouptuts of the secondary educational system using techniques drawn from the theory of production functions in economics. A major concern is to accommodate a wide variety of 'outputs', which, whilst including examination results, are capable of embracing other 'performance indicators'. The initial thrust has been to contrast the interpretations of previous studies using regression analysis with those obtained using data envelope analysis applied to inter-LEA studies. The phase now opening explores the potential at the intra-LEA level.
Published Material: JESSON, D., MAYSTON, D. & SMITH, P. (1987). 'Performance assessment in the education sector: educational and economic perspectives', Oxford Review of Education, Vol 13, No 3, pp.249-266.; JESSON, D. & MAYSTON, D. (1988). 'Developing models of educational accountability', Oxford Review of Education, Vol 14, No 3, pp.321-339.
Status: Sponsored project
Source of Grant: Sheffield University
Date of Research: 1987 - continuing
KEYWORDS: *accountability; educational quality; measurement; performance indicators; school effectiveness; secondary schools*

9/0993
>   Division of Education, 388 Glossop Road, Sheffield S10 2TN
>   0742 768555
>   York University, Language Teaching Centre, Heslington, York YO1 5DD
>   0904 430000
>   Pullin, R. Mr; Rix, D. Mr

The York-Sheffield Russian Project
Abstract: The project aims to: (1) support a network of teacher-based teaching materials groups which will produce new materials to meet the changing needs of Russian at GCSE level and for 11+ beginners' courses; (2) to promote models of teacher development through exchange of ideas and experience, participation in the production of collaborative materials and a series of national and regional inservice courses; and (3) to monitor, evaluate and publicise new developments and initiatives for the consolidation and extension of Russian teaching in British secondary schools.
Published Material: Times Educational Supplement, Modern Languages Extra, November 25th 1988.
Status: Sponsored project
Source of Grant: Nuffield Foundation £15,000
Date of Research: 1988-1992
KEYWORDS: *educational materials; inservice teacher education; Russian studies; second language teaching; teacher development*

South Devon College of Arts and Technology

9/0994
>   Newton Road, Torquay TQ2 5BY
>   0803 213242

Exeter University, School of Education, St Luke's, Heavitree
Road, Exeter EX1 2LU
0392 263263
Megee, M. Mr; *Supervisor:* Evans, D. Mr; Smith, M. Dr
**An approach to music teaching with people with learning
difficulties which emphasises collaborative teaching**
Abstract: The study demonstrates positive changes in the self-esteem
of students with severe and moderate learning difficulties, attending
a weekly group for composing and performing music. The experimental groups consisted of a total of 12 students, aged 16-19
against a control group of six students. Tests used were Piers-Harris;
Gurney's Revised Self-Esteem Inventory and Intellectual Achievement Rating Scale. All the students attend full-time at a local authority
further education college.
Status: Individual research
Date of Research: 1988-1992
KEYWORDS: *further education; moderate learning difficulties;
music activities; music education; self-esteem; severe learning difficulties; special educational needs; teaching methods*

Southampton University

9/0995
Department of Psychology, Highfield, Southampton
SO9 5NH
0703 595000
Hewitt, J. Mr; *Supervisor:* Remington, B. Dr
**Communication training via manual signing for non-speaking
mentally handicapped children**
Abstract: This is an ongoing research programme which aims to
investigate the factors responsible for the development of effective
communication in non-speaking children. Initially, the work focused
both on children with a mental handicap and autistic children, but is
now concerned primarily with mental handicap. Methods usually
involve single-subject experimental designs. The role of receptive
speech on expressive signing and the developments of novel sign
combinations through specialised training methods have been investigated. The current interests of the research staff are in the communicative function of signing and symbol use and the investigation of
transfer between requesting and naming functions.
Published Material: CLARKE, S., REMINGTON, B. & LIGHT, P.
(1988). 'The role of referential speech in sign learning by mentally
retarded children: A comparison of total communication and sign-
alone training', Journal of Applied Behaviour Analaysis, No 21,
pp.419-426.; REMINGTON, B., WATSON, J. & LIGHT, P. (1990).
'Beyond the single sign: A matrix-based approach to teaching productive sign combinations', Mental Handicap Research, No 3, pp.33-
50.; LIGHT, P., WATSON, J. & REMINGTON, B. (1990). 'Beyond
the single sign II: The significance of sign order in a matrix-based
approach to teaching productive sign combinations', Mental Handicap Research, No 3, pp.161-178.; REMINGTON, B. (1991). 'Why
use single subject methods in AAC?'. In: BRODIN, J. & BJORCK-
AKESSON, E. (Eds). 'Methodological issues in research in augmentative and alternative communication', Proceedings of the First
International ISAAC Research Symposium in augmentative and
alternative communication. Stockholm: Swedish Handicap Institute.;
GOODMAN, J., & REMINGTON, B. (1991). 'Teaching communicative signing: Labelling, requesting and transfer of function'. In:
REMINGTON, B. (Ed). The challenge of severe mental handicap: A
behaviour analytic approach. Chichester: J. Wiley and Sons.
Status: Sponsored project
Source of Grant: Economic and Social Research Council
Date of Research: 1978 - continuing
KEYWORDS: *communication aids – for disabled; communication
disorders; manual communication; severe learning difficulties; sign
language; special educational needs; symbolic language*

9/0996
Department of Sociology and Social Policy, Highfield,
Southampton SO9 5NH
0703 595000
Shilling, C. Dr
Vocational education
Abstract: The project is concerned with an investigation into the
structure, organisation and content of vocational education and education-industry relations in England and Wales. The first part of the
proejct involved analysing the historical development of vocational
schooling. The second part concentrated on the actual operation of
vocational schemes with a particular focus on the National Technical
and Vocational Education Initiative (TVEI), the Mini-Enterprises in
Schools Project and a local education authority scheme called the
Schools Vocational Programme. This second part of the research is
based on observation and interviews with project directors, teachers,
students and employers.
Published Material: SHILLING, C. (1989). Schooling for work in
capitalist Britain. Lewes: Falmer Press.; SHILLING, C. (1989). 'The
mini enterprise in schools project: a new stage in education-industry
relations', Journal of Education Policy, Vol 4, No 2, pp.115-124.;
SHILLING, C. & DALE, R. (Eds). (1990). The TVEI story: policy,
practice and preparation for the workplace. Milton Keynes: Open
University Press.; SHILLING, C. (1991). 'Labouring at school: work
experience in the TVEI', Work, Employment and Society, Vol 5, No
1, pp.59-80.
Status: Individual research
Date of Research: 1984-1991
KEYWORDS: *enterprise education; industry-education relationship; technical education; vocational education; work experience*

9/0997
Department of Sociology and Social Policy, Highfield,
Southampton SO9 5NH
0703 595000
Shilling, C. Dr
Educational differentiation and social space
Abstract: Research consists firstly, of a review of the literature on the
role of social space in educational differentiation with particular
reference to the place of space in structuration theory. Secondly, an
ethnographic study has been conducted into the use of space in two
school libraries. Particular attention is given to teacher and pupil
attempts to colonise and regulate this educational space.
Published Material: SHILLING, C. & COUSINS, F. (1990). 'Social
use of the school library: the colonisation and regulation of educational space', British Journal of Sociology of Education, Vol 11, No
4, pp.411-430.; SHILLING, C. (1991). 'Social space, educational
differentiation and gender inequalities', British Journal of Sociology
of Education, Vol 12, No 1, pp.23-45.
Status: Individual research
Date of Research: 1990 - continuing
KEYWORDS: *equal education; personal space; school space*

9/0998
Department of Sociology and Social Policy, Highfield,
Southampton SO9 5NH
0703 595000
Shilling, C. Dr
Supply workers in state schools and the National Health Service
Abstract: This project is concerned with the organisation and work
of supply workers in state schools and the National Health Service,
and is based on interviews with over 70 head/senior teachers, nurse
managers, supply teachers and bank nurses. Research also includes
a review of literature into supply teachers, which is being published
by Educational Research.
Published Material: SHILLING, C. (1991). 'The organisation of
supply workers in state schools and the National Health Service: a
comparison', Journal of Education Policy, Vol 5, No 2, p.127-141.;
SHILLING, C. (1991). 'Permanent supports or temporary props?
Supply workers in state schools and the National Health Service',
Gender and Education, Vol 3, No 1, pp.61-80.; SHILLING, C.
(1991). 'Supply teachers: working on the margins', Educational
Research, Vol 33, No 1, pp.3-12.
Status: Individual research
Date of Research: 1988-1991
KEYWORDS: *health personnel; nurses; substitute teachers; teach-
ing profession*

9/0999
Department of Sociology and Social Policy, Highfield,
Southampton SO9 5NH
0703 595000
London University, King's College, Centre for Educational
Studies, Cornwall House Annexe, Waterloo Road, London
SE1 3TY

071 836 5454
Shilling, C. Dr; Ball, S. Prof.; *Supervisor:* Shilling, C. Dr;
Ball, S. Prof.
New directions in education policy sociology
Abstract: 'New Directions in Education Policy Sociology' is a Nuffield Foundation funded conference taking place in March 1993. It is also intended that the Conference proceedings will (in part) contribute to a book, with the same title, addressing theoretical and methodological issues in the field of education policy sociology.
Status: Sponsored project
Source of Grant: Nuffield Foundation
Date of Research: 1993 - continuing
KEYWORDS: educational policy; sociology of education

9/1000
Department of Teaching Media, Highfield, Southampton
SO9 5NH
0703 595000
Smith, I. Mr; *Supervisor:* Allen, W. Mr
Optimising international links and exchange programmes between departments of photography
Abstract: This project is concerned with the study of links and exchanges as mechanisms for promoting a greater mutual understanding of the nature and structure of college and university courses in photography in Europe. The investigation involves case studies of selected interchange programmes, the establishment of a data base of European courses in photography and an analysis of the characteristics of photographic courses with a view to identifying the potential for a European Scheme for credit accumulation and transfer. The project has reached the stage of having produced a published data base of European courses in photography through the 'Photolink International' scheme which is supported by Kodak Limited and ERASMUS.
Published Material: SMITH, I.R. (1990). 'Directory of photographic education: A European survey', Photolink International.
Status: Sponsored project
Source of Grant: Kodak Limited; ERASMUS
Date of Research: 1988 - continuing
KEYWORDS: international educational exchange; photography

9/1001
Faculty of Educational Studies, Highfield, Southampton
SO9 5NH
0703 595000
Erben, M. Mr
Biography and education
Abstract: The aim of the research is to offer a disquisition on the meaning of biography. This will be realised by supporting a view that the study of biography can develop a hermeneutical conceptualisation of how best knowledge, that can be regarded as educational, is to be obtained and produced. Given that biography is a hermeneutical exercise the manner in which the objective slides into the subjective and vice versa will be developed as the protocol for a successful treatise upon biographical method. The work of Dilthey, Ricoeur, Sartre, Benjamin, Samuel Johnson, and Lacan will be examined to elaborate this exercise in cultural sociology.
Published Material: ERBEN, M. (1991). 'Geneology and sociology', Sociology, Vol 25, No 2, pp.275-292.
Status: Individual research
Date of Research: 1990 - continuing
KEYWORDS: biographies; sociology

9/1002
Faculty of Educational Studies, Highfield, Southampton
SO9 5NH
0703 595000
Ratcliffe, M. Mrs; Fullick, P. Mr; *Supervisor:* Kelly, P. Prof.
Issues in science and decision making
Abstract: With the implementation of the National Curriculum all pupils up to the age of 16 will be expected 'to study scientific controversies' and 'begin to understand the power and limitations of science in solving problems'. There is also a growing need to address the public understanding of science. The objectives of this research are: (1) To identify some of the features of the role of the individual in collective decision making, and to identify the particular thinking skills and capacities which individuals need in order to take decisions about science based issues. This objective to be met through: (a)

literature search from fields of education, sociology, psychology and management; and (b) examination of case studies relating to decision making about science based issues in the public domain; (2) To examine, through action research in classrooms: (a) the ways in which pupils make decisions about aspects of science which affect them personally, and scientific issues which, at the time, may have only a marginal impact on their daily lives; and (b) the ways in which teachers manage this decision making process. Methodology will be observation in classes in the age range 14-18 in order to achieve objective 2. Techniques will include: observation schedules; video analysis; interviews and questionnaires involving both pupils and teachers. It is hoped to develop curriculum materials from this research.
Status: Sponsored project
Source of Grant: Southampton University: School of Education £3,000
Date of Research: 1992 - continuing
KEYWORDS: decision making; National Curriculum; science education; scientific literacy

9/1003
Faculty of Educational Studies, Highfield, Southampton
SO9 5NH
0703 595000
Rolfe, G. Mr; *Supervisor:* Weare, K. Ms
Educating 'desirable attitudes' in nurses
Abstract: This research attempts to discover what attitudes are thought to be 'desirable' in nurses and ways in which desirable attitudes in nurses can be taught and assessed.
Status: Individual research
Date of Research: 1989-1992
KEYWORDS: attitudes; nurse education; nurses

9/1004
Faculty of Educational Studies, Highfield, Southampton
SO9 5NH
0703 595000
Greig, S. Mrs; *Supervisor:* Brumfit, C. Prof.
Spelling: teachers' perceptions, attitudes and expectations
Abstract: This research investigates persistent difficulty with spelling and teachers perceptions of this. The researchers hypothesis is that teachers misunderstand the spelling system and how it is learned and used by pupils, and that if the important features of the system could be explained to teachers with clear and easily followed advice on teaching, spelling, the correction of poor spelling and the marking of written work, their practice would improve and, with it their attitudes to their pupils and to the spelling skill. Higher expectations would follow and would spread to pupils with benefits all round. The method will be to investigate these questions by interview and/or questionnaire with teachers in schools, student teachers and teacher trainers and perhaps try to introduce them to the practices mentioned above and observe the outcome of that.
Status: Individual research
Date of Research: 1989-1992
KEYWORDS: spelling; spelling teaching; teacher attitudes; teaching methods

9/1005
Faculty of Educational Studies, Assessment and Evaluation Unit, Highfield, Southampton SO9 5NH
0703 595000
Clift, P. Mr; Turner, G. Mr; *Supervisor:* Clift, P. Mr
Evaluation of the Southampton University Pilot Appraisal Scheme
Abstract: The aim of the project was to provide information to Southampton University Administration about the working of the pilot scheme for staff appraisal. The methods used were: (i) participant observation of training days; (ii) semi-structured interviews with a random sample drawn from departments involved; and (iii) questionnaires to all staff in the departments involved. The conclusions drawn were: (i) staff perceptions of appraisal and of the University's scheme were uncritical, but half-hearted; (ii) that the professional proximity of the appraisers to the appraisees resulted in little that was new being revealed; (iii) that there had been a lack of tangible and valued outcome; (iv) that the relationship between appraisal and pay and promotion needed urgently to be addressed; (v) that a 'University ethos' of collegial casualness had pervaded the whole exercise; (vi)

that the objectives of appraisal were diverse and unclear. A list of 10 recommendations for the future was put forward.
Published Material: CLIFT, P. & TURNER, G. (1991). University of Southampton Pilot Appraisal Scheme: an evalution. Assessment & Evaluation Unit, School of Education, University of Southampton (mimeo).
Status: Sponsored project
Source of Grant: Southampton University £3,000
Date of Research: 1991-1991
KEYWORDS: *academic staff evaluation; inservice education; programme evaluation; staff development; universities*

9/1006
> Faculty of Educational Studies, Assessment and Evaluation
> Unit, Highfield, Southampton SO9 5NH
> 0703 595000
> Morris, B. Mr; Turner, G. Mr; *Supervisor:* Morris, B. Mr;
> Turner, G. Mr

Evaluation of the Promoting Health in Primary Schools (PHIPS) project
Abstract: Promoting Health in Primary Schools (PHIPS) will plan and undertake a series of ten regional dissemination events focused on Curriculum Guidance 5 (CG5), Health Education Act 1990, which sets out the need for a coherent whole school policy and programme for health education, supported by detailed curriculum guidelines. The aims of these events are to: (1) demonstrate how coherent health education programmes can be managed as an essential aspect of the whole school curriculum; (2) offer a unified response to CG5 through the integration of three major Health Education Authority (HEA) projects: Health for Life; My Body; Happy Heart; and (3) build on, and strengthen the existing dissemination network for health education in England. The evaluation will: (1) provide project teams, regional coordinators and the HEA with information about the effectiveness of each event; (2) provide project teams, regional coordinators and the HEA with information about the outcomes of each event; and (3) provide the HEA with an evaluation of the appropriateness of this model of dissemination for future activities. The regional events will be evaluated using a pre-coded questionnaire. Issues in planning, coordination and impact will be investigated through case studies of three of the regional events which represent the range of approaches chosen throughout the project. The case studies will involve interviews with project managers, team personnel and regional coordinators and the distribution of a more detailed questionnaire to a sample of participants. A report will be submitted to the Health Education Authority in March 1993.
Status: Sponsored project
Source of Grant: Health Education Authority
Date of Research: 1991-1992
KEYWORDS: *curriculum development; health education; primary schools; programme evaluation*

9/1007
> Faculty of Educational Studies, Assessment and Evaluation
> Unit, Highfield, Southampton SO9 5NH
> 0703 595000
> Clift, P. Mr; Morris, B. Mr; *Supervisor:* Clift, P. Mr

An evaluation of the Dorset Local Education Authority Inspectorate
Abstract: The Dorset Local Education Authority (LEA) Advisory Service was converted to an Inspectorate with effect from 1st January 1990, following a period of 'cascaded' training organised by the Centre for Advisor and Inspector Development (CAID). In the summer of 1991, the Unit was invited to design and carry out an evaluation of the work of the Inspectorate to date, reporting to the Chief Inspector, the Chief Education Officer and Elected Members. The issues to be addressed, as agreed with the Chief Inspector are: (i) how effective is the Inspectorate in collecting evidence concerning the quality of education in Dorset schools; (ii) what performance indicators are used by the Inspectorate and how valid are they for judging the educational effectiveness of schools; (iii) how acceptable to schools are the judgements made; (iv) how useful to the LEA administrators and elected members is the evidence of educational effectiveness provided in inspector's reports; (v) how efficient is the internal communication within the Inspectorate; (vi) how effective are role and task differentiation within the Inspectorate; (vii) to what extent and in what ways do the activities of the Inspectorate foster the development of Dorset schools; (viii) how effective is the advisory teacher support offered to schools as a direct consequence of

inspectors' visits; (ix) other issues arising during the investigation. A sample of ten Dorset schools is included (primary, secondary, special) which have been involved in all aspects of the Inspectorate's activity. The main methods of investigation are documentary analysis, interviews with headteachers, governors, Members of the LEA evaluation panel (elected memebers) and inspectors, and questionnaires to all the teachers in the ten schools.
Status: Sponsored project
Source of Grant: Dorset Local Education Authority £10,000
Date of Research: 1991-1992
KEYWORDS: *evaluation; inspection; inspectors of schools; local education authorities*

9/1008
> Faculty of Educational Studies, Centre for Language in
> Education, Highfield, Southampton SO9 5NH
> 0703 595000
> Brumfit, C. Prof.; Mitchell, R. Dr

'Knowledge about language', language learning and the National Curriculum
Abstract: This project aims to investigate the nature of children's understanding of the nature of language and how it works, and how this is developed through experience of English/Modern Languages work in school. Teachers of English and Modern Languages have been encouraged by the Kingman Report, (Department of Education and Science Committee of Inquiry into the Teaching of English Language (1988). Report of the Committee of Inquiry into the Teaching of English Language. London: HMSO), the Language in the National Curriculum (LINC) programme, and National Curriculum programmes for their subjects, to pay more attention to developing children's knowledge about language. Traditionally however, teachers in the different language subjects have dealt with 'Knowledge about Language' (KAL) in rather different ways. Moreover, in spite of much debate, little is known about school age children's resulting knowledge and beliefs about the nature of language, and the relationship between such knowledge and the development of children's practical language skills. Fieldwork consists of case studies carried out during the school year 1991-92 in the English and Modern Languages departments of three Hampshire schools. A period of approximately 8 weeks is being spent in each school, spread over three terms. The focus is on pupils in Year 9; teachers of both subjects are being interviewed, and English/Modern Language classes are being observed and recorded, to learn how and when language matters are discussed, and in what terms. Children will also be interviewed, to explore their developing knowledge about language, and its relationship with classroom discussions and activities. The development of their language skills will also be monitored, through analysis of their day to day work, and possible links with their developing knowledge about language will be explored.
Status: Sponsored project
Source of Grant: Economic and Social Research Council £52,000
Date of Research: 1991 - continuing
KEYWORDS: *English studies; language skills; modern language studies*

9/1009
> Faculty of Educational Studies, Centre for Language in
> Education, Highfield, Southampton SO9 5NH
> 0703 595000
> Mitchell, R. Dr; Grenfell, M. Mr

Evaluation of the Basingstoke Language Awareness Project
Abstract: The Basingstoke Language Awareness Project is a three year project running from 1989-1992, which is providing 'taster' experience of modern language learning for primary school pupils in the six main feeder schools of a Basingstoke secondary school. The project is staffed with four foreign language assistants (FLAs), native speakers of French, German and Spanish. It is funded by local business sponsorship, from accountants KPMG-Peat Marwick McLintock. In 1990-1991 KPMG also sponsored a small scale interim evaluation of the project, by the University of Southampton. The evaluation assessed the aims, structure and methods of the project, and gathered qualitative data on attitudinal outcomes. The evaluation methodology mainly involved interviews with teachers, FLAs and pupils, plus observation of the FLAs at work in the classroom. The evaluation concluded the project was operating successfully overall, thanks to good cross-pyramid cooperation, and documented favourable initial pupil reactions. The final report highlights the special needs of FLAs for systems of support and liaison,

especially with class teachers; it also highlights needs for continuity and progression in the transition to secondary school.
Published Material: MITCHELL, R., MARTIN, C. & GRENFELL, M. (1992). 'University of Southampton Evaluation of the Basingstoke Language Awareness Project: Final Report', Centre for Language in Education Working Paper, University of Southampton.
Status: Sponsored project
Source of Grant: KPMG-Peat Marwick McLintock £5,000
Date of Research: 1990-1991
KEYWORDS: *language teachers; modern language studies; primary schools; programme evaluation; teaching assistants*

9/1010
Faculty of Educational Studies, Centre for Language in Education, Highfield, Southampton SO9 5NH
0703 595000
Mason, K. Ms; *Supervisor:* Brumfit, C. Prof.
Bilingual learners and language provision in the National Curriculum
Abstract: The project surveys existing documentation on multilingual learners in Southampton, attemtping to build as complete as possible a picture of the distribution of multilingual learners and the range of languages represented. Following this survey, one school was chosen for detailed work. This project partly replicates the Linguistic Minorities Project studies on language use, and partly develops further studies on language patterns in the families of respondents. Some effort is made to explore possible future patterns of language distribution in relation to dispersal of speakers of minority languages. The research methodology of the project is carefully described in a booklet (later to be accompanied by seminars and workshops) to enable teachers in other schools to develop similar projects.
Status: Sponsored project
Source of Grant: Southampton University: Research Fund £8,960
Date of Research: 1991-1992
KEYWORDS: *bilingualism; languages; minority groups; mother tongue; multilingualism; National Curriculum*

9/1011
Faculty of Educational Studies, Centre for Language in Education, Highfield, Southampton SO9 5NH
0703 595000
Bilton, L. Miss; *Supervisor:* Mitchell, R. Dr
Adaptation in lecturing styles to audiences with English as a second language
Abstract: Lecturing to audiences in an overseas context where English is a foreign language is expanding, as new universities adopt English as the medium of instruction for science and technology. Expatriate lecturers are on the whole unprepared for their undergraduates' low level of English and consequently much of their effort in planning and delivering lectures is wasted. The aim of this research is to find out what goes on during lectures and where foreign students have particular difficulties in order to make recommendations about the adaptation of lecturing for audience needs.
Status: Individual research
Date of Research: 1989 - continuing
KEYWORDS: *English – second language; English for academic purposes; lecture methods; overseas students; teaching styles*

9/1012
Faculty of Educational Studies, Centre for Language in Education, Highfield, Southampton SO9 5NH
0703 595000
Chappell, D. Miss; *Supervisor:* Mitchell, R. Dr
Native and non-native use of English
Abstract: This is an empirically based study focusing on the structure, nature and use of English by native and non-native speakers in the specific discourse type of information exchange. Data will be gathered from public arenas where transactions between: (i) native/native; (ii) native/non-native; (iii) non-native/non-native speakers take place and, in addition, from within the language learning classroom where activities of a like nature have been set up. The naturally occurring events and classroom tasks will then be analysed at an interactional level and characteristic features of each identified. The use of a psycholinguistic analysis endeavours not only to identify the reasons for participants' interpretive choice during interaction, but also to uncover any underlying relationships between use of these

choices and their effect on the language learning process. In this way it is hoped that such descriptions may inform the understanding of: (1) particular points through and by which language learning takes place; (2) the elements that facilitate such learning; and (3) the conditions under which those elements are best served. The pedagogical implications related to any of the aforementioned aspects include a re-examination of teachers' own choices concerning aims, methodology and materials which may ultimately lead to a re-assessment of the evaluation process at all subsequent levels.
Status: Sponsored project
Source of Grant: Economic and Social Research Council £5,285
Date of Research: 1989-1992
KEYWORDS: *English; English – second language; language usage; mother tongue; verbal communication*

9/1013
Faculty of Educational Studies, Centre for Language in Education, Highfield, Southampton SO9 5NH
0703 595000
Zotou, V, Ms; *Supervisor:* Mitchell, R. Dr
Effective teaching in English as Foreign Language (EFL): a Greek case study
Abstract: Given the dearth of descriptive studies of English as a Foreign Language (EFL) teaching in Greece, the aim of the researcher is to discover the extent to which classroom practice of teachers, judged 'effective' by their fellow professionals and superiors, conforms to a 'normative' model of effective teaching (conceptualised as 'communicative' language teaching), and what are the factors which have shaped their classroom behaviour. Eight main case studies will be conducted in different parts of Greece. Classroom observation will be the main element of each case study. A systematic observation instrument, developed for the study of communicative language teaching will be employed as the main classroom data gathering procedure. The observations will be supplemented with teacher interviews seeking: (a) their views on the nature of effective teaching and the contextual factors promoting/inhibiting it; (b) accounts of practice; and (c) accounts of major influences on their own professional development. In addition, contextual data will be collected from pupils and institutions (including student achievement data). It can be expected that a group of teachers selected in this way will vary considerably in degree of conformity to a normative model of communicative EFL teaching. If so, within-group comparisons will be necessary, in trying to establish: (a) what are the typical classroom practices of the most 'effective' sub-group; and (b) what professional influences and contextual factors have contributed substantially to greater and lesser degrees of 'effectiveness'. Finally, it is hoped to draw conclusions relevant to teacher training and the upgrading of more teachers to 'effective' levels of practice.
Status: Sponsored project
Source of Grant: Greek Ministry of Education
Date of Research: 1988-1991
KEYWORDS: *English – second language; Greece; language teachers; teacher effectiveness*

9/1014
Faculty of Educational Studies, Department of Adult Education, Highfield, Southampton SO9 5NH
0703 595000
Counihan, M. Dr
Concepts in fundamental science: development, interpretation and communication
Abstract: This is a continuing programme of research on fundamental science in the context of adult education. It is concerned with the development and interpretation of concepts, their relevance, and their communication. The central focus is on cosmological and subnuclear phenomenon, and on how these matters can or should be interpreted to improve public understanding of science. The output from this research has taken the form of public course programmes, and is intended to be published in book form.
Status: Individual research
Date of Research: 1977 - continuing
KEYWORDS: *adult education; science education*

9/1015
Faculty of Educational Studies, Department of Adult Education, Highfield, Southampton SO9 5NH
0703 595000

Johnston, R. Dr
Education with unwaged adults as community adult education
Abstract: This thesis focuses primarily on two action-research projects with unwaged adults carried out between 1985 and 1988. The heart of the thesis consists of the published reports of the projects 'Exploring the Educational Needs of Unwaged Adults' and 'Negotiating the Curriculum with Unwaged Adults'. Additional material sets out to put this research into its historical context, to reflect critically on its developing methodology and to learn from it in the context of the nineties. An attempt is made to ground the research in the historical context of the previous debates concerning ideology and curriculum in community-based adult education and their influence on the growth of educational intiatives with unwaged adults, particularly those projects sponsored through Replan in the mid 1980s. The thesis also includes a reflexive methodological critique of the two projects. It concludes by relating the work and findings of the projects to the emerging educational context of the Nineties and identifying the lessons that can be learned for the future development of Community Adult Education.
Published Material: JOHNSTON, R.A. (1987). 'Exploring the educational needs of unwaged adults'. Leicester: NIACE.; JOHNSTON, R.A., JACOBS, M. & MCWILLIAM, I. (1989). 'Negotiating the curriculum with unwaged adults'. London: Further Education Unit.; JOHNSTON, R.A. (1992). 'Education and unwaged adults: relevance, social control and empowerment'. In: ALLEN, G. & MARTIN, I. (Eds). Education and community: the politics of practice. Poole: Cassell.; JOHNSTON, R.A. (1987). 'Outreach work with unemployed and unwaged adults', Adult Education, Vol 60, No 1. pp.58-65.
Status: Individual research
Date of Research: 1985-1991
KEYWORDS: adult education; community education; unemployment

9/1016
Faculty of Educational Studies, Department of Physical Education, Highfield, Southampton SO9 5NH
0703 595000
Evans, J. Dr; Penney, D. Miss; Bryant, A. Miss; *Supervisor:* Evans, J. Dr
The impact of the National Curriculum and Local Management of Schools (LMS) on the provision of sport and physical education in schools
Abstract: The research will be conducted over a three year period to monitor the impact of the National Curriculum and Local Management of Schools (LMS) on the provision of sport and physical education (PE) in schools in England and Wales. The research will be conducted in two phases. The first will employ a qualitative methodology to survey the impact of LMS on the levels and nature of physical education and sport provision for schools. The second will use a qualitative methodology to monitor the effects of LMS and a National Curriculum for PE on processes of teaching and learning in PE and sport in schools.
Status: Sponsored project
Source of Grant: Sports Council; Southampton University; Economic and Social Research Council
Date of Research: 1990 - continuing
KEYWORDS: educational change; local management of schools; National Curriculum; physical education; sports

9/1017
Faculty of Educational Studies, Department of Physical Education, Highfield, Southampton SO9 5NH
0703 595000
Evans, J. Dr
A study of the health education initiatives in physical education
Abstract: The aim of this research is to study the impact of health education initiatives in physical education (PE) on the curriculum and teaching of PE in secondary schools. The study focuses on the curriculum and teaching of PE in one large coeducational comprehensive school. The study is adopting a qualitative methodology (largely employing interview and observation techniques) and is sociological in theoretical orientation.
Status: Sponsored project
Source of Grant: Southampton University Research Fund £500
Date of Research: 1989-1991
KEYWORDS: currciulum development; health education; physical education; secondary education

St Andrews University

9/1018
Department of Psychology, St Andrews, Fife KY16 9AJ
0334 76161
Craigie College of Education, Beech Grove, Ayr KA8 OSR
0292 26031
Johnston, R. Dr; *Supervisor:* Johnston, R. Dr; Holligan, C. Dr
Segmentation ability and patterns of reading failure: the nature of the relationship
Abstract: The aim of this research is to examine: (a) how poor readers recognise words; (b) in what way this is qualitatively distinct from that of normal readers; and (c) why this leads to impaired nonword reading. A study is also being made of poor readers' memory difficulties, and the importance of visual skills to the early stages of reading development.
Status: Sponsored project
Source of Grant: Wellcome Trust £61,000
Date of Research: 1992 - continuing
KEYWORDS: dyslexia; reading difficulties; reading failure; reading skills; word recognition

Staff College

9/1019
Coombe Lodge, Blagdon, Bristol BS18 6RG
0761 462503
Scribbins, K. Mr
Teachers' pay and bargaining machinery in four European countries
Abstract: A study of the effects of educational reform on pay bargaining machinery and the output of negotiations. Pay scales and approaches as well as relativities with other professions will be studied on a comparative basis.
Status: Sponsored project
Source of Grant: Central Bodies Advisory Group/The Staff College £20,000
Date of Research: 1991-1992
KEYWORDS: collective bargaining; comparable worth; teacher employment benefits; teacher salaries

9/1020
Coombe Lodge, Blagdon, Bristol BS18 6RG
0761 462503
Foster, B. Mr
Management training needs of technical institutions in Africa
Abstract: To identify management and management training needs in relation to organisational development for technical institutions in Africa, and to devise appropriate training interventions and resources.
Status: Sponsored project
Source of Grant: The Staff College
Date of Research: 1990-1991
KEYWORDS: Africa; management in education; management studies; technical colleges

9/1021
Coombe Lodge, Blagdon, Bristol BS18 6RG
0761 462503
Pardey, D. Mr
Forecasting student enrolments for further education colleges
Abstract: This research is an analysis of forecasting methodologies used in deriving enrolment projections for further education plans at college and local education authority level.
Status: Sponsored project
Source of Grant: The Staff College
Date of Research: 1990-1991
KEYWORDS: colleges of further education; educational planning; enrolment projections; further education; prediction; student recruitment

9/1022
> Coombe Lodge, Blagdon, Bristol BS18 6RG
> 0761 462503
> Civil, J. Mrs; *Supervisor:* Fineman, S. Dr

Effects of emotion and sexuality in the organizational processes of management
Abstract: This research will look at the effect of emotions and sexuality in the organizational processes of management. Particularly, appraisal, management, structures, interviews, promotions and divisions of labour.
Status: Individual research
Date of Research: 1990 - continuing
KEYWORDS: administration; emotions; employment practices; sex differences; sexuality

9/1023
> Coombe Lodge, Blagdon, Bristol BS18 6RG
> 0761 462503
> Atkinson, D. Mr

English local education authorities schemes of local financial management
Abstract: This research is a comparative analysis of English local education authority funding schemes (schemes of local financial management) for maintained further education colleges which have been prepared in accordance with the Education Reform Act 1988 and the Department of Education and Science Circular 9/88.
Status: Sponsored project
Source of Grant: The Staff College
Date of Research: 1990-1991
KEYWORDS: colleges of further education; educational finance; financial policy; financial support; local education authorities

9/1024
> Coombe Lodge, Blagdon, Bristol BS18 6RG
> 0761 462503
> Gray, L. Mr

Marketing service industries: a comparative study of education and banking
Abstract: This research will involve a comparative study of the education service and banking with reference to the organization of the marketing function, the preparation and use of marketing plans and the relevance of marketing to the development of intangible services.
Published Material: GRAY, L.S. (1991). Marketing Education. Buckingham: Open University Press.
Status: Individual research
Date of Research: 1991-1992
KEYWORDS: marketing; services

9/1025
> Coombe Lodge, Blagdon, Bristol BS18 6RG
> 0761 462503
> Graystone, J. Mr

The new governing bodies for further education colleges
Abstract: This research will involve an investigation of instruments and articles of government of further education colleges in England and Wales, and an analysis of the development needs of the new governors.
Published Material: GRAYSTONE, J.A. & WILLIAMS, D. (1990). Development programmes for further education governors: a guide for providers. London: Further Education Unit.
Status: Sponsored project
Source of Grant: The Staff College
Date of Research: 1990-1991
KEYWORDS: colleges of further education; governing bodies

9/1026
> Coombe Lodge, Blagdon, Bristol BS18 6RG
> 0761 462503
> Gray, L. Mr; Warrender, A-M Mrs; Latcham, J. Mr

Reviewing post-16 provision in four occupational sectors
Abstract: This research will involve a review of current and future demand for post-16 provision of education and training in the sectors of agriculture and horticulture, art and design, caring and the motor vehicle industry.
Status: Sponsored project
Source of Grant: Gloucestershire Local Education Authority £40,000

Date of Research: 1990-1991
KEYWORDS: agricultural education; arts; caregivers; horticulture; industry; school to work transition; sixteen to nineteen education; vocational education

9/1027
> Coombe Lodge, Blagdon, Bristol BS18 6RG
> 0761 462503
> Davies, P. Mr; *Supervisor:* Davies, P. Mr

Choice of further studies at the end of compulsory education
Abstract: The research was based around focus groups and telephone interviews with 396 young people who took GCSEs during 1992, concerning the significant demographic and attitudinal factors which influenced their choice of further studies.
Status: Sponsored project
Source of Grant: Commercial contract
Date of Research: 1992 - continuing
KEYWORDS: choice of subjects; demography; further education; pupil attitudes; sixteen to nineteen education

9/1028
> Coombe Lodge, Blagdon, Bristol BS18 6RG
> 0761 462503
> Gray, L. Mr; Warrender, A-M Mrs

Reducing the cost of technical and vocational education
Abstract: The research project examined policies of national governments and international donor agencies in seeking to reduce the costs and improve the effectiveness of technical education provision at national and local levels. It examined policies concerning equipment provision, the use of centralised workshops, repair and maintenance procedures, and the effective deployment of technical support. It reviewed experiments in encouraging the adoption of competence-based learning strategies, the use of institutionally managed labour market signalling, and the collection, analysis and comparison of cost data within and between training institutions in ways which are compatible with existing administrative systems, and do not demand more sophisticated computerised management information systems. It also looked at project management issues, initial appraisal techniques and the planning framework within which technical and vocational institutions operate. The researchers reviewed the literature on aid projects for technical and vocational education/training, and examined at first hand the work of international donor agencies, and the impact of that work in one African and one Asian country.
Status: Sponsored project
Source of Grant: Overseas Development Administration £20,000
Date of Research: 1991-1992
KEYWORDS: developing countries; development aid; educational finance; programme development; technical education; vocational education

9/1029
> Coombe Lodge, Blagdon, Bristol BS18 6RG
> 0761 462503
> Gray, L. Mr

The functions, purposes and contributions of national education management centres
Abstract: The project will examine the work of national education management centres, in part through visits to a sample of such centres. It will compare their purposes, and relationships to national and local government systems, and funding sources. It will also examine: their functions, with relation to training, consultancy, research, curriculum and management development; their client groups; and their links with other management capabilities across the education sectors. The project will examine the feasibility of building an international network of such centres, will explore the likely costs and benefits, and will seek possible sources of funding for such a network.
Status: Sponsored project
Source of Grant: The Staff College
Date of Research: 1993 - continuing
KEYWORDS: management development; management in education; training centres

9/1030
> Coombe Lodge, Blagdon, Bristol BS18 6RG
> 0761 462503

Warrender, A-M. Mrs; Havard, R. Mr; *Supervisor:*
Havard, R. Mr
Investors in People in post-16 institutions
Abstract: The aim of this research is to identify: the extent to which
post-16 institutions are committed to Investors in People; perceptions
of connection with total quality management and British Standard
5750; and perceptions of support institutions have or are likely to
receive from Training and Enterprise Councils. A survey report will
be available from March 1993.
Status: Sponsored project
Source of Grant: The Staff College
Date of Research: 1992 - continuing
KEYWORDS: *further education colleges; management in education;
quality control; sixteen to nineteen education; staff development*

9/1031
Coombe Lodge, Blagdon, Bristol BS18 6RG
0761 462503
Saunders, R. Mr; *Supervisor:* Gray, L. Mr
**Design of a job evaluation system for use in further education
corporations**
Abstract: Incorporation of further education (FE) colleges will de-
prive them of the services of local authority job evaluation units.
Equal Pay claims where support staff cite academic staff comparators
become increasingly likely. This research aims to design and test a
job evaluation system capable of measuring the comparative value of
all the jobs in a further education corporation to produce an integrated
salary structure. Relevant factors have been selected, defined and
provisionally weighted by analysis of benchmark job descriptions
obtained from four colleges. The resulting job evaluation manual now
needs to be tested in practice by applying it to a range of jobs in one
or more colleges. Outcomes will be described by papers in The Staff
College Mendip Paper series.
Published Material: SAUNDERS, R.C. (1992). Job Analysis and the
preparation of job descriptions. Mendip Paper No 37. Bristol: The
Staff College.
Status: Sponsored project
Source of Grant: The Staff College
Date of Research: 1992 - continuing
KEYWORDS: *comparative worth; employment practices; equal pay;
further education colleges; job analysis; occupational information;
salaries*

9/1032
Coombe Lodge, Blagdon, Bristol BS18 6RG
0761 462503
Further Education Unit, Spring Gardens, Citadel Place,
Tinworth Street, London SE11 5EH
071 962 1266
Graystone, J. Mr; Reece, I. Mr; Bayliss, J. Ms; Evans, S. Ms;
Warrender, A-M Ms; *Supervisor:* Coleman, J. Mrs;
Graystone, J. Mr
**Further education governing bodies and their contribution to a
quality learning service**
Abstract: This project for the Further Education Unit (RP 716): (1)
maps the current composition and characteristics of governing bodies
in further education, with particular interest in their potential for an
impact on curriculum issues; (2) identifies governors' current: (a)
expertise and experience, relevant to further education governance;
and (b) individual commitment to curriculum issues and ways of
working which contribute to the effectiveness of the college as a
learning service; and (3) makes recommendations to further education (FE) colleges for incorporation, having regard for the wider
responsibilities of governing bodies in the future. A short literature
search was carried out, followed by a questionnaire completed by 214
FE colleges in England and Wales. Interviews were then held with
over 50 governors from selected colleges, and five governing body
meetings were observed.
Status: Sponsored project
Source of Grant: Further Education Unit; The Staff College
Date of Research: 1992 - continuing
KEYWORDS: *colleges of further education; educational quality;
governing bodies*

Stirling University

9/1033
Department of Education, Stirling FK9 4LA
0786 467600
Duffield, J. Mrs; *Supervisor:* Riddell, S. Dr; Brown, S. Prof.
**Policy, practice and provision for children with specific
learning difficulties**
Abstract: The project is intended to provide an overview of policy
and provision for children with specific learning difficulties in the
Scottish regions. The central concern is to understand how the
problem is conceptualised by professionals, voluntary organisations
and parents and to analyse the way in which different forms of
provision arise from these conceptualisations. Interviews with principal psychologists, education officers, advisers, voluntary organisations and teacher educators are being undertaken, followed by
surveys of the views of pre-service teachers, inservice teachers and
parents. Case studies of particular ways of meeting the needs of
children with specific learning difficulties are being undertaken
during the final phase of the project.
Status: Sponsored project
Source of Grant: Scottish Office Education Department £44,707
Date of Research: 1990-1992
KEYWORDS: *attitudes; educational policy; learning disabilities;
Scotland; special educational needs*

9/1034
Department of Education, Stirling FK9 4LA
0786 467600
Brown, S. Prof.; Drever, E. Mr; Swann, J. Dr
**The Scottish educational reforms and teachers' theories of
teaching and learning**
Abstract: The Scottish reforms for curriculum, assessment and national testing for 5 to 14 year olds are likely to influence teachers
ideas about teaching and learning. In this context, the project aims to
explore teachers' assumptions about children's learning how teachers
interpret the differences among pupils (in the new atmosphere which
emphasises 'attainment targets') and the ways in which they cater for
these differences. The work focuses on two curriculum areas within
the new reforms: mathematics (which has national testing); and
environmental studies (which does not). Twenty teachers in eight
schools are involved, with classes of 6, 8, 12 and 14 year olds. The
research methods include classroom observation (responsive and
systematic), interviews with teachers (open-ended and semi-structured), an analysis of curriculum documents and of other support.
Particular attention is being paid to the impact of the reforms on
teachers' goals. For instance, do they now emphasise 'progress' more
than 'activity' goals? There is also concern with teachers' conceptions of how pupils influence these goals and the actions taken to
achieve them. The project will explore in depth: teachers' explicit use
of 'attainment targets'; their strategies of assessment and remediation; and evidence about how they think about children's
learning.
Status: Sponsored project
Source of Grant: Economic and Social Research Council £70,370
Date of Research: 1992 - continuing
KEYWORDS: *assessment; curriculum development; educational
change; environmental education; mathematics; National Curriculum; teaching process; teaching profession*

9/1035
Department of Education, Stirling FK9 4LA
0786 467600
Low, L. Mrs; Duffield, J. Mrs; Bankowska, A. Dr;
Supervisor: Brown, S. Prof.; Johnstone, R. Prof.
**Evaluation of national pilot projects: foreign languages in
primary schools (Scotland)**
Abstract: As part of a major government initiative, pilot projects have
been set up to test the feasibility of introducing foreign language
teaching into the primary schools associated with twelve secondary
schools. The commonest model involves collaboration between class
teachers from P4 to P7 and visiting language teachers from the
secondary school. The main aims of the evaluation are: (1) assessment of the linguistic attainments of children involved in the pilot
projects including comparisons with those children not involved; (2)
evaluation of the project courses including commentary on factors

such as the nature of the course and pedagogical methods which influence the linguistic performance of the children involved. The first aim has involved speaking and listening assessments carried out with pairs of pupils in the foreign language. In 1991 these compared 'project' and 'non-project' pupils in S1 and S2. In 1992 attention was on progression from Primary 7 onwards with 'project' pupils only. Within class assessments carried out by teachers have also been analysed. The second aim has been addressed through an interview study with class teachers and others involved at every level in the management of the projects, and a lesson observation study of primary and secondary classes. The result of the evaluation remains confidential until April 1993. An extension, to September 1994, will investigate the gains in linguistic attainments of pupils commencing their foreign language at different stages in the primary school, effective teaching approaches and various wider implications for the organisation of primary and secondary schools.
Published Material: Interim report of Scottish Office Education Department, December 1991.
Status: Sponsored project
Source of Grant: Scottish Office Education Department £172,901
Date of Research: 1991 - continuing
KEYWORDS: *achievement; modern language studies; primary schools; second language learning*

9/1036
Department of Education, Stirling FK9 4LA
0786 467600
Cope, P. Dr; Simmons, M. Mr; *Supervisor:* Cope, P. Dr;
Simmons, M. Mr
Feedback: its effects on procedural and conceptual knowledge for problem solving strategies
Abstract: The aims of the research are: (1) to investigate the effects of changing the instructional environment on the problem-solving strategies of children using Logo microworlds; (2) to measure the effect of such changes of strategy on the development of conceptual knowledge; (3) to determine which aspects of conceptual knowledge relating to rotation and angle will enhance pupils' ability to solve simple geometry problems using a screen turtle; (4) to investigate effective ways of teaching these aspects of rotation and angle. The background to this research is a general concern about the way in which young children interact with a Logo-based system. Effective use of Logo requires the development of mathematical knowledge about basic aspects of turtle geometry such as angle, rotation and distance. Such knowledge is a combination of both procedural and conceptual knowledge and although it is assumed that such knowledge can be developed through the use of Logo itself, this is by no means certain. Ideally, the development of knowledge about turtle geometry is one in which procedural knowledge and conceptual knowledge develop together. But in Logo the constant availability of feedback may have a profound effect on the development of knowledge. There are three phases to the study. Study 1 takes a sample of 60 children aged between 10 and 12. Groups are matched on the basis of a pre-test and thereafter are exposed to different kinds of feedback. Data collection is by taped transcripts and spooled output files. Study 2 takes the most appropriate principles of feedback found in Study 1 to develop structured Logo sessions. Study 3 compares computer based and non-computer based teaching strategies of angle and rotation concepts.
Published Material: COPE, P., SMITH, H. & SIMMONS, M. (1992). 'Misconceptions concerning rotation and angle in LOGO' Journal of Computer Assisted Learning, Vol 8, No 1, pp.16-24.; COPE, P. & SIMMONS, M. (1992). 'Children's exploration of rotation and angle in limited LOGO microworlds', Computers in Education, Vol 16, No 2, pp.133-141.
Status: Sponsored project
Source of Grant: Economic and Social Research Council £11,200
Date of Research: 1991 - continuing
KEYWORDS: *computer-assisted learning; feedback; instructional design; problem solving*

9/1037
Department of Education, Stirling FK9 4LA
0786 467600
Weeden, E. Mrs; *Supervisor:* Drever, E. Mr
Language and primary maths
Abstract: This is an investigation into the language used in primary mathematics texts and the interaction between teachers and pupils, with the emphasis on the pupils' perspective. An initial focus will be

on the materials from the Scottish Primary Mathematics Group, and possibly from the School Mathematics Project.
Status: Individual research
Date of Research: 1988-1991
KEYWORDS: *language of instruction; mathematical vocabulary; mathematics education; primary education; textbooks*

9/1038
Department of Education, Stirling FK9 4LA
0786 467600
Scottish Council for Educational Technology, Dowanhill, 74 Victoria Crescent Road, Glasgow G12 9JN
041 334 9134
Drever, E. Mr
Software reviews: what do teachers need to know?
Abstract: The ways in which teachers gain information and form expectations about 12 to 15 widely used software packages will be studied. The research covers packages used in primary and secondary schools and assesses the extent to which expectations are borne out. Postal questionnaires, interviews and informal classroom observation will be used. Special attention will be given to teachers' views and practices in integrating the packages into the curriculum at classroom level.
Status: Sponsored project
Source of Grant: Scottish Council for Educational Technology £32,809
Date of Research: 1989-1991
KEYWORDS: *computer software; computer uses in education; educational software; teacher attitudes*

Strathclyde University

9/1039
Careers Advisory Service, 16 Richmond Street, Glasgow G1 1XQ
041 522 4400
Graham, B. Miss
Survey of older graduates
Abstract: This is a national survey, by questionnaire of mature graduates' (25+ on graduation) previous experience and qualifications. This includes their: reasons for choice of course and career; experience of job seeking; destinations after employment; opinions of careers services; and of employers' attitudes to older graduates.
Status: Sponsored project
Date of Research: 1990-1991
KEYWORDS: *career choice; careers service; employment opportunities; graduate employment; graduate surveys; mature students*

9/1040
Department of Psychology, Turnbull Building,
155 George Street, Glasgow G1 1RD
041 552 4400
Howe, C. Dr; Tolmie, A. Mr
Conceptual development in primary school science: the design of group tasks
Abstract: The National Curriculum for Science requires primary school teaching to both incorporate group work and focus on conceptual development. Previous studies with primary age groups have shown tasks which expose conceptual conflicts between participants to effectively promote conceptual advance, but there remains scope for additional task constraints which optimise conflict resolution. Three task elements compatible with the prediction-test explanation format used previously, specifically address central aspects of the development of science concepts: (1) the provision of items which constitute critical tests for exclusion of irrelevant factors and isolation of relevant; (2) formulation of law-like statements through rule generation exercises; and (3) identification of law-like statements through rule selection. The two studies planned, in the areas of flotation and cooling, will assess the contribution of these task features to conceptual gain. In each study 120 children between 8 and 12 will be pre-tested using clinical interview techniques to establish initial conceptions. They will then be randomly assigned to groups of four to work on prediction-test explanation problems under one of four conditions. A control condition will present groups with random-

ly ordered items and no additional constraints. A second condition will provide opportunities for critical tests, and the third and fourth conditions will combine critical tests with either rule generation or rule selection. Participants will subsequently be post-tested to obtain measures of conceptual change, in terms of broad level of understanding and movement towards classical conceptions of physical factors. In addition, group sessions will be videotaped to allow identification of on-task behaviours that mark successful learners.

Published Material: HOWE, C.J., RODGERS, C. & TOLMIE, A. (1990). 'Physics in the primary school: peer interaction and the understanding of floating and sinking', European Journal of Psychology of Education, Vol 5, No 4, pp.459-475.; HOWE, C.J., TOLMIE, A. & RODGERS C. (1992). 'The acquisition of conceptual knowledge by primary school children: group interaction and the understanding of motion down an incline', British Journal of Developmental Psychology, Vol 10, Part 2, pp.113-130.; HOWE, C.J., TOLMIE, A. & ANDERSON, A. (1991). 'Information technology and group work in physics', Journal of Computer Assisted Learning, Vol 13, No 3, pp.133-143.

Status: Sponsored project
Source of Grant: Leverhulme Trust £51,000
Date of Research: 1990-1992
KEYWORDS: *concept teaching; group work; primary education; science activities; science education; scientific concepts*

Sunderland University

9/1041

School of Computing and Information Studies, Priestman Building, Green Terrace, Sunderland SR1 3SD
091 515 2000
Moscardini, A. Dr; Curran, D. Dr; Middleton, W. Mr; Bloor, C. Dr; Prior, D. Mr; *Supervisor:* Moscardini, A. Dr

The use of computers to teach mathematics

Abstract: A laboratory has been set up for teaching mathematics to between 300-400 first year undergraduate engineering and science students. The laboratory has replaced a large amount of material previously taught by lectures. The work has also been extended to include teaching the mathematically unadapted and, more recently, teaching the disabled.

Published Material: MIDDLETON, W. (1990). 'Innovative applications of CAL to the teaching of the mathematically unadapted', Conference Proceedings, CAL 90, Barcelona.

Status: Sponsored project
Source of Grant: Training, Enterprise & Education Directorate
Date of Research: 1988 - continuing
KEYWORDS: *computer-assisted learning; computer uses in education; mathematics education*

9/1042

School of Education, Hammerton Hall, Gray Road, Sunderland SR2 7EE
091 515 2000
Dockerty, A. Dr

Primary teachers perception of science concepts

Abstract: The work has evolved from an interest in childrens' perceptions of science concepts. It aims to discover the perceptions of primary school teachers to a range of concepts within the National Curriculum – Science. The investigation uses questionnaires, designed with unambiguous questions, to discover any trends in misconception of important concepts. A pilot study has been completed and new questionnaires are under construction. It is hoped to sample 200-300 individual teachers within 3 local authorities. Preliminary results have shown that most of the participants have serious misconceptions of particle theory and this is being extended to other areas of the National Curriculum. The result of the research will be used to design appropriate inservice packages for primary teachers.

Status: Individual research
Date of Research: 1990-1992
KEYWORDS: *perception; primary school teachers; science education; scientific concepts*

9/1043

School of Education, Hammerton Hall, Gray Road, Sunderland SR2 7EE
091 515 2000
Mercer, D. Mr; *Supervisor:* Constable, H. Dr

Job satisfaction in teaching

Abstract: The research undertaken has involved the development of a methodology suitable for the study, the carrying out of fieldwork based on this methodology and the development of the data obtained into the beginnings of a grounded theory of job satisfaction. In terms of the methodology, three approaches have been developed and made use of as a means of obtaining the data necessary to develop a grounded theory of job satisfaction, a methodological approach first formulated by Glaser & Strauss. These three methods are Life History, Nominal Group Technique and Critical Incident Technique. Of these three, the Critical Incident Technique has proved to be the most productive in that after interviews with 23 secondary headteachers, important categories with regard to job satisfaction have begun to emerge, a crucial first step in the development of substantive and formal grounded theory. Examples of such categories are, for job satisfaction, a sense of personal achievement, the views of significant others, a sense of efficacy, and relations with governors. For job dissatisfaction, work pressure, role conflict, interpersonal relations and self esteem have been identified as being of importance. In total, twenty three and twenty nine respectively of such categories have appeared so far and the next process has begun of condensing these into 'themes'. The emergence of these themes is the second stage in the creation of a theoretical position which explains job satisfaction on the part of secondary headteachers. While data collection is well advanced, it is nevertheless anticipated that perhaps double this number of headteachers will be interviewed to allow for what Glaser & Strauss refer to as 'theoretical saturation'. The research programme has been planned on the assumption that saturation will be achieved by Easter 1993 with fieldwork due to be completed by July 1993. The future progress of the research is indicated by the degree to which the development of substantive theory has already begun. This process will continue as data collection and is guided by what Glaser & Strauss refer to as 'theoretical sampling', i.e. the process of data collection being determined by an analysis of the data already collected. Allied to this, use will be made of the related process of constant comparative analysis which will theoretical notions will be coded, analysed, and re-designed and re-integrated, with such re-design being constantly undertaken as the flow of data emerges from the fieldwork. In this way it is anticipated that a formal theory of job satisfaction will emerge which will identify the key affective features of the job of headteacher. In view of the notable lack of research in this field, this will be a significant development which will increase understanding of a group which has a key part to play in our society.

Published Material: MERCER, D. (1991). 'Professional myopia: job satisfaction and the management of teachers', School Organisation, Vol 11, No 3.

Status: Individual research
Date of Research: 1990 - continuing
KEYWORDS: *job satisfaction; stress – psychological; teacher attitudes; teaching profession*

9/1044

School of Education, Hammerton Hall, Gray Road, Sunderland SR2 7EE
091 515 2000
Mercer, D. Mr

Democratic approaches to initial teacher education

Abstract: This is a study of a variety of student-centred approaches in initial teacher education. These include a democratic learning approach, partnership supervision in the teaching practice and student profiling.

Published Material: MERCER, D. & ABBOTT, I. (1989). 'Democratic learning in initial teacher education: a comparative study', Educational Review, Vol 41, No 1, pp.3-8.; MERCER, D. & ABBOTT, I. (1989). 'Democratic learning in initial teacher education: partnership supervision in the teaching practice', Journal of Education for Teaching, Vol 15, No 2, pp.141-148.

Status: Individual research
Date of Research: 1988-1991
KEYWORDS: *group work; learner centred methods; preservice teacher education*

9/1045
School of Education, Hammerton Hall, Gray Road,
Sunderland SR2 7EE
091 515 2000
Kennard, R. Mr; Adamson, F. Mr
A study of mature entrants to the teaching profession
Abstract: Given their extensive experience of industry, commerce
and life in general, it is popularly assumed that mature students have
much to offer the teaching profession. To what extent is this belief
rooted in reality? Using both qualitative and quantitative approaches
for the collection of data from mature entrants, other school staff and
LEA (local education authority) advisers, the research will attempt
to identify and evaluate the problems they face in training and in
school during the early years of their teaching career. The research
team hope to provide recommendations for institutions with responsibility for the recruitment and training of mature students and for
'good practice' regarding the support of mature probationary teachers
in school.
Status: Sponsored project
Source of Grant: Department of Education and Science £17,600
Date of Research: 1989-1991
*KEYWORDS: mature students; preservice teacher education; prob-
ationary period; student teachers; teaching profession*

9/1046
School of Education, Hammerton Hill, Gray Road,
Sunderland SR2 7EE
091 515 2000
Durham University, School of Education, Leazes Road,
Durham DH1 1TA
091 374 2000
Elliott, J. Mr; *Supervisor:* Coffield, F. Prof.
**Locus of control beliefs in children with emotional and
behavioural difficulties: an exploratory study**
Abstract: The study examines control related beliefs of 240 children
aged between nine and sixteen, and considers the implications of
these beliefs for therapeutic intervention. All subjects have been
referred to the educational psychology service because of perceived
behavioural difficulties, and each child's behaviour is scored on nine
behavioural dimensions. The data used for analysis are drawn from
self-report scales, semi-structured interviews and case files. Both
quantitative (using multivariate techniques) and qualitative modes of
data analysis are employed and the stengths and weaknesses of each
approach are noted. The research challenges many assumptions
contained within the locus of control literature and highlights the
difficulty of adopting findings from nomothetic research for the
purpose of clinical intervention.
Status: Individual research
Date of Research: 1988 - continuing
*KEYWORDS: behaviour disorders; child psychiatry; emotional dis-
turbances; locus of control*

Surrey University

9/1047
Department of Educational Studies, Guildford GU2 5XH
0483 300800
Chadwick, A. Dr; Fisher, J. Dr; Protopapas, G. Mr
**Developing an industrial relations training programme for
Greek supervisors and trade union representatives in
simultaneous process research into training needs**
Abstract: This project is intended to help to develop an industrial
relations training system in Greece for trade union representatives
and managers. It involves: (1) identifying training needs; (2) developing the framework for a training programme; and (3) the implementation of that programme in Greece 'in simultaneous process'. Needs
identification is mainly through consultation with all interested parties and organisations. Programme design and development is ongoing, and evaluation will be by participation and observation, as well
as by response of involved parties. The project is supported by the
Greek government, companies' unions and training organisations.
Status: Sponsored project
Source of Grant: European Community COMETT Programme
Date of Research: 1988-1992
KEYWORDS: Greece; labour relations; supervisors; training; unions

9/1048
Department of Educational Studies, Guildford GU2 5XH
0483 300800
Hobrough, J. Dr; McCann, J. Dr; *Supervisor:* Evans, K. Dr
**The management of the Technical and Vocational Education
Initiative within post-16 institutions in Hampshire**
Abstract: The research programme is designed to analyse the perceptions of the Technical and Vocational Education Initiative (TVEI)
coordinators in relation to management structures adopted within
post-16 institutions. A general/institutional summary is obtained
using interviews, documented by a verified-reporting technique.
Perceptions of senior managers and TVEI coordinators are obtained
using repertory grids, concept maps, and information models. Comparisons between 11-18 schools, sixth form colleges, technical colleges and tertiary colleges will be made. Some comparison between
Hampshire and 'distant' case studies will also be completed.
Status: Sponsored project
Source of Grant: Hampshire Local Education Authority £1,400
Date of Research: 1988-1991
*KEYWORDS: educational administration; sixteen to nineteen edu-
cation; technical education; vocational education*

9/1049
Department of Educational Studies, Guildford GU2 5XH
0483 300800
Germon, S. Mrs; *Supervisor:* Evans, K. Dr
**Technical and Vocational Education Initiative (TVEI) local
evaluation**
Abstract: In setting up the Technical and Vocational Education
Initiative (TVEI), the Manpower Services Commission (MSC) stipu-
lated that each local education authority operating in a pilot scheme
should make arrangements for it to be evaluated by an independent
local evaluator. The purpose of the local evaluation has been to
undertake research into a key aspect of the pilot schemes in operation
and feed back the results to those involved at managerial level, in
order to aid future planning. Local evaluation also gives an independent unbiased viewpoint at 'grassroots' level. Methods have been
mainly questionnaire survey and in depth interview. Topics for
research have varied, responding to local needs, and include: (1)
pupils' perceptions at varying stages during their progress through
TVEI schemes; (2) the employment dimension, in which the value
and use of TVEI to former pupils now in employment, and employers' knowledge and perspectives on TVEI, were investigated; (3)
the impact on TVEI schools and colleges, which explored the outcomes of TVEI in comparison with anticipation, achievements, barriers to change and areas for future development, as perceived by key
participants. These studies, in particular, informed not only the pilot
schemes but also those consortia engaged in developing TVEI extension plans, by highlighting the lessons learned.
Status: Sponsored project
Source of Grant: Surrey, Kingston, Sutton, Berkshire Local Education Authorities: £80,000; West Sussex Local Education Authority
£25,000
Date of Research: 1984-1991
*KEYWORDS: programme evaluation; school to work transition;
technical education; vocational education*

9/1050
Department of Educational Studies, Guildford GU2 5XH
0483 300800
Blackman, S. Dr; Brown, A. Mr
**Evaluation of information technology teacher training
development programme**
Abstract: The Technical and Vocational Education Initiative (TVEI)
Unit funded a major programme (of 8 projects) to help teachers make
more effective use of Information Technology (IT) in teaching and
learning. This project aims to provide formative evaluation and
support to all components of the programme. Methods used include
the use of a rolling feedback strategy to support individual projects
and to facilitate progress of the programme as a whole. The results
of the research will be made available to those outside the programme
at the end of the project.
Published Material: BROWN, A.J. (1992). 'Support for and management of information technology in schools', Proceedings of the
Seventh International Conference on Technology and Education, Vol 2.
Status: Sponsored project
Source of Grant: Training Agency: TVEI Unit £100,000
Date of Research: 1989-1992

KEYWORDS: *information technology; programme evaluation; teacher education; technical education; vocational education*

9/1051

Department of Educational Studies, Guildford GU2 5XH
0483 300800
Reading University, Faculty of Education and Community Studies, Bulmershe Court, Woodlands Avenue, Earley, Reading RG6 1HY
0734 875123
Zufar, K. Mr; *Supervisor:* Pope, M. Prof.

The conceptual ecology of 'Health' and its significance for the science education system in Pakistan

Abstract: This study deals with the conceptual ecology of science students of Pakistan, aged 15-17 years, and their teachers and parents. The concept of health was elicited from the students, their parents and their science teachers by using a technique called 'Interview about pictures'. This involved discussion about the instances and non-instances of health as depicted in line drawings on cards. The repertory grid technique was used to elicit the teachers concepts of good teaching and various science teaching methods. A series of semi-structured interviews was conducted with parents, teachers, health educators, health personnel, religious leaders and community elders. The questions asked were about science and science education, health and health education, religious influence upon education, expectations, problems and suggested solutions. The teachers were selected to represent the male and female population and rural and urban backgrounds. They were also asked to complete an open-ended questionnaire at the end of the field work to ascertain feedback on the effects of the research methods in which they participated.

Status: Individual research
Date of Research: 1985-1991
KEYWORDS: *health education; Pakistan; science education*

Sussex University

9/1052

Institute of Continuing and Professional Education, Sussex House, Falmer, Brighton BN1 9RH
0273 606755
Burke, J. Dr

Research and development in National Vocational Qualifications (NVQs) and the identification of various competencies in teaching and management

Abstract: The National Council for Vocational Qualifications (NCVQ) set up a two year Research Fellowship in April 1989, its three objectives are to: (1) pursue research and development in competency-based learning in support of the emerging model of National Vocational Qualifications (NVQs); (2) publish, disseminate and generally promote research and developments in respect of the above area; and (3) provide consultancy to NCVQ on research and development on specific projects. The major focus of the work in the first year has been on generic competences or core skills. Three papers, dealing with: (a) the reconceptualisation of generic competence; and (b) aspects of problem solving, were published by the NCVQ in Jessup, G. (1990). Several other publications have been produced. The focus of the research in the second year continues on generic competences and involves: (a) supporting the work of the NCVQ in collaboration with the National Curriculum Council (NCC) and School Examinations and Assessment Council (SEAC) and others; (b) working with the Open University Enterprise in Higher Education Project; and (c) providing consultancy for Education Management South East's project on competency in educational management. A fourth area of interest is National Vocational Qualifications and special needs.

Published Material: BURKE, J. (1989). 'Research in competency-based education and training', Competency and Assessment, No 8, pp.12-13.; BURKE, J. (1989). Competency-based education and training. London: Falmer Press.; BURKE, J. (1990). 'Problem solving'. In: JESSUP, G. Common learning outcomes: core skills in A/AS levels and NVQs. London: National Council for Vocational Qualifications, (NCVQ R & D Report No 6).; BURKE, J. (1990). 'Generic units'. In: JESSUP, G. Common learning outcomes: core skills in A/AS levels and NVQs. London: National Council for Vocational Qualifications, (NCVQ R & D Report No 6).; BURKE, J. (1990). 'Towards a framework for problem solving as a common learning outcome'. In: JESSUP, G. Common learning outcomes: core skills in A/AS levels and NVQs. London: National Council for Vocational Qualifications, (NCVQ R & D Report No 6).

Status: Sponsored project
Source of Grant: National Vocational Qualifications £93,000
Date of Research: 1989-1991
KEYWORDS: *competency-based education; minimum competencies; National Vocational Qualifications; skills*

9/1053

Institute of Continuing and Professional Education, Sussex House, Falmer, Brighton BN1 9RH
0273 606755
Northbrook College of Design & Technology, Department of General and Community Education, Broadwater Road, Worthing BN14 8HJ
0903 31445
Angelo, M. Mrs; *Supervisor:* Abbs, P. Dr

Education in active imagination: design and piloting of an open learning course for adult study

Abstract: In the context of an educational system which emphasises the cognitive domain and skills training for business and technical applications, it has become the norm to be imaginally illiterate. Image intelligence is neither recognised nor educated: imagination is culturally stereotyped 'for children, artists or crazies', the expressive disciplines play a marginal role; self-expression, lacking the objective referencing of the traditional 'learning of the imagination', reduces to uncritical self-indulgence. Psychologies of image – Jungian, archetypal and transpersonal – characteristically place a therapeutic framework around their work with imagination. This includes both imagination as process and as place (the 'as if' location of autonomous content names the unconscious or the imaginal). Depth therapies of image are critical of a systematic educative approach, interpreting it as egotistical, manipulative and restrictive. The image of depth education is missing. The research argues for a positive re-valuing of the educational mode, enabling the imaginal discipline of active imagination and guided fantasy to become valid aesthetic studies. It is suggested that a non-egoic directing pattern can be found in the traditional tree of life symbol system of the Renaissance polymath. Understood as the archetype of interrelationships and drawing on the classical art of memory, intrinsic image connections open out for individual exploration. A one-year open learning course has been designed on this basis to provide an imaginal apprenticeship. 24 practical sessions are on tape, guiding an imaginal journey. An accompanying 'travellers diary' is written/drawn weekly. Regular personal tutorials discourage the over-familiar cognitive reductions of image into symptom and explore the cultural amplifications of 'depth-aesthetics'. There have been three piloting years involving small groups meeting on a monthly basis, together with qualitative, individual case studies.

Status: Individual research
Date of Research: 1984-1991
KEYWORDS: *aesthetic education; course content; creative thinking; fantasy; imagination; open education*

9/1054

School of Cognitive and Computing Sciences, Sussex House, Falmer, Brighton BN1 9RH
0273 606755
Del Soldato, T. Ms; *Supervisor:* Du Boulay, J. Dr

Adapting tutoring systems to students' learning styles

Abstract: The purpose of this project is to investigate the possibilities of adapting computer-assisted instruction to students' learning styles. Usually tutoring systems adjust their instructional planning according to what knowledge the learner has acquired, neglecting how the student acquired such knowledge. Several aspects of learning systems (e.g. level of confidence, anxiety, independence vs. need of constant help, toleration to challenge) will be considered by the instructional planner, aiming to motivate the student and enrich the teaching interaction. As a result of this project, the core of a learning style adaptable tutoring system should be implemented.

Status: Sponsored project
Source of Grant: Brazilian Council for Scientific and Technological Development (CNPq)
Date of Research: 1989 - continuing
KEYWORDS: *auto-instructional aids; cognitive style; computer-assisted learning; computer uses in education; learning strategies; teaching machines*

Tavistock Institute of Human Relations

9/1055

Evaluation Development and Review Unit, The Tavistock Centre, 120 Belsize Lane, London NW3 5BA
071 435 7111
Sommerlad, E. Dr
The role of the workplace in the work experience triangle with particular reference to transferable skills
Abstract: Alternance arrangements generally recognise three elements: off-the-job education and training, on the job training and the link between them. The focus of the research is to explore the workplace as an environment for learning and to draw out the implications of workplace diversity for off-the-job education and the links between on the job and off the job. The specific questions being addressed are: (1) What feasibilities do different workplace settings offer for acquiring skills that are transferable? (2) In what ways can the acquisition of transferable skills be maximised in different work settings? (3) How is this mediated or influenced by different labour markets or industrial relations? The research includes: (i) secondary analysis of existing data and literature review; (ii) development of conceptual models and typologies; and (iii) cross-national comparative element (Netherlands and Italy).
Status: Sponsored project
Source of Grant: European Community PETRA Programme £20,000
Date of Research: 1991 - continuing
KEYWORDS: off the job training; on the job training; skill development; transfer of learning; work experience programmes

Teesside University

9/1056

School of Computing and Mathematics, Interactive Systems Research Group, Borough Road, Middlesbrough, Cleveland TS1 3BA
0642 218121
Banerji, A. Mr; *Supervisor:* Barker, P. Prof.; Manji, K. Dr
Design of electronic performance support systems
Abstract: An Electronic Performance Support Systems (EPSS) is an approach to integrating hardware, software and end-user interfaces in order to produce more useful computer-based information delivery systems that embed various types of job performance aid. Essentially, an EPSS is intended to be a computer-based job performance aid that is able to provide 'just-in-time' (JIT) training and an enhanced interactive performance support environment. This environment provides various types of information, data, images, advice, assistance and guidance in order to permit an employee to perform his/her job with minimum support and intervention from others. The concept of JIT training is derived from the JIT inventory control methods adopted by the Japanese and accepted as a new productivity standard. It can be viewed as an evolution of computer based training (CBT) delivery stages – from 'off the job' training through 'prior-to-job-performance' training to the approach of learning while doing a job using an EPSS. Research into basic EPSS techniques has been taking place within the School of Computing and Mathematics at Teesside University. Interest in this area has arisen as a result of the School's organising research into the application of computer-based training and the development of interactive job performance aids. The objective of this current project is to investigate the potential utility of EPSS techniques and to formulate a set of design and fabrication guidelines to facilitate their creation within industrial and commercial environments. The four avenues of investigation currently explored involve: the use of on-line help systems; full-text retrieval packages; expert systems; and intelligent simulation environments, in order to augment the use of CBT within the interactive work environment of an employee. This project will also explore the use of compact disc read-only memory (CD ROM) as a means of embedding and delivering EPSS facilities to end-users.
Published Material: BANERJI, A.K. & SATHYAVASU, M.A. (1990). 'FEDS a computer aided learning approach for training in foregin exchange dealing', Proceedings of Indian Computing Congress ICC 90, Hyderabad, Tata-McGraw Hill, New Delhi.; BAR-

KER, P.G. (1991). 'Computer-based training in India', International Journal of Computers in Adult Education and Training, Vol 2, No 3, pp.213-224.; BARKER, P.G. 'Designing interactive learning systems's, Educational & Training Technology International, Vol 27, No 2, pp.125-145, May.; BARKER, P.G. (1991). 'Developing competence through CBT', paper presented at AETT '91 International Conference, Polytechnic of Wales, Pontypridd, 2-5 April, 1991.
Status: Individual research
Date of Research: 1991 - continuing
KEYWORDS: computer-assisted learning; educational technology; expert systems; optical data discs; training methods

9/1057

School of Computing and Mathematics, Interactive Systems Research Group, Borough Road, Middlesbrough, Cleveland TS1 3BA
0642 218121
Barker, P. Prof.
Design guidelines for electronic books
Abstract: Electronic books based upon the use of digital optical storage (CD ROM) technology are capable of providing many new and novel approaches to the problems of disseminating knowledge and information. They are particularly useful for implementing a wide variety of different types of learning and training activities. Unfortunately, few guidelines currently exist to enable authors of such books to create effective page and book structures. This work is therefore intended to investigate this problem with a view to formulating a set of design guidelines and a collection of fabrication procedures. Three basic optical storage technologies are being studied: basic CD ROM (compact disc read only memory); CD-I (compact disc interactive); and DVI (digital video interactive). Six different categories of electronic book are currently being studied: text books; static picture books; moving picture books; multi-media books; intelligent electronic books; and teleconferencing books. Authoring tools to enable authors to produce these different types of electronic book are also being investigated. To date a number of books have been designed and fabricated. The groups most recent book template is called SPBAN (static picture books with audio narrations). The potential of this category of electronic book as a tool for promoting foreign language learning is currently being investigated.
Published Material: BARKER, P.G. & MANJI, K.A. (1989). 'Designing electronic books', Journal of Artificial Intelligence in Education, Vol 1, No 2, pp.31-42.; BARKER, P.G. (1990). 'Designing, authoring and fabricating electronic books', Proceedings of the Seventh International Conference on Technology and Education, Brussels, Belgium, 20-22 March, pp.291-293.; BARKER, P.G. & MANJI, K.A. (1991). 'Designing electronic books', Educational and Training Technology International, Vol 28, No 4, pp.273-280.
Status: Sponsored project
Source of Grant: Training, Enterprise and Education Directorate £64,000
Date of Research: 1990-1992
KEYWORDS: authoring aids – programming; computer-assisted learning; computer uses in education; electronic books; optical data discs

9/1058

School of Computing and Mathematics, Interactive Systems Research Group, Borough Road, Middlesbrough, Cleveland TS1 3BA
0642 218121
Richards, S. Mr; *Supervisor:* Barker, P. Prof.; Manji, K. Dr
End-user interfaces to electronic books
Abstract: The term 'electronic book' is a metaphor which is used to describe an application which aims to deliver information in an electronic form. The rapid advances in storage technologies, for example Compact Disc Read Only Memory (CD ROM) and Magneto Optical Rewritable Optical Disk (MOROD), have allowed such books to deliver huge quantities of information in a wide variety of presentation media forms. Such developments, along with the advances in: digital information presentation; video and audio compression and decompression in real-time; high resolution colour display devices; and hypermedia information networks, can facilitate the creation of extremely rich and stimulating information delivery environments. The very newness of these technologies has meant that the full capabilities and potentials as applied to electronic books, has as yet not been fully investigated. The current research aims to

develop extremely rich electronic book environments which are capable of tailoring the information which they deliver to individual user requirements. Information will be presented in the form of digital video, sound, animation, hypertext and hyperimages in order to assess the pedagogic impact of such information delivery strategies. This is to be effected by investigating the effectiveness of different page structures based upon the following models: simple page model; composite page model; overlay page model; and the viewport page model. Through the adoption of such a strategy it will then be possible to assess the efficacy of various page structures, presentation media and access techniques within learning and training environments.
Published Material: RICHARDS, S.M. & BARKER, P.G. (1991). 'Page structures for electronic books', Educational and Training Technology International, Vol 28, No 4, pp.291-301.
Status: Sponsored project
Source of Grant: Science and Engineering Research Council; Dean Associates
Date of Research: 1990 - continuing
KEYWORDS: *computer-assisted learning; electronic books; human-computer interaction; hypermedia; information technology; multimedia approach; optical data discs*

9/1059
School of Computing and Mathematics, Interactive Systems Research Group, Borough Road, Middlesbrough, Cleveland TS1 3BA
0642 218121
Lamont, C. Mr; *Supervisor:* Barker, P. Prof.; Manji, K. Dr
Human-computer interfaces to reactive graphical images
Abstract: A reactive graphical image is one that changes its form when pointed at by a computer user using a mouse or a touch screen. Such reactive graphical images can be combined with multimedia presentations (the blending of moving video, sound, and graphics in one display environment) to form the basis of effective interactive multimedia courseware for use in the computer based training (CBT) industries. Work has initially been undertaken to provide custom editors within the PC/PILOT and PROPI authoring environments. A custom editor is designed to enhance the authoring capability of a CBT production environment by allowing parameters to be embedded within a lesson to access external material and devices. Such methods can enhance the usability and training value of a CBT lesson. Initially, custom editors have been built to incorporate videodisc still images or moving video sequences into a lesson, and for displaying graphics images on a remote terminal. However, because videodisc technology is based on analog data, it cannot effectively provide variable speed motion with continued sound synchronisation and effective graphics overlays. Thus the thrust of multimedia technology development is to provide all these features in one digital environment. Future custom editors will be built to take full advantage of this digital video interactive (DVI) technology. Once the full range of graphical custom editors has been designed and built, evaluations will be conducted to assess the quality of design and the usability of the products that are generated. Extensive end-user evaluations will also be conducted in order that a set of models and guidelines which reflect good design practice can be derived from the research.
Status: Sponsored project
Source of Grant: Science and Engineering Research Council; A.P. Chesters and Associates
Date of Research: 1990 - continuing
KEYWORDS: *computer-assisted learning; computer uses in education; educational software; interactive video*

9/1060
School of Computing and Mathematics, Interactive Systems Research Group, Borough Road, Middlesbrough, Cleveland TS1 3BA
0642 218121
Barker, P. Prof.
Database support for multi-media computer assisted learning
Abstract: The multi-media approach to computer-assisted learning (CAL) necessitates the use of human-computer interaction environments that are capable of supporting highly parallel, mixed-mode dialogue. An environment that is able to meet these requirements is often referred to as multi-media workstation. Multi-media CAL workstations provide sophisticated interaction environments for a learner or trainee. These environments usually contain a wide range of interaction peripherals, including a light pen, a keyboard, a barcode reader, one or more concept keyboards, a digitiser, a touch screen, an

image scanner, and so on. In addition to these interaction devices, the workstation might also contain a cluster of local storage peripherals. This study investigates the potential utility of database technology as a support aid within a multi-media workstation environment. Both conventional and intelligent database software resources would be examined. A major objective of the study is to find appropriate means of simplifying both the use and control of a sophisticated workstation that is attached (as an active device) to a distributed wide area computer network system. Such a workstation would be able to act both as a means of facilitating distributed courseware authoring and as a method for the effective realisation of distributed distance learning. In the latter context, it is important to realise that many of the resources used for instruction might either reside at remote host installations or be available locally. The database support facilities embedded within the workstation will therefore need to keep track of those resources which are held locally and those which must be accessed through remote sites. Obviously intelligence in the database will enable the workstation to be connected to the most appropriate host – where a selection exists.
Published Material: BARKER, P.G. & YEATES, H. (1985). Introducing computer assisted learning. Hemel Hempstead: Prentice-Hall International.; BARKER, P.G. (1986). Author languages for CAL. Basingstoke: Macmillan Press.; BARKER, P.G. (1987). 'A practical introduction to authoring for computer assisted instruction'. Part 8: multi-media CAL', British Journal of Educational Technology, Vol 18, No 1, pp.25-40.
Status: Individual research
Date of Research: 1986-1992
KEYWORDS: *computer-assisted learning; database management systems; distance education; educational media; educational technology; multimedia approach; telecommunications*

9/1061
School of Computing and Mathematics, Interactive Systems Research Group, Borough Road, Middlesbrough, Cleveland TS1 3BA
0642 218121
Barker, P. Prof.
Knowledge-based computer assisted learning
Abstract: In the past, most of the conventional approaches to the creation of software for computer assisted learning (CAL) have suffered from a number of significant limitations. One of the most serious of these has been the need to embed the knowledge and skills (that are to be transferred to the student) within particular and discrete items of software. Embedding instructional material within courseware itself can be a source of many difficulties. For example, it leads to a very inflexible approach to the effective utilisation of instructional resources particularly with respect to the creation of software that is adaptable to the particular learning and training needs of individual students. In view of this, the research advocates that a better design principle would involve the creation of a computer resident, shared knowledge-base that acts as a central repository for all the instructional material within a given teaching domain. The knowledge-base is then used to service different types of 'presentation software' that does not embed any specific domain knowledge. Such an approach to the design of courseware could cater for multiple views of knowledge, and hence, the production of effective and adaptable courseware. This research is primarily concerned with an investigation into the potential utility of knowledge-based CAL and the development of appropriate knowledge engineering techniques to support this approach to the development of courseware for use in sophisticated interactive learning systems.
Published Material: BARKER, P.G. (1986). 'Knowledge-based CAL'. In: Proceedings of the Fifth Canadian Symposium on Instructional Technology. Ottawa, Canada, 5-7 May, pp.137-143.; BARKER, P.G. & PROUD, A. (1987). 'A practical introduction to authoring for computer assisted instruction. Part 10: knowledge-based CAL', British Journal of Educational Technology, Vol 18, No 2, pp.140-160.; BARKER, P.G. (1988). 'Knowledge engineering for CAL'. In: LOUIS, F.B. & TAGG, E.D. (Eds). Computers in education: European Conference Proceedings. North-Holland Publishing Company, pp.529-535.
Status: Individual research
Date of Research: 1986-1992
KEYWORDS: *authoring aids – programming; computer-assisted learning; computer uses in education; educational software; expert systems; human-computer interaction*

9/1062
School of Computing and Mathematics, Interactive Systems-Research Group, Borough Road, Middlesbrough, Cleveland TS1 3BA
0642 218121
Barker, P. Prof.
WORM (Write-Once-Read-Many) and CD ROM (Compact Disc Read Only Memory) utility within a CAL (Computer Asssisted Learning) workstation environment
Abstract: Distance learning is concerned with the provision of learning facilities and resources at centres or sites that are remote from those at which these resources are produced. Distributed computer networks provide one mechanism by which distance learning may be realised. However, there are currently many severe limitations associated with the presently available telecommunications facilities with respect to the services available for high speed transmission of large volumes of text, sound and picture material. In due course (with the advent of ISDN (Integrated Service Digital Network)), these limitations are likely to be overcome. However, common access to ISDN over geographically large areas is likely to be some decades away. This feasibility study is therefore concerned with how Write-Once-Read-Many (WORM) and Compact Disc Read Only Memory (CD ROM) discs might be used to help realise some of the goals of distance learning. In particular, it is intended to study how such discs might be used within a CAL workstation learning environment to facilitate the storage of large volumes of textual information and digitised sound and pictorial material. Some of the aspects of optical disc technology (1,2,3) that would be considered in this feasibility study would therefore be the use of: (1) pre-mastered discs (such as conventional dictionaries, reference works, encyclopaedias, picture libraries, etc.) within CAL courseware; and (2) the use of discs created locally (containing image data, sound resources and so on). The first of these studies would involve the fabrication of a multimedia workstation to which is connected one or more CD ROM units. The second study wiould require the workstation to be enhanced through the addition of appropriate image/sound input peripherals, suitable digitisation equipment and, of course, a WORM unit. To support this work an investigation into interfaces and standards would also be necessary.
Published Material: BARKER, P.G. (1985). 'Programming a video disc', Microprocessing and Microprogramming, No 15, pp.263-276.; BARKER, P.G. (1986). 'Video discs in libraries', The Electronic Library, Vol 4, No 3, pp.166-176.
Status: Individual research
Date of Research: 1986-1992
KEYWORDS: computer-assisted learning; computer uses in education; distance education; multimedia approach; optical data discs; telecommunications

Thames Valley University

9/1063
Faculty of Humanities and Languages, 1 The Grove, London W5 5DX
081 579 5000
Roberts, C. Ms; Kapoor, S. Ms; Garnett, C. Mr
Teaching and learning strategies in multi-ethnic further education classrooms
Abstract: The aim of the project is to establish what teaching and learning strategies contribute to the progress and achievement of ethnic minority students in work-related further education classes and to develop some staff training materials. Four London colleges will be visited on a regular basis and the researchers will work closely with four Business and Technical Education Councils (BTEC) lecturers who have agreed to participate in the project as teacher/researchers. Audio and video recordings will be made in the classroom and interviews carried out with lecturers and students. The second part of the project is the development of staff training materials. These will include case studies and a video.
Status: Sponsored project
Source of Grant: Training, Enterprise and Education Directorate £47,000
Date of Research: 1989-1991
KEYWORDS: achievement; educational materials; ethnic groups; further education; learning strategies; performance; teaching methods

9/1064
Faculty of Humanities and Languages, 1 The Grove, London W5 5DX
081 579 5000
Durham University, School of Education, Leazes Road, Durham DH1 1TA
091 374 2000
Roberts, C. Ms; Byram, M. Dr
Cultural studies in advanced language learning: the year abroad in under-graduate courses
Abstract: The aim of this research is to develop a more integrated approach to language and culture on four year language degree courses. At the Thames Valley University this will be done by introducing principles of ethnography in the second year of the degree course. Students will write ethnographies of the target culture while abroad, which will then be evaluated. Two language staff will learn ethnographic approaches and their learning will be documented. They will then develop a new course for the language students.
Status: Sponsored project
Source of Grant: Economic and Social Research Council £44,000
Date of Research: 1990 - continuing
KEYWORDS: cultural education; degree requirements; ethnography; higher education; second language learning; study abroad

Trinity College

9/1065
Carmarthen, Dyfed SA31 3EP
0267 237971
Francis, L. Dr; *Supervisor:* Francis, L. Dr
Monitoring attitudes towards Christianity among secondary school pupils in England
Abstract: A survey of secondary school pupils' attitudes towards Christianity, conducted originally in 1974 has been regularly replicated at four yearly intervals. The data demonstrate the continued drift away from the Christian churches.
Published Material: FRANCIS, L.J. (1989). 'Monitoring changing attitudes towards Christianity among secondary school pupils between 1974 and 1986', British Journal of Educational Psychology, Vol 59, No 1, pp.86-91, February.; FRANCIS, L.J. (1990). 'Monitoring attitudes towards Christianity: the 1990 study', British Journal of Religious Education.
Status: Individual research
Date of Research: 1974-1992
KEYWORDS: attitude change; Christianity; pupil attitudes; religious attitudes; secondary school pupils

9/1066
Carmarthen, Dyfed SA31 3EP
0267 237971
Francis, L. Dr; *Supervisor:* Francis, L. Dr
Television viewing among secondary school pupils
Abstract: The project re-analyses data collected among over 5,000 secondary school pupils regarding television viewing habits. A sequence of analyses has led to a series of focused studies.
Status: Individual research
Date of Research: 1990-1992
KEYWORDS: adolescent attitudes; secondary school pupils; television viewing

9/1067
Carmarthen, Dyfed SA31 3EP
0267 237971
Francis, L. Dr; *Supervisor:* Francis, L. Dr
The measure of neuroticism among 15 and 16 year olds
Abstract: Nearly two hundred 15-16 year old pupils completed four different editions of the Eysenck measures of personality. The data were analysed to examine for sex differences in neuroticism. The findings indicate that Eysenck's neuroticism scales clearly contain two sub-scales, one of which is sex-related and the other of which is not sex-related. This clarification of the construct of neuroticism enables clearer specification of the empirical correlates of scores recorded on the sub-scales.

Published Material: FRANCIS, L.J. & PEARSON, P.R. (1991). 'Religiosity, gender and the two faces of neuroticism', Irish Journal of Psychology, No 12, pp.60-67.
Status: Individual research
Date of Research: 1990-1992
KEYWORDS: adolescents; neurosis; personality measures; personality problems; secondary school pupils; sex differences

9/1068
Carmarthen, Dyfed SA31 3EP
0267 237971
Francis, L. Dr; *Supervisor:* Francis, L. Dr
The social context of prayer among 16 year olds
Abstract: This study examines the influence of home, church and school on an attitudinal predisposition to pray among 711 sixteen year old adolescents attending Roman Catholic, Church of England and county state maintained schools in England. The results are compared with earlier findings among eleven year olds. Among sixteen year olds the influence of church is stronger and the influence of parents is weaker.
Published Material: FRANCIS, L.J. & BROWN, L.B. (1990). 'The predisposition to pray: a study of the social influence on the predisposition to pray among eleven year old children in England', Journal of Empirical Theology, Vol 3, No 2, pp.22-34.; FRANCIS, L.J. & BROWN, L.B. 'The influence of home, church and school on prayer among sixteen year old adolescents in England', Review of Religious Research, (forthcoming).
Status: Individual research
Date of Research: 1990-1992
KEYWORDS: adolescent attitudes; church and education; family influence; parent influence; religious attitudes

9/1069
Carmarthen, Dyfed SA31 3EP
0267 237971
Francis, L. Dr; *Supervisor:* Francis, L. Dr
Small schools and pupil attitudes
Abstract: The project is re-analysing data collected from 82% of the state maintained primary schools in a shire county in order to explore the relationship between school size and pupil attitude towards school. Attitudes are measured by means of semantic differential grids. The data demonstrate that pupils attending schools of sixty or fewer children report a significantly more positive attitude towards school than pupils attending larger schools.
Published Material: FRANCIS, L.J. (1992). 'Primary school size and pupil attitudes: small is happy?' Educational Management and Administration, Vol 20, No 2, pp.100-104.
Status: Individual research
Date of Research: 1989-1992
KEYWORDS: primary school pupils; primary schools; pupil attitudes; school size; small schools

9/1070
Carmarthen, Dyfed SA31 3EP
0267 237971
Francis, L. Dr; *Supervisor:* Francis, L Dr
The influence of Church of England secondary schools on adolescents' attitudes towards the Church
Abstract: Five hundred and forty-six fourth year pupils attending the four county and one Church of England voluntary schools within the same town completed a detailed questionnaire concerning their religious beliefs, practices and attitudes, together with some information regarding parental religiosity. After taking into account the influence of sex, social class and parental religiosity, path analysis indicates that the Church of England school exerts neither a positive nor negative influence on the pupils' religious practice, belief or attitudes.
Status: Individual research
Date of Research: 1991-1992
KEYWORDS: adolescent attitudes; church and education; religious attitudes; secondary school pupils; voluntary schools

9/1071
Carmarthen, Dyfed SA31 3EP
0267 237971
Francis, L. Dr; *Supervisor:* Francis, L. Dr
Church schools in an urban environment
Abstract: This project is re-analysing data collected from over 7,150 Anglican churches to explore the impact of urban church schools on a range of features of urban church life. The presence of a church school is shown to augment slightly the urban church's contact with under 14 year olds through membership of the choir and team of servers. The presence of a church school also increases slightly the number of young confirmands under the age of 14 and the number of 14-17 year olds contacted through church youth groups. There is also a higher number of infant baptisms in parishes which contain a church school.
Status: Individual research
Date of Research: 1989-1992
KEYWORDS: church and education; churches; Protestant churches; urban areas; voluntary schools

9/1072
Carmarthen, Dyfed SA31 3EP
0267 237971
Francis, L. Dr; *Supervisor:* Francis, L. Dr
Measurement of attitudes towards Christianity
Abstract: This project is re-analysing data collected among primary and secondary pupils in England, Scotland and Ireland in order to perfect a reliable and valid short measure of attitude towards Christianity, building on Francis' well established longer Likert scale.
Published Material: FRANCIS, L.J., GREER, J.E. & GIBSON, H.M. 'Reliability and validity of a short measure of attitude towards Christianity among secondary school pupils in England, Scotland and Northern Ireland', Collected Original Resources in Education, (forthcoming).
Status: Individual research
Date of Research: 1991-1992
KEYWORDS: attitude measures; Christianity; pupil attitudes; religious attitudes

9/1073
Carmarthen, Dyfed SA31 3EP
0267 237971
Francis, L. Dr; *Supervisor:* Francis, L. Dr
Secondary school pupils' attitudes towards science and religion
Abstract: This project is analysing data collected from 5,000 secondary school pupils in England to explore the relationships between attitudes to science, religion, creationism and scientism. Attitudes are measured by Likert scales. The findings are discussed against the background of Helmut Reich's theory of the development of complementarity, which enables people to coordinate apparently conflicting statments and to arrive at synoptic points of view.
Published Material: FRANCIS, L.J., GIBSON, H.M. & FULLJAMES, P. (1990). 'Attitudes towards Christianity, creationism, scientism and interest in science among 11-15 year olds', British Journal of Religious Education, Vol 13, No 1, pp.4-17, Autumn.
Status: Individual research
Date of Research: 1989-1992
KEYWORDS: pupil attitudes; religious attitudes; scientific attitudes; secondary school pupils

9/1074
Carmarthen, Dyfed SA31 3EP
0267 237971
Francis, L. Dr; *Supervisor:* Francis, L. Dr
Religion and attitude towards drug use among 13-15 year olds
Abstract: A sample of 4,753 thirteen to fifteen year olds attending the third and fourth year classes of twenty-nine secondary schools completed a questionnaire concerned with attitude towards the use of alcohol, butane gas, glue, heroin, marijuana and tobacco, together with indices of religious affiliation, belief and practice. The data demonstrate that young adolescents' attitudes towards drug use varies considerably from one substance to another and that religiosity is a significant predictor of attitude towards the use of each of the substances included in the survey.
Status: Individual research
Date of Research: 1990-1992
KEYWORDS: adolescent attitudes; drinking; drug abuse; religious attitudes; secondary school pupils; smoking; substance abuse

9/1075
Carmarthen, Dyfed SA31 3EP
0267 237971
Evans, G. Dr; Eynon, A. Mr; *Supervisor:* Evans, G. Dr
Planning for differentiation in the primary classroom
Abstract: This research will explore strategies for plannning for differentiated work. It is intended for children in primary schools to match their abilities and needs.
Status: Sponsored project
Source of Grant: Curriculum Council for Wales
Date of Research: 1990-1991
KEYWORDS: *educational planning; individual needs; individualised methods; primary schools; teaching methods*

9/1076
Carmarthen, Dyfed SA31 3EP
0267 237971
Francis, L. Prof.; *Supervisor:* Francis, L. Prof.; Greer, J. Rev Dr
Secondary school pupils' attitudes towards science and religion (Northern Ireland)
Abstract: This project is re-analysing data collected from 2,000 secondary school pupils attending Catholic and Protestant schools in Northern Ireland in order to explore the relationship between attitudes to science, religion, creationism and scientism. Attitudes are measured by Likert type scales.
Status: Individual research
Date of Research: 1992 - continuing
KEYWORDS: *Northern Ireland; pupil attitudes; religious studies; scientific attitudes; secondary school pupils*

Ulster University

9/1077
Department of Inservice Education, Cromore Road, Coleraine, County Londonderry BT52 1SA
0265 44141
Mallon, P. Mr; *Supervisor:* McGarvey, B. Dr
The impact of curriculum innovation in science in some small rural secondary schools
Abstract: The aim is to identify the range of issues which science teachers in small rural schools were facing in implementing the new Northern Ireland science curriculum at Key Stage 3. Open-ended case studies were conducted initially and then more focused case studies of four schools were carried out over a two-year period. The final report will describe the challenges which the new Science Curriculum is posing to small science departments and the responses being made.
Status: Individual research
Date of Research: 1988 - continuing
KEYWORDS: *Northern Ireland; rural schools; science curriculum; science education; small schools*

9/1078
Department of Inservice Education, Cromore Road, Coleraine, County Londonderry BT52 1SA
0265 44141
McGarvey, B. Dr; Harper, D. Mr; Day, J. Mrs
Differentiated learning in science project
Abstract: The aim of this project is to address the challenges of providing differentiated learning in science by developing and trialling suitable approaches to curriculum planning, teaching and assessing science at Northern Ireland Curriculum Key Stages 1, 2 and 3. Continuity and progression across the primary/secondary school interface will be a particularly important aspect. Two full-time project officers have been appointed and the work is proceeding through four phases: exploration of existing good practice; development work; trials and evaluation; production of guidelines, illustrative materials and INSET (Inservice Education of Teachers) materials.
Status: Sponsored project
Source of Grant: Northern Ireland Curriculum Council £213,378
Date of Research: 1992 - continuing
KEYWORDS: *curriculum development; individualised methods; Northern Ireland; science education*

9/1079
Department of Inservice Education, Cromore Road, Coleraine, County Londonderry BT52 1SA
0265 44141
Austin, R. Dr; *Supervisor:* Austin, R. Dr
Junior Certificate history in the Republic of Ireland: purpose, problems and potential
Abstract: The aim of this study is to explore the ways in which a national curriculum change in the teaching of history in the Republic of Ireland is being implemented in the classroom. A sample of teachers are completing questionnaires, and resource materials are being designed, used and evaluated to measure student reaction to the proposed changes. The research is set in the wider context of the history of curriculum change in the Republic of Ireland and the perceived value and interest of history to young people.
Status: Individual research
Date of Research: 1991 - continuing
KEYWORDS: *curriculum development; history; Ireland*

9/1080
Department of Inservice Education, Cromore Road, Coleraine, County Londonderry BT52 1SA
0265 44141
Chambers, M. Mrs; *Supervisor:* McGarvey, B. Dr
Learning psychiatric nursing skills: the contribution of the ward environment
Abstract: The aim of this study is to ascertain those factors which facilitate student psychiatric nurses in the learning of psychiatric nursing skills. A pilot study of an open-ended nature was conducted on wards, using the Delphi technique, interview and participant observation. The main study, involved more closely focused case studies of the learning experiences of eight students. The final report will compare and contrast the aims of the ward experience and the actual learning opportunities, and will discuss the roles of nursing and nurse education staff in supporting student learning on the ward.
Status: Individual research
Date of Research: 1987 - continuing
KEYWORDS: *Delphi technique; nurse education; psychiatric services*

9/1081
Department of Inservice Education, Cromore Road, Coleraine, County Londonderry BT52 1SA
0265 44141
McGarvey, B. Dr; McMahon, H. Mr; Creighton, N. Mr
The development of a computer-based system for records of achievement in science
Abstract: A computer-based records of achievement system for the Northern Ireland Curriculum Key Stage 3 in Science has been developed, using the Hypercard software of the Apple Macintosh microcomputer. Records are held in the language of the classroom materials and are updated as and when necessary. The system includes the facility to translate records into AT statements of attainment and to display the summary record as a grid or histogram-type display. Trials of the system took place in schools, and an in-house operator manual has been produced.
Status: Individual research
Date of Research: 1990-1991
KEYWORDS: *computer uses in education; Northern Ireland; records of achievement; science curriculum*

9/1082
Department of Inservice Education, Cromore Road, Coleraine, County Londonderry BT52 1SA
0265 44141
Greer, J. Rev.
Science and religion project
Abstract: The aim is to study the relationship between science and religion, with special reference to the problems faced by pupils at school. The sample was composed of 100 pupils from each of 24 grammar schools who completed original questionnaires, which were then revised. Preliminary analysis of data has been carried out and a first draft of a report has been written.
Status: Individual research
Date of Research: 1990-1992
KEYWORDS: *pupil attitudes; religious attitudes; scientific attitudes; secondary school pupils*

9/1083
Faculty of Education, Cromore Road, Coleraine, County Londonderry BT52 1SA
0265 44141
Logan, A. Mr; *Supervisor:* Daws, P. Dr; Livingston, R. Dr
Pupil opinion: a contribution to child-centred theory and to curriculum and staff development
Abstract: The concept of child-centredness in education can be viewed as an aspect of the wider movement to extend human rights to some of those who had hitherto been denied respect as persons; in this instance pupils. The advent of a centralised, statutory curriculum in Britain in the late 1980's has presented child-centredness with a series of challenges. However, pupils in schools, the only bona fide customers in the education system, claim when consulted, that teachers must protect the child-centred dimension in their teaching practice if pupils are to succeed and if learning is to be accessible to them. This thesis argues that one of the most practical and manageable ways of achieving this is to consult with pupils in a meaningful way. The thesis creates a context for the consideration of child-centredness, examines previous research that has been built on pupil views, suggests a model for consultation with pupils and presents their confidential responses. Analysis of the resultant data, especially qualitative data, suggests not only that pupils can respond with intelligence and concern but also that their opinions can inform and enhance the practice of every teacher, regardless of style or philosophy. Finally, this thesis shows that the use of pupil views within a process of curriculum review and staff development can contribute to the theory of child-centredness, adds significantly to teachers' underlying understandings of their job, and helps to ensure effective teaching, happy learning and an improvement in standards.
Status: Individual research
Date of Research: 1984-1991
KEYWORDS: *learner-centred curriculum; learner-centred methods; pupil attitudes; teacher pupil relationship*

9/1084
Faculty of Education, Cromore Road, Coleraine, County Londonderry BT52 1SA
0865 44141
Austin, R. Dr; *Supervisor:* Austin, R. Dr
The European Studies project
Abstract: The European Studies project was set up as a six year curriculum development programme for schools in England, Northern Ireland and the Republic of Ireland. It has been developing programmes of joint work in the curriculum for pupils aged 11-18. Those involved in the 14-16 and 16-18 schemes are also linked to schools in France, Belgium, Denmark, Germany and Scotland. Schools have been using common resources and computer and satellite television links to work together across Europe. From the 93 schools involved in 1991 it is intended that a wider programme of dissemination will be undertaken in 1992.
Published Material: A full list of project reports is available from the researcher.
Status: Sponsored project
Source of Grant: Departments of Education: Northern Ireland and Eire; Departments for Education: England, France, Belgium and Germany
Date of Research: 1986-1992
KEYWORDS: *cross cultural studies; curriculum development; European studies; international cooperation; regional cooperation*

9/1085
Faculty of Education, Department of Adult and Continuing Education, Cromore Road, Coleraine, County Londonderry BT52 1SA
0265 44141
Robinson, A. Mr; Dallat, J. Dr; Livingston, R. Dr
Teaching and learning by video-conferencing
Abstract: The University of Ulster installed a three-campus video-conferencing facility in 1990. The system is designed to permit technician-free operation, once the studios and equipment have been arranged, the tutor controlling robotic cameras on all sites by means of a touch-tablet. The purpose of the study is to evaluate the use of video-conferencing in the teaching of modules of study taken by adult students enrolled in the Postgraduate Diploma in Education (Professional Development) course, on two campuses separated by some 50 miles. Its aims are to consider the effectiveness of the learning that takes place, and the quality of interaction between tutors and students

and among students themselves. Data are gathered through questionnaires, interviews and observation of classes. Results confirmed expectations that tutor input would be largely unaffected by the new medium and also confirmed tutor fears on the difficulties of participant interaction and discussion as compared with conventional teaching. Tutors quickly mastered the operation of the equipment, but the effects of technical shortcomings in the system proved more difficult to overcome. Initial findings are that video-conferencing provides a valuable additional medium of distance education, that it is not directly comparable to face-to-face teaching, and that it requires its own rules of procedure and method of assessment.
Published Material: DALLAT, J., FRASER, G., LIVINGSTON, R. & ROBINSON, A. (1992). 'Teaching and learning by video-conferencing in the University of Ulster', Open Learning, Vol 7, No 2, pp.14-22.
Status: Individual research
Date of Research: 1990 - continuing
KEYWORDS: *distance education; higher education; inservice teacher education; teaching method; teleconferencing*

Ulster University at Jordanstown

9/1086
Shore Road, Newtownabbey, County Antrim BT37 OQB
0232 365131
Crouch, C. Mr
Children and television
Abstract: The research aims to provide a broad picture of children's use and understanding of television. To date, children of primary school age's (i.e. 7 to 11/12) preferences have been explored (sample of 3,700+ from Northern Ireland, England, Australia surveyed) and results have indicated early gender differences; females tending to prefer soap opera programmes increasingly by age. A second wave of research (sample of 1,000 Australian, circa 1,000 Northern Ireland 12 – 12/16 year olds) involves survey by questionnaire on a wide range of issues but with special emphasis on television and learning. These data remain to be analysed.
Published Material: CROUCH, C. (1989). 'Television and primary schoolchildren in Northern Ireland: 1: television programme preferences', Journal of Educational Television, Vol 15, No 13, pp.163-170.; CROUCH, C. (1989). 'Soap in the eyes: primary schoolgirl TV preferences', Metro: Media and Education Magazine, (Australia), No 81, pp.18-22, Summer.; CROUCH, C. (1991). 'The emergence of soap: primary schoolchildren's TV preferences in Northern Ireland, England and Australia', Research in Education, No 46, pp.73-83, November.
Status: Individual research
Date of Research: 1988 - continuing
KEYWORDS: *adolescents; children; television surveys; television viewing*

9/1087
Department of Inservice Education, Shore Road, Newtownabbey, County Antrim, BT37 0QB
0232 365131
Hutchinson, B. Dr
Appraising appraisal: quality control and quality assurance
Abstract: The project is investigating the processes of staff appraisal, quality control and assurance in the University of Ulster. The two principal methods of data collection are: (a) documentary evidence; (b) semi-structured interview. Transcripts of the interviews and the draft report, are cleared with the contributors before the interim and final reports are published. The evidence collected is analysed using the methods of triangulation and critical analysis.
Status: Sponsored project
Source of Grant: Ulster University: Faculty of Education £2,600
Date of Research: 1991-1992
KEYWORDS: *academic staff evaluation; evaluators; higher education; personnel evaluation; teacher evaluation*

9/1088
Regional Curriculum Base, Shore Road, Newtownabbey, County Antrim BT37 0QB
0232 365131

O'Reilly, B. Mr; *Supervisor:* O'Reilly, B. Mr
European adult education directory project (Northern Ireland)
Abstract: The aim of the project is to map out a description of the whole system of adult education in each of the European Community countries, to identify and provide an overview of organisations in the field of general non-vocational adult education and to provide a directory of the findings.
Published Material: O'REILLY, B. & YOUNG, E. (1991). Adult education directory preliminary report: Northern Ireland. Jordanstown: Regional Curriculum Base.
Status: Sponsored project
Source of Grant: European Bureau of Adult Education £2,131
Date of Research: 1991-1992
KEYWORDS: adult education; adult literacy; adult nonvocational education; comparative education; directories

University College of North Wales

9/1089
Department of Psychology, College Road, Bangor, Gwynedd
LL57 2DG
0248 351151
Miles, T. Prof.
Dyslexia and mathematics
Abstract: It is hypothesised that the mathematical difficulties of dyslexics are a consequence of the same anomaly of development which affects their literary skills. It has been shown (Pritchard, et al, 1989) that 15 dyslexic boys aged 12 to 14 had fewer 'number facts' available than a suitably matched control. Work is now in progress on the time needed by dyslexics and matched control to carry out different types of mathematical operations. Data on the mathematical performance of over 12,000 10 year-olds (Child Health and Education Study), including some dyslexics, are in the process of being analysed.
Published Material: MILES, T.R. (1989). 'Dyslexia and mathematics', Ace Reports, No 16, pp.16-20.; PRITCHARD, R.A., MILES, T.R., CHINN, S.J. & TAGGART, A.T. (1989). 'Dyslexia and knowledge of number facts', Links, Vol 14, No 3, pp.17-20.; MILES, T.R. & MILES, E. (Eds). (1991). Dyslexia and Mathematics. London: Routledge.
Status: Individual research
Date of Research: 1988 - continuing
KEYWORDS: dyslexia; learning disabilities; mathematics

9/1090
School of Education, Deiniol Road, Bangor, Gwynedd
LL57 2UW
0248 351151
Baker, C. Dr
The effectiveness of bilingual education in Wales
Abstract: The project will look at the results of computer analysis of the 1991 Census on the Welsh language studying spatial, age, oracy/literacy trends alongside immigration/emigration and the effects on Welsh language educational provision. The major focus of the project will be the relationship of these trends to Welsh medium education and the implications for present and future educational policy. The project will also include: a historical perspective of the growth of bilingual education in Wales 1939 – present; the National Curriculum and Assessment and the implications for bilingual education in Wales; county policies for Welsh language in education and the provision of Welsh medium teaching; recent conflicts and controversies over the Welsh language; perspectives of HMI reports on Welsh medium teaching; Welsh medium curriculum development projects; the provision of Welsh medium education in higher education and further education; Welsh language media and voluntary bodies such as Urdd and Ysgolion Meithrin.
Status: Sponsored project
Source of Grant: University of Wales, Faculty of Education £5,000
Date of Research: 1992 - continuing
KEYWORDS: bilingual education; bilingualism; educational policy; language policy; school effectiveness; Welsh; Welsh studies

9/1091
School of Education, Deiniol Road, Bangor, Gwynedd
LL57 2UW
0248 351151
Baker, C. Dr
Attitudes to the Welsh language and bilingualism
Abstract: The Welsh language has rapidly declined this century. At the turn of the century, some half of the population in Wales spoke Welsh. The Census of 1981 revealed that this figure had dropped to one in five residents in Wales. Attitude to the Welsh language is an important barometer of likely future language trends in Wales. In particular, previous research had indicated that attitudes to Welsh tend to decline during the early and middle teens. The research aims to investigate the reasons for change in attitude to the Welsh language amongst 13 to 16 year olds. An attitude survey of first, second and third year secondary pupils in 1988 will be repeated with the same pupils in 1990. Change in the attitude to Welsh of some 800 pupils will be examined in terms of youth culture, use of mass media, identification models, language and background of the home as well as the school and neighbourhood, type of school attended, self concept, achievement level, gender and age. In addition the research will examine attitude to bilingualism as a concept importantly different from attitude to Welsh
Status: Sponsored project
Source of Grant: Economic and Social Research Council £2,340
Date of Research: 1988-1992
KEYWORDS: attitudes; bilingualism; language policy; language usage; Welsh

9/1092
School of Education, Deiniol Road, Bangor, Gwynedd
LL57 2UW
0248 351151
Williams, I. Prof.; Baker, C. Dr
Evaluation of the National Curriculum assessment of Welsh (GWASG)
Abstract: The aim of this research is to carry out a comprehensive and detailed evaluation of National Curriculum assessment in first language (L1) and second language (L2) Welsh. The research issues can be summarised as: (1) The validity and reliability of teacher assessments (TAs); (2) Comparability, determining influences and patterning in TAs; (3) Variability in teacher interpretations of TAs; (4) Effects of aggregation on standard assessment task scores (SAs); (5) The validity of SAs; (6) Effects of sampling of SAs on assessment outcomes; (7) Comparability, determining influences and patterning in SAs across time; (8) Relationships between assessments and special educational needs pupils; (9) Relationships of assessments across key stages; (10) Quality of formative and summative information provided by the assessments. The process and effectiveness of teachers recording assessments and reporting to parents; (11) Effects of assessments on teaching and assessing L1 and L2 Welsh; (12) Comparability of TAs and SAs. Stability in patterns of difference. Commonality bases; (13) Comparability of assessments from two programmes at National Curriculum Key Stage 3; (14) The manageability of assessments for teachers; (15) Patterns in the take-up of non-statutory National Curriculum Key Stage 1 L2 Welsh materials; (16) Relationship between standardisation of assessment and School Examinations and Assessment Council (SEAC) (and preferably local education authority) training and guidance. Three approaches are being employed. These approaches may be termed the statistical, the representative survey and the expert. First, the assessment data require considerable statistical analysis to investigate issues of validity, reliability, comparability across context and time, patterns and relationships in the data. Second, there are issues requiring a wide-scale survey of teacher, classroom and school practices. By stratified random sampling across Wales, a thoroughly representative elicitation of local procedures and individual viewpoints is necessary. This is achieved by interviewing and questionnaires. Third, the special insights of expert educationists provides a deep and perceptive sensitivity to complement wide consensus viewpoints. A careful and judicious 'purposeful sample' of experts will provide detailed qualitative information to complement the quantitative statistical analysis and the part-qualitative/part quantitative approach of representative surveys. GWASG reports are available from SEAC.
Published Material: GWASG Report. KS3 Welsh First Language Assessment (Cy): Analysis of Assessment Record Booklet Data. Report for School Examinations and Assessment Council/Welsh Office (October 1992).; GWASG Report. KS3 Welsh Second Language Assessment (Ca): Analysis of Assessment Record Booklet

Data. Report for School Examinations and Assessment Council/Welsh Office (October 1992).; GWASG Report. Evaluation of the Bridges Assessment Pack for KS1 Second Language Welsh. Report for School Examinations and Assessment Council/Welsh Office (October 1992).; GWASG Report. KS1: An Analysis of Data from Assessment Record Booklets. Report for School Examinations and Assessment Council/Welsh Office (October 1992).; GWASG Report. National Curriculum Assessment and Welsh Medium Education: Trends in Recent Results. Report for School Examinations and Assessment Council/Welsh Office (October 1992).
Status: Sponsored project
Source of Grant: The Welsh Office £338,000
Date of Research: 1992 - continuing
KEYWORDS: *assessment; mother tongue; National Curriculum; school-based assessment; second language learning; standard assessment tasks; Welsh*

9/1093
School of Education, Deiniol Road, Bangor, Gwynedd LL57 2UW
0248 351151
Rees, W. Dr
Counselling in different settings
Abstract: The aim of this research is to discover whether there is a common core of counselling skills and approaches in different settings. Interviews have been taped and transcribed with hospital chaplains, hospital social workers, probation officers, drugs workers, and student counsellors
Status: Individual research
Date of Research: 1992 - continuing
KEYWORDS: *counselling; counsellor characteristics; counsellor performance; counsellors*

9/1094
School of English and Linguistics, College Road, Bangor, Gwynedd LL57 2DG
0248 351151
Scholfield, P. Mr
Vocabulary rate in course materials for English as a second or foreign language
Abstract: The research consists of analysing the rate of introduction of new vocabulary items, lesson by lesson, in a sample of well known course books for English as a second/foreign language. Using concepts of time series analysis, light is thrown on the patterns of rises and falls to be found. The results are interpreted in the light of learner needs and what the teacher can do when the rate in course materials is inappropriate.
Published Material: SCHOLFIELD, P.J. (1991). 'Vocabulary rate in course books: living with an unstable lexical economy', Proceedings of 5th International Linguistics Symposium, Aristotle University, Thessaloniki.
Status: Individual research
Date of Research: 1989 - continuing
KEYWORDS: *educational materials; English – second language; textbooks; vocabulary development*

9/1095
School of English and Linguistics, College Road, Bangor, Gwynedd LL57 2DG
0248 351151
El Sakran, T. Dr; *Supervisor:* James, C. Dr
Footnotes in academic written discourse: a formal and functional analysis
Abstract: The aim of the study is to investigate the structures of footnotes in academic texts, their different types, their utility to the reader in understanding the texts they accompany, and their disruptive effect on reading comprehension.
Status: Sponsored project
Source of Grant: Egyptian Government Scholarship
Date of Research: 1987-1991
KEYWORDS: *citations – references; reader-text relationship; reading comprehension; text structure*

9/1096
School of Sociology and Social Policy, College Road, Bangor, Gwynedd LL57 2DG

0248 351151
Betts, S. Ms; Garland, P. Ms; *Supervisor:* Betts, S. Ms
Returning to learning: mature students in higher education
Abstract: This research investigates the transitions of students returning to higher education. It considers the pathways and turning points as well as the experiences of mature students in higher education. Most importantly the research highlights gender differences in the pathways and experiences of mature students and seeks to explain these in the wider context of gender divisions in society.
Status: Sponsored project
Source of Grant: University College of North Wales: School of Sociology and Social; Policy £2,000
Date of Research: 1990 - continuing
KEYWORDS: *higher education; mature students; sex differences*

University College of Swansea

9/1097
Centre for Applied Language Studies, Singleton Park, Swansea SA2 8PP
0792 205678
Meara, P. Dr
Word recognition problems among Arabic-speaking learners of English
Abstract: The background of the research lies in the problems Arabic learners of English seem to have in distinguishing English words with similar consonant structure, e.g. broad/bread; curl/cereal. After several initial attempts to design test procedures which would replicate this type of error, a computer-based word-recognition test was developed in which firstly vowels and then secondly consonants were systematically deleted from word stimuli presented to the subjects. The test records response-times and error rates for each subject. Two initial experiments of this type indicated that there was a significant difference between the responses of, on the one hand, Arabic speaking subjects and on the other, native speakers and speakers of European languages written in Roman script. This difference was maintained in the final experiment where Arabic speaking subjects were compared with Japanese, Thai and European language speakers as well as native speakers of English, a total of 131 subjects. In spite of the overall significance of the results of the Arabic speaking group, there were considerable individual differences between subjects; this has prompted the final phase of the study in which it is hoped to design a simple diagnostic test to predict those subjects who are most likely to have word-handling difficulties of the type analysed here. Such a test would have considerable classroom value.
Published Material: RYAN, A. & MEARA, P. (1991). 'The case of the invisible vowels: Arabic speakers reading English words', Reading in a Foreign Language, Vol 7, No 2, pp.531-540.
Status: Individual research
Date of Research: 1987 - continuing
KEYWORDS: *Arabs; English – second language; vowels; word recognition*

9/1098
Centre for Applied Language Studies, Singleton Park, Swansea SA2 8PP
0792 205678
Meara, P. Dr
Lexical behaviour in a second language
Abstract: This project comprises a group of linked studies aimed at improving our understanding of vocabulary acquisition in foreign languages. The project includes: (1) a large scale bibliographical survey; (2) development of lexical tests; and (3) a set of linked PhD projects on lexical difficulties of second language speakers.
Published Material: A list of publications is available from the researcher.
Status: Sponsored project
Source of Grant: Eurocentres; Longmans; TVEI; University of Oxford Local Examinations Delegacy; BBC English
Date of Research: 1981 - continuing
KEYWORDS: *second language learning; vocabulary development*

9/1099
Department of Education, Hendrefoilan, Swansea SA2 7NB

0792 201231
Banks, F. Mr
An evaluation of distance learning Inservice Education of Teachers (INSET) in Wales
Abstract: The problems of geographical isolation and the small number of teachers requiring Inservice Education of Teachers (INSET) in some curriculum areas make distance learning an attractive option for many Welsh local education authorities. The study seeks to illuminate both effective course design and good practice in local education authority (LEA) management of teacher support. Teachers in Wales, from all LEAs, involved in (initially) one distance learning INSET programme have been interviewed about their perceived progress and satisfaction with the course, its delivery, and the extent to which they think the course will alter their practice. An attempt will be made to design an evaluation method which will include a longitudinal study of how teachers change over time following an INSET experience. They were asked to give factual details of patterns of study and use of the materials. The INSET coordinators from the corresponding LEAs have been asked to supply details of the support they are prepared to give to the teachers in terms of fees, expenses, free time, etc., and have been interviewed to gather their opinion of the effectiveness of the programmes.
Status: Sponsored project
Source of Grant: University of Wales: Faculty of Education £3,400
Date of Research: 1989 - continuing
KEYWORDS: *inservice teacher education; programme effectiveness; teacher attitudes; teacher development*

9/1100

Department of Education, Hendrefoilan, Swansea SA2 7NB
0792 201231
Rowe, M. Mr; Tanner, H. Mr; Davies, L. Ms; Morgan-Jones, P. Mr; Prichard, J. Ms
Teacher competencies and professional development
Abstract: Action research is being conducted in Swansea, Aberystwyth and Bangor to develop a framework of competencies for use in initial teacher education. Techniques and documentation are being developed to establish records of achievement for student teachers. The success of the competencies and records of achievement will then be evaluated.
Status: Sponsored project
Source of Grant: University of Wales
Date of Research: 1991 - continuing
KEYWORDS: *competence; competency-based teacher education; preservice teacher education; records of achievement; student teacher*

9/1101

Department of Education, Hendrefoilan, Swansea SA2 7NB
0792 201231
Tanner, H. Mr
The information technology in mathematics project
Abstract: This is a survey of the use of information technology for teaching mathematics in England and Wales. A network of schools has been set up to develop and trial materials and techniques for teaching elements from both the Mathematics and Information Technology (IT) National Curricula. It includes work on spreadsheets, logo and databases.
Status: Sponsored project
Source of Grant: University of Wales
Date of Research: 1989 - continuing
KEYWORDS: *computer uses in education; information technology; mathematics education*

9/1102

Department of Education, Hendrefoilan, Swansea SA2 7NB
0792 201231
Tanner, H. Mr
Teacher assessment of the National Curriculum
Abstract: A network of schools was established to conduct action research into the development of teacher assessment of the National Curriculum in key stage 3. Local education authority advisers were surveyed to establish the extent of guidance offered to teachers. Groups of teachers, trainers and advisers have been meeting to develop guidance materials.
Status: Sponsored project
Source of Grant: University of Wales; Association of Teachers of Mathematics

Date of Research: 1989 - continuing
KEYWORDS: *assessment; National Curriculum; school-based assessment*

9/1103

Department of Education, Hendrefoilan, Swansea SA2 7NB
0792 201231
Hendley, D. Mr; Parkinson, J. Dr; Stables, A. Dr; Tanner, H. Mr; Thomas, B. Mrs
Pupil attitudes to English, Mathematics, Science, Technology and Welsh under the National Curriculum
Abstract: A questionnaire has been developed, using a Likert-type scale, to measure the attitudes of pupils in years 2 and 3 of secondary schools (years 8 and 9 of the National Curriculum) over a period of two years. The degree to which the implementation of the National Curriculum has affected attitudes will be ascertained.
Status: Individual research
Date of Research: 1991 - continuing
KEYWORDS: *National Curriculum; pupil attitudes; secondary schools*

9/1104

Department of Education, Hendrefoilan, Swansea SA2 7NB
0792 201231
Furlong, J. Prof.
The role of the mentor in initial teacher education
Abstract: This is an in-depth study of the work of eight 'mentors' in different programmes of initial teacher education.
Status: Sponsored project
Source of Grant: Paul Hamlyn Foundation £14,000
Date of Research: 1992 - continuing
KEYWORDS: *mentors; preservice teacher education*

9/1105

Department of Education, Hendrefoilan, Swansea SA2 7NB
0792 201231
Kennewell, S. Mr
The differences in teaching and learning styles employed in primary and secondary schools with reference to developing information technology capability
Abstract: This pilot project aims to: (1) identify current approaches to the teaching and learning of information technology (IT) in years 6 and 7 and establish an appropriate observation schedule; (2) examine the nature of changes in approach to learning IT for pupils transferring from primary to secondary school; (3) explore methods of evaluating teaching and learning where IT is involved; and (4) identify teaching approaches and learning materials which will help schools support continuity of learning and enhance progression. The work will specifically consider the development of pupils' mental models for IT systems and processes through practical problem solving. The methods used will include: (1) a questionnaire to year 6 teachers in a sample of primary schools, and year 7 teachers whose pupils learn IT in their lessons in a sample of secondary schools; (2) an ethnographic study of a number of lessons in two secondary and two feeder primary schools; (3) interviews with pupils; and (4) analysis of learning resources.
Status: Sponsored project
Source of Grant: University of Wales: Faculty of Education £1,500
Date of Research: 1992-1992
KEYWORDS: *developmental continuity; information technology; learning strategies; primary secondary education; teaching methods; transfer of learning*

9/1106

Department of Education, Hendrefoilan, Swansea SA2 7NB
0792 201231
Kennewell, S. Mr
Permeating the learning of information technology across the secondary school curriculum
Abstract: Attainment target 5 of the National Curriculum Technology requirement specifies that pupils should develop information technology (IT) capability. The non-statutory guidance suggests strongly that this should be achieved through subjects other than specialist IT/computing lessons. This project aims to identify the extent to which IT had permeated the curriculum of all secondary schools in one Welsh county by mid-1990, and what short-term plans schools had for developing this aspect of the curriculum. Data on individual

curriculum activities involving IT in all subjects were collected within the county and this is being analysed to compare the amount of IT use according to: (a) existing and planned provision; (b) ages of pupils; (c) subjects; (d) course units within each subject; (e) types of IT activity; (f) types of school; and (g) advisory support received.
Status: Sponsored project
Source of Grant: University College of Swansea: Department of Education: 500
Date of Research: 1991-1992
KEYWORDS: *cross curricular approach; information technology; National Curriculum; secondary education; technology education*

9/1107
Department of Education, Hendrefoilan, Swansea SA2 7NB
0792 201231
Jephcote, M. Mr; *Supervisor:* Williams, M. Prof.
Economic awareness as a curriculum entitlement for Welsh pupils
Abstract: The study is to facilitate the development of economic awareness in primary and secondary schools in Wales. The project has curriculum development and curriculum research aspects. On the research side the focus is on the preparation of case studies of individual schools and upon pupils' cognitive growth.
Status: Sponsored project
Source of Grant: Welsh Office; Esme Fairbairn Trust
Date of Research: 1990 - continuing
KEYWORDS: *cross curricular approach; curriculum development; economics education; enterprise education; primary education; secondary education; wales*

9/1108
Department of Education, Hendrefoilan, Swansea SA2 7NB
0792 201231
Tanner, H. Mr; Jones, S. Mrs
The use and practical application of mathematics in a cross curricular context in National Curriculum key stage 4
Abstract: The research examines and develops approaches for teaching and assessing attainment target one of National Curriculum Mathematics in Wales. The research is based initially on the techniques of mathematical modelling and subsequently on applications of mathematics in a cross curricular context. A network of schools in South Wales is conducting action research into the teaching of mathematics through its practical applications. The project aims to: (1) identify relevant approaches to teaching mathematics in a practical context; (2) establish the extent to which the techniques of modelling can be taught in key stage 4; (3) develop materials for use in schools to teach mathematics in a practical context; (4) develop assessment techniques and materials; and (5) consider ways of integrating practical approaches into programmes of study.
Status: Sponsored project
Source of Grant: Welsh Office £64,000
Date of Research: 1991-1992
KEYWORDS: *assessment; attainment tests; cross curricular approach; mathematical models; mathematics education; National Curriculum; secondary education; teaching methods*

9/1109
Department of Education, Hendrefoilan, Swansea SA2 7NB
0792 201231
Tomlinson, S. Prof.
Alternatives in education: an investigation of past, present and future policies in education
Abstract: The aim of this research is to lay the basis for suggesting alternatives to current educational policies by a critical analysis of historical and ideological developments in education from 1944 to 1992. It will include an examination of the nature of and purposes behind the Education Reform Act 1988; an analysis of how the Act and subsequent reforms are working out; and whose interests are being served. The methodology is a library study and 'action research' with the researcher participating in various national political committees and associations concerned with changing educational policies.
Published Material: TOMLINSON, S. (1991). 'Yet another repeat', Times Educational Supplement, 1.11.91.; TOMLINSON, S. & ROSS, A.M. (1991). 'Teachers and parents', Education and Training Paper No 7. London: Institute for Public Policy Research.
Status: Sponsored project
Source of Grant: Leverhulme Trust £20,500

Date of Research: 1990-1992
KEYWORDS: *Education Reform Act 1988; educational change; educational history; educational policy*

9/1110
Department of Sociology and Anthropology, Singleton Park, Swansea SA2 8PP
0792 205678
Adams, S. Ms; *Supervisor:* Harris, C. Prof.
Mature students in higher education
Abstract: The research aims to look into the possible source of insight mature students (especially women) may offer into changing gender relations in the family and in society. There is also the question of why the numbers of mature women students is rising. This can be partly explained by the fact that, due to demographic changes, more mature women are needed in the labour market and access to university is now being made easier for them. It can also be partly explained by women now having more control over their fertility and by changes in women's employment patterns and economic participation rates. The rising numbers may also be partly explained by a change in women's self-perceptions due partially to two decades of activity by the Women's Movement. The researcher is interested in how mature women, particularly those who have experienced a change in self-perception, get on in university. Does higher education deal equitably with the needs of mature male and female students? The research will look at changes in life courses and whether men's life courses affect women's to a far greater extent than vice-versa. It will also investigate how women experience directly the pressures imposed on them to be good wives, mothers, daughters, etc; how they negotiate their own social and sociological reality in this situation; how they negotiate this reality as mature students; and what changes and of what type may occur. Related to this is an analysis of the way in which women are inscribed in unequal, passive and subordinate relations by the State, the law and all the other spheres which have the ability to shape their lives.
Status: Individual research
Date of Research: 1989-1992
KEYWORDS: *gender equality; higher education; mature students; sex differences; women; women's education*

University College of Wales, Aberystwyth

9/1111
Department of Information and Library Studies, Llanbadarn Fawr, Aberystwyth, Dyfed SY23 2AX
0970 622189
Preston, G. Mrs; Barber, J. Mrs; *Supervisor:* Baggs, C. Mr
To initiate a distance learning undergraduate degree course in information and library studies
Abstract: In the light of current moves towards providing greater opportunities for mature adults with non-traditional educational qualifications to gain access to higher education, and the Universities Funding Council's (UFC) programme to encourage flexibility in course provision, it was proposed to set up a research and development programme to initiate a distance learning undergraduate degree course in information and library studies. The aim of the project is to investigate the scope and management of current distance learning provision; to evaluate the relative merits of different methods of course provision, including developments in educational technology; to look at methods of assessment for student-centred learning; and to develop quality control mechanisms appropriate for academic and professional validation. High attrition rates experienced in some models of distance learning provision make it important to assess how inherent problems such as student support and adequate resourcing may be overcome. This will lead to the design of a course aimed at mature non-traditional entrants currently or recently employed in a library or information environment, who wish to gain a professional qualification. The production of student-centred learning packages will involve research into developing Computer Assisted Learning (CAL) and video-conferencing to supplement traditional print-based materials.
Status: Sponsored project
Source of Grant: Universities Funding Council £63,100

Date of Research: 1992 - continuing
KEYWORDS: *distance education; flexible learning; information science; librarianship education; mature students*

University of Central England in Birmingham

9/1112
Faculty of Education, Centre for Advanced Studies in Education, Westbourne Road, Edgbaston, Birmingham B15 3TN
021 331 6130
Cavendish, M. Mr; *Supervisor:* Hellawell, D. Prof.
Going grant-maintained: a case study of change from a management perspective
Abstract: The investigation will cover a three year period (1990-93) during which the researcher's school will become grant-maintained. The intention is to develop an interpretive account of the management of change over the period, examining roles, structures and processes of management.
Status: Individual research
Date of Research: 1992 - continuing
KEYWORDS: *educational administration; educational change; grant maintained schools; school-based management*

9/1113
Faculty of Education, Centre for Advanced Studies in Education, Westbourne Road, Edgbaston, Birmingham B15 3TN
021 331 6130
Brooks, R. Ms; *Supervisor:* Cherrington, D. Prof.; Rowley, K. Mr
Social skills training in the classroom: effects on sociometric status
Abstract: The aims of this research are: (1) To present a review of current sociometric research and materials in the area of children's friendship choices and social adjustment in the classroom; (2) Use sociographic techniques to assess the patterns of specific friendship choices which exist in classes (e.g. popular children, reciprocated pairs, isolates, etc.); (3) Assess the personality and behavioural characteristics of specific 'types' of children (as identified in (2) using the Junior Eysenck and behavioural observations; (4) Intervene to coach the identified 'isolated' children in specific social skills, e.g. asking questions, offering directions to peers; (5) Ascertain what effect(s) the social skill training (as in (4)) has on overall peer acceptance and popularity within the class; (6) Provide an in-depth examination of individual isolates, including the perceptions of friendship, and reasons for sociometric choices made; (7) For individual isolates (as in (6)) examine the family structure, number of siblings, contact with other social networks (e.g. clubs, church) which affect their social experience and competence.
Status: Individual research
Date of Research: 1992 - continuing
KEYWORDS: *intergroup relations; pupil behaviour; social skills; sociometric techniques*

9/1114
Faculty of Education, Centre for Advanced Studies in Education, Westbourne Road, Edgbaston, Birmingham B15 3TN
021 331 6130
Cabral, B. Ms; *Supervisor:* Davis, D. Mr; Cherrington, D. Prof.
Towards a common form of assessment in drama as a methodology and as a performance art
Abstract: The aims of this research are to: (1) Search for a model of assessment for drama in education, both as a methodology and as a performance mode, which represents achievement in drama, not excluding the possibility of achievement in other subject matters as well; (2) Pinpoint the different ways both approaches deal with dramatic conventions and rules, and how these differences interfere in the assessment schemes; (3) Analyse the performance of the reader (audience, self-spectator) as a main element in assessment schemes; (4) Compare the assessment provided by the fellow student (audi-

ence) or by the student himself (self-spectator) with the one provided by the teacher; (5) Analyse the links between the plurality of audience assessment and the possibility of open-ended productions, i.e. a non-closed conclusion to the art-form.
Status: Sponsored project
Source of Grant: Ministry of Education, Brazil
Date of Research: 1992 - continuing
KEYWORDS: *assessment; audience response; drama education; dramatics*

University of Central Lancashire

9/1115
Corporation Street, Preston PR1 2TQ
0772 201201
Brattan, D. Dr
Open learning methods in chemistry
Abstract: Preparation, use of, and evaluation of open learning texts, video and computer based materials, in physical and analytical chemistry. The main aims of this research are to evaluate a change to learning rather than teaching methods and to examine ways of increasing access to higher education. Evaluation will be by interview and questionnaire.
Status: Sponsored project
Source of Grant: University of Central Lancashire/Pickup/Enterprise
Date of Research: 1988 - continuing
KEYWORDS: *chemistry; educational materials; higher education; open education*

9/1116
Corporation Street, Preston PR1 2TQ
0772 201201
Dodd, J. Dr; *Supervisor:* Goulding, K. Prof.
A competence framework in chemistry
Abstract: Recent changes in Business and Technician Education Council (BTEC) policy towards 'competences and transferable skills' call for an urgent response from course teams. The Faculty granted the researcher a six-month secondment (February-August 1992) to make progress in this area. The aim of the project is to develop a competence framework, primarily (but not exclusively) for HND/HNC courses in chemistry – along with supporting materials and delivery systems. The proposed activities are liaison with other course teams in Faculty/University, and with the Faculty Support Group; visits to other institutions (to discover examples of good practice); consultations in industry to provide resource material, and to discuss joint assessment procedures in student placements and works based projects; and the development of related student centred learning materials. The proposed outcomes of the research will be a coherent strategy for a competence framework in BTEC chemistry/science courses; the development of quality materials for use in teaching/learning situations; and the facilitating (and assessment) of transferable skills within the curriculum. Evaluation will take the form of a written report, possibly on educational methods workshop, and some testing on student groups.
Status: Sponsored project
Source of Grant: University of Central Lancashire Faculty of Science
£ 2,500
Date of Research: 1992-1992
KEYWORDS: *Business and Technician Education Council; chemistry education; competency-based education; course objectives; vocational education*

9/1117
Department of Psychology, Preston, Lancashire PR1 2TQ
0772 201201
Wolverhampton Polytechnic, Department of Psychology, Molineux Street, Wolverhampton WV1 1SB
0902 321000
McDonald, M. Ms
Gender roles in adolescent girls
Abstract: A sample of 43 girls aged 10-15 years from the northwest of the United Kingdom were interviewed about their own, and other girls' preferences and choices regarding sports, school subjects, occupations and leisure interests. Their gender-role attitudes were

also examined by means of two other methods: (1) responses to vignettes involving gender-role dilemmas; (2) repertory grids involving supplied and elicited elements. Grids were represented a year later to provide a limited longitudinal design. The interview data has been analysed separately in relation to the four topics. Quantitative analysis showed that the answers for both sports and school subjects departed from established stereotypes. There was little support for the hypothesis that gender-role activities become accentuated at adolescence. Qualitative analysis revealed a number of gender related themes in these answers. The remaining data from the project is being analysed. Supplementary studies have been provided by rating-scale investigations of the gender-stereotyping of school subjects (Archer & Freedman, 1989; Archer & Macrae, 1991), and the research has been integrated into more general theoretical work on gender-role development (Archer, 1984, 1989).
Published Material: ARCHER, J. & FREEDMAN, S. (1989). 'Gender-stereotypic perceptions of academic disciplines', British Journal of Educational Psychology, No 59, pp.306-313.; ARCHER, J. & MACDONALD, M. (1991). 'Gender roles and school subjects in adolescent girls', Educational Research, Vol 33, No 1.; ARCHER, J. (1989). 'Childhood gender roles: structure and development', The Psychologist, No 9, pp.367-370.; ARCHER, J. & MACDONALD, M. (1990). 'Gender roles and sports in adolescent girls', Leisure Studies, No 9, pp.225-240.
Status: Sponsored project
Source of Grant: Lancashire Polytechnic
Date of Research: 1984 - continuing
KEYWORDS: girls; sex differences; sex stereotypes

9/1118
 Corporation Street, Preston PR1 2TQ
 0772 201201
 Manchester University, Department of Psychology, Oxford Road, Manchester M13 9PL
 061 275 2000
 Walker, P. Dr; Hitch, G. Dr; Lewis, C. Dr; *Supervisor:* Walker, P. Dr; Hitch, G. Dr
Cognitive impairments in children with arithmetical learning disabilities
Abstract: This project aims to discover why some children of normal intelligence have great difficulty with elementary arithmetic. In some cases arithmetical difficulties are associated with reading problems, in others they occur in isolation. The project will identify children with arithmetical learning disability and will investigate cognitive impairments in different subgroups using tasks designed to explore working memory, the part of the cognitive system responsible for storing and manipulating temporary information. The hypothesis is that children with specific arithmetical difficulties have impaired working memory for visuo-spatial information, whereas children with learning problems in both arithmetic and reading have impaired working memory for phonological information. These deficits will be analysed in relation to the way working memory normally develops in order to distinguish developmental lag from other kinds of abnormality. The researchers will test the prediction that different kinds of impairment to working memory are related to the kinds of difficulty children experience in simple arithmetic tasks. The results will contribute to diagnosis and assessment of arithmetical learning disabilities, and to the planning of more effective remediation.
Status: Sponsored project
Source of Grant: Medical Research Council £80,000
Date of Research: 1990 - continuing
KEYWORDS: arithmetic; cognitive ability; learning disabilities

9/1119
 Corporation Street, Preston PR1 2TQ
 0772 201201
 University of Northumbria at Newcastle, The Educational Development Service, Ellison Building, Ellison Place, Newcastle upon Tyne NE1 8ST
 091 232 6002
 Cotton, R. Dr; McDowell, L. Ms; *Supervisor:* Cotton, R. Dr; McDowell, L. Ms
Course assessment and its role in the learning process
Abstract: Learning styles and perceptions of the learning environment were investigated for the Higher National Diploma in Science (Applied Biology) students at Lancashire Polytechnic using a previously published questionnaire. The questionnaire was further developed to assess the relative merit of a variety of course work

assessments in promoting learning. This was supported by student interviews. It was concluded that a diversity of assessment types is required to maximise learning from continual assessment.
Published Material: COTTON, R. & MCDOWELL, L. (1990). 'Student experiences of course assessment'. In: FARMER, B., EASTCOTT, D. & LANTZ, B. (Eds). Making learning systems work – aspects of educational and training technology, Vol 23, London: Kogan-Page.; MCDOWELL, L. (1991). 'Course assessment and its role in the learning process'. In: MCDOWELL, L. (Ed). Course evaluation: using students experiences of learning and teaching. Newcastle Polytechnic: The Educational Development Service.
Status: Sponsored project
Source of Grant: Council for National Academic Awards £50,000
Date of Research: 1988-1991
KEYWORDS: assessment; continuous assessment; coursework; learning processes

University of East Anglia

9/1120
 School of Education, Norwich NR4 7TJ
 0603 56161
 Davies, R. Dr
PALM (Pupil Autonomy in Learning with Micros) Extension
Abstract: Between 1988 and 1990, the PALM (Pupil Autonomy in Learning with Micros) project was undertaken to support information technology development in schools using action research methods. The aim was to explore the possibility of improving teaching and learning in the classroom supported by microcomputers. It also aimed to use classroom based action research to investigate and develop pedagogies that were most appropriate for working with the new technologies. The term 'autonomy' was used because its problematic nature served to stimulate enquiry. The extension project is a feasibility study to investigate the extent to which it is possible to disseminate PALM project methods to other local education authorities.
Status: Sponsored project
Source of Grant: National Council for Educational Technology £16,000
Date of Research: 1990-1991
KEYWORDS: computer-assisted learning; computer uses in education; microcomputers; personal autonomy

9/1121
 School of Education, Norwich NR4 7TJ
 0603 56161
 Somekh, B. Ms
INTENT (Initial Teacher Education and New Technology)
Abstract: Project INTENT has been set up as a response to the report, 'Information Technology in Initial Teacher Training' (DES, HMSO (1989)) and the revised criteria of the Council for Accreditation of Teacher Education (1989). It is concerned with supporting development work with information technology (IT) in Initial Teacher Training. It has four main foci: (1) developing the quality of teaching and learning with IT; (2) providing support for lecturers integrating IT across the curriculum for initial teacher training; (3) developing management strategies to enable (1) and (2) above; (4) monitoring the processes of institutional change. In five initial teacher training establishments (two university departments, two colleges and a polytechnic department) a staff development tutor (with no teaching responsibility for the first year) and a senior manager are leading the development process and monitoring its impact. INTENT has an educational rather than a technological focus, and is adopting a research approach to development, believing research and formative evaluation to be essential components of successful development work. In addition to the action-focused research activities at the core of its work, INTENT is supporting individual tutors and lecturers engaging in IT related research, using a range of methodologies. Outcomes will include case studies and associated research reports. There will be an emphasis on sharing the practical and theoretical findings of the project with colleagues in other initial teacher training establishments. During 1991/92 INTENT will produce a series of occasional papers, presenting work from both participating institutions and other initial teacher training establishments.
Status: Sponsored project
Source of Grant: National Council for Educational Technology £113,114

Date of Research: 1990-1992
KEYWORDS: information technology; preservice teacher education

9/1122
School of Education, Norwich NR4 7TJ
0603 56161
Stronach, I. Dr; Frankham, J. Ms; *Supervisor:* Stronach, I. Dr
Parents and teenagers: understanding and improving communication about Human Immunodeficiency Virus/Acquired Immune Deficiency Syndrome (HIV/AIDS)
Abstract: The project will investigate whether and how parents and teenagers discuss matters relating to Human Immunodeficiency Virus/Acquired Immune Deficiency Syndrome (HIV/AIDS) and sexual behaviour. It aims to improve communication within families through the generation of research based educational materials and advice. The study will involve an initial survey of parental attitudes (sample size = 50) and reported behaviour, followed by detailed and voluntary case studies (sample size = 10) of parent/teenager relations in the area. These data will form the basis for the development of educational materials.
Status: Sponsored project
Source of Grant: AIDS Education and Research Trust (AVERT)
£20,000
Date of Research: 1991-1992
KEYWORDS: Acquired Immune Deficiency Syndrome; adolescents; health education; parent attitudes; parent-child relationship; sexually transmitted diseases; speech communication

9/1123
School of Education, Norwich NR4 7TJ
0603 56161
Hayhoe, M. Mr
Adolescents' responses to short stories as representations of other cultures
Abstract: The International Poetry Response Project undertook as one of its themes the investigation of adolescents' means of coping with poems from other cultures which also used English as the main language. The Short Story Response Project will investigate adolescents' understanding of and response to stories from Canada and India which were written in English. Comparison will be made between the views of United Kingdom students and students from the countries from which the stories originate. It is hoped that this pilot study will lead to a major one in two years time.
Status: Sponsored project
Source of Grant: University of East Anglia: School of Education
£350
Date of Research: 1990-1992
KEYWORDS: adolescents; cross cultural studies; reader response; short stories; story telling

9/1124
School of Education, Norwich NR4 7TJ
0603 56161
Brown, C. Mrs
Sex related differences in children's technological achievements in the middle years with special reference to the use of construction materials
Abstract: A study by the Assessment of Performance Unit (APU) showed that experience with construction materials was markedly different in boys and girls. The rise in scientific and technological work in the primary curriculum has made the study of its nature and extent essential. The current study follows on from an initial study in which the gender gap was documented over a period of four years. In this study the quantity and quality of models produced by pupils across the first school age range as a result of specific arrangements facilitating equal access to materials was monitored. Criteria for models made by each year group were drawn up to indicate the range of achievement. The criteria were used to support the teachers, not only in ensuring equal access to materials, but also to structure the work to enable the children to try to meet as many of the criteria as possible. Such structured opportunities were found to narrow the gender gap further than simply ensuring equal access for girls to the construction materials. Consequently a programme offering suggestions for learning opportunities with construction materials was devised for each class in the school. In 1990/91 a class of children who have received such structured opportunities throughout their entire time in the school were again monitored in their final year. The results showed that the gender gap had narrowed further but had not closed. It was decided therefore that the study of this cohort of children, for whom data exists from entry to school at 4+ years, should continue into the middle years. A second phase of data collection began in 1991/92 and findings from that academic year indicate that during that year the performance gap had closed according to the criteria used to assess implementation of science concepts in the models made. It was evident that in the variety of models made and the modification or origination of models the girls still lagged behind the boys. These aspects in addition to the implementation of science concepts will continue to be monitored as the cohort progresses through 1992/93.
Published Material: BROWN, C.A. (1989). 'Girls, boys and technology: getting to the roots of the problem: a study of differential achievement in the early years', School Science Review, Vol 71, No 255, pp.138-142.; BROWN, C.A. (1990). 'Girls, boys and technology: some observations of general progress and of gender related differences in achievement when using construction sets in the early years', School Science Review, Vol 71, No 257, pp.33-40.; BROWN, C.A. (1991). 'What are little girls made of? A study of technology in the early years', Educational Studies, Vol 17, No 1, pp.107-113.; BROWN, C.A. (1991). 'Using construction sets in a primary curriculum', Primary Science Review, No 17, pp.22-24.
Status: Sponsored project
Source of Grant: University of East Anglia
Date of Research: 1991 - continuing
KEYWORDS: construction – process; construction materials; equal facilities; gender equality; primary education; science education; sex differences; technology education

9/1125
School of Education, Norwich NR4 7TJ
0603 56161
Ormell, C. Mr
Analysis of understanding as an educational aim and ways to detect its achievement
Abstract: The research is aimed at answering the question, 'how can we detect whether a child understands something, using objective behavioural methods?'. In most cases, 'understanding x' means 'having a fully assimilated model of x'. The chief assessment method consists of seeing whether children can apply the model swiftly and confidently to new circumstances. The central issue reduces to how to generate suitable 'new circumstances' in the numbers and variety required. To achieve reliability a lot of testing is needed, but this is only acceptable if the child's assessment experiences are also prime learning experiences. This means that the 'circumstances' used need to meet high standards of relevance, interest and memorability from the child's point of view. A major parameter is the degree to which the curriculum is 'liberal'. The more 'liberal' the curriculum the more distant its topics from the child's immediate experience. This makes it harder to devise appropriate 'new circumstances', but unless this problem can be solved, the production of behavioural tests for understanding will fail. The problem has been solved (see Ormell 1988, 1991) by the use of counter-factual and counter-fictional contexts. The project 'Children's application readiness with basic mathematics', applies the general methods devised in this project to the example of mathematics.
Published Material: ORMELL, C.P. (1988). 'Is there a future for liberal education?', Cambridge Journal of Education, Vol 18, No 2, pp.167-177.; ORMELL, C.P. (1991). Behavioural objectives in education. Geelong, Australia: Deakin University Press.; ORMELL, C.P. (1992). 'Behavioural objectives revisited', Educational Research, Vol 34, No 1, pp.23-33.; ORMELL, C.P. (1992). 'Is content good for your health?', Cambridge Journal of Education, Vol 22, No 2, pp.227-242.
Status: Individual research
Date of Research: 1978 - continuing
KEYWORDS: behavioural objective; comprehension; educational objectives; learning experience; test use

9/1126
School of Education, Norwich NR4 7TJ
0603 56161
Wright, D. Mr
Pupils as evaluators of textbooks
Abstract: Textbooks for pupils are reviewed by teachers, not by pupils. Pupils are encouraged nowadays in school to express opinions and to evaluate evidence. The research seeks to experiment with

pupils as reviewers of textbooks and other school books. Pupils in the United Kingdom and Australia are invited to review textbooks and information books. Their written observations are incorporated into articles discussing this new approach. Teachers are involved in evaluating pupils' observations. Results and conclusions will be illuminative, not definitive. Ten provisional conclusions are included in publication (3) below. The findings have implications for teachers and for educational publishers.
Published Material: WRIGHT, D.R. (1987). 'A pupil's perspective on textbooks: issues of motivation and racism'. Internationale Schulbuchforschung, Vol 9, No 2, pp.137-142.; WRIGHT, D.R. (1988). 'Applied textbook research in geography'. In: GERBER, R. & LIDSTONE, J. (Eds). Skills in geographical education. International Geographical Union.; WRIGHT, D.R. (1990). 'The role of pupils in textbook evaluation', Internationale Schulbuchforschung, Vol 12, No 4.
Status: Individual research
Date of Research: 1987 - continuing
KEYWORDS: observation; pupil attitudes; textbook evaluation; textbooks

9/1127
School of Education, Norwich NR4 7TJ
0603 56161
Cockburn, A. Dr
Teaching under pressure
Abstract: Stress in the teaching profession is reaching critical proportions, yet there is very little comprehensible and comprehensive help and advice for teachers. The aim of this study is to produce a practical and insightful guide for trainee, beginning and experienced teachers, on the sources, responses and possible solutions to the negative aspects of stress in their lives. Using a sample of local primary teachers and structured and clinical interview techniques, this investigation will examine teachers' experiences of stress, their awareness of its effects and how, if at all, they manage it.
Status: Sponsored project
Source of Grant: Nuffield Foundation £1,332
Date of Research: 1993 - continuing
KEYWORDS: stress – psychological; stress management; student teachers; teachers; teaching profession

9/1128
School of Education, Norwich NR4 7TJ
0603 56161
Cheltenham and Gloucester College of Higher Education, Faculty of Education and Health, The Park, Cheltenham GL50 2QF
0242 532700
Jones, K. Mr; *Supervisor:* Haylock, D. Dr
The special oral language needs of low attaining pupils in mathematics
Abstract: The research sets out to develop a theoretical framework to help teachers to understand the relationship between various kinds of verbal activity and learning in mathematics, thereby allowing them to determine, more accurately, the special oral language needs of pupils who experience learning difficulties in this area of the curriculum. This is achieved by: examining ways in which researchers have analysed and described models of talk which predominate in mathematics classrooms; critically analysing research which claims that other models of talk facilitate learning in mathematics; enquiring, via a generative analysis of pupils' (N=40) natural language strategies, into the range of verbal activity which appears to promote the breadth of learning intended within recently stated aims of mathematics education. The study also evaluates (via technical action research) the effectiveness of such a framework in allowing teachers, on a principled basis, to plan activities specifically designed to develop children's oral language capabilities in mathematics and, subsequently assess the relative effectiveness of those activities from the point of view of their contribution to the growth of competence in mathematical language performance. The particular focus of the research is the oral language needs of 8- to 10- year old low attaining pupils in numerical problem solving. Whilst supporting the notion that certain forms of discussion might facilitate learning in mathematics, the researcher argues that this is frequently tied to just one aspect of that process, notably the clarification of concepts. Recently stated aims of mathematics education (e.g. National Curriculum Council, 1989) demand a much greater range of learning, each facet of which might, arguably have its own specialised language requirements. The

research enquires into the kinds of verbal activity which appear to promote the full range of learning intended throughout the breadth of the mathematics curriculum.
Published Material: JONES, K. & CHARLTON, T. (1988). 'The special oral languaging needs of low attaining children in mathematics', Links, Vol 12, No 2, pp.22-28.
Status: Individual research
Date of Research: 1985-1991
KEYWORDS: low achievement; mathematics education; oral language; verbal communication; verbal learning

9/1129
School of Education, Norwich NR4 7TJ
0603 56161
Georgetown College, Kentucky, KY 40324, USA 502 863 8011
Brown, G. Prof.; Shaw, G. Dr
Studies of Attention Disordered – Hyperactive (ADHD) children
Abstract: A series of experiments is in progress to explore the cognitive skills of children with attention disorders and hyperactivity. In particular the research is investigating unusual facets of memory and high levels of non-verbal creativity in ADHD (Attention Disordered Hyperactive Children) children. There is also strong evidence of high levels of mixed laterality, left handedness and allergic conditions. Further work is aimed at improving selection procedures of subjects and refining the specially designed measures.
Published Material: SHAW, G.A. & BROWN, G. (1990). 'Laterality and creativity concomitants of attentional problems', Developmental Neuropsychology, Vol 6, No 1, pp.39-59.; SHAW, G.A. & BROWN, G. (1991). 'Laterality, implicit memory and attention disorders', Educational Studies, Vol 17, No 1, pp.15-23.; BROWN, G. (1991). 'Some more equal than others', The Vernon-Wall Lecture to the Education Section of the British Psychological Society, Blackpool, England.
Status: Sponsored project
Source of Grant: University of East Anglia; Georgetown College
Date of Research: 1989 - continuing
KEYWORDS: attention deficit disorder; cognitive ability; hyperactivity; learning disabilities; memory

9/1130
School of Education, Norwich NR4 7TJ
0603 56161
Open University, Walton Hall, Milton Keynes MK7 6AA
0908 652900
Fisher, E. Dr; Elliott, J. Prof.; Mercer, N. Dr
Spoken language and new technology (SLANT)
Abstract: This research aims to contribute to knowledge about the development of children's exploratory and argumentative talk through computer based classroom activities. It is also intended to describe activities which serve this function and the range and quality of exploratory and argumentative talk and to provide information about the role of the teacher in mediating and supporting such activities. It is hoped that this work will make a contribution to educational policy and practice by generating practical suggestions for how computers may be used effectively to stimulate exploratory talk and reasoned arguments in the classroom, with particular reference to the curriculum goals of English and spoken language development across a range of curriculum areas. This research will adopt a social interactionist approach and will draw on VYGOTSKIAN perspectives.
Status: Sponsored project
Source of Grant: Economic and Social Research Council £90,000
Date of Research: 1990-1992
KEYWORDS: classroom communication; computer uses in education; discovery learning; discussion – teaching techniques; information technology; language acquisition

9/1131
School of Education, Norwich NR4 7TJ
0603 56161
University of Minia, Department of Education, El Minia, Egypt
Ormell, C. Mr; Abdel-Ghany, I. Dr
Children's 'application readiness with basic mathematics'
Abstract: 'Application Readiness' is a new idea in mathematics education. It signifies the condition in which a child has assimilated

the applicative potency of a new mathematical concept so well that he/she is able spontaneously (without prompting or cueing) and unselfconsciously to recall and apply that concept to a practical situation needing that concept for its solution. The aims of the research are to clarify the idea of application readiness, to produce tests for it, to improve earlier tests, to trial such tests in schools and evaluate the results. Topics covered so far include basic (natural number) arithmetic up to 99 simple decimals and simple fractions. Recent research has centred on producing large numbers of 'rich, realistic contexts' of the kind needed to test for application readiness, including contexts where there is a mixed teaching/assessment use for the material.

Published Material: ABDEL-GHANY, I. & ORMELL, C.P. (1985). Problem solving with basic mathematics: ten lessons. University of East Anglia: Mathematics Applicable Group.; ORMELL, C.P. (1989). 'Application readiness in mathematics at 10/11'. In: BLUM, W. et al. (Eds). Applications and modelling in learning and teaching mathematics. Maths and its Applications Series. Chichester: Ellis Horwood.; ORMELL, C.P. (1989). 'Application readiness with fractions'. In: BLUM, W. et al. (Eds). Modelling applications, and applied problem solving. Maths and its Applications Series. Chichester: Ellis Horwood.; ORMELL, C.P. (1991). 'Why story maths?', I.M.A. Bulletin.; ORMELL, C.P. (1992). Story maths. Adelaide, Australia: AAMT.

Status: Sponsored project
Source of Grant: Egyptian Bureau, London
Date of Research: 1981 - continuing
KEYWORDS: *mathematical applications; mathematical concepts; mathematics education; test construction*

University of Reading

9/1132
    Department of Arts and Humanities in Education, Bulmershe Court, Woodlands Avenue, Earley, Reading RG6 1HY
    0734 875123
    Richards, B. Dr; Chambers, F. Dr; *Supervisor:* Richards, B. Dr
Oral assessment in modern languages
Abstract: The project is a study of oral testing in French. The aim is to compare the reliability and validity of different assessment criteria currently used by GCSE examining groups and to investigate whether characteristics of teacher-examiners influence their ratings of candidates' performance'. The main focus is on the assessment of 'free conversation'. The project involves: (1) a literature review; (2) a review of the syllabuses, administrative practices and marking schemes of the GCSE examining groups; (3) a survey of current practices in selected schools; (4) development of three sets of criteria for assessing free conversation which reflects different approaches used by examining groups; (5) obtaining tape recordings of 75 children who were examined in the 1990 GCSE examination. This sample represents the full range of oral marks awarded at GCSE; (6) selection of a sub-sample of 30 children from the above to represent the middle ability range; (7) preparation of two versions (two different random orders) of a set of pre-recorded tapes of the 30 children completing a free conversation task; (8) piloting the three sets of assessment criteria and accompanying instructions and mark sheets; (9) assessment by four groups of six teachers representing native and non-native speakers in comprehensive and selective schools, of the 30 conversations on two separate occasions, one month apart; (10) assessment by 22 PGCE Modern Languages students of the 30 conversations; and (11) validation of the GCSE speaking task by using 15-year old children attending two schools in France. Statistical analysis will also be undertaken.
Published Material: CHAMBERS, F. & RICHARDS, B. (1992). 'Criteria for oral assessment', Language Learning Journal, No 5, pp.5-9, September.
Status: Sponsored project
Source of Grant: Reading University Research Endowment Fund £30,000
Date of Research: 1990-1992
KEYWORDS: *assessment; French; General Certificate of Secondary Education; modern language studies; oral tests*

University of Wales College of Cardiff

9/1133
    School of Education, Senghennydd Road, Cardiff CF2 4AG
    0222 874000
    Obeid, S. Mr; *Supervisor:* Nolan, R. Dr
Curriculum development in technical and vocational education in Saudi Arabia related to students' needs, perceptions and expectations
Abstract: This is a study that aims to determine the cause of student wastage in technical and vocational education institutes in Saudi Arabia as a basis of the need for curriculum development.
Status: Sponsored project
Source of Grant: Saudia Arabia Ministry of Education
Date of Research: 1991 - continuing
KEYWORDS: *Arab states; drop out research; student wastage; technical education; vocational education*

9/1134
    School of Education, 42 Park Place, Cardiff CF1 3BB
    0222 834000
    Papatheodorou, T. Ms; *Supervisor:* Ramasut, A. Ms
Teachers' attitudes towards children's behaviour problems in nursery classes in Greece and management strategies used
Abstract: m02 study investigates teachers' attitudes towards children's behaviour problems in nursery classes in Greece and the management strategies used by them. The present research arose out of personal experiences as a nursery school teacher in Greece, together with data collected on behaviour problems in preschool children, which has now prompted this further investigation of teachers' attitudes and coping strategies. From a review of the relevant literature it was found that the age at which children begin to present behavioural problems in schools is getting lower, and that a significant proportion of children who have difficulties on entering school are still having difficulties later in their school life. Furthermore, it is believed that the way teachers view and treat children is of crucial significance in the matter of disruptive behaviour. Additionally, the notion for early intervention which currently dominates education programmes – especially those of nursery education – makes the study of behaviour difficulties in early childhood an urgent and dominant issue in the field. The aims of the study are to examine: (1) the types and prevalence of children's behaviour problems, according to the degree of seriousness; (2) the factors associated with teachers' attitudes towards children's behaviour problems; (3) how teachers manage children's behaviour problems; (4) what kind of help is available to nursery teachers, when children display serious and persistent behaviour problems; (5) how nursery teachers would like/wish to see their nursery school operating in order to prevent or to manage pupils' behaviour problems, more effectively; and (6) some of the theoretical and practical implications of the present study. For the purpose of the study, a questionnaire was constructed, with items elicited from nursery teachers in Greece. The sample of teachers (N=225) was selected from nursery schools located in large urban, small urban and rural areas. Factors such as the type of school and the socioeconomic status of the location were also taken into consideration. Each nursery teacher will complete the questionnaire for the two pupils whom they perceived to exhibit the most serious behaviour problems in their classroom. (Pupils sample N=450)
Status: Sponsored project
Source of Grant: Greek Government
Date of Research: 1991 - continuing
KEYWORDS: *behaviour problems; classroom discipline; discipline; disruptive pupils; Greece; nursery school education; teacher attitudes*

9/1135
    School of Education, Senghennydd Road, Cardiff CF2 4AG
    0222 874000
    Curtis, K. Ms; *Supervisor:* Donald, A. Dr
The role of adult basic education in the re-education of brain injured adults: an investigation into student specific re-learning programmes
Abstract: Although brain injuries are generally perceived to be the prerogative of the medical professions, this thesis presents a role for

the adult basic education service in the re-education of dysphasic adults. The role model is the dysphasia project based in the Rhymney Valley district of Mid Glamorgan's community education service. Emphasis will be placed on the positive assessment of literacy and numeracy skills following brain injury and on student specific re-learning programmes devised for each client. Research methods adopted are literature surveys, interviews and study visits. The thesis includes: (1) an outline of the history of the adult basic education service in England and Wales; (2) an explanation of the causes of the condition known as dysphasia and its effects on language skills; (3) an explanation of the efficacy of dysphasia therapy: the vital role of volunteers, their induction and training for this specialised tuition; (4) an examination of the range of assessment procedures used by medical practitioners and their applicability to adult literacy and numeracy; (5) the assessments devised by the author for use with dysphasics; (6) an explanation of the need for student specific re-learning programmes and work materials, with particular reference to five case studies; and (7) an attempt to evaluate the success of dysphasia therapy and the ethical dilemma experienced by cross-professional approaches to re-education. The various chapters of the thesis combine to guide the educational practitioners along an avenue of rehabilitation not previously explored for sufferers of stroke or head injury.
Status: Individual research
Date of Research: 1991 - continuing
KEYWORDS: *adult basic education; learning disabilities; neurological impairments; special educational needs; speech handicaps*

9/1136
School of Education, 42 Park Place, Cardiff CF1 3BB
0222 874000
Bird, J. Mr; *Supervisor:* Moss, G. Dr
An evaluation of information technology development strategies in South Glamorgan schools
Abstract: The introduction of the National Curriculum has meant a change of course for information technology (IT) education. Information Technology is now statutory and designed to be taught on a cross-curricular basis. The study will follow stages of implementation of IT into the curriculum. The research will be carried out at both primary and secondary levels and issues to be developed will be: local education authority (LEA) advisory roles; policy of school management; actual use; and attitudes of teachers. The research will need to be self-evolving in that the area is constantly undergoing change, and the pressures of time, resources and attitudinal difficulties.
Status: Individual research
Date of Research: 1991 - continuing
KEYWORDS: *cross curricular approach; curriculum development; information technology; National Curriculum*

9/1137
School of Education, 21 Senghennydd Road, Cardiff CF2 4YG
0222 874000
Loudon, M. Mrs; *Supervisor:* Allsobrook, D. Dr
Cardiff Collegiate Faculty of Education: provision of routes to graduate status for certificated teachers
Abstract: The research examines the significance of attainment of graduate status for participants – both providers and students.
Status: Individual research
Date of Research: 1985 - continuing
KEYWORDS: *B. Ed. degrees; graduates; student teachers; teacher certification; teacher education*

9/1138
School of Education, Senghennydd Road, Cardiff CF2 4YG
0222 874000
Loudon, M. Mrs; Williamson, H. Dr; *Supervisor:* Davies, B. Prof.
Youth work curriculum in Wales
Abstract: The aim of this project is to inform the debate on the youth work curriculum in Wales. Twenty-five youth work settings were visited to elicit the views of youth workers and young people on current and future provision.
Status: Sponsored project
Source of Grant: Welsh Office £27,000
Date of Research: 1992 - continuing
KEYWORDS: *community organisations; youth; youth leaders; youth service*

9/1139
School of Education, Senghennydd Road, Cardiff CF2 4AG
0222 874000
Howells, M. Miss; *Supervisor:* Donald, A. Dr
Training for the part-time youth service
Abstract: Most of the face-to-face work in the youth service is carried out by part-time workers. Therefore one way of ensuring good youth work is through the training of the part-time work force. This study describes the development of training for part-time youth work from the Albemarle report to the present, and sets it in the context of the aims of the youth service. Common elements in training are analysed. The social, economic and geographic background of Mid Glamorgan as an example, and the relationship of this with youth service provision are outlined. An investigation, based on a questionnaire and follow-up interview, of the perceptions of their training of 101 participants in the initial training course provided by the county over a period of four years is described. Issues such as the relationship between training and policies and practices; equal opportunities; and communications are discussed. Main findings were that for many of the respondents, the training increased self-confidence and paved the way to new opportunities in employment or in personal life; that the part-time workers concerned brought into the youth service a wide variety of skills which were not always used as fully as they might have been; and that, although there are interesting developments in new forms of training, course-based provision still has a valuable place.
Published Material: HOWELLS, M.J. & DONALD, A. (1992). The contribution made to the youth service by the interests and activities of part-time youth workers. Wales Youth Agency, Occasional Paper, March.
Status: Individual research
Date of Research: 1990 - continuing
KEYWORDS: *part time employment; training; youth service*

9/1140
School of Education, 42 Park Place, Cardiff CF1 3BB
0222 874000
Edwards, M. Mr; *Supervisor:* Donald, A. Dr
The development, monitoring and evaluation of an advanced training course for part-time community education workers
Abstract: This action research/case study concerns the development, monitoring and evaluation of an advanced training course for part-time youth and community workers in South East Wales. The study is designed to reflect on the participants' individual experiences in terms of personal and professional development in the circumstance of a Stage II training course. It attempts to place this innovative and unique course within the context of past and current local education authority training policy and practice. Qualitative data were gathered through participant observation; an analysis of student course journals; evaluation sheets; questionnaires; and tutor/participant meetings. The thesis concludes that there is a need for Welsh statutory youth services to consider the development of progressive training models based on consultation, negotiation and an acceptance of part-time youth worker training needs.
Published Material: LOUDON, M. & EDWARDS, M. (1989). 'The identification of inservice needs of part-time community education workers – a case study', Researching INSET, pp.104-109, September.
Status: Individual research
Date of Research: 1989 - continuing
KEYWORDS: *community organisations; training; youth leaders; youth service*

9/1141
School of Education, 42 Park Place, Cardiff CF1 3BB
0222 874000
Rose, J. Mr; *Supervisor:* Donald, A. Dr
Youth work management policy to practice
Abstract: This study is an investigation into how youth work managers and full- and part-time youth workers within an identified local education authority translate their organisation's youth work policy into practice. It will be concerned with examining the consistency of practice throughout the organisation by trying to determine how quality standards are established and maintained for core elements of the youth work curriculum. It attempts to do this by identifying the political process by which policy is developed and then follows the interpretation of that policy through to the point of delivery with young people. Data are being collected from historical documents relating to policy discussion by the education sub-committee responsible for youth work; and through interviews with the chair of the

relevant education sub-committee, assistant director of youth work, county adviser, part-time youth worker and young people. Questionnaires will also be used to obtain data from area youth workers, full-time youth workers, part-time youth workers and young people.
Status: Individual research
Date of Research: 1991 - continuing
KEYWORDS: *community organisations; policy; youth service*

9/1142
    School of Education, Senghennydd Road, Cardiff CF2 4AG
    0222 874000
    Al-Bassam, A. Mr; *Supervisor:* Richards, J. Dr
Educational resources allocation to primary schools in Saudi Arabia
Abstract: This is an investigation into the sources of education resources to state primary schools in Saudi Arabia, and the relationship with school quality.
Status: Sponsored project
Source of Grant: Saudi Arabian Government
Date of Research: 1991 - continuing
KEYWORDS: *educational finance; educational quality; primary schools; Saudi Arabia*

9/1143
    School of Education, Senghennydd Road, Cardiff CF2 4AG
    0222 874000
    Lapidot, R. Ms; *Supervisor:* Loudon, M. Mrs
Feminisation of teaching: a comparative study of Israel and Chile
Abstract: The mechanisms of feminisation will be examined and the effects on schools' socialising systems will be explored.
Status: Individual research
Date of Research: 1991 - continuing
KEYWORDS: *Chile; comparative education; gender equality; Israel; women's education*

9/1144
    School of Education, 42 Park Place, Cardiff CF1 3BB
    0222 874000
    Gukhool, P. Ms; *Supervisor:* Aspinall, M. Ms
Social and psychological adjustment of educated married women in Mauritius
Abstract: The work concerns a study of the attitudes towards, and difficulties encountered by, educated working women in Mauritius. The investigation involved participatory observation, questionnaire and in-depth questioning of some of the 120 respondents. These were women representing the different racial groups in Mauritius with the emphasis being upon those whose ancestors came from the Indian Sub-Continent, as for historic reasons family attitudes towards their participation in professional work has been slowest to change. Whilst it is being established that attitudes are changing, women are still meeting family and male hostility. However the actual results are not yet available.
Status: Individual research
Date of Research: 1987 - continuing
KEYWORDS: *gender equality; Mauritius; women's education; women's employment*

9/1145
    School of Education, 42 Park Place, Cardiff CF1 3BB
    0222 874000
    Saunders, K. Ms; *Supervisor:* Aspinall, M. Ms
Women and education in Nepal
Abstract: The study examines teacher education and the structure of education in Nepal and questions whether policies will lead to equality in education and employment opportunities for girls and women. The research, spanning the years 1988-90, investigates the situation of female teachers living in Karnali Zone, a remote mountainous region of Mid-West Nepal. In addition, the lives of young girls from the Karnali area are highlighted. Restrictions in attendance at full-time formal school and the introduction of non-formal classes to meet the educational needs of 'out-of-school' girls are discussed. The researcher argues that traditional structures can obstruct equality and suggests that development agencies and educational policy makers sometimes perpetuate the status quo of inequality.
Status: Individual research

Date of Research: 1988 - continuing
KEYWORDS: *educational policy; equal education; gender equality; Nepal; women's education*

9/1146
    School of Education, Senghennydd Road, Cardiff CF2 4AG
    0222 874000
    Nolan, R. Dr
Effectiveness of nurse teacher training related to experience since qualifying
Abstract: This project aims to determine how effective nurse teacher training at University of Wales College of Cardiff and elsewhere was in relation to experience. The sample comprises a random selection of nurse/midwifery teachers who qualified over the past four years taken from college records and via contacts from other centres.
Status: Individual research
Date of Research: 1992 - continuing
KEYWORDS: *nurse education; nurse teachers; programme effectiveness*

9/1147
    School of Education, 42 Park Place, Cardiff CF1 3BB
    0222 874000
    Salkeld, T. Mrs; *Supervisor:* Sutton, R. Dr
The management of cross curricular themes within the National Curriculum
Abstract: Currently there are five cross curricular themes which have been identified as being the most pre-eminent and it is the management of these which is being researched. Curriculum Guidance No. 3 – 'The Whole Curriculum' (National Curriculum Council 1990) points to the importance of the themes being planned and coherent to ensure 'continuity and progression'. The aim of this research is to investigate how schools in Wales are managing staff, structures, teaching and learning to ensure cohesion. Questionnaires will be used to look at staffing structures and the methods used to manage the coordination of the themes. This in itself only indicates the presence of a framework and it will therefore also be necessary to research how learning is being managed. 'What takes place in the classroom?' will form an essential part of the research and will be investigated by a variety of methods. Interviews and questionnaires to both teachers and pupils will be used and examples of pupils' work will be sought. It is recognised from the outset that in the current climate both schools and teachers may still be coming to grips with the necessary re-organisation to keep pace with the changes and therefore the findings of this research will not be finite, but will only reflect 'the current state of play'.
Published Material: SALKELD, T. & SUTTON, R.A. (1991). 'Introducing economic awareness', Economic Awareness, Vol 3, No 2, pp.22-25.
Status: Individual research
Date of Research: 1991 - continuing
KEYWORDS: *cross curricular approach; curriculum development; National Curriculum; school organisation; teaching methods; thematic approach*

University of Wales College of Medicine

9/1148
    Institute of Health Care Studies, Advanced Nursing Section, Heath Park, Cardiff CF4 4XW
    0222 747747
    Cardiff Institute of Higher Education, Faculty of Health & Community Studies, Llandaff Centre, Western Avenue, Cardiff CF5 2SG
    0222 551111
    University of Wales College of Cardiff, School of Education, Senghennydd Road, Cardiff CF2 4AG
    0222 874000
    Tope, R. Mrs; *Supervisor:* Sutton, R. Dr
Integrated interdisciplinary learning of the behavioural sciences in the health and social care professions: a feasibility study

Abstract: Integrated interdisciplinary education in health care and social care is a global issue. Maintaining health, preventing disease and caring for the sick is now so complex a problem that it is impossible for any single health profession to deliver quality care in isolation. In order to enhance an integrated interdisciplinary approach to health care a feasibility study has commenced which examines the behavioural sciences component within the curriculum of 14 health professions. Action research has been adopted as the appropriate methodology. To date a content analysis of the 14 curricula has been completed, which has revealed many potential areas for shared learning. A 'random' stratified sample of teaching staff (N=31) from each discipline, and a student from each year of each discipline (N=42) have been interviewed in order to ascertain their opinions of the potential for shared learning between all the professions. The information obtained from the literature review, the content analysis and the data generated from the structured interviews with the teaching staff and students has formed the basis of a questionnaire which will be distributed to all teaching staff (400) and all students (1,600) in March 1993. It is anticipated that the study will be completed by January 1994.
Status: Sponsored project
Source of Grant: S.E. Wales Inst. of Nursing and Midwifery Education and Cardiff Inst. of Higher Education £1,650; Smith & Nephew Edcuation Scholarship £2,000; Welsh Office Grant £1,500
Date of Research: 1991 - continuing
KEYWORDS: *behavioural sciences; health personnel; health services; interdisciplinary approach; medical education*

Warwick University

9/1149
Centre for English Language Teaching, Coventry CV4 7AL
0203 523523
Khan, J. Ms; *Supervisor:* Henderson, T. Ms; Burgess, R. Prof.
Patterns of bilingualism in some families of Pakistani origin: implications for policy on language education
Abstract: Despite much discussion at policy and institutional levels about the place of community languages in the curriculum, there are very few in-depth studies of the realities of bilingual language use outside the school in minority family or community settings in Britain. Most information available has been gathered by survey methods (e.g. STUBBS, M. (Ed). (1985). The Linguistic Minorities Project – the other languages of England. London: Routledge and Kegan Paul) and does not seek therefore to consider detailed individual profiles or language data. Furthermore, attention is rarely focused on second generation minority group members who have no language problems, who are educationally successful and who do have a bilingual repertoire. This study, in an attempt to make a contribution within such a context, is an ethnographic investigation of intergenerational developments in patterns of bilingualism within a number of families of Pakistani origin. Data are being gathered by extensive interviews, participant observation and recording of a language corpus. Analysis is focusing on patterns of language shift and maintenance, on the wide differences in the range of bilingual skills that exist between young people in different families and on the relationship between use of Punjabi and Urdu, cultural patternings and identity-related issues. Results are contributing to the development of a fine-grained analysis of individual bilingual repertoires. They are potentially very relevant to discussion of language policy in the school curriculum in Britain.
Published Material: STUBBS, M. (Ed). (1985). The other languages of England – The Linguistic Minorities Project. London: Routledge & Kegan Paul
Status: Individual research
Date of Research: 1989-1992
KEYWORDS: *bilingualism; ethnic groups; language across the curriculum; language policy; language usage; minority groups; mother tongue; Pakistanis*

9/1150
Centre for Research in Ethnic Relations, Coventry CV4 7AL
0203 523523
Taylor, P. Mr
Ethnic minorities in higher education
Abstract: The main aims of the project are to: (1) obtain greater knowledge of ethnic minority participation in higher education; (2) study the perceptions formed by these students; and (3) consider the role of higher education institutions in the continuation of discrimination. In order to pursue these aims several different institutions are being studied. Data obtained from various sources (including the Universities Central Council for Admissions (UCCA)) were used to study participation. Consideration of students' experiences and perceptions of higher education will be facilitated by interview and survey material. These studies are to be placed in the context of the institutional policies and practices which affect students, in particular ethnic minorities
Published Material: TAYLOR, P. (1992). 'Ethnic group data and application to higher education', Higher Education Quarterly, Autumn.; TAYLOR, P. (1992). 'Ethnic group data for university entry', Project report for the Committee of Vice-Chancellors and Principals, Coventry: Centre for Research in Ethnic Relations.
Status: Sponsored project
Source of Grant: Economic and Social Research Council
Date of Research: 1991 - continuing
KEYWORDS: *educational discrimination; ethnic minorities; higher education; student recruitment*

9/1151
Centre for Research in Ethnic Relations, Coventry CV4 7AL
0203 523523
Hyder, K. Mrs
The effects of the Education Reform Act 1988 on black communities
Abstract: Pupils of Caribbean background have a long history of educational disadvantage in Britain. The main aim of the study is to examine developments in local authorities and their schools which arise from the Education Reform Act 1988 and which may further disadvantage black pupils. Advantages, disadvantages and the overall effect of the Act will be investigated using a questionnaire to be circulated to all local education authorities in 1993. A second aim of the study is to look in detail at the process of assessment. This is one of the few aspects of the Act with potential benefits for black pupils. The project will examine the hypothesis that the structures and networks developed for assessment will be used by authorities and schools to monitor and respond to inequalities. The third aim is to observe classroom teaching and assessment in order to clarify the more controversial causes of 'underachievement/achievement'. Particular attention will be paid to the role of teacher knowledge and awareness of black children's backgrounds and the mechanisms through which these inform teaching processes and influence academic success. For the second and third aims, the research will focus on a sample of Year Two learners in schools in two authorities. Research methods will include classroom observations and interviews of teachers, pupils and parents.
Status: Sponsored project
Source of Grant: Economic and Social Research Council
Date of Research: 1992 - continuing
KEYWORDS: *achievement; Afro-Caribbean youth; assessment; black pupils; Education Reform Act 1988; equal education; ethnic minorities; low achievement*

9/1152
Faculty of Educational Studies, Coventry CV4 7AL
0203 523523
Abbott, I. Mr
The City Technology College initiative with particular reference to the establishment of a City Technology College on Teesside
Abstract: The study aims to assess the effectiveness and impact of a city technology college on the educational system of a deprived urban area, particularly the effect the college will have on the local education authority schools within the locality. The means of collecting data will include in depth interviews, observation and the use of questionnaires and surveys. Specifically extensive contacts have been made with the institutions and individuals involved in this process. It is expected that a wide range of issues will be identified including the role of the industrial sponsors, the position of the local authority, the effect on schools and colleges, the response of teachers and the impact on parents, pupils and staff involved in the college. The study will be looking at a rapidly developing area and it is expected that it will provide data which will be of use in determining future policy decisions.
Published Material: ABBOTT, I.D. (1991). 'British and American approaches to science and technology', Education and Training, Vol

33, No 1, pp.5-7.; ABBOTT, I.D. (1991). 'School industry links: an American perspective', Head Teachers Review, pp.10-12, Winter.
Status: Individual research
Date of Research: 1989 - continuing
KEYWORDS: city technology colleges; disadvantaged environment; industry education relationship; school-community relationship

9/1153
Faculty of Educational Studies, Coventry CV4 7AL
0203 523523
Johnson, S. Mr; *Supervisor:* Gardner, P. Mr
An inquiry into the role of skills in education
Abstract: This piece of research is a philosophical inquiry into the nature of skills and their prominent position in education with particular reference to general and transferable skills, e.g. problem solving and critical thinking skills, and into the extent to which personal qualities, disposition and virtues can be reduced to and taught as skills. The thesis will also include an inquiry into the role of skills in the teachings of the sophists and the emergence and dominance of skills in contemporary eductional recommendations.
Status: Individual research
Date of Research: 1990 - continuing
KEYWORDS: basic skills; critical thinking; educational philosophy; problem solving; skills; transfer of learning

9/1154
Faculty of Educational Studies, Coventry CV4 7AL
0203 523523
Lewis, A. Dr
Communication between non-handicapped children and pupils with severe learning difficulties
Abstract: This research is investigating the nature of communication between non-handicapped (NH) children and pupils with severe learning difficulties (SLD). The children interact in dyads or triads and each group comprises at least one NH and one SLD child. NH-SLD interaction has been video-recorded for approximately 60 minutes each week throughout a year of weekly integration sessions. Thirty-six NH children (ages ten years, one month to eleven years, one month at the start of the year) and nine pupils with SLD (ages twelve years, four months to fifteen years, eight months at the start of the year) have been involved. Analyses of data is being carried out utilising frameworks developed in an earlier study (Lewis and Carpenter, 1990; Lewis, 1990) involving younger children in NH-SLD dyads.
Published Material: LEWIS, A. (1990). 'Six and seven year old 'normal' children's talk to peers with severe learning difficulties', European Journal of Special Needs Education, Vol 5, No 1, pp.13-23.; LEWIS, A. & CARPENTER, B. (1990). 'Discourse, in an integrated school setting, between six and seven year old non-handicapped children and peers with severe learning difficulties'. In: FRASER, W.I. (Ed) Key issues in mental retardation. London: Routledge.; LEWIS, A. (1991). 'Entitled to learn together?'. In: ASHDOWN, R., CARPENTER, B. & BOVAIR, K. (Eds). Meeting the curriculum challenge. Lewes: Falmer Press.
Status: Sponsored project
Source of Grant: Warwick University: Research and Innovations Fund £1,300
Date of Research: 1990 - continuing
KEYWORDS: communication research; integration studies; severe learning difficulties; special educational needs; verbal communication

9/1155
Faculty of Educational Studies, Coventry CV4 7AL
0203 523523
Lewis, A. Dr
Primary school children's understanding of severe learning difficulties
Abstract: This research investigated non-handicapped (NH) children's understanding of the nature of severe learning difficulties (SLD). The literature on social cognition was reviewed in order to identify developmental changes during middle childhood in understanding about others. As a result of this review two questions about children's understanding of SLD were identified. These two questions were: which cues of SLD are salient for NH children, and do NH children recognise the irrevocability of SLD? Two age groups, 7 and 11 year olds, were selected for interview because research on social cognition (Aboud, 1988; Schneider, 1991) suggests that there

will be marked differences between these two age groups in terms of their understanding of SLD. Nineteen 7 year olds (mean age seven years, two months) were interviewed individually. Thirty-two 11 year olds (mean age eleven years, one month) were interviewed in small friendship groups of four children. All children interviewed had participated in integration projects involving children with SLD. Findings indicated that the 7 year olds were confused about the nature of SLD and tended to believe that children with SLD had transitory sensory, but not cognitive, impairments. The 11 year olds also misunderstood the nature of SLD although they were clearer than the younger children about the irrevocability of SLD. For the 11 year olds, intra-SLD group, as well as inter group (SLD-NH), differences were recognised. These findings are consistent with research into the development of other aspects of social cognition, for example, children's understanding of gender and race.
Published Material: LEWIS, A. 'Integration, education and rights', British Educational Research Journal, (in press).; LEWIS, A. (1992). 'Group child interviews as a research tool', British Educational Research Journal, Vol 18, No 4, pp.413-421.; LEWIS, A. (1993). 'Primary school children's understanding of severe learning difficulties', Educational Psychology, Vol 13, No 1.
Status: Individual research
Date of Research: 1990 - continuing
KEYWORDS: children; comprehension; integration studies; severe learning difficulties; special educational needs

9/1156
Faculty of Educational Studies, Coventry CV4 7AL
0203 523523
Raban, B. Prof.
Evaluation of the National Curriculum core subjects (English) at key stages 1, 2 and 3
Abstract: The aim of this National Curriculum Council (NCC) monitoring programme is to ensure that problems which teachers are facing in implementing National Curriculum English are fully understood, to discover: whether the difficulty lies in the Order; whether it is a question of teacher knowledge and understanding; or whether statement(s) of attainment are pitched inappropriately for pupils within a particular key stage. An analysis of the English Orders will provide a conceptual and practical framework for fieldwork in schools. Between 70-80 schools will be visited in 10 local education authorities (LEAs) throughout England. Teachers, parents and governors will be interviewed. Classrooms will be observed and school documents inspected. Access to key stage 1 standard assessment task data, examples of pupils' work and interviews with LEA personnel will form the body of evidence required to address the issues specified by the NCC.
Status: Sponsored project
Source of Grant: National Curriculum Council £377,000
Date of Research: 1991 - continuing
KEYWORDS: English studies curriculum; evaluation; monitoring; National Curriculum

9/1157
Faculty of Educational Studies, Coventry CV4 7AL
0203 523523
Timmons, G. Mr
Achieving National Curriculum attainment targets in the primary school
Abstract: The aim of the research is to discover whether science attainment targets at key stage 2 of the National Curriculum can be achieved using a study of local history and geography, over a two year period. The research began with 2 classes (9-10 years, 10-11 years), but only the younger class of 30 pupils experienced the full programme. The methods of teaching were those to be found in any good primary school: they were varied, but did involve a good deal of work outside at farms, factories, museums and other enterprises (e.g. a quarry and a brick factory). The children were tested five times in all. About one third of them could be said to have achieved all the targets up to the highest level for key stage 2. About one third achieved a satsifactory level. History and geography targets have also been aimed at, as have some in mathematics and technology.
Published Material: TIMMONS, G., DEVINE, J. & MURPHY, A. (1991). 'Science attainment targets without tears', Education 3-13, Vol 19, No 3, pp.30-36.
Status: Sponsored project
Source of Grant: Warwick University: Research and Innovations Fund £1,900

Date of Research: 1989-1992
KEYWORDS: assessment; attainment tests; local studies; National Curriculum; primary education; school-based assessment; science education

9/1158

Faculty of Educational Studies, Coventry CV4 7AL
0203 523523
Richardson, W. Mr

Participation in education and training: age group 16-19

Abstract: A research seminar will convene on six occasions over two years. Six designated themes are identified: (1) determinants of individuals decisions; (2) qualifications as a predictor of post education destination; (3) funding structures; (4) the status of qualifications; (5) access; (6) quality in teaching and learning
Status: Sponsored project
Source of Grant: Economic and Social Research Council £7,500
Date of Research: 1992 - continuing
KEYWORDS: access to education; further education; sixteen to nineteen education; student participation; tertiary education; vocational education

9/1159

Faculty of Educational Studies, Coventry CV4 7AL
0203 523523
Packwood, A. Ms; *Supervisor:* Raban, B. Prof.

Metaphor as discourse strategy in teacher education

Abstract: A constructivist approach to metaphor has been used to develop an analytic framework. This is then being tested within the context of the discourse analysis of teachers in a classroom situation. The framework of metaphoric analysis will then be evaluated and refined.
Status: Individual research
Date of Research: 1990 - continuing
KEYWORDS: classroom communication; discourse analysis; metaphors; teacher education

9/1160

Faculty of Educational Studies, Coventry CV4 7AL
0203 523523
Troyna, B. Dr

Local management of schools and racial equality

Abstract: The research explores how the recent educational reforms have affected the status of (and commitment to) racial equality issues in a local education authority and a sample of its secondary schools.
Status: Sponsored project
Source of Grant: Commission for Racial Equality £33,000
Date of Research: 1992 - continuing
KEYWORDS: equal education; local management of schools; racial discrimination; racial integration; school-based management; secondary schools

9/1161

Faculty of Educational Studies, Coventry CV4 7AL
0203 523523
Troyna, B. Dr; Siraj-Blatchford, I. Ms

Racial equality and initial teacher education

Abstract: Three case studies of initial teacher education institutions will be undertaken. Using multiple data collection procedures the research will try to establish the salience of racial equality in these institutions.
Status: Sponsored project
Source of Grant: Leverhulme Trust £33,000
Date of Research: 1993 - continuing
KEYWORDS: equal education; institutes of higher education; preservice teacher education; racial discrimination; racial integration

9/1162

Faculty of Educational Studies, Coventry CV4 7AL
0203 523523
Gardner, P. Mr

Ethical absolutism and education

Abstract: A consideration of the implications of ethical absolutism for moral education, especially in a multicultural society.
Published Material: GARDNER, P. (1992). 'Proportional attitudes and multicultural education, or believing others are mistaken'. In: HORTON, J. & NICHOLSON, P. (Eds). Tolerance: philosophy and practice. Aldershot: Avebury Press.; GARDNER, P. (1993). 'Ethical absolutism and moral education', Royal Institute of Philosophy Lectures. Cambridge: Cambridge University Press. (forthcoming).
Status: Individual research
Date of Research: 1992 - continuing
KEYWORDS: ethics; moral education; multiculturalism; relativism – philosophy

9/1163

Faculty of Educational Studies, Coventry CV4 7AL
0203 523523
Gardner, P. Mr

Tolerance and education

Abstract: An inquiry into the nature, value and relevance of tolerance in education today.
Published Material: GARDNER, P. (1992). 'Proportional attitudes and multicultural education, or believing others are mistaken'. In: HORTON, J. & NICHOLSON, P. (Eds). Tolerance: philosophy and practice. Aldershot: Avebury Press.; GARDNER, P. 'Tolerance and education'. In: HORTON, J. (Ed). Liberalism, multiculturalism and toleration. London: Macmillan. (forthcoming).
Status: Individual research
Date of Research: 1992 - continuing
KEYWORDS: attitudes; educational principles

9/1164

Faculty of Educational Studies, Coventry CV4 7AL
0203 523523
Gardner, P. Mr; Pickering, J. Dr

Mature students and higher education

Abstract: Research into how mature students at university perceive younger undergraduates; how they get on in halls of residence; and how course selectors view mature students.
Published Material: GARDNER, P. & PICKERING, J. (1991). 'Learning with yuppies: or, on counselling mature students', Pastoral Care in Education, Vol 9, No 1, pp.13-19.; GARDNER, P. & PICKERING, J. (1992). 'Learning to live with Madonna: or mature students on campus', Pastoral Care in Education, Vol 10, No 4, pp.3-8.; PICKERING, J. & GARDNER, P. (1992). 'Access: a selector's perspective', Journal of Access Studies, Vol 7, No 2, pp.220-233.
Status: Individual research
Date of Research: 1992 - continuing
KEYWORDS: access to education; higher education; mature students; student attitudes; student housing; student recruitment

9/1165

Faculty of Educational Studies, Coventry CV4 7AL
0203 523523
Sikes, P. Dr; Troyna, B. Dr

Life history and initial teacher education

Abstract: Research evidence suggests that many teachers continue, consciously or otherwise, to make important decisions about the organization, orientation and delivery of the formal and informal curricula on grounds which are racist, sexist and discriminatory in a range of other ways. Should we therefore succumb to a system of teacher education/training in which these practices could well be reproduced systematically? Or should we, instead, develop preservice courses geared towards the development of a teaching force which reflects in a critical manner on taken-for-granted assumptions, which can articulate reasons for co-testing some of the conventional wisdoms about pupils, their interests and abilities, and which, ultimately, might influence future cohorts? In contrast to recent calls for the dismemberment of Initial Teacher Education (ITE) courses, as they are presently constituted, the researchers argue for the introduction of life history methods as a strategy for facilitating the transition from pupil to teacher status. The study draws on the researchers' experiences of using this strategy with a group of first year students following an ITE course. Follow-up studies of these students were made throughout their course.
Published Material: TROYNA, B. & SIKES, P. (1989). 'Putting the 'why' back into teacher education', Forum, Vol 32, No 1.; SIKES, P. & TROYNA, B. (1991). 'True stories: a case study in the use of life history in Initial Teacher Education', Educational Review, Vol 43, No 1, pp.3-16.

Status: Individual research
Date of Research: 1988-1992
KEYWORDS: *equal education; preservice teacher education; student attitudes; student teachers; teacher background; teaching profession*

9/1166
Faculty of Educational Studies, Coventry CV4 7AL
0203 523523
Bell, L. Dr
The development of a newly formed comprehensive school
Abstract: This study provides a description of the closure of three comprehensive schools, their amalgamation into one new school, and the strategies used by those within the school to cope with this process. It goes on to examine the initial impact of the Education Reform Act 1988 on the school. The research uses interviews, observation and documentary sources.
Status: Sponsored project
Source of Grant: The Nuffield Foundation £3,000
Date of Research: 1988-1991
KEYWORDS: *closures; comprehensive schools; mergers*

9/1167
Faculty of Educational Studies, Coventry CV4 7AL
0203 523523
Sikes, P. Dr
Motherhood and teaching: a life history investigation
Abstract: Traditionally, it has been seen as 'natural' for women teachers to work with young chldren and to adopt a mother/teacher role. The research focuses on the perceptions and experiences of female primary school teachers and asks such questions as: how do mother teachers perceive their role?; whether they felt there were any links between being a mother and being a teacher and if so what these are and whether or not they felt they affected the way they do their job? The research uses life history method. The sample consists of approximately 15 women. Around one-third are mature students with children on a teacher training course. The reason for including them is to discover whether motherhood had, in any way, motivated them to become teachers. The rest of the sample are practising teachers who were childless when they started teaching. As yet no conclusions have been formally drawn.
Status: Sponsored project
Source of Grant: Warwick University: Research and Innovations Fund £400
Date of Research: 1991 - continuing
KEYWORDS: *mothers; teacher attitudes; teacher background; teacher role; teaching profession; women teachers*

9/1168
Faculty of Educational Studies, Coventry CV4 7AL
0203 523523
Phillips, G. Mr; *Supervisor:* Gardner, P. Mr
Moral knowledge, moral principles and moral education
Abstract: The research is philosophical. It is an inquiry into the possibility of objectivity in moral judgement, with particular reference to theories in moral realism; the nature of reasoning in morality; and the role of knowledge and reason in moral education.
Published Material: PHILLIPS, G. (1990). 'Personal, social and moral education'. In: ENTWISTLE, N. (Ed). A Handbook of Educational Ideas. London: Croom Helm.
Status: Individual research
Date of Research: 1987 - continuing
KEYWORDS: *educational philosophy; ethics; moral education; moral values; realism; reasoning*

9/1169
Faculty of Educational Studies, Coventry CV4 7AL
0203 523523
David, T. Ms
Defining high quality preschool provision in Belgium and Britain
Abstract: Using a variety of research methods (document searches, interviews, observations), the research will explore the views of parents, staff, children and politicians, concerning preschool provision in Belgium and Britain. In particular the research will address issues involved in the rationale underpinning different forms of provision, definitions of quality, and what each situation indicates

about the position of young children in that society. The research will also contribute to debates on research methods. The sample will comprise: 20 parents in each country; 20 children in each country; 20 providers in each country; and politicians representing different political parties in each country.
Status: Sponsored project
Source of Grant: The Nuffield Foundation £2,959
Date of Research: 1991-1992
KEYWORDS: *Belgium; child caregivers; comparative education; parent attitudes; politics education relationship; preschool children; preschool education; young children*

9/1170
Faculty of Educational Studies, Coventry CV4 7AL
0203 523523
Birke, L. Dr; Barr, J. Ms
Women and scientific literacy
Abstract: The project is mapping the extent of understanding in science and science policy among women (with particular attention to ways in which women may have some scientific knowledge but do not identify it as such) and is identifying those issues within science which are of particular interest – actual and potential – to women who have no previous experience of higher education. Outcomes are oriented towards the development of policy and practice, and will be tested through a number of pilot courses.
Status: Sponsored project
Source of Grant: Universities Funding Council
Date of Research: 1990 - continuing
KEYWORDS: *higher education; science education; scientific literacy; women*

9/1171
Faculty of Educational Studies, Centre for Education and Industry, Coventry CV4 7AL
0203 523523
Huddleston, P. Ms; *Supervisor:* Woolhouse, J. Prof.; Tomlinson, J. Prof.
The secondment of professional staff between education and industry
Abstract: The research is concerned with the professional development of outcomes of teacher secondments/placements into business and industry at both individual and institutional level. In particular, the impact of placement experiences on curriculum development is being investigated. The methodology includes questionnaire and personal interviews of teachers who have undertaken placements; longitudinal studies; core studies; and evaluation of placement studies.
Status: Sponsored project
Source of Grant: Goldsmiths' Company of London £165,000
Date of Research: 1988 - continuing
KEYWORDS: *industrial secondments; industry education relationship; teacher development*

9/1172
Faculty of Educational Studies, Centre for Education and Industry, Coventry CV4 7AL
0203 523523
Richardson, W. Mr; Finegold, D. Dr; *Supervisor:* Richardson, W. Mr
The education policies of large companies
Abstract: The project is an analysis of the education policies of large companies in the United Kingdom. Research methods include literature reviews (general and that of specific companies') and interviews with companies' managers. The research characterises the development of companies' education policies, how they are formulated and who is responsible for their operation. Analyses of results is presented in two ways: (a) stages of evolution in a company's relationship with education; (b) variables which shape company behaviour.
Published Material: RICHARDSON, W. & FINEGOLD, D. (1991). 'Making education our business', (interim report). Warwick: Warwick University.
Status: Sponsored project
Source of Grant: British Petroleum £100,000; Department for Education £ 12,500; Department of Employment £12,500
Date of Research: 1989 - continuing
KEYWORDS: *corporate education; industry-education relationship; labour force development*

9/1173
Faculty of Educational Studies, Centre for Education and Industry, Coventry CV4 7AL
0203 523523
Richardson, W. Mr; Finegold, D. Dr; *Supervisor:* Richardson, W. Mr
The relationship of curriculum and workplace change
Abstract: The research poses broad questions about the relationship between curriculum change and changes in skill deployment in the workplace. Specific stress is laid upon the need to incorporate research literature from a number of disciplines (political science, management studies, labour market studies, educational studies); and the main concern is closer analysis of the supply of skilled labour from education and the employers' demand for skilled labour.
Published Material: RICHARDSON, W. (1993). 'The changing nature of work: responses from education'. In WELLINGTON, J. (Ed). The education-work relationship for the future. London: Kogan Page.; RICHARDSON, W. (1994). 'School-business partnerships', The International Encyclopedia of Education. Oxford: Pergamon Press. (forthcoming).
Status: Sponsored project
Source of Grant: British Telecom; Department for Education; Department of Employment
Date of Research: 1990 - continuing
KEYWORDS: *curriculum; employment; industry-education relationship; skills; work-education relationship*

9/1174
Faculty of Educational Studies, Centre for Educational Development, Appraisal and Research, Coventry CV4 7AL
0203 523523
Burgess, R. Prof.; Pole, C. Dr; Sprokkereef, A. Ms; *Supervisor:* Burgess, R. Prof.
Becoming a postgraduate science student
Abstract: This project examines postgraduate training in three disciplinary fields in the sciences: physics, mathematics, and engineering. The key issue to be addressed is: what is the process of becoming a postgraduate science student? Case study data will be collected regarding the first year of postgraduate training in nine departments in the United Kingdom, three in each discipline examined. The aims and objectives of the project are: (1) To provide data on the process of socialization in the first year of postgraduate study. Among the themes to be covered will be: student choice and selection; admission procedures; the selection and focusing of a research topic; taught course work; supervision; monitoring; and assessment; (2) To provide evidence on the range of postgraduate training in the light of the data obtained above; (3) To compare the different types of research training within and between disciplines; (4) To explore the implications of the research evidence for policy and practice regarding research training in the natural sciences in the United Kingdom. The main method of social investigation will be through unstructured interviews and observation. The research will result in nine departmental case studies; three disciplinary case studies; and a thematic report. In the latter comparisons will be made with the work conducted by the Centre for Educational Development, Appraisal and Research (CEDAR) on first year social science postgraduate students.
Status: Sponsored project
Source of Grant: Economic and Social Research Council
Date of Research: 1992 - continuing
KEYWORDS: *graduate study; graduates; science education*

9/1175
Faculty of Educational Studies, Centre for Educational Development, Appraisal and Research, Coventry CV4 7AL
0203 523523
Burgess, R. Prof.; Morrison, M. Ms; *Supervisor:* Burgess, R. Prof.
Teaching and learning about food and nutrition in school: the nation's diet initiative
Abstract: The research is an exploratory case study on teaching and learning about food and nutrition in two primary and two secondary schools. The aim is to examine age, gender, ethnicity and social class in relation to food consumption. It will also contribute more broadly to studies on socialisation and attitude formation, and the use of case study methodology in the sociology of education. Included in the study will be an exploration of the implications of the research evidence for policy and practice on teaching and learning about food and nutrition in schools.
Status: Sponsored project
Source of Grant: Economic and Social Research Council
Date of Research: 1993 - continuing
KEYWORDS: *eating habits; food; health education; nutrition education*

9/1176
Faculty of Educational Studies, Centre for English Language Teaching, Coventry CV4 7AL
0203 523523
Nesi, H. Ms; Tsai, C. Ms; *Supervisor:* Nesi, H. Ms
The development and evaluation of online computer-assisted language learning materials for English for academic purposes
Abstract: The proposed project is to build up a coherent package of English language learning materials which can be accessed by non-native speaker students via the Warwick University network. The programs intended for use are commercially produced, but will be 'authored' by the Centre for English Language Teaching (CELT) staff, with due regard for the students' subject specialisms and levels of expertise. It is anticipated that students will be introduced to the first phase of materials at the beginning of the 1992-1993 academic session, and the use made of the materials will then be monitored by means of Warwick University's Novell 1.12 Netware package, supplemented by questionnaires and interviews with selected subjects. The aim is to discover which types of Computer Assisted Language Learning (CALL) activity are: (a) used most frequently; and (b) judged to be most effective by university-level learners of English for academic purposes. In further phases of the project the intention is to expand and modify the materials in accordance with these findings.
Status: Individual research
Date of Research: 1992 - continuing
KEYWORDS: *computer-assisted language learning; English – second language; English for academic purposes; overseas students; second language learning*

9/1177
Faculty of Educational Studies, Centre for English Language Teaching, Coventry CV4 7AL
0203 523523
Bloor, A. Ms
The linguistic and discourse features of academic writing in English
Abstract: There is a need for objective studies into the nature of academic writing since existing handbooks, based largely on authors' intuitions, often fail to meet learners' needs. The main aims of the present research are to: (1) improve our descriptions of the genres of academic writing in English (for example, research or project reports, journal articles, dissertations); (2) investigate the writing processes employed by successful writers; and (3) (by application) analyse some of the writing problems encountered by inexperienced writers and assist teachers in the task of developing the writing skills of students in further and higher education. The work is of particular relevance to speakers of other languages who are not used to writing in English. The methods employed involve the linguistic and discourse analysis of texts, the evaluation of support materials such as thesauri, and the collation and analysis of the results of previous research projects from around the world, many of which are not available to teachers in Britain.
Published Material: BLOOR, M. & ST JOHN, M.J. (1988). 'Project writing: the marriage of process and product'. In: ROBINSON, P. (Ed). Academic Writing: the Marriage of Process and Product. ELT Documents 129. London: Modern English Publications and The British Council.; BLOOR, M. & BLOOR, T. (1991). 'Cultural expectations and sociopragmatic failure in academic writing'. In: HEATON, B. (Ed). Socio-cultural Issues in EAP. ELT Documents. London: Modern English Publications and The British Council.; NESI, H. (1987). 'Do dictionaries help students write?' In: BLOOR, T. & NORRISH, J. (Eds). Written Language. British Studies for Applied Linguistics. London: Centre for Information on Language Teaching and Research.; NESI, H. (1989). 'How many words is a picture worth?' In: TICKOO, M. (Ed). Learners' Dictionaries: State of the Art. Singapore RELC Anthology Series 23.
Status: Individual research
Date of Research: 1987-1992
KEYWORDS: *authors; discourse analysis; educational materials; writing – composition; writing for publication; writing skills*

9/1178

Faculty of Educational Studies, Department of Continuing
Education, Continuing Education Research Centre, Coventry
CV4 7AL
0203 523523
Lovell, T. Ms; Weller, P. Mr; *Supervisor:* Field, J. Dr
**Performance measurement indicators in research in
continuing education**
Abstract: The project will seek to test the hypothesis that quantitative
analyses of citations can be used to judge quality of research output,
with respect to the field of continuing education. It will involve a
citations count for two leading British-based journals (Studies in the
Education of Adults, and the International Journal of Lifelong Learning).
Status: Individual research
Date of Research: 1990-1991
*KEYWORDS: citation analysis; continuing education; educational
research*

9/1179

Faculty of Educational Studies, Department of Continuing
Education, Continuing Education Research Centre, Coventry
CV4 7AL
0203 523523
Duke, C. Prof.
Continuing education and organisation change in universities
Abstract: This is a study of change in university continuing education
in Britain as a window into change in higher education generally. The
traditional, often marginalised, extramural departments are giving
way to new structures and arrangements. Continuing education is
gaining a much wider meaning and being 'mainstreamed' in policy
and organisation. The research studies these trends and processes, and
considers implications for higher education generally.
Published Material: DUKE, C. (1991). 'Restructuring for better
service in continuing university education', New Education, Vol 13,
No 1, pp.57-68.; DUKE, C. (1991). 'University continuing educa-
tion: identities, prospects and perspectives'. In: FIELDHOUSE, R.
(Ed). The organisation of Continuing Education in Universities.
UDACE.; DUKE, C. (1991). 'Lifelong education and the universities
of the United Kingdom', Higher Education in Europe, Vol XVI, No
1, pp.46-55.
Status: Sponsored project
Source of Grant: Universities Funding Council £30,000; Training,
Enterprise & Education Directorate
Date of Research: 1990 - continuing
*KEYWORDS: adult education; continuing education; higher educa-
tion; organisational change; universities*

9/1180

Faculty of Educational Studies, Department of Continuing
Education, Continuing Education Research Centre, Coventry
CV4 7AL
0203 523523
Weller, P. Mr; *Supervisor:* Field, J. Dr
Competency-based vocational qualifications in the labour market
Abstract: This project investigates the responses of labour market
organisations to the introduction of competency-based vocational
qualifications in the United Kingdom. Its chief concerns are with
trades unions, lobbying bodies and advisory organisations, all of
whom play a role as partners in the labour market, and are reacting
to a standards-based qualifications system which is intended to be
employer-led.
Published Material: FIELD, J. (1991). 'Competency and the pedagogy of labour', Studies in the Education of Adults, Vol 23, No 1,
pp.41-52.
Status: Sponsored project
Source of Grant: Universities Funding Council
Date of Research: 1990-1991
*KEYWORDS: competency-based education; labour market; National
Vocational Qualifications; work-education relationship*

9/1181

Faculty of Educational Studies, Department of Continuing
Education, Continuing Education Research Centre, Coventry
CV4 7AL
0203 523523
Field, J. Dr; *Supervisor:* Field, J. Dr
Policy development and the provision of Access courses
Abstract: During the 1980s, Access courses emerged as a major new
contribution to expanding and broadening participation in higher
education. The project is exploring the process of innovation by
which Access courses were and are still being established; and will
investigate the impact upon decision-making and implementation of
recent changes in the governance and planning of further and higher
education and training (e.g. Training and Enterprise Councils, Access
recognition procedures, the new Funding Councils in further and
higher education, and the single European market for highly skilled
labour).
Published Material: FIELD, J., HARRAGAN, S. & SMITH, G.
(1990). Struggling to learn: the financial situation of Access students.
Derby: Forum for Access Studies.
Status: Sponsored project
Source of Grant: Universities Funding Council £15,000
Date of Research: 1988-1992
*KEYWORDS: Access programmes; access to education; higher edu-
cation; mature students*

9/1182

Faculty of Educational Studies, Department of Science
Education, Coventry CV4 7AL
0203 523523
Harwood, D. Mr
The debriefing process in active learning
Abstract: Previous research has shown that the teacher becomes the
focus of interaction in active learning whenever he or she is present
with the teaching group. This research aims to study the nature of the
teacher's statements and questions during the debriefing porcess and
identify the effects they have upon pupil participation. Teachers who
are experienced in active learning, have volunteered to participate.
The 'debriefing' phase of the lesson will be videotaped and transcribed. As a result of collaboration beteween teacher and researcher,
a commentary will be written to accompany the transcript. Guidelines
for debriefing 'active learning' will be identified.
Published Material: HARWOOD, D.L. (1989). 'The nature of
teacher-pupil interaction in the 'Active Tutorial Work' approach:
using interaction analysis to evaluate student-centred approaches',
British Educational Research Journal, Vol 15, No 2, pp.177-194.;
HARWOOD, D.L. (1991). 'Guidelines for debriefing active learning: an interim report'. Coventry: University of Warwick/Warwick-
shire Local Education Authority. (Available from the author).
Status: Sponsored project
Source of Grant: Warwickshire Local Education Authority £350
Date of Research: 1990 - continuing
*KEYWORDS: classroom communication; learning activities;
teacher-pupil relationship; teacher role; teaching methods*

9/1183

Faculty of Educational Studies, Department of Science
Education, Coventry CV4 7AL
0203 523523
Harwood, D. Mr
**The nature of teacher-student interaction in active and
student-centred approaches: an inservice course in a college of
further education**
Abstract: Student-centred learning has emerged as a parallel, though
related, development to 'active learning'. In this research, tapes and
transcripts of an inservice course for lecturers in a college of further
education are being studied, in order to identify patterns of interaction
in student-centred approaches.
Status: Sponsored project
Source of Grant: Warwick University £300
Date of Research: 1989-1991
*KEYWORDS: active tutorial work; colleges of further education;
learner-centred curriculum; learning activities; teaching methods*

9/1184

Faculty of Educational Studies, Policy Analysis Unit,
Coventry CV4 7AL
0203 523523
Campbell, R. Prof.; Neill, S. Dr
The work of primary school teachers
Abstract: The aim of the project is to analyse the time spent on work
by primary school teachers, using a 29-item coding system and a daily
log of time spent working. The sample comprises one teacher from
each key stage in every primary school in three Midlands local

authorities. The aim is to relate the findings to education policy, especially the implementation of the National Curriculum.
Status: Sponsored project
Source of Grant: Association of Education Committees Trust £10,000
Date of Research: 1991-1992
KEYWORDS: *educational policy; National Curriculum; primary school teachers; teacher workload; time management*

9/1185
Faculty of Educational Studies, Policy Analysis Unit,
Coventry CV4 7AL
0203 523523
Campbell, R. Prof.; Neill, S. Dr
The use of teachers' time
Abstract: The aim of the project is to analyse the time that teachers spend on work, using five broad categories: teaching; preparation; inservice training; administration; and other activities. The analysis is related to education policy, including the delivery of the National Curriculum. Ninety-five key stage 1 teachers, and three hundred secondary school teachers are participating by completing a daily time diary and questionnaire. Analysis is by a specially written program. A sub-sample of twenty-four key stage 1 teachers is being followed up by interviews.
Published Material: CAMPBELL, R.J. & NEILL, S. ST.J. (1990). 'Thirteen hundred and thirty days: final report of a pilot study of teacher time in key stage 1'. Warwick: University of Warwick, Department of Education, Policy Analysis Unit.; CAMPBELL, R.J. et al (1991). 'Workloads, achievement and stress'. Two follow-up studies of teacher time in key stage 1. Warwick: University of Warwick, Department of Education, Policy Analysis Unit.; CAMPBELL, R.J. & NEILL, S. ST.J. (1991). 'The workloads of secondary school teachers'. Final report. Warwick: University of Warwick, Department of Education, Policy Analysis Unit.
Status: Sponsored project
Source of Grant: Assistant Masters and Mistresses Association £15,000
Date of Research: 1990-1991
KEYWORDS: *educational policy; National Curriculum; primary school teachers; secondary school teachers; teacher workload; time management*

9/1186
Faculty of Educational Studies, Coventry CV4 7AL
0203 523523
Reading University, Faculty of Education and Community Studies, Bulmershe Court, Woodlands Avenue, Earley, Reading RG6 1HY
0734 875123
Eggleston, S. Prof.; Lashley, H. Mr
Improving access to education for young black adults
Abstract: The general aim of this research project is to prepare a directory of projects with details of their curriculum arrangements; short term evaluation focusing on quality of training; placement of trainees; content and organization of curriculum; access criteria and opportunity for further advanced training; and jobs obtained. The research work will be organized in Northern and Southern Regions divided by the Midlands; Coventry being the northern limit of the Southern Region and Birmingham/Leicester the southern end of the Northern Region. A base for each regional research associate is provided in London (Southern Region) and Manchester (Northern Region) at the relevant Replan offices. The Directorate and Administration of the project is based at Warwick University.
Status: Sponsored project
Source of Grant: Further Education Unit £37,848
Date of Research: 1987-1992
KEYWORDS: *access to education; black students; ethnic groups; training; vocational education; young adults*

9/1187
Faculty of Educational Studies, Coventry CV4 7AL
0203 523523
University of Wales, College of Cardiff, School of Education, 42 Park Place, Cardiff CF1 3BB
0222 874000
Halpin, D. Dr; Fitz, J. Dr
Self-governance, grant-maintained schools and educational identities

Abstract: The main aim of this research is to explore the extent to which self-governance arising from grant-maintained (GM) status has contributed to innovation and change within education. The specific objectives are: (1) To investigate the impact of self-governance on the distribution of power and control in GM school management structures and practices including its effects on specialisation within the division of labour amongst teaching and non-teaching staff in GM schools and teachers' perceptions of their work and professional status, and its consequences for relations between GM schools and their former local education authorities (LEAs); (2) To compare the management structures and practices found in GM schools with those of other schools in order to: (a) explore the extent to which different forms of self-governance have consequences for the organisation to teaching and learning; and (b) clarify whether the educational experiences offered by GM schools arise from self-governance as much as from perceived financial advantages that GM status may afford; (3) To explore the extent to which organisational differences between GM and other schools foster diversity of pupil experience of schooling and contribute to differentiated and stratified educational identities.
Status: Sponsored project
Source of Grant: Economic and Social Research Council £72,000
Date of Research: 1992 - continuing
KEYWORDS: *educational practices; grant maintained schools; institutional autonomy; institutional characteristics; school-based management*

9/1188
Faculty of Educational Studies, Coventry CV4 7AL
0203 523523
University of Wales College of Cardiff, School of Education, 42 Park Place, Cardiff CF1 3BB
0222 874000
Halpin, D. Dr; Fitz, J. Dr
Opting for grant-maintained status: a study of policy making in education
Abstract: This research aims to explore the origins and implementation of the government's grant-maintained schools policy. The policy will be investigated in the context of other government initiatives, in education and elsewhere, which are intended to enhance competition between providing institutions and to extend 'consumer' choice in the area of public and welfare services. Data collected in the course of the research will aid the conceptualisation of the education policy making process. The project also aims to contribute to current theoretical debates in the area of policy research. The research features the extensive use of interviews with individuals involved in making and implementing policy, both centrally and at local education authority level. In addition, the impact of grant-maintained schools will be investigated by intensive research in selected areas involving research within grant-maintained schools and other adjacent schools as well as interviews with pupils and their parents about their perceptions of schools and education in light of the policy and other related provisions of the Education Reform Act 1988.
Published Material: HALPIN, D. & FITZ, J. (1990). 'Researching grant-maintained schools', Journal of Education Policy, Vol 5, No 2, pp.167-180.; FITZ, J., HALPIN, D. & POWER, S. (1991). 'Grant-maintained schools: a third force in education?', Forum, Vol 33, No 2, pp.36-38.; FITZ, J. & HALPIN, D. (1991). 'From a policy idea to a workable scheme: grant-maintained schools and the DES', International Studies in Sociology of Education, Vol 1.; HALPIN, D., FITZ, J. & POWER, S. (1991). 'Local education authorities and the grant-maintained schools policy', Educational Management and Administration, Vol 19, No 4, pp.233-242.
Status: Sponsored project
Source of Grant: Economic and Social Research Council £49,914
Date of Research: 1989-1992
KEYWORDS: *educational change; grant-maintained schools; institutional autonomy; parent attitudes; school-based management; school-community relationship; school policy*

9/1189
Faculty of Educational Studies, Coventry CV4 7AL
0203 523523
West Glamorgan Local Education Authority, Education Department, County Hall, Swansea SA1 3SN
0792 471111
cunnington, J. Mr; Tomlinson, J. Prof.; Elford, G. Mrs;
Supervisor: Tomlinson, J. Prof.; Cunnington, J. Mr

Tertiary education in West Glamorgan Local Education Authority
Abstract: West Glamorgan Local Education Authority (LEA) sponsored this project to investigate and report upon the effectiveness of their Tertiary Education Policy. The four colleges serve a population of about 360,000 and have 75 per cent of all 16-19 year-old students and 100 per cent 19+ students in further education. The research has included an account of the history of the development of policy 1974-86; the founding of the colleges 1986-89; and a review of the quality of outcomes according to a number of parameters. The report was submitted to West Glamorgan LEA in December 1991 and it is their intention to make copies available to enquirers.
Published Material: TOMLINSON, J., CUNNINGTON, J. & ELFORD, G. (1991). Tertiary education in West Glamorgan Local Education Authority. Coventry: Warwick University/West Glamorgan LEA.
Status: Sponsored project
Source of Grant: West Glamorgan Local Education Authority £20,000
Date of Research: 1989-1991
KEYWORDS: *educational objectives; educational quality; further education; local education authorities; sixteen to nineteen education; tertiary colleges; tertiary education*

West London Institute of Higher Education

9/1190
> Gordon House, 300 St Margaret's Road, Twickenham
> TW1 1PT
> 081 891 0121
> Exeter University, Northcote House, The Queen's Drive,
> Exeter EX4 4QJ
> 0392 263263
> Koshy, V. Ms; *Supervisor:* Ernest, P. Dr

The implementation of the National Curriculum in mathematics: the effects of Key Stage 2 in primary schools
Abstract: The aims of the study are to: (1) find out to what extent changes have been made to the teaching and learning of mathematics in schools as a result of the implementation of the National Curriculum; (2) monitor classroom practice in schools at present, in the National Curriculum context and compare it with what used to be the case, referring to curriculum development documents and surveys. The methodology employed includes questionnaires, interviews and case studies. From the data so far collected the following are noted: (1) there is a marked difference between the responses to questions supplied by teachers on in-service courses in mathematics, and teachers who are not; (2) there is increased awareness of investigative work; (3) group work is being attempted by teachers who use a variety of styles of groups; (4) assessment and record keeping seem to be an area of concern; (5) increased dependence on schemes.
Status: Individual research
Date of Research: 1990 - continuing
KEYWORDS: *change; mathematics education; National Curriculum; primary education; teaching methods*

West Sussex Institute of Higher Education

9/1191
> The Dome, Upper Bognor Road, Bognor Regis PO21 1HR
> 0243 865581
> Ahmed, A. Mr; Oldknow, A. Mr; Williams, H. Ms;
> *Supervisor:* Ahmed, A. Mr

Flexible learning approaches in sixth-form mathematics
Abstract: This project has identified an urgent need to seek ways of establishing long-term productive links with industry and commerce that are self-sustaining, and focus on what education and industry have to offer each other in the context of mathematics. In order that the efforts and resources committed by industry, commerce and education accrue maximum benefit, industry must become an integral

resource for schools and vice-versa. The central aim is to broaden teachers', students' and society's perception of what constitutes the effective learning of a crucial subject such as mathematics and to enable young people, particularly in the 16-19 age range, to gain maximum benefit from their education and training. In particular the strategies and publications developed are designed to: (1) motivate students by offering them access to mathematics being used in both abstract and real contexts; (2) encapsulate 'real-world' situations to encourage the natural interest of students; (3) encourage teachers and students to use resources more effectively, including a wide range of technological devices, databases etc; (4) act as a catalyst for changing classroom approaches to using and applying mathematics; (5) offer students opportunities to encounter mathematics; (6) through challenging tasks, support teachers and students in diagnosis, self-evaluation and record keeping; (7) encourage teachers to become discerning users of support materials; (8) provide opportunities for exploiting the connections that already exist between mathematics and other subject areas; and (9) provide a basis and resource for staff development in order to involve a wider group of teachers in sustained professional development programmes.
Published Material: AHMED, A., OLDKNOW, A.F. & WILLIAMS, H. (1990). Sixth form mathematics. Bognor: West Sussex Institute of Higher Education, Mathematics Centre.; AHMED, A., OLDKNOW, A.F. & WILLIAMS, H. (1990). Mathematics in context. Bognor: West Sussex Institute of Higher Education, Mathematics Centre.; AHMED, A., OLDKNOW, A.F. & WILLIAMS, H. (1990). Using resources. Bognor: West Sussex Institute of Higher Education, Mathematics Centre.; AHMED, A., OLDKNOW, A.F. & WILLIAMS, H. (1990). Using a microcomputer in sixth form mathematics classrooms. Bognor: West Sussex Institute of Higher Education, Mathematics Centre.
Status: Sponsored project
Source of Grant: Training, Enterprise and Education Directorate £190,810
Date of Research: 1989-1991
KEYWORDS: *industry-education relationship; learning activities; mathematics education; mathematics materials; sixteen to nineteen education; sixth form education; teaching methods*

9/1192
> Bishop Otter College, College Lane, Chichester PO19 4PE
> 0243 787911
> Southampton University, Faculty of Educational Studies,
> Highfield, Southampton SO9 5NH
> 0703 575000
> Laws, C. Mr; *Supervisor:* Evans, J. Dr

Individualism and curriculum development in physical education
Abstract: The word individualism is often used by educational writers and teachers without conscious precision as to its meaning. The research project attempts to discover whether teachers' commitment to individualism is expressed in their practice of teaching. Data have been utilized from a four year case study at one secondary school. The emphasis of the research focuses on the interpretative paradigm adopting the qualitative principles associated with ethnography. Initial analysis of data indicates that while individualistic approaches are expressed in the formal intended curriculum, they are not always evident in the practice of teaching. Issues of equality of opportunity, equal worth, and value were recognised by teachers but their practice did not express their commitment to these issues. The capacity of teachers to achieve an individualistic approach in their practice was also related to the distribution of power in schools and the limits inherent in the philosophy of individualism.
Published Material: LAWS, C.J. (1990). 'Individualism and teaching games: a contradiction of terms?', British Journal of Physical Education, Vol 21, No 4, Winter. Research supplement, No 8, pp.2-6.
Status: Individual research
Date of Research: 1986 - continuing
KEYWORDS: *curriculum development; individualism; physical education; teaching methods; theory-practice relationship*

9/1193
> Bishop Otter College, College Lane, Chichester PO19 4PE
> 0243 787911
> Sussex University, Institute of Continuing and Professional
> Education, Sussex House, Falmer, Brighton BN1 9RH
> 0273 606755
> Paton, R. Mr; *Supervisor:* Cooper, B. Mr

Renewal in music and education
Abstract: This is a theoretical and empirical study of musical learning and its role in the changing nature of musical functions and forms. It includes epistemology of music, psychological aspects of musical learning, improvisation and 'holding forms' (containment structures for improvised musical acts). There will be empirical back-up from workshops with students, children and people with learning disabilities, also study of new-style methods and courses elsewhere.
Status: Individual research
Date of Research: 1986 - continuing
KEYWORDS: learning; music; music education

9/1194
        The Dome, Upper Bognor Road, Bognor Regis PO21 1HR
        0243 865581
        Lancaster University, Department of Systems and
        Information Management, Cartmel College, Bailrigg,
        Lancaster LA1 4YW
        0524 65201
        Chambers, F. Mr; *Supervisor:* Lewis, P. Dr
**The evaluation of the management of English Language
Teaching (ELT) overseas aid projects**
Abstract: Using Soft Systems methodology, the investigation develops a consensus model of the purpose of English Language Teaching (ELT) overseas aid which is then used to provide a source for a bank of evaluation questions.
Status: Individual research
Date of Research: 1989-1992
KEYWORDS: databases; development aid; educational objectives; English – second language; English for specific purposes; second language teaching

9/1195
        The Dome, Upper Bognor Road, Bognor Regis PO21 1HR
        0243 865581
        London University, Goldsmiths' College, Faculty of
        Education, Lewisham Way, New Cross, London SE14 6NW
        081 692 7171
        Hill, D. Ms; *Supervisor:* Whitty, G. Prof.
**A comparative study of school-based, school-focused and
college based approaches to teacher education**
Abstract: This research aims to examine and evaluate contemporary developments in teacher education, and to explore the possibilities of developing a left radical analysis of teacher education policy, using a model of the critical reflective practitioner and teacher educator as 'transformative intellectual'. The main objectives of this study are to: (1) ascertain and evaluate the nature of a variety of routes to teacher education; (2) critique radical left, radical right and liberal perspectives on teacher education and schooling; (3) elicit novice teachers' reactions to key elements and issues in their training programmes; (4) identify elements and approaches that facilitate the development of critical reflective approaches to teacher education and schooling; (5) assist in the development of radical left policies for teacher education.
Published Material: HILL, D. (1990). 'Thatcherism, teacher eduation and the suppression of critical thought', Liberal Education and General Educator, Issue 64, pp.36-39, Winter 1989/90.; CLAY, J., COLE, M. & HILL, D. (1990). 'Black achievement in initial teacher education: how do we proceed into the 1990's', Multicultural Teaching, Vol 8, No 3, pp.31-35, Summer.; HILL, D. (1990). 'Local management of schools', New Socialist, October/November.; HILL, D. (1990). 'The Hillcole Group', Forum, Vol 33, No 2, pp.58-59, Spring.; HILLCOLE GROUP (1991). 'What's Left in teacher education?'. In: CHITTY, C. (Ed) Changing the future: redprint for education. London: Tufnell Press.
Status: Individual research
Date of Research: 1990 - continuing
KEYWORDS: political influences; politics-education relationship; teacher education

9/1196
        The Dome, Upper Bognor Road, Bognor Regis PO21 1HR
        0243 865581
        London University, King's College, Centre for Educational
        Studies, Cornwall House Annexe, Waterloo Road, London
        SE1 3TY
        071 836 5454

        Gaine, C. Mr; *Supervisor:* Ball, S. Prof.
Race and education: perspectives of primary B. Ed. students
Abstract: This is a study of the perspectives about race and education held by primary Bachelor of Education (B. Ed.) students, and whether these change in any way during their course, and whether critical or antiracist perspectives persist after two years of working as teachers.
Published Material: GAINE, C. (1987). No problem here. London: Hutchinson Publishing Co.; GAINE, C. (1989). 'On getting equal opportunities policies'. In: COLE, M. (Ed) Education for equality. Basingstoke: Falmer Press.; GAINE, C. (1991). 'The effect of LMS on black children', Multicultural Teaching, Vol 9, No 2, pp.21-22, Spring.
Status: Individual research
Date of Research: 1980 - continuing
KEYWORDS: antiracism education; probationary teachers; racial attitudes; student teacher attitudes; student teachers; teacher education

9/1197
        The Dome, Upper Bognor Road, Bognor Regis PO21 1HR
        0243 865581
        Southampton University, Faculty of Educational Studies,
        Highfield, Southampton SO9 5NH
        0703 595000
        Pinel, A. Mr; *Supervisor:* Briggs, B. Ms
Embedded teacher development
Abstract: The central interest 'embedded teacher development' refers to processes through which teachers develop perceptions of their task, while continuing as classroom practitioners. The major concerns are how they learn more about the capabilities and powers of their pupils and how they attempt to provide more opportunities for the release of these powers through reflecting on and restructuring their approaches to them and to their teaching material. The medium is (mainly) mathematics. The teachers are primary teachers.
Status: Individual research
Date of Research: 1987 - continuing
KEYWORDS: primary school teachers; teacher behaviour; teacher development; teacher role; teaching methods

Westminster College

9/1198
        North Hinksey, Oxford OX2 9AT
        0865 247644
        Bigger, S. Dr
Environmental education in primary teacher education
Abstract: The aims of this research are to: (1) examine issues relating to environmental education as relevant to teacher education for the primary school; (2) design materials, in the form of a handbook, to disseminate to teacher education establishments; and (3) make available to schools for inservice training. The focus of these materials is to combine local with global concerns and include economic and industrial understanding as a sub-theme.
Status: Sponsored project
Source of Grant: Worldwide Fund for Nature UK £5,000
Date of Research: 1991-1992
KEYWORDS: educational materials; environmental education

9/1199
        North Hinksey, Oxford OX2 9AT
        0865 247644
        Prosser, J. Dr
Personal competences in higher education
Abstract: Westminster is one of five colleges/universities trialling a personal competences model for Nottingham Polytechnic (now The Nottingham Trent University). Twenty-five students are using the model, designed originally by the Department of Employment. Both students and supervisors will reflect on the qualities of the model. Data are being collected via document analysis (students keep log books, supervisors keep diaries); semi-structured interviews; and questionnaires. The study has an external evaluator based at Nottingham Polytechnic.
Status: Sponsored project
Source of Grant: Nottingham Polytechnic £4,000
Date of Research: 1991-1992

KEYWORDS: competence; competency-based education; higher education; self evaluation – individuals

9/1200

North Hinksey, Oxford OX2 9AT
0865 247644
Oxford University, Department of Educational Studies,
15 Norham Gardens, Oxford OX2 6PY
0865 274024
Palacio, D. Dr; Lenton, G. Dr; Summers, M. Mr; Kruger, C. Mr
Primary school teachers and science
Abstract: The aim of the project is to produce inservice materials for primary school teachers which will further develop their own understanding of those key conceptual areas of science which are known to be difficult, e.g. force, energy. A constructivist approach to the development of these materials has been adopted by the project team. Initially teachers' understanding in a particular conceptual area was elicited through one-to-one interviews (about 20 interviews per conceptual area) using a technique known as 'interview about instances'. The results of this phase of the project were then used to construct a questionnaire which was given to a larger sample of teachers (about 180 teachers per conceptual area). The results of this, the prevalence phase of the project, were used as a basis for the development of the inservice materials. These materials are designed for use by teachers, preferably in groups of four to five, without recourse to an 'expert' group leader or specialised science equipment.
Published Material: A full list of working papers and publications is available from the researchers.
Status: Sponsored project
Source of Grant: Leverhulme Trust £60,000; University of Oxford £2,500; Westminster College £2,500
Date of Research: 1989 - continuing
KEYWORDS: educational materials; inservice teacher education; primary school teachers; science concepts; science education

9/1201

North Hinksey, Oxford OX2 9AT
0865 247644
Oxford University, Department of Educational Studies,
15 Norham Gardens, Oxford OX2 6PY
0865 274024
Atkinson, S. Ms; *Supervisor:* McIntyre, D. Mr; Lewis, I. Mr
An action research study into the role of a mathematics coordinator in a primary school
Abstract: The role of the mathematics coordinator is explored in the context of school-based Inservice Education of Teachers (INSET). The research looks at changes that took place in a primary school over three years; the ways that teachers coped with change; what the facilitating role of the coordinator involved; and when the facilitating was most successful. The nature of action research is discussed in relation to the feasibility of the concept of teacher-researcher and to the nature of the teacher's 'self' in a demanding situation.
Status: Individual research
Date of Research: 1985 - continuing
KEYWORDS: inservice teacher education; mathematics education; primary school

Wolverhampton University

9/1202

Walsall Campus, Gorway Road, Walsall WS1 3BD
0902 321000
Philps, C. Mrs; *Supervisor:* Crocker, A. Prof.; Thomas, N. Mrs; Stanford, B. Mr
Comparative study of the language development of children with Down's Syndrome placed in mainstream and special schools
Abstract: This is a two-year longitudinal study of a sample of Down's children, half of whom are in mainstream schools and half of whom are in Moderate Learning Difficulty (MLD) schools. The baseline measurements are IQ, language development, social skills and family details. An analysis is to be made of expressive language heard in the context of classroom interaction, playground interaction and, possibly, family interaction with a view to testing the proposition that children placed in mainstream schools initiate more language than those in MLD schools.
Published Material: PHILPS, C. (1984). Elizabeth Joy: a mother's story. Oxford: Lion.; PHILPS, C. & ALEXANDER, P. (1991). Mummy, why have I got Down's Syndrome? Oxford: Lion.; PHILPS, C. & JONES, C. (1986). 'Parental role in portage: a consumer view'. In: DALEY, B. et al (Ed). Portage: the importance of parents. Windsor: NFER-Nelson.
Status: Sponsored project
Source of Grant: Down's Syndrome Association; Wolverhampton Polytechnic
Date of Research: 1990 - continuing
KEYWORDS: Down's Syndrome; expressive language; interaction; language acquisition; mainstreaming; special educational needs; special schools

9/1203

Walsall Campus, Gorway Road, Walsall WS1 3BD
0902 321000
Birley, G. Dr
University examinations in science 1870-1900
Abstract: This research will look at the content of science syllabuses and examination papers set by universities during the period 1870-1900, and relate this to examiners' interests and current scientific developments. The aim is to establish the role of the examinations and the extent to which the examination movement helped to codify scientific disciplines.
Status: Sponsored project
Source of Grant: Royal Society; Wolverhampton University
Date of Research: 1990 - continuing
KEYWORDS: educational history; examination syllabuses; science education; university examinations

9/1204

Walsall Campus, Gorway Road, Walsall WS1 3BD
0902 321000
Jeavons, M. Mrs; *Supervisor:* Crocker, A. Prof.; Birley, G. Dr
Aspects of academic underachievement in the gifted child
Abstract: Five schools catering for a range of children of varying ability and varying socioeconomic background have been selected from one local education authority and children in year three of these primary schools have been given a range of psychometric tests. Those identified as 'gifted' are being observed to measure their interaction with: (a) the teacher; and (b) their peers.
Status: Individual research
Date of Research: 1990 - continuing
KEYWORDS: academic ability; academic failure; gifted; pupil behaviour; underachievement

9/1205

Walsall Campus, Gorway Road, Walsall WS1 3BD
0902 321000
Harrison, R. Miss; *Supervisor:* Kowalski, R. Dr; Crocker, A. Prof.
The role of the college farm in the delivery of the curriculum in non-advanced further education
Abstract: A survey is being made of college farms. The intention of the survey is to establish the role of the farm in facilitating the teaching of practical skills and other aspects of curriculum development in the associated agricultural college.
Status: Individual research
Date of Research: 1990-1992
KEYWORDS: agricultural colleges; agricultural education; colleges of further education; curriculum development; farms; non-advanced further education; vocational education

Y Coleg Normal

9/1206

Ffordd Caergybi, Bangor, Gwynedd LL57 2PX
0248 370171
University College of North Wales, School of Education,
Deiniol Road, Bangor, Gwynedd LL57 2UW

0248 351151
Williams, C. Mr; *Supervisor:* Baker, C. Dr; Jones, G. Mr
An assessment of teaching methodology in bilingual subject area situations in the secondary sector
Abstract: This is a study of successful teaching methods used in subject areas and within the bilingual (Welsh/English) context in the county of Gwynedd. The aim is to produce school based inservice training material based on good practice observed in the classroom, combined with recent research findings in the fields of: (1) language across the curriculum in the bilingual setting; and (2) bilingual teaching. The research will involve observation across a sample of 120 lessons in years 7-9 and in 15-18 secondary schools within the authority, with videotaped evidence of approximately one-third of the lessons. These have been chosen on the basis of: (1) following a Welsh medium class for the whole day (in a variety of language medium settings); (2) following a group of Welsh learners for the whole day (either a whole teaching group or a smaller group within a bilingual class); and (3) observing a specifically stated policy for bilingual development, e.g. both languages within the same lesson, or bilingual development through modular monolingual teaching. Assessment of this variety of teaching methods in a range of bilingual situations will be included in the results and conclusions.
Status: Sponsored project
Source of Grant: Awdurdod Addysg Gwynedd £50,000
Date of Research: 1991 - continuing
KEYWORDS: *bilingual education; bilingual schools; English; secondary education; Welsh*

York University

9/1207
Department of Educational Studies, Heslington, York
YO1 5DD
0904 430000
Metcalfe, C. Mr; *Supervisor:* Lazonby, J. Mr
Case study of staff development in a large comprehensive school
Abstract: The objective of the research is to make a major case study of staff development in a large, purpose-built comprehensive school with a particular focus on the ergence of a scheme of peer counselling as a means of individual and institutional development. The study involves the use of qualitative interview; questionnaires and other forms of research may be used.
Status: Individual research
Date of Research: 1987-1991
KEYWORDS: *comprehensive schools; peer counselling; secondary school teachers; staff development; teacher development*

9/1208
Department of Educational Studies, Heslington, York
YO1 5DD
0904 430000
Robinson, J. Ms; *Supervisor:* Skeggs, B. Dr
A study of the perceptions and responses of young women of South Asian origin to a single-sex access Youth Training Scheme
Abstract: This study is based on a college-based Youth Training Scheme set up in 1987 which was aimed specifically at bilingual young women who were seriously under-represented on existing language-supported courses within a college, situated in a large city of the North of England. The scheme included in the initial stages a number of special provisions to enable the trainees to participate, and has normally involved a gradual transition to 'mainstream' courses during the two-year scheme. The aim of the study is to investigate and analyse the trainees' perceptions of and responses to this kind of provision. The data is being collected by observation of the present trainees and semi-structured interviews with both past (where possible) and present trainees. The findings will be related to the published literature concerning race, gender, education and training. The results and conclusions are expected to relate to the issues surrounding the achievement of equality of opportunity in education and training for young women of South Asian origin.
Status: Individual research
Date of Research: 1989-1991
KEYWORDS: *access to education; bilingual education programmes; ethnic groups; student reaction; women's education; youth programmes*

9/1209
Department of Educational Studies, Heslington, York
YO1 5DD
0904 430000
Davies, I. Mr; *Supervisor:* Lister, I. Prof.
Guidelines for political education
Abstract: There will be three main sections to this research. Firstly, a combination of narrative and analysis which shows the early call for guidelines for political education, the West German example, Department of Education and Science (DES) and Local Education Authority (LEA) guidelines. The researcher will be seeking to illuminate the nature of different guidelines, considering to what extent they address aims, content, methods, evaluation and to suggest how they relate to the recommendations made by key political educators. Secondly, the research will examine the perceptions of guidelines by the producers, by the political educators, by teachers and by gatekeepers who may include heads, governors, LEA officers and a sample of politicians. Finally, the research seeks to enquire how the guidelines help practice and focus on the relation between reality and theory in a number of Local Education Authorities.
Published Material: DAVIES, I. (1988). 'Guidelines for political education', Social Science Teacher, Vol 18, No 2, pp.37-39, Spring.
Status: Individual research
Date of Research: 1987-1992
KEYWORDS: *curriculum development; guidelines; political science studies*

9/1210
Department of Educational Studies, Heslington, York
YO1 5DD
0904 430000
Putsoa, B. Mrs; *Supervisor:* Campbell, R. Dr
Assessing the ability of school leavers in Swaziland to use process skills
Abstract: The study is motivated by the fact that only a minority of school leavers in Swaziland proceed into institutions of higher education at the end of high school. The more fortunate among the remaining majority are either absorbed into professional training institutions or move straight into the adult world of work. The less fortunate join the mainstream of the unemployed. The study aims to find out the extent to which school science may be of use to school leavers in coping cognitively with the experiences they will encounter in the future. Would they rely on the concepts and objective processes that characterize the sciences to interpret the events and situations that arise? This assessment attempts to account for the time and effort spent in teaching and learning science by showing the extent to which it is likely to be used by those who have experienced it. Paper and pencil tests were used in the assessment. A total of 45 questions were designed with the specific purpose of re-enacting the experiences of junior secondary school science and converting them to portray everyday events and experiences in the Swazi environment. Each of the 45 questions was distributed among school leavers in sample schools in such a way that each participating school leaver received 10 questions containing the 10 processes being assessed. The sample comprised all 5th formers in the 20 schools which were selected, so that all regions and types of schools in the country were represented. The sample represented 40% of the target group at the time when the study began, i.e. 1,088 school leavers. The pupils' responses were then analyzed.
Status: Sponsored project
Source of Grant: British Council Technical Assistance to Swaziland
Date of Research: 1988-1991
KEYWORDS: *school leavers; school to work transition; science education; Swaziland; transition education*

9/1211
Department of Language and Linguistic Science, Heslington, York YO1 5DD
0904 430000
University of the West Indies, Mona Campus, Mona, Kingston 7, Jamaica 92 71661 9
Universite Louis Pasteur, Institute Le Bel, 4 rue Blaise Pascal, 67007 Strasbourg, France 88 60 75 50
Warner, A. Dr; Russell, J. Dr; Verma, M. Mr; Christie, P. Dr; Devonish, D. Dr; *Supervisor:* Le Page, R. Prof.; Tabouret-Keller, A. Prof.; Carrington, L. Dr
International group for the study of language standardisation and the vernacularisation of literacy

Abstract: Biennial workshops bring together research workers concerned with the language related educational problems of developing countries, particularly with former colonies of France and Britain, in order to monitor progress with these problems while at the same time using them to refine linguistic sociolinguistic and psycholinguistic insights, theory and stereotypes generally. At each workshop short presentations are made on the application of points in a position paper, and circulated beforehand, to the particular area of each participant. Most of the participants are concerned in some way with teacher training, the formulation of policy and the preparation of descriptions of vernaculars and of teaching materials in the vernaculars. The 1986 York workshop was concerned with the stereotypes concerning 'standardisation', and the volume of abstracts and transcription of discussions was concerned with English, French, German, Italian, Greek, Hindi, Punjabi, Chinese, Swahili, Malay, Bislama, Creole English, Creole French and Sango. The 1988 workshop was concerned with literacy and orthographies for these same language communities with the exception of Italian. The 1990 workshop was concerned with evaluations of historical progress in literacy. In each case the history of the older 'standard languages' will be compared with linguistic evolution in the developing countries in order to illuminate stereotypes about both. The 1992 workshop to be held at Sevres will be concerned with the preparation of chapters for a book seeking to find possible ways forward from the various disasters which have overtaken many of the UNESCO initiatives since publication in 1953 of Monograph VIII 'The use of vernacular languages in education'.

KEYWORDS: art education; children's art; drawing; visual aids

9/1217

Department of Psychology, Heslington, York YO1 5DD
0904 430000
Hulme, C. Dr; Rack, J. Dr; Allinson, N. Mr; Cohen, A. Mr; Snowling, M. Dr

A connectionist model of the development of visual word recognition

Abstract: The project will develop and evaluate a model of the processes involved in learning a sight vocabulary in the early stages of learning to read. The model will be evaluated and refined on the basis of data from studies of children's reading errors and will provide an explicit theoretical account of why good phonological skills aid the rapid learning of a sight vocabulary and how such learning may be impeded in dyslexic children. The research, which depends crucially on collaboration between different disciplines, will also contribute to the development of connectionist modelling techniques by advancing understanding of how to build a prior knowledge into such models, and in applying ideas taken from the study of self-organising neural maps to the modelling of higher level cognitive processes.

Status: Sponsored project
Source of Grant: Economic and Social Research Council; Medical Research Council; SERC – Cognitive Science/Human Computer Interaction Initiative
Date of Research: 1990 - continuing
KEYWORDS: beginning reading; dyslexia; sight method; word recognition

9/1218

English Language Teaching Centre, Heslington, York YO1 5DD
0904 430000
Low, G. Mr; *Supervisor:* Kyriacou, C. Dr

Questionnaire design project

Abstract: The object of the study is to explore the reactions of university students to linguistic aspects of the wording of Likert-type questionnaire items. Items of particular interest are those with 'AGREE/DISAGREE' as rating verbs and 'STRONGLY' or 'COMPLETELY' as adverbs. Three acceptability tests are being designed, involving closer and closer approximations to the task of actually completing a questionnaire. In addition a test has been devised to establish empirically the levels of certain types of salience attached by subjects to sentences in a questionnaire-type environment.

Published Material: LOW, G.D. (1988). 'The semantics of questionnaire rating scales', Evaluation and Research in Education, Vol 2, No 2, pp.69-79.; LOW, G.D. (1991). 'Talking to questionnaires: pragmatic models in questionnaire design'. In: ADAMS, P., HEATON, B. & HOWARTH, P. (Eds). (1991). Review of English Language Teaching 1(2): Socio-Cultural Issues in English for Academic Purposes, pp.118-143. Modern English Publications in association with the British Council.; LOW, G.D., TASKER, I. & LU, H. (1991). 'The wording of bipolar attitude scales in Chinese', Educational Research, Vol 33, No 2, pp.141-150, Summer.
Status: Individual research
Date of Research: 1986 - continuing
KEYWORDS: Likert scales; linguistics; opinions; questionnaires; rating scales; semantics

9/1219

Language Teaching Centre, Heslington, York YO1 5DD
0904 430000
Universitat Munchen, Lehrstuhl fur die Didaktik der Englischen Sprache und Literatur, Schellingstrasse 3, D-8000 Munchen 40, Germany 2180 2995
Green, S. Mr; Hecht, K. Prof.

Learners' language

Abstract: This is an on-going project to investigate learners' language and compare it at all stages with the language of native peers. The project involves German school learners of English and English school pupils in performing three communicative tasks in English, and assessment by native and non-native teachers: (1) a letter writing task; (2) an oral narrative and (3) oral transaction. To date there are 2,490 pupil productions from Germany and England. The productions are analysed from the folowing standpoints: (1) linguistic form; (2) content; (3) communicative effectiveness; (4) strategies; (5) self correction/monitoring; (6) grammatical and lexical competence and performance; (7) the development of communicative competence; (8) assessment/reactions by natives and non-natives. Conclusions are varied.

Published Material: GREEN, P.S. & HECHT, Kh. (1987). 'The influence of accuracy on communicative effectiveness', British Journal of Language Teaching, Vol 25, No 2, pp.79-84, Autumn.; GREEN, P.S. & HECHT, Kh. (1988). 'The sympathetic native speaker – a GCSE role-play for the teacher', Modern Languages, Vol 69, No 1, pp.3-10. March.
Status: Sponsored project
Source of Grant: British Council Academic Linking Scheme £600; European Community £1,400; EC Erasmus £1,400; York University £1,000
Date of Research: 1980 - continuing
KEYWORDS: comparative education; English; German; language tests; modern language studies; native speakers; second language teachers

Author Index

Subject Index

AUTOINSTRUCTIONAL AIDS
9/1054 cognitive style; computer-assisted learning; computer uses in education; learning strategies; teaching machines

B. ED. DEGREES
9/0102 participant satisfaction; preservice teacher education; probationary teachers; student teachers; teaching experience
9/0310 Access programmes; cohort analysis; mature students; preservice teacher education; student development
9/0555 course content; curriculum design; education courses; educational policy; preservice teacher education
9/1137 graduates; student teachers; teacher certification; teacher education

BACHELORS DEGREES
9/0159 course evaluation; preservice teacher education

BASIC SKILLS
9/0610 achievement; adult basic education; adult dropouts; dropout research
9/1153 critical thinking; educational philosophy; problem solving; skills; transfer of learning

BEGINNING READING
9/0253 cognitive processes; reading comprehension; reading rate; reading tests
9/0355 early reading; oral reading; reading skills; teacher-pupil relationship
9/0904 infant school education; reading teaching; teacher-pupil relationship; teaching methods
9/1217 dyslexia; sight method; word recognition

BEHAVIOUR DISORDERS
9/0481 emotional disturbances; special educational needs; statements – special educational needs
9/0710 emotional disturbances; special educational needs; special schools
9/0722 self destructive behaviour; self mutilation; severe learning difficulties; special educational needs
9/0733 child psychiatry; diagnostic assessment; emotional disturbances; special educational needs
9/0735 child psychiatry; diagnostic assessment; emotional disturbances; special educational needs; special schools
9/0763 emotional disturbances; special educational needs; special schools
9/0814 computer-assisted learning; computer uses in education; emotional disturbances; information technology; moderate learning difficulties; special educational needs
9/0815 computer uses in education; information technology; special educational needs; special schools
9/1046 child psychiatry; emotional disturbances; locus of control

BEHAVIOUR MODIFICATION
9/0048 behaviour problems; severe learning difficulties; special education teachers; special educational needs; special schools
9/0734 severe learning difficulties; special educational needs; training

BEHAVIOUR PROBLEMS
9/0046 classroom discipline; classroom management; pupil behaviour; teacher behaviour; teacher-pupil relationship
9/0048 behaviour modification; severe learning difficulties; special education teachers; special educational needs; special schools
9/0147 antisocial behaviour; delinquency prevention; longitudinal studies; secondary school pupils; transfer pupils
9/0200 comparative education; discipline; disruptive pupils; Kenya; secondary schools
9/0538 elective mutism; inhibition; psychopathology
9/0593 emotional problems; reception classes; young children
9/0980 antisocial behaviour; bullying; discipline; discipline policy; pupil behaviour
9/1134 classroom discipline; discipline;

disruptive pupils; greece; nursery school education; teacher attitudes

BEHAVIOURAL OBJECTIVES
9/1125 comprehension; educational objectives; learning experience; test use

BEHAVIOURAL SCIENCES
9/1148 health personnel; health services; interdisciplinary approach; medical education

BELGIUM
9/1169 child caregivers; comparative education; parent attitudes; politics education relationship; preschool children; preschool education; young children

BELIEFS
9/0371 Christianity; mental retardation; religious education; special educational needs

BEREAVEMENT
9/0905 adolescent development; child development; death; moral development; religious attitudes

BERMUDA
9/0289 educational change; teacher attitudes

BILINGUAL EDUCATION
9/1090 bilingualism; educational policy; language policy; school effectiveness; Welsh; Welsh studies
9/1206 bilingual schools; English; secondary education; Welsh

BILINGUAL EDUCATION PROGRAMMES
9/1208 access to education; ethnic groups; student reaction; women's education; youth programmes

BILINGUAL PUPILS
9/0204 ethnic groups; ethnicity; language usage; linguistics; nursery schools; Punjabi; social networks

BILINGUAL SCHOOLS
9/1206 bilingual education; English; secondary education; Welsh

BILINGUALISM
9/0774 Celtic languages; Gaelic; language maintenance; language of instruction; mother tongue; second languages
9/0935 refugees; second language learning
9/1010 languages; minority groups; mother tongue; multilingualism; National Curriculum
9/1090 bilingual education; educational policy; language policy; school effectiveness; Welsh; Welsh studies
9/1091 attitudes; language policy; language usage; Welsh
9/1149 ethnic groups; language across the curriculum; language policy; language usage; minority groups; mother tongue; Pakistanis

BIOGRAPHIES
9/0517 adult education; educational history; extension education; universities; working class
9/1001 sociology

BIRTH
9/0743 age grade placement; age groups; pupil placement; special educational needs; special schools

BLACK PUPILS
9/1151 achievement; Afro Caribbean youth; assessment; Education Reform Act 1988; equal education; ethnic groups; low achievement

BLACK STUDENTS
9/0511 access to education; equal education; ethnic groups; higher education; mature students
9/1186 access to education; ethnic groups; training; vocational education; young adults

BLINDNESS
9/0041 braille; learning disabilities; literacy

education; raised line drawings; sensory aids; special educational needs
9/0044 tactual perception; tactual visual tests; visual impairments
9/0049 architectural education; educational equipment; special educational needs; visual impairments
9/0054 braille; reading teaching; sensory aids; tactile adaptation; tactual perception
9/0055 computer-assisted reading; computer software; computer system design; educational materials; partial vision; visual impairments
9/0056 academic achievement; cognitive development; longitudinal studies; outcomes of education; partial vision; special schools; visual impairments
9/0701 communication problems; higher education; nonverbal communication; special educational needs; visual impairments
9/0849 assessment; mobility aids; partial vision; special educational needs; travel training; visual impairments; visually handicapped mobility
9/0871 braille; human computer interaction; information technology; magnification methods; speech synthesisers; tactile adaptation; visual impairments
9/0873 computer system design; computer uses in education; distance education; human computer interaction; special educational needs; speech synthesisers; visual impairments
9/0879 computer uses in education; optical data discs; special educational needs; speech synthesisers; visual impairments
9/0984 mobility aids; visual impairments; visually handicapped mobility

BOYS
9/0890 educational history; preparatory schools

BRAILLE
9/0041 blindness; learning disabilities; literacy education; raised line drawings; sensory aids; special educational needs
9/0054 blindness; reading teaching; sensory aids; tactile adaptation; tactual perception
9/0871 blindness; human computer interaction; information technology; magnification methods; speech synthesisers; tactile adaptation; visual impairments

BRAIN HEMISPHERE FUNCTIONS
9/0537 dyslexia; handedness; lateral dominance; reading difficulties; visual perception

BULLYING
9/0966 comparative education; discipline policy; discipline problems; material development
9/0978 cooperation; ethnic relations; intergroup relations; intervention; middle school education; pupil behaviour; social isolation
9/0979 discipline problems; playgrounds; pupil behaviour; pupil participation; recreational activities
9/0980 antisocial behaviour; behaviour problems; discipline; discipline policy; pupil behaviour
9/0981 discipline; intervention; mainstreaming; special educational needs
9/0982 discipline problems; playgrounds; pupil attitudes; pupil behaviour; pupil participation; recreational activities
9/0983 antisocial behaviour; family environment; family influence; pupil behaviour

BUSINESS
9/0107 computers; industry; information technology

BUSINESS AND TECHNICIAN EDUCATION COUNCIL
9/1116 chemistry education; competency-based education; course objectives; vocational education

BUSINESS EDUCATION
9/0066 attendance patterns; course evaluation; examination results; outcomes of education; sandwich courses; undergraduate study
9/0131 international studies; undergraduate study
9/0324 curriculum development; higher grade

9/0366 curriculum development; educational objectives; educational philosophy; National Curriculum; work-education relationship

9/0396 European studies

9/0465 educational finance; educational policy; government role; higher education; student numbers

9/0479 educational history; educational policy

9/0509 adult education; Canada; continuing education

9/0513 adult education; educational history; extension education

9/0530 adult education; educational history; extension education

9/0534 adult education; educational history; extension education; intercultural communication; labour education; universities

9/0545 activities; France; outdoor pursuits; physical education

9/0549 computer-assisted learning; computer uses in education; Turkey

9/0557 educational history; educational theories; progressive education

9/0562 industry-education relationship; United States of America; work-education relationship

9/0624 peer evaluation; secondary schools; United States of America; writing – composition; writing skills; writing teaching

9/0653 qualifications; school leavers; school to work transition; sixteen to nineteen education

9/0706 cross cultural studies; educational attitudes; pupil attitudes; Saudi Arabia

9/0707 cross cultural studies; educational attitudes; Japan; pupil attitudes

9/0724 curriculum development; science curriculum

9/0739 pupil attitudes; reading achievement; reading comprehension

9/0818 adult education; China

9/0822 adult education; Taiwan; United Kingdom; universities

9/0833 adult vocational education; disabilities; information technology; Portugal; special educational needs; training; United Kingdom

9/0838 adult education; continuing education; European Community; Germany; United Kingdom; vocational education

9/0840 adult education; continuing education; databases; vocational education

9/0841 China; cultural differences; educational philosophy; United Kingdom

9/0907 educational history; educational quality; school effectiveness; United States of America

9/0936 educational policy; English – second language; multicultural education; multilingualism

9/0966 bullying; discipline policy; discipline problems; material development

9/0986 Education Reform Act 1988; educational change; preservice teacher education; teaching profession; USSR

9/1088 adult education; adult literacy; adult nonvocational education; directories

9/1143 Chile; gender equality; Israel; women's education

9/1169 Belgium; child caregivers; parent attitudes; politics education relationship; preschool children; preschool education; young children

9/1219 English; German; language tests; modern language studies; native speakers; second language teaching

COMPETENCE

9/0070 affective education; individual development; social skills

9/0075 competency-based teacher education; discussion – teaching technique; personal construct theory; repertory grid test; teacher effectiveness

9/0161 adult basic education; employment potential; life skills; mental retardation; moderate learning difficulties; special educational needs; supporting studies

9/0166 assessment; examinations; medical education; medicine; physicians

9/0256 classroom management; preservice teacher education; teacher development; teacher effectiveness

9/0297 English studies; learning; literacy; outcomes of education

9/0958 English studies; linguistic competence; mathematics achievement; mathematics education; Scotland; secondary education; standard grade examinations

9/0964 job performance; knowledge level; museums; standards; vocational education

9/1100 competency-based teacher education; preservice teacher education; records of achievement; student teachers

9/1299 competency-based education; higher education; self evaluation – individuals

COMPETENCY-BASED EDUCATION

9/0155 communication skills; humanities; minimum competencies; modular courses; open education

9/0302 education courses; higher education; masters courses; qualifications; standards

9/0668 higher education; masters courses; National Vocational Qualifications; qualifications; standards

9/1052 minimum competencies; National Vocational Qualifications; skills

9/1116 Business and Technician Education Council; chemistry education; course objectives; vocational education

9/1180 labour market; National Vocational Qualifications; work-education relationship

9/1199 competence; higher education; self evaluation – individuals

COMPETENCY-BASED TEACHER EDUCATION

9/0075 competence; discussion – teaching technique; personal construct theory; repertory grid test; teacher effectiveness

9/0914 preservice teacher education

9/1100 competence; preservice teacher education; records of achievement; student teachers

COMPREHENSION

9/0235 cognitive processes; learning activities; misconceptions; science education

9/0240 learning

9/0247 examination techniques; higher education; learning

9/0441 earth science; oceanography; physical sciences; plate tectonics

9/0449 philosophy of science; science education; scientific concepts; student attitudes

9/0503 acceleration – physics; higher education; mathematics education; mechanics – physics; secondary education

9/0521 mechanics – physics; student development

9/0528 algebra; cognitive processes; mathematical formulas; mathematics education

9/0609 cognitive development; heat; primary education; science education; temperature

9/0622 television; television viewing; visual literacy

9/0629 explanation; historiography; history; imagination

9/0630 computer-assisted learning; computer uses in education; history; thinking skills

9/0945 epistemics; management theories; models

9/1125 behavioural objectives; educational objectives; learning experience; test use

9/1155 children; integration studies; severe learning difficulties; special educational needs

COMPREHENSION TESTS

9/1212 decoding – reading; reading comprehension; remedial programmes

COMPREHENSIVE SCHOOLS

9/0541 educational change; educational history; secondary education

9/1166 closures; mergers

9/1207 peer counselling; secondary school teachers; staff development; teacher development

COMPULSORY EDUCATION

9/0447 attendance; dropouts; law enforcement; social services; truancy

COMPUTER-ASSISTED DESIGN

9/0136 educational media; multimedia approach

9/0473 computer-assisted learning; interactive video; simulation

9/0685 computer graphics; drawing

COMPUTER-ASSISTED LANGUAGE LEARNING

9/0130 educational software; German; translation

9/1176 English – second language; English for academic purposes; overseas students; second language learning

COMPUTER-ASSISTED LEARNING

9/0137 modern language studies; translation

9/0280 cognitive ability; interaction; logo; turtles – robots

9/0336 deafness; hearing impairments; interactive video; special educational needs

9/0471 artificial intelligence; authoring aids – programming; computer software

9/0472 interactive video

9/0473 computer-assisted design; interactive video; simulation

9/0474 artificial intelligence; educational materials; material development

9/0475 artificial intelligence; authoring aids – programming; human computer interaction; simulation

9/0495 educational material evaluation; educational materials; educational software; training

9/0549 comparative education; computer uses in education; Turkey

9/0630 comprehension; computer uses in education; history; thinking skills

9/0814 behaviour disorders; computer uses in education; emotional disturbances; information technology; moderate learning difficulties; special educational needs

9/0869 educational materials; educational media; open education

9/0880 animation; authoring aids – programming; computer uses in education; multimedia approach

9/0881 earth science; educational equipment; microscopes; simulation; special educational needs

9/0884 cooperative learning; computer uses in education; human-computer interaction; learning processes

9/0944 further education students; hypertext; information seeking; information sources

9/1036 feedback; instructional design; problem solving

9/1041 computer uses in education; mathematics education

9/1054 autoinstructional aids; cognitive style; computer uses in education; learning strategies; teaching machines

9/1056 educational technology; expert systems; optical data discs; training methods

9/1057 authoring aids – programming; computer uses in education; electronic books; optical data discs

9/1058 electronic books; human-computer interaction; hypermedia; information technology; multimedia approach; optical data discs

9/1059 computer uses in education; educational software; interactive video

9/1060 database management systems; distance education; educational media; educational technology; multimedia approach; telecommunications

9/1061 authoring aids – programming; computer uses in education; educational software; expert systems; human-computer interaction

9/1062 computer uses in education; distance education; multimedia approach; optical data discs; telecommunications

9/1120 computer uses in education; microcomputers; personal autonomy

COMPUTER-ASSISTED READING

9/0055 blindness; computer software; computer system design; educational materials; partial vision; visual impairments

9/0111 computer uses in education; reading teaching

9/0848 cognitive processes; reading comprehension; reading skills; spelling; word recognition

CONTROLLED SCHOOLS
9/0362 aided schools; church and education; church-state relationship; economics-education relationship; educational administration; educational history; local education authorities; voluntary schools

COOPERATION
9/0002 curriculum development; education support grants; rural schools; school support; small schools; staff development
9/0460 authors; writing – composition
9/0978 bullying; ethnic relations; intergroup relations; intervention; middle school education; pupil behaviour; social isolation

COOPERATIVE EDUCATION
9/0791 school to work transition; vocational education; work-education relationship

COOPERATIVE LEARNING
9/0088 staff development; teacher development
9/0884 computer-assisted learning; computer uses in education; human computer interaction; learning processes

COOPERATIVE PROGRAMMES
9/0550 curriculum enrichment; primary schools; rural areas; rural schools; shared resources and services
9/0897 industry-higher education relationship

COORDINATORS
9/0124 access to education; higher education; mature students; reentry students; student participation

COPING
9/0190 adolescents; Arab states; needs

CORE CURRICULUM
9/0140 curriculum development; educational administration; educational change; educational development; interdisciplinary approach; National Curriculum
9/0789 assessment; English studies; mathematics education; National Curriculum; science education

CORPORATE EDUCATION
9/1172 industry-education relationship; labour force development

CORPORATE SUPPORT
9/0417 educational finance; industry-further education relationship; industry-higher education relationship; sponsorship

COST EFFECTIVENESS
9/0711 developing countries; educational economics; educational finance; efficiency
9/0804 career counselling; evaluation; vocational guidance

COUNSELLING
9/1093 counsellor characteristics; counsellor performance; counsellors

COUNSELLING SERVICES
9/0578 higher education; pastoral care – education; student counselling; student needs
9/0810 higher education; mature students; student counselling

COUNSELLING TECHNIQUES
9/0179 communication skills; counsellor training; course evaluation

COUNSELLOR CHARACTERISTICS
9/1093 counselling; counsellor performance; counsellors

COUNSELLOR PERFORMANCE
9/1093 counselling; counsellor characteristics; counsellors

COUNSELLOR TRAINING
9/0179 communication skills; counselling techniques; course evaluation

COUNSELLORS
9/1093 counselling; counsellor characteristics; counsellor performance

COURSE CONTENT
9/0030 communication disorders; distance education; language handicaps; speech handicaps; teacher education
9/0138 educational materials; Italian; modern language studies; multimedia approach
9/0555 B. Ed. degrees; curriculum design; education courses; educational policy; preservice teacher education
9/1053 aesthetic education; creative thinking; fantasy; imagination; open education

COURSE EVALUATION
9/0060 education courses; preservice teacher education; teacher education curriculum
9/0066 attendance patterns; business education; examination results; outcomes of education; sandwich courses; undergraduate study
9/0159 bachelors degrees; preservice teacher education
9/0179 communication skills; counselling techniques; counsellor training
9/0515 professional continuing education; quality assurance; quality control
9/0520 curriculum development; deafness; interdisciplinary approach; special educational needs; thinking skills
9/0532 economics-education relationship; educational administration; educational economics; entrepreneurship; further education
9/0868 distance education; open universities; student attitudes; surveys

COURSE OBJECTIVES
9/1116 Business and Technician Education Council; chemistry education; competency-based education; vocational education

COURSES
9/0719 industrial training; market research; marketing; technical education; telecommunications

COURSEWORK
9/0716 General Certificate of Secondary Education; projects – learning activities; pupil experience; pupil projects; sex differences; social influences
9/1119 assessment; continuous assessment; learning processes

CRAFT DESIGN TECHNOLOGY
9/0583 achievement; assessment; design education; technology education

CREATIVE DEVELOPMENT
9/0922 computer uses in education; concept formation; learning processes

CREATIVE THINKING
9/1053 aesthetic education; course content; fantasy; imagination; open education

CREATIVE WRITING
9/0032 English studies curriculum; literary genres; National Curriculum; writing – composition; writing skills

CREATIVITY
9/0208 comparative education; France; handwriting; writing research; writing skills

CREDIT TRANSFER
9/0105 European Community; insurance occupations; qualifications; transfer policy

CREDITS
9/0120 experiential learning; industry-higher education relationship; job placement; work-education relationship
9/0795 school to work transition; training; Training and Enterprise Councils; vocational education; vocational guidance

CRITICAL READING
9/0461 reading; student development; study skills; writing – composition; writing skills

9/0750 literary criticism; text structure

CRITICAL THINKING
9/1153 basic skills; educational philosophy; problem solving; skills; transfer of learning

CRITICISM
9/0007 art activities; art education; cross curricular approach
9/0150 art education; comparative education; degrees – academic; fine arts; Greece
9/0317 art education; curriculum development; design education; Scottish Certificate of Education; standard grade examinations
9/0364 argument; higher education; sixth form education; writing processes; writing skills
9/0365 argument; learning; National Curriculum; teaching methods; writing processes; writing skills
9/0383 argument; narration; persuasive discourse; writing – composition; writing research; writing skills; writing teaching

CROSS CULTURAL STUDIES
9/0116 economic change; lifestyle; political attitudes; social change; students
9/0154 art education; comparative education; ethnography; Japan
9/0594 ethnic studies; ethnocentrism; history; teacher attitudes; teaching methods; USSR
9/0706 comparative education; educational attitudes; pupil attitudes; Saudi Arabia
9/0707 comparative education; educational attitudes; Japan; pupil attitudes
9/0977 job satisfaction; motivation; school to work transition; socialisation; vocational adjustment; work attitudes; youth employment
9/1084 curriculum development; European studies; international cooperation; regional cooperation
9/1123 adolescents; reader response; short stories; story telling

CROSS CURRICULAR APPROACH
9/0007 art activities; art education; criticism
9/0043 special education teachers; special educational needs; support services; team teaching
9/0101 art; art history; cognitive development; mathematics; spatial ability
9/0157 employment; enterprise education; preservice teacher education; primary education; pupil attitudes
9/0178 Cameroon; English – second language; language of instruction; mathematics education
9/0777 construction – process; construction industry; industry-education relationship; vocational education
9/1106 information technology; National Curriculum; secondary education; technology education
9/1107 curriculum development; economics education; enterprise education; primary education; secondary education; Wales
9/1108 assessment; attainment tests; mathematical models; mathematics education; National Curriculum; secondary education; teaching methods
9/1136 curriculum development; information technology; National Curriculum
9/1147 curriculum development; National Curriculum; school organisation; teaching methods; thematic approach

CULTURAL ACTIVITIES
9/0018 curriculum; European Community; sciences

CULTURAL AWARENESS
9/0196 English – second language; German; modern language studies; textbook evaluation
9/0205 classroom communication; foreign culture; modern language studies
9/0219 Arab states; English – second language; foreign culture; native speakers; second language learning

CULTURAL DIFFERENCES
9/0841 China; comparative education; educational philosophy; United Kingdom

9/0731 communication aids – for disabled; hearing aids; hearing impairments; psychological evaluation

9/0932 access to education; disabilities; hearing impairments; mainstreaming; special educational needs

DEATH
9/0905 adolescent development; bereavement; child development; moral development; religious attitudes

DECISION MAKING
9/0728 cognitive processes; professional education
9/0729 cognitive processes; professional autonomy
9/1002 National Curriculum; science education; scientific literacy

DECODING – READING
9/1212 comprehension tests; reading comprehension; remedial programmes

DEGREE REQUIREMENTS
9/1064 cultural education; ethnography; higher education; second language learning; study abroad

DEGREES – ACADEMIC
9/0150 art education; comparative education; criticism; fine arts; Greece
9/0341 higher education; measurement objectives; organisational effectiveness; performance indicators; programme effectiveness
9/0468 main subjects; Postgraduate Certificate in Education; preservice teacher education
9/0894 academic staff; careers; educational history; outcomes of education; socioeconomic background; university students

DELINQUENCY PREVENTION
9/0147 antisocial behaviour; behaviour problems; longitudinal studies; secondary school pupils; transfer pupils

DELPHI TECHNIQUE
9/1080 nurse education; psychiatric services

DEMOCRACY
9/0361 change; comparative education; development education; politics education relationship

DEMOGRAPHY
9/1027 choice of subjects; further education; pupil attitudes; sixteen to nineteen education

DEPARTMENTS OF EDUCATION
9/0681 inner city; preservice teacher education; probationary teachers; teacher appointment; teacher distribution

DEPTH PERCEPTION
9/0863 cognitive ability; drawing; problem solving; spatial ability; visual perception

DEPUTY HEADTEACHERS
9/0708 equal opportunities – jobs; sex discrimination; sex role; women

DESIGN
9/0919 art; Postgraduate Certificate of Education; preservice teacher education; probationary teachers; programme effectiveness; student teachers

DESIGN EDUCATION
9/0153 A level examinations; learner characteristics; personality
9/0317 art education; criticism; curriculum development; Scottish Certificate of Education; standard grade examinations
9/0582 information technology; inservice teacher education; National Curriculum; standard assessment tasks; technology education
9/0583 achievement; assessment; craft design technology; technology education
9/0851 curriculum development; National Curriculum; technology education

DEVELOPING COUNTRIES
9/0008 development education; environmental education
9/0027 educational administration; educational environment; educational finance
9/0045 educational administration; educational policy; politics education relationship; school systems
9/0326 distance education; masters degrees; masters dissertations
9/0348 English – second language; second language teaching
9/0372 Arab states; development education; educational policy
9/0711 cost effectiveness; educational economics; educational finance; efficiency
9/0713 comparative analysis; educational administration; educational finance; financial policy
9/0727 community development; development education; economic development; rural development
9/1028 development aid; educational finance; programme development; technical education; vocational education
9/1211 language policy; language standardisation; literacy; mother tongue

DEVELOPMENT AID
9/1028 developing countries; educational finance; programme development; technical education; vocational education
9/1194 databases; educational objectives; English – second language; English for specific purposes; second language teaching

DEVELOPMENT EDUCATION
9/0008 developing countries; environmental education
9/0361 change; comparative education; democracy; politics education relationship
9/0372 Arab states; developing countries; educational policy
9/0727 community development; developing countries; economic development; rural development

DEVELOPMENT PLANS
9/0670 educational administration; planning; primary schools

DEVELOPMENTAL CONTINUITY
9/0089 English literature; higher education; sixteen to nineteen education; teaching methods
9/0592 ability; child development; longitudinal studies; personality development
9/0788 curriculum development; local education authorities; National Curriculum; primary secondary education
9/1105 information technology; learning strategies; primary secondary education; teaching methods; transfer of learning

DEVELOPMENTAL PSYCHOLOGY
9/0476 educational history; educational theories; intellectual development; intelligence; Piagetian theory

DIAGNOSTIC ASSESSMENT
9/0588 assessment; colleges of further education; disabilities; further education; moderate learning difficulties; special educational needs
9/0733 behaviour disorders; child psychiatry; emotional disturbances; special educational needs
9/0735 behaviour disorders; child psychiatry; emotional disturbances; special educational needs; special schools

DIALECT STUDIES
9/0623 Jamaican Creole; language policy; language role; language usage; native speakers; secondary schools; sociolinguistics
9/0925 language variation; sociolinguistics

DIRECTORIES
9/0796 educational research; environmental education
9/1088 adult education; adult literacy; adult nonvocational education; comparative education

DISABILITIES
9/0098 institutional evaluation; mainstreaming; special educational needs; United States of America
9/0174 groups; medical services; needs; psychologists; special educational needs
9/0238 communication aids – for disabled; educational materials; special educational needs
9/0319 access to education; curriculum development; educational discrimination; equal education; higher education; race
9/0368 mainstreaming; physical education; special educational needs
9/0588 assessment; colleges of further education; diagnostic assessment; further education; moderate learning difficulties; special educational needs
9/0607 Cerebral Palsy; motor reactions; perceptual handicaps; perceptual motor coordination; special educational needs
9/0762 foster care; foster children; foster family; severe learning difficulties; voluntary agencies
9/0813 adult vocational education; adults; computer literacy; information technology; sheltered workshops; special educational needs; training centres
9/0816 adult basic education; adults; computer literacy; information technology; special educational needs
9/0817 adults; computer literacy; information technology; special educational needs; training centres
9/0824 communications; computer networks; training; wide area networks
9/0833 adult vocational education; comparative education; information technology; Portugal; special educational needs; training; United Kingdom
9/0932 access to education; deafness; hearing impairments; mainstreaming; special educational needs
9/0949 employment practices; equal opportunities – jobs; teacher employment; teacher recruitment

DISADVANTAGED
9/0422 moderate learning difficulties; special educational needs; support services

DISADVANTAGED ENVIRONMENT
9/0221 academic achievement; school effectiveness; social status
9/1153 city technology colleges; industry-education relationship; school-community relationship

DISCIPLINE
9/0057 antisocial behaviour; disruptive pupils; pupil behaviour; pupil placement
9/0200 behaviour problems; comparative education; disruptive pupils; Kenya; secondary schools
9/0956 classroom discipline; classroom management; discipline policy; primary schools; pupil behaviour; Scotland; secondary schools
9/0980 antisocial behaviour; behaviour problems; bullying; discipline policy; pupil behaviour
9/0981 bullying; intervention; mainstreaming; special educational needs
9/0989 educational quality; inner city; pupil behaviour; school effectiveness; urban schools
9/1134 behaviour problems; classroom discipline; disruptive pupils; Greece; nursery school education; teacher attitudes

DISCIPLINE POLICY
9/0321 adolescents; antisocial behaviour; discipline problems; disruptive pupils; girls
9/0956 classroom discipline; classroom management; discipline; primary schools; pupil behaviour; Scotland; secondary schools
9/0966 bullying; comparative education; discipline problems; material development
9/0980 antisocial behaviour; behaviour problems; bullying; discipline; pupil behaviour

DISCIPLINE PROBLEMS
9/0321 adolescents; antisocial behaviour; discipline policy; disruptive pupils; girls

GREECE
9/0150 art education; comparative education; criticism; degrees – academic; fine arts
9/0462 mathematics education; mathematics teachers; teacher education
9/0531 geometry education; mathematics education; problem solving
9/1013 English – second language; language teachers; teacher effectiveness
9/1047 labour relations; supervisors; training; unions
9/1134 behaviour problems; classroom discipline; discipline; disruptive pupils; nursery school education; teacher attitudes

GROUP COUNSELLING
9/0335 individual development; peer counselling; primary education; social development

GROUP DISCUSSION
9/0625 classroom communication; nondirective methods; peer groups; primary school pupils

GROUP EXPERIENCE
9/0951 adult education; community education; community programmes; groups; intergroup relations

GROUP WORK
9/0358 computer uses in education; microcomputers; primary schools; problem solving
9/0433 classroom communication; discussion – teaching technique; speech communication; teacher-pupil relationship
9/0581 discussion; interaction; intergroup education; learning activities
9/0643 computer uses in education; teaching methods
9/1040 concept teaching; primary education; science activities; science education; scientific concepts
9/1044 learner-centred methods; preservice teacher education

GROUPS
9/0174 disabilities; medical services; needs; psychologists; special educational needs
9/0421 community involvement; school-community relationship
9/0951 adult education; community education; community programmes; group experience; intergroup relations

GUIDANCE OBJECTIVES
9/0797 career counselling; evaluation methods; measurement techniques; vocational guidance

GUIDELINES
9/1209 curriculum development; political science studies

HANDEDNESS
9/0537 brain hemisphere functions; dyslexia; lateral dominance; reading difficulties; visual perception

HANDWRITING
9/0208 comparative education; creativity; France; writing research; writing skills
9/0603 motor development; perceptual motor coordination; reading; speech
9/0617 educational materials
9/0893 infant school pupils; reading; spelling; writing skills

HEADTEACHERS
9/0029 educational change; local management of schools; school-based management
9/0084 management information systems; office automation; school organisation; school secretaries
9/0091 management in education; mentors
9/0096 primary schools; school organisation; teaching profession
9/0139 management development; principals; United States of America
9/0187 leadership; leadership styles; local management of schools; management in education; school-based management
9/0552 administrator role; educational change;

role conflict; school-based management; secondary schools; teacher role
9/0561 educational history
9/0748 curriculum development; National Curriculum; school organisation
9/0854 career development; careers; teaching profession
9/0862 career development; sex differences; teaching profession
9/0938 change; local management of schools; primary schools; role conflict; stress variables; time management

HEALTH
9/0290 child psychology; physical activities; physical activity level
9/0665 primary health care; primary school pupils

HEALTH ACTIVITIES
9/0215 educational materials; exercise; health promotion; heart rate; physical activities; primary school pupils
9/0216 educational materials; exercise; health promotion; physical activities; primary school pupils

HEALTH EDUCATION
9/0171 medical services; patient education; pharmacists; pharmacy
9/0654 Acquired Immune Deficiency Syndrome; homeless people
9/0655 Acquired Immune Deficiency Syndrome; evaluation; training
9/0656 Acquired Immune Deficiency Syndrome; educational materials
9/0661 Acquired Immune Deficiency Syndrome; secondary schools
9/0662 Acquired Immune Deficiency Syndrome; educational materials
9/0679 Acquired Immune Deficiency Syndrome; colleges of further education; sexually transmitted diseases; tertiary colleges
9/0704 Acquired Immune Deficiency Syndrome; sex education
9/0773 human body; primary education
9/0793 school policy; sex education
9/0832 teacher education; training; tutors
9/1006 curriculum development; primary schools; programme evaluation
9/1017 curriculum development; physical education; secondary education
9/1051 Pakistan; science education
9/1122 Acquired Immune Deficiency Syndrome; adolescents; parent attitudes; parent-child relationship; sexually transmitted diseases; speech communication
9/1175 eating habits; food; nutrition education

HEALTH PERSONNEL
9/0169 cancer; doctor-patient relationship; medical education; medical services; professional continuing education
9/0657 Acquired Immune Deficiency Syndrome; educational materials; evaluation
9/0998 nurses; substitute teachers; teaching profession
9/1148 behavioural sciences; health services; interdisciplinary approach; medical education

HEALTH PROMOTION
9/0203 adolescents; drug abuse; drug education; illegal drug use
9/0215 educational materials; exercise; health activities; heart rate; physical activities; primary school pupils
9/0216 educational materials; exercise; health activities; physical activities; primary school pupils

HEALTH SERVICES
9/1148 behavioural sciences; health personnel; interdisciplinary approach; medical education

HEARING AIDS
9/0731 communication aids – for disabled; deafness; hearing impairments; psychological evaluation

HEARING IMPAIRMENTS
9/0035 deafness; educational experience;

mainstreaming; primary secondary education; social experience; special educational needs; transition education
9/0315 deafness; early reading; home-school relationship; prereading experience; preschool children; reading; reading difficulties
9/0333 deafness; special educational needs; teaching methods
9/0336 computer-assisted learning; deafness; interactive video; special educational needs
9/0524 communication skills; deafness; hearing therapy; special schools; total communication
9/0730 deafness; special educational needs
9/0731 communication aids – for disabled; deafness; hearing aids; psychological evaluation
9/0932 access to education; deafness; disabilities; mainstreaming; special educational needs

HEARING THERAPY
9/0524 communication skills; deafness; hearing impairments; special schools; total communication

HEART RATE
9/0215 educational materials; exercise; health activities; health promotion; physical activities; primary school pupils

HEAT
9/0609 cognitive development; comprehension; primary education; science education; temperature

HELPLESSNESS
9/0477 motivation; self-esteem; special educational needs

HIGHER EDUCATION
9/0006 comparative education; institutional evaluation; self evaluation – groups
9/0079 educational policy; graduate study
9/0081 cognitive processes; cognitive psychology; epistemology; learning processes; memory
9/0082 performance indicators
9/0089 developmental continuity; English literature; sixteen to nineteen education; teaching methods
9/0113 homosexuality; lesbianism; student needs
9/0114 expectation; student attitudes; student experience
9/0124 access to education; coordinators; mature students; reentry students; student participation
9/0125 Access programmes; programme evaluation
9/0135 educational materials; literature; politics; undergraduate study
9/0188 curriculum development; English – second language; English for specific purposes; Jordan; science education; technology education
9/0197 Arabic studies; pupil attitudes; sixth forms
9/0223 access to education; educational change; further education; sixteen to nineteen education
9/0226 further education; school to work transition; unemployment; vocational education; youth employment
9/0236 employment opportunities; graduate employment; labour market; mature students; women's employment
9/0245 educational innovation; learning strategies; teaching methods
9/0247 comprehension; examination techniques; learning
9/0249 learning motivation; learning strategies; mathematics achievement; sixteen to nineteen education; undergraduate study
9/0266 mathematics education; student attitudes; student evaluation of teacher performance; teaching methods
9/0301 profiles; records of achievement; resumes – personal; self evaluation – individuals; skill development
9/0302 competency-based education; education courses; masters courses; qualifications; standards
9/0319 access to education; curriculum development; disabilities; educational discrimination; equal education; race

MODERN LANGUAGE STUDIES
9/0013 comparative education; pupil attitudes
9/0137 computer-assisted learning; translation
9/0138 course content; educational materials; Italian; multimedia approach
9/0196 cultural awareness; English – second language; German; textbook evaluation
9/0205 classroom communication; cultural awareness; foreign culture
9/0288 preservice teacher education; student teachers
9/0328 learning motivation; Scotland; second language teaching
9/0350 primary education; problems; second language teaching; teaching methods
9/0445 educational objectives; French
9/0519 language attitudes; language teachers; learning motivation
9/1008 English studies; language skills
9/1009 language teachers; primary schools; programme evaluation; teaching assistants
9/1035 achievement; primary schools; second language learning
9/1132 assessment; French; General Certificate of Secondary Education; oral tests
9/1219 comparative education; English; German; language tests; native speakers; second language teaching

MODULAR COURSES
9/0155 communication skills; competency-based education; humanities; minimum competencies; open education
9/0224 certification; comparative education; curriculum; labour market; vocational education
9/0228 curriculum research; National Certificate – Scotland; Scotland; secondary education; sixteen to nineteen education
9/0953 curriculum development; higher grade examinations; qualifications; Scotland

MONITORING
9/0689 education consultants; programme evaluation; technical education; vocational education
9/0769 evaluation; inspection; local education authorities; schools
9/1156 English studies curriculum; evaluation; National Curriculum

MORAL DEVELOPMENT
9/0905 adolescent development; bereavement; child development; death; religious attitudes

MORAL EDUCATION
9/0367 Education Reform Act 1988; individual development; National Curriculum; primary schools; religious education; social development
9/0402 philosophy; values education
9/0559 curriculum development; educational philosophy; individual development; physical education; religious education
9/0920 educational philosophy; Taiwan
9/1162 ethics; multiculturalism; relativism – philosophy
9/1168 educational philosophy; ethics; moral values; realism; reasoning

MORAL VALUES
9/1168 educational philosophy; ethics; moral education; realism; reasoning

MOTHER TONGUE
9/0774 bilingualism; Celtic languages; Gaelic; language maintenance; language of instruction; second languages
9/0827 history; nationalism; politics; religion; Wales; Welsh
9/1010 bilingualism; languages; minority groups; multilingualism; National Curriculum
9/1012 English; English – second language; language usage; verbal communication
9/1092 assessment; National Curriculum; school-based assessment; second language learning; standard assessment tasks; Welsh
9/1149 bilingualism; ethnic groups; language across the curriculum; language policy; language usage; minority groups; Pakistanis

9/1211 developing countries; language policy; language standardisation; literacy

MOTHERS
9/0001 access to education; community education; preschool education; young children
9/0673 child development; cognitive development; day care; emotional development; preschool children; social development; women's employment
9/1167 teacher attitudes; teacher background; teacher role; teaching profession; women teachers

MOTIVATION
9/0064 Access programmes; educational experience; mature students; men; working class
9/0477 helplessness; self-esteem; special educational needs
9/0480 sex differences; sexual identity; teacher-pupil relationship
9/0755 achievement; orientation; physical education
9/0977 cross cultural studies; job satisfaction; school to work transition; socialisation; vocational adjustment; work attitudes; youth employment

MOTOR DEVELOPMENT
9/0058 cerebral palsy; conductive education; evaluation; psychomotor skills
9/0100 primary school pupils; sex differences
9/0117 moderate learning difficulties; movement education; special educational needs; teaching process
9/0425 special educational needs; special schools
9/0603 handwriting; perceptual motor coordination; reading; speech
9/0604 child development; neurological impairments; perceptual handicaps; premature infants; special educational needs

MOTOR REACTIONS
9/0607 cerebral palsy; disabilities; perceptual handicaps; perceptual motor coordination; special educational needs

MOVEMENT EDUCATION
9/0117 moderate learning difficulties; motor development; special educational needs; teaching process

MULTICULTURAL EDUCATION
9/0038 imagery; religious differences; religious education
9/0072 educational administration; educational change; educational innovation; educational planning; primary schools
9/0076 antiracism education; educational policy; equal education; local education authorities
9/0077 intercultural programmes; international baccalaureate; international education; international schools
9/0151 art education; curriculum development; Japan
9/0552 ethnic groups; primary schools
9/0705 antiracism education; ethnic groups
9/0776 antiracism education; Education Reform Act 1988; educational planning; equal education; local education authorities
9/0906 centralisation; educational practices; international education; National Curriculum
9/0936 comparative education; educational policy; English – second language; multilingualism
9/0942 databases; resource materials

MULTICULTURALISM
9/0744 cultural interrelationships; ethnic groups; ethnic relations; school policy; secondary schools
9/1162 ethics; moral education; relativism – philosophy

MULTILINGUALISM
9/0916 English; minority groups; teaching methods
9/0936 comparative education; educational policy; English – second language; multicultural education

9/1010 bilingualism; languages; minority groups; mother tongue; National Curriculum

MULTIMEDIA APPROACH
9/0136 computer-assisted design; educational media
9/0138 course content; educational materials; Italian; modern language studies
9/0880 animation; authoring aids – programming; computer-assisted learning; computer uses in education
9/1058 computer-assisted learning; electronic books; human-computer interaction; hypermedia; information technology; optical data discs
9/1060 computer-assisted learning; database management systems; distance education; educational media; educational technology; telecommunications
9/1062 computer-assisted learning; computer uses in education; distance education; optical data discs; telecommunications

MULTIPLE DISABILITIES
9/0761 access to education; adult basic education; adult learning; intelligence differences; severe learning difficulties

MULTISENSORY ROOMS
9/0543 severe learning difficulties; special educational needs; special schools

MUSEUMS
9/0964 competence; job performance; knowledge level; standards; vocational education

MUSIC
9/0193 learning; music education; songs; young children
9/0901 art; art activities; art education; dance; drama; primary education
9/1193 learning; music education

MUSIC ACTIVITIES
9/0994 further education; moderate learning difficulties; music education; self-esteem; severe learning difficulties; special educational needs; teaching methods

MUSIC CURRICULUM
9/0921 educational history; inspectors – of schools; music education

MUSIC EDUCATION
9/0119 National Curriculum; primary school teachers
9/0193 learning; music; songs; young children
9/0261 computer uses in education; educational technology
9/0262 computer uses in education; educational technology
9/0644 music techniques; musical instruments; psychomotor skills
9/0645 applied music; computer uses in education; perception
9/0915 consultants; inservice teacher education; music teachers; primary school teachers
9/0921 educational history; inspectors – of schools; music curriculum
9/0994 further education; moderate learning difficulties; music activities; self-esteem; severe learning difficulties; special educational needs; teaching methods
9/1193 learning; music

MUSIC TEACHERS
9/0577 professional development; professional training; teacher education
9/0915 consultants; inservice teacher education; music education; primary school teachers

MUSIC TECHNIQUES
9/0644 music education; musical instruments; psychomotor skills

MUSICAL INSTRUMENTS
9/0644 music education; music techniques; psychomotor skills

9/0485 professional recognition; status need; teacher attitudes; teachers; teaching profession

NON ADVANCED FURTHER EDUCATION
9/1205 agricultural colleges; agricultural education; colleges of further education; curriculum development; farms; vocational education

NON WESTERN LANGUAGES
9/0252 Arabic; Chinese languages; educational materials; Japanese; second language learning

NONCONFORMITY
9/0369 church and education; church-state relationship; educational history; educational legislation; religion and education

NONDIRECTIVE METHODS
9/0625 classroom communication; group discussion; peer groups; primary school pupils

NONDISCRIMINATORY EDUCATION
9/0444 educational policy; equal education; gender equality

NONFICTION
9/0325 English studies; literature studies; reading
9/0917 English studies; literature studies; secondary education

NONFORMAL EDUCATION
9/0507 adult education; continuing education; evaluation; mature students; rural areas

NONTRADITIONAL EDUCATION
9/0332 models; performance; physical education; sports; teaching methods

NONVERBAL COMMUNICATION
9/0701 blindness; communication problems; higher education; special educational needs; visual impairments

NORTHERN IRELAND
9/1076 pupil attitudes; religious education; scientific attitudes; secondary school pupils
9/1077 rural schools; science curriculum; science education; small schools
9/1078 curriculum development; individualised methods; science education
9/1081 computer uses in education; records of achievement; science curriculum

NUMBER CONCEPTS
9/0608 arithmetic; cognitive development; numbers; numeracy; primary education

NUMBERS
9/0608 arithmetic; cognitive development; number concepts; numeracy; primary education

NUMERACY
9/0202 employer attitudes; graduate employment; graduates; mathematical ability; work-education relationship
9/0608 arithmetic; cognitive development; number concepts; numbers; primary education

NURSE EDUCATION
9/0010 information needs; information seeking; nurses
9/0172 distance education; professional continuing education; professional development
9/0428 management studies
9/0533 career choice; nursing; qualifications; recruitment; selection; student motivation
9/0658 Acquired Immune Deficiency Syndrome
9/0663 Acquired Immune Deficiency Syndrome; nurses; sexually transmitted diseases
9/0790 Acquired Immune Deficiency Syndrome; educational materials; information needs; nurses
9/0808 change; Cyprus
9/1003 attitudes; nurses
9/1080 Delphi technique; psychiatric services
9/1146 nurse teachers; programme effectiveness

NURSE TEACHERS
9/1146 nurse education; programme effectiveness

NURSERY SCHOOL EDUCATION
9/0296 early childhood education; preschool education; regional characteristics; regional planning
9/0947 aesthetic education; art activities; art appreciation
9/1134 behaviour problems; classroom discipline; discipline; disruptive pupils; Greece; teacher attitudes

NURSERY SCHOOL PUPILS
9/0786 infant school pupils; reading; reading readiness; reception classes; tests

NURSERY SCHOOLS
9/0033 dyslexia; language handicaps; phonics; phonology; preschool children; speech tests
9/0034 phonology; preschool children; preschool education; speech handicaps
9/0204 bilingual pupils; ethnic groups; ethnicity; language usage; linguistics; Punjabi; social networks
9/0318 computer uses in education

NURSES
9/0010 information needs; information seeking; nurse education
9/0663 Acquired Immune Deficiency Syndrome; nurse education; sexually transmitted diseases
9/0790 Acquired Immune Deficiency Syndrome; educational materials; information needs; nurse education
9/0998 health personnel; substitute teachers; teaching profession
9/1003 attitudes; nurse education

NURSING
9/0533 career choice; nurse education; qualifications; recruitment; selection; student motivation

NUTRITION EDUCATION
9/1175 eating habits; food; health education

OBSERVATION
9/1126 pupil attitudes; textbook evaluation; textbooks

OCCUPATIONAL ASPIRATION
9/0976 private education; work attitudes

OCCUPATIONAL INFORMATION
9/1031 colleges of further education; comparable worth; employment practices; equal pay; job analysis; salaries

OCCUPATIONS
9/0802 career counselling; careers teachers; teaching profession; training; vocational education teachers; vocational guidance

OCEANOGRAPHY
9/0441 comprehension; earth science; physical sciences; plate tectonics

OFF THE JOB TRAINING
9/1055 on the job training; skill development; transfer of learning; work experience programmes

OFFICE AUTOMATION
9/0084 headteachers; management information systems; school organisation; school secretaries

ON THE JOB TRAINING
9/0489 employee attitudes; training; work education relationship
9/1055 off the job training; skill development; transfer of learning; work experience programmes

OPEN EDUCATION
9/0155 communication skills; competency-based education; humanities; minimum competencies; modular courses
9/0470 communications; distance education; networks; teleconferencing

9/0869 computer-assisted learning; educational materials; educational media
9/1053 aesthetic education; course content; creative thinking; fantasy; imagination
9/1115 chemistry; educational materials; higher education

OPEN ENTRY
9/0040 Education Reform Act 1988; educational administration; educational change; educational finance; grant maintained schools; parent choice; school-based management

OPEN UNIVERSITIES
9/0715 distance education; Saudi Arabia; women's education
9/0866 adult students; distance education; humanities; mature students; student attitudes
9/0867 computer uses in education; distance education; microcomputers
9/0868 course evaluation; distance education; student attitudes; surveys
9/0877 distance education; international educational exchange; teleconferencing

OPINIONS
9/0403 attitudes; further education; higher education; industry; school leavers; school to work transition; surveys
9/1218 Likert scales; linguistics; questionnaires; rating scales; semantics

OPPORTUNITIES
9/0144 access to education; action research; special educational needs; training
9/0847 educational policy; equal education; justice; social attitudes

OPTICAL DATA DISCS
9/0879 blindness; computer uses in education; special educational needs; speech synthesisers; visual impairments
9/1056 computer-assisted learning; educational technology; expert systems; training methods
9/1057 authoring aids – programming; computer-assisted learning; computer uses in education; electronic books
9/1058 computer-assisted learning; electronic books; human-computer interaction; hypermedia; information technology; multimedia approach
9/1062 computer-assisted learning; computer uses in education; distance education; multimedia approach; telecommunications

ORACY
9/0807 information technology; National Curriculum; teacher attitudes
9/0924 oral language; programme evaluation; speech communication

ORAL LANGUAGE
9/0924 oracy; programme evaluation; speech communication
9/1128 low achievement; mathematics education; verbal communication; verbal learning

ORAL READING
9/0355 beginning reading; early reading; reading skills; teacher-pupil relationship

ORAL TESTS
9/1132 assessment; French; General Certificate of Secondary Education; modern language studies

ORGANISATIONAL CHANGE
9/1179 adult education; continuing education; higher education; universities

ORGANISATIONAL CLIMATE
9/0311 attitude measures; institutes of higher education; institutional environment; student attitudes; teacher attitudes

ORGANISATIONAL EFFECTIVENESS
9/0341 degrees – academic; higher education; measurement objectives; performance indicators; programme effectiveness
9/0430 educational objectives; institutional evaluation; performance indicators

9/0914 competency-based teacher education
9/0919 art; design; Postgraduate Certificate of
Education; probationary teachers; programme
effectiveness; student teachers
9/0967 mature students; secondary school
teachers; student recruitment; student teacher
attitudes; student teachers
9/0974 curriculum; probationary teachers;
programme evaluation; student teachers;
teacher education; teaching experience
9/0986 comparative education; Education
Reform Act 1988; educational change;
teaching profession; USSR
9/1044 group work; learner-centred methods
9/1045 mature students; probationary period;
student teachers; teaching profession
9/1100 competence; competency-based teacher
education; records of achievement; student
teachers
9/1104 mentors
9/1121 information technology
9/1161 equal education; institutes of higher
education; racial discrimination; racial
integration
9/1165 equal education; student attitudes; student
teachers; teacher background; teaching
profession

PRIMARY EDUCATION
9/0017 reading difficulties; reading teaching;
remedial programmes; remedial reading;
special educational needs
9/0020 inservice teacher education; preservice
teacher education; science education; student
teachers
9/0157 cross curricular approach; employment;
enterprise education; preservice teacher
education; pupil attitudes
9/0160 gender equality; projects – learning
activities; sex differences
9/0199 religious education
9/0212 computer uses in education; gifted;
individualised methods; Jordan; mathematics
9/0260 assessment; English studies; National
Curriculum; writing evaluation; writing skills
9/0268 history; National Curriculum
9/0281 National Curriculum; parent attitudes;
parent-school relationship; science education
9/0335 group counselling; individual
development; peer counselling; social
development
9/0350 modern language studies; problems;
second language teaching; teaching methods
9/0414 science education; science experiments
9/0464 learning activities; practical science;
science education; teaching methods;
technology education
9/0467 history studies; National Curriculum;
school-based assessment
9/0501 drama education; dramatics; learning
processes; theatre arts
9/0560 geography education; mathematics
education; navigation; orientation;
orienteering; outdoor pursuits
9/0564 elementary schools; inservice teacher
education; process education; science
education; skill development; United States of
America
9/0565 science education; science teachers;
teacher role; United States of America
9/0568 science education
9/0605 primary schools; reading strategies;
reading teaching; teacher effectiveness;
teaching methods
9/0608 arithmetic; cognitive development;
number concepts; numbers; numeracy
9/0609 cognitive development; comprehension;
heat; science education; temperature
9/0635 attendance; India; learning motivation;
socioeconomic background
9/0766 attainment tests; history studies; National
Curriculum; standard assessment tasks
9/0770 assessment; National Curriculum; science
education
9/0772 assessment; attainment tests; educational
testing; inservice teacher education; standard
assessment tasks
9/0773 health education; human body
9/0783 assessment; English studies; mathematics
achievement; National Curriculum; science

education; standard assessment tasks; Welsh
studies
9/0785 assessment; mathematics achievement;
National Curriculum; science education;
standard assessment tasks
9/0901 art; art activities; art education; dance;
drama; music
9/0910 curriculum development; tourism; travel
9/1037 language of instruction; mathematical
vocabulary; mathematics education; textbooks
9/1040 concept teaching; group work; science
activities; science education; scientific
concepts
9/1107 cross curricular approach; curriculum
development; economics education; enterprise
education; secondary education; Wales
9/1124 construction – process; construction
materials; equal facilities; gender equality;
science education; sex differences; technology
education
9/1157 assessment; attainment tests; local
studies; National Curriculum; school-based
assessment; science education
9/1190 change; mathematics education; National
Curriculum; teaching methods

PRIMARY HEALTH CARE
9/0665 health; primary school pupils

PRIMARY SCHOOL CURRICULUM
9/0015 history; information technology
9/0071 educational change; infant school
curriculum; infant school education; National
Curriculum; standard assessment tasks
9/0209 educational theories
9/0354 curriculum research; specialisation

PRIMARY SCHOOL PUPILS
9/0100 motor development; sex differences
9/0215 educational materials; exercise; health
activities; health promotion; heart rate;
physical activities
9/0216 educational materials; exercise; health
activities; health promotion; physical activities
9/0611 primary school teachers; primary schools;
teacher-pupil relationship
9/0625 classroom communication; group
discussion; nondirective methods; peer groups
9/0665 health; primary health care
9/1069 primary schools; pupil attitudes; school
size; small schools

PRIMARY SCHOOL TEACHERS
9/0090 inservice teacher education; teacher
development
9/0119 music education; National Curriculum
9/0194 professional development; teacher
attitudes
9/0611 primary school pupils; primary schools;
teacher-pupil relationship
9/0909 classroom communication; teacher
behaviour; teacher-pupil relationship; teaching
methods
9/0915 consultants; inservice teacher education;
music education; music teachers
9/0928 inservice teacher education; mathematics;
teacher attitudes
9/1042 perception; science education; scientific
concepts
9/1184 educational policy; National Curriculum;
teacher workload; time management
9/1185 educational policy; National Curriculum;
secondary school teachers; teacher workload;
time management
9/1197 teacher behaviour; teacher development;
teacher role; teaching methods
9/1200 educational materials; inservice teacher
education; scientific concepts; science education

PRIMARY SCHOOLS
9/0011 probationary teachers; teacher induction
9/0016 assessment; profiles; pupil responsibility;
records of achievement; school reports; self
evaluation – individuals
9/0072 educational administration; educational
change; educational innovation; educational
planning; multicultural education
9/0093 local education authorities;
mainstreaming; special educational needs;
teacher development

9/0096 headteachers; school organisation;
teaching profession
9/0181 measurement; measurement equipment;
science activities; science education
9/0283 classroom management; classroom
research
9/0286 access to education; Education Reform
Act 1988; parent choice
9/0318 children's literature; fiction; story reading
9/0344 physical activities; physical education;
Scotland
9/0357 reading strategies; silent reading;
sustained silent reading
9/0358 computer uses in education; group work;
microcomputers; problem solving
9/0367 Education Reform Act 1988; individual
development; moral education; National
Curriculum; religious education; social
development
9/0375 educational change
9/0382 educational environment; educational
equipment; educational facilities; play;
playgrounds; recreational facilities
9/0384 Education Reform Act 1988; educational
change; educational legislation; educational
planning; school size; small schools
9/0413 school boards – Scotland;
school-community relationship; school
governing bodies
9/0550 cooperative programmes; curriculum
enrichment; rural areas; rural schools; shared
resources and services
9/0551 ethnic groups; multicultural education
9/0605 primary education; reading strategies;
reading teaching; teacher effectiveness;
teaching methods
9/0611 primary school pupils; primary school
teachers; teacher-pupil relationship
9/0670 development plans; educational
administration; planning
9/0726 educational administration; educational
environment; management in education
9/0738 locus of control; mainstreaming; self-
esteem; socialisation; special educational needs
9/0749 assessment; formative evaluation;
reading; reading achievement; school-based
assessment
9/0767 computer software; information
technology; local education authorities;
National Curriculum; technology education
9/0805 educational change; National Curriculum
9/0908 change strategies; educational
administration; educational change;
school-based management; school
organisation; staff-school relationship
9/0938 change; headteachers; local management
of schools; role conflict; stress variables; time
management
9/0956 classroom discipline; classroom
management; discipline; discipline policy;
pupil behaviour; Scotland; secondary schools
9/1006 curriculum development; health
education; programme evaluation
9/1009 language teachers; modern language
studies; programme evaluation; teaching
assistants
9/1035 achievement; modern language studies;
second language learning
9/1069 primary school pupils; pupil attitudes;
school size; small schools
9/1075 educational planning; individual needs;
individualised methods; teaching methods
9/1142 educational finance; educational quality;
Saudi Arabia
9/1201 inservice teacher education; mathematics
education

PRIMARY SECONDARY EDUCATION
9/0035 deafness; educational experience; hearing
impairments; mainstreaming; social
experience; special educational needs;
transition education
9/0788 curriculum development; developmental
continuity; local education authorities;
National Curriculum
9/0970 curriculum development; programme
evaluation
9/1105 developmental continuity; information
technology; learning strategies; teaching
methods; transfer of learning

9/0525 ability; pupil projects; secondary education; technology education

9/0716 coursework; General Certificate of Secondary Education; pupil experience; pupil projects; sex differences; social influences

PROTESTANT CHURCHES

9/0860 church and education; feminism; language usage; power structure

9/1071 church and education; churches; urban areas; voluntary schools

PSYCHIATRIC SERVICES

9/1080 Delphi technique; nurse education

PSYCHIATRY

9/0168 distance education; medical education; professional continuing education

9/0170 distance education; management development; medical education; pharmacology

PSYCHOLINGUISTICS

9/0572 language acquisition; language handicaps; learning disabilities

PSYCHOLOGICAL EVALUATION

9/0003 cognitive development; cognitive measurement; emotional disturbances

9/0731 communication aids – for disabled; deafness; hearing aids; hearing impairments

PSYCHOLOGICAL TESTING

9/0569 educational history; France; intelligence tests; psychology

PSYCHOLOGISTS

9/0174 disabilities; groups; medical services; needs; special educational needs

PSYCHOLOGY

9/0059 educational theories; learning theories; teacher education; teaching experience; teaching practice; teaching process

9/0569 educational history; France; intelligence tests; psychological testing

PSYCHOMOTOR SKILLS

9/0058 cerebral palsy; conductive education; evaluation; motor development

9/0644 music education; music techniques; musical instruments

PSYCHOPATHOLOGY

9/0538 behaviour problems; elective mutism; inhibition

PUBLIC EDUCATION

9/0478 educational administration; educational history; educational policy; secondary education; tripartite system

PUBLICATIONS

9/0313 educational materials; environmental education; outdoor education; resource materials

9/0314 educational materials; environmental education; social studies

PUNJABI

9/0204 bilingual pupils; ethnic groups; ethnicity; language usage; linguistics; nursery schools; social networks

PUPIL ATTITUDES

9/0013 comparative education; modern language studies

9/0031 animals; laboratory animals; National Curriculum; science education

9/0042 educational experience; exceptional persons; special educational needs

9/0108 school health services

9/0157 cross curricular approach; employment; enterprise education; preservice teacher education; primary education

9/0197 Arabic studies; higher education; sixth forms

9/0230 outcomes of education; technical education; vocational education

9/0379 general studies; pastoral care – education; sixth form colleges

9/0400 material development; parent attitudes; school effectiveness; self evaluation – groups; teacher attitudes

9/0706 comparative education; cross cultural studies; educational attitudes; Saudi Arabia

9/0707 comparative education; cross cultural studies; educational attitudes; Japan

9/0739 comparative education; reading achievement; reading comprehension

9/0753 aesthetic values; dance; physical education; sports

9/0982 bullying; discipline problems; playgrounds; pupil behaviour; pupil participation; recreational activities

9/0990 learning experience; pupil-school relationship; school effectiveness; secondary education; secondary school pupils; teaching process

9/1027 choice of subjects; demography; further education; sixteen to nineteen education

9/1065 attitude change; Christianity; religious attitudes; secondary school pupils

9/1069 primary school pupils; primary schools; school size; small schools

9/1072 attitude measures; Christianity; religious attitudes

9/1073 religious attitudes; scientific attitudes; secondary school pupils

9/1076 Northern Ireland; religious education; scientific attitudes; secondary school pupils

9/1082 religious attitudes; scientific attitudes; secondary school pupils

9/1083 learner-centred curriculum; learner-centred methods; teacher-pupil relationship

9/1103 National Curriculum; secondary schools

9/1126 observation; textbook evaluation; textbooks

PUPIL BEHAVIOUR

9/0046 behaviour problems; classroom discipline; classroom management; teacher behaviour; teacher-pupil relationship

9/0057 antisocial behaviour; discipline; disruptive pupils; pupil placement

9/0334 stress – psychological; stress management; stress variables

9/0956 classroom discipline; classroom management; discipline; discipline policy; primary schools; Scotland; secondary schools

9/0978 bullying; cooperation; ethnic relations; intergroup relations; intervention; middle school education; social isolation

9/0979 bullying; discipline problems; playgrounds; pupil participation; recreational activities

9/0980 antisocial behaviour; behaviour problems; bullying; discipline; discipline policy

9/0982 bullying; discipline problems; playgrounds; pupil attitudes; pupil participation; recreational activities

9/0983 antisocial behaviour; bullying; family environment; family influence

9/0989 discipline; educational quality; inner city; school effectiveness; urban schools

9/1113 intergroup relations; social skills; sociometric techniques

9/1204 academic ability; academic failure; gifted; underachievement

PUPIL DEVELOPMENT

9/0115 inservice teacher education; programme evaluation; self concept

9/0572 assessment; pupil evaluation; reception classes; school entrance age; screening tests

PUPIL EVALUATION

9/0572 assessment; pupil development; reception classes; school entrance age; screening tests

PUPIL EXPERIENCE

9/0716 coursework; General Certificate of Secondary Education; projects – learning activities; pupil projects; sex differences; social influences

PUPIL NEEDS

9/0024 ability identification; educational planning; literacy

PUPIL NUMBERS

9/0025 long range planning; prediction; regional planning

PUPIL PARTICIPATION

9/0237 educational policy; participation; physical education; social influences; sports

9/0899 individual development; mathematics achievement; mathematics education; sex differences

9/0979 bullying; discipline problems; playgrounds; pupil behaviour; recreational activities

9/0982 bullying; discipline problems; playgrounds; pupil attitudes; pupil behaviour; recreational activities

PUPIL PLACEMENT

9/0057 antisocial behaviour; discipline; disruptive pupils; pupil behaviour

9/0743 age grade placement; age groups; birth; special educational needs; special schools

PUPIL PROJECTS

9/0525 ability; projects – learning activities; secondary education; technology education

9/0716 coursework; General Certificate of Secondary Education; projects – learning activities; pupil experience; sex differences; social influences

9/0883 animation; computer uses in education

PUPIL RESPONSIBILITY

9/0016 assessment; primary schools; profiles; records of achievement; school reports; self evaluation – individuals

PUPIL-SCHOOL RELATIONSHIP

9/0933 educational environment; educational philosophy; pastoral care – education; pupil welfare

9/0990 learning experience; pupil attitudes; school effectiveness; secondary education; secondary school pupils; teaching process

PUPIL WELFARE

9/0933 educational environment; educational philosophy; pastoral care – education; pupil-school relationship

QATAR

9/0195 technical education; vocational education; work education relationship

QUALIFICATIONS

9/0105 credit transfer; European Community; insurance occupations; transfer policy

9/0302 competency-based education; education courses; higher education; masters courses; standards

9/0426 computer system design; information systems; vocational education; youth opportunities

9/0516 European Community; professional associations; professional continuing education; Single European Market

9/0533 career choice; nurse education; nursing; recruitment; selection; student motivation

9/0596 National Vocational Qualifications; vocational education

9/0653 comparative education; school leavers; school to work transition; sixteen to nineteen education

9/0668 competency-based education; higher education; masters courses; National Vocational Qualifications; standards

9/0953 curriculum development; higher grade examinations; modular courses; Scotland

QUALITY ASSURANCE

9/0515 course evaluation; professional continuing education; quality control

QUALITY CONTROL

9/0299 educational quality; industry-higher education relationship; vocational education; work-education relationship

9/0515 course evaluation; professional continuing education; quality assurance

9/0671 child caregivers; child minding; day care; day care centres; preschool children

9/1030 colleges of further education; management in education; sixteen to nineteen education; staff development

Subject Index

REFUGEES
9/0935 bilingualism; second language learning

REGIONAL CHARACTERISTICS
9/0296 early childhood education; nursery school education; preschool education; regional planning

REGIONAL COOPERATION
9/1084 cross cultural studies; curriculum development; European studies; international cooperation

REGIONAL PLANNING
9/0025 long range planning; prediction; pupil numbers
9/0296 early childhood education; nursery school education; preschool education; regional characteristics

RELATIVISM – PHILOSOPHY
9/1162 ethics; moral education; multiculturalism

RELIABILITY
9/0087 assessment; moderation – marking; National Curriculum; school-based assessment; validity

RELIGION
9/0080 family life; nationalism; state schools
9/0827 history; mother tongue; nationalism; politics; Wales; Welsh

RELIGION AND EDUCATION
9/0210 educational theories; Islamic education
9/0274 Education Reform Act 1988; school worship; symbolism
9/0369 church and education; church-state relationship; educational history; educational legislation; nonconformity
9/0857 Islamic education; Muslims; religious cultural groups; women's education
9/0858 Islamic education; Muslims; religious cultural groups; women's education

RELIGIOUS ATTITUDES
9/0905 adolescent development; bereavement; child development; death; moral development
9/1065 attitude change; christianity; pupil attitudes; secondary school pupils
9/1068 adolescent attitudes; church and education; family influence; parent influence
9/1070 adolescent attitudes; church and education; secondary school pupils; voluntary schools
9/1072 attitude measures; christianity; pupil attitudes
9/1073 pupil attitudes; scientific attitudes; secondary school pupils
9/1074 adolescent attitudes; drinking; drug abuse; secondary school pupils; smoking; substance abuse
9/1082 pupil attitudes; scientific attitudes; secondary school pupils

RELIGIOUS CONFLICT
9/0177 Christianity; church and education; community relations; educational history; interfaith relations; religious differences; social change

RELIGIOUS CULTURAL GROUPS
9/0857 Islamic education; Muslims; religion and education; women's education
9/0858 Islamic education; Muslims; religion and education; women's education

RELIGIOUS DIFFERENCES
9/0038 imagery; multicultural education; religious education
9/0177 Christianity; church and education; community relations; educational history; interfaith relations; religious conflict; social change

RELIGIOUS EDUCATION
9/0038 imagery; multicultural education; religious differences
9/0039 educational materials
9/0050 adult education; capitalism; Christianity; church and education; secularisation

9/0199 primary education
9/0271 assessment; National Curriculum
9/0367 Education Reform Act 1988; individual development; moral education; National Curriculum; primary schools; social development
9/0371 beliefs; Christianity; mental retardation; special educational needs
9/0559 curriculum development; educational philosophy; individual development; moral education; physical education
9/1076 Northern Ireland; pupil attitudes; scientific attitudes; secondary school pupils

REMEDIAL PROGRAMMES
9/0017 primary education; reading difficulties; reading teaching; remedial reading; special educational needs
9/1212 comprehension tests; decoding – reading; reading comprehension
9/1214 reading achievement; reading difficulties; reading skills

REMEDIAL READING
9/0017 primary education; reading difficulties; reading teaching; remedial programmes; special educational needs

REPERTORY GRID TEST
9/0075 competence; competency-based teacher education; discussion – teaching technique; personal construct theory; teacher effectiveness

RESEARCH
9/0158 databases; local management of schools

RESEARCH METHODOLOGY
9/0535 sample size

RESEARCH OPPORTUNITIES
9/0648 financial support; social science research; social sciences
9/0651 financial support; grants; social science research

RESEARCH TOOLS
9/0637 models; statistical analysis
9/0641 computer software; models; statistical analysis; United States of America

RESIDENTIAL CARE
9/0175 child welfare; community services; Scotland; social services; social work

RESIDENTIAL INSTITUTIONS
9/0721 deaf blind; further education; institutional evaluation; severe learning difficulties; special educational needs

RESOURCE-BASED LEARNING
9/0308 educational innovation; resource materials; teaching methods

RESOURCE MATERIALS
9/0308 educational innovation; resource-based learning; teaching methods
9/0313 educational materials; environmental education; outdoor education; publications
9/0942 databases; multicultural education

RESUMES – PERSONAL
9/0302 higher education; profiles; records of achievement; self evaluation – individuals; skill development

RETENTION – PSYCHOLOGY
9/0640 assessment; job skills; mastery tests; vocational education

ROLE CONFLICT
9/0552 administrator role; educational change; headteachers; school-based management; secondary schools; teacher role
9/0938 change; headteachers; local management of schools; primary schools; stress variables; time management

ROLE MODELS
9/0300 peer teaching; student-school relationship; Wales

ROLE OF EDUCATION
9/0891 citizenship; citizenship education; identity; nationalism; Zambia

ROMAN CATHOLIC CHURCH
9/0360 Catholic schools; church and education; church-state relationship; educational history; educational policy

RURAL AREAS
9/0507 adult education; continuing education; evaluation; mature students; nonformal education
9/0550 cooperative programmes; curriculum enrichment; primary schools; rural schools; shared resources and services

RURAL DEVELOPMENT
9/0727 community development; developing countries; development education; economic development

RURAL SCHOOLS
9/0002 cooperation; curriculum development; education support grants; school support; small schools; staff development
9/0550 cooperative programmes; curriculum enrichment; primary schools; rural areas; shared resources and services
9/1077 Northern Ireland; science curriculum; science education; small schools

RUSSIAN STUDIES
9/0993 educational materials; inservice teacher education; second language teaching; teacher development

SAFETY EDUCATION
9/0934 traffic safety

SALARIES
9/1032 colleges of further education; comparable worth; employment practices; equal pay; job analysis; occupational information

SAMPLE SIZE
9/0535 research methodology

SANDWICH COURSES
9/0066 attendance patterns; business education; course evaluation; examination results; outcomes of education; undergraduate study

SAUDI ARABIA
9/0706 comparative education; cross cultural studies; educational attitudes; pupil attitudes
9/0715 distance education; open universities; women's education
9/1142 educational finance; educational quality; primary schools

SCALING
9/0690 academic achievement; performance factors; school effectiveness; social environment; socioeconomic influences

SCHEMATA – COGNITION
9/0548 English – second language; reading comprehension; teaching methods

SCHOOL-BASED ASSESSMENT
9/0087 assessment; moderation – marking; National Curriculum; reliability; validity
9/0275 academic records; parent aspiration; parent-school relationship
9/0467 history studies; National Curriculum; primary education
9/0746 assessment; inservice teacher education; reading achievement
9/0769 assessment; formative evaluation; primary schools; reading; reading achievement
9/0952 assessment; technology education
9/0955 action research; assessment; educational research
9/1092 assessment; mother tongue; National Curriculum; second language learning; standard assessment tasks; Welsh
9/1102 assessment; National Curriculum
9/1157 assessment; attainment tests; local studies; National Curriculum; primary education; science education

child welfare; family environment; foster
children; home-school relationship; low
achievement

SOCIAL SKILLS
9/0070 affective education; competence;
individual development
9/0456 moderate learning difficulties; problem
solving; severe learning difficulties; special
educational needs
9/1113 intergroup relations; pupil behaviour;
sociometric techniques

SOCIAL STATUS
9/0221 academic achievement; disadvantaged
environment; school effectiveness

SOCIAL STUDIES
9/0314 educational materials; environmental
education; publications
9/0957 examinations; investigations; learning
activities; Scotland; standard grade
examinations

SOCIAL WORK
9/0175 child welfare; community services;
residential care; Scotland; social services

SOCIAL WORK STUDIES
9/0420 law related education

SOCIALISATION
9/0738 locus of control; mainstreaming; primary
schools; self-esteem; special educational
needs
9/0977 cross cultural studies; job satisfaction;
motivation; school to work transition;
vocational adjustment; work attitudes; youth
employment

SOCIALIST COUNTRIES
9/0839 adult education; citizenship education;
political influences; social change; voluntary
agencies

SOCIOECONOMIC BACKGROUND
9/0635 attendance; India; learning motivation;
primary education
9/0894 academic staff; careers; degrees –
academic; educational history; outcomes of
education; university students

SOCIOECONOMIC INFLUENCES
9/0631 educational benefits; educational history;
elementary education; social history; women's
education; working class
9/0690 academic achievement; performance
factors; scaling; school effectiveness; social
environment
9/0912 educational history; educational
legislation; educational theories; educational
trends; elementary education; politics
education relationship

SOCIOLINGUISTICS
9/0623 dialect studies; Jamaican Creole;
language policy; language role; language
usage; native speakers; secondary schools
9/0925 dialect studies; language variation

SOCIOLOGY
9/1001 biographies

SOCIOLOGY OF EDUCATION
9/0163 educational theories
9/0999 educational policy

SOCIOMETRIC TECHNIQUES
9/1113 intergroup relations; pupil behaviour;
social skills

SONGS
9/0193 learning; music; music education; young
children

SPATIAL ABIITY
9/0539 cognitive processes; mainstreaming;
special educational needs

SPATIAL ABILITY
9/0101 art; art history; cognitive development;
cross curricular approach; mathematics
9/0768 memory; perceptual development
9/0771 assessment; memory
9/0863 cognitive ability; depth perception;
drawing; problem solving; visual perception

SPECIAL EDUCATION TEACHERS
9/0043 cross curricular approach; special
educational needs; support services; team
teaching
9/0048 behaviour modification; behaviour
problems; severe learning difficulties; special
educational needs; special schools

SPECIAL EDUCATIONAL NEEDS
9/0017 primary education; reading difficulties;
reading teaching; remedial programmes;
remedial reading
9/0035 deafness; educational experience; hearing
impairments; mainstreaming; primary
secondary education; social experience;
transition education
9/0041 blindness; braille; learning disabilities;
literacy education; raised line drawings;
sensory aids
9/0042 educational experience; exceptional
persons; pupil attitudes
9/0043 cross curricular approach; special education
teachers; support services; team teaching
9/0048 behaviour modification; behaviour
problems; severe learning difficulties; special
education teachers; special schools
9/0049 architectural education; blindness;
educational equipment; visual impairments
9/0052 aspiration; lifestyle; skills; visual
impairments; vocational education
9/0067 assessment; examinations; general
certificate of secondary education; low
achievement
9/0086 comparative education; educational
materials; mainstreaming; teacher education
9/0092 mainstreaming; secondary schools;
support staff
9/0093 local education authorities;
mainstreaming; primary schools; teacher
development
9/0095 curriculum development; individual
needs; mainstreaming; mixed ability; writing
teaching
9/0098 disabilities; institutional evaluation;
mainstreaming; United States of America
9/0117 moderate learning difficulties; motor
development; movement education; teaching
process
9/0144 access to education; action research;
opportunities; training
9/0161 adult basic education; competence;
employment potential; life skills; mental
retardation; moderate learning difficulties;
supporting studies
9/0174 disabilities; groups; medical services;
needs; psychologists
9/0238 communication aids – for disabled;
disabilities; educational materials
9/0277 mainstreaming; secondary education;
support services
9/0304 city technology colleges; dyslexia;
educational materials; learning disabilities;
teaching methods
9/0312 dyslexia; learning disabilities; reading
difficulties; teacher education
9/0333 deafness; hearing impairments; teaching
methods
9/0336 computer-assisted learning; deafness;
hearing impairments; interactive video
9/0368 disabilities; mainstreaming; physical
education
9/0371 beliefs; Christianity; mental retardation;
religious education
9/0386 communication aids – for disabled;
communication disorders; programme
evaluation; workshops
9/0387 communication aids – for disabled;
communication disorders; physical disabiities;
workshops
9/0422 disadvantaged; moderate learning
difficulties; support services
9/0423 aphasia; language handicaps; learning

disabilities; services
9/0425 motor development; special schools
9/0454 computer system design; computer uses
in education; severe learning difficulties
9/0456 moderate learning difficulties; problem
solving; severe learning difficulties; social
skills
9/0477 helplessness; motivation; self-esteem
9/0481 behaviour disorders; emotional
disturbances; statements – special educational
needs
9/0520 course evaluation; curriculum
development; deafness; interdisciplinary
approach; thinking skills
9/0539 cognitive processes; mainstreaming;
spatial abiity
9/0543 multisensory rooms; severe learning
difficulties; special schools
9/0588 assessment; colleges of further education;
diagnostic assessment; disabilities; further
education; moderate learning difficulties
9/0589 access to education; adult education;
educational finance; further education; local
education authorities
9/0597 support teachers; teachers
9/0604 child development; motor development;
neurological impairments; perceptual
handicaps; premature infants
9/0606 cluster grouping; educational
cooperation; special schools
9/0607 cerebral palsy; disabilities; motor
reactions; perceptual handicaps; perceptual
motor coordination
9/0613 computer uses in education; human
computer interaction; interaction; severe
learning difficulties
9/0618 cluster grouping; educational
cooperation; special schools
9/0619 educational policy
9/0701 blindness; communication problems;
higher education; nonverbal communication;
visual impairments
9/0709 further education; mainstreaming; visual
impairments
9/0710 behaviour disorders; emotional
disturbances; special schools
9/0714 Down's Syndrome; mainstreaming
9/0721 deaf blind; further education; institutional
evaluation; residential institutions; severe
learning difficulties
9/0722 behaviour disorders; self destructive
behaviour; self mutilation; severe learning
difficulties
9/0730 deafness; hearing impairments
9/0732 communication disorders; National
Curriculum; speech handicaps
9/0733 behaviour disorders; child psychiatry;
diagnostic assessment; emotional disturbances
9/0734 behaviour modification; severe learning
difficulties; training
9/0735 behaviour disorders; child psychiatry;
diagnostic assessment; emotional disturbances;
special schools
9/0736 curriculum development; National
Curriculum; severe learning difficulties
9/0738 locus of control; mainstreaming; primary
schools; self-esteem; socialisation
9/0740 dyslexia; learning disabilities
9/0743 age grade placement; age groups; birth;
pupil placement; special schools
9/0763 behaviour disorders; emotional
disturbances; special schools
9/0765 assessment; moderate learning
difficulties; National Vocational
Qualifications; trainees; youth opportunities
9/0780 school leavers; services; transition
education; youth
9/0781 educational planning; educational policy;
educational practices; local education
authorities
9/0813 adult vocational education; adults;
computer literacy; disabilities; information
technology; sheltered workshops; training centres
9/0814 behaviour disorders; computer-assisted
learning; computer uses in education;
emotional disturbances; information
technology; moderate learning difficulties
9/0815 behaviour disorders; computer uses in
education; information technology; special
schools

277

9/1070 adolescent attitudes; church and education; religious attitudes; secondary school pupils

9/1071 church and education; churches; Protestant churches; urban areas

VOWELS
9/0083 phonetics; reading research; reading skills

9/1097 Arabs; English – second language; word recognition

WALES
9/0300 peer teaching; role models; student-school relationship

9/0598 curriculum development; economics education; enterprise education; teacher education

9/0827 history; mother tongue; nationalism; politics; religion; Welsh

9/1107 cross curricular approach; curriculum development; economics education; enterprise education; primary education; secondary education

WELL BEING
9/0448 educational objectives; educational philosophy; quality of life

WELSH
9/0811 educational television; infant school education; programme evaluation; second language learning

9/0827 history; mother tongue; nationalism; politics; religion; Wales

9/1090 bilingual education; bilingualism; educational policy; language policy; school effectiveness; Welsh studies

9/1091 attitudes; bilingualism; language policy; language usage

9/1092 assessment; mother tongue; National Curriculum; school-based assessment; second language learning; standard assessment tasks

9/1206 bilingual education; bilingual schools; English; secondary education

WELSH STUDIES
9/0783 assessment; English studies; mathematics achievement; National Curriculum; primary education; science education; standard assessment tasks

9/0801 assessment; attainment tests; National Curriculum; standard assessment tasks

9/1090 bilingual education; bilingualism; educational policy; language policy; school effectiveness; Welsh

WIDE AREA NETWORKS
9/0824 communications; computer networks; disabilities; training

WOMEN
9/0708 deputy headteachers; equal opportunities – jobs; sex discrimination; sex role

9/1110 gender equality; higher education; mature students; sex differences; women's education

9/1170 higher education; science education; scientific literacy

WOMEN TEACHERS
9/0176 educational history; sex differences; sex role; women's education

9/0295 career development; institutes of higher education; teacher evaluation; teaching profession; women's employment

9/1167 mothers; teacher attitudes; teacher background; teacher role; teaching profession

WOMEN'S EDUCATION
9/0112 educational history; educational policy; France; teaching profession

9/0176 educational history; sex differences; sex role; women teachers

9/0377 Nigeria

9/0459 educational history; training; women's employment

9/0514 Access programmes; continuing education; educational benefits; educational objectives

9/0631 educational benefits; educational history; elementary education; social history; socioeconomic influences; working class

9/0715 distance education; open universities; Saudi Arabia

9/0806 mature students; preservice teacher education; student behaviour; student teacher attitudes; student teachers

9/0819 Asians; community education; ethnic groups; youth service

9/0857 Islamic education; Muslims; religion and education; religious cultural groups

9/0858 Islamic education; Muslims; religion and education; religious cultural groups

9/1110 gender equality; higher education; mature students; sex differences; women

9/1143 Chile; comparative education; gender equality; Israel

9/1144 gender equality; Mauritius; women's employment

9/1145 educational policy; equal education; gender equality; Nepal

9/1208 access to education; bilingual education programmes; ethnic groups; student reaction; youth programmes

WOMEN'S EMPLOYMENT
9/0236 employment opportunities; graduate employment; higher education; labour market; mature students

9/0295 career development; institutes of higher education; teacher evaluation; teaching profession; women teachers

9/0459 educational history; training; women's education

9/0673 child development; cognitive development; day care; emotional development; mothers; preschool children; social development

9/1144 gender equality; Mauritius; women's education

WOMEN'S STUDIES
9/0498 girls; leisure time; recreational activities

WORD RECOGNITION
9/0848 cognitive processes; computer-assisted reading; reading comprehension; reading skills; spelling

9/1018 dyslexia; reading difficulties; reading failure; reading skills

9/1097 Arabs; English – second language; vowels

9/1217 beginning reading; dyslexia; sight method

WORK ATTITUDES
9/0976 occupational aspiration; private education

9/0977 cross cultural studies; job satisfaction; motivation; school to work transition; socialisation; vocational adjustment; youth employment

WORK-EDUCATION RELATIONSHIP
9/0120 credits; experiential learning; industry-higher education relationship; job placement

9/0195 Qatar; technical education; vocational education

9/0202 employer attitudes; graduate employment; graduates; mathematical ability; numeracy

9/0291 flexible learning; further education

9/0299 educational quality; industry-higher education relationship; quality control; vocational education

9/0305 engineering education; engineers; graduate employment

9/0306 career development; engineering education; engineers; training

9/0365 comparative education; curriculum development; educational objectives; educational philosophy; National Curriculum

9/0412 educational materials; enterprise education

9/0466 enterprise education; higher education; programme evaluation

9/0489 employee attitudes; on the job training; training

9/0554 technical education; vocational education

9/0562 comparative education; industry-education relationship; United States of America

9/0791 cooperative education; school to work transition; vocational education

9/0803 career choice; career counselling; career development; enterprise education; higher education; vocational guidance

9/0836 adult vocational education; employment; job skills; job training

9/0842 curriculum evaluation; economics-education relationship; Hong Kong; technical education; training; vocational education

9/0852 enterprise education; further education

9/1173 curriculum; employment; industry-education relationship; skills

9/1180 competency-based education; labour market; National Vocational Qualifications

WORK EXPERIENCE
9/0106 employer attitudes; job placement; student employment

9/0809 industry-higher education relationship; management studies; placement

9/0996 enterprise education; industry-education relationship; technical education; vocational education

WORK EXPERIENCE PROGRAMMES
9/1055 off the job training; on the job training; skill development; transfer of learning

WORKING CLASS
9/0064 Access programmes; educational experience; mature students; men; motivation

9/0482 educational history; educational policy; educational principles; school systems; secondary education; secondary modern schools; tripartite system

9/0517 adult education; biographies; educational history; extension education; universities

9/0518 adult education; educational history; educational policy; extension education

9/0631 educational benefits; educational history; elementary education; social history; socioeconomic influences; women's education

WORKS SCHOOLS
9/0494 adult basic education; adult literacy

9/0508 adult education; labour force development

9/0829 adult education

WORKSHOPS
9/0386 communication aids – for disabled; communication disorders; programme evaluation; special educational needs

9/0387 communication aids – for disabled; communication disorders; physical disabiities; special educational needs

9/0687 experiential learning; interpersonal competence; learning experience; preservice teacher education; student teachers

WORLD STUDIES
9/0590 citizenship education; conservation – environment; environmental education; futures – of society; global approach

WRITING – COMPOSITION
9/0032 creative writing; English studies curriculum; literary genres; National Curriculum; writing skills

9/0373 narration; persuasive discourse; secondary education; writing research

9/0383 argument; criticism; narration; persuasive discourse; writing research; writing skills; writing teaching

9/0460 authors; cooperation

9/0461 critical reading; reading; student development; study skills; writing skills

9/0624 comparative education; peer evaluation; secondary schools; United States of America; writing skills; writing teaching

9/0757 examinations; linguistic performance; undergraduate students; writing evaluation

9/0845 adult education; authors; community education; leadership training

9/1177 authors; discourse analysis; educational materials; writing for publication; writing skills

WRITING EVALUATION
9/0260 assessment; English studies; National Curriculum; primary education; writing skills

9/0757 examinations; linguistic performance; undergraduate students; writing – composition